The Supreme Court and the Attitudinal Model Revisited

This book, authored by two leading scholars of the Supreme Court and its policy making, systematically presents and validates the use of the attitudinal model to explain and predict Supreme Court decision making. In the process, it critiques the two major alternative approaches to Supreme Court decision making: the legal and rational choice models.

Using the U.S. Supreme Court Data Base, the justices' private papers, and other sources of information, the book analyzes the appointment process, certiorari, the decision on the merits, opinion assignments, and the formation of opinion coalitions. The book provides the definitive presentation of the attitudinal model as well as an authoritative critique of the legal and rational choice models. The book thoroughly reflects research done since the 1993 publication of its predecessor, as well as decisions and developments in the Supreme Court, including the momentous decision of *Bush v. Gore*.

Jeffrey A. Segal is Professor of Political Science at SUNY Stony Brook. Recent publications include *Majority Rule or Minority Will* (1999) with Harold Spaeth, winner of the C. Herman Pritchett Award of the American Political Science Association for best book in law and judicial politics published in 1999.

Harold J. Spaeth is Professor of Political Science at Michigan State University. His publications include *Stare Indecisis* (1995), with Saul Brenner.

The Supreme Court and the Attitudinal Model Revisited

JEFFREY A. SEGAL
State University of New York, Stony Brook

HAROLD J. SPAETH
Michigan State University

PUBLISHED BY THE PRESS SYNDICATE OF THE UNIVERSITY OF CAMBRIDGE
The Pitt Building, Trumpington Street, Cambridge, United Kingdom

CAMBRIDGE UNIVERSITY PRESS
The Edinburgh Building, Cambridge CB2 2RU, UK
40 West 20th Street, New York, NY 10011-4211, USA
477 Williamstown Road, Port Melbourne, VIC 3207, Australia
Ruiz de Alarcón 13, 28014 Madrid, Spain
Dock House, The Waterfront, Cape Town 8001, South Africa

http://www.cambridge.org

First published 2002

Printed in the United Kingdom at the University Press, Cambridge

Typeface Sabon 10/13 pt. *System* QuarkXPress [BTS]

A catalog record for this book is available from the British Library.

Library of Congress Cataloging in Publication Data

Segal, Jeffrey Allan.
The Supreme Court and the attitudinal model revisited / Jeffrey A. Segal, Harold J. Spaeth.
p. cm.
Includes bibliographical references and index.
ISBN 0-521-78351-8 (hb) – ISBN 0-521-78971-0 (pbk.)
1. United States. Supreme Court. 2. Constitutional law – United States. 3. Constitutional history – United States. 4. Judicial process – United States. I. Spaeth, Harold J. II. Title.
KF8742 .S43 2002
347.73′26–dc21

2001052978

ISBN 0 521 78351 8 hardback
ISBN 0 521 78971 0 paperback

In memory of my parents, Eli and Billie Segal

Jeffrey A. Segal

For Jean

Harold J. Spaeth

Contents

List of Illustrations

List of Tables

Preface

Like *The Supreme Court and the Attitudinal Model*, the purpose of this book is to scientifically analyze and explain the Supreme Court, its processes, and its decisions from an attitudinal perspective. While changes in judicial policy over the past ten years would have warranted an updated second edition to our original work, changes in public scholarship require something more.

Two specific changes bear initial mention. First is the rise of rational choice scholarship on the Court, as intuitively exemplified by Lee Epstein and Jack Knight's *The Choice Justices Make*[1] and formally exemplified by John Ferejohn and Charles Shipan's "Congressional Influence on Bureaucracy,"[2] an article more influential in the judicial studies than in either the congressional or bureaucratic literatures.

Second is the rise in the testing of legal variables. Various critics of *The Supreme Court and the Attitudinal Model* have noted that our evidence against the legal model consisted solely of anecdotal evidence. Based on what we hope is a more refined explanation of the legal model, we now provide tests of at least some of its tenets.

The result is a newly titled book that in name and substance will be familiar to readers of *The Supreme Court and the Attitudinal Model*, but which nevertheless provides important new material.

[1] (Washington, D.C.: Congressional Quarterly Press, 1998). Or see Forrest Maltzman, James F. Spriggs II, and Paul J. Wahlbeck, *The Collegial Game* (New York: Cambridge University Press, 2000).

[2] John Ferejohn and Charles Shipan, "Congressional Influence on Bureaucracy," 6 *Journal of Law and Economics* 1 (1990).

Chapter 1, "Supreme Court Policy Making": The book begins with an explanation of what courts do and why their activity results in policy making. The chapter is updated to take into account, first, the historic *Bush v. Gore* decision, and second, the changes in the relationship between the federal and state judicial systems wrought by the Supreme Court's invigoration of the sovereign state immunity doctrine.

Chapter 2, "Models of Decision Making: The Legal Model": In the first book, we relied exclusively on the Court's view of the legal model, ignoring the modern scholarly literature on legal decision making. We rectify this omission with a discussion of the legalistic positions taken from scholars in political science, economics, and law.

Chapter 3, "Models of Decision Making: The Attitudinal and Rational Choice Models": In the original book we had no discussion of the application of rational choice theory to Supreme Court decision making. This now burgeoning field receives extensive analysis in this chapter, with particular attention paid to the so-called separation-of-powers model. We have also updated our discussion of the attitudinal model.

Chapter 4, "A Political History of the Supreme Court": In keeping with the Court's policy-making role, we present in Chapter 4 a political history of the Court, one which outlines the ideological considerations that have motivated the thrust of the Court's decisions since its inception. This chapter has been updated to include discussion of the Rehnquist Court's attack on congressional authority, in terms not only of state sovereign immunity, but of the commerce clause as well.

Chapter 5, "Staffing the Court": This chapter concerns the nomination and confirmation of the justices. We identify the factors affecting their nomination and present a brief case study of the five failed nominations between the effort to elevate Abe Fortas to the chief justiceship and the withdrawal of Douglas Ginsburg from consideration. We also pay special attention to the barely successful Thomas nomination. An aggregate analysis of all nominations is provided, followed by an individual-level focus on the votes of senators on the twenty-six nominations between Earl Warren and Stephen Breyer. We have also added a section on the impact of presidential appointments on judicial policy making.

Chapter 6, "Getting into Court": This chapter describes the legal requirements litigants must meet to gain access to the Court, and the procedures and criteria the justices employ to select the cases they choose to decide. In the first book, we provided no original research in this chapter. Now, we provide extensive original research, taking advantage of newly coded data from the justices' docket books. This enables us to provide tests of reversal strategies and prediction strategies and to test the Court's role as a hierarchical superior in the federal judicial system.

Chapter 7, "The Decision on the Merits: The Legal Model": One of the main criticisms of the original book was that we provided no tests of the legal model. In this chapter we provide extensive systematic tests of the Court's use of *stare decisis*, in both its everyday form and what we label its crisis form, and a more limited discussion of the role of text and intent.

Chapter 8, "The Decision on the Merits: The Attitudinal and Rational Choice Models": We demonstrate that the components of the attitudinal model – the facts of the case and the ideology of the justices – successfully explain and predict the votes of Supreme Court justices. We also provide extensive analysis of rational choice theory's separation-of-powers model.

Chapter 9, "Opinion Assignment and Opinion Coalitions": This chapter has been rewritten to include a wealth of new data and a variety of new tests on the writing and opinion coalition behavior of the justices. We make extensive use of newly available data from the justices' docket books and reformulate the way in which we test opinion assignment hypotheses. We demonstrate that attitudinal considerations coexist with egalitarian concerns to govern majority opinion assignments by the chief justice. We then consider opinion coalitions. Unfortunately, a majority opinion coalition does not always form. When this happens, only a nonauthoritative judgment of the Court results. We investigate the reasons for these judgments by determining which justices are responsible for the resulting breakdown in collegiality. We also investigate opinion coalitions generally: Who joins with whom and why.

Chapter 10, "The Supreme Court and Constitutional Democracy": This chapter updates the material we previously presented and adds a substantial new section on the impact of public opinion on the Court's decisions.

Chapter 11, "Conclusions": This chapter includes discussions of the new postpositive legalist position, the future potential of the rational-choice model, and the continued vitality of the attitudinal model in light of the Rehnquist Court's continued, and perhaps unmatched, activism.

In consideration of the substantial additions that we made, cuts were made as well. The new book no longer contains a chapter on the impact of judicial decisions. Everyone interested in impact is going to read

Rosenberg's book,[3] regardless of what we might say. The new book no longer contains the methodological appendix on logit analysis, as the technique is far more common today. And we no longer provide the extensive descriptive analysis of the justices' voting behavior; the widespread availability of the Supreme Court database and other published sources means that this sort of information is available to almost anyone at any time.

Assessment of the operation of any theoretically grounded model requires highly reliable data. Although we have utilized data from a variety of sources, we have most frequently depended on those contained in the U.S. Supreme Court Judicial Database and its offshoots, projects conceived and designed for multiinvestigator use by Harold Spaeth, who compiled the data therein with the financial assistance of the National Science Foundation. The data, of known reliability, are updated regularly and encompass a wide range of variables that bear on the behavior of the Court and the individual justices. These encompass background, chronological, substantive, outcome, and voting and opinion variables. The offshoots of the original database include the conference voting of the justices of the Vinson, Warren, and Burger Courts, and a flipping of all the data in all the databases so that the unit of analysis becomes the individual justice rather than the Court's cases.[4]

Except for our treatment of the Court's political history, we generally concentrate on the activity, decisions, and policies of the last half of the twentieth century, with the most specific attention paid to the Rehnquist Court. We do so for two reasons. Though antiquarianism has its place, it ought not upstage the here and now, at least not in an arena as dynamic as that of the Court. Second, the database on which we primarily rely dates from the beginning of the Vinson Court in 1946; hence, the focus on activity since then. But we do not totally ignore the nineteenth century in testing our theory, as our work on precedent demonstrates.

We acknowledge the assistance of other scholars without whose help this book could never have been written: Michael F. Altfeld, Sara C. Benesh, Saul Brenner, Charles M. Cameron, Albert D. Cover, Lee Epstein, Timothy M. Hagle, Thomas H. Hammond, Robert Howard, John N. Jacob, Ellen Lazarus, Donald R. Songer, Thomas G. Walker, and

[3] Gerald Rosenberg, *The Hollow Hope: Can Courts Bring about Social Change?* (Chicago: University of Chicago Press, 1991), p. 180.

[4] All databases and their documentation may be downloaded at the website of Michigan State University's Program for Law and Judicial Politics: www.ssc.msu.edu/~pls/pljp.

Stephen Wermiel. For better or for worse, the day of the solitary scholar buried behind the stacks of a library or the equipment of a laboratory who successfully advances human knowledge sans personal interaction and collaboration with others is history. We gratefully thank these individuals whose wisdom, understanding, and knowledge have so appreciably enhanced ours – deficient though ours remains.

This is the third Cambridge University Press book that we have coauthored. Along with their predecessors, plus a fourth of which Spaeth is the coauthor, we continue to find the Press and its staff congenial, cooperative, and fully competent. In this regard, we especially thank Lewis Bateman, our editor, and Stephanie Sakson, our production editor and copyeditor. They display a light and unobtrusive touch – antithetically bureaucratic – that hallmark the editorial excellence so characteristic of Cambridge University Press.

A goodly bit of the research that appears on the following pages was undertaken with the financial support of the National Science Foundation through grants SES-8313733, SES-8812935, SES-8842925, SES-9112755, SBR-9320284, SBR-9519335, SBR-9614000, and SES-9910535. We profusely thank the NSF. Without its support, our knowledge and understanding of the Court would have remained largely anecdotal and impressionistic.

October 2001

Jeffrey A. Segal
Harold J. Spaeth

1

Introduction

Supreme Court Policy Making

If the fatuousness characteristic of Pollyanna had continued to rose-color anyone's attitude toward the U.S. Supreme Court, the decision in *Bush v. Gore* must have been mind-boggling.[1] More neatly than we might have imagined, the Court's three most conservative justices – William Rehnquist, Antonin Scalia, and Clarence Thomas – overruled the Florida Supreme Court's interpretation of Florida law and declared that Florida's recount violated the equal protection clause. The Court's two other conservatives, less extremely so than their colleagues – Anthony Kennedy and Sandra Day O'Connor – agreed with the equal-protection violation and ruled with the triumvirate that the current recount was illegal and set a deadline (two hours hence!) that made any subsequent recount impossible. Two moderates, David Souter and Stephen Breyer, found equal protection problems with the recount but thought the problems solvable; whereas the Court's most liberal members, Ruth Bader Ginsburg and John Paul Stevens, who usually support equal protection claims, found nothing wrong with the recount. As we declared in 1993, "... if a case on the outcome of a presidential election should reach the Supreme Court ... the Court's decision might well turn on the personal preferences of the justices."[2]

The justices in the majority, who historically have resisted Fourteenth Amendment claims far more than their colleagues, rested their decision

[1] 148 L Ed 2d 388 (2000). Because of the frequency of references to this decision, we avoid further use of its citation. Keep in mind that this reference appears first.

[2] Jeffrey A. Segal and Harold J. Spaeth, *The Supreme Court and the Attitudinal Model* (New York: Cambridge University Press, 1993), p. 70.

on a blithely asserted violation of the equal protection clause. Unbroken precedent had held that such a violation requires purposeful discrimination, but clearly this pattern did not preclude the majority from reaching its preferred outcome. And never mind that this attack on federalism came from the same five justices who by the same identical vote have granted the states and their courts, under the guise of states' rights, immunity from the provisions of a variety of progressive federal laws, for example, disabled persons,[3] violence against women,[4] age discrimination in employment,[5] overtime pay,[6] and gun-free school zones.[7]

While *Bush v. Gore* may appear to be the most egregious example of judicial policy making, we suggest that it is only because of its recency. Our history is replete with similar examples, although perhaps none as shamelessly partisan. One that took less liberty with legal language perhaps, but nonetheless engendered a fierce conflict that has not yet dissipated, is *Roe v. Wade*.[8] Included within the right to privacy – which is nowhere mentioned in the Constitution – and which in turn is imbedded in the due process clauses, is a woman's right to terminate her pregnancy. The majority then proceeded to write a detailed legislative specification of when and under what conditions an abortion was constitutional.

Although we live in a representative democracy, the extent to which either representation or democratic elections have force and effect depends on the will of a majority of the nine unelected, lifetime-serving justices. These justices decide whether abortions should be allowed, death penalties inflicted, same-sex marriage legitimated, and, every century or so, who shall become President.[9] Although the justices conventionally claim for public consumption that they do not make public policy, that they merely interpret the law, the truth conforms to Chief Justice (then Governor) Charles Evans Hughes's declaration, "We

[3] *Board of Trustees v. Garrett*, 148 L Ed 2d 866 (2001).
[4] *United States v. Morrison*, 146 L Ed 2d 658 (2000).
[5] *Kimel v. Florida Board*, 145 L Ed 2d 522 (2000).
[6] *Alden v. Maine*, 144 L Ed 2d 636 (1999).
[7] *United States v. Lopez*, 514 U.S. 549 (1995). [8] 410 U.S. 113 (1973).
[9] In 1876, five justices of the Supreme Court served on a congressional commission to resolve 21 disputed electoral votes. The two Democratic justices on the commission voted to give each disputed vote to the Democrat Tilden, while the three Republican justices voted to give each disputed vote to the Republican Hayes. The congressional members of the commission, split evenly between Democrats and Republicans, similarly voted a straight party line. Thus did the justices of the Supreme Court legitimize what was, at the time, the most fraudulent presidential election in U.S. history.

are under a Constitution, but the Constitution is what the judges say it is."[10]

This chapter focuses on why the Supreme Court, along with other American courts, makes policy. We initially present a set of reasons for judicial policy making. Though these reasons are crucial to our understanding of the institution's importance, they do not tell us anything about the considerations that cause the justices to make the choices that produce the Court's policies. We take up those factors in Chapters 2 and 3, which describe and evaluate three models of Supreme Court decision making: the legal, the attitudinal, and the rational choice. While *Bush v. Gore* undoubtedly serves as a prime example of attitudinal decision making, we cannot generalize from a single case. Thus, we carefully evaluate these models in Chapters 2 and 3 and throughout the book, with our most specific tests presented in Chapters 8 and 9.

WHAT COURTS DO

To explain why justices act as they do, we begin with a specification of what courts themselves do. From the most general and nontechnical standpoint, they resolve disputes. Not all disputes, of course, only those that possess certain characteristics. The party initiating legal action must be a "proper plaintiff," and the court in which the dispute is brought must be a "proper forum," that is, it must have the authority – the jurisdiction – to resolve the dispute. Thus, for example, courts generally, and the federal courts in particular, may resolve only a "case" or "controversy."[11] We detail the specific characteristics that enable a litigant to be a proper plaintiff and those pertaining to the proper forum in Chapter 6.

The process whereby courts resolve disputes produces a decision. This decision, unless overruled by a higher court, is binding on the parties to the dispute. If a higher court does overrule the trial or a lower appellate

[10] Quoted in Craig Ducat and Harold Chase, *Constitutional Interpretation*, 4th ed. (New York: West, 1988), p. 3.

[11] For all practical purposes, the two terms are synonymous. A "case" includes all judicial proceedings, while a "controversy" is a civil matter. As Justice Iredell pointed out in the lead opinion in *Chisholm v. Georgia*, 2 Dallas 419 (1792), at 432: "it cannot be presumed that the general word, 'controversies' was intended to include any proceedings that relate to criminal cases. . . ." Although the Eleventh Amendment nullified the Court's decision in *Chisholm v. Georgia*, Iredell's distinction survives.

court, then its decision replaces the earlier one. A court's decision, binding the litigants, is authoritative in the sense that nonjudicial decision makers, such as legislators or executive officials, cannot alter or nullify it.[12]

Judicial authority, however, is not subverted by the possibility that the legislature may at some point in the future alter the law that the court applied to the case it decided. Examples of congressional overrides abound. As an extreme example, the Civil Rights Act of 1991 overturned six highly charged Supreme Court decisions that were handed down between May 1 and June 15, 1989.[13] Even though a congressional overruling does not subvert judicial authority, the Supreme Court not uncommonly disapproves of Congress's efforts to undo the interpretation it has given to congressional enactments.[14] Thus, for example, a seventh decision handed down during the six-week period mentioned above[15] required Congress "to pass the same statute *three times* to achieve its original goal."[16] And though Congress eventually won this battle, it had less success on another aspect of the same issue that conflicted the *Dellmuth* Court: the authority of Congress to abrogate the states' immunity from being sued in the federal courts. This is the so-called sovereign immunity doctrine, an ancient judge-made rule that rests on the notion that the divinely ordained sovereign (historically, a king or queen) could do no wrong, and therefore could not be sued for the very simple and logical reason that courts exist to right wrongs. *Dellmuth* concerned the Education of the Handicapped Act and the ability of parents of a handicapped child to obtain reimbursement for private school tuition pending the outcome of state administrative proceedings. The Court said the parents could obtain no relief in the federal courts. Notwithstanding this series of cases that Congress overturned, the Court

[12] This assumes, of course, that the court in question had authority to resolve the dispute in the first place. If, e.g., a court were to decide a matter for which a legislative or executive agency has ultimate responsibility, its decision lacks authority.

[13] *Price Waterhouse v. Hopkins*, 490 U.S. 228; *Finley v. United States*, 490 U.S. 545; *Ward's Cove Packing Co. v. Atonio*, 490 U.S. 642; *Martin v. Wilks*, 490 U.S. 755; *Lorance v. AT&T Technologies*, 490 U.S. 900; and *Patterson v. McLean Credit Union*, 491 U.S. 164.

For a more general discussion, see William N. Eskridge, Jr., "Overriding Supreme Court Statutory Interpretation Decisions," 101 *Yale Law Journal* 331 (1991).

[14] On the other hand, and also not uncommonly, the justices *invite* Congress to alter the Court's interpretation of its legislation. See, e.g., Rehnquist's concurrence, joined by Scalia and Kennedy, in *Ortiz v. Fibreboard Corp.*, 144 L Ed 2d 715 (1999), at 752.

[15] *Dellmuth v. Muth*, 491 U.S. 223 (1989).

[16] Eskridge, *op. cit.*, n. 13, *supra*, p. 410.

did not meekly accede – at least not where sovereign immunity is concerned.[17]

If action by Congress to undo the Court's interpretation of one of its laws does not subvert judicial authority, a fortiori neither does the passage of a constitutional amendment, for example, the Twenty-Sixth Amendment reducing the voting age to eighteen and thereby undoing the decision in *Oregon v. Mitchell*,[18] which held that Congress could not constitutionally lower the voting age in state elections. Furthermore, not only does a constitutional amendment not subvert judicial authority, courts themselves – ultimately, the Supreme Court – have the last word when determining the sanctioning amendment's meaning. Thus, the Court is free to construe any amendment – whether or not it overturns one of its decisions – as it sees fit, even though its construction deviates appreciably from the language or purpose of the amendment.

Consider, for example, the Fourteenth and Sixteenth Amendments. The former clearly overturned the Court's decision in *Scott v. Sandford*[19] and was meant to give blacks legal equality with whites. Scholars disagree about other objectives the amendment may have had, but it does appear that the prohibition of sex discrimination was not among them.[20] Nonetheless, in 1971 the Court held that the equal protection clause of the Fourteenth Amendment encompassed women.[21] As for the Sixteenth Amendment, it substantially, but not completely, reversed the Court's decisions in *Pollock v. Farmers' Loan and Trust Co.*, which declared unconstitutional the income tax that Congress had enacted in 1894.[22] In 1913, the requisite number of states ratified an amendment that authorized Congress to levy a tax on income "from whatever source derived." The language is unequivocal. Yet for the next twenty-six years the

[17] This discord between Court and Congress over sovereign immunity has not abated, but has rather intruded itself into other areas of litigation. Thus, e.g., in *United States v. Nordic Village*, 503 U.S. 30 (1992), the Court ruled that a corporate officer's use of funds purloined from his bankrupt employer to pay his federal taxes could not be recovered by the corporation's bankruptcy trustee, notwithstanding that the relevant federal statute rather clearly waives the sovereign immunity of the United States. In an uncharacteristically strident dissent, Justice Stevens, joined by Justice Blackmun, castigated the majority for its "love affair" with the "thoroughly discredited" doctrine, which the Court itself has noted is a "persistent threat to the impartial administration of justice." 503 U.S. at 42–43.

For a contextual discussion of sovereign immunity, see the section on sovereign immunity in this chapter.

[18] 400 U.S. 112 (1970). [19] 19 Howard 393 (1857).

[20] See *Bradwell v. State*, 16 Wallace 130 (1873). [21] *Reed v. Reed*, 404 U.S. 71 (1971).

[22] 157 U.S. 429 (1895) and 158 U.S. 601 (1895).

Supreme Court ruled that this language *excluded* the salaries of federal judges. Why the exclusion? Because Article III, section 1, of the original Constitution orders that judges' salaries "not be diminished during their continuance in office." Though it is an elementary legal principle that later language erases incompatible earlier language, the justices ruled that any taxation of their salaries, and those of their lower court colleagues, would obviously diminish them.[23] Finally, in 1939, the justices overruled their predecessors and magnanimously and unselfishly allowed themselves to be taxed.[24]

Judges as Policy Makers

The authoritative character of judicial decisions results because judges make policy. This statement may have once appeared heretical – as well as demeaning to judges – because it conflicts with the unsophisticated view that judges are objective, dispassionate, and impartial in their decision making. But the Warren Court's liberal activism, followed not long after by the Rehnquist Court's conservative activism (topped off by *Bush v. Gore*) certainly must have dampened the remaining remnants of such a notion. Actually, even the justices themselves recognize that they make policy, for example, "The majority's analysis . . . is motivated by its policy preferences."[25] Policy making is certainly not a subversive activity. It merely involves choosing among alternative courses of action, where the choice binds the behavior of those subject to the policy maker's authority. Phrased more succinctly, a policy maker authoritatively allocates resources.

Even so, judges are reluctant to admit the obvious. Consider *Gregory v. Ashcroft*,[26] which required the Court to directly answer the question of whether judges make policy. The Age Discrimination in Employment Act exempts appointed state court judges from its ban on mandatory

[23] See *Evans v. Gore*, 253 U.S. 245 (1920), and *Miles v. Graham*, 268 U.S. 501 (1925).

[24] *O'Malley v. Woodrough*, 307 U.S. 277 (1939). The subjection of federal judges "to a general tax . . . merely [recognizes] . . . that judges are also citizens, and that their particular function in government does not generate an immunity from sharing with their fellow citizens the material burden of the government whose Constitution and laws they are charged with administering." *Id.* at 282.

[25] *Gustafson v. Alloyd Co.*, 513 U.S. 561 (1995), at 27. The statement spanned the Court's ideological spectrum: written by the conservative Justice Thomas, and joined by his fellow conservative, Justice Scalia, as well as two who frequently dissociate themselves from them, Ginsburg and Breyer.

[26] 501 U.S. 452 (1991).

retirement, and the Court construed the relevant language – "appointees . . . 'on a policymaking level' " – to encompass judges. But not without considerable waffling. The majority noted that exemption requires judges only to function on a policy-making level, not that they "actually make policy." And though "[i]t is at least ambiguous whether a state judge is an 'appointee' on the policymaking level," nonetheless "we conclude that the petition[ing judges] fall presumptively under the policymaking exception."[27] Justices White and Stevens, concurring in the result, had no hesitance to call a spade a spade. Using Webster's definition of policy, they concluded by quoting the lower court whose decision the Supreme Court reviewed: "[E]ach judge, as a separate and independent judicial officer, is at the very top of his particular 'policymaking' chain, responding . . . only to a higher appellate court."[28]

Unfortunately, the justices further muddied matters in another case decided on the same day as *Gregory v. Ashcroft.* The issue was the retroactive application of a decision that declared unconstitutional a state statute that discriminatorily taxed liquor produced out of state.[29] The six-member majority required four opinions to state their varied positions, none of which commanded more than three votes.[30] Justice White continued the realistic thrust of his *Ashcroft* opinion by acerbically criticizing the opinion of Justice Scalia, which read:

> I am not so naive (nor do I think our forebears were) as to be unaware that judges in a real sense "make" law. But they make it *as judges make it*, which is to say *as though* they were "finding" it – discerning what the law *is*, rather than decreeing what it is today *changed to*, or what it will *tomorrow* be. Of course, this mode of action poses difficulties of a . . . practical sort . . . when courts decide to overrule prior precedent.[31] (emphasis in original)

White replied:

[27] *Id.* at 466, 467.

[28] *Id.* at 485. Justice Blackmun, whom Marshall joined, dissented, refusing to accept Webster's definition as authoritative: "I hesitate to classify judges as policymakers. . . . Although some part of a judge's task may be to fill in the interstices of legislative enactments, the *primary* task of a judicial officer is to apply rules reflecting the policy choices made by, or on behalf of, those elected to legislative and executive positions." At 487, n. 1. The dissent relied on the opinion of Judge Amalya Kearse of the Second Circuit, who flatly asserted, "The performance of traditional judicial functions is not policy making." Linda Greenhouse, "Justices to Hear Retirement Age Case," *New York Times*, November 27, 1990, p. A12. Judge Kearse's opinion, and one from the Eastern District of Virginia, are the only ones that held judges not to be policy makers. The majority of lower courts, holding to the contrary, are listed at 482, note 2.

[29] *Bacchus Imports Ltd v. Dias*, 468 U.S. 263 (1984).

[30] *James B. Beam Distilling Co. v. Georgia*, 501 U.S. 529 (1991).

[31] *Id.* at 549.

. . . even though the Justice is not naive enough (nor does he think the Framers were naive enough) to be unaware that judges in a real sense "make" law, he suggests that judges (in an unreal sense, I suppose) should never concede that they do and must claim that they do no more than discover it, hence suggesting that there are citizens who are naive enough to believe them.[32]

The foregoing evidence, such as it is, suggests that the fairy tale of a discretionless judiciary survives. Post–*Bush v. Gore* polls persistently indicate that the bulk of the public simply will not allow themselves to be confused by the fact of judicial policy making.

Although the typical judicial decision will only authoritatively allocate the limited resources at issue between the parties to a lawsuit, the resources allocated at appellate court levels commonly affect persons other than the litigants. Appellate courts support their decisions with opinions precisely because of their broader impact, so that persons who find themselves in similar situations may be apprized of the fate that may befall them if they engage in actions akin to those of the relevant litigant.

Do note, however, that trial court decisions may also have wide-ranging policy effects. Few cases are appealed; as a result, unappealed decisions become as authoritative as those of a supreme court. Multi-party litigation is becoming increasingly common. A class of thousands of human or legal persons may institute a single lawsuit, the decision in which binds all participants, for example, all taxpayers in the State of California, or all stockholders of General Motors. Organizations frequently sue or are sued as surrogates for their members, for example, the Sierra Club or the Teamsters Union. A lawsuit brought by or against the United States or a state or local government may have very broad and pervasive effects.

Courts make policy only on matters which they have authority to decide, that is, within their jurisdiction. The subjects of the jurisdiction of American courts range from the banal to matters of utmost societal importance. As an eminent Canadian jurist phrases it:

Reading through an American constitutional law text is like walking through modern human existence in an afternoon. From a woman's control of her own body to the Vietnam war and from desegregation of schools to drunken drivers, it is hard to imagine a facet of American existence that has not been subjected to constitutional scrutiny.[33]

[32] *Id.* at 546.

[33] Bertha Wilson, "The Making of a Constitution," 71 *Judicature* 334 (1988).

In the case of the Supreme Court, its jurisdiction has sufficient breadth to allow it to address novel issues: thus, the right to die and assisted suicide,[34] the internet transmission of patently offensive communications to minors,[35] the propriety of subjecting an incumbent President to civil damages litigation,[36] and the question of whether a city could restrict admission to certain dance halls to persons between fourteen and eighteen years of age.[37] On the other hand, the Court's jurisdiction does not preclude it from considering such trifling matters as the escheat to the tribe of fractional land allotments of deceased Indians. Thus,

> Tract 1305 is 40 acres and produces $1,080 in income annually. It is valued at $8,000. It has 439 owners, one-third of whom receive less than $0.05 in annual rent and two-thirds of whom receive less than $1. . . . The common denominator used to compute fractional interests in the property is 3,394,923,840,000. The smallest heir receives $0.01 every 177 years. If the tract were sold (assuming the 439 owners could agree) for its estimated $8,000 value, he would be entitled to $0.000418.[38]

Without dissent, the Court declared the Act of Congress decreeing escheat unconstitutional because it took property without the payment of just compensation. If a more trivial dispute ever produced a declaration of congressional unconstitutionality, we are unaware of it.

Consider also the matter of punitive damages. Since the founding of the Republic, tort – personal injury – law, with its concepts of due care, fault, and liability, has been the province of the states. Moreover, the law of torts is overwhelmingly judge-made (i.e., common-law) rather than legislatively enacted. Notwithstanding, the Supreme Court injected itself into the issue of punitive damages – albeit negatively – in *Browning-Ferris Industries v. Kelco Disposal*,[39] ruling that $6 million in punitive damages on top of a measly $51,000 in compensatory damages did not violate the excessive fines clause of the Eighth Amendment where government neither prosecuted the action nor received any share of the awarded damages. Two justices – Stevens and O'Connor – held to the contrary. Five years later, the justices ruled that Oregon's constitutional provision that denied its courts the authority to review jury verdicts for excessiveness violated the due process clause of the Fourteenth

[34] E.g., *Washington v. Glucksberg*, 521 U.S. 702 (1997), and *Vacco v. Quill*, 521 U.S. 793 (1997).

[35] *Reno v. ACLU*, 521 U.S. 844 (1997).

[36] *Clinton v. Jones*, 520 U.S. 681 (1997).

[37] *Dallas v. Stanglin*, 490 U.S. 19 (1989).

[38] *Hodel v. Irving*, 481 U.S. 704 (1987).

[39] 492 U.S. 257 (1989).

Amendment.[40] Finally, the Court directly addressed the constitutionality of a jury's award. An award of $2 million was granted to the purchaser of a $40,000 – new – car that had been repainted unbeknownst to the purchaser. Over the dissents of Ginsburg, Rehnquist, Scalia, and Thomas, the majority ruled the damages grossly excessive and thus in violation of due process.[41]

The jurisdiction that American courts have derives from the constitution that established them and/or from legislative enactments. Because judges' decisions adjudicate the legality of contested matters, judges of necessity make law. Even so, Americans find it unsettling to admit to judicial policy making because we have surrounded judicial decisions with a panoply of myth, the essence of which avers that judges and their decisions are objective, impartial, and dispassionate. In the language of Chief Justice John Marshall:

> Judicial power, as contradistinguished from the power of the laws, has no existence. Courts are the mere instruments of the law and can will nothing. When they are said to exercise a discretion, it is a mere legal discretion, a discretion to be exercised in discerning the course prescribed by law; and, when that is discerned, it is the duty of the court to follow it. Judicial power is never exercised for the purpose of giving effect to the will of the judge; always for the purpose of giving effect to the will of the legislature....[42]

Until *Bush v. Gore*, this statement had a thin veneer of plausibility. But since the decision awarding the presidency to Bush, everyone not totally disconnected from reality now recognizes that "Judges make law."[43] Everyone, that is, except judges.

Consider the language of Justice Scalia, whom many deem the most intelligent of today's justices:

> The very framing of the issue that we purport to decide today – whether our decision ... shall "apply" retroactively – presupposes a view of our decisions as *creating* the law, as opposed to *declaring* what the law already is. Such a view is contrary to that understanding of "the judicial Power," US Const, Art III, Sec. 1, cl 1, which is not only the common and traditional one, but which is the only one that can justify courts in denying force and effect to the unconstitutional enactments of duly elected legislatures.... To hold a governmental act to be

40 *Honda Motor Co. v. Oberg*, 512 U.S. 415 (1994). Justices Ginsburg and Rehnquist dissented.

41 *BMW v. Gore*, 517 U.S. 559 (1996).

42 *Osborn v. Bank of the United States*, 9 Wheaton 738 (1824), at 866.

43 Wilson, *op. cit.*, n. 33, *supra*, p. 334.

unconstitutional is not to announce that we forbid it, but that the *Constitution* forbids it. . . .[44]

Apparently, intelligence does not preclude self-deception. But perhaps we render too harsh a judgment. Scalia may simply believe a bit of "spin" should color an occasional opinion. Even so, Scalia's remarks are puzzling. If it is he and his colleagues in whom the Constitution speaks, and not vice-versa, how could he consistently assert a few paragraphs later in the same opinion that he might not adhere to what "the *Constitution* forbids"? Thus:

stare decisis – that is to say, a respect for the needs of stability in our legal system – would normally cause me to adhere to a decision of this Court already rendered as to the unconstitutionality of a particular type of state law.[45]

Note the use of the phrase "a decision of this Court." Scalia presumably distinguishes between "what the *Constitution* forbids" or commands and the Court's decisions. Some of the latter must contain only matters that a majority of lawmaking justices forbid or command. Scalia has provided no objective criteria for determining in which decisions the Constitution speaks and which merely voice the willful utterances of a biased majority. Perhaps those from which he dissents?

Relatedly, consider the Court's decision in *Printz v. United States*.[46] A better example of judicial doublespeak probably doesn't exist. Over the objections of four justices, the Court's five conservatives declared unconstitutional the highly publicized Brady Handgun Violence Prevention Act, which required local law enforcement authorities to conduct background checks on prospective handgun purchasers. Scalia wrote the Court's opinion. One may sensibly assume that when the Court declares congressional action unconstitutional, it will at least partially rest its decision on the document's language. Virtually always does it do so. Enhancing the probability of such an outcome are the words of the opinion's author who asserted – as quoted above – that to be legitimate such action must be forbidden by the Constitution, and not merely result from judicial fiat. Does the author practice what he preaches? Of course not. One searches the language of *Printz* in vain for reference to the constitutional language on which the opinion rests. Instead, the reader is instructed to fixate on the "structure of the Constitution" in order to divine "a principle" governing the case.[47] And – *voila!* – digging deeply,

[44] *American Trucking Assns. v. Smith*, 497 U.S. 167 (1990), at 291. Emphasis in original.
[45] *Id.* at 204. [46] 521 U.S. 848 (1997). [47] *Id.* at 934.

Scalia unearths what he calls "the very *principle* of separate state sovereignty."[48] We may call it S-cubed, created by a judicial activist piously masquerading as a devoted adherent of the words of the Constitution.

REASONS FOR JUDICIAL POLICY MAKING

Few nations empower its courts to resolve so broad a range of disputes as does the United States. Neither do most nations concede to their courts such authoritative decision making. Furthermore, in making their decisions, their courts do so with a minimum of interference from other governmental bodies or officials. That is not to say that Congress, the presidency, bureaucrats, state governments, or the public at large meekly accept whatever courts decree. Not at all. Sound and fury directed at a particular court – or at courts in general – frequently characterize political discourse. But the sound and fury typically signify nothing more than the alleviation of the frustration of adversely reacting segments of the body politic, as Congress's annual remonstrations about flag burning and school prayer clearly demonstrate.[49]

Why do American judges have such virtually untrammeled policy-making authority? Five interrelated factors provide an answer: fundamental law, distrust of governmental power, federalism, separation of powers, and judicial review. Because they are so closely interconnected, we cannot empirically judge their relative importance. Rather, they appear to function as so many parts of a seamless web.

Fundamental Law

The original English colonizers of New England brought with them the concept of a fundamental law: the idea that all human and governmental action should accord with the word of God or the strictures of nature as the leadership of the particular settlement decreed.[50] These individuals had left Europe because they were unwilling or unable to conform to the teachings of England's established church. Their arrival in America did not produce religious harmony. Much of the settlement of Rhode

[48] *Id.* at 943. [49] Eskridge, *op. cit.*, n. 13, *supra.*

[50] Kermit L. Hall, *The Magic Mirror: Law in American History* (New York: Oxford University Press, 1989), pp. 12–17, 24–27.

Island and Connecticut, for example, resulted from the expulsion of dissenters from Plymouth and Massachusetts Bay.

The overtly religious motivations that inspired the founding of new settlements was reflected in the charters and constitutions that their inhabitants devised. Although the theocratic parochialism of the early colonies, if not of specific towns and villages within each of them, had largely vanished by the beginning of the Revolutionary War, the notion of a fundamental law had not, but instead retained its vitality.[51]

The environment in which the colonists found themselves did not lend itself to the stabilizing influences of the Old World. Religious diversity flourished. Dissenters – with or without a theomanic preacher – merely had to move a few miles west to establish their own kindred community. The process of westward settlement produced marked social and economic turbulence, which continued throughout the nineteenth and into the twentieth century and persists still. The industrial and technological revolutions transformed a society of yeoman farmers and artisans into one of urban employees. Culturally, well before the Revolution, the original English settlers had been supplemented by substantial numbers from The Netherlands, Germany, Scotland, and Ireland, to say nothing of the forcible importation of African slaves. The cultural diversity that resulted became vastly more eclectic with the mass immigration of the latter half of the nineteenth and the early years of the twentieth centuries.

The changes in life style and status that these and associated forces have wrought preclude the establishment of a fixed and stable religious, social, economic, or cultural system. Indeed, Americans generally view change in these areas of human activity to be desirable, considering them synonymous with progress and freedom. Only in the political realm do we view drastic change as undesirable.

This schizoid orientation reflects the reality of American life. No one can function well in an unduly dynamic environment. To a substantial extent, human beings are creatures of habit. Economic misfortune, the unexpected breakup of personal relationships, and the demolition of cherished beliefs produce trauma. Life becomes frightening to those who find events in the saddle riding herd on them. But the political sphere appeared to be an arena amenable to stability. Consciously or otherwise, this was the goal that the Framers set for themselves when they gathered in Philadelphia in the summer of 1787: to transpose the

[51] See Edward S. Corwin, *The "Higher Law" Background of American Constitutional Law* (Ithaca: Cornell University Press, 1955).

religious notion of a fundamental law into a secular context, to enshrine the Constitution that they intended to create as a secular substitute for Holy Writ.

The fact that the Constitution has lasted longer than that of any other nation evidences the Framers' success. Its long life has added political stability to the distinguishing features of American life. Although a resurrected Framer might be appalled at the size of the governmental system he helped create, he most assuredly would recognize the workings of what he had wrought. Other societies may achieve stability through an established church, to which the citizenry pay at least pro forma obeisance, or through the hierarchical social control that a hereditary caste or group exercises. Alternatively, the economic system may prove unchanging, as in a nonindustrialized society where subsistence farming occupies all but a privileged elite. Or national boundaries may coincide with ethnic or tribal lines, insuring cultural homogeneity. In these environments, the political sphere provides the vehicle for change. Radical regime changes, bloody or otherwise, become commonplace. Not so in the United States. The Constitution and its system of government furnish us with our link to the invariant.

Distrust of Governmental Power

A second reason for judicial policy making inheres in our historic distrust of governmental power, especially that exercised from a central level. Like the concept of fundamental law, this factor also dates from the colonial era. Americans viewed British insistence that they defray the costs of the French and Indian War, which ended in 1763, as inimical to their rights and liberties. Opposition to these policies led to the onset of the Revolutionary War, which coincided with an internal struggle for control of the newly formed governments that the patriots (i.e., the non-Loyalists) established in each of the colonies. This internal struggle roughly pitted the socioeconomic elite, such as it was, against the rural yeomanry and urban artisans. It was continuing apace when the Framers convened in Philadelphia in 1787.

Unsettled economic conditions that persisted beyond the end of the Revolution severely strained the governmental capabilities of both the Continental Congress and the individual states. The Articles of Confederation, which took effect in 1781, made no provision for a chief executive or a federal judiciary; the Continental Congress had no power to levy taxes; nor could it exercise any of its limited powers over individuals; amendment of the Articles required unanimous approval of the thirteen state legislatures. A number of states yielded to debtor demands and printed large quantities of paper money that they issued as legal tender, while others enacted stay laws that extended the period of time during which debtors could legally pay their creditors. To protect their own interests, some states imposed tariffs and other trade barriers that inhibited the free flow of interstate commerce. Of the money that Congress requested to defray the costs of the Confederation and the Revolutionary War, the states paid so little that Congress could not meet the interest payments on the national debt.

Support for strengthening the governmental system came from a number of sources: leaders who believed that the power of a single state to prevent change endangered them all, merchants and shipowners concerned about commercial restrictions, frontiersmen threatened by Indian attacks, and veterans and members of the Continental Congress who had developed national loyalties. Of the fifty-five delegates to the Constitutional Convention, thirty-nine had served in Congress; at least thirty were veterans; eight had signed the Declaration of Independence; and all were experienced in the politics of their respective states.

They clearly recognized that any effort to replace the Articles of Confederation with a more capable government required the creation of a system that no single interest or "faction" (to use the word then in vogue) could control or dominate, one that – from the broadest standpoint – neither the "haves" nor the "have nots" could become master of. The governmental capability of the federal level had to be strengthened, whereas that of the states required diminution. The hoped-for result was a system in which neither level would do much governing. The federal government would be empowered to defend the Union, coin money, operate a postal system, regulate interstate commerce, and – needless to say – levy taxes. The states would be saddled with restrictions to prevent them from interfering with the responsibilities given to the federal level, as Article I, section 10, illustrates.

The federal government did not escape similar strictures. Section 9 of Article I, for example, contains eight clauses of "thou shalt nots" that specify things that Congress may not do.

In short, the Framers limited the powers of government in two distinctly different ways. First, they severely limited what government could do. Second, they specified in considerable detail the *way* in which government could exercise the powers that it did possess. Thus, Article III stipulates that persons accused of committing a federal crime, other than impeachment, be tried by a jury, and Article I, section 7, details the procedure whereby a bill becomes a law. The sum total of these substantive and procedural limitations on the exercise of power paradigmatically evidences the "constitutionalism" of the Constitution.[52]

The resulting system gained the support of the major elements of American society, though not without a sharp and hard-fought struggle. The lower socioeconomic echelons stood to benefit from limited government because they lacked experience in the affairs of state. Some had been deprived of the right to vote or hold public office because of property qualifications. Others, though entitled to vote and hold office, lacked the political seasoning of their more experienced neighbors. Their preference for states' rights and local self-government made them suspicious of what might become a strong and efficient centralized government. If not in their own experience, in that of their ancestors, government had been a vehicle of oppression and tyranny. For the many who lived along the frontier, the utility of a federal government was limited to an occasional band of cavalry to pacify unruly natives.

Nor were the landed gentry and mercantile interests necessarily opposed to a government invulnerable to any group's effective control. They chiefly feared loss of position on the socioeconomic ladder. As long as governmental power was not used against them, they sensibly assumed that they could perpetuate their position in society, given their education and wealth and the status that accompanied it.

Consequently, for self-interested reasons that varied from one group and interest to another, the Jeffersonian ideal that that government is best that governs least quickly became an article of faith for Americans generally. Subsequent developments insured its retention: The lure of the frontier and the opportunities it provided individuals to begin again, the immigrating refugees of the nineteenth and twentieth centuries for whom government was synonymous with tyranny and oppression, the Darwinian thesis of the survival of the fittest, the gospel of wealth, and rugged individualism all paid homage to the concept of limited government.

Federalism

In addition to rigorously circumscribing the powers of government, the Framers divided those that were provided between the national govern-

[52] For a classic treatment of constitutionalism, see Charles H. McIlwain, *Constitutionalism: Ancient and Modern*, rev. ed. (Ithaca: Cornell University Press, 1947).

ment and the states. For the most part, certain powers are delegated to the federal government, while others are reserved for the states. Some, however, are shared, such as the power to tax.

The constitutional language that pertains to this geographical division of power sorely lacks precision. As a result, the Supreme Court has confronted a constant stream of litigation that has required the justices to determine the relative power of the federal government vis-à-vis the states. The Court's first major case, *Chisholm v. Georgia*,[53] concerned federal-state relations. Constitutional language tilts resolution of these conflicts in favor of the federal government, for example, the supremacy clause (Article VI, section 2):

> This Constitution, and the laws of the United States which shall be made in pursuance thereof; and all treaties made, or which shall be made, under the authority of the United States, shall be the supreme law of the land; and the Judges in every State shall be bound thereby, anything in the Constitution or laws of any State to the contrary notwithstanding.

The resolution of federal-state conflicts also tilts in favor of the federal government because the Supreme Court has arrogated to itself the authority to ultimately decide these disputes. It did so early in the nineteenth century, in a pair of landmark decisions, *Martin v. Hunter's Lessee* and *Cohens v. Virginia*.[54]

But do not infer that resolution necessarily advantages Washington at the expense of the states. It does not, as we see below. The tilt results only because a federal entity – the Supreme Court – has the last word. The Court's decisions have caused the degree of centralization/decentralization to vary from one period to another. Indeed, during the late nineteenth and early twentieth centuries when the Court was writing the doctrines of laissez-faire economics into the Constitution, the justices rather even-handedly struck down antibusiness regulations regardless of the governmental level from which they emanated.

Apart from the operation of the justices' personal policy preferences, the limited jurisdiction of the federal courts and the separate constitutional existence of the state judicial systems have enabled the states to resist rather successfully a variety of centralizing tendencies. We address these matters in the next major section of this chapter, "The Federal and State Judicial Systems."

[53] 2 Dallas 419 (1793). [54] 1 Wheaton 304 (1816) and 6 Wheaton 264 (1821).

Separation of Powers

Separation of powers compartmentalizes government into three separate chambers, in the sense that each exercises powers distinct from the others and does so with its own personnel. The effect of this arrangement precludes any branch from compelling action by the other two. Instead, separation of powers institutionalizes conflict, particularly between Congress and President. To prevent one branch from overpowering another, each is provided with certain powers that functionally belong to one of the other branches. These are the so-called checks and balances. Thus, the President constitutionally possesses the legislative power to veto Congress's actions, while the Senate participates in the selection of executive officials through the constitutional requirement of advice and consent. Both check the courts: the President by nominating judges, and Congress by consenting to their selection (Senate only) and determining their number and jurisdiction. The courts, in turn, check the President and Congress through the power of judicial review, which we discuss below.[55]

The Framers were most concerned about the exercise of legislative power. To lessen their fears, they divided Congress into two separate chambers, the Senate and the House of Representatives, with the membership chosen from distinct constituencies (except for those states that have only a single representative) and with a different term of office. They required that a bill pass both houses with identical provisions, down to the last comma, before it could be sent to the President for signature or veto. The judiciary, by contrast, escaped relatively unscathed. The Framers did not view the courts as a threat to the constitutionalism they so carefully crafted.[56] They were more concerned lest the judges

[55] In exercising their power of judicial review, the Supreme Court and the lower federal courts primarily rest their decisions on constitutional provisions other than separation of powers. Once in a great while, however, the basis for decision is the language pertaining to separation of powers. It is used when the court in question views the action taken by the other branch as intruding on the realm of judicial power and responsibility. Thus, e.g., *Plaut v. Spendthrift Farm*, 514 U.S. 211 (1995), in which the Court voided an effort by Congress forcing the federal courts to retroactively reopen securities fraud cases that the courts had authoritatively resolved. Justice Scalia, reputedly deferential to the "democratic" branches of government, wrote the Court's opinion. Justices Stevens and Ginsburg dissented.

[56] Nonetheless, the courts sometimes get caught up in the crossfire resulting from the adolescent game of chicken that the President and Congress often play. Though it may strain credulity, their failure to resolve how the census in the year 2000 should be conducted

become subservient to either of the other branches. To insure the judiciary's independence, the Framers created a selection process that neither the President nor Congress could control, and provided judges with lifetime tenure and with no reduction in salary. But because both branches are involved – the President nominating candidates and the Senate deciding whether to confirm them or not – this divided responsibility encourages delay, especially when one party controls the Senate and the other the presidency.[57]

Separation of powers enables the Supreme Court to resolve authoritatively such justiciable disputes as pit Congress and the President against one another.[58] A politically charged example concerned the Gramm–Rudman Balanced Budget and Deficit Reduction Act of 1985. Congress assigned one of its own employees, the comptroller general, responsibility for determining the cuts needed to reduce the budget deficit. By a 7-to-2 vote, the Supreme Court declared the provision unconstitutional because a person removable by Congress was given the executive power to estimate, allocate, and order the spending cuts required to satisfy the deficit targeted by the law. The Court ruled that since Congress could remove the comptroller general from office, he was "subservient" to it.[59] The fact that Congress had never done so during the sixty-five years of the office's existence did not sway the majority from their deductively predetermined outcome.

Notwithstanding the publicity that attended this decision, the dispute turned on a trivial technicality. The Court did not void the fallback provision that allows the regular legislative process to effectuate the cuts;

almost forced the courts to shut down on June 15, 1999, because of a congressionally imposed budgetary deadline. The courts became involved because longstanding budget committee procedures fund the courts together with several executive branch departments, including the Department of Commerce, which includes the Census Bureau. Fortuitously, Congress passed an emergency supplemental appropriation which the President signed on May 21 that enabled him to fund the war then going on in Kosovo. Buried within it was a provision to continue funding the federal courts. See Thomas Baker, "Courts as Drive-By Victims," *National Law Journal*, June 21, 1999, p. A22.

57 Wendy L. Martinek, Mark Kemper, and Steven Van Winkle, "To Advise and Consent: The Senate and Lower Federal Court Nominations, 1997–1998," 62 *Journal of Politics* (2002) [forthcoming].

58 Many such disputes are "political questions." The plaintiff lacks standing to sue because the Court believes the matter, though within the courts' subject matter jurisdiction, should be resolved by the "political" branches of government themselves. We discuss this matter in the section on standing to sue in Chapter 5.

59 *Bowsher v. Synar*, 478 U.S. 714 (1986), at 727. The dissenters were White and Blackmun.

neither does the decision preclude Congress from merely repealing the provision that allows it to remove the comptroller, or from bestowing the comptroller's power on an official whom Congress can remove only through impeachment. Either of these options would make the official "executive" rather than "legislative." This arguably is a distinction without a difference.

No technicality marred the decision in *Clinton v. New York City*[60] in which the Court declared unconstitutional the line-item veto. Although Congress consciously gave the President authority to veto single spending items and specific tax breaks, thereby strengthening the presidency in its dealings with Congress, the Court said Congress could not do so, ruling that the President could veto only all of the provisions in a bill, not just some of them.

The creation of the judiciary as an independent coordinate branch of the government has appreciably promoted the policy-making capabilities of federal judges in general, and that of the Supreme Court in particular. Absent functional independence, the judges would likely be viewed – along with other government officials – as mere politicians and bureaucrats. Their efforts to distinguish themselves and their activities as principled, even-handed, and nonpartisan would likely be unsuccessful, with the result that the public would view them as on all fours with the persons of minimal competence and dubious ethics who engage in the dirty business of politics.

Judicial Review

The most striking evidence of judicial independence is a court's exercise of the power of judicial review. Although the power to declare an action of the other branches of government incompatible with the content of the fundamental law is nowhere specified in the Constitution, its exercise comports with the motivations and concerns that led to the drafting and ratification of the document.

First, if the Constitution is to be the fundamental law of the land, some body must be able to decide whether the actions of government conform to it. Such decisions may theoretically be made by Congress and/or the President. After all, they do take the same oath as federal judges to preserve, protect, and defend the Constitution of the United

[60] 141 L Ed 2d 393 (1998).

States. But the competition between Congress and President that separation of powers engenders may cause either of them to take a less than objective view of the constitutionality of their own conduct as opposed to that of the other branch. Unseemly squabbles would likely result. How much better to leave such decisions to the judges. Not only are they independent of the other branches, but their lifetime appointment also insulates them from factious electoral pressures.

Second, inasmuch as separation of powers ensures conflict between the executive and legislative branches, does it not make sense to position the judiciary, which, as we have seen, is beholden to neither of them, as the balance of power?

Third, given the federal system, a decision maker is also needed to authoritatively resolve disputes between the federal government and the states. The opacity of the constitutional provisions governing their relationship magnifies the need for such an "umpire." To allow the "political" branches of the federal government or the states themselves to resolve such disputes would unduly centralize or decentralize governmental authority depending on which level makes the decisions.

The Enunciation of the Doctrine of Judicial Review

John Marshall, newly ensconced as chief justice, seized the opportunity that the case of *Marbury v. Madison*[61] presented and formally enunciated the doctrine of judicial review. In the closing days of John Adams's administration, the Federalist-controlled Congress passed an act that provided for forty-two new judges. Adams quickly nominated ardent Federalists to these positions, and on March 3, 1801, the last day of the Adams administration and the last day of the lame-duck holdover Congress, the Senate approved the nominations. The appointments would have legal effect when each nominee received a sealed commission of office from Secretary of State John Marshall, who was then serving in that position as well as chief justice.

Not all the commissions were delivered by the appointed hour of midnight. Jefferson's Secretary of State, James Madison, refused to deliver the remainder. William Marbury, one of the nonrecipients, went directly to the Supreme Court and requested a writ of mandamus that would order Madison to deliver him his commission. Marbury argued that the Judiciary Act of 1789 gave the Supreme Court original jurisdiction to issue such writs.

[61] 1 Cranch 137 (1803).

In the political context of the time, Marshall and Jefferson were bitter rivals. The crushing Federalist defeat in the election of 1800 gave Jefferson the upper hand. Marshall realistically feared impeachment. Hence, his need to behave strategically. Given his druthers, he would have awarded Marbury his commission, in addition to voiding the provision of the Judiciary Act of 1789.[62]

Marshall, speaking for a unanimous Court, ruled that Marbury had a right to the commission, but the Court had no power to order its delivery. Section 13 of the Judiciary Act, which purportedly expanded the Court's original jurisdiction, was unconstitutional because the Constitution specifies the Court's original jurisdiction, with all other matters being heard only on appeal. The issuance of writs of mandamus does not appear among the listed subjects of original jurisdiction. By expanding the Court's original jurisdiction, the Judiciary Act violated the Constitution.

Given this decision, it appeared that the judicial branch was not the enemy the Jeffersonians thought it to be. Arguably, Jefferson himself did not view judicial review all that disapprovingly. Moreover, the *Marbury* decision provided no inkling of the impact judicial review would have on subsequent events.

According to elementary canons of judicial ethics, Marshall, as the individual responsible for the controversy that gave rise to the lawsuit, should have recused himself.[63] Marshall, however, realized that no better opportunity to formulate judicial review would occur.[64] The case, aptly described as a "trivial squabble over a few petty political plums,"[65] should never have been decided by the Supreme Court in the

[62] Jack Knight and Lee Epstein, "On the Struggle for Judicial Supremacy," 30 *Law and Society Review* 87 (1996).

[63] Special Committee on Standards of Judicial Conduct, "Code of Judicial Conduct," in *Code of Professional Responsibility and Code of Judicial Conduct* (Chicago: American Bar Assn., 1978), pp. 62, 63.

[64] Marshall theoretically could have declared the Jeffersonian Act that reduced the size of the federal judiciary and increased its tasks unconstitutional, instead of upholding it, in *Stuart v. Laird*, 1 Cranch 299 (1803). But that would have been tactically most unwise. Knight and Epstein, *op. cit.*, fn. 62, *supra*, pp. 111–12. Subsequent events proved Marshall correct. Not until 54 years later, in *Scott v. Sandford*, 19 Howard 393 (1857), did the Court declare another act of Congress unconstitutional. Unlike *Marbury v. Madison*, the decision in that case, which led directly to the Civil War, hardly conduced to the continued vitality of judicial review.

[65] John A. Garraty, "The Case of the Missing Commissions," in John A. Garraty, ed., *Quarrels That Have Shaped the Constitution* (New York: Harper and Row, 1964), p. 13.

first place. As Marshall's opinion makes clear, in bringing his case to the Supreme Court, Marbury entered the wrong forum and should merely have been directed to the appropriate federal district court. Marshall, however, did not allow either legal or ethical niceties to deprive him of his opportunity.

Marshall held that any action by Congress to expand the Court's original jurisdiction to include subjects not specified in the Constitution was unconstitutional.[66] The fact that the First Congress enacted the Judiciary Act of 1789 and that a disproportionate number of its members had been delegates to the Constitutional Convention – Marshall, significantly, not among them – did not give Marshall pause. Clearly, if any group of persons knew the meaning and intention of the Constitution's provisions, it was the members of the First Congress. Furthermore, the provision of the Judiciary Act declared unconstitutional was authored by Oliver Ellsworth, Marshall's predecessor as chief justice. The irony of a chief justice of the United States, a member of the First Congress, and a delegate to the Constitutional Convention violating his oath of office by writing a statute that contravened the fundamental law of which he was also an author apparently did not strike Marshall as at all peculiar, notwithstanding that Ellsworth, like Marshall, was a dyed-in-the-wool Federalist.

Even more mind-boggling is the fact that nothing in the language of the statute – section 13 of the Judiciary Act of 1789 – even remotely suggests an expansion of the Supreme Court's original jurisdiction! After listing the cases in which the Supreme Court might exercise original jurisdiction, the statute catalogs the matters over which the Court has appellate jurisdiction:

> The supreme court shall also have appellate jurisdiction from the circuit courts and the courts of the several states, in the cases herein after specially provided for. And shall have power to issue writs of prohibition to the district courts when proceeding as courts of admiralty and maritime jurisdiction; and writs of MANDAMUS, in cases warranted by the principles and usages of law, to any courts appointed, or persons holding office, under the authority of the United States.

[66] Significantly, Marshall's decision did not require executive action for its enforcement. Furthermore, he ruled against a member of his own political party. Madison and the Jeffersonians won the battle (although not the war, as history has shown). From the perspective of the average citizen, what better evidence of the objectivity and impartiality of judicial decision making!

This is the only language that concerns Marbury's case. Marshall clearly had absolutely nothing to declare unconstitutional![67] He simply formulated the doctrine of judicial review without applying it to any specific statutory language. As further evidence of this fact, nowhere in *Marbury v. Madison* does Marshall quote the foregoing language. This may well be the only case in the Court's Reports in which the prevailing opinion does not cite the language declared unconstitutional. The only reference to the provision antecedes Marshall's opinion of the Court where the Reporter, William Cranch, in recording the testimony of the witnesses and the arguments of the attorneys, notes that Marbury's attorney, Charles Lee, made mention of it.[68]

In the course of his opinion, Marshall tenders a view of judicial competence and integrity in which he presents arguments and makes assertions that humiliate and debase the other branches. These assertions, the reader should note, are ones that Americans have unquestioningly come to accept. Thus,

> It is a proposition too plain to be contested, that the constitution controls any legislative act repugnant to it; or, that the legislature may alter the constitution by an ordinary act.[69]

Of course. The statement is logically impeccable. But consider the implications: that Congress, aided if not necessarily abetted by the President, is fully capable of acting unconstitutionally. Query: Why do we not make the same presumption about the justices themselves?

Marshall returns to the foregoing argument when he writes that those who controvert the principle that the Constitution is the fundamental law

> must close their eyes on the constitution, and see only the law.
>
> This doctrine would subvert the very foundation of all written constitutions. . . . It would declare that if the legislature shall do that which is expressly forbidden, such act, notwithstanding the express prohibition, is effectual.[70]

Again, this is an indisputable proposition. But again consider the implication: Marshall assumes that Congress would consciously and deliber-

[67] In support of our assertion, see Charles Warren, *The Supreme Court in United States History* (Boston: Little, Brown, 1922), I, 242, and William W. Van Alstyne, "A Critical Guide to Marbury v. Madison," 1969 *Duke Law Journal* 1, at 15.

[68] 1 Cranch 137, at 148. Marshall's opinion begins at the end of p. 153.

[69] *Id.* at 177. [70] *Id.* at 178.

ately behave unconstitutionally, even though, as we have seen, Congress did nothing of the sort here. If we couple this fact with Marshall's deviousness and his dubious ethics, can we say the same of the Court? Might it not be as appropriate, if not more so, to consider the possibility that the justices might void a constitutional law or uphold an unconstitutional one, or intrude themselves into matters in which they precedentially had no business, for example, *Bush v. Gore*?[71]

In a final argument, Marshall lays logic aside and, with an indignant flourish, rhetorically poses the ethical question:

> Why otherwise does it [the Constitution] direct the judges to take an oath to support it? This oath certainly applies in an especial manner, to their conduct in their official character. How immoral to impose it on them, if they were to be used as the instruments, and the knowing instruments, for violating what they swear to support! . . .
>
> Why does a judge swear to discharge his duties agreeably to the constitution of the United States, if that constitution forms no rule for his government?[72]

The fact that all federal officials take the same oath gave Marshall no more pause than it gives us today. What is sauce for the goose is NOT sauce for the gander. Only politicians betray their oaths of office, not judges. If the doctrine of judicial review did not congruently fit the Framers' concept of fundamental law and their – and our – distrust of elected officials, would we not direct the logic and implications of Marshall's reasoning – to say nothing of his behavior here – against the Court itself?

[71] By adhering to its self-created political question doctrine, first applied in the 1849 case of *Luther v. Borden*, 7 Howard 1, which states that the Court will not decide matters more appropriate for resolution by the states or the other branches of the federal government. See the section on legal requirements for getting into court in Chapter 6. One would be hard put to find in the Court's annals a more extreme example of chutzpah insultingly denigrating of readers' intelligence than the closing paragraph of the per curiam opinion of the Rehnquist Five:

> None are more conscious of the vital limits on judicial authority than are the members of this Court, and none stand more in admiration of the Constitution's design to leave the selection of the President to the people, through their legislatures, and to the political sphere. When contending parties invoke the process of the courts, however, it becomes our unsought responsibility to resolve the federal and constitutional issues the judicial system has been forced to confront.

148 L Ed 2d 388 (2000), at 402.

[72] *Op. cit.*, n. 68, *supra*, at 179.

The Mythology of Judging

Given our acceptance of judicial supremacy as evidenced by the doctrine of judicial review and the other reasons supporting authoritative judicial and Supreme Court policy making, why do we find it necessary to surround courts and judges with myth? Assertions that judicial decisions are objectively dispassionate and impartial are obviously belied by the fact that different courts and different judges do not decide the same question or issue the same way, to say nothing of the fact that appellate court decisions – particularly, those of the United States Supreme Court – typically contain dissenting votes. So, too, a single personnel change may fundamentally alter the course of constitutional law.

Insofar as judicial and Supreme Court policy making are concerned, mythology basically exists because judges play God with regard to the life, liberty, and property of those who appear before them. No matter the issue – trivial or earthshaking – the final decision rests with a court. But mere mortals ought not engage in autotheistic activity. And so mythology is born. Judges are said not to have discretion in the matter of principles;[73] they do not announce their decisions; it is, rather, the law or the Constitution speaking through them that dictates the outcome. If any policy results, fundamental law and governmental actions compatible therewith have mandated it, not the judge. Judges, therefore, are objective, dispassionate, and impartial. To ensure that facts do not becloud the myth, we adopt an ostrich posture.

To support the mythology, devices have been created to inculcate respect and reverence for judges. Secrecy and mystery shroud the decision-making process. Thus, we garb judges in distinctive dress. And although society attires some governmental personnel other than judges characteristically – the military, police, and some postal workers – none wears a black robe, the most solemn and mysterious of outfits. Courthouses and courtrooms replicate churches and temples. Instead of altars, they contain elevated benches to which all who enter must look *up*. The proceedings are ritualized, accompanied by pomp and ceremony, and conducted (at least before the decline of legalistic jargon) in a language largely unintelligible to laypersons. The religious imagery evoked in Chief Justice Taft's statements about the utility of the judicial robe typify the matter:

[73] See, e.g., Ronald Dworkin, *Taking Rights Seriously* (Cambridge, Mass.: Harvard University Press, 1988), p. 47.

It is well that judges should be clothed in robes, not only, that those who witness the administration of justice should be properly advised that the function performed is one different from, and higher than, that which a man discharges as a citizen in the ordinary walks of life; but also, in order to impress the judge himself with the constant consciousness that he is a high priest of the temple of justice and is surrounded with obligations of a sacred character that he cannot escape. . . .[74]

Hence the dominance of the judiciary. Governmental affairs become judicial affairs in the sense that their outcome often depends on a court's decision, most authoritatively those of the United States Supreme Court. Aided and abetted by a mythology that blunts criticism and insulates them from the hue and cry, judges blithely do their thing, obligated to none but themselves. As enigmatic technicians, as so many Delphic oracles, they objectively dispense revealed truth and wisdom. As one astute commentator irreverently observed:

Like oysters in our cloisters we avoid the storm and strife.
Some President appoints us, and we're put away for life.
When Congress passes laws that lack historical foundation,
We hasten from a huddle and reverse the legislation.
The sainted Constitution, that great document for students,
Provides an airtight alibi for all our jurisprudence.
So don't blame us if now and then we seem to act like bounders;
Blame Hamilton and Franklin and the patriotic founders.[75]

THE FEDERAL AND STATE JUDICIAL SYSTEMS

As a result of federalism, the United States has two separate and autonomous court systems: those of the states and that of the federal government. The subject-matter jurisdiction of the federal courts is limited to "federal questions" – those whose resolution depends on a provision of the Constitution, an act of Congress, or a treaty of the United States[76] – and cases that arise under "diversity of citizenship" –

[74] William Howard Taft, *Present Day Problems* (New York: Dodd, Mead, 1908), pp. 63–64. Judge Jerome Frank candidly and incisively critiqued the symbolism surrounding judicial decision making as "the cult of the robe" in his classic *Courts on Trial* (New York: Atheneum, 1963), pp. 254–61.

[75] Arthur Lippmann, "Song of the Supreme Court," *Life Magazine*, August 1935, p. 7.

[76] The Constitution also gives the Supreme Court jurisdiction "to controversies between two or more States" and "to all cases affecting ambassadors, other public ministers and consuls." Such disputes need not concern any constitutional provision or federal statute or treaty. They rarely occur, however, and when they do they take on the character of a local or purely private dispute, not one of broad public policy significance.

those that do not contain a federal question, but which may yet be heard in a federal court if the parties are residents of different states. By contrast, the jurisdiction of the state courts covers a much wider range of subjects. This results in concurrent state court jurisdiction over many matters that are also appropriate for resolution by the federal courts. The opposite situation, however, does not obtain: the federal courts do not have concurrent jurisdiction with the state courts over matters that do not contain a federal question or involve diversity of citizenship.[77] In other words, the federal courts lack exclusive jurisdiction, except over such peculiarly federal matters as admiralty and maritime cases and federal crimes, with the result that plaintiffs commonly have a choice of forums in which to bring their cases.[78]

To apportion jurisdictional responsibility between itself and the lower federal courts on the one hand, and the state courts on the other, the Supreme Court utilizes three constitutional provisions – the supremacy clause, the Eleventh Amendment's doctrine of sovereign immunity, and the full faith and credit clause – plus three policies of its own design – comity, an adequate and independent state ground for decision, and the rules governing choice of law. A discussion of each follows.

National Supremacy

The existence of concurrent jurisdiction produces conflict. This conflict typically pits the Supreme Court against the courts of the various states.

[77] Minor exceptions exist. The federal courts may constitutionally exercise "supplementary jurisdiction"; i.e., ancillary and pendent jurisdiction. See the Judicial Improvements Act of 1990, 28 *U.S. Code* 1367. If a jurisdictionally sufficient claim exists, either party, as well as third parties, may join with that jurisdictionally sufficient claim other jurisdictionally *in*sufficient claims that any of them may have if these additional claims "derive from a common nucleus of operative fact." *United Mine Workers v. Gibbs*, 383 U.S. 715 (1966), at 725. If the federal trial court finds that this condition exists, the multiple claims will be joined with the others and the entire dispute decided. This policy lessens piecemeal litigation and promotes judicial economy.

Pendent jurisdiction involves joining state law claims to a jurisdictionally sufficient federal question, whereas ancillary jurisdiction involves joining claims of persons other than the original plaintiff to the lawsuit, e.g., the respondent's counterclaim or those of a third party who alleges an interest in the property that the lawsuit concerns.

Chapter 6 contains a more detailed description of ancillary and pendent jurisdiction as part of our discussion of the jurisdiction of the federal courts.

[78] This does not mean that when the federal or state or local governments initiate litigation they cross jurisdictional lines to do so. Neither federal nor local prosecutors, for example, have authority to file charges in any court other than those of which they are officers.

To resolve these conflicts, the Framers provided for the supremacy of federal law, but did not say who shall decide such cases. The First Congress eliminated this omission and, in the famous section 25 of the Judiciary Act of 1789, authorized the Supreme Court to review state court decisions that involved a federal question.

Except for the Supreme Court and its original jurisdiction,[79] Congress creates the lower federal courts and determines – within the subject matter specified in Article III, section 2, clause 1 – which courts may decide what sorts of cases. In authorizing the Supreme Court to review state court decisions that contained a federal question, Congress withheld Supreme Court review until the losing litigant had exhausted all remedies under state law, typically, a final judgment[80] by the state supreme court.

This jurisdictional grant, however, did not settle matters. Congress had not seen fit to provide the federal trial courts with jurisdiction to hear federal questions, preferring to leave such matters to the state courts. Not until after the Civil War did Congress invest the federal courts with first instance federal question jurisdiction. As a result, such cases were heard in the state courts. State court judges did not take kindly to Supreme Court review of their decisions, alleging that though they were bound by the supremacy clause, they were not obliged to adhere to the Supreme Court's interpretation of the Constitution, acts of Congress, or treaties of the United States. They asserted that to be so bound would materially impair state sovereignty and the independence of state courts.

In what is arguably the most important decision it has ever made, *Martin v. Hunter's Lessee*, the Supreme Court unequivocally rejected the states' contentions:

> Judges of equal learning and integrity, in different states, might differently interpret a statute, or a treaty of the United States, or even the constitution itself. If there were no revising authority to control these jarring and discordant judgments, and harmonize them into uniformity, the laws, the treaties, the constitution of the United States would be different in different states, and might, perhaps, never have . . . the same construction, obligation, or efficacy, in any two states. The public mischiefs that would attend such a state of things would be

[79] "In all cases affecting ambassadors, other public ministers and consuls, and those in which a State shall be party, the Supreme Court shall have original jurisdiction." Article III, section 2, clause 2.

[80] A "final judgment" typically means any decree or order from which an appeal lies. See, e.g., Rule 54(a) of the Federal Rules of Civil Procedure.

truly deplorable . . . the appellate jurisdiction must continue to be the only adequate remedy for such evils.[81]

Precisely. Without such power, each provision of the Constitution, every act of Congress, and treaty would have a different meaning in each of the fifty states. The United States would be no more united than the United Nations. Each state would be as sovereign as any petty principality or third world polity. What constitutes taxable income, the status of women and minors, the meaning of due process and equal protection, the scope and applicability of the First Amendment, the reasonableness of searches and seizures, whether the Constitution recognizes any kind of right to privacy would vary from state to state as each of fifty autonomous state supreme courts decreed.

Note further that this link, this bit of glue, that binds the fifty states into a single entity couples together only the courts at the top of each hierarchy: the state and federal supreme courts. And note that the 176 operative words in section 25 of the Judiciary Act of 1789 emanate from Congress, and what Congress grants, Congress may revoke. Indeed, until well after the Civil War, bills were regularly introduced to do just that.[82]

The federal courts use the writ of habeas corpus sparingly. Although the Warren Court had opened this door rather widely in the mid-1960s in decisions such as *Dombrowski v. Pfister*,[83] in which a civil rights organization enjoined state officials from prosecuting it under the state's subversive activities statutes, the Burger Court substantially closed it by the early 1980s.[84]

[81] 1 Wheaton 304 (1816), at 348.

[82] To be completely accurate, we should also note the existence of an alternative link between the federal and state court systems, which dates from 1867: the use of the writ of habeas corpus. *United States Code*, Sections 2241–55. Persons convicted of crime under state law who allege that their convictions violate the federal Constitution may petition the federal district court where they are incarcerated to review their state court convictions. To do so, convicts must have complied with the state's contemporaneous objection rule, which requires them to raise their federal question at the time the evidence is introduced. If the state court fails to give full and fair consideration to their federal question, they may petition the federal district court in the locale where the state court sits for a writ of habeas corpus once they have exhausted their appeals under state law.

[83] 380 U.S. 479 (1965).

[84] See, e.g., *Stone v. Powell*, 428 U.S. 465 (1976); *Engle v. Isaac*, 456 U.S. 107 (1982); *United States v. Frady*, 456 U.S. 152 (1982). The Rehnquist Court barred it further in *McCleskey v. Zant*, 481 U.S. 279 (1991), a ruling that essentially limited state prisoners to a single habeas petition, and in *Coleman v. Thompson*, 501 U.S. 722 (1991), which held that state prisoners' failure to comply with the state's procedural requirements forfeits their right to bring a habeas petition in federal court.

The System of Comity

The decision in *Martin v. Hunter's Lessee*, discussed above, did not make the state courts superfluous to the resolution of federal questions for two reasons. First, the Supreme Court accepts review of an exceptionally small proportion of state court decisions, whether or not they arise on writ of habeas corpus. Rejected cases, as well as those that the Supreme Court affirms, become the law at least in the state of the court that decided the matter.[85] Second, mindful of the tender sensibilities of the states and their judges (whose sensibilities are markedly less pronounced than they were prior to the Civil War), the Supreme Court has devised a system of comity for the purpose of minimizing conflict between the two judicial systems.

The vehicle whereby the Court implements comity is the abstention doctrine, "whereby the federal courts 'exercising a wise discretion,' restrain their authority because of 'scrupulous regard for the rightful independence of the state governments' and for the smooth working of the federal judiciary."[86] Thus, the abstention doctrine requires the federal courts to avoid intruding themselves into ongoing state judicial proceedings or otherwise duplicating litigation already begun in a state court. Exceptions are narrowly confined. State proceedings may be enjoined on a showing of "irreparable injury" that is "both great and immediate."[87] A plaintiff is not likely to meet this standard in other than extreme cases of bad faith prosecution or official harassment. Efforts to remove a state-initiated case from a state to a federal court are governed by equally stringent criteria.[88]

Normally, once state proceedings have commenced, litigants must almost always avail themselves of and exhaust the state's administrative and judicial remedies before they take their federal questions into a federal court. Accordingly, determination of the constitutionality of state laws and regulations rests initially with the state courts themselves. If the state courts resolve the federal questions their cases contain compatibly with federal law, the basis for Supreme Court review disappears.

85 The Supreme Court, of course, is not precluded from hearing and deciding the same issue if and when a subsequent case is properly brought to its attention.
86 *Railroad Commission of Texas v. Pullman Co.*, 312 U.S. 496 (1941), at 501.
87 *Younger v. Harris*, 401 U.S. 37 (1971), at 46.
88 E.g., *Johnson v. Mississippi*, 421 U.S. 213 (1975); *Arizona v. Manypenny*, 451 U.S. 232 (1981).

But do recognize that the federal component of cases that begin in the state courts is typically only one of a number of legal questions that the case contains. Federal jurisdiction extends only to the federal question; state law governs the others. Hence, if the Supreme Court does overturn the state court's ruling on a federal question, almost always will the Supreme Court remand the case for further state court proceedings. The reason is that state law, rather than the federal question, may determine the outcome of the case. A classic example occurred in *Williams v. Georgia*.[89] The state convicted a black man of murder. On petition to the Supreme Court, the justices ruled that Georgia had used an unconstitutional method of selecting jurors, one that racially identified potential jurors before they were chosen, thus insuring that only whites were seated. Following remand, the Georgia Supreme Court unanimously reaffirmed its original decision, holding that the state's contemporaneous objection rule required litigants to object to courtroom action at the point in the proceedings at which it occurs. Williams's attorney had failed to do so. The U.S. Supreme Court rebuffed a petition for further review. Though the justices provided no explanation, the reason is clear: Contemporary objection rules work no discrimination; as a result, their operation involves no federal question. The upshot: Williams was duly electrocuted.

Apart from the deference that comity pays to the state courts, abstention also impedes prompt federal court protection of federal rights. According to Justice Douglas, who opposed abstention more than any of his colleagues, "We do a great disservice when we send . . . tired and exhausted litigants into the desert in search of this Holy Grail that is already in the keeping of the federal court."[90]

Sovereign Immunity

Until the onset of the Rehnquist Court in 1986, the doctrine of sovereign immunity had far less effect on the relationships between the state and federal courts than the system of comity and the abstention doctrine. Since then, however, the Court has used the doctrine to appreciably expand the range of authoritative state court policy making.

Sovereign immunity, the immunity from liability that government has for its actions, has its genesis as an ancient English concept that pre-

[89] 349 U.S. 375 (1955).

[90] *Harris County Commissioners Court v. Moore*, 420 U.S. 77 (1975), at 91.

cluded citizens from suing the king or queen because no one had power to enforce any judgment against them. In reaction to the Court's 1793 decision in *Chisholm v. Georgia*, discussed above, allowing nonresidents to sue a state in the federal courts, Congress proposed and the states ratified the Eleventh Amendment in 1798, which decreed: "The judicial power of the United States shall not be construed to extend to any suit in law or equity, commenced or prosecuted against one of the United States by citizens of another State, or by citizens or subjects of any foreign State."[91] Note that the explicit prohibition on suits from those outside the state would almost certainly appear to allow suits from a state's own citizens.

In 1908, the Court sensibly construed the amendment compatibly with the supremacy clause. Citizens could sue state officials for money damages for injury inflicted on them, although not sue the state itself.[92] Accordingly, immunity applied only to the states as states, not to local governments or to officials of either state or local governments. Thus, the central purpose of the amendment – protection of the state's money – remained safe from confiscation.

Note, however, that where the states *qua* states are concerned, appellate jurisdiction does exist notwithstanding that the "case began in state court as a suit brought against one State . . . by citizens of another," and though "in hearing this case, [a federal court] would be exercising the 'Judicial power of the United States,'" and though the State "has not waived its right to object to the exercise of that power," the justices nonetheless "unanimously h[o]ld that the 'Eleventh Amendment does not constrain the appellate jurisdiction of the Supreme Court over cases arising from state courts.'"[93] Why? Because "when a state court takes cognizance of a case, the State assents to appellate review by this [Supreme] court of the federal issues raised in the case 'whoever may be the parties to the original suit, whether private persons, or the state itself.'"[94]

[91] Do note, however, that though the federal government does not have immunity under the Eleventh Amendment, it does have common law sovereign immunity as decreed by the Supreme Court. The scope and criteria governing the federal government's immunity are essentially the same as that governing the states. See *Department of the Army v. Blue Fox*, 142 L Ed 2d 718 (1999), and *West v. Gibson*, 144 L Ed 2d 196 (1999).

[92] *Ex parte Young*, 209 U.S. 123.

[93] *South Central Bell v. Alabama*, 143 L Ed 2d 258 (1999), at 265, quoting from *McKesson Corp. v. Florida Division of Alcoholic Beverages and Tobacco*, 496 U.S. 18 (1990), at 31.

[94] *Id.*

In 1964, the Warren Court ruled that if a state intruded into a sphere of federal regulation – for example, intellectual property – they subjected themselves to federal liability, including money damages.[95] The Burger Court complemented this ruling by holding that the Fourteenth Amendment permits Congress to impose money damages on states who deprive persons of their civil rights.[96] Subsequently, the Burger Court required Congress to provide an "express statement" of its intent to abrogate sovereign immunity.[97]

But then the Rehnquist Court turned the constitutional worm. It not only resurrected a disputed 1890 decision holding that the amendment applies to suits by a state's own citizens, it further ruled that Congress cannot use its Article 1 power to abrogate state immunity because the Eleventh Amendment postdates the provisions of the original Constitution and because the Article I (section 8) powers do not limit the states.[98] The Fourteenth Amendment, however, empowers Congress to protect civil rights against state action and does postdate the Eleventh Amendment. No problem, decreed the Court. It read into the pertinent constitutional language the words "remedial" and "proportionate." Only federal legislation imposing remedies proportionate to a documented pattern of state violations may be enacted.[99]

Three decisions handed down at the end of the 1998 term that declared two federal laws unconstitutional and explicitly overruled one precedent and silently voided another illustrate the extent to which federal supremacy has become federal descendency. States are immune to suits by their own employees for violations of federal labor law, by patent owners for infringement by states and their instrumentalities – for example, state universities – and by businesses injured by unfair competition.[100] Accordingly, if a state wrongs somebody, resident or not,

[95] *Parden v. Terminal R. Co.*, 377 U.S. 184. The Rehnquist Five overruled this decision as part of its states' rights crusade in *College Savings Bank v. Florida Prepaid*, 144 L Ed 2d 605 (1999).

[96] *Fitzpatrick v. Bitzer*, 427 U.S. 445 (1976).

[97] *Atascadero State Hospital v. Scanlon*, 473 U.S. 234 (1984).

[98] *Seminole Tribe v. Florida*, 517 U.S. 44 (1996). See also *Hans v. Louisiana*, 134 U.S. 1 (1890).

[99] *City of Boerne v. Flores*, 521 U.S. 507 (1997).

[100] *Florida Prepaid v. College Savings Bank*, 144 L Ed 2d 575 (1999); *College Savings Bank v. Florida Prepaid*, 144 L Ed 2d 605 (1999); and *Alden v. Maine*, 144 L Ed 2d 636 (1999). It will be interesting to observe whether Congress will repass the voided legislation in altered form so as to gain the approval of the nay-saying Rehnquist Five. If Congress does so, it will lessen the bizarre result of these decisions. The majority did

no remedy may right that wrong according to Justices Rehnquist, O' Connor, Scalia, Kennedy, and Thomas unless the state willingly submits to suit. Not only may a state not be sued in federal court, neither may it be sued in its own courts. As a result, a state laboratory may copy a patented product and peddle it to whomever it wishes, and the patent owner has no redress against the state for infringement. Similarly, a state university may reproduce a copyrighted textbook, sell it to students, and pay the author nothing.[101]

How is this possible, given that the Constitution expressly authorizes Congress, not the states, to regulate patents and copyrights? According to the Rehnquist Five: Because royal English immunity fundamentally applies in an immutable fashion to the principle of federalism, a principle moreover that the structure of the Constitution embodies. The legacy of John C. Calhoun apparently remains alive and well, even though the only one of the five with a Southern origin is Clarence Thomas.

The Court wreaked further carnage on federal authority in *Board of Trustees v. Garrett* by declaring unconstitutional provisions in the Americans with Disabilities Act that allowed state and local employees to sue their states for failure to comply with the act's provisions.[102] The vote, needless to say, pitted the Rehnquist Five against the others. But the majority did not merely expand state immunity further, it also constricted congressional authority by requiring it to convincingly prove that states themselves engaged in patterns of deliberate unconstitutional discrimination. Justice Breyer, in an acerbic dissent, pointed out the obvious: that Congress is not a court and, hence, draws general, not specific, conclusions. In this case, Congress based its findings on a dozen hearings and thirty-nine pages of examples of official state acts of discrimination against the disabled. Rehnquist dismissively derided them as

not say that Congress can't impose minimum wage and maximum hour laws on state governments, but only that state employees, unlike all others, can't sue to enforce these rights. Neither did the majority rule that states are not subject to the patent and trademark laws, but only that intellectual property owners can't sue states when they pirate inventions, books, or software. See Charles Fried, "Supreme Court Folly," *New York Times*, July 6, 1999, p. A21.

The precedent overruled *sub silentio* – *Garcia v. San Antonio Metropolitan Transit Authority*, 469 U.S. 528 (1985) – had itself overruled a nine-year-old precedent.

101 Financially straitened state colleges and universities might consider selling Microsoft Windows to alleviate their condition.

102 148 L Ed 2d 866 (2001). On the morning of the day that the decision was announced, our article anticipating the decision also appeared: "Supreme Court 5 Are on Power Trip," *Newsday*, February 21, 2001, p. A31.

"unexamined, anedotal accounts" not worthy of the status of legislative findings.[103]

The Five have not restricted their limits on national supremacy to state immunity. We may trace the genesis of the Court's states' rights posture to *United States v. Lopez*[104] where the same five justices declared unconstitutional the Gun-Free School Zones Act, which prohibited firearm possession in a school or within 1000 feet of school property. Although the basis for decision was the interstate commerce clause rather than the Eleventh Amendment, the effect on the diminution of federal authority was the same, indeed, perhaps more so. The Court had not ruled that a federal law exceeded Congress's commercial authority since 1936 when it voided minimum wage and maximum hour regulations in coal mining.[105]

Directly antecedent to the 1999 decisions was the factually picayune dispute in *Seminole Tribe v. Florida*.[106] Again, the same Rehnquist Five voided another federal law – the Indian Gaming Regulatory Act – that imposed on states a duty to bargain in good faith with Indian tribes about gambling. Not only did the Five use the Eleventh Amendment to void the law, it also overruled another precedent – this one of seven years' vintage.[107]

The Full Faith and Credit Clause

A constitutional provision that has had relatively little impact on federal-state relationships thus far is the full faith and credit clause of Article IV, section 1: "Full faith and credit shall be given in each State to the public acts, records, and judicial proceedings of every other State." A long line of decisions has construed the clause to apply only to final state court judgments in civil, not criminal, cases. These judgments have the same force and effect in the courts of other states as they do in the rendering state, provided that the original court had not exercised jurisdiction over a nonresident defendant in a way that violates due process of law.[108] A federal statute requires the same of federal courts.

[103] *Id.* at 894–918, 881. [104] 514 U.S. 549 (1995).

[105] *Carter v. Carter Coal Co.*, 298 U.S. 238. [106] 517 U.S. 44 (1996).

[107] *Pennsylvania v. Union Gas Co.*, 491 U.S. 1 (1989). The conservative coalition originally lost this case because it antedated the appointment of Justice Thomas, the fifth vote needed to form states' rights majorities.

[108] A state court's decision over a nonresident defendant does not violate due process if it meets the "minimum contacts" test of *International Shoe Co. v. Washington*, 326 U.S.

Most such cases concern commercial transactions, insurance, and various forms of compensation. These are automatically enforced. Not so those that pertain to child custody, support, and spousal alimony. These lack the necessary finality to trigger full faith and credit because they are subject to ongoing modification as the best interests of the benefited party require, for example, a minor child.[109] As the Supreme Court recently observed: "Because courts entering custody orders generally retain the power to modify them, courts in other States were no less entitled to change the terms of custody according to their own views of the child's best interest."[110] The Supreme Court, of course, is free to alter its stance and subject domestic relations to the operation of the clause. Its failure to do so enables litigants to avoid or alter their responsibilities by the simple expedient of crossing a state line.

Lurking on the horizon is the matter of same-sex marriage. If a state were to legitimize such,[111] would other states be required to recognize such a relationship and afford the partners the rights and privileges it accords those in a conventional marital relationship? A recent decision may shed some light: *Baker v. General Motors.*[112] As part of a settlement between a former employee and GM, the employee agreed to a permanent injuction forbidding him to testify as an expert witness in litigation against GM. The employee was subsequently subpoenaed as an expert witness in Missouri litigation brought by the children of a woman who died in a GM vehicle that caught fire after a collision. In a unanimous decision, the Supreme Court echoed the posture it assumes in cases that limit the capacity of state courts to subject out-of-state defendants to their jurisdiction, ruling that Michigan courts lack the power to

310 (1945). If defendants are not present in the forum state, the court has personal jurisdiction over them if they have had "certain minimum contacts with it such that the maintenance of the suit does not offend 'traditional notions of fair play and substantial justice.'" 326 U.S. at 316. The jurisdictional problems that out-of-state defendants pose are described in the section of Chapter 6 that pertains to jurisdiction over the parties.

109 In *Ford v. Ford*, 371 U.S. 187 (1962), e.g., the Supreme Court unanimously ruled that a Virginia custody decree that gave custody to the parents of three minor children for only a specific part of the year did not prevent the mother from filing suit in a South Carolina court for full custody.

110 *Thompson v. Thompson*, 484 U.S. 174 (1988), at 180.

111 Vermont has enacted a civil union law that creates same-sex marriages in all but name. See Carey Goldberg, "Vermont Gives Final Approval to Same-Sex Unions," *New York Times*, April 26, 2000, p. A12; "Protecting the Civil Union Law," *National Law Journal*, December 25, 2000–January 1, 2001, p. A16.

112 522 U.S. 222 (1998).

compel out-of-state litigants in courts of another state to comply with a Michigan decision totally at variance from the laws and decisions of the other forty-nine states. The upshot: a public policy exception that allows states to ignore the noncriminal policies and judicial decisions of other states and their courts. Whether it will be applicable to same-sex marriage remains undetermined.

Adequate and Independent State Grounds for Decision

From a policy-making standpoint, this aspect of the relationship between the federal and state courts differs markedly from the Court's use of comity and the abstention doctrine. Whereas comity views the state courts as conscientious and competent to decide federal questions, the Court's use of adequate and independent state grounds for decision cuts both ways. On the one hand, it allows the Court to view state judges as devious decision makers who employ their own laws and constitutional provisions to concoct policies at variance with those mandated by the Supreme Court. On the other, it permits state court decisions to escape review by the Supreme or other federal courts when a majority of the justices so prefer.

Historically, the Supreme Court had supplemented the abstention doctrine with the self-imposed assumption that if a state court decision contained a federal question that was intermixed with questions of solely state concern,[113] the state court's decision rested "on an adequate and independent state ground." In other words, if the state court did not clearly indicate that its decision was based on state, as opposed to federal, law, the Supreme Court simply assumed that the state court decided the case on the basis of its own law.

In 1983, in a run-of-the-mill vehicular search and seizure case, the Burger Court reversed its historic policy and ruled that when

> . . . a state court decision fairly appears to rest primarily on federal law, or to be interwoven with the federal law, and when the adequacy and independence of any possible state law ground is not clear from the face of the opinion, we will accept . . . that the state court decided the case the way it did because it believed that federal law required it to do so.[114]

[113] For an example of a case with mixed state and federal questions, see *Williams v. Georgia*, discussed above.

[114] *Michigan v. Long*, 463 U.S. 1032 (1983), at 1040–1041. The Court upheld a police protective search of those portions of the passenger compartment of an automobile in

To overcome this new – and contradictory – presumption, the state court bore the burden of demonstrating that the federal cases and authorities that it cited in its opinion did "not themselves compel the result that the [state] court has reached," but were used only for "guidance." How might the state court meet this burden? "If the state court decision indicates clearly and expressly that it is alternatively based on *bona fide separate*, adequate, and independent grounds, we, of course, will not undertake to review the decision" (emphasis added).[115] Not only must state courts apparently issue a plain statement denying reliance on federal law, but they must also persuade the justices that this reliance is genuine. The addition of the word "separate" to "bona fide," "adequate," and "independent" should enable the justices to review any state court decision they wish so long as it makes reference to some federal authority.[116]

Why did the moderately conservative Burger Court, with a reputation of deference to the states, suddenly change its tune?

Analysis of decisions in which the majority used *Michigan v. Long* to review state court decisions shows it to be a means to overturn liberal state decisions upholding the rights of persons accused or convicted of crime, particularly those involving unreasonable searches and seizures.[117] Indeed, Justice Powell in his docket sheets for *Long*, which are on file at the Washington and Lee Law School Library, quotes Justice Rehnquist as saying: "We should not invite state courts to avoid Supreme Court review by basing decisions on state grounds. We could end up with fifty state courts being final on many issues." A more candidly antistate assertion is hard to imagine, emanating as it does from the Court's preeminent (verbal) supporter of state "sovereignty." It clearly presaged the action of the Rehnquist Five in *Bush v. Gore*. But observe that Rehnquist's assertion of judicial supremacy does not impede the states' freedom to do their thing, if doing their "thing" accords with the values of the conservative majority.

which a weapon could be placed or hidden. The police had stopped to investigate after Long's car had swerved into a ditch. The search yielded a pouch containing marijuana.

115 *Id.* at 1041.

116 *Bush v. Gore* bodes well to become a classic example of this, as well as other, aspects of federal-state judicial relationships.

117 In its three remaining terms after *Long*, the Burger Court used the ruling as authority to review state court decisions in ten cases. Eight of them overturned liberal state court decisions, five of which concerned searches and seizures, and one each jury instructions, double jeopardy, and the due process rights of prisoners.

The Rehnquist Court has continued to use *Long* as the Burger Court did.

Choice of Law

As we have noted, in cases where federal and state law conflict, the Constitution mandates the supremacy of federal law. But what of those cases in which no controlling federal law exists? These rarely concern federal questions, but they do regularly pertain to cases arising under "diversity of citizenship."[118] This results because Article III, section 2, extends federal court jurisdiction to cases "between citizens of different States." The Framers apparently thought that the parties in these cases should have a choice of forum because of the possibility of prejudice against the out-of-state litigant.[119] The substantive issues in these cases are those that, absent diversity jurisdiction, are grist for state judicial mills: commercial transactions, contracts, torts, and property. Since 1789, Congress has required the federal courts to apply the "law of the several states" to the resolution of these disputes.

The Supreme Court initially defined the "law of the several states" to mean only their statutes and constitutions, not their judge-made, or common, law.[120] Given that legislatures enacted little law before the twentieth century, and that constitutions paid more attention to limitations on the scope of governmental power than they did to its exercise, the range of common law was extensive. Consequently, the federal courts were individually free to make their own law to resolve diversity cases. Litigants engaged in forum shopping in order to evade the state or federal court whose law did not support the shopper's contentions and/or to find the court whose law best presaged a favorable outcome.

In 1938, the Court overruled *Swift v. Tyson* and held that the federal courts' creation of common law derogated states' rights.[121] The refusal of federal courts, sitting in diversity, to follow the common law of the

[118] We discuss diversity jurisdiction in Chapter 6.

[119] Nowhere in the pages referencing diversity jurisdiction in the "Index by Clauses of the Constitution," in James H. Hutson, ed., *Supplement to Max Farrand's The Records of the Federal Convention of 1787* (New Haven: Yale University Press, 1987), pp. 350–51, does a statement of the reasons for diversity jurisdiction appear.

[120] *Swift v. Tyson*, 16 Peters 1 (1842).

[121] *Erie Railroad v. Tompkins*, 304 U.S. 64 (1938). The facts of the case provide a classical illustration of forum shopping. Tompkins, a Pennsylvania resident, brought a tort action for injuries suffered by something projecting from a passing train while he walked along the Erie's tracks. The railroad was a New York corporation. Tompkins chose to file in the New York federal district court because Pennsylvania common law viewed persons walking along a railroad right of way as trespassers. The New York federal court favored the rule of *Swift v. Tyson*. It therefore exercised its own independent judgment and held the railroad liable.

state in which they are located is an unconstitutional assumption of power:

> ... whether the law of the State ... be declared by its Legislature in a statute or by its highest court in a decision is not a matter of federal concern. There is no federal general common law. Congress has no power to declare substantive rules of common law applicable in a State whether they be local in their nature or "general," be they commercial law or a part of the law of torts. And no clause in the Constitution purports to confer such a power upon the federal courts.[122]

Thus ended the preference that *Swift v. Tyson* and its progeny had effectively accorded the out-of-state litigant.[123]

Summary

Use of these six considerations governing the relationship between the state and federal court systems not only affects their relative autonomy, but also enables the Court to adapt its policy making to the substantive personal policy preferences of its members. Thus, for example, the willingness of the Burger and Rehnquist Courts' conservative majority to subordinate considerations of federalism to its substantive policy preferences insofar as adequate state grounds for decision are concerned should occasion no surprise. Matters of procedure, whether they be a court-created rule or a constitutional provision, are regularly invoked when the majority supports the merits of the lower court's decision. The justices, of course, do defer, but they do not do so blindly. Justices who are conservative on criminal procedure (Rehnquist, Burger, O'Connor, Powell, White, Blackmun, Scalia, Kennedy, and Thomas) apparently thought the Court's traditional standard of review unduly hindered them from reversing liberal state court decisions. They therefore changed the rules of the game in *Michigan v. Long* so that their substantively conservative policy preferences could continue to be accommodated.[124]

[122] *Id.* at 78.

[123] The Rehnquist Court's decisions have incrementally supported a broadened scope and applicability of diversity jurisdiction. See *Newman-Green v. Alfonzo-Larrain*, 490 U.S. 826 (1989); *Freeport-McMoRan v. K N Energy*, 498 U.S. 426 (1991); *Caterpillar v. Lewis*, 519 U.S. 61 (1996); and *Lords Landing Condominium Owners v. Continental Insurance Co.*, 520 U.S. 893 (1997).

[124] The constitutional provisions and Court-made policies governing the relationship between the state and federal courts are not the only instruments that the Court utilizes to justify and rationalize its policy preferences. As we discuss in Chapter 10, at least as important is the deference, or lack of it, that judicial restraint and judicial activism provide.

Conversely, if disaffected litigants wish to force the states to conform to federal legislative policies, the reinvigorated Eleventh Amendment and its doctrine of sovereign state immunity nicely blocks such efforts. Consequently, the Court can and does systematically defy the adage by having its cake and eating it also.

And it does not necessarily matter if – in reaching a conservative objective – obeisance is paid to considerations of federalism. The latter is an instrumental value and, as such, subordinates itself to substantive objectives.

But this is nothing new. Early in the twentieth century the Court conducted its first and only criminal trial, a procedure that necessarily rested on the Court's original jurisdiction. This jurisdiction, which the Constitution specifically limits to "Cases affecting Ambassadors, other public Ministers, and those in which a State shall be Party," did not extend to the relevant parties in this case: a county sheriff, his deputy, and four private persons whom the Court accused of disregarding its order that the execution of a black man convicted of raping a white woman be stayed pending the Court's review. When the sheriff heard that a mob had formed, he gave his deputies the night off and stood idly by while the mob broke into the jail, seized the black, and lynched him. The Court ruled that the defendants, especially the sheriff, "aided and abetted" the mob and convicted them of contempt.[125] Making the case even more noteworthy is the fact that the opinion of the three dissenters emphasized the sheriff's character and reputation without the slightest objection to the Court's exercising jurisdiction or even a passing reference to considerations of federalism.[126]

CONCLUSIONS

This chapter has specified the five interrelated features of the Constitution that enable the federal courts in general, and the Supreme Court in particular, to function as authoritative policy makers. The view of Americans that the Constitution is the fundamental law establishes it as the benchmark from which the legitimacy of all governmental action is to

[125] *United States v. Shipp*, 214 U.S. 386 (1909), at 423.

[126] *Id.* at 426–38. Also see Mark Curriden and LeRoy Phillips, Jr., *The Turn-of-the-Century Lynching That Launched 100 Years of Federalism* (New York: Faber and Faber, 1999); Willard L. King, *Melville Weston Fuller* (Chicago: University of Chicago Press, 1967), pp. 323–27; LeRoy Phillips, Jr., "Fighting for a Client Who Was Lynched 94 Years Ago," *National Law Journal*, March 20, 2000, p. A14.

be judged. The popular belief that that government is best that governs least has produced an abiding distrust of government, politicians, and bureaucrats. That distrust, however, does not extend to judges and their decisions. The constitutional division of governmental power between the states and Washington, as well as that among the three branches of the federal government, requires some entity to resolve the conflicts that such division and separation produces. By its enunciation of the doctrine of judicial review in *Marbury v. Madison*, the Supreme Court arrogated to itself the authority to guard against subversion of the fundamental law and to concomitantly resolve the conflicts that federalism and separation of powers produce.

Because the Constitution limits the subject-matter jurisdiction of the federal courts, on the one hand, and provides for the existence of autonomous state courts, on the other, the Supreme Court has had to share policy making with the courts of the individual states. Apportionment of this jurisdictional responsibility rests on three constitutional provisions – the supremacy clause, sovereign immunity, and full faith and credit – and three criteria of the Supreme Court's own creation: the system of comity, adequate and independent state grounds for decision, and the rules governing whether state or federal law should be used to resolve a given dispute. By subjecting their initial formulation to redefinition, the Supreme Court has been able to increase or decrease its policy-making capacity vis-à-vis the state courts to conform to the justices' fluctuating preferences toward centralization/decentralization and their substantive support of liberal or conservative policies.

2

Models of Decision Making

The Legal Model

In the next two chapters, we present three distinct models of Supreme Court decision making: the legal model, the attitudinal model, and the rational choice model. While we apply these models throughout the text, we present the clearest tests of them in Chapters 7 and 8, which cover the decision on the merits.

ABOUT MODELS

Before discussing these models, it may be useful to discuss what a model is and why it is used. We start with the premise that the real world is extraordinarily complex. While natural phenomena may often reduce perfectly to formulae such as $E = mc^2$, the causes of human behavior are typically much more complex and intermeshed. For example, why did the Court find for Roe and not Wade in its 1973 decision striking abortion laws?[1] We readily imagine that we could write an entire book on why the justices did so. Following that, we could write a similar book about *Brown v. Board of Education*,[2] *Marbury v. Madison*,[3] or any number of similarly important cases. We expect that we would learn a lot in researching and writing such a book, and that readers might learn a bit in reading it.

This approach to learning, the case study approach, involves learning as much as possible about as little as possible. While one can profit from this sort of immersion in detail, several shortcomings result as well. First,

[1] *Roe v. Wade*, 410 U.S. 113 (1973). [2] 347 U.S. 484 (1954).
[3] 1 Cranch 137 (1803).

the complexity of human behavior could occasion years of studying a particular decision and still not result in full comprehension. Given that individuals rarely understand their own decisions, it is immeasurably more difficult to fully understand the decisions of others. Second, we quickly forget the facts we learn about a single decision, as students who cram for exams readily know. Third, the causes of one particular case may not be generalizable to the rest of judicial politics. The litigation strategy of the NAACP Legal Defense Fund may have been crucial in *Brown v. Board of Education*. Is that generally the case? Marshall's decision in *Marbury v. Madison* may have been influenced by fears of political repercussions.[4] Do such considerations frequently concern the Court? The simple yet accurate answer is that while the detailed study of a single event may provide a useful description of events, it does not and cannot explain action independent of that event with any degree of confidence.

As an alternative to case studies, the modeling approach also recognizes the complexity of the world around us; nevertheless it postulates that attempting to learn everything about one thing may not be the best approach to knowledge. Instead, whether quantitatively or qualitatively, modelers attempt to examine the most explanatory aspects of a wider range of behavior.[5] Learning the most important factors that affect thousands of decisions might be far more beneficial than learning all there is to know about a single decision.

This is where models come in. A model is a simplified representation of reality; it does not constitute reality itself. Models purposefully ignore certain aspects of reality and focus instead on a select and often related set of crucial factors. Such simplifications provide a useful handle for understanding the real world that reliance on more exhaustive and descriptive approaches does not. For instance, journalistic accounts of presidential elections discuss thousands of factors that might have influenced the final results. Consider, instead, a retrospective voting model where voters evaluate the performance of the incumbent party and vote accordingly. While this could be tested in a variety of ways, imagine that 80 percent of the variance in post–World War II presidential elections

[4] Jack Knight and Lee Epstein. "On the Struggle for Judicial Supremacy," 30 *Law and Society Review* 87 (1996).

[5] For a critique of the ability of models to explain judicial behavior, see Michael McCann, "Causal versus Constitutive Explanations (or, On the Difficulty of Being So Positive ...)," 21 *Law and Social Inquiry* 457 (1996).

can be explained by changes in real disposable income during the incumbent's regime. If so, then this simple retrospective model gives us an extraordinarily useful tool for explaining and understanding not just one but a series of presidential elections.

From the viewpoint of a social scientist, a successful model achieves two often contradictory goals: It explains the behavior in question, and it does so parsimoniously. A model that does not validly and reliably explain and predict the behavior in question obviously has little value. But an unduly complex model that explains behavior may be almost as worthless, for it fails to give us the handle on reality that models provide. Unfortunately, the goals of explanation and parsimony are often contradictory, for the more complex one's model, the more behavior one can "explain." For instance, a justice's vote in a particular equal protection case may result from an encounter the justice had with a member of the group in question earlier in the day. A vote in another case might depend on a different random event. We could potentially expand the "explanatory" power of a model by including these idiosyncratic factors, but the resulting complexity would effectively make the model useless. Useful models ignore idiosyncratic factors and highlight instead variables that explain a high percentage of the behavior in question.[6]

Because models simplify reality, we cannot judge them as true or false, for, strictly speaking, all models are false in that they purposefully exclude idiosyncratic and trivial factors that may marginally influence the behavior in question. Rather, we judge models by whether they are useful in helping us understand that behavior. Internal consistency, coherence, explanatory ability, and parsimony are all hallmarks of a good model. Ultimately, though, model evaluation is a comparative exercise. Because no model explains everything, the crucial question becomes whether it does a better job than its competitors in meeting these criteria.

Requisite to a model's explanatory ability is that it must be *falsifiable* or testable. That is, the model must be able to state a priori the potential conditions that, if observed, would refute the model. For example, if a judicial rational choice model did not state the goals of judges in advance, then almost any systematic behavior would comport with the model, for some goal would almost always be consistent with the behav-

[6] Though models typically aim at uncovering the most important aspects of decisions or behavior, some models may purposefully highlight one aspect of a decision in full knowledge that other aspects may be as or more important.

ior being studied. Or if precedents exist on both sides of a case, a legal model based on precedent so long as the judges followed one precedent or another would not be falsifiable. To complete the picture, an attitudinal model that measures the justices' attitudes by their voting behavior and then explains their votes by their attitudes would similarly be unfalsifiable. In these situations, it is nearly impossible to imagine evidence that would refute the model. As a result, the evidence gathered would not constitute a test of the model, for a test requires the possibility of failure. Of course, a mere a priori statement of conditions that would refute the model does not end the matter. With regard to attitudes, for example, a rigorous definition that strongly portends falsifiability is essential, one, moreover, that is tested by a measure that makes failure highly probable statistically.

Legal scholars[7] and Supreme Court justices often fail to comprehend falsifiability. In *Daubert v. Merrell Dow*[8] Justice Blackmun accurately wrote for the Court:

> Ordinarily, a key question to be answered in determining whether a theory or technique is scientific knowledge . . . will be whether it can be (and has been) tested. "Scientific methodology today is based on generating hypotheses and testing them to see if they can be falsified; indeed, this methodology is what distinguishes science from other fields of human inquiry." . . . See also C. Hempel, Philosophy of Natural Science 49 (1966) ("[T]he statements constituting scientific explanation must be capable of empirical test"); K. Popper, Conjectures and Refutations: The Growth of Scientific Knowledge 37 (5th ed., 1989) ("[T]he criterion of the scientific status of a theory is its falsifiability, or refutability, or testability").[9]

Not bad. But then Justice Rehnquist, whose intellectual gifts are praised by even his staunchest critics, replied: "I defer to no one in my confidence in federal judges; but I am at a loss to know what is meant when it is said that the scientific status of a theory depends on its 'falsifiability,' and I suspect some of them will be, too."[10]

Whether federal judges understand this or not, the point is rather simple. If no potential conditions exist by which a model can be wrong, then empirical evidence is irrelevant to the model's validity. Since scientific evidence requires empirical support, the model is of no scientific value. And if *almost* no potential conditions exist that would falsify a

[7] See, esp., the Law and Courts listserv, Digest 179, June 7, 1997, and Digest 180, June 8, 1997, questioning the need and desirability of falsifiable models. http://www.Lawcourts-l@usc.edu.

[8] 509 U.S. 579 (1993). [9] *Id.* at 593. [10] *Id.* at 600.

model, such that almost all potentially observable behavior is consistent with the model, the model is falsifiable, but trivially so. The more potential behavior that is inconsistent with a model, and the more plausible that behavior is, the more leverage that model provides.

As a necessary criterion for the validity of a model, falsifiability will take on special significance when we discuss the legal model, as we do next.

THE LEGAL MODEL

The legal model ranges from the mechanical jurisprudence in vogue through the early twentieth century[11] to the more sophisticated variants that we mention below. What typically connects these variants together is the belief that, in one form or another,[12] the decisions of the Court are substantially influenced by the facts of the case in light of the plain meaning of statutes and the Constitution, the intent of the Framers, and/or precedent.[13] To various degrees, jurists, legal scholars, and political scientists propound variants of the legal model.

Of course, judges still subscribe to the legal model, at least for public consumption. In addition to the comments of Justices Marshall and Scalia, as quoted in Chapter 1, we add those of Judge Harry Edwards

[11] Essentially, mechanical jurisprudence posits the existence of a single correct answer to legal questions that judges are to find. According to one legal authority, "*most* contemporary scholars no longer adhere to the strict determinate formalist model." Frank Cross, "Political Science and the New Legal Realism: A Case of Unfortunate Interdisciplinary Ignorance," 92 *Northwestern University Law Review* 251 (1997) at 255. Emphasis added.

Modern legal scholars who argue that law is determinate include: Richard S. Markovits, *Matters of Principle: Legitimate Legal Argument and Constitutional Interpretation* (New York: New York University Press, 1998), who claims "internally-correct answers to all legal questions" (p. 1); Kent Greenawalt, *Law and Objectivity* (New York: Oxford University Press, 1992), who argues that "any extreme thesis that the law is always or usually indeterminate is untenable" (p. 11); and, arguably, Ronald Dworkin, whose work we discuss in detail below.

[12] To postpositive legalists, the only required influence of law is a subjective influence that resides within the justice's own mind. See, e.g., Steven J. Burton, *Judging in Good Faith* (Cambridge: Cambridge University Press, 1992). Needless to say, this internal program is essentially nonfalsifiable (in the postpositive vision of the world, this is not a vice) and provides almost no leverage as to which decisions judges will actually make. We discuss this further in the final chapter.

[13] In addition to text, intent, and precedent, *The Supreme Court and the Attitudinal Model* included balancing as well. On further reflection, balancing strikes us as a standard of review akin to the Preferred Freedoms Doctrine (see Chapter 4) rather than a component of the legal model.

of the D.C. Court of Appeals, who asserts that "it is law – and not the personal politics of individual judges – that controls judicial decision making in most cases resolved by the court of appeals."[14] According to Judge Wald of the same court, "there is little time or inclination to infuse the decision making process with personal ideology."[15]

Nonjurists also mouth such notions.[16] Consider, for example, the writings of Ronald Dworkin, arguably this generation's preeminent legal theorist. In *Taking Rights Seriously*, Dworkin disputes the notion that judges freely exercise discretion. While recognizing that precedent only inclines judges toward certain conclusions, rather than commands them, he nevertheless disputes the notion that judges "pick and choose amongst the principles and policies that make up [this] doctrine,"[17] or that judges apply "extra-legal" principles (e.g., no man shall profit from his own wrong) "according to his own lights."[18]

Precedent plays an important role in *Taking Rights Seriously*, and that role becomes paramount in hard cases, those where no preexisting rule of law exists.[19] Dworkin argues that legal positivists err in claiming that judges legislate new rights in such cases, and again denies that they exercise discretion. "It remains the judge's duty, even in hard cases, to *discover* what the rights of the parties are, not to invent new rights retrospectively."[20]

When a new case falls clearly within the scope of a previous decision, the earlier case has an "enactment force" that binds judges. But even when novel circumstances appear, earlier decisions exert a "gravitational force" on judges.[21] This is not mechanical jurisprudence, as judges may disagree as to what the gravitational force is. Yet to Dworkin, judges must *find* the *correct* answer. And though his theory of precedent requires a judge's answer to "reflect his own intellectual and philosophical

[14] Harry T. Edwards, "Public Misperceptions Concerning the 'Politics' of Judging: Dispelling Some Myths About the D.C. Circuit," 56 *University of Colorado Law Review* 619 (1985) at 620.

[15] Patricia M. Wald, "A Response to Tiller and Cross," 99 *Columbia Law Review* 235 (1999) at 237. Both Edwards and Wald, though, assert that nonlegal factors have a substantially greater impact on Supreme Court decisions than those of the Courts of Appeals.

[16] This section derives in part from Harold J. Spaeth and Jeffrey A. Segal, *Majority Rule or Minority Will: Adherence to Precedent on the U.S. Supreme Court* (New York: Cambridge University Press, 1999), pp. 8–15.

[17] Ronald Dworkin, *Taking Rights Seriously* (Cambridge, Mass.: Harvard University Press, 1988), p. 38.

[18] *Id.* at 39. [19] *Id.* at 110–15. [20] *Id.* at 81, emphasis added. [21] *Id.* at 111.

convictions in making that judgment, that is a very different matter from supposing that those convictions have some independent force in his argument just because they are his."[22]

We do not wish to misrepresent Dworkin's position. He does not adhere to a purely legalistic perspective. While the requirement of finding a fit between past cases to the current one will "eliminate interpretations that some judges would otherwise prefer, so that the brute facts of legal history will in this way limit the role any judge's personal concoctions can play in his decisions," "different judges will set this threshold differently."[23] Nor is he oblivious to institutional factors. Higher courts generally deviate from strict precedent, the *obligation* to follow past decisions, but nevertheless are subject to the gravitational pull of weak precedent.[24] Overall, though, the notions that the judge's job is to find correct answers to hard legal questions, and that precedents guide this search, indicate that stare decisis plays a vital role in judicial decision making.

Support for the legal model, though to a lesser degree, survives not just in the precedential world of Ronald Dworkin, but in the writings on text and intent that appear in the eclectic world of modern legal scholars. While we do not review these scholars' works in detail, we note the following.

Bruce Ackerman's *We the People* argues that the Supreme Court's role in American history has been to provide a synthesis between constitutional transformations (such as that following the Civil War) and past practices (e.g., the Founders' Constitution). Thus, to Ackerman, the notorious *Lochner* decision[25] represents not conservative justices reaching conservative results, but justices "exercising a preservationist function, trying to develop a comprehensive synthesis of the meaning of the Founding and Reconstruction out of the available legal materials."[26]

[22] *Id.* at 118. This quote concerns Dworkin's mythical judge Hercules, but Dworkin applies the technique to human judges as well (p. 130). One might argue that we are turning a normative argument into an empirical one. In our defense, Dworkin frequently mixes and matches what he thinks judges actually do with what he thinks they ought to do. For example, "judges are agreed that earlier decisions have gravitational force" (1978, p. 112), and "judges characteristically feel an obligation to give what I call 'gravitational force' to past decisions" (Dworkin 1986, p. viii) are empirical statements, not normative ones.

[23] Ronald Dworkin, *Law's Empire* (Cambridge, Mass.: Harvard University Press, 1988), p. 255.

[24] *Id.* at 401.

[25] *Lochner v. New York*, 198 U.S. 45 (1905).

[26] Bruce Ackerman, *We the People: Foundations* (Cambridge, Mass.: Harvard University Press, 1991), p. 101.

Similarly, to Howard Gillman, a postpositive scholar,[27] the *Lochner* Court "was, to a large extent, giving voice to the founders' conception of appropriate and inappropriate policymaking."[28]

Among more modern justices, Hugo Black, of course, is the exemplar of "originalist" jurisprudence: "In interpreting the Constitution [Black] followed the plain meaning of the words and the intent of the framers";[29] "Hugo Black, with a 'near religious fervor' for most of his tenure on the Court, fought and argued to base his and the Court's constitutional interpretation on the literal text itself. . . . Always at war against judicial roaming in the murky 'natural law' ether of substantive rights . . . Black tried to interpret constitutional phrases in accordance with the intent of the Framers and the history of the clause or amendment."[30] More subtly, Leslie Goldstein argues that Black "utilized a moderately textualist jurisprudence . . . guided primarily by the wording of the constitutional text and its structure."[31]

So too for the Court's most conservative justices. Davis states that Rehnquist's behavior on the Court cannot be explained by his conservative ideology. Rather, she claims, Rehnquist is a legal positivist, one who believes that "lawmaking is a prerogative of legislators rather than judges. . . . In an attempt to adhere to the law as an empirical fact, a positivist jurist limits his or her interpretation of the Constitution to the meaning of the words or the text or intent of its authors."[32] "The school of thought of which Chief Justice Rehnquist is the most prominent adherent would deny for the most part the validity of any tradition except that already frozen in the founding events."[33] Without accepting Scalia's words at face value, David Schultz and Christopher Smith note that "Scalia's uniqueness stems from his notable role as the Court's most consistent, forceful advocate of constitutional interpretation according to the original meaning intended by the

[27] See n. 12, *supra*.

[28] Howard Gillman, *The Constitution Besieged: The Rise and Demise of Lochner Era Police Power Jurisprudence* (Durham: Duke University Press, 1993), p. 20.

[29] Sue Davis, *Justice Rehnquist and the Constitution* (Princeton, N.J.: Princeton University Press, 1989), pp. 23–24.

[30] Howard Ball and Phillip J. Cooper, *Of Power and Right* (New York: Oxford University Press, 1992), pp. 318–19.

[31] Leslie Goldstein, *In Defense of the Text* (Savage, Md.: Rowman and Littlefield, 1991), p. 41.

[32] Davis, *op. cit.*, n. 29, *supra*, p. 24.

[33] H. Jefferson Powell, "Symposium: The Republican Civic Tradition: Reviving Republicanism," 97 *Yale Law Journal* 1703 (1998), at 1703–4.

framers."[34] According to Smith, "Thomas seeks to base his opinions on the original intent of the Framers of the Constitution, Bill of Rights, and subsequent constitutional amendments. His opinions are replete with references to the primacy of the Framers' intentions. He treats these intentions as the compelling directives that dictate the outcomes and reasoning in cases."[35]

More generally, Herman Pritchett, who assertively "blazed a trail"[36] that behavioral judicial scholars have followed for fifty years, retreated from his assumption that the justices' votes are "motivated by their own preferences"[37]:

> [P]olitical scientists, who have done so much to put the "political" in "political jurisprudence" need to emphasize that it is still "jurisprudence." It is judging in a political context, but it is still judging; and judging is still different from legislating or administering. Judges make choices, but they are not the "free" choices of congressmen.... There is room for much interpretation in the texts of constitutions, statutes, and ordinances, but the judicial function is still interpretation and not independent policy making. It is just as false to argue that judges freely exercise their discretion as to contend they have no policy functions at all. Any accurate analysis of judicial behavior must have as a major purpose a full clarification of the unique limiting conditions under which judicial policy making proceeds.[38]

Prominent rational choice theorists, who typically conceive of justices as primarily interested in policy outcomes (see Chapter 3), clearly hold open the possibility that judges have legal considerations as goals, and not just constraints.[39] Other economic-minded scholars argue, like

[34] David A. Schultz and Christopher E. Smith, *The Jurisprudential Vision of Justice Antonin Scalia* (Lanham, Md.: Rowman and Littlefield, 1996), p. 80.

[35] Christopher E. Smith, "Clarence Thomas: A Distinctive Justice," 28 *Seton Hall Law Review* 1 (1997), p. 9.

[36] Glendon Schubert, *Judicial Decision Making* (New York: Free Press of Glencoe, 1963), p. v.

[37] C. Herman Pritchett, *The Roosevelt Court* (New York: Macmillan, 1948), p. xii.

[38] C. Herman Pritchett, "The Development of Judicial Research," in Joel Grossman and Joseph Tanenhaus, eds., *Frontiers of Judicial Research* (New York: Wiley, 1969), p. 42. In the aftermath of *Bush v. Gore*, any limitation on "independent policy making," free "exercise of... discretion," and "unique limiting conditions" would seem no more substantial than phlogiston. For what it may be worth, Justice Stevens, joined by Brennan and Marshall, identify Pritchett as an "historian" in *Allegheny County v. Greater Pittsburgh ACLU*, 492 U.S. 573 (1989), at 646, n. 1.

[39] John Ferejohn and Barry Weingast, "A Positive Theory of Statutory Interpretation," 12 *International Review of Law and Economics* 263 (1992), and Lewis Kornhauser, "Modeling Collegial Courts II: Legal Doctrine," 8 *Journal of Law, Economics, and Organization* 441 (1992).

Dworkin, that the goal of judges is to find the "correct" answer to legal questions.[40]

Finally, modern political theorists argue that Supreme Court decision making can best be understood as a *constitutive* process, by which "members of the Supreme Court believe that they are required to act in accordance with particular institutional and legal expectations and responsibilities."[41] Thus, "justices must be principled in their decision-making process."[42]

> At the core of a constitutive approach to Supreme Court decision making are the following six major premises: First, the Court does not follow elections or politics, but views itself as autonomous from direct and indirect political pressure. Second, justices do not follow personal policy wants. Third, respect for precedent and principled decision making are central to Supreme Court decision-making. . . .[43]

And so on.

In contrast, we argue that the legal model and its components serve only to rationalize the Court's decisions and to cloak the reality of the Court's decision-making process. We begin with an analysis of plain meaning.

Plain Meaning

Plain meaning applies not only to the language of statutes and constitutions, but also to the words of judicially formulated rules. It simply holds that judges rest their decisions in significant part on the plain meaning of the pertinent language.[44] So if Article I, section 10, of the Constitution declares that no state shall pass any law impairing the obligation of contract, then the Court should consistently strike laws that do so.

[40] Lewis Kornhauser, "Adjudication by a Resource-Constrained Team: Hierarchy and Precedent in a Judicial System," 68 *Southern California Law Review* 1605 (1995).

[41] Ronald Kahn, "Interpretive Norms and Supreme Court Decision Making: The Rehnquist Court on Privacy and Religion," in Cornell W. Clayton and Howard Gillman, eds., *Supreme Court Decision Making: New Institutionalist Approaches* (Chicago: University of Chicago Press, 1999), p. 175.

[42] *Id.* at 176.

[43] *Id.* at 177–78. Needless to say, the decision in *Bush v. Gore* could not have happened in such a world.

[44] Note that no correlation need exist between plain meaning and intelligibility. Not infrequently, even the Court so admits. Thus, "It may be well to acknowledge at the outset that it is quite impossible to make complete sense of the provision at issue here." *Asgrow Seed Co. v. Winterboer*, 513 U.S. 179 (1995), at 185–86.

Alternatively, courts should not judicially create rights that the Constitution does not explicitly contain.

For several reasons, construction through plain meaning possesses a chameleonic quality that spans the color spectrum. First, English as a language lacks precision. Virtually all words have a multiplicity of meanings, as the most nodding acquaintance with a dictionary will attest. Meanings, moreover, may directly conflict. For example, the common legal word "sanction" means to reward as well as to punish. The penumbral quality of a given word, especially in combination with others, insures wide-ranging discretion by those charged with construing the overall meaning of the pertinent set of words. Second, legislators and framers of constitutional language typically fail to define their terms: legislators because of the need to effect a compromise, framers because of their inability to anticipate the future. Third, one statutory or constitutional provision or court rule may conflict with another. And while some language may be clearer than others, the meaning of words under construction in the types of cases heard by the Supreme Court, as we see below, is likely to be particularly opaque. Fourth, identical words in the same or different statutes need not have the same meaning.[45]

A commonly used example of plain meaning pertains to the operative language of the Mann Act, a classic bit of congressional morals legislation.[46]

> ... any person who shall knowingly transport or cause to be transported, or aid or assist in obtaining transportation for, or in transporting, in interstate or foreign commerce ... any woman or girl for the purpose of prostitution or debauchery, or for any other immoral purpose, or with the intent and purpose to induce, entice, or compel such woman or girl to become a prostitute or to give herself up to debauchery, or to engage in any other immoral purpose ... shall be deemed guilty of a felony.[47]

[45] Justice Blackmun, writing also for Brennan and Marshall, provides several examples in *Sullivan v. Stroop*, 496 U.S. 478 (1990), at 489–90.

[46] We trust that the irony of Congress's concern with morals legislation is not lost on the reader.

The Court, of course, also legislates morality – e.g., *Barnes v. Glen Theater*, 501 U.S. 560 (1991), which permits state and local governments to outlaw nude dancing – and, according to many, also immorality – c.f., *United States v. Playboy Entertainment Group*, 146 L Ed 2d 865 (2000), declaring unconstitutional the Communications Decency Act of 1996 that restricted sexually explicit cable TV programs to late-night hours.

[47] 18 *United States Code Annotated* 398, section 2. The Court held the statute constitutional as an appropriate exercise of Congress's power to regulate interstate commerce in *Hoke v. United States*, 227 U.S. 308 (1913).

The first case concerned three men who transported their mistresses across a state line. By a vote of 5 to 3, the Court affirmed their convictions on the basis that the phrase "immoral purpose" included persuading a woman to become a "concubine and mistress," even though the venture was nonremunerative.[48] The second case involved a madam and her husband who took two of their employees with them on a vacation to Yellowstone National Park, crossing state lines on the way. The employees did not work until after they returned from vacation. By a 5-to-4 vote, the Court reversed the employers' convictions, ruling that there was no immoral purpose inasmuch as the purpose of the trip "was to provide innocent recreation and a holiday" for their employees.[49] The final case pertained to a group of polygamous Mormons who had transported their several wives across state lines. Justice Douglas, speaking for himself and four of his colleagues, ruled, "The establishment or maintenance of polygamous households is a notorious example of promiscuity." Justice Murphy demurred: "etymologically, the words 'polygyny' and 'polygamy' are quite distinct from 'prostitution' 'debauchery' and words of that ilk."[50] Presumably, the crucial consideration for Douglas, who was married four times, is that plural wives are permissible so long as a man has them consecutively, rather than concurrently.

At the constitutional level, an oft-cited example of plain meaning concerns the creative use that the Marshall and Taney Courts made of the word "citizens," as it is used with reference to the diversity jurisdiction of the federal courts. To avoid subjecting fledgling American business enterprise to the potentially harsh mercies of out-of-state courts, Marshall ruled that a corporation was a "citizen" notwithstanding that no dictionary defined it as such. Marshall reasoned that inasmuch as corporations are artificial entities created by law, one should look to the human reality behind the legal facade, the stockholders.[51] And if they were all domiciled in a state different from that of the other party to the litigation, diversity existed.[52]

Marshall's creative solution worked well as long as American business remained localistic. But once a corporation's stockholders no longer

[48] *Caminetti v. United States*, 242 U.S. 470 (1917), at 483.
[49] *Mortensen v. United States*, 322 U.S. 369 (1944), at 375.
[50] *Cleveland v. United States*, 329 U.S. 14 (1946), at 19, 26.
[51] *Bank of the United States v. Deveaux*, 5 Cranch 84 (1810). For the details of diversity jurisdiction, see Chapter 6.
[52] *Strawbridge v. Curtis*, 3 Cranch 267 (1806).

resided in a single state, the corporation lost its access to the federal courts unless – this time compatibly with lexicographic plain meaning – diversity was complete, that is, no party on one side of the dispute held citizenship in the same state as a party on the other side of the dispute. In 1845, the Taney Court, not noted for its support of either business or federal power, rescued business from the specter of localistic tyranny. Observing that *Deveaux* and *Strawbridge* had "never been satisfactory to the bar," and that Marshall himself had "repeatedly expressed regret that those decisions had been made," the Court ruled the words of the Constitution did not prohibit Congress from giving "the courts jurisdiction between citizens in many other forms than that in which it has been conferred."[53] Hence, for purposes of federal jurisdiction, a corporation was a citizen of the state of its incorporation. The result:

> the most remarkable fiction in American law. A conclusive and irrebuttable presumption . . . that all stockholders of a corporation were citizens of the state in which the corporation was chartered. By operation of this fiction, every one of the shareholders of General Motors Corporation is a citizen of Delaware despite the fact that there are more shareholders than there are Delawareans.[54]

One need not retreat to cases of ancient vintage to document the deficiencies of plain meaning as an explanation of the Court's decisions. Three from a four-month period of 1990 nicely suffice. The question in the first case was the meaning of the words "adjustment" and "recovery" with regard to the Social Security Act's old age benefits. The majority defined the terms to the recipient's detriment; the dissenters conversely. The majority supported its construction by defining the words as they are defined in another section of the statute. The majority said this approach is "reasonable, if not necessary," while confessing that its definition is not "an inevitable interpretation of the statute, but it is assuredly a permissible one."[55]

[53] *Louisville, Cincinnati and Charleston Railroad Co. v. Letson*, 2 Howard 497 (1845), at 555, 554. To shore up its creative use of "citizens," the Court peremptorily asserted that its decision "will be admitted by all to be coincident with the policy of the Constitution." *Id.* at 556. Note also that the Court's reliance on plain meaning enabled it to severely constrict the applicability of Marshall's decisions in *Deveaux* and *Strawbridge*, thereby illustrating the ability of one application of the plain meaning model to undo another.

[54] John P. Frank, *Justice Daniel Dissenting* (Cambridge: Harvard University Press, 1964), p. 219.

[55] *Sullivan v. Everhart*, 494 U.S. 83 (1990), at 92, 93.

The dissenters, in an opinion of equal length, asserted that the majority's construction is "inconsistent with both common sense and the plain terms of the statute" and supplemented their linguistic analysis by concluding that the majority's interpretation "defeat[s] clear congressional intent." The dissent does admit, albeit grudgingly, "that students of language could justify" the majority's result if intent were ignored.[56]

The second case, decided by the same voting alignment as the first (Rehnquist, White, O'Connor, Scalia, and Kennedy vs. Brennan, Marshall, Blackmun, and White), presented the question of whether a "child's insurance benefits" under one provision of the Social Security Act constituted "child support" under another title of the same act. The majority turned not to Webster but to Black's Law Dictionary to determine the "common usage" of child support. The dissenters did the opposite. The majority, however, ruled the common usage of child support "to have become a term of art," and "any attempt to break down the term into its constituent words is not apt to illuminate its meaning."[57]

Whether the supplementation of plain meaning with "term of art" warrants segmenting this version of the legal model into two distinct subtypes will apparently need to await future legalistic developments and usage. But be this as it may, the dissenters again supplemented their focus on "ordinary English usage" with reference to its purpose.[58]

The third case not only illustrates an additional shortcoming of plain meaning, it also demonstrates the inutility of the major alternative model to plain meaning: legislative intent.[59] The case turned on the meaning of the phrase "noncurriculum related student group," as used in a federal statute that requires public schools to give student religious groups equal access to school facilities that other extracurricular groups have. The majority held that the statute did not violate the establishment clause of the First Amendment, but that a high school's refusal to allow students to form a Christian club did violate the law.

The prevailing opinion observed that not only did the act fail to define "noncurriculum related student group," even the law's sponsors did not know what it meant.[60] Given the inadequacy of both plain meaning and intent to resolve the problem, the majority simply rested its judgment on

[56] *Id.* at 96, 103, 106. [57] *Sullivan v. Stroop*, 496 U.S. 478 (1990), at 483.
[58] *Id.* at 496, 486.
[59] *Westside Community Schools v. Mergens*, 496 U.S. 226 (1990).
[60] *Id.* at 237, 243. The dissenting opinion also agreed with this assertion. At 281.

the "logic" of a 1981 decision. In dissent, Justice Stevens targeted yet another deficiency of plain meaning:

> The Court relies heavily on the dictionary's definition of "curriculum." . . . That word, of course, is not the Act's; moreover the word "noncurriculum" is not in the dictionary. Neither Webster nor Congress has authorized us to assume that "noncurriculum" is a precise antonym of the word "curriculum." "Nonplus," for example, does not mean "minus" and it would be incorrect to assume that a "nonentity" is not an "entity" at all.[61]

As a final example, we cite the Court's own words in an important First Amendment freedom case to further falsify plain meaning as a reliable guide to why the Court decides a case the way it does. The Court begins by quoting itself to the effect that "above all else, the First Amendment means that government has no power to restrict expression because of its message, its ideas, its subject matter, or its content." This unequivocal language is followed by citations to seven cases that arose in seven different contexts, in addition to the one that the Court was quoting. Immediately thereafter, the following language appears:

> This statement, read literally . . . would absolutely preclude any regulation of expressive activity predicated in whole or in part on the content of the communication. But we learned long ago that broad statements of principle, no matter how correct in the context in which they are made, are sometimes qualified by contrary decisions before the absolute limit of the stated principle is reached.[62]

In short, plain meaning does not explain the Court's decisions because the justices plainly do not necessarily mean what they say. Nor do they provide criteria that inform analysts when they intend to act as snolly-

[61] *Id.* at 291.

[62] *Young v. American Mini Theatres*, 427 U.S. 50 (1976), at 65. But the justices are willing to quarrel with one another. Thus, in an otherwise unexceptional case, *Conroy v. Aniskoff*, 507 U.S. 511 (1993), Justice Scalia chided the majority for not adhering to the statutory language "which is entirely clear, and if that is not what Congress meant then Congress has made a mistake and Congress will have to correct it." At 528. The majority, through Justice Stevens, feigned disbelief that Scalia would "conclude that we have a duty to enforce the statute as written even if fully convinced that every Member of the enacting Congress, as well as the President who signed the Act, intended a different result." At 518, n. 12. Note also that Scalia believes that even a "wretchedly drafted statute" should be applied "as written." *United States v. Granderson*, 511 U.S. 39 (1994), at 60.

gosters or pseudologists. Indeed, they go further still and indicate that plain meaning sometimes ought not be used at all:

> We have understood the Eleventh Amendment to stand not so much for what it says, but for the presupposition of our constitutional structure which it confirms: that the States entered the federal system with their sovereignty intact; that the judicial authority in Article III is limited by this sovereignty.[63]

Akin to equivocation about the First Amendment is the longstanding rule that the Constitution's absolute prohibition on laws impairing the obligation of contract is not to be read literally. Rather, the Court will uphold such laws, so long as they are reasonable. "Laws which restrict a party to those gains reasonably to be expected from the contract are not subject to attack under the Contract Clause, notwithstanding that they technically alter an obligation of contract."[64]

Rights not explicitly found in the Constitution, such as travel and privacy, are currently upheld with the strictest scrutiny.[65] This is not to say that the justices decided these cases incorrectly. We only note that if the Court can regularly read rights out of the Constitution that it explicitly contains while simultaneously reading into the Constitution rights that it does not explicitly embrace, then the plain meaning rule fails as an explanation of what the Court has done. Indeed, not only has no one systematically demonstrated that plain meaning influences the decisions of Supreme Court justices, no proponent has even suggested a falsifiable test for this component of the legal model. Such a demonstration, of course, need not mean that a justice or justices follow plain meaning in every case. Rather, falsifiability simply requires, for example, that some method of determining plain meaning in some cases be established a priori;[66] corroboration of the model might require, for example, that, ceteris paribus, justices must systematically react positively in some meaningful degree to such arguments. Of this, we have no evidence.

[63] *Blatchford v. Native Village of Noatak*, 501 U.S. 775 (1991), at 779. The author of *Blatchford*? Justice Scalia, the Rehnquist Court's self-proclaimed literalist.

[64] *El Paso v. Simmons*, 379 U.S. 497 (1965), at 515.

[65] *Shapiro v. Thompson*, 394 U.S. 618 (1969); *Griswold v. Connecticut*, 381 U.S. 479 (1965).

[66] This, of course, seems to require that plain meaning itself be meaningfully definable. That, unfortunately, is often not the case. Consider the following situation: Two statutes with "virtually identical language" nonetheless had "vastly different meanings." Why? Because, according to Justice Thomas's concurrence, a statute's plain meaning in this case at least "depends upon ... [its] policy objectives and legislative history." *Fogarty v. Fantasy Inc.*, 510 U.S. 517 (1994), at 522, 535, 538.

Legislative and Framers' Intent

Legislative and Framers' intent refers to construing statutes and the Constitution according to the preferences of those who originally drafted and supported them. The sole substantive difference between these two types of intent is that the former pertains to the interpretation of statutes, while the latter construes constitutional provisions. As guides to the justices' decisions, neither improves upon plain meaning. Indeed, as we saw above, and as we further observe below, these two versions not infrequently support an opposite result in cases before the Court. Inasmuch as the Court provides no empirically supportable basis for choosing meaning over intent, or vice-versa, a justice's choice of one in preference to the other necessarily rests on considerations other than the model itself.[67]

The Normative View

The belief that the text of the Constitution or the intent of the Framers should bind Supreme Court justices is known as interpretivism or originalism. According to John Hart Ely, interpretivism is the "insistence that the work of the political branches is to be invalidated only in accordance with an inference whose starting point, whose underlying premise, is fairly discoverable in the Constitution."[68] Thus, an interpretivist would support the constitutionality of the death penalty, despite the Eighth Amendment's ban on cruel and unusual punishment, because the Fifth Amendment explicitly permits capital punishment.[69] Similarly, interpretivists might argue that the Sixth Amendment's trial by jury means a

[67] The Court, however, does typically "begin with the text." *Gollust v. Mendell*, 501 U.S. 115 (1991), at 121. Also see *Demarest v. Manspeaker*, 498 U.S. 184 (1991): "In deciding a question of statutory construction, we begin of course with the language of the statute." At 187. And if, in the majority's "view, the plain language ... disposes of the question before us," intent will not be assessed (*Toibb v. Radloff*, 501 U.S. 157 (1991), at 160); with some exceptions, of course: "When we find the terms of a statute unambiguous, judicial inquiry should be complete except in rare and exceptional circumstances." *Freytag v. Commissioner*, 501 U.S. 868 (1991), at 873. This language also appears in *Demarest v. Manspeaker*, at 190.

[68] *Democracy and Distrust* (Cambridge: Harvard University Press, 1980), p. 2.

[69] The Fifth Amendment explicitly or implicitly condones the death penalty in three separate phrases. (1) "No person shall be held to answer for a capital or otherwise infamous crime, unless on a presentment or indictment of a grand jury ...," (2) "nor shall any person be subject for the same offence to be twice put in jeopardy of life or limb ...," (3) "nor be deprived of life, liberty or property without due process of law. ..."

The second clause above presumably suggests to interpretivists that not only is capital punishment acceptable, but dismemberment is as well.

unanimous jury of twelve citizens, because that's what the word "jury" meant in 1791.[70]

While Supreme Court justices generally deny that their own opinions go beyond a fair-minded interpretation of the text of the Constitution or the intent of the Framers, elementary common sense establishes the opposite. In 1905, the Supreme Court declared that New York did not have the right to limit the hours bakers could work. The case, *Lochner v. New York*,[71] rested on a right to contract that the Court found implicit in the Fourteenth Amendment's due process clause. Of course, the amendment says nothing about the right to contract. Moreover, the liberty guaranteed by the amendment is certainly not absolute. For these reasons, among others, *Lochner* received heavy criticism, and thirty-two years later the Court overruled it.[72]

In 1965, the Court overturned a Connecticut law that prohibited anyone in the state, married or otherwise, from using contraceptives.[73] The Court's majority opinion, written by Justice Douglas, created a general right to privacy. The decision did not rest on any specific constitutional clause, but instead on the "penumbras and emanations" of the First, Third, Fourth, Fifth, Ninth, and Fourteenth Amendments. Like the right to contract, the right to privacy can nowhere be found in the Constitution. Neither, for that matter, can the right to marry or bear children.

The arguments for and against interpretation of the Constitution bound to the intent of the Framers have dominated legalistic critiques of the Supreme Court in past years. This partially results because the Court struck down antiabortion laws in forty-six of the fifty states in *Roe v. Wade*[74] and nearly overruled this decision in *Webster v. Reproductive Services*.[75] The *Roe* opinion, like those in *Lochner* and *Griswold*, has only imperceptible ties to the text of the Constitution or the intent of the Framers.

Additionally, interpretivism was seized upon as an issue by Reagan's Attorney General, Edwin Meese. According to Meese, the Court must follow a "Jurisprudence of Original Intention. . . . Those who framed the Constitution chose their words carefully; they debated at great length the most minute points. The language they chose meant something. It is incumbent upon the Court to determine what that meaning

[70] Raoul Berger, *Death Penalties* (Cambridge, Mass.: Harvard University Press, 1982).
[71] 198 U.S. 45. [72] *West Coast Hotel v. Parrish*, 300 U.S. 379 (1937).
[73] *Griswold v. Connecticut*, 381 U.S. 479. [74] 410 U.S. 113 (1973).
[75] 492 U.S. 490 (1989).

was."[76] Meese, though, was less concerned about original intent than he was the creation of a conservative jurisprudence. He attacked the application of the Bill of Rights to the states, noting that those rights originally limited only the national government. His tale of wrongful incorporation jumps from *Barron v. Baltimore*,[77] in which Chief Justice Marshall accurately asserted that the Framers did not intend the Bill of Rights to apply to the states, to *Gitlow v. New York*,[78] which first incorporated a noneconomic provision of the Bill of Rights, without mentioning the intervening ratification of the Fourteenth Amendment, whose first section was thought by at least some of its proponents to overrule *Barron*.[79] Relatedly, one might also wonder why Meese opposed federal and state affirmative action programs. He contested the former on constitutional grounds even though no constitutional provision explicitly requires the national government to provide equal protection, and he opposed state affirmative action although no proponent of the Fourteenth Amendment ever stated that the amendment could be used to protect white Americans.[80]

An interpretivist almost as harsh as Meese, but with more scholarly credentials, is Raoul Berger.[81] Berger's best-known book, *Government by Judiciary*,[82] argues that the framers of the Fourteenth Amendment did not intend to incorporate the Bill of Rights, protect voting rights, or desegregate public schools. He quotes Representative James Wilson (R-Iowa) that "civil rights . . . do not mean that all citizens shall sit on juries, or that their children shall attend the same schools." Berger then declares that "Wilson's statement is proof positive that segregation was excluded from the scope" of the Fourteenth Amendment, as if a single statement by a single congressman could be proof of anything.[83]

[76] Edwin Meese, Speech before American Bar Association, reprinted in *The Great Debate* (Washington D.C.: Federalist Society, 1986), p. 9. Like judges, politicians prevaricate. As we noted in Chapter 1, diversity jurisdiction, hardly a minute matter, lacks any reference in any report of the Constitutional Convention.

[77] 7 Peters 243 (1833). [78] 268 U.S. 652 (1925).

[79] *Adamson v. California*, 332 U.S. 46 (1947), at 71–72. Justice Black attached a lengthy appendix to his dissenting opinion that supports full incorporation. At 92–123.

The first case to incorporate a provision of the Bill of Rights into the Constitution was *Chicago, Burlington and Quincy R. Co. v. Chicago*, 166 U.S. 266 (1897), which requires government to pay owners just compensation for taking their property.

[80] Meese, *op. cit.*, n. 76, *supra*, pp. 7–8.

[81] But see Bruce Ackerman's devastating critique of Berger's misuse of historical documents: *We the People: Foundations* (Cambridge, Mass.: Harvard University Press, 1991), pp. 334–36.

[82] (Cambridge, Mass.: Harvard University Press, 1977). [83] *Id.* pp. 119–20, 120.

Former Supreme Court nominee Robert Bork provides the best normative defense of interpretivism. According to Bork, interpretivism solves the Madisonian problem of protecting minority rights without interfering with democratic rule.

One essential premise of the Madisonian model is majoritarianism. The model has also a counter-majoritarian premise, however, for it assumes there are some areas of life a majority should not control. There are some things a majority should not do to us no matter how democratically it decides to do them. These are areas properly left to individual freedom, and coercion by the majority in these aspects of life is tyranny.

Some see the model as containing an inherent, perhaps an insoluble, dilemma. Majority tyranny occurs if legislation invades the areas properly left to individual freedom. Minority tyranny occurs if the majority is prevented from ruling where its power is legitimate. Yet, quite obviously, neither the majority nor the minority can be trusted to define the freedom of the other. This dilemma is resolved in constitutional theory, and in popular understanding, by the Supreme Court's power to define both majority and minority freedom through the interpretation of the Constitution. Society consents to be ruled undemocratically within defined areas by certain enduring principles believed to be stated in, and placed beyond the reach of majorities, by the Constitution.

But this resolution of the dilemma imposes severe requirements upon the Court. For it follows that the Court's power is legitimate only if it has, and can demonstrate in reasoned opinions that it has, a valid theory, derived from the Constitution, of the respective spheres of majority and minority freedom. If it does not have such a theory but merely imposes its own values, or worse if it pretends to have a theory but actually follows its own predilections, the Court violates the postulates of the Madisonian model that alone justifies its power. It then necessarily abets the tyranny either of the majority or of the minority.[84]

From these premises Bork argues that the Court must "stick close to the text and history (of the Constitution), and their fair implications and not construct new rights."[85] His reading of the text and history of the Constitution leads him to conclude that the *Griswold* decision is unprincipled, that state courts can enforce racially discriminatory contracts despite the equal protection clause,[86] and that the First Amendment provides no protection whatsoever for scientific, literary, or artistic expression.[87] These views had much to do with the Senate's refusal to confirm Bork to the Supreme Court in 1987.

[84] Robert Bork, "Neutral Principles and Some First Amendment Problems," 47 *Indiana Law Journal* 1 (1971), 3.

[85] *Id.* at 8. [86] See *Shelley v. Kraemer*, 334 U.S. 1 (1948).

[87] Bork, *op. cit.*, n. 84, *supra*, pp. 27–30.

Despite the use of interpretivism by right-wing politicians and legal scholars, it is not necessarily a conservative doctrine. The Supreme Court justice who most consistently argued for interpretation bound to the text and history of the Constitution was Hugo Black, a most forceful advocate for freedom of communication and the incorporation of the Bill of Rights as binding on the states. He defended the former through the plain meaning of the First Amendment and the latter through his reading of the intent of the framers of the Fourteenth Amendment.[88] To Black, reading rights out of the Constitution posed a far greater danger to American freedoms than reading rights into it.

Additional arguments for the interpretivist position – as noted by legal historian Raoul Berger – are found in the writings of James Madison and Thomas Jefferson. According to Madison, "if the sense in which the Constitution was accepted and ratified by the Nation . . . be not the guide in expounding it, there can be no security for a consistent and stable government."[89] According to Jefferson, "our peculiar security is in the possession of a written constitution. Let us not make it a blank paper by construction."[90]

Finally, interpretivists question the alternatives to interpretivism. They argue that if the Constitution does not authoritatively guide the Court's decisions, the policy preferences of the judicial majority will control. Where is the legitimacy of a rule by nine unelected people who do nothing more than decide cases based on their own values?

Alternatively, Justice William Brennan claims:

> A position that upholds constitutional claims only if they were within the specific contemplation of the Framers in effect establishes a presumption of resolving textual ambiguities against the claim of constitutional right. It is far from clear what justifies such a presumption against claims of right. Nothing intrinsic in the nature of interpretation – if there is such a thing as the nature of interpretation – commands such a passive approach to ambiguity. This is a choice no less political than any other; it expresses antipathy to claims of minority rights against the majority. Those who would restrict claims of right to the values of 1789 specifically articulated in the Constitution turn a blind eye to social progress and eschew adaptation of overarching principles to changes of social circumstance.[91]

An obvious case to criticize on these grounds is *Olmstead v. United States*, in which Chief Justice Taft declared that the Fourth Amendment's

[88] On freedom of speech, see *Barenblatt v. United States*, 360 U.S. 109 (1959). On the incorporation of the Bill of Rights, see *Adamson v. California*, 332 U.S. 46 (1947).
[89] Berger, *op. cit.*, n. 82, *supra*, p. 364. [90] Id. [91] *Id.* at 15.

protection against unreasonable searches and seizures did not extend to wiretaps on telephone wires because such activity was not within "the meaning of the 4th Amendment."[92] Similarly, Justice Black argued in a later wiretapping case that the Court's duty is "to carry out as nearly as possible the original intent of the Framers."[93] Did the Framers intend to prohibit wiretapping? Obviously not, so to Black and other interpretivists, the Constitution leaves such activity outside the purview of searches and seizures.

Though in an entirely different case, Brennan responded that such questions ought not be decided by divining the intent of the Framers. "A more fruitful inquiry, it seems to me, is whether the practices here challenged threaten those consequences which the Framers deeply feared."[94] If wiretapping of one's home in search of evidence without probable cause and a warrant threatens the type of personal privacy protected by the Fourth Amendment, then the amendment should forbid wiretapping.

Finally, it is not clear that the Framers intended that their intent be binding. Virtually every constitutional clause lacks definition. What are the Eighth Amendment's cruel and unusual punishments, or the Fourteenth Amendment's due process and equal protection? No doubt many of the framers of these amendments had certain "conceptions" of what the language meant. But according to constitutional theorist Ronald Dworkin, the "concepts" of due process, equal protection, and cruel and unusual punishments are written into the Constitution, not their conception:

> Suppose I tell my children simply that I expect them not to treat others unfairly. I no doubt have in mind examples of the conduct I mean to discourage, but I would not accept that my "meaning" was limited to these examples, for two reasons. First I would expect my children to apply my instructions to situations I had not and could not have thought about. Second, I stand ready to admit that some particular act I had thought was fair was in fact unfair, or vice versa, if one of my children is able to convince me of that later; in that case I should want to say that my instructions covered the case he cited, not that I had changed my instructions. I might say that I meant the family to be guided by the concept of fairness, not by any conception of fairness I might have had in mind.[95]

More devastating to the interpretivist cause is the position of James Madison. "As a guide to expounding and applying the provisions of the

[92] 277 U.S. 438 (1928), at 466. [93] *Berger v. New York*, 388 U.S. 41 (1967), at 87.
[94] *Abington Township v. Schempp*, 374 U.S. 203 (1963), at 236.
[95] *Taking Rights Seriously* (Cambridge, Mass.: Harvard University Press, 1977), p. 134.

Constitution, the debates and incidental decisions of the Convention can have no authoritative character."[96] "Thus the dilemma: If one believes the 'intent' of the framers is binding, one must not consider that form of intent as binding."[97]

The Empirical Reality

Whatever the merits of the normative arguments for or against intent, its application to the real world is a separate matter. Because many of those who ought to know better believe that intent really explains the justices' behavior, it behooves us to demonstrate the falsity of such belief, as well as its fatuousness, by reference not only to the justices' words but to the writings of commentators as well. And indeed, as we show below, choice based on group intent may be inconsistent and illogical.

The first question that needs answering is whether the concept of the "intent of the framers" is at all meaningful.[98]

Needless to say, the Constitution's framers never conceived of most issues the Court faces today, from affirmative action to workers' compensation. Moreover, even for issues familiar to them, the notion of group intent may be meaningless. To wit: It is well established, via mathematical proof, that every method of social or collective choice – every arrangement whereby individual choices are pooled to arrive at a collective decision – violates at least one principle required for reasonable and fair democratic decision making.[99]

[96] James Madison, *Letters and Other Writings of James Madison* (Philadelphia: Lippincott, 1865), III, 228. See also H. Jefferson Powell, "The Original Understanding of Original Intent," 98 *Harvard Law Review* 885 (1985); and Joseph M. Lynch, *Negotiating the Constitution: The Earliest Debates over Original Intent* (Ithaca, N.Y.: Cornell University Press, 1999), all of which come to the same conclusion.

[97] Walter Murphy, James Fleming, and William Harris II, *American Constitutional Interpretation* (New York: Foundation Press, 1986), p. 305.

[98] We thank Thomas H. Hammond of Michigan State University for his help in this section of the book.

[99] Kenneth Arrow, *Social Choice and Individual Values*, 2nd ed. (New Haven: Yale University Press, 1963); William H. Riker, *Liberalism Against Populism* (San Francisco: W. H. Freeman, 1982), ch. 5; Frank H. Easterbrook, "Ways of Criticizing the Court," 95 *Harvard Law Review* 802 (1982).

These desirable principles can be summarized in six seemingly innocuous rules: (1) Individuals are free to order their preferences as they see fit. (2) A winning choice may not be a loser, and vice versa; i.e., if the voters prefer A to B and B to C, A must defeat C. (3) An outcome may not be imposed regardless of whether the citizenry approves of it or not. (4) If unanimity prevails for one option over another, the less preferred option cannot win. (5) Identical preference patterns may not produce different results. (6) No individual may function as a dictator. For a fuller statement of these conditions, see

TABLE 2.1. *Hypothetical Choices of Three Legislators among Three Alternatives*

	Legislator		
	1	2	3
First choice	A	C	B
Second choice	B	A	C
Third choice	C	B	A

To achieve a meaningful choice, the preferences of the decision makers must conform to decision rules that reflect the actors' sense of reasonableness. In American society, this tends to mean majority rule (or at least plurality rule, with the winner being the choice that garners more votes than any other option). Equal weight is accorded the vote of each participant, that is, one person, one vote. Further, among a range of choices – for example, A, B, C – each decision maker must be free to order them preferentially as he or she sees fit. Any system that precludes a person from choosing a particular preference order is dictatorial, and hence morally unacceptable, unfair, and undemocratic. In exercising such choice, an option that no one chooses may not be imposed. Conversely, if everybody prefers A to B, then B may not become the social choice.

However, majority rule under these minimal conditions can produce cyclical judgments. Consider, for example, a panel of three legislators (or framers) with the preferences shown in Table 2.1. Legislator 1 prefers alternative A to alternative B, and also prefers alternative B to alternative C. Legislator 2 prefers alternative C to A, and A to B. Legislator 3 prefers alternative B to C, and C to A.

Assume legislators make their decisions by majority rule. Alternative A loses because legislators 2 and 3 together prefer C. Alternative B loses because legislators 1 and 2 together prefer A. And to make matters complete, alternative C loses because legislators 1 and 3 together prefer B. The result is a social preference cycle among the three alternatives: alternative A defeats alternative B, alternative B defeats alternative C, but alternative C defeats alternative A. Because Congress (or the Framers)

Riker, *Liberalism Against Populism*, pp. 116–19, and Easterbrook, "Ways of Criticizing the Court," pp. 823–31.

are a "they," not an "it,"[100] legislative preferences, and therefore intent, may well be intransitive.

This cycling need not necessarily occur. If legislator 3 prefers B to A, and C least of all, alternative A will win because it defeats both B and C. In this case, legislators 1 and 2 prefer A to B, and legislators 1 and 3 prefer A to C. C now becomes the least preferred option because 1 and 3 prefer B to C. But nothing prevents cycling from occurring, and as the size of the group increases from three members to, say, fifty-five (the number who attended the Constitutional Convention), the likelihood of cyclical preferences increases dramatically.[101] Cycling is always a potential problem, not just for legislatures, but for courts as well.[102]

Organizations can create rules that can limit the likelihood of cyclical results, for example, by arbitrarily keeping items off the agenda.[103] But this in no way limits the intransitivity of preferences. And if preferences are intransitive, the notion of group intent becomes illusory at best.

But even if preferences are not intransitive, group intent remains problematic. After all, who were the Framers? All fifty-five of the delegates who showed up at one time or another in Philadelphia during the summer of 1787? Some came and went.[104] Only thirty-nine signed the final document. Some probably had not read it. Assuredly, they were not all of a single mind. Apart from the delegates who refused to sign, should not the delegates to the various state conventions that were called to

[100] Kenneth A. Shepsle, "Congress Is a 'They,' Not an 'It': Legislative Intent as Oxymoron," 12 *International Review of Law and Economics* 239, 244 (1992).

[101] See Peter Ordeshook, *Game Theory and Political Theory* (New York: Cambridge University Press, 1986); cf. Bradford Jones, Benjamin Radcliff, Charles Taber, and Richard Timpone, "Condorcet Winners and the Paradox of Voting: Probability Calculations for Weak Preference Orders," 89 *American Political Science Review* 137 (1995), who demonstrate nonmonotonic likelihoods with weak preference structures.

[102] Professor, now Judge, Easterbrook provides a realistic example. See "Ways of Criticizing the Court," 95 *Harvard Law Review* 802 (1982), at 815–16. Extensive cycling would mean that the Court's decisions would have little relationship to the preferences of its justices. The Court, though, has various means that severely limit the actuality of cycling. See Maxwell L. Stearns, *Constitutional Process: A Social Choice Analysis of Supreme Court Decision Making* (Ann Arbor: University of Michigan Press, 2000).

[103] Kenneth A. Shepsle and Barry R. Weingast, "Structure-Induced Equilibrium and Legislative Choice," 37 *Public Choice* 503 (1981).

[104] Yates, e.g., whose notes "are next in importance" to Madison's. His notes cease with July 5, thereby omitting the crucial last two and a half months of the Convention. Max Farrand, ed., *The Records of the Federal Convention of 1789*, rev. ed. (New Haven: Yale University Press, 1966), I, xv, xiv.

ratify the Constitution also be counted as Framers? Unfortunately, commentators exclude these persons from consideration.

The intent of framers of constitutional amendments also lacks specification. For example, while Radical Republican Senator Charles Sumner (R-Mass.) insisted that "separate education deprived blacks of their Fourteenth Amendment rights,"[105] Lyman Trumbull (R-Ill.) viewed equal protection as covering only what were then considered civil rights: "the right to go and come; the right to enforce contracts; the right to convey his property; the right to buy property – those general rights that belong to mankind everywhere."[106] "So, two of the leading figures of the Thirty-ninth Congress fundamentally differed about what the Amendment they had enacted meant."[107]

This leads to our second question: If group intent is problematic, whose intent do we examine?

According to Berger, the most important source is the draftsman, the person who wrote the bill, amendment, or clause.[108] Yet Berger himself frequently disregards or disparages the latitudinal interpretations of the Fourteenth Amendment by section 1 coauthor John Bingham (R-Ohio) in favor of more limited constructions by less consequential Republican proponents of the bill. Alternatively, McNollgast argues that the intent of the pivotal coalition member, the one with the ability to make or break the deal, should matter most.[109] More often than not, these differences give any justice worthy of his or her robes the ability to find some framer who supports his or her positon.

But supposing we could determine whose intent mattered most, even the notion of individual intent can be problematic. Justice Scalia wrote precisely in a leading case that considered the constitutionality of a state statute:

> The number of possible motivations, to begin with, is not binary, or indeed even finite. In the present case, for example, a particular legislator need not have voted for the Act either because he wanted to foster religion or because he wanted to improve education. He may have thought the bill would provide jobs for his district, or may have wanted to make amends with a faction of his party he had alienated on another vote, or he may have been a close friend of the bill's sponsor, or he may have been repaying a favor he owed the Majority Leader, or he may

[105] Judith Baer, *Equality under the Constitution* (Ithaca: Cornell University Press, 1983), p. 96.

[106] *Id.* [107] *Id.* at 97. [108] Berger, *op. cit.*, n. 82, *supra*, p. 365.

[109] McNollgast, "Positive Canons: The Role of Legislative Bargains in Statutory Interpretation," 80 *Georgetown Law Journal* 705 (1992).

have hoped the Governor would appreciate his vote and make a fundraising appearance for him, or he may have been pressured to vote for a bill he disliked by a wealthy contributor or a flood of constituent mail, or he may have been seeking favorable publicity, or he may have been reluctant to hurt the feelings of a loyal staff member who worked on the bill, or he may have been mad at his wife who opposed the bill, or he may have been intoxicated and entirely unmotivated when the vote was called, or he may have accidentally voted "yes" instead of "no," or, of course, he may have had (and very likely did have) a combination of some of the above and many other motivations. To look for the sole purpose of even a single legislator is probably to look for something that does not exist.

Putting that problem aside, however, where ought we to look for the individual legislator's purpose? We cannot . . . assume that every member present . . . agreed with the motivation expressed in a particular legislator's pre-enactment floor or committee statement. . . . Can we assume . . . that they all agree with the motivation expressed in the staff-prepared committee reports . . . [or] post-enactment floor statements? Or post-enactment testimony from legislators, obtained expressly for the lawsuit? . . . media reports on . . . legislative bargaining? All these sources, of course, are eminently manipulable.

. . . If a state senate approves a bill by a vote of 26 to 25, and only one intended solely to advance religion, is the law unconstitutional? What if 13 of 26 had that intent? What if 3 of the 26 had the impermissible intent, but 3 of the 25 voting against the bill were motivated by religious hostility or were simply attempting to "balance" the votes of their impermissibly motivated colleagues? Or is it possible that the intent of the bill's sponsor is alone enough to invalidate it – on a theory, perhaps, that even though everyone else's intent was pure, what they produced was the fruit of a forbidden tree[?][110]

Despite all of these problems, let us assume for argument's sake that legislative intent does exist. The next question becomes: Can we find it?

Obviously, any assessment of intent must depend on the record that the authors of the language left. This record varies as between constitutional and statutory language, as well as from one constitutional provision or statute to another. In the case of the original Constitution, we have only a "carelessly kept" journal; plus Madison's notes, which he edited in 1819, thirty-two years after the events he reports; and a smattering of scattered notes from eight of the delegates to the Constitutional

[110] *Edwards v. Aguillard*, 482 U.S. 578 (1987), at 636–38. Also see parallel language by Justice Stevens in *Rogers v. Lodge*, 458 U.S. 613 (1982), at 642–43.

The other justices essentially disagree with Scalia's anti-intent position because "common sense suggests that inquiry benefits from reviewing additional information rather than ignoring it." *Wisconsin Public Intervenor v. Mortier*, 501 U.S. 597 (1991), at 611, n. 4.

Convention.[111] None of these documents identifies the Framers' intentions in even the most rudimentary fashion.

Apart from their fragmentary character, even official records meant to convey intent may falsify and mislead. The Congressional Record is a prime case in point. Until 1978, members of Congress were free to add to, subtract from, edit, and insert remarks they never uttered on the floor of the House or the Senate, notwithstanding the law that requires the Record to be "substantially a verbatim report of the proceedings of Congress."[112]

The upshot? Partisans on both sides of most every major constitutional issue have been able to support their contentions by equally plausible references to the Framers' intent. And given that the records pertaining to congressional legislation are much more voluminous than those of constitutional provisions, our observation applies to acts of Congress a fortiori. Grist for this mill includes the debates that preceded passage of the legislation; majority and minority committee reports; the statements and views of sponsors of the legislation; testimony and comments of individual legislators, government officials, and interested private entities given at committee and subcommittee hearings; and previous court decisions interpreting the statute.

According to former Senator John C. Danforth (R-Mo.), for example: "Any judge who tries to make legislative history out of the free-for-all that takes place on the floor of the Senate is on very dangerous ground."[113] Lower federal court judges do not disagree. According to Alex Kozinski of the Ninth Circuit Court of Appeals: "Legislative history can be cited to support almost any proposition, and frequently is."[114]

[111] Max Farrand, ed., *The Records of the Federal Convention of 1789*, rev. ed. (New Haven: Yale University Press, 1966), I, xiii. The eight delegates, in addition to Madison, were Robert Yates, Rufus King, James McHenry, William Pierce, William Paterson, Alexander Hamilton, Charles Pinckney, and George Mason.

[112] Marjorie Hunter, "Case of the Missing Bullets," *New York Times*, May 15, 1985, p. 24. This change presumably decreased the likelihood that 112 pages of events could appear on a day when the Senate had met for only eight seconds, and the House not at all. *Id.* For other examples of how Congress doctors its official records, see Harold J. Spaeth, *Supreme Court Policy Making* (San Francisco: W. H. Freeman, 1979), p. 72, and the references cited therein.

[113] Robert Pear, "With Rights Act Comes Fight to Clarify Congress's Intent," *New York Times*, November 18, 1991, p. A1.

[114] *Id.* An additional quotation from this same article explains why legislative history covers the waterfront of intent: " 'I would like to add some legislative history at the end of my remarks,' Representative Henry J. Hyde, Republican of Illinois, said as he casually dropped a 9,000-word interpretive memorandum into the Congressional Record."

Former Supreme Court Justice William Brennan summarized these problems well:

There are those who find legitimacy in fidelity to what they call "the intentions of the Framers." In its most doctrinaire incarnation, this view demands that Justices discern exactly what the Framers thought about the question under consideration and simply follow that intention in resolving the case before them. It is a view that feigns self-effacing deference to the specific judgments of those who forged our original social compact. But in truth it is little more than arrogance cloaked as humility. It is arrogant to pretend that from our vantage we can gauge accurately the intent of the Framers on application of principle to specific, contemporary problems. All too often, sources of potential enlightenment such as the records of the ratification debates provide sparse or ambiguous evidence of the original intention. Typically, all that can be gleaned is that the Framers themselves did not agree about the application or meaning of particular constitutional provisions, and hid their differences in cloaks of generality. Indeed, it is far from clear whose intention is relevant – that of the drafters, the congressional disputants, or the ratifiers in the states? – or even whether the idea of an original intention is a coherent way of thinking about a jointly drafted document drawing its authority from a general assent of the states. And apart from the problematic nature of our sources, our distance of two centuries cannot but work as a prism refracting all we perceive. One cannot help but speculate that the chorus of lamentations calling for interpretation faithful to "original intention" – and proposing nullification of interpretations that fail this quick litmus test – must inevitably come from persons who have no familiarity with the historical record.[115]

More succinctly, the deficiencies of interpretivism have led one critic so far as to assert that "the case for constitutional interpretation bound strictly to text and history is only slightly stronger than the case for the proposition that we inhabit a flat earth."[116]

The use to which intent may be put is perhaps best illustrated by cases in which the Court molds intent to create conflicts with plain meaning. We begin with the first major affirmative action case, *Regents of the University of California v. Bakke*. Four justices ruled that the quota system established by the medical school of the University of California at Davis violated the plain words of Title VI of the Civil Rights Act of 1964, which says, "No person in the United States shall, on the ground of race, color, or national origin, be excluded from participation in, be denied benefits of, or be subjected to discrimination under any program

[115] William Brennan, "Speech at Georgetown University," reprinted in *The Great Debate* (Washington, D.C.: Federalist Society, 1986), pp. 14–15.

[116] Lief Carter, *Contemporary Constitutional Lawmaking* (New York: Pergamon Press, 1985), p. 41.

or activity receiving federal financial assistance." They cited the rule that a constitutional issue should be avoided if a case can fairly be decided on statutory grounds[117] and concluded that the "ban on exclusion is crystal clear. Race cannot be the basis for excluding anyone from participation in a federally funded program." Four other justices held these words not to mean what they said because Title VI was enacted "to induce voluntary compliance with the requirement of nondiscriminatory treatment." That being so, "It is inconceivable that Congress intended to encourage voluntary efforts to eliminate the evil of racial discrimination while at the same time forbidding the voluntary use of race-conscious remedies." Justice Powell split the difference, ruling that race could be one of a number of factors governing admission to the medical school, but it could not be the only factor.[118]

In the next affirmative action case that the Court addressed, *Steelworkers v. Weber*, the liberals were able to create a majority opinion that positioned meaning and intent adversely to one another. At issue was the meaning of Title VII of the same 1964 Civil Rights Act that *Bakke* concerned,[119] which makes it unlawful for an employer "to discriminate . . . because of . . . race." Over the objections of the two dissenters – Rehnquist and Burger – who said that the employers' quota system was plainly illegal, the five-member majority ruled the system legal because, citing an 1892 decision,

> It is a "familiar rule that a thing may be within the letter of the statute and yet not within the statute, because not within its spirit, nor within the intention of its makers."[120]

Within the spirit? We leave such answers to mystics. But within the intention of its makers? Not if we abide by the specific statements of the bill's chief sponsors, as Rehnquist demonstrates in his legally compelling dissent. Nevertheless, the majority brushed this aside, arguing that it "would be ironic indeed if a law triggered by . . . concern over centuries of racial injustice . . . constituted the first legislative prohibition of all voluntary, private, race-conscious efforts to abolish . . . racial segregation."[121]

The message is clear: If all else fails, simply dust off this language and apply it to destroy both plain meaning of laws and specific statements

[117] The rule cited here is, of course, directly antithetical to Marshall's decision in *Marbury v. Madison*, discussed in Chapter 1.

[118] 438 U.S. 265 (1978), at 412, 418, 336, 319–20.

[119] *Bakke* concerned Title VI.

[120] 443 U.S. 193 (1979), at 199–200, 201.

[121] *Id.* at 204.

of intent.[122] Though its use has been sporadic, by no means does this maxim have applicability only to affirmative action cases. Four years prior to *Steelworkers v. Weber*, the Court used it to deny a union's request for a jury when it was tried for criminal contempt even though the pertinent statute said that the accused shall enjoy a jury trial in "all cases of contempt."[123]

By no means does the Court always find it necessary to use the maxim when it wishes to rationalize policy on the basis of intent rather than plain meaning. It is able to do so very nicely without even a passing reference to it. As an example, consider *Maryland v. Craig* where the majority said that the confrontation clause of the Sixth Amendment does not mean what it says because the purpose of the clause is to ensure that evidence admitted against the accused is reliable and subject to "rigorous adversarial testing."[124] The four dissenters focused on the obvious:

> Whatever else it may mean in addition, the defendant's constitutional right "to be confronted with witnesses against him" means, always and everywhere, at least what it explicitly says: the " 'right to meet face to face all those who appear and give evidence at trial.' "[125]

Note should also be made that the Court has at its disposal additional rules of its own creation that allow it to disregard both plain meaning and intent, without replacing either of them with another variant of the legal model. Chief among such devices are the Ashwander Rules that Justice Brandeis formulated in a case of the same name. One such rule reads as follows:

> When the validity of an act of the Congress is drawn in question, and even if a serious doubt of constitutionality is raised, it is a cardinal principle that this Court will first ascertain whether a construction of the statute is fairly possible by which the question may be avoided.[126]

It conveniently enables the Court to concurrently disregard plain meaning and intent in order to concoct an alternative interpretation of

[122] The majority's view of intent contradicts not only the plain meaning of the act but the dissenters' view of intent as well. Rehnquist makes a compelling case, buttressed by numerous quotes from floor leader Hubert Humphrey (D-Minn.), that the intent of the framers of Title VII was to abolish *all* race-preferential treatment.

[123] *Muniz v. Hoffman*, 422 U.S. 454 (1975), at 457.

[124] 497 U.S. 836 (1990), at 857.

[125] *Id.* at 862.

[126] *Ashwander v. Tennessee Valley Authority*, 297 U.S. 288 (1936), at 348. Though the Ashwander Rules were formulated in a dissenting opinion, that has not precluded their use by judges at all levels of the judicial hierarchy to rationalize their decisions.

statutory language of which the majority approves. Two examples will suffice: In *Webster v. Reproductive Services*[127] the Supreme Court construed a Missouri statute limiting abortion rights. One section requires doctors to perform such tests "as are necessary to make a finding" of viability on fetuses over twenty weeks of gestational age. As fetuses at twenty weeks have no lung capacity and thus lack viability, the statute, according to the lower court, required superfluous tests and thus imposed "unnecessary and significant health risks for both the mother and the fetus."[128] To interpret the statute in a way that would avoid constitutional difficulties, the plurality simply said that the statute did not absolutely require the mandated tests.

A second example involves a key provision of the Bankruptcy Reform Act of 1978, which makes certain household goods and personal possessions automatically exempt from the blanket liens that finance companies standardly obtain as security for consumer loans. On the basis of such liens, the creditor company would seize the property of debtors who filed for bankruptcy. To avoid deciding whether the retroactive application of the provision would take creditors' property without due process of law, the Court unanimously rewrote the language, notwithstanding congressional intent, to deny protection to consumers who incurred their debts prior to the statute's enactment.[129]

Given the variety of reasons that legislative intent may not exist, and the problems of finding it in those cases where it does exist, perhaps we ought to discard completely judicial efforts to fathom intent. If legislative preferences are meaningless as social choices, interpretivism as a guide to judicial decision becomes unintelligible. So also strictures that courts and judges should exercise judicial restraint, a subject we discuss in Chapter 10.

Like plain meaning, not only has no one systematically demonstrated that legislative or framers' intent influences the decisions of Supreme Court justices, no proponent of intent has even suggested a falsifiable test for this component of the legal model.

[127] 492 U.S. 490 (1989). [128] 851 F2d 1071, at 1075.

[129] *United States v. Security Industrial Bank*, 459 U.S. 70 (1982). A variation of the quoted Ashwander Rule was used to sustain the constitutionality of a statute conditioning minors' access to abortion: "Where fairly possible courts should construe a statute to avoid a danger of unconstitutionality." *Ohio v. Akron Reproductive Health Center*, 497 U.S. 502 (1990), at 514. Unlike the Ashwander Rules, which were formulated in an opinion to which only the author – Brandeis – subscribed, this one had the support of a second justice, Burger, in addition to its author, Powell. *Planned Parenthood Assn. v. Ashcroft*, 462 U.S. 476 (1983), at 493.

Precedent

Precedent, or stare decisis, quite simply means adherence to what has been decided. Today's decisions are linked with those handed down yesterday. The law thereby develops a quality of connectedness, an appearance of stability. But no more than plain meaning and intent does precedent restrict the justices' discretion in the types of cases that come before the Court; nor does its use explain any better why the justices decided a particular case in favor of one party rather than the other.

Unlike plain meaning and the variations on intent, judges use precedent as an ostensible explanation for virtually every decision they make. Though it may appear in isolation from other aspects of the legal model, it much more often buttresses the meaning or the intent that the Court ascribes to the statute or the constitutional provision at issue. That is, the justices will support their judgment that a legal or constitutional provision means this rather than that by citing a number of previous decisions. As a result, the frequency accorded precedent far surpasses that accorded any other aspect of the legal model.

Precedent parallels meaning and intent in its application to both statutory construction and constitutional interpretation. As the justices unanimously explained:

> Adherence to precedent is, in the usual case, a cardinal and guiding principal of adjudication, and "[c]onsiderations of stare decisis have special force in the area of statutory interpretation, for here, unlike in the context of constitutional interpretation, the legislative power is implicated, and Congress remains free to alter what we have done."[130]

But in cases concerning constitutional interpretation, the Court is more openly willing to reexamine its precedents because the Constitution is rarely amended and also – according to Chief Justice Taney – to ensure that the reasoning on which such decisions depend remains cogent.[131] Justice Scalia recently restated the justification for the individual justice to discount constitutional precedents:

> With some reservation concerning decisions that have become so embedded in our system of government that return is no longer possible . . . I agree with Justice

[130] *California v. Federal Energy Regulatory Commission*, 495 U.S. 490 (1990), at 499.

[131] *Mitchell v. W. T. Grant Co.*, 416 U.S. 600 (1974), at 628; *Passenger Cases*, 7 Howard 283 (1849), at 470. Three recent Courts adhere to this stricture, deviating but little from one another, as Table 2.2, below, shows. They overturned constitutional decisions approximately twice as often as they did nonconstitutional ones.

Douglas: "A judge looking at a constitutional decision may have compulsions to revere past history and accept what was once written. But he remembers above all else that it is the Constitution which he swore to support and defend, not the gloss which his predecessors have put on it." Douglas, Stare Decisis, 49 Colum L Rev 735, 736 (1949).[132]

Although precedent is typically presented as an obligatory norm, except that constitutional issues are always open – theoretically – for reconsideration, the justices have rarely acceded to those of which they disapprove.[133] Justice Stevens – in dissent, of course – provides a candid rationale for nonadherence to precedents of which a justice disapproves:

Despite my respect for *stare decisis*, I am unwilling to accept *Seminole Tribe* as controlling precedent. First and foremost, the reasoning of that opinion is so profoundly mistaken and so fundamentally inconsistent with the Framers' conception of the constitutional order that it has forsaken any claim to the usual deference or respect owed to decisions of this Court. *Stare decisis*, furthermore, has less force in the area of constitutional law. . . . Finally, by its own repeated overruling of earlier precedent, the majority has itself discounted the importance of *stare decisis* in this area of the law. The kind of judicial activism manifested in cases like *Seminole Tribe, Alden v. Maine* . . . represents such a radical departure from the proper role of this Court that it should be opposed whenever the opportunity arises.[134]

Though precedent, like plain meaning and intent, looks backward, it does not appreciably restrict judicial discretion, for a number of reasons. First, and most basic, precedents lie on both sides of most every controversy, at least at the appellate level. If losing litigants at trial did not have authority to support their contentions, no basis for appeal would exist. Even judges themselves recognize this fact. Judge Frank M. Coffin of the U.S. Court of Appeals for the First Circuit said: "Precedent is certainly real and we learn to live with it. But if precedent clearly governed, a case would never get as far as the Court of Appeals: the parties would settle."[135]

That view was echoed by Judge Frank H. Easterbrook of the United States Court of Appeals for the Seventh Circuit, in Chicago.

[132] *South Carolina v. Gathers*, 490 U.S. 805 (1989), at 835.

[133] See Spaeth and Segal, *op. cit.*, n. 16, *supra.*

[134] *Kimel v. Florida Board of Regents*, 145 L Ed 2d 522 (2000), at 551–52.

[135] Linda Greenhouse, "Precedent for Lower Courts: Tyrant or Teacher," *New York Times*, January 29, 1988, p. 12.

"Given that litigation is so expensive, why are parties willing to take their cases up?" he asked. "It's because precedent doesn't govern. Precedent covers the major premise. But the mind-set of the judge governs the minor premise."[136]

As further evidence that precedents exist to support the contentions of both parties, merely consult any appellate court case containing a dissenting opinion. This, as well as the majority opinion, will likely contain a substantial number of references to previously decided cases. Reference to these cases will undoubtedly show that those cited by the majority support its decision, while those specified by the dissent bolster its contrary judgment. The same can be said for cases without dissent, as any reading of the litigants' briefs will demonstrate.

As an example, consider the first two campaign spending cases that the Rehnquist Court decided. In the first case, by a 5-to-4 vote, the justices declared unconstitutional a provision of the Federal Election Campaign Act as applied to a nonprofit corporation formed for "prolife" purposes.[137] Not only did the corporation not need to set up a political action committee through which its funds must be filtered, it also has a First Amendment right to spend its own money directly. The majority as well as the dissenters located an abundance of precedents to support their respective contentions. The second case held that government not only could prohibit nonprofit corporations from contributing money directly to political candidates, but it also could forbid them from spending their own money on behalf of candidates. Because the three conservatives who held that the restrictions violated the First Amendment – Kennedy, O'Connor, and Scalia – were able simply to cite the precedents used in the preceding case, plus that decision itself, as authority for their position, it might superficially appear that the majority would not fare as well precedent-wise. Not so. The Court has taken a very dim view of censorship, which is what the statute at issue decreed, authorizing it only with respect to the military, prisoners, and minor children. Moreover, the Court has consistently stated that political speech is entitled to special protection. Indeed, Justice Marshall, in his opinion of the Court, admitted as much:

Certainly, the use of funds to support a political candidate is "speech"; independent campaign expenditures constitute "political expression 'at the core of our electoral process and of the First Amendment freedoms.' "[138]

[136] *Id.*
[137] *Federal Election Commission v. Massachusetts Citizens for Life*, 479 U.S. 238 (1986).
[138] *Austin v. Michigan Chamber of Commerce*, 494 U.S. 652 (1990), at 657.

Nevertheless, Marshall had no difficulty finding seven cases to support the law's constitutionality, including several citations to the majority opinion in *Massachusetts Citizens for Life* itself![139]

A second issue may be briefly adumbrated to further illustrate precedent's ability to serve contradictory masters simultaneously: the conditioning of government action in such a way that it inhibits the free exercise of religion. On the one hand, government may not deny individuals benefits (e.g., unemployment compensation for refusing to work on the Sabbath). But on the other, government may deny welfare benefits to an individual who refuses, for religious reasons, to show a social security number, or to construct a road that defiles government land that had traditionally been used by an Indian tribe for religious purposes.[140]

Not uncommonly, the majority itself will note the existence of alternative lines of precedent. The Court's landmark decision in *Griswold v. Connecticut* provides a most instructive example.[141] Not only did the majority identify alternative sets of precedents, it did so in a decision that shattered legal precedent by establishing a new right to privacy based substantially on a heretofore unused provision of the Constitution: the Ninth Amendment.[142] In ruling unconstitutional a law that criminalized a married couple's use of birth control, the Court rejected a discredited line of largely overruled cases.[143] Instead, the majority candidly recognized the lack of textual authority for its holding:

> The association of people is not mentioned in the Constitution nor in the Bill of Rights. The right to educate a child in a school of the parents' choice – whether public or private or parochial – is also not mentioned. Nor is the right to study any particular subject or any foreign language. Yet the First Amendment has been construed to include certain of those rights.[144]

139 *Id.* at 658–66.

140 *Sherbert v. Verner*, 374 U.S. 398 (1963), and *Hobbie v. Florida Unemployment Appeals Commission*, 480 U.S. 136 (1987), versus *Bowen v. Roy*, 476 U.S. 693 (1986), and *Lyng v. Northwest Indian Cemetery Protective Assn.*, 485 U.S. 439 (1988). Also see *Employment Division, Oregon Dept. of Human Resources v. Smith*, 494 U.S. 872 (1990), upholding the denial of unemployment benefits to persons who used peyote for religious purposes.

141 381 U.S. 479 (1965).

142 It is especially instructive to note that the Court's precedent-shattering decision did *not* require it to formally overrule any precedent. It shattered precedent by creation, not destruction.

143 I.e., "Overtones of some arguments suggest that Lochner v. New York, 198 U.S. 45, should be our guide." 381 U.S. at 481–82.

144 *Id.* at 482.

The Court then proceeded to cite twelve cases to document the quoted language, which cases also became the authority for the right that its decision created.

As a more recent, but equally innovative, example of precedent's ability to use past decisions to create new and innovative law, consider *Cruzon v. Director, Missouri Department of Health*, in which the Court created a constitutional right to die.[145] To document the principle underlying the decision – "that a competent person has a constitutionally protected liberty interest in refusing unwanted medical treatment" – and thereby sustain the Court's ruling, Chief Justice Rehnquist cited five cases as precedent: one pertaining to compulsory vaccination, another to search and seizure, a third to forcible medication of prisoners, and the final pair to mandatory behavior modification and the confinement of children.[146]

A second reason why precedent does not restrict judicial discretion is because it consists of two components: the court's decision and the material facts that the court took into account in arriving at its decision. Because the facts in two appellate cases invariably differ, and the degree of factual similarity and dissimilarity between any two given cases involves an intensely personal and subjective judgment, judges may pick and choose among precedents to find those that accord with their policy preferences, while simultaneously asserting that these are also the ones that best accord with the facts of the case at hand.

Third, jurists disagree over what constitutes a precedent. One school accepts the previously mentioned considerations: decision, plus material facts. The other ascertains the ratio decidendi, the underlying principle on which the case was decided. Defining the ratio decidendi in an intersubjectively transmissible fashion seems all but impossible; it does appear, however, to turn on a fairly basic principle, one typically more global than the rule of law that the court cites as authority for its decision.

Two cases involving the inheritance rights of illegitimate children provide an instructive example of this approach to precedent. The cases not only came from the same state, Louisiana, each was decided incompatibly with the other, thereby providing courts and judges with authority to rule in favor of or against the children depending on the decision maker's subjective preferences. The first case held that the five illegitimate children of a woman could sue for damages because of her wrongful death

[145] 497 U.S. 261 (1990). [146] *Id.* at 278–80.

due to negligent medical treatment. Starting "from the premise that illegitimate children are not 'nonpersons'" (an obvious statement if there ever was one!) the Court ruled the statute prohibiting such actions unconstitutional because "[t]he rights asserted here involve the intimate, familial relationship between a child and his own mother."[147] The second case, decided three years later, saw the three dissenters from the first case join with Nixon's first two appointees, Burger and Blackmun, to rule that Louisiana could constitutionally prohibit acknowledged illegitimate offspring from sharing their father's estate equally with his legitimate children. "Levy did not say . . . that a State can never treat an illegitimate child differently from legitimate offspring." The law has a rational basis: "promoting family life and of directing the disposition of property left within the State."[148] As a consequence, the Court has a perfectly good precedent on both sides of the matter: if it wishes to rule in favor of illegitimates, *Levy* and its progeny nicely suffice;[149] if it does not, *Labine* is preferable.[150]

Clearly then, precedent as a component of the legal model provides virtually no guide to the justices' decisions. All that one can say is that precedent is a matter of good form, rather than a limit on the operation of judicial policy preferences. A court should lard its opinions with precedents, but doing so will not inhibit the exercise of discretion. And even if the court should confront a situation with but a single line of precedents – perhaps because it has decided only one case in point – it has devices that enable it to deviate from what has been decided, and to do so, moreover, compatibly with good legal form.

There are four such devices – obiter dicta, distinguishing a precedent, limiting (or extending) a precedent in principle, and overruling a precedent. The first two technically do not alter the scope of the precedent involved; the latter two do.

Obiter Dicta

Obiter dicta, or simply dicta, indicate that specified portions of the opinion in a previously decided case consist of surplus language. As such,

[147] *Levy v. Louisiana*, 391 U.S. 68 (1968), at 70, 71.

[148] *Labine v. Vincent*, 401 U.S. 532 (1971), at 536.

[149] See *Weber v. Aetna Casualty & Surety Co.*, 406 U.S. 164 (1972); *Gomez v. Perez*, 409 U.S. 535 (1973); *New Jersey Welfare Rights Organization v. Cahill*, 411 U.S. 619 (1973); *Jimenez v. Weinberger*, 417 U.S. 628 (1974); and *Trimble v. Gordon*, 430 U.S. 762 (1977).

[150] See *Mathews v. Lucas*, 427 U.S. 495 (1976); *Norton v. Mathews*, 427 U.S. 524 (1976); *Fiallo v. Bell*, 430 U.S. 787 (1976); and *Lalli v. Lalli*, 439 U.S. 259 (1978).

the reasoning contained in those portions do not control decision in the case at bar. An oft-cited example concerns the power of the President to remove federal officials from office. Congress had authorized the President to remove postmasters short of their four-year term of office only with the advice and consent of the Senate. In 1920, Woodrow Wilson removed the Portland, Oregon, postmaster without Senate approval. In a lengthy opinion, William Howard Taft, the only person to occupy the White House and a seat on the Supreme Court, ruled that the President could remove any and all executive officials at will.[151] With the establishment of executive agencies during the early New Deal whose officials exercised quasilegislative and quasijudicial power, the question of presidential removal arose again. The Court thereupon declared *Myers* applicable only to those executive officials who exercised purely executive power. Congress could restrict the President's removal power of all other federal officials.[152]

Distinguishing a Precedent

The other method of avoiding adherence to precedent without formally altering the precedent in question distinguishes the precedent. Its use merely requires the court to assert that the facts of the case before it sufficiently differ from the situational aspects of the precedent. The cases concerning the inheritance rights of illegitimates illustrate the matter well, particularly *Lalli v. Lalli*, where the plurality took especial pains to distinguish the situation therein from *Trimble v. Gordon*, which had been decided eighteen months earlier.[153] *Lalli* concerned a New York law that bars illegitimates from inheriting their fathers' estates unless the intestate father had gone to court and received judicial recognition of his paternity within two years of the child's birth. The *Trimble* majority had declared unconstitutional an Illinois law that allowed illegitimates to inherit only from intestate mothers, not fathers. The *Lalli* plurality stated that the New York law "is different in important respects" from the Illinois statute because "even a judicial determination of paternity was insufficient to permit inheritance" in Illinois, while "the marital status of the parents is irrelevant" to New York. "A related difference" pertains to their respective purposes. The Illinois law was "a means of encouraging legitimate family relationships," while "no such justifi-

[151] *Myers v. United States*, 272 U.S. 52 (1926).
[152] *Humphrey's Executor v. United States*, 295 U.S. 602 (1935).
[153] 439 U.S. 259 (1978), and 430 U.S. 762 (1977).

cation" supports the New York law. Its purpose, instead, "is to provide for the just and orderly disposition of property at death."[154]

Limiting a Precedent in Principle

The first and less drastic of the two methods of formally altering precedent limits them in principle. A classic example concerns the matter of taxpayers' suits. Initially, the Court flatly prohibited them as a means of challenging the purpose for which federal funds were spent. Given that there are millions of federal taxpayers, their individual interests are minute and indeterminable. Any individual taxpayer therefore suffers only an indirect injury at best. Access to the federal courts, however, requires direct and substantial injury.[155] Forty-five years later, the Court qualified this policy by carving out an exception to the flat ban. If the taxpayer challenged Congress's expenditure on the basis that it exceeded some specific constitutional limitation on Congress's power to tax and spend money (in this case, the establishment clause of the First Amendment), then the taxpayer has standing to sue.[156]

A woman's right to an abortion provides a second example. In *Roe v. Wade*,[157] the Court held that during the first trimester of pregnancy a woman had an untrammeled right to an abortion. Subsequent decisions have qualified the holding in *Roe*, however, to read that women have a right to an abortion without undue governmental interference.[158]

Overruling Precedent

The other way in which a court may formally alter precedent is to overrule it. Because of the other means available to manipulate precedent, none of which shatters the appearance of consistency and predictability of judicial decision making to the extent that overruling does, it rarely occurs. On the other hand, when the Court does overrule precedent, it tends to say so in a rather straightforward fashion. Thus, we may determine the frequency of overruling. As Table 2.2 shows, the Supreme Court has overruled its own precedents only 128 times between the 1953 and 2000 terms. By comparison, it has declared more than four times as many laws unconstitutional during this same period.

[154] 439 U.S. at 266, 267, 268. [155] *Frothingham v. Mellon*, 262 U.S. 447 (1923).
[156] *Flast v. Cohen*, 392 U.S. 83 (1968). [157] 410 U.S. 113 (1973).
[158] *Maher v. Roe*, 432 U.S. 464 (1977); *Webster v. Reproductive Health Services*, 492 U.S. 490 (1989).

TABLE 2.2. *Precedents Overruled, 1953–2000 Terms*

Court	*N*	Constitutional	Nonconstitutional	Percent constitutional	Overrulings per term
Warren	43	29.0	14.0	67.4	2.7
Burger	46	29.5	16.5	64.1	2.6
Rehnquist	39	26.0	13.0	66.7	2.6
TOTALS	128	84.5	43.5	66.0	2.7

Even so, when the Court decides to overrule itself, it not uncommonly will do so – *mirabile dictu* – on the basis of precedent itself. In 1961, for example, the Court ruled that no person could be convicted on the basis of evidence secured from an unreasonable search or seizure, thereby overruling a 1949 decision that allowed state officials to use such evidence.[159] The Court noted that it had just prohibited the states from using the fruits of a coerced confession and cited that decision[160] as its authority to overrule *Wolf*: "Why should not the same rule apply to what is tantamount to coerced testimony by way of unconstitutional seizure of goods, papers, effects, documents, etc.[?]"[161]

A more recent example concerns a choice of law question: the extent to which state rather than federal law governs a state's title to riverbeds within its boundaries. In 1973, the Court ruled that such controversies must be resolved on the basis of federal law.[162] Four years later, the Court overruled itself: "Since one system of resolution of property disputes has been adhered to from 1845 until 1973, and the other only for the past three years, a return to the former would more closely conform to the expectations of property owners than would adherence to the latter."[163]

Finally, one should not assume that when a court does adhere to precedent no policy change can occur. Not uncommonly adherence to precedent will not only alter the Court's policy, but also expand the scope of the precedent to which the Court is adhering. A recent example concerns the direct purchaser rule, which limits those who may bring an action for the violation of the antitrust laws. The Court had held that only direct

159 *Wolf v. Colorado*, 338 U.S. 25 (1949). 160 *Rogers V. Richmond*, 365 U.S. 534 (1961).
161 *Mapp v. Ohio*, 367 U.S. 643 (1961), at 656.
162 *Bonelli Cattle Co. v. Arizona*, 414 U.S. 313 (1973).
163 *Oregon ex rel. State Land Board v. Corvallis Sand & Gravel Co.*, 429 U.S. 363 (1977), at 382.

purchasers suffer a redressible injury, not their customers, who are indirect purchasers.[164] The rationale for the rule was problems of proof and apportionment of damages. But the Court applied the rule even where state law required the direct purchaser – here a public utility that had purchased gas from a producer and the pipeline that transported it – to pass its costs on to its ratepayers, and to which the rule's rationale accordingly did not apply. As the dissent observed:

> ... I cannot agree with the rigid and expansive holding that in no case, even in the utility context, would it be possible to determine in a reliable way a pass-through to consumers of an illegal overcharge that would measure the extent of their damage.[165]

While precedent seems no more likely to explain the Supreme Court's decisions than plain meaning or intent, we have developed systematic tests for its operationalization, which we present in Chapter 7. To the extent that the doctrine of stare decisis is falsifiable, it also turns out to be false.

We conclude the section on the legal model with the following comment from Judge Richard Posner:

> There is a tremendous amount of sheer hypocrisy in judicial opinion writing. Judges have a terrible anxiety about being thought to base their opinions on guesses, on their personal views. To allay that anxiety, they rely on the apparatus of precedent and history, much of it extremely phony.[166]

We now leave what Posner states to be the phony world of precedent and history, and examine what we believe to be the real world of attitudes and values.

[164] *Hanover Shoe, Inc. v. United Shoe Machinery Corp.*, 392 U.S. 481 (1968), and *Illinois Brick Co. v. Illinois*, 431 U.S. 720 (1977).

[165] *Kansas v. Utilicorp United Inc.*, 497 U.S. 199 (1990), at 225.

[166] Linda Greenhouse, "In His Opinion," *New York Times*, September 26, 1999, p. A13.

3

Models of Decision Making

The Attitudinal and Rational Choice Models

The legal model, as Chapter 2 explains, holds that the Supreme Court decides disputes before it in light of the facts of the case vis-à-vis precedent, the plain meaning of the Constitution and statutes, and the intent of the framers. We have shown that both litigants generally have precedents supporting them and each side typically alleges that either the plain meaning of the legal provisions at issue and/or the intent of the law makers supports its position. If various aspects of the legal model can support either side of any given dispute that comes before the Court, and the quality of these positions cannot be reliably and validly measured a priori, then the legal model hardly satisfies as an explanation of Supreme Court decisions. By being able to "explain" everything, in the end it explains nothing.

THE ATTITUDINAL MODEL

We move now to an alternative explanation of the Court's decisions, the attitudinal model. The attitudinal model represents a melding together of key concepts from legal realism, political science, psychology, and economics.[1] This model holds that the Supreme Court decides disputes in light of the facts of the case vis-à-vis the ideological attitudes and values of the justices. Simply put, Rehnquist votes the way he does because he is extremely conservative; Marshall voted the way he did because he was extremely liberal.

[1] See Forrest Maltzmann, James Spriggs, and Paul Wahlbeck, *The Collegial Game* (New York: Cambridge University Press, 2000), ch. 1.

The Legal Realists

The attitudinal model has its genesis in the legal realist movement of the 1920s. The movement, led by Karl Llewellyn and Jerome Frank, among others, reacted to the conservative and formalistic jurisprudence then in vogue. According to the classical legal scholars of the time, law was

> a complete and autonomous system of logically consistent principles, concepts and rules. The judge's techniques were socially neutral, his private views irrelevant; judging was more like finding than making, a matter of necessity rather than choice.[2]

Legal jurisprudence had hardly advanced since the great British jurist Sir William Blackstone wrote in the eighteenth century that judges "are the depositories of the laws; the living oracles, who must decide in all cases of doubt." He is sworn

> to determine, not according to his own private judgment, but according to the known laws and customs of the land; not delegated to pronounce a new law, but to maintain and expound the old one. Yet this rule admits of exception, where the former determination is most evidently contrary to reason; much more if it be clearly contrary to the divine law. But even in such cases the subsequent judges do not pretend to make a new law, but to vindicate the old one from misrepresentation. For if it be found that the former decision is manifestly absurd or unjust, it is declared, not that such a sentence was bad law, but that it was not law.[3]

Against this nescient theory of a static law that judges merely find rather than make, the legal realists argued that lawmaking inhered in judging. According to Karl Llewellyn, the first principle of legal realism is the "conception of law in flux, of moving law, and of judicial creation of law."[4]

Judicial creation of law did not result because bad jurists sought power for themselves, but as inevitable fallout from an ever-changing society. According to Jerome Frank:

> The layman thinks that it would be possible so to revise the law books that they would be something like logarithm tables, that the lawyers could, if only they would, contrive some kind of legal sliderule for finding exact legal answers. . . .

[2] Yosal Rogat, "Legal Realism," in Paul Edwards, ed., *The Encyclopedia of Philosophy* (New York: Macmillan, 1972), p. 420.

[3] Quoted in Walter F. Murphy and C. Hermann Pritchett, eds., *Courts, Judges and Politics*, 4th ed. (New York: Random House, 1986), pp. 14, 15.

[4] Karl Llewellyn, "Some Realism about Realism – Responding to Dean Pound," 44 *Harvard Law Review* 1237 (1931).

> But the law as we have it is uncertain, indefinite, subject to incalculable changes. This condition the public ascribes to the men of law; the average person considers either that lawyers are grossly negligent or that they are guilty of malpractice, venally obscuring simple legal truths in order to foment needless litigation, engaging in a guild conspiracy of distortion and obfuscation in the interest of larger fees. . . .
>
> Yet the layman errs in his belief that this lack of precision and finality is to be ascribed to lawyers. The truth of the matter is that the popular notion of the possibilities of legal exactness is based upon a misconception. The law always has been, is now, and will ever continue to be, largely vague and variable. And how could this be otherwise? The law deals with human relations in their most complicated aspects. The whole confused, shifting helter-skelter of life parades before it – more confused than ever, in our kaleidoscope age.
>
> Even in a relatively static society, men have never been able to construct a comprehensive, eternalized set of rules anticipating all possible legal disputes and settling them in advance. Even in such a social order no one can foresee all the future permutations and combinations of events; situations are bound to occur which were never contemplated when the original rules were made. How much less is such a frozen legal system possible in modern times. . . . Our society would be straight-jacketed were not the courts, with the able assistance of lawyers, constantly overhauling the law and adapting it to the realities of ever-changing social, industrial and political conditions.[5]

If judges necessarily create law, how do they come to their decisions? To the legal realists, the answer clearly is not to be found in "legal rules and concepts insofar as they purport to describe what either courts or people are actually doing."[6] Judicial opinions containing such rules merely rationalize decisions; they are not the causes of them.

Without clear answers to how judges actually made decisions, the legal realists called for an empirical, scientific study of law,[7] taking as dictum the statement of Oliver Wendell Holmes, Jr., that "the prophecies of what courts will do in fact, and nothing more pretentious, are what I mean by law." "The object of our study, then, is prediction."[8]

The Behavioralists

Scholars responded only slowly to the call for scientific study of law. Jerome Frank attempted to use the theories of Sigmund Freud and Jean

[5] Jerome Frank, *Law and the Modern Mind* (New York: Coward-McCann, 1949), pp. 5–7.

[6] Llewellyn, *op. cit.*, n. 4, *supra*, p. 1237.

[7] Hessel Yntema, "Legal Science and Reform," 34 *Columbia Law Review* 209 (1934).

[8] Oliver Wendell Holmes, "The Path of the Law," 10 *Harvard Law Review* 460–61, 457 (1897). While an effective counsel need not be able to explain decisions as long as he can predict them, for social scientists, explanation is paramount.

Piaget to explain judicial decisions, but understandably little has come of this line of work.

Meanwhile, the heretofore misnomered discipline of political science began to test its theories scientifically. This movement, known as behavioralism, argued that

1. Political science can ultimately become a science capable of prediction and explanation. . . .
2. Political science should concern itself primarily, if not exclusively, with phenomena which can actually be observed. . . .
3. Data should be quantified and "findings" based upon quantifiable data. . . .
4. Research should be theory oriented and theory directed.[9]

Among early behavioral works was a 1948 book by C. Herman Pritchett entitled *The Roosevelt Court*. It systematically examined dissents, concurrences, voting blocs, and ideological configurations from the Court's nonunanimous decisions between 1937 and 1947. Pritchett did not provide a theory of Supreme Court decision making, yet he made the assumptions behind his work quite explicit. "This book, then, undertakes to study the politics and values of the Roosevelt Court through the nonunanimous opinions handed down by the justices" and acknowledged that the justices are "motivated by their own preferences."[10]

The Psychological Influence

Glendon Schubert, drawing on the work of psychologist Clyde Coombs, first provided a detailed attitudinal model of Supreme Court decision making.[11] Schubert assumed that case stimuli and the justices' values could be ideologically scaled. To illustrate: Imagine a search and seizure whose constitutionality the Court must determine. Assume the police searched a person's house with a valid warrant supported by probable cause. There were no extenuating circumstances. The search uncovers an incriminating diary. Now imagine a second search, similar to the first in that probable cause existed, but in which the police failed to obtain a warrant. Again, there were no extenuating circumstances.

[9] Albert Somit and Joseph Tanenhaus, *The Development of Political Science* (Boston: Allyn and Bacon, 1967), pp. 177–78.

[10] (New York: Macmillan, 1948), pp. xii, xiii.

[11] Clyde Coombs, *A Theory of Data* (New York: Wiley, 1964); Glendon Schubert, *The Judicial Mind* (Evanston: Northwestern University Press, 1965). See also Glendon Schubert, *The Judicial Mind Revisited* (New York: Oxford University Press, 1974).

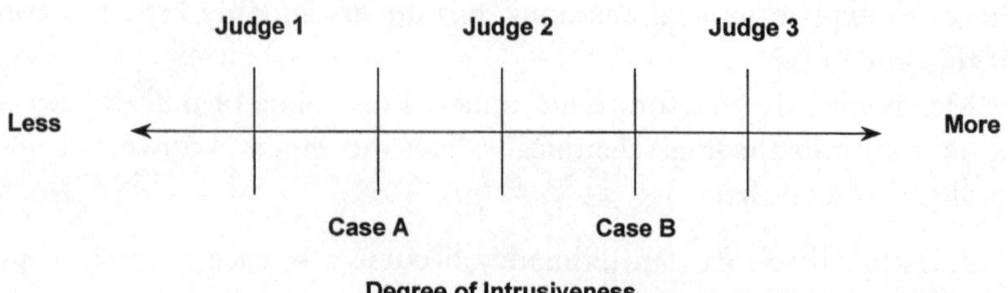

FIGURE 3.1. Justices and cases in ideological space.

According to Schubert, one can place these searches in ideological space. Since the search without a warrant can be considered less libertarian than the search with the warrant, we place the first search to the left of the second search. This is diagrammed in Figure 3.1, where A represents the first search and B the second. Presumably, any search and seizure will locate on the line; depending on case characteristics the search will be to the left of A, between A and B (inclusive), or to the right of B. The less prior justification (probable cause or warrant) and the more severe the intrusion (home vs. car, or full search vs. frisk), the further to the right the search will fall. The more prior justification and the less intrusive the search, the further to the left it will be. The points on the line where the searches lie are referred to as j-points.

Next, we place the justices in ideological space. Consider three justices, 1, 2, and 3, who are respectively liberal, moderate, and conservative. They could easily be ranked on an ideological scale, with 1 on the left, 2 in the middle, and 3 on the right.

With some additional information we might be able to go a bit further and say that justice 1 is so liberal that he or she would not even uphold the search in the first case, perhaps because he believes that police may not search and seize "mere evidence," such as papers and diaries.[12] Thus we could place justice 1 to the left of case A. Justice 2 might not be quite so strict as justice 1; he or she would uphold the search of the home with a warrant, but would not uphold the warrantless search. Thus we could place justice 2 to the right of case A but to the left of case B. Finally, justice 3 might find the warrant requirement fairly unimportant and would uphold any search he or she considered reasonable. Since prob-

[12] See, e.g., Justice Douglas's concurrence in *Berger v. New York*, 388 U.S. 41 (1967), at 64.

able cause supported both searches, both are reasonable. Thus we could place justice 3 to the right of case B. The justices are placed in ideological space with the cases in Figure 3.1.

Schubert refers to the positions of the justices as their "ideal points" (i-points), though as we see below the term is a misnomer. According to Schubert, a justice would vote to uphold all searches that are dominated by (i.e., are to the left of) the justice's ideal point and would vote to strike all searches that dominate (i.e., are to the right of) the justice's ideal point. If this is the situation, though, the i-points represent not the ideal points of each justice, but the indifference point. Justice 1 upholds all searches to the left of her indifference point, rejects all searches to the right of her indifference point, and is indifferent whether searches at that point are upheld or overturned.

In addition to Schubert, Harold Spaeth investigated the influence of attitudes on the justices' behavior in a series of articles and monographs. Relying on the work of psychologist Milton Rockeach, Spaeth defined his central concept, an attitude, as a relatively enduring "interrelated set of beliefs about an object or situation. For social action to occur, at least two interacting attitudes, one concerning the attitude object and the other concerning the attitude situation must occur."[13] The objects are the direct and indirect parties to the suit; the situations are the dominant legal issue in the case.

In focusing on attitudes, Spaeth's work begins at a microanalytic level. For example, Spaeth and Peterson gather the Court's decisions into discrete sets of cases, each of which is organized on the basis of the "attitude situation" within which the "attitude object" is encountered. These are categorized as specifically in content as the decisions of the Court permit. The theory on which the model is based assumes that sets of these cases that form around similar objects and situations will correlate with one another to form issue areas (e.g., criminal procedure, First Amendment freedoms, judicial power, federalism) in which an interrelated set of attitudes – that is, a value – will explain the justices' behavior (e.g., freedom, equality, national supremacy, libertarianism).[14]

[13] Harold J. Spaeth, *An Introduction to Supreme Court Decision Making: Revised Edition* (New York: Chandler Publishing, 1972), p. 65.

[14] Harold J. Spaeth and David J. Peterson, "The Analysis and Interpretation of Dimensionality: The Case of Civil Liberties Decision Making," 15 *American Journal of Political Science* 415 (1971).

The Economics Influence

While building on Spaeth's earlier psychological works, David Rohde and Harold Spaeth provide an explanation why the justices are able to engage in attitudinal behavior.[15] Whereas Schubert viewed the attitudinal model as a general model of political decision making,[16] Rohde and Spaeth, influenced by the application of economic notions of rationality to political decisions, recognize that decisions depend on goals, rules, and situations. While their definitions may have been updated in more recent years, the economics influence is obvious.

Goals

To Rohde and Spaeth, goals simply mean that "actors in political situations are outcome oriented; when they choose among a number of alternatives, they pick the alternative that they perceive will yield them the greatest net benefit in terms of their goals."[17] To Rohde and Spaeth:

> the primary goals of Supreme Court justices in the decision-making process are *policy goals*. Each member of the Court has preferences concerning the policy questions faced by the Court, and when the justices make decisions they want the outcomes to approximate as nearly as possible those policy preferences.[18]

Rules

Next, they contend that an actor's choices will depend on the rules of the game, "the various formal and informal rules and norms within the framework of which decisions are made. As such, they specify which types of actions are permissible and which are impermissible, the circumstances and conditions under which choice may be exercised, and the manner of choosing."[19]

The Supreme Court's rules and structures, along with those of the American political system in general, give life-tenured justices enormous latitude to reach decisions based on their personal policy preferences. Members of the Supreme Court can further their policy goals because they lack electoral or political accountability, have no ambition for higher office, and comprise a court of last resort that controls its own caseload. While the absence of these factors may hinder the personal

[15] David W. Rohde and Harold J. Spaeth, *Supreme Court Decision Making* (San Francisco: W. H. Freeman, 1976).

[16] Schubert, 1965, *op. cit.*, n. 11, *supra*, pp. 15–21.

[17] Rohde and Spaeth, *op. cit.*, n. 15, *supra*, p. 70. [18] *Id.* at 72. [19] *Id.* at 71.

policy-making capabilities of lower court judges or judges in other political systems, their presence enables the justices to engage in "rationally sincere behavior."[20]

We start our elaboration of these issues with the fact that unlike most other appellate courts, the Supreme Court *controls its own docket*. While this does not guarantee that the justices will vote their policy preferences, it is a requisite for their doing so. Many meritless cases undoubtedly exist that no self-respecting judge would decide solely on the basis of his or her policy preferences. If a citizen sought to have President Clinton's midnight pardons declared unconstitutional, and if the Supreme Court had to decide the case, we would not expect the votes in the case to depend on whether the justices favored the particular pardons. But because the Supreme Court does have control over its docket, the justices would refuse to decide such a meritless case. Those that the Court does decide tender plausible legal arguments on both sides.

Echoing our position on the discretion inherent in judicial lawmaking, Judge Richard Posner declares:

> Where the Constitution is clear, for example in entitling each state to two senators regardless of population, there is no need for judicial review to determine whether there has been a violation. The violation would be obvious, and (save in an extraordinary crisis) the people would be indignant. Where the Constitution is unclear, judicial review is likely to be guided by the political prejudices and the policy preferences of the judges rather than by the Constitution itself. The text is so old, and the controversies over its meaning are so charged with political significance, that constitutional "interpretation" in doubtful cases (the only cases likely to be litigated) is bound to be creative and discretionary rather than constrained and interpretive.[21]

With regard to *electoral accountability*, many state court judges are subject to electoral sanctions. Such judges do indeed react to factors such as public opinion at least in highly salient areas.[22] But in low visibility areas and especially in cases that contain a federal question, state supreme courts do not appear to follow public wants, according to a

[20] Jeffrey A. Segal, "Separation of Power Games in the Positive Theory of Law and Courts," 91 *American Political Science Review* 28 (1997).

[21] Richard A. Posner, "Appeal and Consent," *The New Republic*, August 16, 1999, pp. 36–40 at 37.

[22] James Kuklinski and John Stanga, "Political Participation and Governmental Responsiveness," 73 *American Political Science Review* 1090 (1979); James Gibson, "Environmental Constraints on the Behavior of Judges," 14 *Law and Society Review* 343 (1980); Paul Brace and Melinda Gann Hall, "Neo-Institutionalism and Dissent in State Supreme Courts," 52 *Journal of Politics* 54 (1990).

recent study.[23] The evidence on life-tenured federal court judges, however, suggests no such influence, including those who sit on the Supreme Court.[24]

Relatedly, justices are virtually immune from *political accountability*. Congress can impeach Supreme Court justices, but this has happened only once and the vote to remove failed.[25] The Court's appellate jurisdiction totally depends on Congress and Congress may alter it as it sees fit. Rarely, though, has Congress used this power to check the justices.[26] Overall the negative political consequences, electoral or otherwise, of limiting judicial independence far outweigh whatever short-run policy gains Congress might gain by reining in the Court. Nevertheless, we do note that there is some evidence that two Justices, Roberts in 1937 and Harlan in 1959, reversed previously unpopular decisions in the face of threats by Congress, but such examples are rare indeed. Moreover, while the President appoints the justices, he has no authority over them once they are confirmed. *United States v. Nixon* forcefully illustrates this point, where three Nixon appointees joined a unanimous Court requiring the President to relinquish the Watergate tapes, and thus delivered the coup de grace that forced Nixon to resign.[27]

This is not to say that a lack of political finality necessarily characterizes all Supreme Court decisions. Congress can overturn judicial interpretations of statutory language and amendments can undo constitutional interpretation. Nevertheless, the fact that the President and the Senate choose the justices means that the justices' preferences will rarely be out of line with that of the dominant political coalition at the time of their individual selection. And even if on some matters they are, the difficulty of overriding Supreme Court decisions, even statutory

[23] Sara C. Benesh and Wendy L. Martinek, "State-Federal Judicial Relations: The Case of State Supreme Court Decision Making in Confession Cases," paper presented at Federalism and the Courts: A National Conference, Athens, Ga., February 2001, and Sara C. Benesh and Wendy L. Martinek, "State Court Decision Making in Confession Cases," 23 *Justice System Journal* (2002) [forthcoming]. The authors' findings in both indicate that the new institutionalism may be relatively inoperative in other than high-salience areas like abortion and death penalty.

[24] E.g., Micheal Giles and Thomas G. Walker, "Judicial Policy-Making and Southern School Segregation," 37 *Journal of Politics* 917 (1975). See Chapter 10, *infra*, for further discussion.

[25] The justice was Samuel Chase, a Federalist, whom the Jeffersonians impeached in 1804.

[26] One such instance occurred after the Civil War when Congress denied the Court authority to hear appeals of persons detained by the military authorities. The Supreme Court complied with Congress's decision in *Ex parte McCardle*, 7 Wallace 506 (1869).

[27] 418 U.S. 683 (1974).

ones,[28] in a decentralized legislative environment means that the Court typically has little to fear from Congress. We detail these and other factors that protect the Court from Congress when we discuss the rational choice model, below.

Moreover, the supermajorities needed to propose and ratify an amendment make constitutional overruling vastly more difficult. Constitutional amendments have overturned only five Supreme Court decisions: the Eleventh Amendment (1798) overturned *Chisholm v. Georgia*,[29] which had allowed individuals to sue states in federal courts; the Fourteenth Amendment (1868) overturned *Scott v. Sandford*,[30] which had declared blacks ineligible for United States citizenship; the Sixteenth Amendment (1913) overturned *Pollock v. Farmer's Loan and Trust Company*,[31] which had voided the federal income tax; the Nineteenth Amendment (1920) overruled *Minor v. Happersett*,[32] which precluded the Fourteenth Amendment from guaranteeing women's suffrage; and the Twenty-sixth Amendment (1971) overturned *Oregon v. Mitchell*,[33] which had struck a federal law permitting eighteen-year-olds to vote in state elections.

With regard to *ambition*, lower court judges may desire higher office and thus be influenced by significant political others. Lobbying for a Supreme Court seat from the lower courts, through speeches or through written opinions, is not uncommon. One interested in reaching the High Court could hardly vote his or her personal policy preferences on abortion during the Bush administrations if those preferences were prochoice. Lower court judges might also be interested in other political positions besides the Supreme Court. Howell Heflin (D-Ala.) went from the Supreme Court of Alabama to the United States Senate. Thus we cannot assume that those interested in higher office will necessarily vote their personal policy preferences.

Efforts to seek higher office – assuming that such exists – is most improbable for today's justices. During the first decade of the Court's existence, members used the office as a stepping stone to run for positions such as governor,[34] but today few – if any – positions have more power, prestige, and security than that of Supreme Court justice. Three

[28] See Beth Henschen, "Statutory Interpretations of the Supreme Court," 11 *American Politics Quarterly* 441 (1983).

[29] 2 Dallas 419 (1793). [30] 19 Howard 393 (1857).

[31] 157 U.S. 429, 158 U.S. 601 (1895).

[32] 88 U.S. 162 (1874). [33] 400 U.S. 112 (1970).

[34] The first chief justice, John Jay, twice ran for governor of New York while on the Supreme Court and left the bench when he finally won.

times during the twentieth century members have resigned for alternative (or at least the potential of alternative) political positions, but in only one case was the move for a potentially higher office. That occurred in 1916, when Charles Evans Hughes resigned in order to seek the presidency. The other two cases occurred in 1942, when the exigencies of World War II led President Roosevelt to ask James Byrnes to become Director of Economic Stabilization, and 1965, when President Johnson convinced Arthur Goldberg to become United Nations Ambassador in order, Goldberg believed, to negotiate an end to the Vietnam War.

Finally, the Supreme Court is the *court of last resort*. Other judges are subject to courts superior to their own. Unless they wish to be reversed, they must follow the legal and policy pronouncements of higher courts. Though the evidence is mixed, examination of appellate court decisions in several different issue areas shows little overtly noncompliant behavior.[35] The Supreme Court, of course, sits at the pinnacle of both the federal and state judicial systems. No court overrules it.[36]

Situations

Because few areas in political life can be well represented by unconstrained choice, judicial scholars have carefully limited the attitudinal model in its pure form to the one area where it most plausibly applies: the decision on the merits. More broadly, attitudinal works have gone beyond the unconstrained-choice model when examining factors such as the vote on certiorari, formation of the majority opinion, opinion assignment, and so on. In these areas, attitudinalists expect that attitudes will be a crucial factor shaping decisions, but not the only factor. Such works have extended the pure model by *starting* with notions of attitudes, values, and policy goals and intuitively deriving hypotheses therefrom based on the rules and situations facing the Court. Thus as far back as 1959 Glendon Schubert argued that the justices' certiorari decisions would depend on their beliefs as to what would happen on the

[35] See Donald R. Songer, "An Overview of Judicial Policymaking in the United States Courts of Appeals," in John B. Gates and Charles A. Johnson, eds., *The American Courts: A Critical Assessment* (Washington, D.C.: Congressional Quarterly, 1990), and Sara C. Benesh, *The U.S. Court of Appeals and the Law of Confessions: Perspectives on the Hierarchy of Justice* (New York: LFB Scholarly Publishing, 2002).

[36] In approximately one fifth of the decisions in which it overruled its own precedents, the Warren, Burger, and Rehnquist Courts *affirmed* the lower court's decision that overruled it! See Malia Reddick and Sara C. Benesh, "Norm Violation by the Lower Courts in the Treatment of Supreme Court Precedent: A Research Framework," 21 *Justice System Journal* 117 (2000).

merits.[37] In the 1970s Rohde and Spaeth examined the likelihood of minimum winning opinion coalitions while incorporating the anomaly of decision making under threat situations.[38] And in this book's predecessor volume we showed that opinion writers frequently have to move beyond their sincere preferences if they hope to obtain a majority opinion, especially in closely divided cases. On the merits, though, the attitudinal model has produced clear and convincing evidence of the overwhelming importance of the justices' attitudes and values, as we demonstrate in Chapter 8.

THE RATIONAL CHOICE MODEL

The final model we consider is the rational choice model, which we discussed briefly above in terms of its influence on the attitudinal model. The rational choice paradigm represents an attempt to apply and adapt the theories and methods of economics to the entire range of human political and social interactions. Because of the scope of this paradigm, innumerable rational choice models that rest on a common set of assumptions exist. While scholars might quibble about the core of rational choice, we adopt William Riker's statement of its essence:

1. Actors are able to order their alternative goals, values, tastes and strategies. This means that the relation of preference and indifference among the alternatives is transitive. . . .
2. Actors choose from available alternatives so as to maximize their satisfaction.[39]

The first statement requires that individuals can rank alternatives, such that an individual either prefers one alternative to another or is indifferent between them. For example, a justice might prefer, say, reversing a lower court decision to not hearing the case (i.e., denying cert), and might prefer not hearing the case to affirming it. Moreover, individual

[37] Glendon Schubert, *Quantitative Analysis of Judicial Behavior* (Glencoe, Ill.: Free Press, 1959).

[38] Rohde and Spaeth, *op. cit.*, n. 15, *supra*, chs. 8 and 9.

[39] William H. Riker, "Political Science and Rational Choice," in James E. Alt and Kenneth A. Shepsle, eds., *Perspectives on Positive Political Economy* (New York: Cambridge University Press, 1990), p. 172. We note, additionally, that there may be serious differences among rational choice theorists about noncore assumptions. We rely primarily, though not exclusively, on the writings of William Riker, who more than anyone created the field of positive political theory (the application of rational choice theory to political phenomena).

preferences are transitive, such that if the justice prefers reversing to denying cert, and denying cert to affirming, then the justice must prefer reversing to affirming.

The second statement requires only that the actor attempt to maximize satisfaction. Actors are allowed to make errors that frustrate their goals because they lack information about the consequences of their decisions, about the preferences of others, and so on. Nor are there any limits as to what brings actors satisfaction; no goals are ruled out.

This breadth, we note, means that while specific rational choice models can be falsified, as scholars invariably state the goals assumed to motivate their specific models, rational choice theory itself, for the most part, cannot be.[40] If any goals are allowed, then there must always be goals that can explain the behavior in question. For example, Riker argues that even suicide can be consistent with rational choice theory.[41] Moreover, as Riker recognizes, the allowance of incomplete information means that even for a specific goal, all choices, even the most foolish ones, can be deemed rational because they may result from incomplete information.[42]

Maximizing satisfaction requires rational foresight, the consideration of the consequences of one's decisions. For example, justices often engage in error-correction, voting to hear a case if they disapprove of a lower court decision in the hope of reversing it. But if a justice casts a decisive vote to grant cert in a disfavored case but the Court affirms the decision, voting to grant will have harmed her goals, as she would have been better off if cert had been denied. When an actor considers the ramifications of his or her actions in a game-theoretic situation and makes the best response to that situation given available information, that actor may be said to have behaved strategically. This may involve acting in accordance with one's sincere preferences, or it may involve acting in a sophisticated manner, that is, against one's sincere preference in order to obtain a better result. For example, if the justice believed that the Court would reverse the lower court decision, then the strategic choice would be his or her sincere preference: to grant cert. But if the justice thought the Court would affirm the lower court decision, then the strategic choice would

[40] Taking actions that defeat one's goals would seem to qualify, but Riker and Ordeshook argue that if one's behavior is contrary to one's stated goals, then we should disbelieve the stated goals and give credence only to the behavior. See *An Introduction to Positive Political Theory* (Englewood Cliffs, N.J.: Prentice Hall, 1973), p. 21.

[41] *Id.*, and Riker, *op. cit.*, n. 39, *supra*, p. 173.

[42] Riker, *id.*

be to vote to deny cert in order to prevent the disfavored lower court decision from being affirmed by the Supreme Court.

Unlike the intuitions that frequently influence behavioral models, rational choice theorists typically insist that hypotheses and explanations derive from mathematical and/or logical deductions.[43] Thus to Bruce Bueno de Mesquita, scientific knowledge cannot be attained "without the abstract, rigorous exercise of logical proof."[44]

The goal of logical proof in rational choice theory is the finding of equilibrium. An outcome in equilibrium is a stable outcome, one that no player has any incentive to unilaterally shift away from. While there are different types of equilibria, the broadest and most widely used, Nash equilibria,[45] represent a best response to the other player's best response. For a classic example, consider Anthony Downs's conclusion that in a two-party system in which voters vote ideologically, the party closer to the median voter will win. If the median voter is at 50 on a ideological scale of 0 to 100, and the left party is at 30 while the right party is at 60, the right party will capture the votes of all citizens to the right of 45, the midpoint between 30 and 60. Since this includes the median, the party will win a majority. But the parties' positions are not in equilibrium, as the left party's best response to a right party at 60 is not to remain at 30. Let's say the party moves to 45, while the right party stays where it is. In the next election, the left party will win, as it captures all voters to the left of 52.5. A right party at 60 is not a best response to a left party at 45, so the right party then moves closer to the middle, which induces the left party to move toward the center. Eventually, both parties will converge on 50. This equilibrium is each party's best response to the other party's best response.

Equilibria, as with the logical proofs from which they derive, are crucial to most rational choice theorists. They represent "a prediction,

43 David Austen-Smith and Jeffrey S. Banks, *Positive Political Theory I* (Ann Arbor: University of Michigan Press, 1999), p. xi; Michael Laver, *The Politics of Private Desires: The Guide to the Politics of Rational Choice* (New York: Penguin Books, 1981), p. 11; Riker and Ordeshook, *op. cit.*, n. 40, *supra,* pp. 9–12. Alternatively, see Lee Epstein and Jack Knight, "Toward a Strategic Revolution in Judicial Politics: A Look Back, a Look Ahead," 53 *Political Research Quarterly* 625 (2000).

44 Bruce Bueno de Mesquita, "Toward a Scientific Understanding of International Conflict: A Personal View," 29 *International Studies Quarterly* 121 (1985), p. 129.

45 We include under "Nash equilibria" its various refinements, such as subgame-perfect equilibria, perfect Bayesian equilibria, sequential equilibria, perfect equilibria, and trembling hand equilibria.

for a prespecified circumstance, about the choices of people and the corresponding outcomes. This prediction generally takes the form of 'if the institutional context of a choice is . . . and if people's preferences are . . . then the only choices and outcomes that can endure are . . .'" (ellipses in original).[46] To Riker they are absolutely essential to both social science theory[47] and explanation, providing necessary and sufficient conditions for choices to occur.[48] Note, though, that Epstein and Knight dispute the centrality of equilibrium analysis for rational choice models, labeling the positions taken by each side of this debate a play "to its competitive advantage."[49]

While we agree with Epstein and Knight that equilibrium analysis is not the only way to "do" rational choice theory, equilibrium analysis is rational choice theory's most powerful tool and is clearly *the* comparative advantage that rational choice theory has over other theories.

The Supreme Court and Rational Choice Theory

The Supreme Court rational choice arena may be divided into two camps: an internal camp that focuses on the interactions among the justices and an external camp that focuses on constraints imposed on the Court by other political actors. For better or worse, the leading internal rational choice studies of the Supreme Court, such as Walter Murphy's masterful *Elements of Judicial Strategy*,[50] have not availed themselves of the exceptional power that equilibrium analysis provides. The consequences of this for Murphy's work, in terms of the possibility of a rational choice theory of the Court, are laid out by Edward Schwartz, who tries to explain why Murphy's work did not achieve the prominence of Riker's, Downs's, or Thomas Schelling's:

> All three of these authors produced very specific behavioral predictions within their books. Some of these predictions were more credible than others, but even those that seem most incorrect spawned attempts to refine the theory in order

[46] Peter C. Ordeshook, *Game Theory and Political Theory* (New York: Cambridge University Press, 1986), p. xii.

[47] Riker, *op. cit.*, n. 39, *supra*, p. 175. [48] *Id.* at 177.

[49] Epstein and Knight, *op. cit.*, n. 43, *supra*, p. 642.

[50] (Chicago: University of Chicago Press, 1964). Our list of leading rational choice works on the Court also includes Lee Epstein and Jack Knight's award-winning *Choices Justices Make* (Washington, D.C.: Congressional Quarterly Press, 1998), and Forrest Maltzman, James F. Spriggs II, and Paul J. Wahlbeck's award-winning *The Collegial Game* (New York: Cambridge University Press, 2000).

to produce results more in accord with observed behavior. Murphy, however, only identified strategies that might be pursued under some circumstances. Often, such a pronouncement is immediately followed by a disclaimer that the contrary strategy might be more appropriate under other circumstances. The problem is that he derives no tight predictions about exactly when we should expect to see certain behaviors as opposed to others.

To wit, from the chapter on "Marshalling the Court," Murphy writes "[a justice] would probably feel it unethical to appeal to the strong personal dislike of one justice for another, though there may have been occasions when such an appeal would have been effective." Murphy is just stating that sometimes we will observe a strategy and sometimes we won't.

In the same section, Murphy suggests that "when a new justice comes to the Court, an older colleague might try to charm his junior brother." Might? Well, when will he and when won't he? We now understand from game theory that such overtures are likely to be perceived as "cheap talk" absent some costly signal attached thereto. The book is filled with such lukewarm or fuzzily conditional recommendations about strategies that the justices can employ. A scholar reading the book is likely to emerge from the experience, as I did, wondering exactly what Murphy thought Supreme Court justices actually do, given that he seems to believe that almost any tactic might be useful (or not), depending upon the circumstances.

Why does Murphy come across so wishy-washy where Downs, Riker and Schelling appear bold, decisive and challenging? The answer lies in understanding the importance of deriving equilibrium predictions. Downs, Riker and Schelling actually write down models, solve them and derive equilibria – Murphy does not. Without attention to finding combinations of judicial strategies that formed in equilibrium, it was not possible for Murphy to generate hypotheses about exactly what kind of strategies we should expect to observe the justices pursuing.

Absent such predictions and hypotheses there's not much for subsequent scholars to sink their teeth into. Murphy all but admitted that any behavior might be a good strategy, so it was not possible to refute or corroborate his theory. All that Murphy managed to do was to provide a laundry list of strategic concerns for the justices to think about. He left to others the job of matching desirable strategies with particular scenarios.[51]

Schwartz, a rational choice theorist, goes on to declare:

Schubert, on the other hand, offers a tight internally consistent theory of judicial behavior. It was possible to apply this theory to available data and investigate whether it predicted actual judicial practice. Scholars like Rohde and Spaeth (1976) latched onto Schubert's theory, improved upon it, and spawned the attitudinal model that enjoys a position of prominence within the judicial politics community to this day.[52]

[51] Edward Schwartz, "The New Elements of Judicial Strategy," unpublished manuscript, Harvard University, 1997, pp. 18–20.

[52] *Id.* at 20.

Similar to Murphy's work, the most prominent of the recent rational choice works on the Supreme Court do not derive or adapt equilibrium solutions, for example, they do not demonstrate that interactions among the justices constitute a best response to a best response, or alternative equilibrium solutions. Consider, for example, various works that consider multiple opinion drafts as evidence of strategic behavior.[53] While this seems to make sense, this hypothesis fails to account for the likelihood that if delay is costly, a rational opinion writer will preemptively accommodate her coalition. Indeed, the adaptation of at least one prominent class of bargaining models would lead to the conclusion that the best response of the opinion writer is to write a first draft that leaves the fifth most distant member of the coalition just barely at the point where she prefers signing on to concurring separately.[54]

To date, the top journals of political science have published less than a handful of studies that derive or examine equilibrium behavior of judges,[55] though economics journals, of course, have published

[53] Paul J. Wahlbeck, James F. Spriggs II, and Maltzman, "Marshalling the Court: Bargaining and Accommodation on the U.S. Supreme Court," 42 *American Journal of Political Science* 294 (1997); and Epstein and Knight, *op. cit.*, n. 50, *supra*, ch. 3.

[54] Ariel Rubinstein, "Perfect Equilibrium in a Bargaining Model," 50 *Econometrica* 97 (1982). See also Maltzman, Spriggs, and Wahlbeck, *op. cit.*, n. 50, *supra*, ch. 4.

[55] Accepting the *American Political Science Review*, the *American Journal of Political Science*, and the *Journal of Politics* as the top journals, we count to date one case study (Robert Clinton, "Game Theory, Legal History, and the Origins of Judicial Review," 38 *American Journal of Political Science* 285 (1994)), one analysis of certiorari (Charles M. Cameron, Jeffrey A. Segal, and Donald R. Songer, "Strategic Auditing in a Political Hierarchy: An Informational Model of the Supreme Court's Certiorari Decisions," 94 *American Political Science Review* 109 (2000)), and one comparative study (Georg Vanberg, "Legislative-Judicial Relations: A Game-Theoretic Approach to Constitutional Review," 45 *American Journal of Political Science* 346 (2001)) that derive equilibria. Two others test equilibrium predictions derived elsewhere (David Rohde, "Policy Goals and Opinion Coalitions in the Supreme Court," 16 *American Journal of Political Science* 208 (1972), and Jeffrey A. Segal, "Separation of Powers Games in the Positive Theory of Law and Courts," 91 *American Political Science Review* 28 (1997)).

There is also a growing rational choice literature on the behavior of juries. For example, Fedderson and Pesendorfer conclude that unanimous juries are *more* likely to convict the innocent or acquit the guilty than majority-rule juries. See Timothy Fedderson and Wolfgang Pesendorfer, "Convicting the Innocent: The Inferiority of Unanimous Jury Verdicts under Strategic Voting," 92 *American Political Science Review* 23 (1998). Gerardi concludes that as jury size increases, unanimous juries almost never convict. In his prime example, the probability of acquitting the guilty is greater than 0.5 for five-person juries and almost 0.67 for twelve-person juries. See Dino Gerardi, "Jury Verdicts and Preference Diversity," 94 *American Political Science Review* 395 (2000). Needless to say, empirical support is lacking for both sets of findings.

more.[56] Moreover, while there are some internal equilibrium models out there,[57] these models have not been empirically tested.

Because the internal works are either consistent with earlier attitudinal works or, at least, not inconsistent with them (see pp. 86–97), and because these works generally do not test equilibrium predictions, which are central (and to some, essential) to rational choice theory, we focus on the external works. This external literature formally derives and tests equilibrium predictions that directly contradict the attitudinal model. The prime subject of most of these articles has been the separation-of-powers model originally formulated by Brian Marks.[58]

The Marksist Separation-of-Powers Model

Separation-of-powers models examine the degree to which the courts must defer to legislative majorities in order to prevent overrides that result in policy worse than what the court might have achieved through more sophisticated behavior. In the landmark work, Brian Marks carefully examined the placement of preferences in Congress that prevented *Grove City College v. Bell*[59] from being overturned prior to 1986.[60]

[56] See, e.g., Thomas J. Miceli, "Optimal Prosecution of Defendants Whose Guilt Is Uncertain," 6 *Journal of Law, Economics and Organization* 189 (1990); Edward P. Schwartz, "Policy, Precedent, and Power: A Positive Theory of Supreme Court Decision Making," 8 *Journal of Law, Economics and Organization* 219 (1992); Lewis A. Kornhauser, "Modeling Collegial Courts I: Path Dependence," 12 *International Review of Law and Economics* 169 (1992); and Gregory A. Caldeira, John R. Wright, and Christopher J. W. Zorn, "Strategic Voting and Gatekeeping in the Supreme Court," *Journal of Law, Economics and Organization* (1999).

Of these articles, only the model in the Caldeira et al. article has been tested empirically.

[57] See, e.g., Thomas H. Hammond, Chris W. Bonneau, and Reginald S. Sheehan, "Toward a Rational Choice Spatial Model of Supreme Court Decision Making: Making Sense of Certiorari, the Original Vote on the Merits, Opinion Assignment, Coalition Formation and Maintenance, and the Final Vote on the Choice of Legal Doctrine," paper presented at the 1999 annual meeting of the American Political Science Association, Atlanta, Ga.

[58] We exclude from consideration here the hundreds of articles in "law and economics" that attempt to demonstrate the economic efficiency, or lack thereof, of judicial decisions.

[59] 465 U.S. 555 (1984).

[60] Brian A. Marks, "A Model of Judicial Influence on Congressional Policymaking: *Grove City College v. Bell*," working papers in Political Science, P-88-7, Hoover Institution, Stanford University, 1988. Senate Judiciary Committee Chair Orrin Hatch (R-Utah) kept override legislation bottled up in his committee.

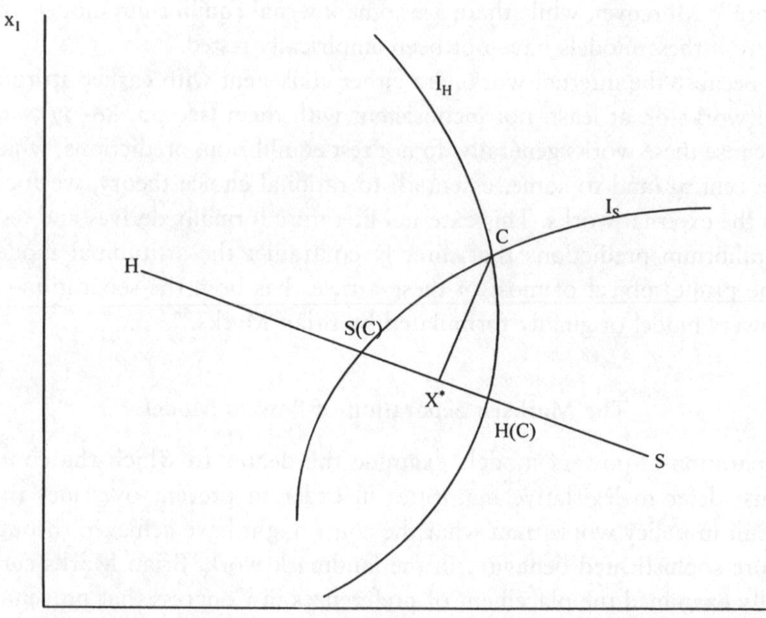

FIGURE 3.2. The neo-Marksist model. H: House ideal point; S: Senate ideal point; C: Court ideal point; I_H: House indifference curve; I_S: Senate indifference curve; S(C): point on set of irreversible decisions where Senate is indifferent to Court ideal point; H(C): point on set of irreversible decisions where House is indifferent to Court ideal point; X*: equilibrium.

Consistent with the attitudinal model, Marks claimed that the justices simply voted their ideal points. Building on his work, subsequent neo-Marksist theorists argued that if the Court exercised rational foresight, it would not always choose its ideal point.[61] We present a standard representation of these models.

Consider the example in Figure 3.2, where the Court must decide a case in two-dimensional policy space. The game is played as follows. First, the Court makes a decision in (x_1, x_2) policy space. Second, the House and Senate can override the Court decision if they agree on an alternative. H, S, and C represent the ideal points of the House, Senate,

[61] See, e.g., John Ferejohn and Charles Shipan, "Congressional Influence on Bureaucracy," 6 *Journal of Law, Economics and Organization* 1 (1990); and Rafael Gely and Pablo T. Spiller, "A Rational Choice Theory of Supreme Court Decision Making with Applications to the *State Farm* and *Grove City* Cases," 6 *Journal of Law, Economics and Organization* 263 (1990).

and Court, respectively. The line segment HS represents the set of irreversible decisions. That is, no decision on that line can be overturned by Congress, because improving the position of one chamber by moving closer to its ideal point necessarily worsens the position of the other. Alternatively, any decision off of HC – call it x – can be overturned, because there will necessarily be at least one point on HC that both H and C prefer to x. Imagine, for example, a Court decision at the Court's ideal point, C. The arc I_S represents those points where the Senate is indifferent to this decision. And, obviously, the Senate prefers any point inside the arc to any point on the arc (or, obviously, outside the arc). Similarly, I_H represents those points where the House is indifferent to the Court's decision. Thus, both the House and Senate prefer any point between S(C) (the point on the set of irreversible decisions where the Senate is indifferent to the Court's decision) and H(C) (the point on the set of irreversible decisions where the House is indifferent to the Court's decision) to a decision at C.

What, then, should a strategic Court do in this situation? If the Court rules at its ideal point (or, indeed, any place off the set of irreversible decisions), Congress may overturn the Court's decision and replace it with something that is necessarily worse from the Court's perspective. For example, if the Court rules at C, then Congress's result will be someplace between S(C) and H(C). The trick for the Court is to find the point on the set of irreversible decisions that is closest to its ideal point. By the Pythagorean Theorem, it accomplishes this by dropping a perpendicular onto the line. Thus, rather than voting sincerely at C and ending up with a policy someplace between S(C) and H(C), the Court rules at X*, the point between S(C) and H(C), indeed, the point between H and S, that it prefers the most. This is the equilibrium result.

The separation-of-powers games vary in a variety of details, such as the number of issue dimensions, the number of legislative chambers, the influence of committees, and the existence of presidential veto. But regardless of the specific assumptions made, these models (with the important exception of Marks) assume that the Court will construe legislation as close to its ideal point as possible without getting overturned by Congress.

The separation-of-powers models, like all models, make a series of assumptions about the behavior in question. What is noteworthy about the simplifications is that they typically make it easier to conclude that the Court will defer to congressional preferences. These assumptions involve the Supreme Court, Congress, and interactions between the two. We begin with assumptions about the Court.

Perfect and Complete Information

Virtually every separation-of-powers model assumes the justices have perfect and complete information about the preferences of Congress.[62] Implicitly, these models also assume complete information about Congress's transaction and opportunity costs (which are, in fact, assumed to be zero).[63] If a policy-seeking Court knew that a particular decision would cause Congress to worsen the result, it boggles the imagination to conclude that the Court wouldn't make the necessary compromises to obtain a better final outcome. But the Court, at best, will have some form of probability distribution as to the preferences of Congress, with some vague inkling about the costs and benefits to Congress of override (based on its preferences and loss function). If the justices typically believe they face a Congress unlikely to override their decisions,[64] then they will be significantly more likely to vote their sincere preferences.

Enforced Statutory Interpretation

Nearly unanimous are the separation-of-powers modelers in their decisions to treat the level of interpretation as exogenously determined. Nevertheless, in many cases the Court can opt out of statutory mode and find constitutional bases for its decisions.[65] Consider, for example, a Court intent on striking private affirmative action plans. William Eskridge argues that in *United Steelworkers v. Weber*[66] the Court had such preferences but was deterred by a Congress that might have overridden such action.[67] If we forget that a divided Court had upheld the constitutionality of affirmative action just one year earlier[68] and thus could not have been that opposed to affirmative action, we still have the possibility that a conservative Court could have opted into constitutional mode. Following *Shelley v. Kraemer*,[69] the Court could have ruled that

[62] Daniel B. Rodriguez, "The Positive Political Dimensions of Regulatory Reform," 72 *Washington University Law Quarterly* 1 (1994), p. 95.

[63] Alternatively, we could view this as perfect information about whether the Court is facing a Congress that will override if the Court rules outside the set of irreversible decisions, which Congress always would.

[64] William N. Eskridge, Jr., "Overriding Supreme Court Statutory Interpretation Decisions," 101 *Yale Law Journal* 331 (1991), p. 365.

[65] Pablo T. Spiller and Matthew L. Spitzer, "Judicial Choice of Legal Doctrines," 8 *Journal of Law, Economics and Organization* 8 (1992).

[66] 443 U.S. 193 (1979).

[67] William N. Eskridge, Jr., "Reneging on History? Playing the Court/Congress/President Civil Rights Game," 79 *California Law Review* 613 (1991).

[68] *Regents v. Bakke*, 438 U.S. 265 (1978). [69] 334 U.S. 1 (1948).

such private contracts, though legal, could not be judicially enforced. Restricting the Court to statutory mode underestimates the Court's freedom to act.

Unidimensional Issues

The standard separation-of-powers model not only forces the Court to reach decisions statutorily, it also forces the Court to reach decisions in a unidimensional policy space. Unlike the congressional committee system, no corresponding method prevents the Court from bundling issues. Indeed, Court cases often contain multiple dimensions. One likely result is that a strategic Court, through what Riker has labeled "heresthetics,"[70] can reframe and/or bundle issues so as to protect itself from reversal. For example, the Supreme Court recently required a state institution to provide funding for a Christian newspaper.[71] Surprisingly, the howls of outrage that might typically accompany such a decision did not occur. The reason, no doubt, is that the Court packaged the case as a freedom of speech issue. If the University of Virginia generally provides funding to other student newspapers, it cannot deny funding to one because of its religious slant. The Court's preemptive ability to strategically manipulate issues protects it from congressional overrides.

We next consider separation-of-powers assumptions about Congress.

Costless Legislation/Salience

The separation-of-powers models treat the enactment of legislation as costless. Needless to say, Congress incurs both transaction costs and opportunity costs. At the very least, this expands the Court's discretionary zone, and thus makes it less likely for the Court to defer to Congress for fear of being overturned.

Limited Veto Points

How legislation gets passed is vitally important to the separation-of-powers model. Theoretically, the gist of the model merely requires chamber medians, as in Figure 3.2. Of course, the addition of committees, presidential veto, and so on would greatly increase the model's correspondence to reality, without altering the fundamental understanding

[70] William H. Riker, "The Heresthetics of Constitution-Making: The Presidency in 1787, with Comments on Determinism and Rational Choice," 78 *American Political Science Review* 1 (1984).

[71] *Rosenberger v. University of Virginia* 515 U.S. 819 (1995).

of the model. Nevertheless, understanding the actual extent to which the Court must defer to Congress requires greater realism. Specifically, as the number of places where legislation can be kept off the floor increases, the Court's discretionary zone increases. Thus, under a potentially more realistic view of the legislative process, the Court's ability to act sincerely might be guaranteed most of the time.

For example, according to some views of congressional procedure, relevant committee chairs are capable of bottling up legislation. Indeed, Marks's study of *Grove City* gives full credit/blame to killing override legislation to Senate Judiciary Chairman Orrin Hatch. Eskridge also finds committee chairs to have special influence over their committees' actions.[72]

To the extent that this view of the legislative process is correct, the set of irreversible decisions is likely to be much greater than currently modeled by the standard separation-of-powers models. Between 1956 and 1986, either James Eastland (D-Miss.) or Strom Thurmond (R-S.C.) headed the Senate Judiciary Committee, except for Ted Kennedy's two-year reign in 1979–1980. Eastland's Americans for Democratic Action scores while chair averaged 12.1, while Thurmond's averaged 2.5.[73] Meanwhile, either Emanuel Celler (D-N.Y.) (1955–72) or Peter Rodino (D-N.J.) (1973–88) headed the House Judiciary Committee during this period. Both were liberals whose ADA scores averaged in the 80s. If override legislation requires the support of both judiciary chairs, then the Court was effectively immune from congressional interference. Thus, the Supreme Court has significantly more discretion than these models suggest.

Finally, we consider assumptions about Congress/Court interactions.

Last Licks

The separation-of-powers models discussed above and below vary as to the inclusion of Presidents, agencies, and second chambers of Congress. However, they do not vary in that they always give Congress the final move. Ferejohn and Weingast note that

> if we can say nothing else with certainty, we can say that there is no "last word" in politics. No person or individual ever gets to say what the law is finally; Congress can and often does react to Court decisions, as can agencies and the pres-

[72] Eskridge, *op. cit.*, n. 67, *supra*, pp. 625, 635.

[73] Michael J. Sharp, *The Directory of Congressional Voting Scores and Interest Group Ratings* (New York: Facts on File Publications, 1988).

ident. Each actor in the political and legal setting – president, agency, Congress, litigants, court – can take new courses of action, devise new interpretations or enact new statutes. This capacity to react is a fundamental feature of the political process.[74]

Obviously, giving Congress the final move is completely arbitrary and, moreover, biases the outcome toward congressional influence. As Ferejohn and Weingast suggest, if Congress overturns a statutory decision of the Court, the Court nonetheless interprets the meaning and the validity of the remedial legislation. For example, the Supreme Court responded to Congress's decision to override *Lampf v. Gilbertson*[75] by declaring pertinent parts of the override unconstitutional.[76] In at least one series of Court decisions-overrides-reinterpretations-reoverrides, "Congress had to pass the same statute three times to achieve its original goal."[77] While Congress might win such battles more often than not, the standard separation-of-powers models underestimate the Court's freedom to act by completely eliminating the Court's ability to react to congressional action.

Exogenous Judicial Preferences

The separation-of-powers literature treats judicial preferences as if they were exogenously determined, which often allows them to be far to the right or left of congressional and/or presidential preferences. While it might not be unusual to find particular Supreme Court justices whose preferences lie outside the set of irreversible decisions, it would be rare, indeed, to find that the President and the Senate consistently nominate and approve people who are well to the left or to the right of their preferences (see Chapter 5). This is especially true when seats that may affect the median position of the Court are at stake.[78] Thus, under Robert Dahl's formulation,[79] the Supreme Court follows the preferences of the dominant electoral coalition not because of deference (whether strategic or otherwise) to its preferences, but because the coalition chooses the

[74] John Ferejohn and Barry Weingast, "A Positive Theory of Statutory Interpretation," 12 *International Review of Law and Economics* 263 (1992), at 263. Despite their cogent argument, Ferejohn and Weingast then proceed to give Congress the last word.

[75] 501 U.S. 350 (1991). [76] *Plaut v. Spendthrift Farm*, 514 U.S. 211 (1995).

[77] Eskridge, *op. cit.*, n. 64, *supra*, p. 410.

[78] Peter H. Lemieux and Charles H. Stewart III, "Advise? Yes. Consent? Maybe. Senate Confirmation of Supreme Court Nominations," paper presented at the annual meeting of the American Political Science Association, Washington, D.C., 1988.

[79] Robert Dahl, "Decision-Making in a Democracy: The Supreme Court as a National Policy-Maker," 6 *Journal of Public Law* 179 (1957).

Court and they thus have similar preferences. By modeling judicial preferences as exogenous, the separation-of-powers models significantly overestimate the need for sophisticated voting.

In sum, we have made a strong enough case to cast theoretical doubt on the standard separation-of-powers model. These doubts could be erased – indeed, should be erased – if empirical evidence supports the model. But to date, the empirical evidence refutes the model. We examine this evidence in detail in Chapter 8.

SUMMARY AND CONCLUSIONS

In Chapter 1 we examined why the Supreme Court necessarily makes authoritative policy. In Chapters 2 and 3 we examined the three different models that attempt to explain how justices make policy.

We initially considered the legal model, which holds in one form or another that justices make decisions influenced by the facts of the case in light of plain meaning, the intent of the framers, and precedent. While the Court uses these factors to justify its decisions, they do not explain their outcome.

Plain meaning assumes a mathematical exactness in the use of English that simply does not exist. Yet even when the constitutional language is fairly clear, the Court may behave arrogatingly, reading into the document rights that are not explicitly there, and reading out of the Constitution rights that it explicitly contains. Supporters of legislative or framers' intent must recognize the sparseness of the historical record: that however "framer" is defined, different framers had different intentions; that intent often conflicts with plain meaning; and, most notably, that the framers did not claim such prescience that only their motivations could rightfully bind future generations. Precedent also fails as an explanation of judicial decisions. In appellate cases legitimate precedents exist on both sides of controversies, allowing justices to abide by precedent no matter which position they take. And even when the weight of authority leans heavily toward one side, several legalistic methods enable courts and judges to avoid literal adherence to precedent. Justices can even cite precedents to avoid adhering to precedent.

Against the legal model we present the attitudinal model, which holds that justices make decisions by considering the facts of the case in light of their ideological attitudes and values. The attitudinal model, as developed by Glendon Schubert and David Rohde and Harold Spaeth, emanated from the criticisms of the classical legal model made by the legal realists in the 1920s, the need for empirical tests as demanded by the behavioral school of political science that began to flower in the 1950s, the psychological theories of Clyde Coombs and Milton Rokeach, and the institutional concerns of the rational choice model.

Attitudinalists argue that because legal rules governing decision making (e.g., precedent, plain meaning) in the cases that come to the Court do not limit discretion; because the justices need not respond to public opinion, Congress, or the President; and because the Supreme Court is the court of last resort, the justices, unlike their lower court colleagues, may freely implement their personal policy preferences as the attitudinal model specifies.[80]

Finally, we considered the rational choice model. While the attitudinal model derives in part from the rational choice model, there are several distinctions worth noting.

First, the rational choice model has an extraordinarily powerful tool for explaining interactions between players: equilibrium analysis. But, unfortunately, beyond the questionable separation-of-powers games, these equilibrium solutions have rarely been used to study actual judicial behavior. The results from the extant literature, by and large, derive from strategic intuitions that have not differed markedly from earlier works by Schubert, Rohde and Spaeth, and others.[81] This isn't to say that there hasn't been extremely good work in this area;[82] rather, it is to say that work to date has not taken advantage of what makes rational choice theory powerful.

Second, while the attitudinal model limits the justices to policy goals, rational choice theory allows any goals whatsoever. For example, Ferejohn and Weingast posit the possibility of legal concerns, such as fidelity to legislative intent, as goals that judges might seek.[83] We believe

[80] This is not to say that the goals of lower court judges (especially other appellate court judges) differ from Supreme Court justices but, rather, that the constraints on reaching those goals differ. See Reddick and Benesh, *op. cit.*, n. 36, *supra*. Indeed, even highly esteemed judges themselves have publicly acknowledged the dominance of their personal policy preferences in arriving at their decisions. See Richard A. Posner, "What Do Judges and Justices Maximize? (The Same Thing Everybody Else Does)," 3 *Supreme Court Economic Review* 1 (1993).

[81] Glendon Schubert, *op. cit.*, n. 37, *supra,* section IV; Rohde and Spaeth, *op. cit.*, n. 15, *supra*, 1976, chs. 8 and 9; Robert Boucher and Jeffrey A. Segal, "Supreme Court Justices as Strategic Decision Makers: Offensive Grants and Defensive Denials on the Vinson Court," 57 *Journal of Politics* 824 (1995).

[82] See, e.g., Epstein and Knight, *op. cit.*, n. 50, *supra*; and Maltzmann, Spriggs, and Wahlbeck, *op. cit.*, n. 50, *supra.*

[83] Ferejohn and Weingast, *op. cit.*, n. 74, *supra.*

that viewing justices as policy seekers provides enormous leverage in understanding their behavior. We also consider it more than ironic that rational choice theorists, whose field includes social choice theory, should model concepts such as "legislative intent," as if group intent exists.

Third, the attitudinal model differs from traditional rational choice models in terms of how the decision on the merits plays out. To rational choice theorists, the Court typically must defer to Congress in statutory cases.[84] Some leading scholars argue that even in constitutional cases, where override is virtually impossible,[85] the Court must frequently defer to the elected branches. According to one set of proponents, rational choice perspectives

> argue that because justices take into account the preferences of the ruling regime (even if they do not necessarily share those preferences) and . . . the actions they expect the regime to take, the Court's decisions typically will never be far removed from what contemporary institutions desire . . . .
>
> This does not mean, however, that the Court will never . . . strike down federal laws. Indeed, if preferences of the contemporary regime and of the Court support those weapons, the Court will feel free to deploy them.[86]

If this is the rational choice perspective on when the Court can invoke judicial review, then that perspective is seriously mistaken, as the Court's willingness to strike down school prayer, Bible readings, flag protection statutes, the Gun Free School Zone Act, the Religious Freedom Restoration Act, and so on amply demonstrate. Nor should one assume that such behavior occurs either infrequently or disproportionately in cases of little moment. One day after declaring the Religious Freedom Restoration Act unconstitutional on the basis that Congress temerariously had the audacity to contravene the sacred principle of separation of powers and tell the Court what constitutes the free exercise of religion,[87] the jus-

[84] William N. Eskridge, Jr., *op. cit.*, n. 64, *supra*.

[85] A constitutional amendment requires two thirds of each chamber of Congress and three quarters of the states. Alternatively, Congress can attempt to attack the Court's independence, e.g., by adding to the size of the Court or limiting the Court's jurisdiction. But concerns over judicial independence, if not by congresspersons themselves, then by their constituents, severely limit Congress's use of this tool to the most extraordinary situations, such as Reconstruction.

[86] Lee Epstein and Thomas Walker, "The Role of the Supreme Court in American Society: Playing the Reconstruction Game," in Lee Epstein, ed., *Contemplating Courts* (Washington, D.C.: Congressional Quarterly Press, 1995), pp. 323–24; see also Epstein and Knight, *op. cit.*, n. 50, *supra*, pp. 150–54.

[87] In *City of Boerne v. Flores*, 526 U.S. 507 (1997).

tices voided two additional acts of Congress: the Communications Decency Act, which prohibited knowing transmission via telecommunication of "indecent" or "patently offensive" material to minors,[88] and the Brady bill, which required local law enforcement officials to check the background of those transferring handguns.[89] The Court replicated its behavior one year later, declaring unconstitutional another three acts of Congress, two of which were of lesser importance than those of 1997. The Court, moreover, provided a bit more breathing room: voiding the laws over a three-day period rather than only over two days.[90]

Consider the following summary by Linda Greenhouse at the close of the Court's 1998 term:

> The Supreme Court rules.
>
> That was the message of a term in which the Court asserted its power over every branch and level of government, few of which emerged unchanged from the encounter.
>
> Most dramatically, the Court reconfigured the federal-state balance of power in three decisions that carved out a broad sphere of immunity for the states from the reach of federal law. Those decisions had a subtext with even more far-reaching implications, indicating the Court's unwillingness to credit Congress its own view not only of the way legislation should be written but even of the justification for federal legislation at all in areas where Congress has deemed it preferable to switch the states into a uniform, nationwide rule of law.
>
> Nor was the Court any more solicitous of the executive branch, rejecting the Clinton Administration's plan for conducting the 2000 census and insisting that there was no alternative to the traditional headcount for apportioning seats in the House of Representatives. Looking to the states, the court invalidated California's two-tiered welfare policy that disadvantaged new arrivals, a policy the new federal welfare law had authorized. . . .
>
> "This is a court that doesn't defer to government at any level," Walter Dellinger, an acting Solicitor General earlier in the Clinton Administration said

[88] In *Reno v. ACLU*, 521 U.S. 844 (1997).

[89] In *Printz v. United States*, 521 U.S. 898 (1997).

[90] A 1992 law requiring forfeitures grossly disproportionate to criminal offenses violates the excessive fines clause of the Eighth Amendment (*United States v. Bojakajian*, 141 L Ed 2d 314 (1998)); the Line Item Veto Act, authorizing the President to strike certain spending and tax benefit provisions from legislation he otherwise approved, violates the presentment clause of Article I (*Clinton v. New York City*, 141 L Ed 2d 393 (1998)); and a provision of the Coal Industry Retirement Health Benefit Act of 1992 that required coal industry operators who had signed labor agreements to fund retiree health care benefits violates the takings clause of the Fifth Amendment (*Eastern Enterprises v. Apfel*, 141 L Ed 2d 451 (1998)).

the other day. "The Court is confident it can come up with the right decisions, and it believes it is constitutionally charged with doing so."[91]

Consistent with what we more systematically demonstrate below to be the Court's actual behavior, attitudinalists believe the structure of the American political system virtually always allows the justices to engage in rationally sincere behavior on the merits.

[91] Linda Greenhouse, "The Justices Decide Who's in Charge," *New York Times*, June 27, 1999, sec. 4, p. 1. The decision in *Bush v. Gore* unimpeachably established the accuracy of the source Greenhouse quoted, Walter Dellinger, and – for that matter – of Greenhouse herself.

4

A Political History of the Supreme Court

This chapter presents an overview of the role the Court has played as an authoritative policy maker during the course of American history. The mythology described in Chapter 1 that surrounds the Court and its decisions has decreed that the only proper perspective from which to view the Court is a legalistic one, namely, the legal model that we critiqued in Chapter 2. To place the model that we employ – the attitudinal one – in a proper perspective, we present this historical summary.

THE FIRST SUPREME COURT

The eleven years before John Marshall became chief justice are typically viewed as the first Supreme Court. If we adhere to the modern practice of identifying Courts by their chief justice, two Courts preceded Marshall: the Jay Court from 1790 to 1795, and the Ellsworth Court from 1796 to 1800. Neither of them left a legacy akin to that of their successor Courts. By our count, these two Courts decided a grand total of only sixty-one cases, an average of less than six per year.

These Courts, however, did not want for eminent members. Jay himself was the third author of *The Federalist Papers*. Three of the five other original members served in the Constitutional Convention, as did Chief Justice Ellsworth and William Paterson, the author of the New Jersey Plan, whom Washington nominated in 1793. The others all supported ratification of the Constitution. Indeed, all of Washington's and Adams's nominees staunchly supported the Constitution and the federal government in its conflicts with the states.

The fact that six of the twelve justices who antedated Marshall resigned to take positions that by today's standards are of much lower status than service on the Court has certainly affected our judgment of the first two Courts. Jay left to accept the governorship of New York, while Ellsworth resigned to continue his career as a foreign diplomat. Indeed, when President Adams nominated Jay for a second term as chief justice after Ellsworth's resignation, Jay supplemented his declination for health reasons with the statement that the Court lacked "the energy, weight, and dignity which are essential to its affording due support to the national government."[1]

Nonetheless, the pre-Marshall Court was not a political nullity even though it did not decide a single case in five of its first twenty-two terms in addition to the August 1794 term – to which the Reports make no reference whatsoever[2] – and even though its first major decision produced such a storm of protest that a constitutional amendment was quickly proposed and ratified to overturn it. This case, *Chisholm v. Georgia*,[3] held that persons not resident in a state could nonetheless sue that state in federal court. Though the appropriately labeled Federalist Party controlled all three branches of the federal government, states' rights sentiments were sufficiently strong to occasion the decision's repeal through the Eleventh Amendment. While the Eleventh Amendment has generated little controversy over most of its life, it has substantially roiled the policy waters in which the Rehnquist Court has attempted to steer a conservative course.

Notwithstanding its lack of status, the early Court did decide one indisputably landmark case: *Calder v. Bull*,[4] which authoritatively defined for the next 200 years (and still counting) the scope of ex post facto laws, one of a very few matters that the Constitution separately prohibits the state and federal governments from enacting. Statutes retroactively criminalizing conduct that was innocent when performed

[1] Elder Witt, ed., *The Supreme Court and Its Work* (Washington: Congressional Quarterly, 1981), p. 114.

[2] The Court's reporter, A. J. Dallas, at 2 Dallas 479, explained the lack of cases during the August 1793 term as follows: "The malignant fever, which during this year, raged in the city of Philadelphia [where the Court was sitting], dispersed the great body of its inhabitants, and proved fatal to thousands, interrupted, likewise, the business of the courts; and I cannot trace, that any important cause was agitated in the present term." Similar conditions may explain the absence of any entries for the August 1794 term.

[3] 2 Dallas 419 (1793). [4] 3 Dallas 386 (1798).

are unconstitutional, as are those that retroactively enhance criminal punishments. The Court also rendered a second definitive judgment which, though important, was rather self-evident, given the language of the supremacy clause of the Constitution: that U.S. treaties overrode the provisions of conflicting state laws.[5]

From a political perspective, however, the Court's use of the legalistic doctrine of standing to sue, and the case or controversy requirement of Article III on which it largely rests, were of greater importance than either of these decisions. In refusing to decide a matter if its decision were susceptible of review by either Congress or the President because "[s]uch revision and control . . . [is] radically inconsistent with the independence of that judicial power which is vested in the courts,"[6] the Supreme Court formulated a flexible doctrine that enabled it – when so inclined – to avoid controversies better resolved extrajudicially. One year later, it extended this principle by refusing to render an advisory opinion at President Washington's request concerning United States policies toward certain European nations.[7] The Court, therefore, astutely coupled its concern for judicial independence with self-serving self-restraint. The Court linked its concern for judicial independence with fastidious attention to proper procedure by requiring, inter alia, that the residence of the parties in cases arising under diversity jurisdiction be clearly spelled out, and that all matters must be brought to trial compatibly with the regular process of law.[8]

THE MARSHALL COURT

Unquestionably, John Marshall dominated his Court as no other justice has. Indeed, given the influence he exerted, one may plausibly argue that no person has had a greater effect on the course of American life – political or otherwise – than he. Under his aegis, the Marshall Court established three enduring legacies: the doctrine of judicial supremacy, national supremacy, and an expansive view of federal power vis-à-vis that of the states.

[5] *Ware v. Hylton*, 3 Dallas 199 (1796). [6] *Hayburn's Case*, 2 Dallas 409 (1792), at 410.

[7] Charles Warren, *The Supreme Court in United States History* (Boston: Little Brown, 1922), I, 108–11.

[8] *Bingham v. Cabot*, 3 Dallas 382 (1797); *Dewhurst v. Coulthard*, 3 Dallas 409 (1799).

Judicial Supremacy

Judicial supremacy is rooted in the doctrine of judicial review that Marshall formulated and applied in *Marbury v. Madison*, which we discussed at some length in Chapter 1. Although Marshall availed himself of no other opportunities to declare unconstitutional an act of Congress, and the second instance of its use, *Scott v. Sandford*, proved to be counterproductive, precipitating as it did the Civil War, the doctrine nonetheless survived full-blown and intact.

As we observed in Chapter 1, Marshall's tactics in deciding *Marbury* raise serious questions of propriety and decorum, and his arguments in the opinion of the Court demean the integrity of the other branches of government. Nonetheless, the decision gained sufficient acceptance among the American public to become warp and woof of the constitutional fabric. In great part, this may have resulted from the political aspect of the decision. Marshall, after all, did rule against his political party and its well-known strategy, following its defeat in the election of 1800, to retreat into the judicial branch from whence it could lick its wounds preparatory to fighting another day. Second, the decision did not require enforcement. It automatically had force and effect without the need for executive action. Though Jefferson, Madison, and company were well aware of the constitutionally subordinate position in which *Marbury v. Madison* placed the legislative and executive branches, the average person, legally unsophisticated, likely saw the decision as a victory for principle over political expediency and as an additional buttress to the system of limited government crafted by the Framers. And, indeed, given Jefferson's ambivalence about judicial review,[9] he may have realized it could serve as a meaningful check on rambunctious tendencies in the other branches.

National Supremacy

The second and third bequests of Marshall's legacy are closely interrelated: national supremacy and an expansive interpretation of the scope of federal power.

Although they may superficially appear inseparable, this is not true in fact. Beginning with the Taney Court and continuing – largely without

[9] Jack Knight and Lee Epstein, "On the Struggle for Judicial Supremacy," 30 *Law and Society Review* 87 (1996), 110–11.

interruption – until the famous "switch in time" in 1937, the instruments of national supremacy were used to curb and confine the exercise of federal power and, during the heyday of laissez-faire, that of the states as well. Decisions of the Rehnquist Court during the 1990s resurrected some nineteenth- and early twentieth-century limitations on federal power. But unlike the earlier periods, the effect of the Rehnquist Court decisions – as we see below – expanded the sphere of state authority.

From a political standpoint, Marshall's effort to establish national supremacy met with truculent opposition. Although Article VI of the Constitution reads unequivocally, it nonetheless ran counter to deeply held states' rights sentiments. Marshall faced markedly less opposition to judicial review or the broad definition of federal power, even though the relevant constitutional language in these regards is either nonexistent or opaque. Furthermore, neither of these latter two values contradicted others of equal force.

National supremacy required three major decisions to provide it with a firm foundation. In *Fairfax's Devisee v. Hunter's Lessee*,[10] the Court reversed a ruling of Virginia's supreme court concerning title to lands possessed by British subjects under provisions of the Jay Treaty of 1794. Virginia refused to accede to the Court's decision, arguing that though it was bound by the supremacy clause of the Constitution, it need not adhere to the Supreme Court's interpretation thereof. As a result of Virginia's noncompliance, the case returned to the Supreme Court three years later.[11] Construing the language in the Judiciary Act of 1789 that authorizes Supreme Court review of state court decisions containing a federal question, the Court ruled that if a state were free to determine the compatibility of its own actions with those of the federal government, any given provision of the Constitution, act of Congress, or U.S. treaty would likely mean something different in each state. The uniformity of federal law would be chimerical along with the unity of the United States.

But not until the decision in *Cohens v. Virginia*[12] did the states' rights forces yield. Congress had authorized the District of Columbia to

[10] 7 Cranch 603 (1813).

[11] *Martin v. Hunter's Lessee*, 1 Wheaton 305 (1816). Marshall did not participate in this case or its predecessor, because he and his brother were themselves financially interested in the land in dispute.

[12] 6 Wheaton 264 (1821).

conduct a lottery for the purpose of financing public improvements. Virginia forbade lotteries, unlike most states today. Its authorities arrested two District residents and convicted them of selling lottery tickets. Virginia protested the sellers' appeal of their case to the Supreme Court, arguing that when a state is party to a lawsuit, the Supreme Court has only original, not appellate, jurisdiction. Marshall, participating in this case, ruled that when a state took action against individuals who defended themselves on the basis of federal law, the Supreme Court did, indeed, have appellate jurisdiction. Addressing the merits, Marshall again displayed the political astuteness that served him in such good stead in *Marbury v. Madison*, and ruled that Congress did not intend the sale of lottery tickets outside the District of Columbia. Those who did so acted at their peril. Again, as in *Marbury*, Marshall won the war by losing the battle. Virginia had no court order to resist or disobey.

Federal Power Vis-à-Vis That of the States

Two distinct lines of cases characterize this aspect of Marshall's legacy: a set of decisions that broadly construes the scope of federal power – particularly, the necessary and proper and the interstate commerce clauses, and a second set that concomitantly confines the scope of state power within a narrow compass. A pair of cases from each line illustrates the Marshall Court's policy position.

Unlike the establishment of national supremacy, but like the creation of judicial review, Marshall needed only one decision to settle the scope of federal power. The original charter of the Bank of the United States had expired the year before the War of 1812 began. The need for renewal had become painfully apparent during the course of the war as a result of the financial stringencies that afflicted the federal government. By the time Congress got around to rechartering the bank in 1816, the economy was too far gone for the bank to save it. Indeed, a number of the bank's branches made financial conditions worse by engaging in speculation, mismanagement of funds, and shady business practices.[13] In reaction, the states attempted to oust the bank from their territory by state constitutional prohibition or taxation. One such state was Maryland, whose legislature imposed a hefty tax that the State's courts upheld.

[13] The savings and loan banking scandals of the 1980s and 1990s have an ancient, if less than honorable, lineage.

The case, *M'Culloch v. Maryland*, contained two questions requiring a judicial answer: Did Congress have the power to establish a national bank and, if so, could a state tax it? Although the Constitution nowhere makes reference to a bank, it does allow Congress to raise taxes, borrow money, regulate commerce, wage war, and raise and support armies and navies. From these expressly delegated powers, Marshall inferred the power to establish a national bank. "[I]t may with great reason be contended" that on the exercise of these powers "the happiness and prosperity of the nation so vitally depends." If so, "ample means for their execution" must be available.[14] These means he found in the necessary and proper clause of Article I, section 8, clause 18:

> Let the end be legitimate, let it be within the scope of the constitution, and all means which are appropriate, which are plainly adapted to that end, which are not prohibited, but consist with the letter and spirit of the constitution, are constitutional.[15]

Famous words, these, as well known and as oft-cited as those of any opinion. And though more than a century would elapse after Marshall's death in 1835 before this language overcame occasional nit-picking treatment,[16] no Court has ever formally qualified it.

Marshall answered *M'Culloch*'s other question in the negative, basing his response on the supremacy clause. To allow the states to tax instrumentalities of the federal government "involves the power to destroy."[17] Half a century later, the Court even-handedly concluded that the federal government could not tax the employees, property, or activities of the states.[18] The resulting scheme of intergovernmental tax immunity was not dismantled until the eve of World War II. Its major modern remnant exempts from federal taxation income derived from state and municipal bonds.

Marshall used the first interstate commerce clause case – *Gibbons v. Ogden* – as his vehicle to assert an expansive concept of federal power, and, as in *Marbury v. Madison*, his opinion decided far more than what was needed to reach a decision. The controversy concerned a conflict over the licensing of steamboats between New York and Congress and was readily resolvable on the basis of the supremacy clause. But again

[14] *M'Culloch v. Maryland*, 4 Wheaton 316 (1819), at 408. [15] *Id.* at 421.

[16] E.g., *Adair v. United States*, 208 U.S. 161 (1908); *Hammer v. Dagenhart*, 247 U.S. 251 (1918); and *Adkins v. Children's Hospital*, 261 U.S. 525 (1923).

[17] 4 Wheaton, at 431. [18] *Collector v. Day*, 11 Wallace 113 (1871).

Marshall seized his opportunity and eagerly leapt where others had not yet trod.

He began by defining commerce not only as "traffic, but it is something more; it is intercourse."[19] Noting that the key constitutional word is commerce "among" the several states, he defined it as "inter-mingled with. A thing which is among others, is intermingled with them." Therefore, "Commerce among the states cannot stop at the external boundary line of each state, but may be introduced into the interior."[20]

Did this mean that the states had no power at all over commerce, especially if Congress had acted?

> It is not intended to say that these words comprehend that commerce which is completely internal, which is carried on between man and man in a state, and which does not extend to or affect other states. Such a power would be inconvenient, and is certainly unnecessary.[21]

Note that Marshall did not write that Congress has no power to regulate "completely internal" commerce, only that such power is "inconvenient" and "unnecessary." But he does go on to say that "[t]he completely internal commerce of a state, then, may be considered as reserved to the state itself."[22]

Particularly in light of hindsight, Marshall's position was clear. The commerce "among the several States" that Congress might regulate did not stop at a state line, and it certainly was not limited to business activities. And though Marshall's language did not foreclose all state regulation, any incompatibility would be resolved by the preference that the supremacy clause accords the federal government.

Independently of the expansive interpretation given federal powers, the Marshall Court narrowly construed those of the states. The primary basis was the language of Article I, section 10, that forbids a state to "pass any . . . law impairing the obligation of contracts." It should occasion no surprise that the first case to construe the contract clause was the first decision to void a state law: *Fletcher v. Peck*.[23]

In 1795, enterprising schemers bribed the kakistocratic Georgia legislature into selling virtually all of Alabama and Mississippi for the munificent sum of $500,000. One year later, a new legislature revoked the grant. Meantime, the purchasers sold some of their ill-gotten gains to speculators and prospective settlers. Although the resulting litigation

[19] *Gibbons v. Ogden*, 9 Wheaton 1 (1824), at 189. [20] *Id.* at 194. [21] *Id.*
[22] *Id.* at 195. [23] 6 Cranch 87 (1810).

did not involve a bona fide "case or controversy" – which the Constitution limits federal courts to deciding – Marshall again disregarded jurisdictional limitations, as he did in *Marbury v. Madison.*[24]

Emphasizing the harm that good-faith purchasers would suffer, Marshall equated a land grant with a contract by asserting that a grant "implies a contract" which estops the grantor from reneging.[25] As for the inclusion of public grants within the compass of the contract clause, Marshall simply asserted that "[t]he words themselves contain no such distinction. They are general, and are applicable to contracts of every description."[26] Nine years later, Marshall extended the scope of the contract clause still further, ruling that corporate charters were also protected from abridgment.[27]

These decisions effectively positioned vested property rights alongside those that the Constitution explicitly protected from governmental abrogation and presaged the use later Courts made of the Fourteenth Amendment to protect private property from commercially hostile governmental regulation. If the individualistic tenor of American life needed constitutional sanction, decisions such as *Fletcher v. Peck* and *Dartmouth College* convincingly provided it.

THE CIVIL WAR ERA

Although the division between North and South became increasingly institutionalized in the years following the death of Chief Justice Marshall in 1835, the Court did not directly address the slavery question until 1857. Before then, its major decisions, like those of the Marshall Court, concerned the supremacy, interstate commerce, and contract clauses.

The Taney Court

No more than the Burger Court undid the decisions of the Warren Court did the Taney Court undo those of the Marshall Court. Expectations that the leveling influences of Jacksonian Democracy would curtail vested

[24] The case was a friendly suit, a collusive action between parties whose real interests coincided. See C. Peter Magrath, *Yazoo: Law and Politics in the New Republic* (New York: Norton: 1966). Justice Johnson, in his concurring opinion in *Fletcher v. Peck*, also alluded to its feigned character. 6 Cranch, at 147–48.

[25] *Id.* at 137. [26] *Id.* [27] *Dartmouth College v. Woodward*, 4 Wheaton 518 (1819).

property rights and commercial interests and expand the sphere of states' rights went largely unrealized. President Jackson himself saw six of his nominees, including Chief Justice Taney, seated on the High Court. Not since Washington had a single President been responsible for the appointment of a majority of the justices.

Two rulings typify the Taney Court's handling of the policy issues that characterized the Marshall Court. In *Charles River Bridge v. Warren Bridge*,[28] Taney ruled that states could reserve the right to alter, amend, or repeal corporate charters, and that no implied powers exist in the provisions of a public grant to a private organization. A corporation has only those specifically bestowed. Any ambiguity should be resolved in favor of the public. In drawing the foregoing line between private enterprise and government regulation, the Taney Court did not markedly deviate from Marshall's position. Marshall himself had observed that corporations are artificial entities created by law. As creatures of the law, they have only the powers their charters expressly confer.

In *Cooley v. Board of Port Wardens*,[29] the Taney Court spelled out the Marshall Court's ruling in *Gibbons v. Ogden*. Labeling their common position "selective exclusiveness," the majority held that Congress's power to regulate commerce was complete and to some extent exclusive. Only those subjects that "are in their nature national, or admit of only one uniform system, or plan of regulation, may justly be said to be of such a nature as to require exclusive regulation by Congress."[30] The states might regulate other matters if their regulations did not conflict with those of Congress.

The Case of *Scott v. Sandford*

The reputation of the Taney Court is thoroughly colored by its decision in *Scott v. Sandford*.[31] Its other contributions pale by comparison. Not only did the decision precipitate the Civil War, the self-inflicted wound that the ruling produced all but destroyed the public's perception of the Court as objective, dispassionate, and impartial.

Dred Scott, a slave, sought his freedom on his return to Missouri, a slave state, as a result of several years' residence in Wisconsin, a nonslave territory under the Missouri Compromise of 1820. After

[28] 11 Peters 420 (1837). [29] 12 Howard 299 (1852). [30] *Id.* at 319.
[31] 19 Howard 393 (1857).

losing in the state supreme court, Scott brought suit in federal court, alleging that since he and his owner were citizens of different states, the federal court had jurisdiction. When the case reached the Supreme Court, each justice wrote his own opinion. Taney's was dispositive. Because no black – slave or free – could be an American citizen, no black could sue in a federal court. The reason: At the time the Constitution was adopted, blacks were

> considered as a subordinate and inferior class of beings, who had been subjugated by the dominant race, and whether emancipated or not, yet remained subject to their authority, and had no rights or privileges but such as those who held the power and the government might choose to grant them.[32]

Did no constitutional provision protect blacks? Again Taney said no: "[F]or more than a century" blacks had

> been regarded as beings of an inferior order; and altogether unfit to associate with the white race . . . and so far inferior, that they had no rights which the white man was bound to respect; and that the negro might justly and lawfully be reduced to slavery for his benefit. He was bought and sold, and treated as an ordinary article of merchandise and traffic, whenever a profit could be made by it. This opinion was at that time fixed and universal in the civilized portion of the white race.[33]

As a plain, unvarnished statement of unadulterated racism, Taney's statement expressed a view shared by millions of Americans who did possess American citizenship. But might not language in the Declaration of Independence refute the "universal" perception of black inferiority? Specifically, the references to "all men" being "created equal," and the business about all men being "endowed by their Creator with certain inalienable rights"? Again Taney said no. "The language of the Declaration of Independence is equally conclusive."

> . . . it is too clear for dispute, that the enslaved African race were not intended to be included, and formed no part of the people who framed and adopted this Declaration; for if the language, as understood in that day, would embrace them, the conduct of the distinguished men who framed the Declaration of

[32] *Id.* at 404–5.

[33] *Id.* at 407. If Taney's statement applies only to "the civilized portion of the white race," one may wonder what lesser status blacks might have been accorded by *uncivilized* whites, a qualification that certainly applied to slaveholders generally.

Independence would have been utterly and flagrantly inconsistent with the principles they asserted; and instead of the sympathy of mankind, to which they so confidently appealed, they would have deserved and received universal rebuke and reprobation.[34]

If doubt had existed, by a vote of 7 to 2 the justices made it pellucid that the Constitution formed a government of, by, and for white males alone. The die was cast. Only civil war could alter the Court's decree. Four years later hostilities began, and three years after they ended the Fourteenth Amendment was ratified permanently, interring the most rebarbative decision in the Court's history.[35]

Given the ruling that Scott was not a citizen, the majority should simply have dismissed the case for want of jurisdiction. Instead, Taney took a page from Marshall's book on devious deviations from proper judicial procedure and declared the Missouri Compromise, which banned slavery in certain territories, unconstitutional. Note may also be made that the Constitution in Article IV, section 3, explicitly authorizes Congress to "make all needful rules and regulations respecting the territory or other property belonging to the United States."

[34] *Id.* at 409, 410. Hard to believe, perhaps. But not only is the quoted language accurate, it also displays the utter malleability of logic in general, and legal logic in particular. Good is bad, and unmitigated evil is actually just and moral.

[35] One may quarrel about this being the most repulsive decision in the Court's history. Other racial alternatives are *Plessy v. Ferguson* and *Korematsu v. United States*, both of which are discussed later in this chapter, and *Elk v. Wilkins*, 112 U.S. 94 (1884), which, paralleling *Scott v. Sandford*, declared that Native Americans, even those who had left the jurisdiction of Indian reservations, could not be citizens of the United States. This notwithstanding the plain words with which the Fourteenth Amendment begins: "All persons born or naturalized in the United States and subject to the jurisdiction thereof, are citizens of the United States. . . ." *Plessy*, of course, has also been interred, as a result of *Brown v. Board of Education.* Not so *Korematsu* or *Elk*, though the latter was legislatively overturned by the Indian Citizenship Act of 1924.

We learned of the Elk case as a result of Segal's effort to answer his daughter Michelle's question for her fourth-grade social studies class: "When did American Indians get the right to vote?" We assumed the Fifteenth Amendment would have settled the matter, if not the Fourteenth, but Lexis pointed to the Elk case, which, according to Shepards, had not been overturned. The only constitutional law book on our shelves that mentioned *Elk* also says nothing about it having been overturned. See John E. Nowak, Ronald D. Rotunda, and J. Nelson Young, *Constitutional Law* (St. Paul, Minn.: West, 1978), p. 588. Pursuing the matter further, we phoned Professor Regina P. Branton of Rice University, who informed us that the Indian Citizenship Act of 1924 had legislatively overruled *Elk*.

Segal had assumed that around eleventh or twelfth grade his daughter might ask him math and science questions to which he might not know the answer. But certainly not a question emanating from a fourth-grade social studies class!

RECONSTRUCTION

Following its decision in *Scott v. Sandford*, the power and influence of the Court hit bottom. The decision revolted large segments of the public, especially in the North. Congress displayed its contempt by altering the Court's size three times within a decade, all for purely political purposes. But with the end of the Civil War, the Court began to regain some of its lost luster. Lincoln placed five persons on the Court whom history highly regards: Noah Swayne, Samuel Miller, David Davis, Stephen Field, and the new chief justice, Salmon P. Chase. The American bar, newly organized and increasingly influential, regularly paid it homage. The justices themselves mostly kept to the middle of the ideological road, ratifying the policies of other officials rather than initiating their own.

Only once during this time did the Court shoot itself in the foot: over the matter of legal tender. In an effort to finance the Civil War, Congress had enacted legislation that substituted paper money for gold as legal tender. In 1870, by a 4-to-3 vote, the Court held the legislation unconstitutional for the payment of debts that antedated the law's enactment in 1862.[36] One year later, the three dissenters, joined by two new appointees, reversed the earlier ruling and held that the Congress properly exercised the powers implied in the necessary and proper clause.[37] The Court managed to escape relatively unscathed, however, because criticism fell on President Grant for interfering with the independence of the judiciary by "packing" the Court.[38]

Military Justice

Although the Court refused to decide the constitutionality of military tribunals during the Civil War, on the basis that Congress had not given it jurisdiction to do so,[39] it effectively reversed itself once the war was over. In a two-part ruling, the Court unanimously held that the President lacks power to try civilians by military tribunals during wartime in places where the civil courts are open and functioning and, by a 5-to-4 vote, that the combined war powers of President and Congress did not

[36] *Hepburn v. Griswold*, 8 Wallace 603. Ironically, Chief Justice Chase, while secretary of the treasury in Lincoln's administration, proposed and implemented the issuance of paper money as legal tender to finance the Civil War. As chief justice, he voted against its constitutionality.

[37] *Knox v. Lee*, 12 Wallace 457 (1870). [38] Warren, *op. cit.*, n. 7, *supra*, III, 243–49.

[39] *Ex parte Vallandigham*, 1 Wallace 243 (1864).

constitutionally authorize such tribunals where the regular courts were open.[40]

In a case that also arose from the actions of a military tribunal, but with ramifications that went beyond military justice, the Court meekly deferred to Congress and upheld a law that revoked its jurisdiction over a certain matter even though the case was already argued and awaiting decision.[41] Scholars have used *Ex parte McCardle* as an example of the operation of the rational choice, or strategic, model we discussed in Chapter 2.[42] However, the Court has always deferred to Congress when it has constricted federal court jurisdiction. Thus, for example, in 1932, Congress revoked the authority of the federal courts to issue injunctions in labor disputes. Up to that time, business had obtained such injunctions to criminalize strikes, thus impeding labor's ability to bargain collectively. Moreover, the facts of the *Milligan* and *McCardle* cases do not support the strategic model particularly well.[43]

Civil Rights

The Court first confronted the Fourteenth Amendment in the *Slaughterhouse Cases*[44] in 1873. Curiously, the case had nothing to do with blacks, but rather with a monopoly that Louisiana had granted to a slaughterhouse. Other butchers complained that the act put them out of business. Although the due process and equal protection clauses have been more litigated than any others in the Constitution, the provision of the Fourteenth Amendment on which the majority focused – the privileges and immunities clause – has been little used. The Amendment created no new rights, said the Court, but only allowed Congress, if it is so minded, to legislatively protect the handful of privileges and immunities that peculiarly derive from federal rather than state citizenship. The right to own and operate a butcher shop was not among them.[45]

[40] *Ex parte Milligan*, 4 Wallace 2 (1866).

[41] *Ex parte McCardle*, 7 Wallace 506 (1869). Congress presumably feared that if the Court were to decide the case, it might declare Congress's efforts to reconstruct the South unconstitutional.

[42] Lee Epstein and Thomas G. Walker, "The Role of the Supreme Court in American Society: Playing the Reconstruction Game," in Lee Epstein, ed., *Contemplating Courts* (Washington, D.C.: Congressional Quarterly, 1995), pp. 315–46.

[43] See Chapter 8.

[44] 16 Wallace 36.

[45] The Court's decision in *Saenz v. Roe*, 143 L Ed 2d (1999), may signal the provision's reinvigoration. The justices voided a California law awarding lower welfare benefits to

The first major Fourteenth Amendment decision that directly concerned blacks was the *Civil Rights Cases* of 1883.[46] The Court had previously gutted congressional legislation designed to protect blacks who exercised their right to vote under the Fifteenth Amendment.[47] Over the dissent of Justice Harlan, a former slave owner, the same fate befell congressional legislation designed to outlaw discrimination in places of public accommodation. The amendment does not apply to private discrimination, said the justices, only that resulting from affirmative state action.

The decision in the *Civil Rights Cases* did not end the matter, of course. The racism that Chief Justice Taney had so ably rationalized in *Scott v. Sandford* was not to be eradicated simply because the bloodiest war in United States history had been fought and three constitutional amendments ratified. By legitimating white supremacy and the strict segregation and blatant discrimination mandated by Jim Crow legislation, the Court effectively declared these events null and void until the middle of the twentieth century, when a later Court partially undid what its predecessors had wrought. In the meantime, the nation still needed a constitutional doctrine to rationalize and justify white supremacy. Thirteen years later the Court provided it in *Plessy v. Ferguson* when the justices – with Justice Harlan again dissenting – formulated the separate but equal doctrine.[48] Thereafter, no sanction would befall even the most flagrantly discriminatory state action so long as the governmental facilities or actions in question were separate, regardless of inequality.

FIGHTING THE WELFARE STATE

Following the Civil War, the United States, previously an agrarian society, became one of the world's industrial giants. As the Court reneged on the promises of the Fourteenth Amendment, it began to focus its attention on the economy.

recent residents. Related cases decided in 1969 and 1982 had relied on a "right to travel," a provision, like the "separate state sovereignty" (S-cubed) discussed in Chapter 1, nowhere appears in the Constitution. The *Saenz* Court provided no reason for its reliance on the privileges and immunities clause.

[46] 109 U.S. 3.

[47] In *United States v. Reese*, 92 U.S. 214 (1876), and *United States v. Cruikshank*, 92 U.S. 542 (1876).

[48] 163 U.S. 537 (1896).

> ... as capitalism expanded, it impinged on the lives of individuals as never before; as it became the most important fact in American life, it became the most troublesome fact as well. Men began to say, first from scattered quarters, then in a steadily augmenting chorus, that the power of government should be used to control this giant, to mitigate the harm to individual and collective welfare that it might do if left unchecked. And conversely, others began to say, with a vengeance and volume far greater than in the past, that the giant would serve the community best if it were allowed to go its own way, that governmental tinkering with the economy was both futile and mischievous, that laissez faire should be the watchword of the day.[49]

More often than not the Supreme Court threw its lot with the plunderbunds who favored laissez-faire. We examine the three main areas where the Court applied the gospel of wealth: taxation, commerce, and substantive due process.

Taxation

The Articles of Confederation provided the Continental Congress no direct authority to tax individuals. States could be solicited, but they could not be compelled to pay. This was one of the many deficiencies in the Articles that led to the calling of the Constitutional Convention in 1787.

The Framers of the Constitution granted Congress certain tax powers. Article I, section 8, clause 1, declares that "Congress shall have the power to lay and collect taxes, duties, imposts, and excises." The Framers restricted this broad tax power in three ways: duties, imposts, and excises must be uniform (Article I, section 8); capitation and other "direct" taxes must be levied proportionate to population (Article I, section 2; Article I, section 9); and no tax or duty could be placed on goods exported from any state (also Article I, section 9).

The first federal income tax was levied during the Civil War. The Supreme Court upheld it as an excise tax, not a direct tax, and thus one not subject to apportionment. Declared the Court: "[D]irect taxes, within the meaning of the Constitution, are only capitation taxes . . . and taxes on real estate."[50]

In 1894, Congress enacted the Wilson-Gorman Tariff Act, which placed a tax of 2 percent on the income of individuals and corporations

[49] Robert McCloskey, *The American Supreme Court* (Chicago: University of Chicago Press, 1960), pp. 102–3.

[50] *Springer v. United States*, 102 U.S. 586 (1880), at 602. The ruling sustained the 1796 precedent, *Hylton v. United States*, 3 Dallas 171.

from rents, interest, dividends, salaries, and profits over $4,000. Progressive and populist elements hailed the tax as a great victory. So much did the plunderbund fear the tax that they told the Court that the act was part of a "'Communist march' against the rights of property."[51] In April of 1895, the Court declared in *Pollock v. Farmers' Loan and Trust*[52] that the tax on rents was in reality a tax on land and thus a direct tax that must be apportioned. Taxes on municipal bonds were invalidated on the grounds of intergovernmental immunity. With Justice Jackson ill, the Court split 4 to 4 on the constitutionality of the income tax. When Jackson recovered, the case was reargued. Jackson joined those who thought the income tax constitutional, but Justice Shiras switched, invalidating the tax.[53] According to Supreme Court historian Robert McCloskey, the direct tax clause "provided the judges with an objective formulation of their prejudice in favor of wealth."[54]

In a final blow to the act, the Court also struck the tax on business profits and employment income. It did not find such taxes unconstitutional; rather, it asserted that Congress would not have taxed these sources of income if it could not also tax dividends, interest, and rent. The *Pollock* decisions led to the ratification of the Sixteenth Amendment, one of five times an amendment undid a decision of the Court (see Chapter 3). The Amendment simply states, "The Congress shall have power to lay and collect taxes on incomes, from whatever source derived, without apportionment among the several States, and without regard to any census or enumeration." As noted in Chapter 1, the language did not prevent the members of the Court from exempting themselves and their lower bench colleagues from its operation on the ground that the Constitution prohibits any lowering of judicial salaries. As we see below, the amendment also did not prevent the Court from voiding taxes by labeling them constitutionally prohibited *non*taxes.

Interstate Commerce and Other National Powers

The same year that the Supreme Court ruled the income tax unconstitutional, 1895, it rendered two additional decisions that supported laissez-faire. One week after the second *Pollock* ruling, the Court upheld

[51] C. Herman Pritchett, *The American Constitution*, 3rd ed. (New York: McGraw-Hill, 1977), p. 168.

[52] 157 U.S. 429. [53] *Pollock v. Farmers' Loan and Trust Co.*, 158 U.S. 601 (1895).

[54] *Op. cit.*, n. 49, *supra*, p. 141.

an injunction prohibiting railroad workers, led by Eugene Debs, from obstructing the nation's railroads, and thus interstate commerce.[55] In effect, the Court declared the Pullman strike of 1894 illegal.

The Court's ruling in *Debs* was not the result of any principled belief in broad national powers over interstate commerce, such as Chief Justice Marshall had expressed in *Gibbons v. Ogden*. Typically, a cramped construction better enabled the Court to achieve a result consistent with its laissez-faire philosophy. The first relevant case, *United States v. E. C. Knight Co.*,[56] was decided a few months before the *Pollock* and *Debs* cases. It involved enforcement of the Sherman Antitrust Act, enacted by Congress in 1890, which made "every contract, combination . . . or conspiracy in restraint of trade or commerce among the several states, or with foreign nations . . . illegal."[57] The Department of Justice sought to break up the American Sugar Refining Company, which, through acquisitions, controlled over 98 percent of the nation's sugar refining.

The Court conceded that the sugar trust was an illegal monopoly. The relevant question, rather, was whether Congress had the authority to suppress monopolies. The Court said it did not. First, the Court asserted that the protection of life, health, and property is part of the police power, which belongs exclusively to the states. When monopolies burden the citizens of a state, the state's legislature must remedy the wrong. Second, while the Court recognized that Congress had plenary authority to regulate interstate commerce, it denied that the manufacture of 98 percent of the nation's sugar in several different states by one company constituted commerce. Drawing a distinction between manufacturing and commerce, the Court declared that "[c]ommerce succeeds to manufacture, and is not a part of it."[58] Monopolistic production affects commerce only indirectly, and thus is beyond the power of Congress to regulate. The Court subsequently held that mining and agriculture also preceded commerce and, like manufacturing, were beyond congressional regulation.

The Court's commerce clause decisions did not invariably support business, however. In 1905, for example, it ruled that fixing prices through collusion at a stockyard violated the Sherman Act even though the activity took place within a single state. The Court held the activity to be part of "a current of commerce among the States"[59] that started with the raising of cattle and ended with the final retail sale. Other busi-

[55] *In re Debs*, 158 U.S. 564. [56] 156 U.S. 1 (1895). [57] *Id.* at 6. [58] *Id.* at 12.
[59] *Swift and Co. v. United States*, 196 U.S. 375, at 398–99.

nesses did not deserve protection because of their incompatibility with the Puritan ethic that underlay laissez-faire economics. Thus, the Court held the commerce clause a perfectly appropriate vehicle for prohibiting the interstate sale of lottery tickets.[60] But such decisions were exceptions to the rule. More typical rulings invalidated the Child Labor Act of 1916, which prohibited the shipment of goods across state lines produced by children under the age of fourteen, or by those between fourteen and sixteen who worked more than forty-eight hours per week.[61] According to the Court's 5-to-4 decision, Congress could not use the commerce power to regulate the conditions of production, because the Tenth Amendment reserved the matter to the states. The Court distinguished *Hammer* from the lottery case because the goods intended for interstate commerce were not in and of themselves harmful. Thus Congress could ban the sale of lottery tickets across state lines, but not goods made by child labor.

In reaction, Congress enacted a law that imposed a tax of 10 percent on the net profits of firms that hired children under the age of fourteen. With the passage of the Sixteenth Amendment, such taxing authority seemed clearly within Congress's power. Nevertheless, the Court struck the law on the ground that the imposition was not a tax, but a penalty.[62] Like Humpty Dumpty in *Through the Looking Glass*, words mean what the Court chooses them to mean – neither more nor less.[63]

With the onset of the Great Depression in 1929, the demand for federal regulation increased. When Franklin Roosevelt took office in 1933, he immediately proposed "New Deal" legislation to revive the national economy. Although the legislation sailed through Congress, it failed to receive Court approval.

First to fall was the National Industrial Recovery Act (NIRA), which required business and government to establish codes of fair competition that would result in higher prices and, so the government hoped, better

[60] *Champion v. Ames*, 188 U.S. 321 (1903).

[61] *Hammer v. Dagenhart*, 247 U.S. 251 (1918).

[62] *Bailey v. Drexel Furniture*, 259 U.S. 20 (1922).

[63] " 'The question is,' said Alice, 'whether you *can* make words mean so many different things.'

" 'The question is, said Humpty Dumpty, 'which is to be master – that's all.' " The Supreme Court has obviously sided with Humpty. See Lewis Carroll, *Alice's Adventures in Wonderland and Through the Looking Glass* (New York: Oxford University Press, 1971), p. 190.

wages and lower unemployment. In 1935, the Court struck down a provision that allowed (but did not require) the President to prohibit the transportation in interstate commerce of oil produced in excess of state and federal regulations.[64] With only Justice Cardozo dissenting, the Court ruled the provision to be a standardless delegation of legislative power that left the decision of whether to ban such shipments entirely to the President's discretion.

The Court considered the remainder of the NIRA later in 1935. Although the act would expire in three weeks, the Court nevertheless agreed to review it in *Schechter Poultry v. United States*.[65] The Schechter brothers owned slaughterhouses in New York that butchered out-of-state chickens. In violation of the authorized codes of fair competition, the brothers allegedly filed false sales and price reports and sold diseased chickens.

The Court voided the NIRA on two grounds. First, the establishment of codes of fair competition by businesses working with the executive branch unlawfully delegated legislative powers. More troublesome to Roosevelt was the second part of the Court's opinion, which declared that the statute went beyond Congress's commerce power. Though out-of-state farmers supplied the chickens, their slaughter and sale occurred after "the flow of interstate commerce had ceased. The poultry had come to a permanent rest within the state."[66] Indeed they had. Once again, the Court ruled the effect on interstate commerce merely indirect and thus beyond the scope of the commerce clause. President Roosevelt criticized the Court for "relegat[ing] us to the horse-and-buggy definition of interstate commerce."[67]

Also struck was the Agricultural Adjustment Act of 1933.[68] The act attempted to increase depressed farm prices by subsidizing farmers who agreed to reduce crop production. Funds to pay the farmers came from a tax levied on the processors of the relevant commodities. Even though the Constitution gives Congress the power to tax for the general welfare, the Court ruled that the taxing and spending provisions of the act,

[64] *Panama Refining Co. v. Ryan*, 293 U.S. 388 (1935).

[65] 295 U.S. 495 (1935). Inasmuch as the act was generally perceived to be an ineffective solution to the nation's economic woes, no substantial effort had been made to extend it.

[66] *Id.* at 543.

[67] Gregory Caldeira, "Public Opinion and the Supreme Court: FDR's Court-Packing Plan," 81 *American Political Science Review* 1139 (1987), at 1141.

[68] *United States v. Butler*, 297 U.S. 1 (1936).

because they regulated agricultural production, violated the Tenth Amendment.

One of the biggest blows to the New Deal came in the 1936 case *Carter v. Carter Coal Co.* The Court's decision invalidated the Bituminous Coal Conservation Act, which attempted to stabilize the coal industry by allowing a commission to set minimum and maximum prices. Maximum hour and minimum wage standards were also established. Coal producers were subject to a 15 percent sales tax from which they would be largely exempt if they abided by the commission's standards.

The Court's opinion focused on the scope of the commerce clause. While in *Schechter* the attempted focus of regulation came *after* commerce allegedly ended, here the focus occurred *before* commerce began. According to the Court,

> . . . the word "commerce" is the equivalent of the phrase "intercourse for the purposes of trade." Plainly, the incidents leading up to and culminating in the mining of coal do not constitute such intercourse. The employment of men, the fixing of their wages, hours of labor and working conditions, the bargaining in respect of these things – whether carried on separately or collectively – each and all constitute intercourse for the purposes of production, not of trade. The latter is a thing apart from the relation of employer and employee, which in all producing occupations is purely local in character. Extraction of coal from the mine is the aim and the completed result of local activities. Commerce in the coal mined is not brought into being by force of these activities, but by negotiations, agreements, and circumstances entirely apart from production. Mining brings the subject-matter of commerce into existence. Commerce disposes of it.[69]

By intruding into employer-employee relations the act also interfered with the rights that the Tenth Amendment reserved to the states. Thus by an idiotropic reading of the commerce clause, the Court throttled much of the New Deal.

Freedom of Contract

The preceding section shows that when the federal government attempted to regulate working conditions, the Court ruled that such legislative powers belonged to the states, not the federal government. When the states tried to regulate hours worked and wages paid, the Court generally ruled such state legislation violated "freedom of contract," which the Court decreed to be implicit in the due process clause of the

[69] 298 U.S. 238, at 303–4.

Fourteenth Amendment. Because these decisions are based on the subjects of state regulation, not the procedures states use, commentators classify these cases under the oxymoronic rubric "substantive due process."

The idea behind substantive due process – that courts may void government action even though it does not violate any explicit constitutional provision – traces at least to *Calder v. Bull*.[70] There the Court upheld a Connecticut law against the claim that it constituted an ex post facto law. Speaking for himself, Justice Chase declared that he could not

> subscribe to the omnipotence of a state legislature, or that it is absolute and without controul; although its authority should not be expressly restrained by the constitution, or fundamental law of the state. . . . To maintain that our federal or state legislature possesses such powers, if they had not been expressly restrained, would, in my opinion, be a political heresy altogether inadmissable in our free republican governments.[71]

The first known instance of a law being struck on the grounds of substantive due process occurred in an 1856 case, *Wynehamer v. People*.[72] The New York Court of Appeals declared that a law prohibiting the sale of liquor deprived saloon keepers of their property.

The judicial and economic impact of *Wynehamer* was quickly felt:

> In less than twenty years from the time of its rendition the crucial ruling in *Wynehamer* was far on the way to being assimilated into the accepted constitutional law of the country. The "due process" clause, which had been intended originally to consecrate a mode of procedure, had become a constitutional test of ever reaching reach of the substantive content of legislation. Thus was the doctrine of vested rights brought within the constitutional fold.[73]

The first case in which the Supreme Court voided a state law on substantive due process grounds was the 1897 decision in *Allgeyer v. Louisiana*.[74] The Court invalidated a statute that prohibited Louisiana companies from purchasing marine insurance from out-of-state businesses that did not comply with Louisiana regulations. The Court overturned Allgeyer's conviction for purchasing the insurance because

> the statute is a violation of the fourteenth amendment of the federal constitution, in that it deprives the defendants of their liberty without due process of law. . . . The "liberty" mentioned in that amendment means, not only the right of a citizen to be free from the mere physical restraint of his person, as by incar-

[70] 3 Dallas 386 (1798). [71] *Id.* at 387–89. [72] 13 N.Y. 378.

[73] Edward S. Corwin, *Liberty against Government* (Baton Rouge: Louisiana State University Press, 1948), pp. 114–15.

[74] 165 U.S. 578.

ceration, but the term is deemed to embrace the right of the citizen to be free to . . . enter into all contracts which may be proper, necessary and essential to his carrying out a successful conclusion the purposes above mentioned.[75]

Whatever one may think of laissez-faire economics as public policy, its constitutional basis is problematic. Reasonable people disagree whether the term "liberty" in the Fourteenth Amendment includes freedom of contract. But whatever the scope of this liberty, it is far from absolute. The Court simply sought a result and reached it by the most convenient means possible, even though this meant reading into the Constitution nonexistent language.

A decision eleven years earlier magnified the consequences of *Allgeyer*: that corporations were "persons" within the meaning and protections of the Fourteenth Amendment.[76] Hence, states could not limit the freedom of either individuals or corporations to contract.

However nugatory the substance of the *Allgeyer* decision might seem – allowing companies to let out-of-state contracts hardly seems momentous – the scope of the new right to contract became apparent in *Lochner v. New York*.[77] Under its police powers, the state had enacted a maximum-hour law limiting bakers to ten hours of work per day and sixty hours of work per week. In a 5-to-4 decision the Court ruled that the law interfered with freedom of contract. Rejecting evidence that long hours were injurious to bakers, the Court declared that the "real object and purpose were simply to regulate the hours of labor between the master and his employees."[78] Never mind that when the federal government enacted such regulations, the Court ruled that only the states could do so. Justice Holmes argued in dissent that this case

is decided upon an economic theory which a large part of the country does not entertain. . . . The Fourteenth Amendment does not enact Mr. Herbert Spencer's Social Statics. . . . A constitution is not intended to embody a particular economic theory, whether of paternalism and the organic relation of the citizen to the state or of *laissez faire*.[79]

On the authority of *Lochner* the Supreme Court invalidated federal and state laws barring employers from prohibiting workers to join labor unions.[80] In the state case the Court acknowledged that it is "impossible to uphold freedom of contract and the right of private

[75] *Id.* at 589.
[76] *Santa Clara County v. Southern Pacific R. Co.*, 118 U.S. 394 (1886).
[77] 198 U.S. 45 (1905). [78] *Id.* at 64. [79] *Id.* at 75.
[80] *Adair v. United States*, 208 U.S. 161 (1908), and *Coppage v. Kansas*, 236 U.S. 1 (1915).

property without at the same time recognizing as legitimate those inequalities of fortune that are a necessary result of the exercise of those rights."[81]

The Court did not always uphold freedom of contract, however. In 1908 it sustained a law limiting women to ten hours of work per day in factories or laundries because a "woman's physical structure, and the functions she performs in consequence thereof, justify special legislation."[82] In 1917 the Court upheld a maximum hour law for factory workers of both sexes without mentioning *Lochner*.[83] More often than not, though, state social legislation was invalidated. Thus, in *Wolff Packing Co. v. Court of Industrial Relations*[84] the Court struck a Kansas statute requiring binding arbitration of labor-management disputes when they threatened public well-being. In *Adkins v. United States*[85] the Court voided a law setting minimum wages for women and children in the District of Columbia.

Following the onset of the Great Depression in 1929, the need for state regulation became acute. The validity of such legislation continued to depend on judicial approval. On the Supreme Court, a trifurcated alignment emerged: a four-person conservative coalition consisting of James McReynolds, Willis Van Devanter, George Sutherland, and Pierce Butler; a three-person liberal alliance of Oliver Wendell Holmes (replaced in 1932 by Benjamin Cardozo), Louis Brandeis, and Harlan Stone; and the two swing voters, Chief Justice Charles Evans Hughes and Justice Owen Roberts. In 1934 Hughes and Roberts joined the liberals to uphold a New York law regulating the price of milk,[86] but in 1935 and 1936 they joined forces with the conservatives in a series of important cases. Shortly after concluding that the national government infringed on states' rights by regulating wages and prices, the Court ruled that New York's attempt to regulate minimum wages for women violated due process. By a 5-to-4 vote (Hughes split with Roberts and voted with the dissenters) the Court declared that "the State is without power by any form of legislation to prohibit, change or nullify contracts between employers and adult women workers as to the amount of wages to be paid."[87] As one commentator remarked:

[81] *Coppage v. Kansas*, 236 U.S. 1 (1915), at 17.
[82] *Muller v. Oregon*, 208 U.S. 412 (1908), at 420.
[83] *Bunting v. Oregon*, 243 U.S. 426 (1917). [84] 262 U.S. 522 (1923).
[85] 261 U.S. 525 (1923). [86] *Nebbia v. New York*, 291 U.S. 502.
[87] *Morehead v. New York ex rel. Tipaldo*, 298 U.S. 587 (1936), at 611.

The argument of the Chief Justice, who dissented, that the *Adkins* precedent need not be followed because of "material differences" in the two laws; the argument of Stone, Brandeis, and Cardozo, also dissenting, that precedent since *Adkins*, and "what is more important, reason" support state power to control wages, had no weight for five men now thoroughly deluded by the notion that the welfare state could be judicially throttled and the brave old world of their youth restored.[88]

The Court-Packing Plan

By the middle of 1936 it was obvious that the Court would allow neither the federal nor the state governments to relieve the misery caused by the Depression. President Roosevelt made little issue of the Supreme Court in his 1936 reelection campaign, but following his landslide victory he contrived a bold move. On February 5, 1937, he proposed a court reform bill, ostensibly designed to improve judicial efficiency. The bill would allow the President to appoint one new justice for each gerontocratic member over seventy who chose not to resign. Given the ages of the justices, this would have amounted to six new appointments. Though many of the Court's decisions were unpopular, the notion of judicial independence was not. The press vilified the plan and the public opposed it.[89] Progressive forces failed to rally behind the bill; Southern Democrats joined Republicans in opposition to it.[90]

The Court itself played no small role in defusing the plan.[91] On March 29, 1937, by a 5-to-4 vote the justices overturned forty years of freedom-of-contract doctrine. Noting that the law in question allegedly violated the right to contract, the Court majority speculated

> What is this freedom? The Constitution does not speak of freedom of contract. It speaks of liberty and prohibits the deprivation of liberty without due process of law. In prohibiting that deprivation the Constitution does not recognize an absolute and uncontrollable liberty. . . . Liberty under the Constitution is thus necessarily subject to the restraints of due process, and regulation which is reasonable in relation to its subject and is adopted in the interests of the community is due process.[92]

[88] McCloskey, *op. cit.*, n. 49, *supra*, pp. 166–67. [89] Caldeira, *op. cit.*, n. 67, *supra*.

[90] David Adamany, "Legitimacy, Realigning Elections, and the Supreme Court," 1973 *Wisconsin Law Review* 790 (1973).

[91] Recent scholarship concludes that this was not a strategic retreat, but where the Court was headed with or without congressional interference. See Barry Cushman's award-winning book, *Rethinking the New Deal Court: Structure of a Constitutional Revolution* (New York: Oxford University Press, 1998).

[92] *West Coast Hotel Co. v. Parrish*, 300 U.S. 379, at 391.

Then on April 12, another 5-to-4 vote upheld the National Labor Relations Act, which guaranteed the right of labor to bargain collectively and authorized the National Labor Relations Board to prevent unfair labor practices. The case, *National Labor Relations Board v. Jones and Laughlin Steel Corp.*,[93] declared that a steel company, centered in Pittsburgh, with coal mines in Michigan, Minnesota, and Pennsylvania; warehouses in Chicago, Detroit, Cincinnati, and Memphis; and factories in New York and New Orleans conducted business in interstate commerce. Rejecting the dichotomy between manufacture and commerce, the Court instead asked whether steel production had a substantial effect on commerce. Clearly it did.

Three subsequent decisions illustrate the scope of this ruling that returned the definition of interstate commerce to what it had been in John Marshall's time. In the first, *Wickard v. Filburn*,[94] the Court upheld a penalty on a farmer for harvesting twelve acres of unauthorized wheat that he grew for his own consumption. The Court pointed out that the excess wheat, when considered with all other wheat grown throughout the country for home consumption, could have a substantial effect on the price of wheat destined for interstate commerce. In the second case, the Court upheld the constitutionality of the Civil Rights Act of 1964, which prohibits discrimination in places of public accommodation, because of the effect such discrimination had on interstate commerce.[95] The most recent concerned a conspiracy among ophthalmologists at a local hospital to eliminate one competing practitioner. This said the majority restrains trade and commerce among the several states sufficient to violate the Sherman Antitrust Act.[96]

Finally, on May 24, 1937, a third 5-to-4 vote declared the Social Security Act to be within the tax powers of Congress.[97] This effectively overruled the limits on the taxing power decreed by the Butler case. In all three decisions, Hughes and Roberts joined the three liberals to uphold the state or federal action in question. Because of the negative impact these decisions had on support for Roosevelt's plan, they became known as "the switch in time that saved nine."

[93] 301 U.S. 1 (1937). [94] 317 U.S. 111 (1942).

[95] *Heart of Atlanta Motel v. United States*, 379 U.S. 241 (1964), and *Katzenbach v. McClung*, 379 U.S. 294 (1964).

[96] *Summit Health Ltd. v. Pinhas*, 500 U.S. 322 (1991).

[97] *Steward Machine Co. v. Davis*, 301 U.S. 548.

Roosevelt's plan became fully superfluous when Justice Van Devanter resigned on May 18, 1937. Instead of a shaky 5-to-4 majority, the Court would soon have its first Roosevelt appointee and with it a 6-to-3 majority. Roosevelt lost the battle to enlarge the Court, but of course, he had won the war.

THE CIVIL LIBERTIES AGENDA

At the same time that the Supreme Court began to remove itself from managing the nation's economic affairs, it began to pay closer attention to the noneconomic rights and liberties of the Bill of Rights and the Civil War amendments. One of the first hints of the Court's switch from a defender of economic freedoms to a defender of other civil rights and liberties came in *U.S. v. Carolene Products Co.*[98]

The Preferred Freedoms Doctrine

The Carolene Products case involved the constitutionality of the Filled Milk Act of 1923, which prohibited the interstate shipment of skimmed milk with oil-based fillers. Justice Stone, writing for the majority, made it clear that the Court would only minimally scrutinize such statutes:

> Regulatory legislation affecting ordinary commercial transactions is not to be pronounced unconstitutional unless in light of the facts made known or generally assumed it is of such a character as to preclude the assumption that it rests upon some rational basis within the knowledge and experience of the legislators.[99]

At this point Stone inserted a footnote that has shaped the Supreme Court's doctrinal developments to this day:

> There may be a narrower scope for operation of the presumption of constitutionality when legislation appears on its face to be within a specific prohibition of the Constitution, such as those of the first ten amendments, which are deemed equally specific when held to be embraced within the Fourteenth. . . .
>
> It is unnecessary to consider now whether legislation which restricts those political processes which can ordinarily be expected to bring about repeal of undesirable legislation, is to be subjected to more exacting judicial scrutiny under the general prohibitions of the Fourteenth Amendment than are most other types of legislation. . . .
>
> Nor need we inquire whether similar considerations enter into the review of statutes directed at particular religious . . . or national . . . or racial minorities

[98] 304 U.S. 144 (1938). [99] *Id.* at 152.

> ... whether prejudices against discrete and insular minorities may be a special condition, which tends seriously to curtail the operation of those political processes ordinarily thought to be relied upon to protect minorities, and which may call for a correspondingly more searching judicial inquiry.[100]

Thus the formulation of what is known as the "preferred freedoms doctrine." Under this doctrine, the Court assumes legislation constitutional unless it facially abridges a provision of the Bill of Rights, restricts access to normal political processes (e.g., the right to vote), or violates the equal protection rights of "insular minorities." If so, then the presumption of constitutionality does not obtain. The state can overcome the presumption of unconstitutionality if a law is "narrowly tailored" to sustain a "compelling" governmental interest.

As an example of this doctrine, consider the decision in *Regents of the University of California v. Bakke*.[101] The University of California Medical School at Davis had an affirmative action plan that reserved sixteen of its 100 seats for members of certain minority groups. The remaining eighty-four seats were open to people of all races. Bakke, a rejected white applicant, had higher admissions scores than many admitted under the affirmative action plan. The judgment of the Supreme Court, written by Justice Powell, subjected the school's admission policy to strict scrutiny (even though Bakke was not a member of a "discrete and insular minority") because it created a racial classification. Powell then considered whether California had a compelling interest in its special admission program. California argued that it had a compelling interest in (1) reducing the historic deficit of minority doctors, (2) countering the effects of societal discrimination, (3) increasing the number of doctors who would practice in poor communities, and (4) obtaining the benefits of a diverse student body.

Powell asserted that the first argument served no compelling governmental interest; this was discrimination for discrimination's sake. Powell suggested that redressing societal discrimination constituted such an interest, but as there was no evidence that Davis had previously discriminated against minorities in its admissions process, the state's interest did not justify the violation of an innocent party's rights. Powell recognized a compelling interest in increasing health-care services to poor communities, but noted that the university did not narrowly draw its program to meet that goal: No evidence showed that those admitted under the affirmative action program had shown special interest in prac-

[100] *Id.* at 152–53. [101] 438 U.S. 265 (1978).

ticing in low-income communities. Powell, however, did find a compelling interest in Davis's desire for a diverse student body, but that the quota system again failed of narrow drafting. As an alternative, he suggested that a program that took race into account, but did not impose a quota, would be constitutionally permissible.

Incorporation of the Bill of Rights

A Court interested in following a civil liberties agenda must have jurisdiction over individual rights, most of which involve actions by state and local governments. Under the language of the original Constitution, the federal government was chiefly barred from abridging individual rights. States were prohibited only from passing bills of attainder, ex post facto laws, and impairing the obligation of contracts. The Bill of Rights, ratified in 1791, only limited the exercise of national power. So if Virginia wished to establish a state religion, or if New Jersey wished to punish persons who criticized government policies, nothing in the federal Constitution prevented their doing so.

The Supreme Court affirmed the inapplicability of the Bill of Rights to the states in the 1833 case of *Barron v. Baltimore*.[102] Marshall's unanimous decision categorically rejected Barron's claim that the Fifth Amendment or, indeed, any of the Bill of Rights, applied to the states. Marshall noted that people of the United States established the Constitution for the governance of the United States, not for that of the respective states. If people wanted protection from their state governments, the state constitutions could so provide. Textually, the original Constitution speaks generally when it refers to the national government and specifically mentions the states in those instances where limits on power are applicable to them. He therefore gave effect to the plain language of the Bill of Rights.

The potential application of the Bill of Rights to the states began with the passage of the Fourteenth Amendment, which says in part that "[n]o State shall make or enforce any law which shall abridge the privileges or immunities of citizens of the United States; nor shall any State deprive any person of life, liberty, or property, without due process of law." Despite the statements of some of the framers that they meant the privileges and immunities clause to overturn *Barron* and apply the Bill of Rights to the states, the Supreme Court gave the clause a very limited construction, as we saw in the discussion of the *Slaughterhouse Cases*.

[102] 7 Peters 243.

To this day, the privileges and immunities clause does not significantly limit the behavior of state governments. A recent decision, however, may presage a change.[103]

To the extent that the Bill of Rights does currently bind the states, it does so through the due process clause. The first case to focus on whether this provision made any of the Bill of Rights binding on the states was *Hurtado v. California*.[104] California allowed indictment by information presented to a magistrate, rather than by a grand jury. Hurtado, who had been indicted and convicted of murder, argued that indictment by information violated due process. The Supreme Court ruled in a 7-to-1 decision that (1) the due process clause in the Fourteenth Amendment means the same thing as the due process clause in the Fifth Amendment; (2) if due process in the Fifth Amendment included the requirement of indictment by grand jury, then the grand jury clause of the Fifth Amendment would be superfluous; and (3) nothing in the Constitution should be considered such. (This logic, though, did not prevent the Court from ruling that the Fourteenth Amendment's due process clause prohibited states from taking property without just compensation, even though the Fifth Amendment requires due process and prohibits uncompensated property taking.[105]) John Marshall Harlan dissented in *Hurtado*, arguing that the Fourteenth Amendment incorporated the Bill of Rights, and thus the right to indictment by grand jury. Following the *Hurtado* majority's logic, the Court ruled in 1900 that the due process clause did not prevent the states from employing an eight-person jury,[106] and in 1908 that nothing in the Fourteenth Amendment precluded compelled self-incrimination.[107] Harlan dissented alone in these cases, also.

[103] *Saenz v. Roe*, 143 L Ed 2d 689 (1999). California sought to restrict new residents to the welfare benefit they would have received in their previous state of residence. The Supreme Court had voided two similar efforts – in 1969 and 1982 – on the basis of a "right to travel," language which nowhere appears in the Constitution. Only Rehnquist and Thomas dissented. Not only did the decision void the California law, but it also struck a 1996 amendment to the Social Security Act and left the *Slaughterhouse Cases* teetering on a tottery foundation. Whether it will tumble into the abyss of discarded decisions remains to be seen. But if it does, we may expect to see the rise of a new jurisprudence of human rights, one more tightly tied to the text of the Constitution than was the case at the end of the twentieth century.

Other than the *Slaughterhouse Cases*, the only other decision based on the privileges and immunities clause was *Colgate v. Harvey*, 296 U.S. 404 (1935), which was overruled in 1940 by *Madden v. Kentucky*, 309 U.S. 83.

[104] 110 U.S. 516 (1884).

[105] *Chicago, B. & Q. Railway Co. v. Chicago*, 166 U.S. 226 (1897).

[106] *Maxwell v. Dow*, 176 U.S. 581. [107] *Twining v. New Jersey*, 211 U.S. 78.

The Court reversed the logic of these decisions in its opinion in *Gitlow v. New York*.[108] Gitlow, a left-wing radical, was convicted under a New York statute that made it a crime to advocate the forceful overthrow of government. Though the Supreme Court upheld his conviction, it also ruled without dissent that "freedom of speech and of the press – which are protected by the First Amendment from abridgment by Congress – are among the fundamental personal rights and 'liberties' protected by the due process clause of the 14th Amendment from impairment by the states."[109] Soon thereafter the Court added freedom of religion and assembly.[110]

In *Palko v. Connecticut*,[111] the Court set the standard for incorporation that survives to this day. Justice Cardozo, writing for the majority, declared the due process clause to incorporate only those provisions of the Bill of Rights that are "implicit in the concept of ordered liberty" or "so rooted in the traditions and conscience of our people to be ranked as fundamental."[112] Today, most of the provisions of the Bill of Rights have been incorporated through this doctrine: the First, Fourth, and Sixth Amendments; the Fifth Amendment, except for the right to indictment by grand jury; and the Eighth Amendment protection against cruel and unusual punishments. Not binding are the Eighth Amendment protections against excessive bail and fines (but probably only because no appropriate case has reached the Court); and Amendments Two (right to bear arms), Three (right not to have soldiers quartered in private homes in peacetime), and Seven (right to jury trials in civil suits where the amount in controversy exceeds $20).

First Amendment Freedoms

The Court's initial concern with the First Amendment occurred as the result of antisubversive legislation enacted by Congress during World War I. To determine whether the statements of persons convicted under these laws were constitutionally protected, the Court, speaking through Justice Holmes, formulated the clear and present danger doctrine.[113] The

[108] 268 U.S. 652 (1925). [109] *Id.* at 666.

[110] *Hamilton v. Regents of the University of California*, 293 U.S. 245 (1934); *De Jonge v. Oregon*, 299 U.S. 353 (1937).

[111] 302 U.S. 319 (1937). [112] *Id.* at 325. Neither phrase was defined then or since.

[113] In *Schenck v. United States*, 249 U.S. 47 (1919). Also see *Frohwerk v. United States*, 249 U.S. 204 (1919); *Debs v. United States*, 249 U.S. 211 (1919); and *Abrams v. United States*, 250 U.S. 616 (1919).

doctrine, however, provided no protection for the challenged communications because these were wartime cases and "[w]hen a nation is at war many things that might be said in time of peace are such a hindrance to its effort that their utterance will not be endured so long as men fight."[114]

In 1951 the Supreme Court upheld Smith Act convictions of Eugene Dennis and associates for organizing the Communist Party of the United States and advocating the overthrow of the government,[115] despite the fact that no overt acts of violence or revolution were alleged. In 1956, however, a more liberal Court ruled in *Pennsylvania v. Nelson*[116] that the Smith Act preempted the states' authority to regulate subversive activity, despite the fact that the title of the United States Code in which Congress placed the Smith Act specifically states that "nothing in this title shall be held to take away or impair the jurisdiction of the courts of the several States, under the laws thereof."[117] The following year the Court struck at the House Un-American Activities Committee (HUAC) by invalidating a contempt conviction of a labor leader for refusing to name associates who had worked for the Communist Party,[118] and severely limited Smith Act prosecution of those who organized the Communist Party.[119]

Congress reacted by attempting to limit the Court's authority. In July 1957, Senator William Jenner (R-Ind.) introduced a bill to limit the Supreme Court's appellate jurisdiction over a variety of antisubversive laws. The compromise bill passed by the committee kept the Court's appellate jurisdiction intact with a minor exception, but reversed the *Nelson* and *Yates* decisions. When the bill reached the Senate floor in August 1958, it was defeated by a 49-to-41 vote.

Two of the Court's decisions helped reduce any further congressional threat. In *Barenblatt v. United States*, the Court distinguished the *Watkins* decision and upheld the authority of HUAC.[120] The same day the Court limited the Nelson case and upheld the authority of states to investigate subversive activities aimed at them.[121] Both cases were decided 5 to 4 and in both cases Justice Harlan switched from his earlier liberal position. This helped reduce the pressure on the Court, much as Owen Roberts's switch had in 1937.

[114] 249 U.S. 47, at 52. [115] *Dennis v. United States*, 341 U.S. 494. [116] 350 U.S. 497.
[117] Title 18, U.S. Code, section 3231. [118] *Watkins v. United States*, 354 U.S. 178 (1957).
[119] *Yates v. United States*, 354 U.S. 298 (1957). [120] 360 U.S. 109 (1959).
[121] *Uphaus v. Wyman*, 360 U.S. 72 (1959).

Not until 1969 did the Court give clear and present danger its plain meaning: Government may not "forbid or proscribe advocacy of the use of force or of law violation except where such advocacy is directed to inciting or producing imminent lawless action and is likely to incite or produce such action."[122]

Not all communication receives constitutional protection, however. Obscenity,[123] fighting words,[124] and defamatory statements[125] do not because the Court considers them to lack "redeeming social value." At the other extreme, the Court generally accords political communication more protection than that dealing with other subjects.[126] Decisions of the Warren, Burger, and Rehnquist Courts have extended First Amendment protection to symbolic speech (e.g., demonstrations, flag burning),[127] the right to silence,[128] and commercial communications (e.g., advertising).[129]

Among the First Amendment's freedoms, historically the least subject to governmental restriction has been the free exercise of religion. Individuals acting under religious auspices may constitutionally engage in certain otherwise illegal activities. Thus, ordinances prohibiting door-to-

[122] *Brandenburg v. Ohio*, 395 U.S. 444 (1969), at 447.

[123] *Roth v. United States*, 354 U.S. 476 (1957); *Miller v. California*, 413 U.S. 15 (1973); *Jenkins v. Georgia*, 418 U.S. 153 (1974).

[124] *Terminiello v. Chicago*, 337 U.S. 1 (1949); *Cohen v. California*, 403 U.S. 15 (1971).

[125] *New York Times v. Sullivan*, 376 U.S. 254; *Gertz v. Welch*, 418 U.S. 323 (1974); *Time v. Hill*, 385 U.S. 374 (1967); *Cox Broadcasting Corp. v. Cohn*, 420 U.S. 469 (1975); *Dun & Bradstreet, Inc. v. Greenmoss Builders Inc.*, 472 U.S. 749 (1985).

[126] E.g., *Brown v. Hartlage*, 456 U.S. 45 (1982). "It is designed and intended to remove governmental restraints from the arena of public discussion, putting the decision as to what views shall be voiced largely into the hands of each of us, in the hope that use of such freedom will ultimately produce a more capable citizenry and more perfect polity and in the belief that no other approach would comport with the premise of individual dignity and choice upon which our political system rests." *Cohen v. California*, 403 U.S. 15 (1971), at 24. "There can be no doubt that the expenditures at issue in this case [an expenditure of more than $1,000 by an independent political committee to further the election of a presidential candidate who has opted to receive public financing of his general election campaign] produce speech at the core of the First Amendment." *Federal Election Commission v. National Conservative Political Action Committee*, 470 U.S. 480 (1985), at 493.

[127] *Edwards v. South Carolina*, 372 U.S. 229 (1963); *Tinker v. Des Moines School District*, 393 U.S. 503 (1969); *Boos v. Barry*, 485 U.S. 312 (1988); *United States v. Eichman*, 496 U.S. 310 (1990).

[128] *NAACP v. Alabama*, 357 U.S. 449 (1958); *Shelton v. Tucker*, 364 U.S. 479 (1960).

[129] *Virginia State Board of Pharmacy v. Virginia Citizens Consumer Council*, 425 U.S. 748 (1976); *Bates v. State Bar of Arizona*, 433 U.S. 350 (1977); *First National Bank of Boston v. Bellotti*, 435 U.S. 765 (1978).

door solicitation in order to protect the right to privacy must exclude those distributing or selling religious materials, and communities may not require a license of those so engaged. A constitutional right to proselytize exists. Courts may not ascertain the truth or falsity of religious beliefs, and unconventional beliefs and denominations are as protected as traditional ones. The Amish may not be compelled to send their children to high school. No one may be compelled to salute the flag or display a state-mandated ideological message inimical to his or her religious beliefs. Individuals may not be denied unemployment compensation for refusing to work on their Sabbath day or to manufacture weapons. Congress may constitutionally authorize religious institutions to affirmatively discriminate against women and nonbelievers.[130] Of course, not all action is immunized. Bigamy is a crime whether or not one is a Mormon, and Indians are forbidden to use peyote.[131]

In reaction to the Rehnquist Court's use of a mere rationality standard in the Indian peyote case, Congress enacted the Religious Freedom Restoration Act in 1993, which reinstituted the strict scrutiny standard: no governmental restriction on religious activity unless it furthered a compelling governmental interest and did so in the least restrictive fashion. The peyote case majority, in a Scalia opinion, had held that neutral laws of general applicability could be applied to religious activities even though the law lacked a compelling governmental interest. For a Republican Congress to take umbrage at a conservative Supreme Court decision is virtually unheard of. Moreover, not a single member of the House of Representatives and only three senators voted against the act. Notwithstanding, when a challenge to the act reached the Court,[132] six justices disdainfully declared it unconstitutional, not because of anything

[130] *Cantwell v. Connecticut*, 310 U.S. 296 (1940); *Murdock v. Pennsylvania*, 319 U.S. 105 (1943); *United States v. Ballard*, 322 U.S. 78 (1944); *Saia v. New York*, 334 U.S. 558 (1948); *Kunz v. New York*, 340 U.S. 290 (1951); *Cruz v. Beto*, 405 U.S. 319 (1972); *Wisconsin v. Yoder*, 406 U.S. 205 (1972); *West Virginia State Board of Education v. Barnette*, 319 U.S. 624 (1943); *Wooley v. Maynard*, 430 U.S. 705 (1977); *Thomas v. Review Board of the Indiana Employment Security Division*, 450 U.S. 707 (1981); *Hobbie v. Florida Unemployment Appeals Comn.*, 480 U.S. 136 (1987); *Corporation of the Church of Latter-Day Saints v. Amos*, 483 U.S. 327 (1987).

For decisions producing an opposite result when religion was not present, see *Kovacs v. Cooper*, 336 U.S. 77 (1949); *Feiner v. New York*, 340 U.S. 315 (1951); *Breard v. Alexander*, 341 U.S. 622 (1951).

[131] *Reynolds v. United States*, 98 U.S. 145 (1879); *Native American Church of Navajoland v. Arizona Corporation Comn.*, 405 U.S. 901 (1972); *Employment Division, Oregon Dept. of Human Resources v. Smith*, 494 U.S. 872 (1990).

[132] In *City of Boerne v. Flores*, 138 L Ed 2d 624 (1997).

having to do with religion but because Congress trespassed upon the Court's prerogatives and thereby violated the doctrine of separation of powers. Brandishing *Marbury v. Madison*, the majority imperiously trumpeted that it alone authoritatively construed the Constitution. The fact that a less activist Court could have exercised restraint and viewed the act as a statutory right to religious exemptions seems not to have crossed the justices' minds.[133] As we explain in a subsequent section of this chapter, we view the Court's apparent subordination of free exercise to a less preferred position among the panoply of First Amendment freedoms a function of its hostility toward Congress and the executive branch, rather than any religious animus.

In establishment clause cases the Supreme Court originally echoed Thomas Jefferson's sentiment for a "wall of separation" between church and state. Thus the Warren Court voided organized classroom prayer[134] and devotional Bible readings.[135] Public outrage followed. A New York congressman called the prayer decision "the most tragic decision in the history of the United States."[136] A Georgia congressman declared that first the Court "put the Negroes in the schools – now they put God out."[137] Yet the Court persisted in keeping explicitly sectarian influences out of public schools. More than forty years after the Scopes Monkey Trial the Court voided an Arkansas law that prohibited the teaching of evolution at public schools or universities[138] and, nineteen years later, over the dissents of Rehnquist and Scalia, struck down a follow-up law that required schools to teach "creation science" if they also chose to teach evolution.[139]

The Court has accommodated secular aid to parochial schools more than it has allowed religious influences in public schools. States may

[133] Although the *Boerne* decision rested on a constitutional basis, readers may nonetheless benefit from a rereading of the separation-of-powers model discussed in Chapter 2. *Boerne* also bears on the matter of judicial activism/restraint, the subject of Chapter 10.

[134] *Engel v. Vitale*, 370 U.S. 421 (1962). More recently, a Texas school district policy of student-led prayer before football games was voided in *Santa Fe Independent School District v. Doe*, 147 L Ed 2d 295 (2000).

[135] *Abington School District v. Schempp*, 374 U.S. 203 (1963).

[136] Quoted in Fred Friendly and Martha Elliott, *The Constitution: That Delicate Balance* (New York: Random House, 1984), p. 109.

[137] *Id.* The kakistocrat used the pejorative Southern equivalent of "Negroes."

[138] *Epperson v. Arkansas*, 393 U.S. 97 (1968).

[139] *Edwards v. Aguillard*, 482 U.S. 578 (1987). Amazingly, we have not seen the last of this issue. See Pam Belluck, "Board for Kansas Deletes Evolution from Curriculum," *New York Times*, August 12, 1999, p. A6.

provide bus transportation[140] and loan educational materials to parochial school students.[141] Although the Court voided plans to supplement the salaries of parochial school teachers,[142] it overruled subsequent decisions that prohibited public school teachers from being sent into parochial schools during regular school hours to teach certain secular subjects.[143] The Court also allows states to provide tuition tax credits to parents who send their children to private schools.[144]

Establishment clause cases aside, the law of the First Amendment appears reasonably well settled. Though these cases frequently generate much political controversy, as in the flag-burning cases,[145] typically judicial resolution not only cools the fervor that formerly affected them, but it does so with relatively little fluctuation in the Court's established policies.

Criminal Procedure

The Bill of Rights provides extensive protection for the rights of persons accused of crime, including a prohibition on unreasonable searches and seizures, self-incrimination, and the right to counsel, and a ban on cruel and unusual punishment. For all but the last of these, the leading decisions date from the Warren Court (1953–69).

The fundamental Fourth Amendment question concerns the use of evidence obtained by an unreasonable search and seizure. In 1914, the Supreme Court ruled that such evidence could not be admitted in federal trials. It declared that without such a rule, Fourth Amendment protections would be "of no value, and, so far as those thus placed are concerned, might as well be stricken from the Constitution."[146]

Because most crimes are state matters, this federal exclusionary rule was of minor significance. In 1949, though, the Supreme Court made the Fourth Amendment binding on the states.[147] The Court specifically ruled that Colorado had violated the Fourth Amendment rights of Dr. Julius

140 *Everson v. Board of Education*, 330 U.S. 1 (1947).

141 *Mitchell v. Helms*, 147 L Ed 2d 660 (2000). The case was decided by a judgment of the Court and overruled two precedents from the mid-1970s.

142 *Lemon v. Kurtzman*, 403 U.S. 602 (1971).

143 *Agostini v. Felton*, 521 U.S. 203 (1997), overruling *Aguilar v. Felton*, 473 U.S. 402 (1985) and *Grand Rapids v. Ball*, 473 U.S. 373 (1985).

144 *Mueller v. Allen*, 463 U.S. 388 (1983).

145 *Texas v. Johnson*, 491 U.S. 397 (1989); *United States v. Eichman*, 496 U.S. 310 (1990).

146 *Weeks v. United States*, 232 U.S. 383 (1914), at 393.

147 *Wolf v. Colorado*, 338 U.S. 25.

Wolf by illegally seizing his appointment book, which was then used to convict him of conspiracy to commit an abortion. Nevertheless, the majority opinion rejected the extension of the exclusionary rule to the states, thus upholding Wolf's conviction and a one-to-five-year prison term.

The Court overruled its 1949 decision twelve years later in the first of the Warren Court's many landmark criminal rights decisions. The case in question, *Mapp v. Ohio*,[148] involved the warrantless search of the home of Dollree Mapp, who was believed to be harboring a man wanted for bombing the house of an alleged numbers racketeer, future boxing promoter Don King. The police found no fugitive but did seize some pornographic pictures. Mapp was arrested and convicted of violating Ohio's obscenity statute. Speaking for a five-person majority, Justice Clark declared that the Constitution requires states to abide by the *Weeks* exclusionary rule, which precludes admission of illegally seized evidence at trial.

This controversial decision came under attack in the 1970s and 1980s by the more conservative Burger Court, four of whose members were chosen by President Nixon precisely because they did not support expansion of the rights of persons accused of crime. The rallying cry against the exclusionary rule originated with a dissenting statement by Judge (later Justice) Benjamin Cardozo: "The criminal is to go free because the constable has blundered."[149] The Burger Court refused to extend the rule to grand jury hearings,[150] civil cases,[151] habeas corpus relief,[152] or deportation hearings.[153] In 1984 the Court created a good-faith exception to the exclusionary rule, whereby illegally obtained evidence would not be suppressed if the police acted in objective good faith.[154] Given the increasing conservatism of the Rehnquist Court, the exclusionary rule rests on extremely shaky ground.

The Fifth Amendment's protection against self-incrimination was an understandable reaction against British attempts to coerce confessions, as in Star Chamber proceedings. Prior to the 1960s, the Supreme Court decided on a case-by-case basis whether the accused's will was overborne by physical or psychological duress.[155] Such determinations were not

[148] 367 U.S. 643 (1961). [149] *People v. Defore*, 242 N.Y. 13 (1926), at 21.

[150] *United States v. Calandra*, 414 U.S. 338 (1974).

[151] *United States v. Janis*, 428 U.S. 433 (1976). [152] *Stone v. Powell*, 428 U.S. 465 (1976).

[153] *Immigration and Naturalization Service v. Lopez-Mendoza*, 468 U.S. 1032 (1984).

[154] *United States v. Leon*, 468 U.S. 897.

[155] E.g., *Brown v. Mississippi*, 297 U.S. 278 (1936); *Ashcraft v. Tennessee*, 322 U.S. 143 (1944); *Fikes v. Alabama*, 352 U.S. 191 (1957); *Jackson v. Denno*, 378 U.S. 368 (1964).

easily made, especially when "facts" about the interrogation itself were often in dispute. Despair over the case-by-case approach led the Court to seek a prophylactic rule that it hoped would put an end to involuntary confessions. The vehicle for this new rule was the 1966 case *Miranda v. Arizona*,[156] which more than any other typifies Warren Court activism in the realm of criminal procedure. Under *Miranda*, police must inform suspects prior to any custodial interrogation that (1) they have the right to remain silent; (2) if they choose to speak anything they say may be used against them; (3) they have the right to an attorney; and (4) if they cannot afford an attorney one will be provided them.

Not surprisingly, this rule also came under attack by the Burger Court. It ruled in two cases that though incriminating statements made without *Miranda* warnings could not be used in the prosecution's case-in-chief, they could be used to impeach the credibility of witnesses if they took the stand and contradicted anything they had said prior to receiving their *Miranda* warnings.[157] In 1984 the Court created a public safety exception to *Miranda*, holding that the accused's response to a question about the whereabouts of a gun hidden in a grocery store could be used in evidence even though no warnings had been given.[158] Despite these exceptions, the *Miranda* rule itself remains in place.[159]

The right to counsel received strong support from the Court as early as 1932. In *Powell v. Alabama*,[160] the Court required the states to provide indigent criminal defendants with counsel under certain conditions. The case involved seven illiterate black youths who, after a fight with several white youths on a train, were falsely accused of raping two white girls. In a lynch-mob atmosphere, the youths were convicted in a series of one-day trials. The presiding judge had appointed all members of the local bar to defend them at their arraignment, but no one stepped forward to do so until the day of the trial. In reversing their convictions, the Supreme Court noted that

> during perhaps the most critical period of the proceedings against these defendants, that is to say, from the time of their arraignment until the beginning of

[156] 384 U.S. 436.

[157] *Harris v. New York*, 401 U.S. 222 (1971); *Oregon v. Hass*, 420 U.S. 714 (1975).

[158] *New York v. Quarles*, 467 U.S. 649.

[159] At the end of its 1999 term, not only did the Court flatly reaffirm *Miranda*, stating that it has "become part of our national culture," but it also voided an act of Congress that had attempted to overrule it. *Dickerson v. United States*, 147 L Ed 2d 405 (2000), at 419.

[160] 287 U.S. 45 (1932).

their trial, when consultation, thorough-going investigation and preparation were vitally important, the defendants did not have the aid of counsel in any real sense, although they were as much entitled to such aid during that period as at the trial itself.[161]

The Court not only declared that the right to counsel begins at arraignment, but they also ruled that given the capital nature of the offense and the status of the defendants, a constitutional right to appointed counsel existed.[162] *Powell* further suggested that all indigent defendants should be afforded counsel; nevertheless, the ruling limited itself to capital cases where the defendants were unable to defend themselves because of illiteracy or other extenuating circumstances. In 1942 the Court ruled that the Constitution provided no unequivocal right to appointed counsel, only a right conditioned on the facts of each case.[163]

In 1963 the Warren Court overruled the 1942 decision. The case, *Gideon v. Wainright*,[164] involved the trial and conviction of an individual for breaking into and entering a pool hall with intent to commit a crime. Gideon had requested an attorney at his trial but was refused since Alabama provided appointed counsel only in capital cases. The justices ruled unanimously that states must afford indigent defendants appointed counsel in all felony cases.

The *Gideon* decision has fared reasonably well under the Burger and Rehnquist Courts. In 1972 the justices ruled that no indigent person could be jailed without court-appointed counsel or an intelligent waiver thereof.[165] On the other hand, while the Warren Court had pushed the entitlement to counsel back from the time of indictment to the time of arrest,[166] and extended the right to include the presence of an attorney at lineups,[167] the Burger Court declined to combine the two rules and extend the right to counsel to preindictment lineups.[168] The majority in the 5-to-4 decision included all four Nixon appointees.

161 *Id.* at 57.

162 Alabama subsequently retried four of the defendants, all of whom were again found guilty. Charlie Weems received a 75-year sentence in 1937 and was paroled in 1943; Andrew Wright received a 99-year sentence in 1937 and was paroled in 1944; Haywood Patterson received a 75-year sentence in 1936, escaped prison in 1948, and was later arrested and convicted for manslaughter; and Clarence Norris was convicted on retrial, sentenced to death, but had his sentence commuted to life. He was paroled in 1944.

163 *Betts v. Brady*, 316 U.S. 455.

164 372 U.S. 335.

165 *Argersinger v. Hamlin*, 407 U.S. 25.

166 *Escobedo v. Illinois*, 378 U.S. 478 (1964).

167 *United States v. Wade*, 388 U.S. 218 (1967).

168 *Kirby v. Illinois*, 406 U.S. 682 (1972).

The most frequently litigated Eighth Amendment issue during the past twenty years has been the constitutionality of the death penalty. Unlike the *Mapp*, *Miranda*, or *Gideon* decisions, not until the Burger Court were latitudinal interpretations of the clause made.

The Court first upheld the death penalty in 1878,[169] and in 1890 it upheld electrocution on the mistaken assumption that the electric chair produced instantaneous and painless death.[170] Punishments are cruel and unusual, declared the Court, when they involve torture or a lingering death. In 1947 the Court even upheld the reelectrocution of a black youth who survived his first appointment with the chair.[171]

No successful challenge to the death penalty occurred before 1972. Then, in *Furman v. Georgia*,[172] a highly fractured Court declared unconstitutional capital punishment imposed at the untrammeled discretion of jurors. Justices Marshall and Brennan thought the death penalty always unconstitutional: Marshall because it is "morally unacceptable to the people of the United States at this time in their history,"[173] and Brennan not only because "its rejection by contemporary society is total," but because it is "severe," "degrading," and fails to respect murderers for "their intrinsic worth as human beings."[174] Douglas thought the death penalty as applied discriminated against minorities and the poor, a contention that the Court rejected in 1987. Stewart and White, without emphasizing race or class, also believed the death penalty to be cruel and unusual because it was arbitrarily and capriciously imposed on some and not on others. Along with Douglas, they reserved judgment on the constitutionality of mandatory death sentences. The four Nixon appointees dissented, claiming no constitutional violation in the death penalty in general or as imposed.

In response to *Furman*, thirty-five states and Congress reimposed the death penalty, some making it mandatory, others imposing guidelines for juries. In July 1976 the Court responded by declaring mandatory capital punishment to be just as arbitrary as the totally discretionary death penalties struck in *Furman*,[175] but upholding the death penalty if juries are provided guidelines.[176] Brennan and Marshall dissented, again arguing that death is always cruel and unusual. Given overwhelming

[169] *Wilkerson v. Utah*, 99 U.S. 130. [170] *In re Kemmler*, 136 U.S. 436.
[171] *Louisiana ex rel. Francis v. Resweber*, 329 U.S. 459 (1947).
[172] 408 U.S. 238. [173] *Id.* at 360. [174] *Id.* at 305.
[175] *Woodson v. North Carolina*, 428 U.S. 280. [176] *Gregg v. Georgia*, 428 U.S. 153.

legislative support and massive public approval,[177] Marshall nevertheless argued that if only others knew as much about capital punishment as he did, they would find it "shocking, unjust, and unacceptable."[178]

The biggest blow to death penalty abolitionists since 1976 occurred when the Rehnquist Court rejected a claim that the death penalty was imposed in a racially discriminatory manner.[179] The abolitionists based their major claim on the race not of the convict but of the victim. A Georgia study of 2,000 murders found that killing a white person made one 4.3 times more likely to receive the death penalty than killing a black person, even after controlling statistically for dozens of other factors. The Court nevertheless ruled that even if the death penalty were discriminatorily imposed, petitioners would have to prove intentional bias.

The Rehnquist Court has continued to support the death penalty, upholding the states' right to apply it to a retarded adult with the mental age of six and a half years[180] and to a youth of sixteen at the time of the murder.[181] The Court also upheld the death penalty in the context of the felony murder rule, for example, for two sons who helped their father escape from jail and kidnap a family, even though the father murdered the kidnap victims without the direct aid or prior knowledge of his sons.[182]

Equal Protection

With its decision in *Plessy v. Ferguson*,[183] the equal protection clause became a dead letter insofar as black America was concerned. The

[177] Thomas R. Marshall, *Public Opinion and the Supreme Court* (Boston: Unwin Hyman, 1989).

[178] *Gregg v. Georgia*, 428 U.S. 153 (1976), at 232.

[179] *McCleskey v. Kemp*, 481 U.S. 279 (1987).

[180] *Penry v. Lynaugh*, 492 U.S. 392 (1989). The Supreme Court reversed the death sentence because the trial court judge did not inform the jury that it could consider the defendant's retardation a mitigating factor. In November 2000 the Court again granted cert in the case to review the specific juror instructions granted, without reconsidering its rule allowing the execution of the mentally retarded. *Penry v. Johnson*, 150 L Ed 2d 9 (2001).

At age nine, a state psychologist tested Penry's IQ at 56. At twelve he was institutionalized at the Mexia State School for the Mentally Retarded. At fifteen he could not read simple words such as "dress," "drum," or "flag." Yet the prosecutor in his case still insists that Penry is not mentally retarded. For a harrowing account of the Penry case, see Raymond Bonner and Sara Rimer, "Mentally Retarded Man Facing Texas Execution Draws Wide Attention," *New York Times*, November 12, 2000, p. 34.

[181] *Stanford v. Kentucky*, 492 U.S. 361 (1989).

[182] *Tison v. Arizona*, 481 U.S. 137 (1987).

[183] 163 U.S. 537 (1896).

separate but equal doctrine that *Plessy* formulated paid no heed to plain meaning; courts focused only on separation, not on whether the governmental facilities were "equal." Thus, the Court upheld the discontinuance of black high schools, but not white ones, on the basis that an injunction against funding the white schools would only make matters worse and, in any event, not help black students.[184] Similarly, the Court sustained segregation in all schools, public as well as private, for the nocuously paralogical reason that state-chartered private schools were creatures of the state to which the due process clause did not apply.[185]

Not until 1954 did the Court appreciably temper its – and America's – racist hypocrisy by overruling separate but equal and replacing it one year later with a requirement that school desegregation proceed "with all deliberate speed."[186] Mindful that its decision almost caused the South to rise again, evidenced by a vogue in hooded sheets and burning crosses, the Court gave the federal district courts primary responsibility for applying its mandate. Fifteen years later, the Burger Court's first formal decision capped this phase of desegregation by ordering immediate termination of dual school systems.[187] But desegregation in the South did not produce desegregation in the North. Violations of equal protection require purposeful governmental action. None occurs where discrimination is only the unintended effect of governmental action, or where no state action at all has occurred.[188] Moreover, if a northern district does engage in intentional discrimination (e.g., Detroit), a judicially ordered remedy may not extend beyond the boundary of the district or districts that acted unconstitutionally even though the districts themselves are creatures of the state.[189] Arguably, then, from a constitutional standpoint,

[184] *Cumming v. Richmond County Board of Education*, 175 U.S. 528 (1899).

[185] *Berea College v. Kentucky*, 211 U.S. 45 (1908).

[186] *Brown v. Board of Education*, 347 U.S. 484 (1954); 349 U.S. 294 (1955).

[187] *Alexander v. Holmes County Board of Education*, 396 U.S. 19 (1969). The Burger Court's ruling was presaged by *Bradley v. Richmond School Board*, 382 U.S. 103 (1965), in which the Warren Court declared, "Delays in desegregating school systems are no longer tolerable." At 105.

[188] As in a civil service examination, where far more blacks than whites fail to pass. See *Washington v. Davis*, 426 U.S. 229 (1976), for an example. Housing segregation is commonly cited as an example of nongovernmental or private discrimination, notwithstanding community zoning ordinances. On the other hand, the equal protection clause does reach some private acts of discrimination if they require judicial action for enforcement, e.g., restrictive housing covenants (*Shelley v. Kraemer*, 334 U.S. 1 (1948)) or a white mother's loss of child custody because after her divorce she married a black (*Palmore v. Sidoti*, 466 U.S. 429 (1984)).

[189] *Milliken v. Bradley*, 418 U.S. 717 (1974).

a double standard still exists: Discrimination against blacks remains much more permissible than that disadvantaging whites.

The Court has complemented the limited reach of equal protection with equally restrictive limitations on the action that the state and federal governments may *voluntarily* take under other constitutional provisions to alleviate the persistence of racism in American society. To pass constitutional muster, affirmative action programs may set only goals, not quotas. Race may be only one among a number of factors that determine eligibility. Moreover, the Court presumes the program unconstitutional unless the responsible governmental officials can show that it serves a compelling governmental interest (which, post-*Bakke*, excludes promoting diversity, which is now only an important governmental interest[190]) and is narrowly tailored to remedy past evidence of discrimination.[191]

Needless to say, what is sauce for the black goose is not sauce for the white gander. Affirmative action programs – including those with quotas – that benefit whites do not violate the equal protection clause. Thus, public educational institutions typically give preferential treatment to children of alumni; seniority systems may constitutionally contain a last hired, first fired policy; and the states may subsidize suburban school students much more generously than those who live in inner-city ghettos or rural slums.[192]

Apart from affirmative action, American racism is markedly less systematic than it was during the heyday of white supremacy and Jim Crow. Congress has enacted a number of major civil rights laws that have

[190] *Adarand Constructors, Inc. v. Pena*, 515 U.S. 200 (1995).

[191] *Regents of the University of California v. Bakke*, 438 U.S. 265 (1978); *Wygant v. Jackson Board of Education*, 476 U.S. 267 (1986); *Richmond v. Croson Co.*, 488 U.S. 469 (1989).

[192] *Regents of the University of California v. Bakke*, 438 U.S. 265 (1978); *Firefighters Local Union v. Stotts*, 467 U.S. 561 (1984); *San Antonio School District v. Rodriguez*, 411 U.S. 1 (1973).

The measures of "intelligence" we use were originally devised to identify students in need of special assistance. Following World War I these tests were correlated with race and sex on the assumption that white males were smartest and all others intellectually inferior. Aspects of "intelligence" that did not advantage white males were deleted: social skillfulness, memory, wit. These have real-world correlates, unlike the tests that maintain white dominance. E.g., the "verbal ability" exam used to screen police department candidates in *Washington v. Davis* (see n. 188 above) bore no relationship to the qualities needed for good policing. See Robert L. Hayman, Jr., *The Smart Culture: Society, Intelligence, and Law* (New York: New York University Press, 1998), pp. 246, 259, 185, 183.

effectively outlawed discrimination in places of public accommodations[193] and in voting,[194] and to some limited extent in housing.[195] Although the Court delayed resolution of the most pathological of white America's racial fears – miscegenation – for thirteen years after it overruled the separate but equal doctrine, when it did void prohibitions on interracial marriage, it did so on a dual basis – due process as well as equal protection – in a most felicitously titled unanimous decision: *Loving v. Virginia*.[196]

The Court has offset somewhat the disparate treatment accorded blacks by extending the equal protection clause to other groups and classes. Notwithstanding what the framers of the Fourteenth Amendment may have intended, women, aliens, indigents, illegitimates, the mentally ill, the physically handicapped, and the elderly may not be subject to unreasonably discriminatory governmental action.[197] And although the courts do not scrutinize laws and policies that classify people on these bases – with the exception of state laws that discriminate on the basis of alienage[198] – with the closeness imparted to racial classifications, all have received a measure of judicial inspection. With the exception of indigents, on whom the Warren Court looked favorably, beneficial treatment has primarily resulted from the policy making of the moderately conservative Burger Court. Women, for example, were

[193] *Heart of Atlanta Motel v. United States*, 379 U.S. 241 (1964); *Katzenbach v. McClung*, 379 U.S. 294 (1964).

[194] *South Carolina v. Katzenbach*, 383 U.S. 301 (1966). In light of the Florida voters disqualified in the 2000 presidential election for various reasons, this statement may warrant qualification.

[195] *Jones v. Mayer Co.*, 392 U.S. 409 (1968).

[196] 388 U.S. 1 (1967). On the eve of the Court's decisions in *Brown v. Board of Education*, in the mid-1950s, approximately three dozen states had criminalized interracial marriage, thereby providing rather strong evidence – if any were needed – that legally sanctioned white supremacy flourished throughout the United States and not just in the South.

But old habits die hard. It took more than 30 years after *Loving* for South Carolina to act. On November 3, 1998, the citizens of that state voted to repeal the state's ban on interracial marriage by a vote of 566,165 (62%) to 347,687 (38%).

[197] "Unreasonable" and its opposite, "reasonable," are key words not only in the interpretation of the equal protection clause but in all facets of our law. Their utility results because their determination, like beauty, rests in the eye of the beholder (i.e., judge and/or jury). They thus afford decision makers a veneer of objectivity with which to rationalize their decisions. As Justice Rehnquist has said, speaking for the Court, "The most arrogant legal scholar would not claim that all of these cases applied a uniform or consistent test under the Equal Protection Clause." *Railroad Retirement Board v. Fritz*, 449 U.S. 166 (1980), at 177 (n.).

[198] *Bernal v. Fainter*, 467 U.S. 216 (1984).

"regarded as the center of home and family life" in the Warren Court's only sex discrimination case and as such properly subject to ostensibly protective disabling legislation: in this case, automatic exemption from jury service, notwithstanding the constitutional right to an impartial jury.[199] Not until 1975 did the Court admit – over the dissent of Justice Rehnquist – that "[n]o longer is the female destined solely for the home and the rearing of the family, and only the male for the marketplace and the world of ideas."[200]

But since the mid-1970s the Court has addressed a stream of sex discrimination cases sufficiently variegated to warrant a separate constitutional standard: "skeptical scrutiny" that those "seek[ing] to defend gender-based government action must demonstrate an 'exceedingly persuasive justification' for that action."[201] Thus, the Court voided the male-only admission policy of the Virginia Military Institute, unanimously construed the congressional prohibition against sex discrimination to apply to same-sex workplace harassment, and made employers vicariously liable for their supervisors' conduct.[202] On the other hand, by a 5-to-4 vote the Court declared unconstitutional the Violence Against Women Act that permitted victims of rape, domestic violence, and other crimes "motivated by gender" to sue their attackers in federal court. Nothing in the Constitution gave Congress the authority to so legislate, said Rehnquist and his four conservative colleagues, even though thirty-six states joined a brief supporting the law, while only one (Alabama) opposed it.[203]

Reapportionment

Despite the Warren Court's pathbreaking decisions in civil rights and criminal procedure, Chief Justice Warren believed that "reapportionment, not only of state legislatures, but of representative government in this country, is perhaps the most important issue we have had before the Supreme Court."[204]

[199] *Hoyt v. Florida*, 368 U.S. 57 (1961), at 62.
[200] *Stanton v. Stanton*, 421 U.S. 7, at 14–15.
[201] *United States v. Virginia*, 518 U.S. 515 (1996).
[202] *Id.; Oncale v. Sundowner Offshore Services*, 140 L Ed 2d 201 (1998); *Burlington Industries v. Ellerth*, 141 L Ed 2d 633 (1998); *Faragher v. Boca Raton*, 141 L Ed 2d 662 (1998).
[203] *United States v. Morrison*, 146 L Ed 2d 658 (2000).
[204] Quoted in David W. Rohde and Harold J. Spaeth, *Supreme Court Decision Making* (San Francisco: W. H. Freeman, 1976), p. 178.

Prior to the Warren Court's decisions on reapportionment, the Supreme Court had let stand arrangements whereby some congressional or state legislative districts might have ten or twenty times the population of other districts. For instance, in *Colegrove v. Green*[205] the Supreme Court dismissed an Illinois congressional reapportionment suit. The judgment of the Court, written by Felix Frankfurter, ruled reapportionment a nonjusticiable political question best solved by the democratic process. He admonished the courts "not to enter this political thicket."[206]

Reliance on democratic political processes is singularly poor advice when the problem at hand is minority control of that process through malapportionment. The 20 percent of the population that controls 55 percent of the legislative seats will not likely vote to undo their domination, any more than small states will allow the number of senators to vary from one state to another. With a liberal Warren Court majority firmly in place, the Court ruled that federal courts can take jurisdiction over reapportionment suits.[207] Two years later, the Court decided the merits of federal and state reapportionment cases. In *Wesberry v. Sanders*[208] the Court declared that the Constitution's command that representatives be chosen "by the People of the several States" means that each person's vote must be worth the same; in other words, one person, one vote. Thus, congressional districts within a given state must contain an equal number of people. Then, in *Reynolds v. Sims*,[209] the Court ruled that state legislative districts must be of approximately equal size. Despite the example of the U.S. Senate, even the upper house of state legislatures had to be apportioned on a one-person, one-vote basis.[210] The Court later extended its ruling to virtually all governmental units, such as school districts and sewer boards.[211]

A new dimension of the apportionment controversy involves race: specifically, the constitutionality of so-called majority-minority congressional districts, that is, those drawn so as to contain a majority of minority residents. In a series of five decisions decided between 1993 and 1997, a minimum winning coalition of the same five justices – Rehnquist, O'Connor, Scalia, Kennedy, and Thomas – has held such a practice

[205] 328 U.S. 549 (1946). [206] *Id.* at 556. [207] *Baker v. Carr*, 369 U.S. 186 (1962).
[208] 376 U.S. 1 (1964). [209] 377 U.S. 533 (1964).
[210] *Lucas v. Forty-Fourth General Assembly*, 377 U.S. 713 (1964).
[211] *Avery v. Midland County*, 390 U.S. 474 (1968); *Hadley v. Junior College District*, 397 U.S. 50 (1970).

neither constitutional nor mandated by the Voting Rights Act of 1965. In the last of these five decisions, the majority observed that the reduction of Georgia's majority-minority districts from three to one did not result in the defeat of the blacks who represented the former black districts.[212] On the other hand, the same five justices *upheld* the constitutionality of voting plans that deliberately discriminate against blacks so long as the plan does not leave blacks worse off than before.[213] Worms eventually do turn, however. Such was the case when the Madame in the Middle, Justice O'Connor, joined forces with the Stevens Four to permit the use of race as a factor in legislative districting so long as it is not the "dominant and controlling" one.[214] Political considerations, such as advantaging an incumbent, are permissible though they largely involve black voters. The upshot seems to be that in redistricting state legislatures and drawing congressional boundaries, racial gerrymandering may be engaged in – either to black or other minority advantage or detriment – so long as some "political" label is given the redrawing.

The Right to Privacy

Probably no better evidence of the adaptability of the Constitution to changing circumstances and conditions exists than the right to privacy. A number of constitutional provisions pertain to privacy, though not in so many words: the ban on unreasonable searches and seizures, the self-incrimination clause, the First and Ninth Amendments, and the due process clauses of the Fifth and Fourteenth Amendments. Among the most important privacy rights are those grounded in the freedom of association safeguarded by the First Amendment and the substantive due process liberties that pertain to marriage, family relationships, abortion, sexual activities, and the right to die.

The Court has positioned the right to associational privacy above human equality insofar as bona fide private organizations are concerned. "Members only" policies are constitutional as long as they are not hung on places of public accommodations or places that do not engage in intimate private relationships, such as large-membership all-male service

[212] *Abrams v. Johnson*, 521 U.S. 74 (1997). The others were *Shaw v. Reno*, 509 U.S. 630 (1993); *Miller v. Johnson*, 515 U.S. 900 (1995); *Shaw v. Hunt*, 517 U.S. 899 (1996); and *Bush v. Vera*, 517 U.S. 952 (1996).

[213] *Reno v. Bossier Parish School Board*, 145 L Ed 2d 845 (2000).

[214] *Husat v. Cromartie*, 149 L Ed 2d 430 (2001).

clubs.[215] Consequently, B'nai B'rith need not accept *goyim* or the Knights of Columbus non-Catholics. The Society of Mayflower Descendants may deny membership to members of the Mafia, and the Daughters of the American Revolution may exclude the significant others of those who invaded Grenada and Panama in the 1980s and Iraq in the 1990s. Social, sexual, racial, and religious exclusiveness – snobbery, if you will – is constitutionally protected for those engaged in truly private affairs, but government may mandate openness otherwise.

A landmark decision concerning marital privacy and family rights is *Griswold v. Connecticut*, in which the Court voided "an uncommonly silly law" that made it a crime for any person – including married couples – to use, assist, or counsel another to use "any drug, medicinal article or instrument for the purpose of preventing conception."[216] Relying on the Ninth and Fourteenth Amendments, the majority stated that "specific guarantees in the Bill of Rights have penumbras, formed by emanations from those guarantees that help give them life and substance. . . . Various guarantees create zones of privacy." They concluded:

> We deal with a right of privacy older than the Bill of Rights – older than our political parties, older than our school system. Marriage is a coming together for better or for worse, hopefully enduring, and intimate to the degree of being sacred. It is an association that promotes a way of life, not causes; a harmony in living, not political faiths; a bilateral loyalty, not commercial or social projects. Yet it is an association for as noble a purpose as any involved in our prior decisions.[217]

Notwithstanding the fundamental character of the rights surrounding child and family relationships, the Court has upheld the constitutionality of compulsory sterilization laws. "In order to prevent our being swamped with incompetence," said Justice Holmes, "it is better for all the world, if instead of waiting to execute degenerate offspring for crime, or to let them starve for their imbecility, society can prevent those who are manifestly unfit from continuing their kind. . . . Three generations of imbeciles are enough."[218] At the time Holmes wrote, capital punishment was utilized with considerably greater frequency than it is today, and public welfare was not available as a way of life. Nonetheless, public

[215] Compare *Moose Lodge v. Irvis*, 407 U.S. 163 (1972), with the two Rehnquist Court sex discrimination cases, *Rotary International v. Rotary Club of Duarte*, 481 U.S. 537 (1987); and *New York State Club Assn. v. New York City*, 487 U.S. 1 (1988).

[216] 381 U.S. 479 (1965), at 480. The reference to the silliness of the law appears in Justice Stewart's dissent, at 527.

[217] *Id.* at 484, 486.

[218] *Buck v. Bell*, 274 U.S. 200 (1927), at 207.

squeamishness has largely made compulsory sterilization a dead letter, even though at least ten states authorize their judges to sterilize the mentally retarded.[219]

The right of a woman to secure an abortion without undue governmental interference has existed since the Burger Court's decision in *Roe v. Wade*.[220] Fear that conservative replacements of the liberal Brennan and Marshall would produce *Roe*'s overruling proved unfounded when O'Connor, Kennedy, and Souter jointly authored an opinion of the Court, which was joined by Stevens and Blackmun (*Roe*'s author), that reaffirmed adherence to *Roe*.[221] Subsequent decisions have focused not on the right to an abortion as such, but rather on abortion procedures and the efforts of opponents to disrupt abortion clinics.[222] The right, a classic example of substantive due process, rests among the liberties that government may not deprive persons of. The *Roe* decision, an extreme example of an opinion that takes the form of judicial legislation, also exemplifies a rarity among court-made rules, one whose application is absolutely pellucid. Relying upon the common law and the plain meaning of the operative word in the due process clause, the Court held that the constitutional right to life only protects persons, and personhood commences with birth.[223] When life begins – with the production of sperm, or an egg, at conception, at implantation, or at some later point – is constitutionally irrelevant. Though one may correctly argue that an all but delivered fetus is better endowed with potential life than a person born acephalously, or a raving maniac, or a senescent victim of Alzheimer's disease, and that the Court's equation of personhood with birth is arbitrary, it is indisputable that the latter have been born, and a fetus by definition has not. Willy-nilly, they are persons protected by the Constitution.

Not all activities that persons engage in under the rubric of privacy or personal autonomy are equally protected. The Burger Court, in one of its last decisions, sharply distinguished conventional sexual activities

[219] Rorie Sherman, "Involuntary Sterilization Gains," *National Law Journal*, March 7, 1988, p. 3. Stephen Jay Gould argues that the Buck in the case of *Buck v. Bell* was not mentally defective, and that her case was rather "a matter of sexual morality and social deviance.... Who really cared whether ... [she was] of normal intelligence; she was the illegitimate child of an illegitimate woman. Two generations of bastards are enough." "Carrie Buck's Daughter," 7 *Natural History* 14 (July 1984), at 17.

[220] 410 U.S. 113 (1973).

[221] In *Planned Parenthood v. Casey*, 505 U.S. 833 (1992).

[222] E.g., *Stenberg v. Carhart*, 147 L Ed 2d 743 (2000); *Hill v. Colorado*, 147 L Ed 2d 597 (2000).

[223] 410 U.S. at 157–59.

from those engaged in by consenting adult homosexuals. Only choices fundamental to heterosexual life – marriage, procreation, child rearing, and family relationships – are constitutionally protected. Although the law at issue flatly banned oral and anal sex regardless of marital status or sexual orientation, the majority rewrote the statute to apply only to homosexuals and, as so construed, justified its ruling because "[p]roscriptions against that conduct have ancient roots" and at the time the Fourteenth Amendment was ratified, "all but five of the 37 States in the Union had criminal sodomy laws."[224] More recently, over the dissent of the Court's three most conservative members (Rehnquist, Scalia, and Thomas), the Court voided a Colorado amendment that not only repealed existing laws protective of gays but also prohibited their future enactment. "The resulting disqualification," said the Court, "is unprecedented in our jurisprudence." The amendment does not "deprive homosexuals of special rights. To the contrary, the amendment imposes a special disability on those persons alone." The "disadvantage imposed is born of animosity toward the class of persons affected."[225]

On the next privacy issue that the Court confronted, the right to die, the majority contradicted its sodomy case assertion that "[t]he Court is most vulnerable and comes nearest to illegitimacy when it deals with judge-made constitutional law having little or no cognizable roots in the language or design of the Constitution,"[226] by holding that persons who make their wishes clearly known have a constitutional right to terminate life-sustaining care: "The principle that a competent person has a constitutionally protected liberty interest in refusing unwanted medical treatment may be inferred from our prior decisions."[227] However, the right to die does not extend to assisted suicide.[228]

[224] *Bowers v. Hardwick*, 478 U.S. 186 (1986), at 200–201, 214–16, 190, 192, 193. In rebuttal, one of the dissenting opinions cogently observed that "neither history nor tradition could save a law prohibiting miscegenation from constitutional attack," even though the states treated it as a crime akin to sodomy. 478 U.S., at 216.

[225] *Romer v. Evans*, 517 U.S. 620 (1996), at 633, 631, 634. But the Rehnquist Five ruled the Boy Scouts have a First Amendment right to exclude gays from membership. *Boy Scouts of America v. Dale*, 147 L Ed 2d 554 (2000).

[226] 478 U.S. at 194.

[227] *Cruzan v. Missouri Health Department*, 497 U.S. 261 (1990), at 278. Although the Court ruled that the petitioning party failed to provide clear and convincing evidence of her desire at trial, as Missouri law required, on remand the trial judge allowed the plaintiff's family to cease pumping chemical nutrition and water into her body. Six months after the Supreme Court's ruling, she died.

[228] *Washington v. Glucksberg*, 521 U.S. 702 (1997), and *Vacco v. Quill*, 521 U.S. 793 (1997).

THE SUPREME COURT AND THE DISTRIBUTION OF POWER, 1936–2000

The movement toward a civil liberties agenda that began with the Carolene Products case did not end the Supreme Court's role as arbiter of power among the three branches of government. Five cases dealing with executive, legislative, and judicial powers during this period deserve special attention because of the role they may play in the resolution of future national controversies: *United States v. Curtiss-Wright Export Corporation*,[229] *Korematsu v. United States*,[230] *Youngstown Sheet and Tube Co. v. Sawyer*,[231] *United States v. Nixon*,[232] and *Immigration and Naturalization Service v. Chadha*.[233] Though they have lain largely dormant since their announcement, lack of use does not mean irrelevance.

The Curtiss-Wright Case

A joint resolution of Congress had authorized the President to prohibit arms sales to warring Paraguay and Bolivia. Following its indictment for violating the embargo, Curtiss-Wright sued to have the resolution invalidated as an unlawful delegation of power to the executive. The Court's decision not only upheld the resolution but broadly defined the foreign affairs powers of the President. Distinguishing domestic powers, which are delegated to the national government by the Constitution, from foreign powers, which reside wholly in the national government, the justices held that within the national government the foreign powers vest almost exclusively in the presidency.

> In this vast external realm with its important, complicated, delicate and manifold problems, the President alone has the power to speak or listen as representative of the nation. He *makes* treaties with the advice and consent of the Senate; but he alone negotiates. Into the field of negotiation the Senate cannot intrude; and Congress itself is powerless to invade it.[234]

Given the breadth of his foreign powers, the Court suggested that the President could have imposed the embargo even without congressional authorization.

> It is important to keep in mind that we are here dealing not alone with an authority vested in the President by an exertion of legislative power, but with such an

229 299 U.S. 304 (1936). 230 323 U.S. 214 (1944). 231 343 U.S. 579 (1952).
232 418 U.S. 683 (1974). 233 462 U.S. 919 (1983). 234 299 U.S., at 319.

> authority plus the very delicate plenary and exclusive power of the President as sole organ of the federal government in the field of international relations – a power that does not require as a basis of its exercise an act of Congress. . . .[235]

The broad dicta of *Curtiss-Wright* were progressively tested in both the Japanese internment and the Steel Seizure cases.

The Japanese Internment Cases

Two months after Japan attacked Pearl Harbor, President Roosevelt issued an executive order allowing the military to remove American citizens of Japanese descent from the West Coast and place them in "relocation centers." Congress ratified the President's order the following month.[236] No similar actions were taken against German- or Italian-Americans, even though the United States had also declared war against those nations.[237] Indeed, no charges of disloyalty or subversion were ever filed against any Japanese-Americans, many of whom fought bravely for their country in World War II. The pressure for the relocation came not from fear of an invasion but from members of California farm associations envious of the fertile land owned and cultivated by Japanese-Americans and from the state's then governor who, eleven years later, became chief justice of the United States: Earl Warren.

The Supreme Court upheld Roosevelt's orders in two decisions. In *Hirabayashi v. United States*[238] the justices sustained the dusk-to-dawn curfew imposed on Japanese-Americans by the military under the President's power as commander-in-chief. Far more damaging was the decision in *Korematsu v. United States*, which upheld their detention. Though noting a difference between the curfew in *Hirabayashi* and the relocation in *Korematsu*, the majority declared itself "unable to conclude that it was beyond the war power of Congress and the Executive to

[235] *Id.* at 319–20.

[236] The Japanese in Hawaii were not interned, even though it had been attacked at Pearl Harbor. Unlike the Japanese on the West Coast, those in Hawaii provided the unskilled and "stoop" labor essential to the operation of the Hawaiian economy that self-respecting whites would not perform. Bigotry, and its attendant hypocrisy, thus took a back seat to economic well-being.

[237] American treatment of Italian-American citizens during World War II was not completely above board. While the United States interned about 1,600 Italian nationals, it also forced about 10,000 American citizens of Italian descent to move from their homes in California coastal communities to inland abodes. See James Brooke, "After Silence, Italians Recall the Internment," *New York Times*, August 11, 1997, p. A10.

[238] 320 U.S. 81 (1943).

exclude those of Japanese ancestry from the West Coast war area at the time they did."[239] The decision, very much the law of the land today, means that a mere allegation of military necessity suffices to warrant the summary incarceration of any individual or group without any judicial determination of wrongdoing whatsoever.[240]

The Steel Seizure Case

While *Curtiss-Wright* involved presidential action subsequent to congressional authorization, and *Korematsu* involved presidential action followed by congressional ratification, the Steel Seizure case, *Youngstown Sheet and Tube Co. v. Sawyer*, involved unilateral presidential action that expressly contradicted congressional policy. Here, finally, the Court placed limits on presidential action related to foreign affairs.

The relevant facts are these: In December 1951, during the Korean War, the United Steelworkers Union announced plans to strike. Several attempts at federal mediation failed. On April 4, 1952, the Union announced an April 9th strike deadline. Because of the indispensability of steel production to the war effort, President Truman issued an executive order directing the secretary of commerce to take possession of the steel mills and keep them running. Under the United States flag, the workers returned to work. The steel companies filed suit.

Justice Black's majority opinion noted that the Constitution grants "all legislative powers" to Congress, not the President. As Congress had enacted no law authorizing such seizures, the President could not be

[239] 323 U.S., at 217–18.

[240] On the eve of the Persian Gulf War, reports such as the following appeared in the media:

> Federal law enforcement agencies have ... vastly stepped up intelligence-gathering activities directed at Iraqis and other allied Arab groups in this country, Administration officials said today....
>
> Today, the Federal Bureau of Investigation ordered its agents throughout the country to interview business and community leaders of Arab descent, asking for information about possible terrorist activities by Iraqis....
>
> Some Arab representatives expressed the fear that a war could excite the same kind of hysteria that led Government officials to intern more than 110,000 Americans of Japanese ancestry during World War II, but officials insisted that no such plans had been considered or approved.

"Scrutiny of Iraqis Stepped Up in U.S.," *New York Times*, January 8, 1991, p. A1. Note that the officials referred to in the last sentence above did not suggest that any such plan would be unconstitutional or illegal. Whether the "War" against terrorism, ongoing as we write, will produce similar reports or action remains to be seen.

acting under his constitutional authority to take "care that the laws be faithfully executed." Nor could the action be authorized under the President's authority as commander-in-chief, as the steel mills were not part of a theater of war. Had Truman's actions been upheld, it is not clear what, if any, limits would exist on unilateral presidential action in matters related to foreign affairs.

The Watergate Tapes Case

The President can conflict not only with Congress, as in the Steel Seizure case, but also with the judiciary. Unfortunately for the President, the judiciary itself decides the outcome of such conflicts.

On March 1, 1974, a grand jury indicted seven top aides to President Nixon for activities related to the Watergate burglary and cover-up. Nixon himself was named as an unindicted coconspirator. Following the indictments, Watergate Special Prosecutor Leon Jaworski sought and obtained a subpoena ordering Nixon to provide him with tape recordings and other evidence. Nixon refused to supply all the materials requested. The case quickly reached the Supreme Court, where Nixon's lawyer argued that executive privilege protected the requested conversations and asserted that the President might not comply with a decision of the Supreme Court that was not definitive.[241]

The threat of noncompliance was a tactical mistake. By questioning the Court's authority, Nixon all but guaranteed himself a definitive decision. While other Presidents, such as Lincoln, successfully stood up to the Supreme Court, Richard Nixon in the summer of 1974 was in no position to do so. In a unanimous decision, the Court restated the position of Chief Justice Marshall in *Marbury v. Madison*: It is emphatically the province and the duty of the judiciary to say what the law is. After deciding that the courts alone had the authority to rule on the question of executive privilege, the Supreme Court found that such a right exists, but that it cannot outweigh the need to provide subpoenaed evidence in a criminal trial.

Following the decision, Nixon reluctantly agreed to turn over the tapes, which showed him to have directed the Watergate cover-up from the beginning. Shortly thereafter, in the face of imminent impeachment by the House of Representatives, Nixon resigned.

[241] Bob Woodward and Scott Armstrong, *The Brethren* (New York: Simon and Schuster, 1979), pp. 305–7.

The Legislative Veto Case

As the role of the national government expanded during Franklin Roosevelt's New Deal, and again during Lyndon Johnson's Great Society, Congress found itself without the institutional capacity to make all the legislative decisions required of it. Thus, it doesn't have the inclination or capability to regulate the stock market and so it delegates the task to the Securities and Exchange Commission. It doesn't have the scientific wherewithal to set nuclear energy policy and delegates these decisions to the Nuclear Regulatory Commission. Such delegation is inevitable in any complex society.

When Congress delegates authority to the executive branch or independent agencies, a certain degree of responsiveness is lost. The federal bureaucrats whom Congress provides with quasilawmaking powers are obviously unelected. In an attempt to keep some control over the authority it delegates, Congress enacted since 1932 almost 200 statutes that provided for one- or two-house vetoes of independent agency or executive branch decisions. The best-known example is the War Powers Act, which limits the President's right to go to war without congressional authorization to ninety days.

In *Immigration and Naturalization Service v. Chadha*,[242] the Court struck down the legislative veto on two grounds. A one-house veto violates the constitutional requirements that a law must be enacted by both houses of Congress and presented to the President for signature or veto. By contrast, the two-house veto violates only the presentment clause. In its decision the Court voided 196 federal laws – more than it had in its previous history – and severely limited Congress's ability to oversee the bureaucracy to which it has delegated enormous power.

We may expect an increase in the frequency of conflicts among the legislative, executive, and judicial branches, and not just with regard to the conduct of foreign policy and the exercise of the war powers that the Constitution divides between President and Congress. With the Balkanization of the world resulting from the end of the Cold War and the spread of terrorist activities to all corners of the globe, long-dormant ethnic and religious animosities have flared anew. Some of these have already threatened the United States, response to which has become and will continue to be major matters of public concern. There is no reason

[242] 462 U.S. 919 (1983). Also see Barbara Hinkson Craig, *Chadha* (Berkeley: University of California Press, 1990).

to expect that resulting controversies will be any less likely than those of the past to ultimately come to the Court for resolution. And though heated confrontation ensues, we may expect the Court, as usual, to emerge supreme.

The Distribution of Power at the Millennium

Two decisions on the threshold of the twenty-first century indisputably highlighted the dominance of the Supreme Court in the governance of the United States: the Line Item Veto case and *Bush v. Gore.*

Notwithstanding the endemic conflict between the legislative and executive branches, a Republican-controlled Congress enacted legislation in 1996 that gave a Democratic President authority to veto portions of tax and spending legislation rather than its entirety. The President could therefore veto the objectionable provisions of a statute while authorizing enactment of the remainder. The law was an attempt to limit "pork barrel" appropriations whereby members of Congress figuratively scratch one another's backs by favorably voting for pet capital expenditure projects and attaching them as riders to crucial budgetary bills that enable the government to continue operating.

Even though a self-effacing Congress unprecedentedly renunciated a major bulwark against presidential power, the Supreme Court characteristically intruded itself into the matter and, by a 6-to-3 vote, declared the Line Item Veto Act unconstitutional.[243] Recognizing the Constitution's silence "on the subject of unilateral Presidential action that either repeals or amends parts of duly enacted statutes," the majority nonetheless asserted that "[t]here are powerful reasons for construing constitutional silence . . . as equivalent to an express prohibition."[244] And what might these reasons be? (1) "The 'finely wrought' procedure" of the presentment clause of the Constitution, which is all of sixty-nine words in length,[245] and (2) the words of George Washington (not exactly known heretofore as a constitutional scholar) that the presentment clause required him either to "approve all the parts of a Bill, or reject it in toto."[246]

[243] *Clinton v. New York City*, 141 L Ed 2d 393 (1998). [244] *Id.* at 414, 415.

[245] *Id.* at 414. "Every Bill which shall have passed the House of Representatives and the Senate, shall, before it becomes a Law, be presented to the President of the United States; If he approve he shall sign it, but if not he shall return it, with his Objections, to that House in which it shall have originated, who shall enter the Objections at large on their Journal, and proceed to reconsider it."

[246] *Id.* at 415.

In a related vein, the Court, prior to the Line Item Veto case, had considered the constitutionality of the Independent Counsel Act, enacted in 1974 in the aftermath of Watergate and renewed in 1994. With only Justice Scalia in dissent, and Kennedy not participating, the Court upheld the law against a variety of challenges based on the structure of American government. Scalia's dissent pointed out the obvious, which the Monica Lewinsky affair and Clinton's impeachment made all too clear: that independent counsels are "principal" officers of the executive branch for whom the Constitution requires presidential nomination and senatorial confirmation, and not "inferior" officers named by a panel of three judges. The latter, Scalia pointed out, require a superior, who manifestly does not exist. Hence, independent counsels lack accountability and are superior to everyone – the Supreme Court, of course, excluded. As Chapter 1 explains, ours is a government of limited powers characterized by checks and balances. The Independent Counsel Law mandates the investigation of persons, not crimes – thus inviting cancerous accretion. Answering to no one, special prosecutors operate with an unlimited budget and under no time constraints.

In 1995, the justices apparently realized how far they had drifted from constitutional moorings into uncharted waters and united behind Scalia in an opinion that requires "inferior" officers to be supervised by others whom the President has nominated and the Senate confirmed.[247] Whether this decision tacitly overruled *Morrison v. Olson*[248] became a moot point when Congress, in June 1999, unremorsefully allowed the Independent Counsel Act to die a natural death.

But the most telling decision about the distribution of power – not only at the millennium but arguably at any point in our nation's history – was the midnight decision in *Bush v. Gore*.[249] Although partisan decisions have typified the Court since the days of John Marshall, the partisanship displayed itself along ideological lines as we have documented in this chapter and as we do more specifically in Chapter 8. But in *Bush v. Gore* one may accurately say that never in its history has a majority of the Court behaved in such a blatant *politically* partisan fashion.

[247] *Edmund v. United States*, 520 U.S. 651 (1997). [248] 487 U.S. 654 (1988).

[249] 148 L Ed 2d 388 (2000). The decision was actually handed down at 10:15 P.M. EST. For a Court whose formal decisions almost invariably antedate noon, midnight is only a mild exaggeration.

We consider the best all-around treatment of *Bush v. Gore* to be Howard Gillman, *The Votes That Counted: How the Court Decided the 2000 Presidential Election* (Chicago: University of Chicago Press, 2001).

The Court's five most conservative members, Rehnquist, O'Connor, Scalia, Kennedy, and Thomas, ruled, first, that disparate standards for recounting Florida's ballots violated the equal protection clause, while the two most liberal justices, Ginsburg and Stevens, refused, atypically, to find an equal-protection violation.

The majority's position was particularly curious, for heretofore government action could violate equal protection only by showing purposeful intent to discriminate. But more basically, if counties may not constitutionally count their own ballots, how can it be constitutional for judges and juries applying totally subjective standards to deprive persons of life, liberty, and property? As Justice Stevens observed in his dissent, the standard that the Florida Supreme Court prescribed – "the intent of the voter" – can hardly "lead to results any less uniform than . . . the 'beyond a reasonable doubt standard' employed everyday by ordinary citizens in courtrooms across the country." Note further that this standard, mandated by the U.S. Supreme Court as a key element of due process, is completely undefinable in any intersubjectively transmissible sense.[250]

Second, the Court ruled that the time needed to carry out a recount under a proper single standard had expired. But the Court itself had stopped the recount in advance of its decision, thus aiding and abetting Bush's attempt to run out the clock. The Court "reasoned" in the initial summary judgment that a recount of the votes prior to its decision would do irreparable harm to Bush, perhaps by informing the world how Florida voters tried to vote. Of course, the real irreparable harm was done to Gore, who faced an impossible deadline of the Court's making.

The Court's reasoning in *Bush v. Gore* on the deadline can be described only as ingenuously preposterous. Time had run its course because of an old federal law that state certification of its vote was valid if filed on the date of the Court's decision, December 12. But states commonly disregard this date, and several did so in the 2000 election. The date serves only as a "safe harbor" precluding nonjudicial manipulation of the election outcome. Any state is free to disregard the afforded protection in the interest of a complete and fair vote count. The choice is the state's and, as such, raises no federal question, the only basis on which the Court could exercise its jurisdiction.

[250] Walter F. Murphy and C. Herman Pritchett, *Courts, Judges, and Politics*, 4th ed. (New York: Random House, 1986), pp. 358–59. Also see Jerome Frank, *Courts on Trial* (New York: Atheneum, 1963), pp. 108–45.

The Court's cunning is further revealed by considering *Bush v. Gore* in the context of *Bush v. Palm Beach County Canvassing Board*,[251] which it had remanded to the Florida Supreme Court just one week earlier. The decision declared that the state court owed the Florida legislature unusual deference due to Article II's command that electors shall be chosen "in such Manner as the Legislature thereof may direct."

That decision undoubtedly led to the Florida Supreme Court's decision in *Bush v. Gore* not to add specificity to the legislature's requirement that the ultimate test in recounts shall be the "intent of the voter." Thus, if the Florida Supreme Court leaves that standard in place, as it did, then the U.S. Supreme Court finds an equal protection problem. But *Bush v. Palm Beach* makes it abundantly clear that had the Florida Supreme Court added specificity to that standard, the Court would have found an Article II problem. Heads, Bush wins; tails, Gore loses.

Moreover, though Bush had raised an equal protection issue in the Palm Beach case, along with several others, the Court made absolutely no reference to it, thereby misleading the Florida court, who could have attempted to resolve the matter in time. But if the justices could have successfully done so, Gore may have won and the justices inclined to retire – reportedly, Rehnquist and O'Connor – would have had to wait at least four more years – God willing – before an acceptable President occupied the White House.

The majority's intrusion stands the Constitution on its head: Presidents have had the power to select the Court's members. Now the worm has turned: the justices select the President. In doing so, the majority has been subject to unusually acerbic criticism, especially from sources noted for their restraint and respect. Thus, Linda Greenhouse, who covers the Supreme Court for the *New York Times*, quotes a distinguished conservative legal scholar and former University of Michigan Law School dean, Terrance Sandalow, as describing the stay of the Florida court "an unmistakably partisan decision without any foundation in the law." The Pulitzer Prize-winning author and *Times* columnist Anthony Lewis wrote that "[d]eciding a case of this magnitude with such disregard for reason . . . would be a terrible price to pay." The Brennan Center for Justice at the New York University School of Law compiled comments from a variety of news sources: The decision is a "partisan and ideological assault on democracy"; the Rehnquist Court has "punctured the

251 148 L Ed 2d 366 (2000).

myth that the Court is above politics"; stopping the recount "stopped democracy."[252]

SUMMARY AND CONCLUSIONS

Our survey has outlined the ideological considerations that have motivated the thrust of the Court's decisions since its inception. Clearly, it has not marched to the beat of alien or enigmatic drums, even though those drums have typically beaten a stridently partisan cadence. In the process, the justices have demonstrated that the elements of the legal model – plain meaning, intent, and precedent – have enabled them to pursue logically incompatible objectives with authoritative aplomb. Thus, notwithstanding the atavistic activism of divine-right monarchism that the Rehnquist Five displayed in *Bush v. Gore* to produce an arrogantly anti–states' rights decision, these same five justices, as detailed in Chapter 1, patently effected a states' rights posture in a series of eight minimum winning votes over a four-and-a-half-year period for the purpose of formalistically redefining federal-state relationships.[253]

The majority in these cases clearly disconnected from history. In the Printz case the Court ruled that Congress cannot "commandeer" state officials into doing federal work. Yet, dating back to the first Congress, it had repeatedly done exactly that. As *Federalist* 27 argues, "The legislatures, courts and magistrates, of the respective members, will be incorporated into the operations of the national government as far as its just and constitutional authority extends; and will be rendered auxiliary to the enforcement of its laws." While *The Federalist* is not fundamental law, we are aware of no Supreme Court decision that more directly contradicts an explicit statement from the Papers.

Moreover, one needn't delve very deeply into the three volumes of Farrand's *Records of the Federal Convention of 1787* and its *Supplement*[254] to learn that the primary motivation for convening were com-

252 "Collision with Politics Risks Court's Legal Credibility," *New York Times*, December 11, 2000, p. A1. "A Failure of Reason," *New York Times*, December 16, 2000, p. A31. "Court Pester E-lert," www.brennancenter.org, December 14, 2000.

253 *United States v. Lopez*, 514 U.S. 549 (1995); *Seminole Tribe v. Florida*, 517 U.S. 44 (1996); *Idaho v. Coeur d'Alene Tribe*, 521 U.S. 261 (1997); *Printz v. United States*, 521 U.S. 898 (1997); *Florida Board v. College Bank*, 144 L Ed 2d 575 (1999); *College Savings Bank v. Florida Board*, 144 L Ed 2d 605 (1999); *Alden v. Maine*, 144 L Ed 2d 636 (1999); and *Kimel v. Florida Board of Regents* 145 L Ed 2d 522 (2000).

254 (New Haven: Yale University Press, 1966, 1987).

plaints about the lack of federal authority. References to "state sovereign immunity" imply precedence over the public will and hark back to the debased argument of John C. Calhoun and other secessionists. Scalia's opinion in *College Savings Bank* epitomizes irony. The justice who views himself as acolytically faithful to plain meaning impudently construes the Eleventh Amendment to mean more than it reads: that state immunity nullifies certain constitutional provisions.

Notwithstanding a few aberrational decisions, the values that motivated Warren and Burger Court policy making in the areas of civil liberties and civil rights – freedom and equality – continue to explain the voting of the incumbent justices. In matters economic, the justices whose service began on the Burger and Warren Courts appear to decide cases on considerations other than the New Deal economics that motivated their predecessors. A degree of libertarianism has emerged, coupled with attitudes toward the decision making of administrative agencies and the federal courts, along with the mentioned considerations pertaining to federal-state relationships.[255]

In other areas, the Court's recent policy making has provided it with a means to decide cases that heretofore had been the province of the state courts. Until 1983, the Court would not review cases containing intermixed questions of state and federal law unless the party invoking the Court's jurisdiction could show that the state court's decision rested on federal, rather than state, law. The Court reversed its policy, however, and decreed that it would presume that state courts based their decisions on federal law in cases containing intermingled questions of federal and state law.[256] Two effects have resulted. First, the Court has used *Long* to reach out and reverse state court decisions with which its conservative majority disapproves, particularly in the area of criminal procedure. Second, the threat of *Long* has forced liberally oriented state courts to rely on their own constitutional provisions instead of those in the federal Constitution in order to protect and safeguard individual rights and liberties.[257]

To avoid the first effect, we expect the state courts to use their own common, statutory, and constitutional law as the basis for an ever-increasing proportion of their decisions, not only in the area of civil

[255] See Chapter 6. [256] *Michigan v. Long*, 463 U.S. 1032 (1983).

[257] Harold J. Spaeth, "Justice Sandra Day O'Connor: An Assessment," in D. Grier Stephenson, Jr., ed., *An Essential Safeguard* (Westport, Conn.: Greenwood Press, 1991), pp. 92–95.

liberties, but also rather broadly across the board. Thus, for example, in the aftermath of the Court's ruling that education is not a fundamental right protected by the Constitution,[258] states began to look to their own constitutional and statutory provisions to equalize the financing of public education. Within a generation, virtually all of the states addressed this matter, and though their involvement produced mixed results, what is significant is that responsibility for the resolution of this major policy issue rests with the individual states rather than Washington.[259] Reliance on state law will not appreciably diminish the relevance of the Court's policy making, but rather will signal the emergence of the state courts from the shadow of the Supreme Court and a substantial increase in the importance of state constitutional law, the amount of which will depend on the ideological distance separating a given state's courts from the Marble Palace. The Court, of course, is not solely dependent on *Long* in order to review state court decisions. Even if a state court exclusively relies on its own law, the Supreme Court may still rule the matter one that the states are preempted from regulating, either because Congress has already acted or because the matter is suited only for uniform national regulation. But because the Supreme Court will be dominated well into the twenty-first century by justices who couple their conservatism on substantive issues with support of the states (except where other more politically important considerations, such as determining the outcome of a presidential election, are at stake), we expect much more authoritative policy making on matters of major national moment by the state courts than has occurred at any previous time in the nation's history.[260]

As for *Bush v. Gore*, we doubt that this decision will preclude the Court from perpetuating its position as the authoritative policy maker on any subject that it decides to address. Thus, though we do agree in part with the judgment of another august commentator in a journal that heretofore respected the Court and its decisions, we disagree that the fallout from *Bush v. Gore* will diminish the Court's stature:

[258] *San Antonio Independent School District v. Rodriguez*, 411 U.S. 1 (1973).

[259] For a summary of this development, see Rorie Sherman, "Tackling Education Financing," *National Law Journal*, July 22, 1991, pp. 1, 22–23.

[260] In support of our judgment, see Ronald K. L. Collins, "Reliance on State Constitutions," 63 *Texas Law Review* 1095 (1985); Ronald K. L. Collins, "State Constitutional Law," *National Law Journal*, September 29, 1986, p. S-1; Barry Latzer, "The Hidden Conservatism of the State Court 'Revolution,'" 74 *Judicature* 190 (1991); William Glaberson, "State Courts Sweeping Away Laws Curbing Suits for Injury," *New York Times*, July 16, 1999, pp. A1, A13.

> ... by not even bothering to cloak their willfulness in legal arguments intelligible to people of good faith who do not share their views, these four vain men and one vain woman have not only cast a cloud over the presidency of George W. Bush. They have, far more importantly, made it impossible for citizens of the United States to sustain any kind of faith in the rule of law as something larger than the self-interested political preferences of William Rehnquist, Antonin Scalia, Clarence Thomas, Anthony Kennedy, and Sandra Day O'Connor.[261]

Whether the public views the justices as motivated by partisanship or by what passes for legal reasoning, it will not likely alter its view of the Court as other than supreme. If a choice were to be made among President, Congress, and Court as to which branch should rule, we continue to put our money on the justices. And the fact that legalists' faith in the rule of law may go the way of phlogiston will not affect the popular conviction that the emanations from the Marble Palace alone safeguard the American way of life, and not the pestiferous effluent generated by the "political" branches of government.

[261] Jeffrey Rosen, "Disgrace," *The New Republic*, December 25, 2000, p. 18.

5

Staffing the Court

On July 1, 1987, President Ronald Reagan nominated Robert Bork, U.S. Circuit Court Judge for the District of Columbia, to the Supreme Court. Bork, former professor at Yale Law School and erstwhile Solicitor General of the United States, had been confirmed to what is reputedly the nation's second most prestigious court by a unanimous vote of the Senate. In November 1986, Senate Judiciary Committee Chairman Joseph Biden (D-Del.) told the *Philadelphia Inquirer* that if a well-qualified conservative like Bork were nominated for the Supreme Court, "I'll have to vote for him, and if the groups tear me apart, that's the medicine I'll have to take."[1] Yet eleven months later Biden's Judiciary Committee followed his lead and voted 9 to 5 against Bork. Less than three weeks after that, the full Senate concurred, 58 to 42. History will undoubtedly regard the rejection of the radical-rightist Bork as the biggest legislative failure of the Reagan administration.

To the extent that the legal model requires justices to find the "correct" answer to legal questions,[2] it should not matter much whom the President nominates or whether the Senate confirms, given a requisite modicum of legal training and intelligence. Differences might result, say, from followers of intent versus followers of text, but there would be overwhelming agreement on the basic principles of government. However, if the Court largely bases its decisions on the attitudes and

[1] *Philadelphia Inquirer*, November 16, 1986, p. A13.

[2] See Lewis Kornhauser, "Adjudication by a Resource-Constrained Team: Hierarchy and Precedent in a Judicial System," 68 *Southern California Law Review* 1605 (1995), for recent approaches to such models.

values of the justices, then clearly "the most important appointments a President makes are those to the Supreme Court of the United States."[3]

Following Nixon's contention, a case can be made that among the most important *decisions* a President makes are his nominations to the Supreme Court. What, for example, among Eisenhower's decisions compares to his appointments of Earl Warren, John Harlan, Potter Stewart, and William Brennan? What among John Adams's compares to his nomination of John Marshall? In this chapter, we examine the process by which Presidents nominate and senators confirm or reject appointees to the Supreme Court.

PRESIDENTIAL SELECTION

Article II, section 2, clause 2, of the United States Constitution gives the President the power, "by and with the Advice and Consent of the Senate," to appoint "Judges of the supreme Court." Despite the wording of this clause, the role of the Senate in Supreme Court nominations has been limited to consent; Presidents have sought advice only in the naming of lower court judges, especially those to the district courts, particularly when there is a senator of the President's party from the state in which the court is located. If the senator disapproves of the President's nominee, he or she can invoke "senatorial courtesy" and block the nomination. This process has not applied to the Supreme Court for nearly a century, nor was it ever intended to. According to Alexander Hamilton in number 66 of *The Federalist Papers*,

> There will, of course, be no exertion of *choice* on the part of the Senate. They may defeat one choice of the Executive and oblige him to make another; but they cannot themselves *choose* – they can only ratify or reject the choice he may have made. They might even entertain a preference to some other person at the very moment they were assenting to the one proposed, because there might be no positive ground of opposition to him; and they could not be sure, if they withheld their assent, that the subsequent nomination would fall upon their own favorite.[4]

Modern Presidents usually delegate the initial phases of the selection process to the attorney general, chief of staff, or other top advisers.

[3] Richard Nixon, "Transcript of President's Announcements," *New York Times*, October 22, 1971, p. 24.

[4] Alexander Hamilton, James Madison, and John Jay, *The Federalist* (New York: Mentor, 1961), p. 405.

Recommendations from politicians, legal professionals, and interest groups are filtered through the Justice Department's Office of Legal Policy.[5] The President's advisers then pass the names of one or more top candidates to the FBI for exhaustive investigative checks.[6] The final choice is the President's, but the influence of others can be felt. Reagan Attorney General Edwin Meese lobbied hard, first for Robert Bork and next for Daniel Ginsburg, against a more moderate position urged by Chief of Staff Howard Baker. Nixon's choice of Harry Blackmun was obviously influenced by Blackmun's childhood friend, Chief Justice Warren Burger. Former President William Howard Taft lobbied successfully for his own appointment to the chief justiceship.[7]

Factors Affecting Nomination

Presidential selection undoubtedly involves complex choices. We may, nevertheless, be able to explain the type of person nominated. Moreover, some recent work even models whom the President chooses. First, though, we examine some of the factors that influence presidential selection.

Partisanship and Ideology

Given the Supreme Court's role as a national policy maker, it would boggle the mind if Presidents did not pay careful attention to the ideology and partisanship of potential nominees. This factor has been crucial from the Republic's beginning, with President Washington nominating eleven consecutive Federalists to the Court. Overall, 128 of 147 nominees (87 percent) have come from the President's party.[8] Simple parti-

[5] David O'Brien, *Storm Center* (New York: Norton, 1986), p. 53.

[6] Nescience rather than competence apparently characterizes many of these investigations. E.g., the FBI's failure to uncover references in 1983 speeches of Bush's nominee, Clarence Thomas, that praised the anti-Semitic black leader Louis H. Farrakhan, head of the Nation of Islam, while Thomas was chair of the Equal Employment Opportunities Commission. See Pete Applebome, "Black Conservatives: Minority within a Minority," *New York Times*, July 13, 1991, pp. A1, A7.

[7] See Henry F. Pringle, *The Life and Times of William Howard Taft* (New York: Farrar and Rinehart, 1939), II, ch. 50.

[8] The data here and below were derived by the authors and are current through the end of the millennium. We exclude from consideration two nominations: William Paterson, whose first nomination in 1793 was temporarily withdrawn so that he could officially resign from the Senate, and Homer Thornberry, whose nomination in 1968 was conditional on Fortas's promotion to chief justice. This leaves us with 147 nominations, the number we use throughout this chapter.

sanship paints an incomplete picture. In his discussions with Senator Henry Cabot Lodge about Democrat Horace Lurton, President Theodore Roosevelt observed that "the nominal politics of the man have nothing to do with his actions on the bench. His *real* politics are all important." Roosevelt had earlier sought assurances from Lodge that Oliver Wendell Holmes was "in entire sympathy with our views" before nominating him to the Supreme Court.[9]

In more recent times, presidential candidate Richard Nixon campaigned in 1968 on the promise to appoint justices who would support the "peace forces" of society instead of those who favored the rights of accused criminals. His appointees have been consistently conservative on criminal procedure. Ronald Reagan's 1980 campaign platform included support for judicial nominees who were harsh on crime, opposed abortion, and favored school prayer. In 1986, Reagan argued that

> the proliferation of drugs has been part of a crime epidemic that can be traced to, among other things, liberal judges who are unwilling to get tough with the criminal element in this society. . . . We don't need a bunch of sociology majors on the bench. What we need are strong judges who will aggressively use their authority to protect our families, communities and way of life; judges who understand that punishing wrongdoers is our way of protecting the innocent; judges who do not hesitate to put criminals where they belong, behind bars.[10]

Political Environment

While a rational President will wish to nominate someone with views as close to his as possible, political reality might make such a choice difficult. A President who chooses an unconfirmable nominee will lose more than he will gain.

A classic example of a President "trimming his sails" to avoid a battle with the Senate was Ford's nomination of John Paul Stevens. Ford, who became President following Nixon's resignation, entered office with the lowest initial approval ratings of any President since George Gallup began polling. That low level of popularity fell even further when Ford pardoned Nixon for any crimes he may have committed during his administration. When Justice Douglas resigned, Ford faced a Senate that consisted of sixty-two Democrats and thirty-eight Republicans. Further, Ford had to replace the Court's most liberal justice, one whom Ford

[9] Henry Cabot Lodge, *Selections from the Correspondence of Theodore Roosevelt and Henry Cabot Lodge, 1894–1918* (New York: Scribner's, 1925) II, 228; I, 519.

[10] "Reagan Aims Fire at Liberal Judges," *New York Times*, October 9, 1986, p. A32.

himself had tried to impeach while House Minority Leader.[11] Under these circumstances, the conservative Ford pragmatically chose the moderate Stevens rather than conservatives such as Robert Bork or J. Clifford Wallace.[12]

Prior Experience

All 147 individuals nominated to the high bench have been attorneys. Virtually all have had experience in public affairs of one sort or another, including several as senators, governors, and one as a former President. Most commonly, they have previously served as jurists. Four of the five justices on the first Supreme Court had prior judicial experience. Overall, 93 of the 147 nominees (63 percent) have occupied judicial positions. This overall rate masks strong partisan differences: 73 percent of Republican nominees have had prior experience, versus only 50 percent of Democratic nominees.

Region

The Judiciary Act of 1789 divided the nation into six circuits, then corresponding to the number of seats on the Supreme Court. As the number of circuits increased, so also did the number of justices. Until the end of the nineteenth century, each justice served in a dual capacity: as a circuit court judge and as a member of the Supreme Court. The assumption from the beginning was that the justice would reside within the circuit he served: The Judiciary Act of 1802 explicitly refers to "the justice of the supreme court residing within the said circuit."[13] Thus began the tradition of regional representation.

When circuit riding ended in 1891, the need for regional representation lessened. In fact, Lincoln ignored regional "rules" during the Civil War, and though such practices were revived after the war, "by the late 1880's presidents disregarded it with increasing frequency."[14] In 1930,

[11] Ford's charges against Douglas concerned Douglas's publication of excerpts from his book, *Points of Rebellion*, in the *Evergreen Review*, a magazine that featured sexually explicit material. During the failed impeachment effort, Ford declared that "an impeachable offense is anything a majority of the House of Representatives considers [it] to be at a given moment of history." See Harold J. Spaeth, *Supreme Court Policy Making* (San Francisco: W. H. Freeman, 1979), p. 114.

[12] David O'Brien, "The Politics of Professionalism: President Gerald Ford's Appointment of Justice John Paul Stevens," 21 *Presidential Studies Quarterly* 103 (1991).

[13] Act of April 29, 1802, 2 Stat. 156–57.

[14] Richard Friedman, "The Transformation in Senate Response to Supreme Court Nominations," 5 *Cardozo Law Review* 1 (1983), 50.

though, Hoover declined to nominate Judge Benjamin Cardozo on the ground that two New Yorkers were sitting on the Court, one of whom was Jewish. When another vacancy occurred, Justice Stone, one of the New Yorkers, offered to resign if that would secure Cardozo's nomination.[15] Hoover then selected Cardozo without calling Stone's bluff.

The most recent use of regionalism was Nixon's attempt to nominate a Southerner to replace Justice Black in 1971. Nixon hoped that doing so would win him electoral support from conservative Southerners who traditionally voted Democratic. The "Southern strategy" resulted in the failed nominations of Clement Haynsworth and G. Harrold Carswell, and the successful nomination of Lewis Powell.

Religion, Race, and Sex

Of the 147 people nominated to the Supreme Court, 145 have been white, 145 have been male, and 126 have been Protestant. The only African-Americans to date are Thurgood Marshall and Clarence Thomas; the sole females are Sandra Day O'Connor and Ruth Bader Ginsburg. Though it is often claimed that no Hispanics have served on the Court,[16] it is not clear why Benjamin Cardozo, a Sephardic Jew of Spanish heritage, should not count. Ethnically, virtually all of the white Protestant nominees have been Anglo-Saxon. Antonin Scalia was the first Italian-American. Of the twenty-one non-Protestants named to date, nine were Jewish, twelve Roman Catholic.[17]

The first Catholic named to the Court was Roger Taney, who was nominated, defeated, and renominated in 1835, and finally confirmed in

[15] Walter F. Murphy, *Elements of Judicial Strategy* (Chicago: University of Chicago Press, 1964), p. 76.

[16] E.g., O'Brien, *op. cit.*, n. 5, *supra*, p. 66; Stephen Wasby, *The Supreme Court in the Federal Judicial System* (Chicago: Nelson-Hall, 1988), p. 117. John Schmidhauser, who is the "dean" of studies of judicial backgrounds, also states that no Hispanics have served on the Court; instead, he labels Cardozo "Iberian." See his *Judges and Justices* (Boston: Little, Brown, 1979), p. 60. Our research indicates Schmidhauser's label to be accurate. Cardozo's family background is Spanish *and* Portuguese, and at the beginning of the twentieth century his family attended a Spanish-Portuguese synagogue. See George S. Hellman, *Benjamin N. Cardozo: American Judge* (New York: McGraw Hill, 1940), ch. 1.

[17] The numbers are based on nominations, not nominees. Thus Taney (Catholic) and Fortas (Jewish) are counted twice.

A focus on religious background is becoming increasingly fatuous. Justice Thomas, whom we count as a Protestant, was born of Protestant parents, raised a Roman Catholic, attended an Episcopalian church at the time of his nomination (thus our categorization), and has recently returned to Catholicism.

1836. A second Catholic, Edward White, was not named until 1894. Since then, for all but eight years, at least one Catholic has sat on the Court. Following Murphy's death in 1949, no Catholic sat until Brennan's appointment in 1956, which resulted in part from direct lobbying by Cardinal Spellman for a Catholic on the Court.[18] Three Catholics served simultaneously during the 1988 and 1989 terms: Brennan, Scalia, and Kennedy. A so-called Jewish seat existed from 1916, when Louis Brandeis was confirmed, until 1969 when Abe Fortas resigned. Douglas Ginsburg, who is Jewish, was nominated by Reagan in 1987 but withdrew following allegations that he smoked marijuana while on the faculty of Harvard Law School.[19] President Bush's choice of Clarence Thomas as Thurgood Marshall's successor did not surprise us. Indeed, we predicted as much on Marshall's statement at the end of the 1990 term that he would retire when a successor was confirmed.[20] It seems a virtual certainty that the Court will always count at least one woman among its number in the future.

Friendship and Patronage

Sometimes it's not what you know, it's whom you know. About three-fifths of those named to the Supreme Court personally knew the President who nominated them.[21] Most of Washington's appointees, for instance, had personal ties to him.[22] Harry Truman nominated four close friends: Harold Burton, Fred Vinson, Tom Clark, and Sherman Minton. Lyndon Johnson named his longtime crony, Abe Fortas, as associate justice and failed in his attempt to have him elevated to chief justice. Had Fortas been confirmed to the latter position, another friend of Johnson's, Homer Thornberry, would have been selected to fill Fortas's seat. Occasionally, though, the tie between President and potential nominee is not particularly close. Richard Nixon knew William Rehnquist from the latter's work at the Justice Department, but Nixon thought Rehnquist's

[18] David Alistair Yalof, *Pursuit of Justices* (Chicago: University of Chicago Press, 1999), ch. 3.

[19] Linda Greenhouse, "High Court Nominee Admits Using Marijuana and Calls It a Mistake," *New York Times*, November 6, 1987, p. 1; Linda Greenhouse, "Cabinet Official Advises Ginsburg to Give Up Quest," *New York Times*, November 7, 1987, p. 1.

[20] On News 12, a local Long Island television station, June 29, 1991.

[21] Updated from Robert Scigliano, *The Supreme Court and the Presidency* (New York: Free Press, 1971), p. 95.

[22] Henry Abraham, *Justices and Presidents*, 2nd ed. (New York: Oxford University Press, 1985), p. 72.

name was "Renchler" and referred to him in a prenomination taped conversation as a "clown."[23]

A position on the Supreme Court may also be used to pay political debts. In 1952, Earl Warren, seeing his chances for obtaining the Republican presidential nomination falter, threw his support and that of the California delegation to General Eisenhower rather than Eisenhower's rival, Senator Robert Taft of Ohio. One year later, Eisenhower nominated Governor Warren to replace Chief Justice Fred Vinson. Similarly, Kennedy's friend, Byron White, best known as an All-American football player, received a seat on the Supreme Court in 1962, two years after organizing Citizens for Kennedy-Johnson.

Explaining Presidential Choice

As the nomination of Byron White exemplifies, reasons almost always exist that can explain, after the fact, why a President chose a particular person. Far more difficult is the task of explaining a priori whom the President selects, or even the characteristics (e.g., ideology) of the nominee.

According to one analysis, Presidents interested in maintaining their popularity and prestige will attempt to avoid losing the confirmation battle, if at all possible.[24] Therefore, if one places the median senator, the President, and potential nominees on a liberal-conservative ideological spectrum, the President should always nominate someone in the space between himself and the Senate, rather than a nominee outside that range.

Presidents usually nominate individuals within this range, but occasionally they do not. One example is when a President has very strong policy concerns about the Court. If the Court is very liberal and the President is conservative, the President might attempt to balance the liberalism of the Court with someone more conservative than himself, even if that person locates outside the President-Senate interval. Similarly, if the Court is very conservative and the President is liberal, the President might attempt to balance the conservatism of the Court with a nominee more liberal than himself (and the Senate). Overall, a model

23 David Rosenbaum, "Tapes Say Nixon Saw Plot in Pentagon Papers' Release," *New York Times*, June 6, 1991, p. B11.

24 Charles Cameron, Albert D. Cover, and Jeffrey A. Segal, "Supreme Court Nominations and the Rational Presidency," paper presented at the 1990 annual meeting of the American Political Science Association, San Francisco.

using the ideology of the President, median senator, and Supreme Court explains 80 percent of the variance in the ideology of presidential nominees.

More recently, Moraski and Shipan argue that while the ideology of the President, the ideology of the median senator, and the ideology of the Court all should influence the type (ideology) of the person selected by the President, they should have different influences under different political regimes.[25] For example, if the President falls between the Senate and the median justice, only the President's ideology should matter, as the Senate prefers someone at the President's ideal point to the status quo. But if the Court median lies between the Senate and the President, then the President will be constrained by the Senate and only the Court median will matter.

While the previous two studies have attempted to explain the ideology of the person nominated, one recent work goes further and attempts to explain the actual person who is nominated.[26] Conditional on a short list gleaned from presidential papers and biographical sources, Presidents are more likely to choose colleagues[27] and those with political experience, but only during unified government. Alternatively, Presidents are more likely to choose a person with lower court experience during divided government. Additionally, ceteris paribus, the President is more likely to choose a person who hails from a large state if that state supported the President in the previous election. Perhaps due to the inherent selection effects in such a study, the authors find that copartisans are no more likely to be chosen than opposition party members.[28]

SENATE CONFIRMATION

Following nomination by the President, the American Bar Association (ABA) conducts its own inquiry of the nominee, rating him or her along

[25] Byron J. Moraski and Charles R. Shipan, "The Politics of Supreme Court Nominations: A Theory of Institutional Constraints and Choices," 43 *American Journal of Political Science* (1999), 1069.

[26] Christine Nemachek and Paul J. Wahlbeck, "The President's Choice of a Supreme Court Nominee," paper presented at the 1998 annual meeting of the Midwest Political Science Association, Chicago, Ill.

[27] The authors define a colleague as someone who served in the President's Cabinet, served with the President in Congress, or came from the President's state.

[28] Persons from the opposition party are undoubtedly less likely to make it onto the President's short list, and if they do, it may well be because they are ideologically aligned with the President despite partisan labels, e.g., Nixon and Powell.

a qualified/not qualified dimension. The ABA prescreened lower court appointees prior to nomination until President George W. Bush abolished the practice. It does not screen Supreme Court nominees until the President announces his choice.

The bar's involvement in Supreme Court nominations has been controversial. In 1969, it initially and unanimously ranked Haynsworth "highly qualified," then reconsidered and reaffirmed its judgment by a divided vote. In 1970, it labeled Carswell "qualified," though even his supporters thought him mediocre. For a short period of time following the Haynsworth debacle, the Nixon administration gave the ABA the right to prescreen potential nominees. This practice ended when ABA votes against potential nominees Mildred Lillie and Herschel Friday were leaked to the press. When Nixon nominated Lewis Powell and William Rehnquist in 1972, he did not apprize the ABA until after he had sent their names to the Senate Judiciary Committee. In 1975, President Ford gave the ABA a list of names that included John Paul Stevens, who received the committee's top ranking. Reagan discontinued the prescreening practice and gave the ABA no advance word on Sandra O'Connor. The committee found O'Connor "qualified," and Scalia and Rehnquist "highly qualified." Robert Bork received ten "highly qualified" votes, one vote "not opposed," and four votes "not qualified." Even before Anita Hill's sexual harassment charges, Clarence Thomas received but a "qualified" rating from twelve of the committee's fifteen members; two thought him unqualified, and one did not vote. Of twenty-three nominees, Thomas is the first who failed to receive at least a unanimous "qualified" rating or a majority superior rating.[29]

Following the submission of a nominee's name to the Senate, the Judiciary Committee holds hearings. The committee will hear testimony from the legal community, interest groups, and the nominee. Nominees did not appear before the committee prior to 1925, and the practice did not become established until the mid-1950s. Often nominees refuse to answer substantive legal questions because to do so would compromise their presumed open-mindedness when such cases came before the Court. This avoids the appearance of partiality, not partiality itself, for it is not clear why the communication of a prior view biases one less than a flat refusal to communicate one's position. Such silence, though, does serve

[29] "Thomas: The Least Qualified Nominee So Far?," *National Law Journal*, September 16, 1991, p. 5. Also see Neil A. Lewis, "A.B.A. Is Split on Fitness of Thomas for High Court," *New York Times*, August 28, 1991, p. A1.

to keep nominees out of political trouble. For instance, had nominee Souter stated his views on abortion, he would have instantly alienated half of the Senate. Nevertheless, the Judiciary Committee has generally recommended nominees who have refused to talk substance. Thus Clarence Thomas refused to admit that he had ever discussed the merits of *Roe v. Wade* with anyone at any time.

The great exception to strategic silence is the Bork nomination. Bork had criticized certain Supreme Court decisions so outspokenly that he could not avoid telling senators under oath what he had repeatedly told the rest of the world in articles and speeches. Though Bork attempted to assume a moderate stance at the hearings, his previous writings and speeches, some of which he made only weeks before his nomination, led many to believe that his moderation was part of a "confirmation conversion" that would not last once he joined the Court.

If the Judiciary Committee does not table a nomination, it goes to the full Senate for consideration. The nomination will be debated on the floor, and unless filibustered, as was the second Fortas nomination, the full chamber will vote on it. Confirmation requires a simple majority.

Of the 147 nominees whom the Senate considered through the end of the millennium, 122 (83 percent) have been confirmed. Not all of the 122 have served; seven declined their seat. Robert Harrison, for instance, declined Washington's appointment in order to become chancellor of Maryland, and John Jay declined reappointment due to the Court's low prestige.[30]

Of the twenty-seven rejections, the Senate formally repudiated twelve, failed to act on five, indefinitely postponed four, and forced the President to withdraw six.[31] We list the rejected nominees in Table 5.1.

To gain insight into the factors that lead to rejection, we take three approaches. First, we examine the five nominations that failed between 1968 and 1999, along with the almost-failed nomination of Clarence Thomas in 1991. Then, we conduct a systematic analysis of the factors affecting rejection since 1789. Finally, we examine the roll-call votes of senators between the nomination of Earl Warren in 1953 and Stephen Breyer in 1994.

[30] Elder Witt, ed., *The Supreme Court and Its Work* (Washington: Congressional Quarterly, 1981), pp. 4, 74.

[31] The six withdrawn candidates include Daniel Ginsburg, who withdrew because of misgivings as much within the Reagan administration as within the Senate.

TABLE 5.1. *Rejected Supreme Court Nominees*

Name	President	Year[a]	Vote
John Rutledge	Washington	1795	10–14
Alexander Wolcott	Madison	1811	9–24
John Crittenden	J. Q. Adams	1828	Postponed
Roger Taney	Jackson	1835	Postponed
John Spencer	Tyler	1844	21–26
Reuben Walworth	Tyler	1844	Withdrawn
Edward King	Tyler	1844	Postponed
Edward King	Tyler	1844	Withdrawn
John Read	Tyler	1845	No action
George Woodward	Polk	1845	20–29
Edward Bradford	Fillmore	1852	No action
George Badger	Fillmore	1853	Postponed
William Micou	Fillmore	1853	No action
Jeremiah Black	Buchanan	1861	25–26
Henry Stanbery	Johnson	1866	No action
Ebenezer Hoar	Grant	1869	24–33
George Williams	Grant	1873	Withdrawn
Caleb Cushing	Grant	1874	Withdrawn
Stanley Matthews	Hayes	1881	No action
William Hornblower	Cleveland	1893	24–30
Wheeler Peckham	Cleveland	1894	32–41
John Parker	Hoover	1930	39–41
Abe Fortas[b]	Johnson	1968	45–43[c]
Clement Haynsworth	Nixon	1969	45–55
G. Harrold Carswell	Nixon	1970	45–51
Robert Bork	Reagan	1987	42–58
Douglas Ginsburg	Reagan	1987	Withdrawn

[a] Year is year nominated.

[b] Fortas's rejection led to the withdrawal of the nomination of Homer Thornberry, who was to take Fortas's place as associate justice.

[c] Vote on cloture failed to reach two thirds' majority. Nomination subsequently withdrawn.

The Case Studies

Between 1930 and 1967, Presidents nominated twenty-four consecutive persons to the Supreme Court without a single rejection. Thereafter, the Senate rejected five of the next fifteen nominees. We examine the five rejections in sequence.

Abe Fortas

Following Lyndon Johnson's theft of the Democratic Senate nomination in the Texas primary in 1948,[32] he called on attorney Abe Fortas to prevent a legal maneuver by his opponent, former Governor Coke Stevenson, to keep Johnson off the November ballot. Fortas's successful efforts resulted in a close personal and professional relationship that culminated in Johnson's naming Fortas to the Supreme Court in 1965. Fortas remained a close adviser of Johnson's while on the Court. According to one report, "few important Presidential problems are settled without an opinion from Mr. Justice Fortas."[33]

In June 1968, Chief Justice Warren announced his retirement from the Court, effective at Johnson's pleasure. Johnson declared that the retirement would not take effect until "such time as a successor is qualified."[34] This in essence told the Senate that if they didn't approve Warren's successor, Warren would simply stay on as chief justice, but it also allowed Senate opponents to claim that no actual vacancy existed. Ironically, Fortas may have suggested the contingent retirement scenario to Johnson.[35]

Johnson named Fortas to replace Warren, and another Johnson crony, Homer Thornberry, to occupy Fortas's place as associate justice.

The timing of the vacancy worked against Fortas. By the summer of 1968 a presidential election was only months away. In and out of Washington, Johnson's popularity was plummeting. Republicans and Southern Democrats had every reason to believe that if they defeated the Fortas nomination, Richard Nixon would make the new appointment. Historically, Supreme Court nominees have fared poorly during the fourth year of a President's term in office. Johnson was particularly weak during his fourth year because he had already announced his decision not to seek a second term. Presidential threats would not be effective; presidential promises could not be kept.

The second factor to work against the nomination was Fortas's and the Warren Court's liberal ideology. In his four terms, Fortas had supported the liberal position in civil liberties cases over 80 percent of the

[32] Robert A. Caro, *The Years of Lyndon Johnson: Means of Ascent* (New York: Knopf, 1990), chs. 13–16.

[33] *Newsweek*, July 8, 1968, p. 18.

[34] "Warren-Johnson Letters," *New York Times*, June 27, 1968, p. A30.

[35] John Massaro, *Supremely Political* (New York: State University of New York, 1990), p. 41.

time, aligning himself with a bloc that included Warren, Douglas, Marshall, and Brennan.[36] Members of the Judiciary Committee during the hearings grilled Fortas about liberal decisions he had rendered,[37] and even for some that antedated his tenure.[38]

The third factor to work against the promotion of Fortas concerned a matter of ethics. The hearings disclosed that he had accepted a £15,000 fee for teaching a nine-week seminar at American University. The money was raised by Fortas's former law partner, Paul Porter, from wealthy businessmen involved in litigation that could come before the Supreme Court. Additionally, some senators questioned the propriety of Fortas's close relationship with Johnson. These considerations enabled conservative senators to oppose Fortas without appearing partisan.[39]

The motion to confirm Fortas never came up for a direct vote because of a filibuster on the Senate floor. The vote to invoke cloture shows the influence that ideology had on the nomination. The simple correlation between the support scores of senators compiled by Americans for Democratic Action (ADA), which measures how liberal senators vote, and their vote to invoke cloture is 0.79. Though there were forty-five votes to invoke cloture and only forty-three opposed, this was far less than the two thirds then needed to end Senate debate. With a direct vote on Fortas precluded, Johnson withdrew the nomination.

Clement Haynsworth

Following Richard Nixon's election, Warren announced his unconditional resignation at the end of the 1968 term. On May 21, 1969, Nixon named Warren Burger to replace him. Burger was confirmed on June 9 with little controversy. Meanwhile, a *Life* magazine story in May 1969 disclosed that in 1966 Fortas had accepted £20,000 as part of an annual "consulting" fee from Louis Wolfson, a millionaire businessman later convicted of stock manipulations. Though Fortas returned the money

[36] Jeffrey A. Segal and Harold J. Spaeth, "Decisional Trends on the Warren and Burger Courts: Results from the Supreme Court Data Base Project," 73 *Judicature* (1989) 103.

[37] E.g., *Brown v. Louisiana*, 383 U.S. 131 (1966), which vacated the breach of peace conviction of blacks engaged in a stand-in at a segregated library.

[38] *Mallory v. United States*, 354 U.S. 449 (1957), which overturned the conviction and death sentence of an alleged rapist who confessed after a seven-hour unarraigned interrogation. Mallory was subsequently convicted of another rape in 1960, and died in a shootout with police following yet another rape in 1972.

[39] Donald Songer, "The Relevance of Policy Values for the Confirmation of Supreme Court Nominees," 13 *Law and Society Review* 927 (1979).

and accepted no future handouts from Wolfson, the ensuing controversy forced him to resign.

On August 18, 1969, Nixon chose Circuit Court of Appeals Judge Clement Haynsworth, a Democrat from South Carolina, to replace Fortas. The selection of Haynsworth was part of Nixon's "Southern strategy," by which he hoped to win the votes of conservative white Southern Democrats in 1972.

Haynsworth at first appeared certain of confirmation. Though the Democrats controlled the Senate, a working majority of Republicans and conservative Southern Democrats existed. Confidence in Haynsworth began to erode when Judiciary Committee hearings focused on cases decided by Haynsworth in which he had a direct financial interest. One case concerned parties who had direct business dealings with a company in which he had a substantial stake. In another, Haynsworth bought stock in a company after deciding a case involving the company but before the decision was announced. While Haynsworth gained but few dollars from these decisions, his behavior made him an easy target for one nominated to restore high ethical standards.

Similar to the Fortas case, Haynsworth's ideological opponents viewed the ethics charges as most serious. Liberals alleged that Haynsworth had compiled an antiunion, anti–civil rights record as an appellate judge. On the union front, Haynsworth had ruled that businesses could shut down specific factories solely for the purpose of punishing union activity.[40] He also ruled that unions could not use authorization cards as a means to determine whether it had the support of a majority of a company's employees.[41] As for civil rights, Haynsworth had allowed private hospitals receiving federal funds to discriminate racially.[42] He also upheld "freedom of choice" school plans, where students were allowed to choose the schools they would attend with the inevitable result that the schools remained segregated.[43]

Liberal opposition to Haynsworth produced vigorous lobbying. On November 21, 1969, the Senate rejected Haynsworth by a vote of 55 to 45. According to Nixon aide John Ehrlichman, Haynsworth "was not confirmed because of a highly expert, expensive and intensive lobbying campaign by organized labor and civil rights groups."[44] The correlation

[40] *Darlington Manufacturing Company v. NLRB*, 325 F.2d 682 (1963).
[41] *N.L.R.B. v. S.S. Logan Packing Company*, 386 F.2d 562 (1967).
[42] *Simkins v. Moses H. Cone Memorial Hospital*, 323 F.2d 959 (1964).
[43] *Green v. County School Board*, 372 F.2d 338 (1967).
[44] Quoted in Massaro, *op. cit.*, n. 35, *supra*, p. 22.

between ADA scores and the votes supporting Haynsworth was −0.79.

G. Harrold Carswell

In angry reaction to Haynsworth's defeat, Nixon nominated G. Harrold Carswell, a little-known federal judge from Florida who had graduated from a local Southern law school. So poorly qualified was he that the Dean of the Yale Law School was moved to declare that he "presents more slender credentials than any nominee put forth this century."[45] Carswell was reversed significantly more frequently – 40 percent – than the average district court judge in the Fifth Circuit, the circuit in which he served.[46] So deficient were Carswell's qualifications that his Senate floor leader, Roman Hruska (R-Neb.), declared, "Even if he were mediocre, there are a lot of mediocre judges, and people and lawyers. They are entitled to a little representation, aren't they, and a little chance."[47] Even Nixon administration insiders considered him a "boob" and a "dummy."[48]

Carswell's record as a federal judge and as a private citizen made him far more suspect on civil rights than Haynsworth. One of his decisions delaying implementation of desegregation explicitly deviated from higher court rulings; another made it virtually impossible to challenge segregation in public reform schools.[49] In 1956, Carswell, then a United States attorney, had helped transform a public golf club built with federal funds into a private club in order to avoid desegregation. While a U.S. attorney, he also helped charter a Florida State University booster club with membership limited to "any white person." But the most damaging blow to Carswell's candidacy occurred when a Florida television station found film of a 1948 speech in which he declared, "I yield to no man as a fellow candidate or as a fellow citizen in the firm vigorous belief in the principles of White Supremacy, and I shall always be so governed."[50] The defense of Carswell continued, though. William Rehnquist, then an assistant attorney general, later commented that Carswell's support for white

[45] U.S. Senate, *Hearings on the Nomination of G. Harrold Carswell, of Florida, to Be Associate Justice of the Supreme Court of the United States*, 91st Congress, 2nd Session, 1970, p. 242.

[46] Massaro, *op. cit.*, n. 35, *supra*, p. 6.

[47] Warren Weaver, Jr., "Carswell Nomination Attacked and Defended as Senate Opens Debate on Nomination," *New York Times*, March 17, 1970, p. A21.

[48] Massaro, *op. cit.*, n. 35, *supra*, p. 116. [49] *Id.*, pp. 3–4.

[50] *New York Times*, "Excerpts from Carswell Talk," January 22, 1970, p. A22.

supremacy amounted to no more than "some rather thin evidence of personal hostility toward blacks."[51]

Given the case against Carswell, the vote against him was surprisingly close, 51 to 45. More than two thirds of the Republicans supported Carswell, as did fewer than a third of the Democrats. The correlation between ADA scores and pro-Carswell voting was −0.84. If Nixon had had a Republican Senate majority, Carswell would have been confirmed.

Robert Bork

As noted at the beginning of the chapter, President Reagan nominated Bork to the seat vacated by the retirement of Justice Powell in 1987. Bork first came to public attention on October 20, 1973, when as Solicitor General he fired Watergate Special Prosecutor Archibald Cox at President Nixon's request after Attorney General Elliott Richardson and Deputy Attorney General William Ruckleshaus had refused to do so. Richardson resigned in protest of Nixon's order; Ruckleshaus was fired for refusing to obey. Bork executed Nixon's order, which later became known as the Saturday Night Massacre.

The turning point in Bork's confirmation came not in 1987 when he was nominated, but in 1986 when partisan control of the Senate switched from the Republicans to the Democrats. Reagan had worked feverishly to retain Republican control of the Senate. At campaign stops in Missouri and Alabama, he echoed concerns he first raised in North Carolina:

> Today, Senators Strom Thurmond and Jim Broyhill are in a majority on the Senate Judiciary Committee, overseeing judicial appointments. Without Jim Broyhill and a Republican Senate majority, that job will be turned over to Teddy Kennedy and Joe Biden.... You can strike a blow against drugs, thugs and hoodlums by casting your vote for Jim and keeping him as a force for law and order in the United States Senate. The future of our country, its safety and security, is in our hands.[52]

On November 4, 1986, the Democratic Party won twenty of thirty-four open Senate seats, taking a decisive 55-to-45 majority. Behind a huge black vote, Democrats won Republican seats in Alabama, Florida, Georgia, and North Carolina.[53]

[51] Massaro, *op. cit.*, n. 35, *supra*, p. 109.
[52] "Reagan Aims Fire at Liberal Judges," *New York Times*, October 9, 1986, p. A32.
[53] Lena Williams, "Blacks Cast Pivotal Ballots in Four Key Senate Races, Data Show," *New York Times*, November 6, 1986, p. A33.

On the day of Bork's nomination, Ted Kennedy set the tone for the campaign to follow:

> Robert Bork's America is a land in which women would be forced into back alley abortions, blacks would sit at segregated lunch counters, rogue police could break down citizen's doors in midnight raids, writers and artists could be censored at the whim of the government, and the doors of the federal courts would be shut on the fingers of millions of citizens.[54]

Interest groups opposed to Bork joined the fray. The People for the American Way, the Women's Legal Defense Fund, the Alliance for Justice, and the National Abortion Rights Action League immediately went on the attack. The AFL-CIO joined the anti-Bork forces in August 1987 along with the American Civil Liberties Union, which dropped its fifty-one-year-old policy of noninvolvement in Supreme Court nominations. Planned Parenthood ran advertisements that read, "State controlled pregnancy? It's not as far fetched as it sounds. Carrying Bork's position to its logical end, states could not ban or require any method of birth control, impose family quotas for population purposes, make abortion a crime, or sterilize anyone they choose."[55]

Opponents' allegations stemmed from Bork's published writings on and off the bench. In 1963, Bork declared that the proposed Civil Rights Act, which prohibited race discrimination in places of public accommodations, invoked a "principle of unsurpassed ugliness."[56] Most of the fodder, though, came from a 1971 article in which Bork criticized Supreme Court rulings that created a right to privacy, struck down prohibitions on the use of birth control by married people, voided state court enforcement of racial covenants, and declared unconstitutional malapportioned state legislative districts.[57] He also argued that the equal protection clause of the Fourteenth Amendment should be limited to racial discrimination, to the exclusion, for instance, of sexual discrimination, and that the First Amendment is entirely inapplicable to scientific, literary, or artistic speech.[58]

[54] James Reston, "Kennedy and Bork," *New York Times*, July 5, 1987, sec. 4, p. 15.

[55] "Robert Bork's Position on Reproductive Rights," *New York Times*, September 13, 1987, p. B9.

[56] Robert Bork, "Civil Rights – A Challenge," *The New Republic*, August 31, 1963, p. 22.

[57] Robert Bork, "Neutral Principles and Some First Amendment Problems," 47 *Indiana Law Journal* 1 (1971), at 8–11, 15–17, 18–19.

[58] *Id.* at 11–12, 20–35.

During the Judiciary Committee hearings Bork repudiated many of his previous views. He did not, however, recant his views on the right to privacy. Moreover, his newly found moderation was seen as part of a "confirmation conversion," which impeached his credibility without softening his right-wing image.

Public pressure on the Senate to vote against Bork was enormous. Senator John Breaux (D-La.), who was first elected in 1986, told the *New York Times* that "many Southern Democrats were elected by black votes and that his black supporters were making the Bork vote a 'litmus test' issue. 'You can't vote maybe.' "[59] Constituent pressure was so great that even John Stennis, onetime leader of Southern segregationists, voted against Bork.

Bork was defeated by a 58-to-42 vote. Ideology played a huge role – the correlation between ADA scores and the confirmation vote was –0.83, but so did partisanship and interest group pressure.[60] Because of constituent pressure, the anti-Bork coalition included moderate and conservative Southern Democrats who otherwise might have supported him. Some 96 percent of the Democrats opposed Bork, while 87 percent of the Republicans supported him.

Douglas Ginsburg

During the floundering Bork campaign, President Reagan threatened to nominate someone liberals would abhor just as much as Bork if Bork were rejected.[61] He attempted to accomplish that with the nomination of Douglas Ginsburg, a former Harvard Law Professor who had served for fourteen months on the District of Columbia Circuit Court of Appeals. Unfortunately for Ginsburg's opponents, he had left no paper trail that tied him to unpopular views, à la Bork. A potential scandal inhered in a Ginsburg vote on a cable television contract decided while Ginsburg held $140,000 in another cable company directly benefited by the ruling. That story soon became secondary when Nina Totenberg of National Public Radio reported that Ginsburg smoked marijuana with some of his students while at Harvard. The antidrug, anticrime, "just

[59] Steven Roberts, "White House Says Bork Lacks Votes for Confirmation," *New York Times*, September 26, 1987, p. 1.

[60] On interest group influence, see Gregory A. Caldeira and John R. Wright, "Lobbying for Justice: Organized Interests, Supreme Court Nominations, and the United States Senate," 42 *American Journal of Political Science* 499 (1998).

[61] *New York Times*, October 14, 1987, p. A1.

say 'no'" administration quickly dropped its support of the nominee, who then asked Reagan not to forward his nomination to the Senate.

Clarence Thomas

Though the Senate narrowly confirmed Clarence Thomas, his confirmation battle evidences the crucial variables associated with the five rejected nominees: ideologically motivated opposition spurred by serious questions as to the nominee's qualifications.

At the end of the 1990 Supreme Court term, Thurgood Marshall announced his intent to retire at such point that a successor was confirmed to take his place.[62] Marshall, a towering figure as a litigator for the NAACP Legal Defense Fund, Inc., influenced the Court more before he became a justice than after. He made history as a member of the Court more for what he was – the first African-American to sit on the tribunal – than for anything he did while there. Faced with replacing him, President Bush quickly nominated Clarence Thomas to the Court. In reply to charges that Bush nominated Thomas because he was black, Bush responded that Thomas was "the best man for the job on the merits. And the fact that he's a minority, so much the better."[63]

Clarence Thomas was an outspoken conservative who curried favor in the Reagan and Bush administrations by speaking forcefully against affirmative action. Under Reagan he served as director of the civil rights office in the Department of Education and then as Chairman of the Equal Employment Opportunity Commission (EEOC). President Bush nominated him to the United States Circuit Court for the District of Columbia, the same Court on which Warren Burger, Antonin Scalia, Robert Bork, and Daniel Ginsburg served prior to their Supreme Court nominations.

Liberal interest groups immediately expressed concern about his Supreme Court nomination. Civil rights groups were alarmed by his long opposition to affirmative action. Indeed, the NAACP executive board voted unanimously, with one abstention, to oppose the nominee. Women's groups were outraged by a speech in which Thomas seemingly endorsed using the Constitution to outlaw abortion. Senior citizens

62 As the Thomas confirmation dragged on, Marshall chose to retire rather than serve into the 1991 term.

63 John E. Yang and Sharon LaFraniere, "Bush Picks Thomas for Supreme Court," *Washington Post*, July 2, 1991, p. A1, at A6.

complained that Thomas let over 1,000 age discrimination suits lapse during his tenure at EEOC.

Moreover, Thomas's qualifications came increasingly under question. Though Thomas had graduated from Yale Law School, university officials admitted that he was admitted only because of the school's affirmative action program,[64] the same sort of program Thomas now condemned. Thomas's career on the federal bench was short (one and a half years) and undistinguished. As noted above, the ABA could do no better than give him a rating of "qualified."

At the first round of confirmation hearings, Thomas attempted a middle ground between the stonewall of Souter and the conversion of Bork. Thomas refused to state where he stood on abortion and even tried to suggest that he had never really thought about the issue. Yet at the same time he tried to disown his previous statements on fetal rights. He also, for the first time in his career, managed to praise affirmative action programs. This, of course, led to Democratic charges of a Bork-like confirmation conversion.

Not the conservative ideology, nor the interest group opposition, nor the questions of qualifications were enough to bring Thomas down. Four days before the scheduled October 8 vote, only about forty senators opposed the nominee. Then, on October 6, Timothy Phelps of *Newsday*[65] and Nina Totenberg of National Public Radio reported that a law school professor in Oklahoma, Anita Hill, told Senate Judiciary Committee staffers that Thomas sexually harassed her in the early 1980s while she worked for him at the Department of Education and later at the EEOC. Hill, who had spoken to the committee on condition of confidentiality, was drawn out by the media after someone on or working for the committee leaked the story.

The Senate delayed the vote for a week in order to give the Judiciary Committee time to consider the charges. It would take a book-length manuscript to recount the charges and countercharges leveled at the hearings. Most persuasive from Hill's side was the fact that she told several people of the alleged harassment at the time it occurred. Most persuasive from Thomas's side was the fact that Hill never filed a complaint against Thomas at the time and actually followed him from the Department of Education to the EEOC.

[64] "Judge Thomas Takes the Stand," *New York Times*, September 8, 1991, sec. 4, p. 18.

[65] "The Thomas Charge: Law Prof Told FBI That He Sexually Harassed Her at EEOC," *New York Times*, October 6, 1991, p. 7.

Democrats and Republicans treated the hearings quite differently from one another. "The Democrats made a pass at figuring out what had happened in the case. The Republicans tried to win. While the Democrats were pronouncing themselves flummoxed by two diametrically opposing stories, the Republicans had already launched a scorched-earth strategy against Professor Hill."[66] Bush himself endorsed the policy to attack Hill.[67] Thus Arlen Specter (R-Pa.) charged Hill with committing perjury; Orrin Hatch (R-Utah) accused her of concocting her story in coordination with liberal interest groups; and Alan Simpson (R-Wyo.) even questioned her sexual proclivities.[68] The Democrats, either not understanding that the Republicans were playing hardball or unable to compete in the game, never asked Thomas about his alleged penchant for watching pornographic movies, which would have corroborated part of Hill's testimony; didn't call other witnesses who claimed that Thomas had harassed them; and didn't introduce into evidence the positive results of Hill's lie detector test.[69]

The final vote for Thomas was 52 to 48. Again, charges relating to the qualifications of the nominee were acted upon only by those ideologically opposed to the nominee: The correlation between ADA scores and the vote on the Thomas nomination was –0.81. Partisanship was similarly in evidence: forty-one of forty-three Republicans supported Thomas; forty-six of fifty-seven Democrats opposed him. These five rejections, plus Thomas, lead to the following tentative conclusions. First, the probability of rejection is greatest when the President is in a weak position. Every rejection occurred either when the nominating President was in the fourth year of his term of office or when his party did not control the Senate. Second, qualifications play a crucial role in confirmation politics. Every rejected nominee, with the possible exception of Bork, confronted a serious question of ethics or competence. Third, the role of qualifications is largely interactive. Lack of qualifications leads only ideologically opposed Senators to vote against the

66 Maureen Dowd, "Going Nasty Early Helps G.O.P. Gain Edge on Thomas," *New York Times*, October 15, 1991, p. A1.

67 Andrew Rosenthal, "White House Role in Thomas Defense," *New York Times*, October 14, 1991, p. A1.

68 Anthony Lewis, "Time of the Assassins," *New York Times*, October 14, 1991, p. A19; William Safire, "The Plot to Savage Thomas," *New York Times*, October 14, 1991, p. A19.

69 That lie detectors are not allowed as courtroom evidence is largely irrelevant. Hearsay is generally not allowed, either; yet no objections to hearsay were raised during the committee hearings.

nominee. Fourth, electoral politics influence confirmation voting. Interest groups and constituents have an impact.

These conclusions are tentative, as they are based only on case studies of rejected nominees. To assess the impact of these and other variables on confirmation voting, we turn to more systematic analyses. We start with an aggregate analysis that examines confirmation decisions since 1789. Because we lack reliable information about relevant variables for many eighteenth- and nineteenth-century nominees, we supplement the aggregate analysis with an individual-level focus on the votes of senators, starting with the nomination of Earl Warren.

An Aggregate Analysis

From 1789 through 2000, some 147 people have been nominated to the Supreme Court,[70] of whom the Senate has confirmed 122 (83 percent). Published research suggests that the Senate's decision to confirm particular nominees can be explained by partisan and institutional politics between the Senate, on the one hand, and the President or the Court, on the other.[71]

From this framework we test several hypotheses about the confirmation process. First, a pro-Senate bias should manifest itself rather simply; namely, the Senate should be more likely to confirm those nominees who are U.S. senators than those who are not.

Second, an anti-President bias should most likely surface under divided government, which, for our purposes, occurs when the President's party does not control the Senate (e.g., Reagan and Bork, Nixon and Haynsworth/Carswell), and during the fourth year of the President's term of office (e.g., Johnson and Fortas), except for the period between reelection and the start of a new term. Presidents in the fourth year are likely to have minimal influence over senators of either party.

A President's strength may also depend on his electoral base. For instance, one presidential scholar has found moderate relationships

[70] As mentioned in note 8, this list excludes William Paterson, whose nomination was withdrawn by President Washington so that Paterson could officially resign from the Senate, and Homer Thornberry, whose nomination for associate justice became moot when the Senate refused to promote Abe Fortas to chief justice. It does include Douglas Ginsburg, who was nominated, but whose name was never officially forwarded to the Senate. Ginsburg asked President Reagan not to forward his name after revelations that Ginsburg had smoked marijuana while a professor at Harvard Law School.

[71] Jeffrey A. Segal, "Senate Confirmation of Supreme Court Justices: Partisan and Institutional Politics," 49 *Journal of Politics* 998 (1987).

between a President's electoral strength in a congressional member's home district and the congressional member's support for the President's policies.[72] If this relationship also holds for the Senate, then the larger the President's previous electoral victory, the more likely his nominees are to be confirmed. Although the President and vice-president are elected as a team, the electoral coalition may not remain loyal if the vice-president succeeds to office through the death or resignation of the President. Thus, elected Presidents should more readily secure confirmation of their nominees than succession Presidents. John Tyler, for instance, the successor to William Henry Harrison, failed in four consecutive attempts to secure confirmation of his nominees.

While the Senate might add to its prestige by confirming one of its own, it may particularly damage the President by rejecting those closest to him, such as members of his cabinet. Similarly, an anti-Court motivation can manifest itself by a refusal to promote an associate justice to chief justice (e.g., Fortas).

We begin with a bivariate analysis of our hypotheses. First, we find little independent support for a pro-Senate bias in confirmation voting. The Senate has confirmed eight out of nine of its own (89 percent), but this proportion is virtually indistinguishable from the 81 percent of nonsenators whom the Senate has confirmed.

Substantial support is found for antipresidential motivations, however. Only 56 percent of nominees (14 of 25) have been confirmed in the fourth year of a President's term, versus 87 percent in the first three years (106 of 122). Similarly, the Senate has confirmed only 59 percent of nominees under divided government (23 of 39), as compared with 90 percent when the President's party controlled the Senate (97 of 108). Additionally, elected Presidents appear to fare substantially better (86 percent) than succession Presidents (53 percent). Nevertheless, such success does not depend on the size of the President's electoral coalition. The correlation between the percent of the President's electoral college vote and Senate approval or disapproval is slightly negative, –0.15. Nominees politically close to the President fare especially poorly: 29 percent of current Cabinet members have been rejected versus only 17 percent of non-Cabinet nominees.

Finally, the simple relationship between promotion from associate justice to chief justice lacks strength. Some 82 percent of nonjustices have

[72] George C. Edwards, *Presidential Influence in Congress* (San Francisco: W. H. Freeman, 1980).

TABLE 5.2. *Logit Estimates of Aggregate Confirmation Votes*

Variable	Maximum likelihood estimate	Standard error	Significance level[a]	Impact
U.S. Senate	0.07	1.38	n.s.	–
Fourth year	−1.56	0.58	0.01	−0.034
Divided	−1.91	0.61	0.01	−0.042
Succession	−0.055	0.69	n.s.	–
Electoral College	−0.001	0.01	n.s.	–
Cabinet	−1.54	0.66	0.01	−0.33
AJ to CJ	−1.80	0.99	0.05	−0.40
Constant	4.03	0.92	0.01	0.98[b]

Notes: Percent reduction in error: 30.
[a] N.s. = not significant.
[b] Probability of confirmation when all independent variables equal zero.

been confirmed, as compared with only 71 percent of promoted associate justices.

To determine the independent impact of each variable while controlling for all other variables, we conduct a logit analysis of the 147 aggregate-level Senate confirmation decisions. The dependent variable is whether the Senate confirms a particular nominee; the independent variables are the factors specified above. Table 5.2 presents the results.

The results include the "impact," or substantive significance, of each variable. This is calculated by measuring the difference in the probability of confirmation when that variable is present as opposed to its absence. We measure the impact from a baseline of a 0.82 prior probability of confirmation, the mean confirmation rate.[73] For instance, divided government decreases by 0.42 the probability of a nominee's confirmation, while the fourth year of a President's term lowers the probability of confirmation by 0.34. These are clearly substantial effects.

The results indicate a fair degree of support for the aggregate confirmation model. Four out of the seven variables in the model reach statistical significance. Overall, the model predicts 87 percent of the

[73] Because the logit model is nonlinear, the impact on predicted probabilities will vary based on starting points. Moreover, the nonlinearity means that we cannot simply add together the impact of more than one variable from the same baseline.

confirmation votes correctly, for a 30 percent reduction in error.[74] In addition to divided government and fourth-year effects, nomination from the President's Cabinet and promotion from associate justice to chief justice substantially lowers the likelihood of confirmation, as predicted.

The model, of course, distorts reality to some extent. We treat Senate confirmation votes as single units when in fact they consist of as many as 100 individual voters, each of whom faces a distinct decision calculus. Additionally, crucial factors that might influence confirmation votes, such as the ideology or qualifications of the nominee, are excluded. Because of data limitations, we cannot measure such factors for all confirmation votes. Nevertheless, we can measure most of the factors that influence confirmation from the nomination of Earl Warren in 1953 to that of Stephen Breyer in 1994.

An Individual-Level Analysis

Any examination of the individual votes of senators must begin with an explanation of their motivations. First and foremost, senators should be concerned with reelection. Though it may be too much to claim that senators are "single-minded seekers of reelection," to use David Mayhew's description of U.S. representatives,[75] one cannot long enjoy the perquisites of Senate life if one's roll-call behavior systematically antagonizes one's constituents.

Scientific analyses of confirmation voting usually suggest that public concern over nominees turns on the nominees' perceived judicial ideology and perceived qualifications. Ideologically proximate nominees should be perceived as attractive; poorly qualified nominees unattractive; and ideologically distant and poorly qualified nominees very unattractive.

Beyond these factors, the President may take an active role in the confirmation process, particularly if the confirmation becomes controversial. The President will generally have more political resources to deploy and can use them more effectively when his party controls the Senate and when he is not in the final year of his term. In addition, presidential

[74] The percent reduction in error statistic compares the error rate from the model to the error rate by predicting the modal value every time.

[75] *Congress: The Electoral Connection* (New Haven: Yale University Press, 1974), p. 17.

resources are likely to impact members of his own party more than those of the other party. We also include the President's popularity, which has been extensively linked to executive success in the legislative arena.[76]

Finally, we account for organized interest groups, representing as they do more active citizens and potential campaign contributions. Historical evidence clearly indicates that lobbying has influenced the confirmation process. For example, Peter Fish argues that the rejection of Judge Parker in 1930 was due in large part to the activity of organized labor and the NAACP.[77] The nomination of Haynsworth brought forth a torrent of interest group activity, which in turn was exceeded by the almost frenetic mobilization of groups during the Bork nomination.

Data and Variables

The dependent variable consists of the 2,451 confirmation votes cast by individual senators from the nomination of Earl Warren through the nomination of Stephen Breyer.

Nominee Ideology and Qualifications

To determine perceptions of nominees' qualifications and judicial philosophy, we use a content analysis from statements in newspaper editorials from the time of the nomination until the Senate voted.[78] The analysis used four of the nation's leading papers, two with a liberal stance, the *New York Times* and the *Washington Post*, and two with a more conservative outlook, the *Chicago Tribune* and the *Los Angeles Times*. Table 5.3 reports the results. Qualifications range from 0 (most unqualified) to 1 (most qualified). Ideology ranges from 0 (extremely conservative) to 1 (extremely liberal).

As indicated elsewhere, the data are reliable and appear to be valid.[79] The ideology scores meet the strictest test for validity, predictive validity. As we demonstrate in Chapter 8, the ideology scores correlate at 0.79 with the overall ideological direction of the votes the approved nominees later cast on the Court.

[76] George C. Edwards, *At the Margins: Presidential Leadership of Congress* (New Haven: Yale University Press, 1989).

[77] "Spite Nominations to the United States Supreme Court: Herbert Hoover, Owen J. Roberts, and the Politics of Presidential Vengeance in Retrospect," 77 *Kentucky Law Journal* 545 (1989).

[78] Charles M. Cameron, Albert D. Cover, and Jeffrey A. Segal, "Senate Voting on Supreme Court Nominees: A Neoinstitutional Model," 84 *American Political Science Review* 525 (1990).

[79] *Id.*

TABLE 5.3. *Nominee Margin, Vote Status, Ideology, and Qualifications*

Nominee	Year	Pres's Status[a]	Margin	Qual[b]	Ideol[c]
Warren	1954	Strong	96–0[d]	0.74	0.75
Harlan	1955	Weak	71–11	0.86	0.88
Brennan	1957	Weak	95–0[d]	1.00	1.00
Whittaker	1957	Weak	96–0	1.00	0.50
Stewart	1959	Weak	70–17	1.00	0.75
White	1962	Strong	100–0[d]	0.50	0.50
Goldberg	1962	Strong	100–0[d]	0.92	0.75
Fortas, 1st time	1965	Strong	100–0[d]	1.00	1.00
Marshall	1967	Strong	69–11	0.84	1.00
Fortas, 2nd time	1968	Weak	45–43[e]	0.64	0.85
Burger	1969	Weak	74–3	0.96	0.12
Haynsworth	1969	Weak	45–55	0.34	0.16
Carswell	1970	Weak	45–51	0.11	0.04
Blackmun	1970	Weak	94–0	0.97	0.12
Powell	1971	Weak	89–1	1.00	0.17
Rehnquist, 1st time	1971	Weak	68–26	0.89	0.05
Stevens	1975	Weak	98–0	0.96	0.25
O'Connor	1981	Strong	99–0	1.00	0.48
Rehnquist, 2nd time	1986	Strong	65–33	0.40	0.05
Scalia	1986	Strong	98–0	1.00	0.00
Bork	1987	Weak	42–58	0.79	0.10
Kennedy	1988	Weak	97–0	0.89	0.37
Souter	1990	Weak	90–9	0.77	0.33
Thomas	1991	Weak	52–48	0.41	0.16
Ginsburg	1993	Strong	96–3	1.00	0.68
Breyer	1994	Strong	87–9	0.55	0.48

[a] The President is labeled "Strong" in a non-election year in which the President's party controls the Senate, and "Weak" otherwise.
[b] Qualifications [Qual] are measured from 0.00 (least qualified) to 1.00 (most qualified).
[c] Ideology [Ideol] is measured from 0.00 (most conservative) to 1.00 (most liberal).
[d] Voice vote.
[e] Vote on cloture – failed to receive necessary two-thirds' majority.
Source: Updated from Cameron, Cover, and Segal, "Senate Voting on Supreme Court Nominees: A Neoinstitutional Model," 84 *American Political Science Review* 526 (1990).

Ideological Distance

Ideological distance is the absolute value of the distance between nominee ideology and the senator's ideology.[80]

[80] To do this we first divide ADA scores by 100, which puts the scores on a 0 to 1 scale. While the scaling analysis by Cameron, Cover, and Segal (1990) suggests a further

Presidential Strength and Same Party Status

We measure presidential strength as a dummy variable that takes the value "1" when the President's party controls the Senate and the President is not in the fourth year of his term, and zero otherwise. We measure "same party" as a dummy variable that takes the value "1" when a senator is of the same party as the President and zero otherwise.

Presidential Popularity

We measure the President's popularity as the percent of people who approve of the job the incumbent is doing as measured by the Gallup survey prior to the Senate vote.

Interest Group Activity

In the best of all possible situations we would have senator-level data on the amount of lobbying by organized interests dating back to 1954. Such data are largely unavailable.[81] Thus, while recognizing that some senators will be lobbied more than others, we choose a variable that measures lobbying activity with respect to each nominee, the number of organized interests presenting testimony for ("interest group pro") and against the nominee ("interest group con") at the Senate Judiciary Committee hearings. Though this process treats all groups as fungible, we know that some groups are more powerful than others. Unfortunately for the purposes of political research, the Constitution protects the membership lists of organized interests. Despite this problem, we presume that the more opposition a nominee has, the less support he or she will have, and, alternatively, the more organized support for a nominee, the more support he or she will have.

Results

Again, we first present the bivariate results and then proceed to the multivariate analysis. The substantive results, though, are largely the same. We present both because those without extensive statistical backgrounds may find the logit analysis daunting, while those with such a background may be skeptical of bivariate results. Those preferring bivariate analyses

rescaling of ADA scores to make them more comparable to the nominee ideology scores, we find, as did the original authors, that further scaling makes almost no difference in the results. Thus we leave the scales as they are.

[81] But see Caldeira and Wright, *op. cit.*, n. 60, *supra*.

TABLE 5.4. *Confirmation Voting by Nominee Qualifications ($\gamma = 0.81$)*

Vote	Qualifications		
	Low	Moderate	High
No	187 47.5%	167 17.9%	24 2.1%
Yes	207 52.5%	765 82.1%	1,112 97.9%

can skip the multivariate section; those preferring more multivariate analyses can skip the bivariate section.

We begin our examination with the influence of qualifications. While we expect that ideology should strongly affect votes, other nominee characteristics also influence senators. If they did not, it would be impossible to explain how certain strong liberals (e.g., Brennan) and conservatives (e.g., Scalia) breezed through the Senate. Senators may find it difficult, for instance, to justify opposition to highly qualified nominees. As our qualifications variable is skewed toward the high end, we classify nominees as highly qualified if their qualifications score from the content analysis is greater than 0.90, moderately qualified if their score is greater than or equal to 0.50 and less than 0.90, and unqualified if their score is less than 0.50. We see in Table 5.4 a strong positive relationship between qualifications and votes. Senators voted for highly qualified nominees 98 percent of the time, for moderately qualified nominees 82 percent of the time, and for lesser-qualified nominees but 53 percent of the time. In other words, if 100 votes are cast, a poorly qualified nominee will receive forty-five fewer votes on average than a highly qualified nominee. We can measure the strength of the bivariate relationship by looking at its gamma value, a measure of association that runs from −1.0 (perfect negative relationship) through 0.0 (no relationship) to 1.0 (perfect positive relationship). A gamma value of 0.81 indicates that senators are much more likely to vote for nominees who are perceived as well qualified.

We next examine ideology or, more explicitly, the ideological distance between a senator and the nominee, recognizing that a senator's "ideology," as ranked by groups such as the ADA, represents a variety of

TABLE 5.5. *Confirmation Voting by Constituent Ideological Distance ($\gamma = -0.79$)*

	Distance		
Vote	Close	Moderate	Far
No	29 2.4%	121 17.0%	228 42.8%
Yes	1,177 97.6%	591 83.0%	305 57.2%

TABLE 5.6. *Confirmation Voting by Qualifications and Distance (% pro)*

	Ideological distance		
Qualifications	Near	Medium	Distant
High	99.3 (602)	97.3 (299)	94.8 (231)
Medium	97.6 (422)	83.0 (317)	44.9 (187)
Low	91.8 (182)	38.5 (96)	1.7 (115)

Note: Number in parentheses is total votes in that category. Thus, 99.3 percent of the 602 votes for ideologically close, highly qualified nominees were positive.

ideological influences, including party and, perhaps most important, constituents. To examine this relationship we categorize senators and nominees as liberal, moderate, and conservative using the data described above. Senators should be most likely to vote for nominees who are ideologically close to them (e.g., liberals and liberals) and least likely to vote for nominees who are ideologically distant from their constituents (e.g., liberals and conservatives). This is exactly what we find. We see in Table 5.5 the percentage of senators voting for ideologically proximate, ideologically moderate, and ideologically distant nominees. Overall, senators voted almost 98 percent of the time for nominees who were ideologically close to them, 83 percent of the time for nominees who were of moderate distance, and but 57 percent of the time for nominees who were ideologically distant. A gamma value of –0.79 indicates that senators are much less likely to vote for nominees who are ideologically distant from them.

What is perhaps most interesting about ideology is the manner in which it interacts with qualifications. Table 5.6 examines the percentage

TABLE 5.7. *Confirmation Voting by Presidential Status ($\gamma = 0.64$)*

	Status	
Vote	**Weak**	**Strong**
No	322 21.6%	56 5.8%
Yes	1,171 78.4%	913 94.2%

Note: President is "weak" under divided government and/or in the fourth year of his term of office.

of "yes" votes cast by senators by both constituent ideological distance and qualifications. The results couldn't be clearer. Senators are willing to vote for highly qualified candidates regardless of ideological distance. They are also willing to vote for ideologically close nominees regardless of qualifications. Charges against Fortas no more influenced liberals than charges against Thomas did conservatives. But when nominees are both distant and poorly qualified, opposition is virtually certain.

Confirmation votes occur in the political world, not in a vacuum. The most important player in this political world is the President, who is expected to use his influence to secure a successful nomination. The President's resources will be lower, and thus he will have less influence, when he is in the final year of his term and when his party does not control the Senate. In fact, Presidents have secured over 94 percent of the votes on the average when they are in a strong position vis-à-vis the Senate and less than 79 percent of the votes when in a weak position ($\gamma = 0.64$) (see Table 5.7). Thus, a weakly positioned President can cost his nominee an average of fifteen votes. Additionally, the President's influence is likely to be lower on members of the opposition party. Senators of the President's party support his nominees with 94 percent of their votes, while senators of the opposition party do so only 76 percent of the time ($\gamma = 0.66$) (see Table 5.8). Additionally, popular Presidents – those with approval ratings greater than 70 – average 98 percent of the votes, while unpopular Presidents – those with approval ratings less than 50 – average only 83 percent ($\gamma = 0.30$). This indicates that an unpopular President costs a nominee an average of fifteen votes (see Table 5.9).

Finally, we expect interest groups to influence the votes of senators. When nominees face fierce opposition by organized interests at

TABLE 5.8. *Confirmation Voting by Presidential Partisanship (γ = 0.66)*

Vote	Partisanship	
	Opposing	Same
No	302	76
	24.4%	6.2%
Yes	934	1,149
	75.6%	93.8%

TABLE 5.9. *Confirmation Voting by Presidential Approval (γ = 0.30)*

Vote	Approval		
	Low	Moderate	High
No	151	216	11
	21.5%	18.8%	2.4%
Yes	694	932	458
	78.5%	81.2%	97.7%

TABLE 5.10. *Confirmation Voting by Interest Group Opposition (γ = −0.64)*

Vote	Opposition		
	None	Moderate	High
No	20	129	229
	2.7%	13.9%	29.1%
Yes	729	798	557
	97.3%	86.1%	70.9%

confirmation hearings – for example, Haynsworth and Bork – they receive on average 71 percent of the votes, but when they have no opposition, they average 97 percent of the votes (γ = −0.64) (see Table 5.10). Because supportive interest group mobilization arises largely in reaction to interest group mobilization against nominees, there is little likelihood of a bivariate relationship between votes and positive group support. In

TABLE 5.11. *Dependent and Independent Variables*

Variable	Mean	Minimum	Maximum	Standard deviation
Vote	0.85	0.00	1.00	0.36
Distance	0.39	0.00	1.00	0.28
Qualifications (lack of)	0.21	0.00	0.89	0.25
Qualifications * Distance	0.08	0.00	0.83	0.14
Strong President	0.39	0.00	1.00	0.49
President Popularity	58.37	40.00	79.00	11.14
Same Party	0.50	0.00	1.00	0.50
Interest Group +	5.39	0.00	21.00	6.56
Interest Group −	6.29	0.00	32.00	7.85

fact, none is found: $\gamma = -0.12$. However, if we control for other factors, interest group support should help a nominee.

Because our bivariate tables do not readily allow us to control for the influence of other factors, and because they do not allow us to predict individual results based on the complete set of specified factors, we move to a multivariate analysis of our confirmation model.

We estimated the model using logit analysis. The independent variables are the original interval-level measures discussed above. Table 5.11 presents the means, ranges, and standard deviations of the dependent and independent variables. Table 5.12 provides the results of the logit equation.[82]

Before discussing the results, we need to explain the nature of the interaction between the lack of qualifications ("unqual") and ideological distance ("dist"). If we temporarily just consider these variables and their interaction, the equation reduces to

$$\text{Prob } Y_I = 1 = -2.27 * \text{UNQUAL} - 4.33 * \text{DIST} - 9.61 * \text{DISTQUAL}.$$

The coefficients for UNQUAL and DIST are sometimes referred to as "main effects," but that is misleading in the case of interval-level variables. In this equation, there is neither a main effect for UNQUAL nor for DIST. Rather, the *slope* of UNQUAL depends on the *value* of DIST and the *slope* of DIST depends on the *value* of UNQUAL. Thus, the slope of UNQUAL

[82] Because the votes are unlikely to be independent of one another, we use robust standard errors. We further guard against correlated errors by declaring clusters by nominee. Previous work demonstrates no significant clustering within senators. See Segal, Cameron, and Cover, *op. cit.*, n. 78, supra.

TABLE 5.12. *Logit Estimates of Individual-Level Confirmation Model*

Variable	Maximum likelihood estimate	Standard error	Impact[a]
Constant	1.19	0.55	–
Distance	–4.33[b]	1.20	–[c]
Qualifications (lack of)	–2.27[d]	1.53	–[c]
Distance × Qualifications	–9.61[e]	2.69	–[c]
Strong President	1.82[e]	0.31	0.36
Same Party	1.33[f]	0.55	0.29
President Popularity	0.07[e]	0.02	0.21
Interest Group +	0.02	0.07	0.04
Interest Group –	–0.06[g]	0.04	–0.12
χ^2/df		845/2442	
Proportion predicted correctly		0.94	
Proportionate reduction error		0.60	

[a] "Impact" measures the change in probability of a yes vote given a one unit change in Strong President and Same Party, and a one standard deviation change in President popularity and the Interest Group variables for an undecided ($p = 0.5$) senator.
[b] Significant at $p < 0.001$ for all values of Qualifications.
[c] See Table 5.13.
[d] Qualifications significant at $p < 0.10$ when Distance = 0, and significant at $p < 0.001$ when Distance = 1.
[e] Significant at $p < 0.001$.
[f] Significant at $p < 0.01$.
[g] Significant at $p < 0.10$.

equals –2.27 when and only when DIST equals 0. If DIST equals 0.5, the equation becomes

$$\text{Prob } Y_1 = 1 = -2.27 * \text{UNQUAL} - 4.33 * 0.5 - 9.61 * 0.5 * \text{UNQUAL}$$

which reduces to

$$\text{Prob } Y_1 = 1 = 2.16 - 7.08 * \text{UNQUAL}$$

Thus, when DIST equals 0.5, the slope of UNQUAL is –7.08. This means that the slope and significance level of DIST reported in the table is valid only when UNQUAL equals 0, and the slope and significance level of UNQUAL reported in the table is valid only when DIST is set at 0. Further interpretation is required (and provided) to assess the impact of these variables at levels of their counterparts other than 0.

The impact of the remaining variables is a bit more straightforward. For the dummy variables Same Party and Strong President, we measure the change in the probability of voting to confirm as that variable changes from 0 to 1 for an undecided senator. Both variables have a strong impact on Senate voting (0.29 and 0.36, respectively) even after controlling for other factors. For the interval-level independent variables, Presidential Popularity and the two interest group variables, the "impact" column measures the change in the probability of a "yes" vote given a one-standard-deviation change in each independent variable for an undecided senator.

Unquestionably, no one-to-one relationship between presidential popularity and confirmation approval exists. President Nixon, for instance, was at the height of his popularity when Haynsworth and Carswell were rejected (65 and 63 percent approval, respectively). President Johnson's approval rating was only at 39 percent when Thurgood Marshall was confirmed. Yet it is also true that Johnson's approval ratings were almost as low when Fortas was rejected as chief justice (42 percent), and President Reagan was near his second-term low when Bork was defeated (50 percent). On average, the difference between an average President (e.g., 58 percent approval) and a popular one (e.g., 70 percent approval) increases the likelihood that an undecided senator will vote "yes" from 0.50 to 0.71.

Additionally, strong interest group mobilization against a nominee can hurt a candidate, while interest group mobilization for a nominee appears to have no impact. The Bork nomination provides an interesting example. Seventeen organized groups testified against Bork at the Judiciary Committee hearings; twenty supported him, but negative pressure has much more influence. In probabilistic terms, a moderate-to-conservative Southern senator who would have voted for Bork with a probability of 0.90 without any interest group pressure would have voted for him at a probability of only 0.57 after the intensive interest group mobilization.

As qualifications and ideological distance interact with one another, we examine their joint impact in Table 5.13 and Figure 5.1.

Reading across Table 5.13, we see the impact of ideological distance at different levels of qualifications. At the highest levels of qualifications (1.0), ideological distance has little effect: For the closest nominees, the probability of a yes vote is greater than 0.99, while for the most distant nominees, the probability of a yes vote is still a substantial 0.93. At slightly lower levels of qualifications (0.75), ideological distance has a

TABLE 5.13. *Joint Impact of Qualifications and Ideological Distance on the Probability of Voting to Confirm*

	Ideological distance				
Qualifications	**0.00**	**0.25**	**0.50**	**0.75**	**1.00**
1.00	0.99	0.99	0.99	0.98	0.93
0.75	0.99	0.99	0.95	0.79	0.41
0.50	0.99	0.97	0.77	0.26	0.03
0.25	0.99	0.91	0.37	0.03	0.00
0.00	0.99	0.76	0.09	0.00	0.00

substantial effect: For the closest nominees, the probability of a yes vote is still greater than 0.99, while for the most distant nominees, the probability of a yes vote drops precipitously to 0.41. At even lower levels of qualifications, increased ideological distance is devastating. For example, if qualifications are as low as 0.25, ideological soulmates will still vote for a nominee (probability equals 0.99), but by the time ideological distance equals 0.75, there is virtually no chance of a positive vote.

Reading down Table 5.13, we see the impact of qualifications at different levels of ideological distance. At the lowest levels of ideological distance (0.0), qualifications has no effect: For all close nominees, the probability of a yes vote is greater than 0.99. At slightly higher levels of ideological distance (0.25), qualifications have a substantial effect: For the most qualified nominees, the probability of a yes vote is still greater than 0.99, while for the least qualified nominees the probability of a yes vote drops to 0.76. At moderate levels (0.50) of ideological distance and above, qualifications have a devastating impact. For example, if distance equals 0.75, highly qualified nominees still have a 0.98 chance of gaining a senator's vote. But by the time qualifications are as low as 0.50, there's about a 0.26 chance of a yes vote.

Figure 5.1 presents a graphical view of these data. The plane on the right measures ideological distance from 1.0 (most distant) to 0.0 (least distant). The plane on the left represents the *lack* of qualifications. Those at 0 on that plane are most qualified; those at 1.0 are least qualified. The height of the graph represents the probability of a senator voting to confirm. Thus, the far back corner represents a probability of voting for

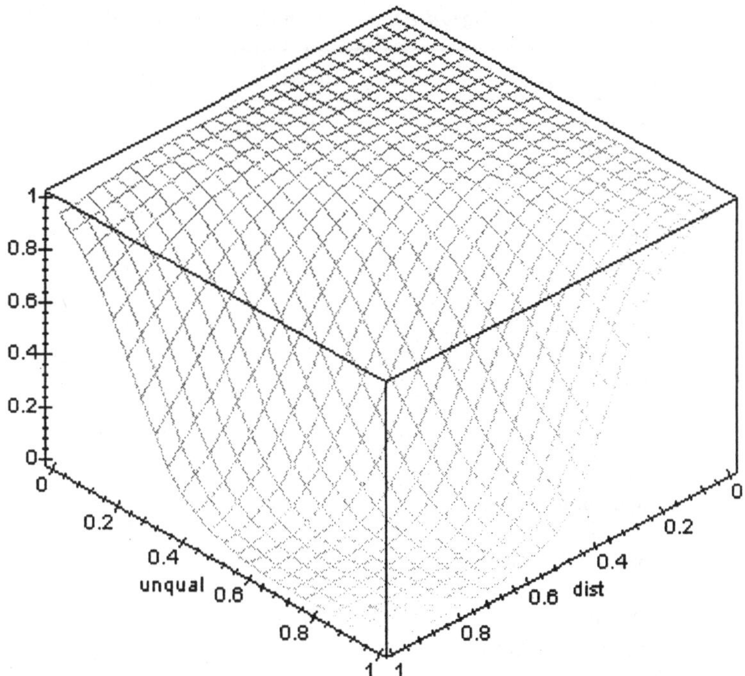

FIGURE 5.1. Probability of voting to confirm for given levels of UNQUAL and DIST.

an ideologically close, well-qualified nominee at about 1.0. At all levels of DIST for UNQUAL = 0 (i.e., the highest qualifications) the probability of a yes vote remains close to 1. Similarly, at all levels of qualifications for DIST = 0, the probability remains around 1. But as we move from the back corner to the front corner of the graph, the probability of a yes vote drops sharply.

In sum, the most important finding of the model is that ideologically close senators will vote to confirm a nominee regardless of the nominee's qualifications, that highly qualified nominees will receive yes votes from even the most distant nominees, but that ideologically distant senators will refuse to support nominees as soon as substantial questions about the nominee's qualifications arise.

Overall, the results for the model are quite impressive. All of the estimated logit coefficients are of the predicted sign, are of reasonable magnitudes, and are highly significant. The model predicts 94 percent of the votes correctly, for a 60 percent reduction in error.

TABLE 5.14. *Actual versus Predicted "No" Votes*[a]

Nominee	Actual	Predicted
Warren	0	0
Harlan	11	1
Brennan	0	0
Whittaker	0	0
Stewart	17	0
White	0	0
Goldberg	0	0
Fortas, 1st time	0	0
Marshall	11	5
Fortas, 2nd time	43	48
Burger	3	0
Haynsworth	55	48
Carswell	51	50
Blackmun	0	0
Powell	1	0
Rehnquist, 1st time	26	25
Stevens	0	0
O'Connor	0	0
Rehnquist, 2nd time	33	35
Scalia	0	0
Bork	58	38
Kennedy	0	0
Souter	9	14
Thomas	48	56
Ginsburg	3	0
Breyer	9	0

[a] Mean absolute error 3.77; *r* actual vs. predicted 0.95.

Beyond the parameter estimates, the model does an excellent job in predicting confirmation outcomes. Table 5.14 presents the actual and predicted "no" votes for every confirmation from Earl Warren (1954) through Stephen Breyer (1994).

Overall, the model's mean absolute error is but 3.77 votes per confirmation. The correlation between actual and predicted no votes is 0.95. On a nomination-level basis, the model underpredicts the low levels of opposition to the Harlan, Stewart, Marshall, Bork, and Breyer nominations. In the first three cases, conservative Southern senators voted against nominees who strongly supported desegregation. Though most of the opposition to Bork is predicted, he did considerably worse than expected given his high qualifications. On the other hand, the model predicts 50 votes against Carswell, almost exactly the 51 no votes he received.[83]

PRESIDENTIAL INFLUENCE

Few Presidents had the potential opportunity to influence the Supreme Court that Ronald Wilson Reagan did. The conservative Republican reached out again and again to social conservatives, calling for the return of school prayer and the overruling of *Roe v. Wade*.[84] Fate smiled upon the fortieth President, granting him four appointees to the High Court and hundreds of appointees to the lower federal courts. Yet the Supreme Court he left was no more conservative than the one he inherited. Moreover, despite his appointees, the twentieth century ended with organized school prayer still unconstitutional and *Roe v. Wade* the law of the land.

In contrast, the more moderate Richard Nixon had a much greater impact in pulling the Court to the right. The Warren Court, he declared in his 1968 campaign, had gone too far in protecting the criminal forces in society, as opposed to the peace forces. He wanted "strict constructionists" who would not read their preferred views of public policy into law. Nixon won the election, earning the opportunity, like Reagan, to name four new justices to the Supreme Court.[85]

Nixon, though, was successful in ways that Reagan was not. Though the Burger Court placed limits on the death penalty, it upheld its constitutionality provided that procedural safeguards were followed;[86] it limited the reach of the *Mapp*[87] and *Miranda* decisions;[88] increased the ability of states to ban obscene materials;[89] refused to equalize state spending between school districts;[90] refused to extend the right to privacy to homosexual conduct;[91] and allowed programs within colleges and

[83] With only 96 votes cast, the analysis correctly categorizes the nomination as a rejection.

[84] "Reagan Aims Fire at Liberal Judges," *New York Times*, October 9, 1986, p. A11.

[85] This section is based in part on Jeffrey A. Segal and Robert Howard, "Justices and Presidents," in Steven A. Shull, ed., *Presidential Policymaking* (New York: M. E. Sharp, 1999).

[86] *Gregg v. Georgia*, 428 U.S. 153 (1976).

[87] *Stone v. Powell*, 428 U.S. 465 (1976) and *United States v. Leon*, 468 U.S. 897 (1984).

[88] *New York v. Quarles*, 467 U.S. 649 (1984).

[89] *Miller v. California*, 413 U.S. 15 (1973).

[90] *San Antonio v. Rodriguez*, 411 U.S. 1 (1973).

[91] *Bowers v. Hardwick*, 478 U.S. 186 (1986).

universities to discriminate without fear of the entire school losing federal funds.[92]

Nevertheless, a variety of factors limited the conservative thrust of the Burger Court. First, outside of criminal justice, Nixon was not exceptionally conservative on social issues, and we would not necessarily expect his justices to be universally conservative, either. Moreover, we could not have expected him to have paid attention to issues such as privacy and abortion before they became salient issues for the Court.

Second, like most Presidents, Nixon did not get to place a majority of justices on the Court. William Rehnquist has voted liberally in civil liberties cases just 21 percent of the time, far lower than any other justice sitting on the Court at the time of Rehnquist's appointment.[93] This helped make for a more conservative Court, but even four nominees did not give President Nixon a guaranteed winning coalition on the Court. In fact, power devolved to the moderate swing justices.

Third, justices who fit ideologically on one end of the spectrum may change over time, a situation exemplified by the career of Nixon appointee Harry Blackmun. Similarly, David Souter's scores jumped from 41.5 under Bush to over 60 under Clinton. Justice Stevens has become increasingly liberal with each administration, while Byron White became increasingly conservative.

Fourth, no justice, however ideologically concordant with his or her appointing President, will support the President on every issue. Warren Burger wrote the majority opinion in support of racial busing,[94] opposing the view of President Nixon. Reagan appointees Sandra Day O'Connor and Anthony Kennedy (along with David Souter) coauthored the judgment of the Court upholding the right of a woman to have an abortion.[95]

Thus, though the Burger Court clearly reversed the trend of increasingly liberal Warren Court decisions, it was the Burger Court that first created abortion rights,[96] protected women under the Fourteenth

[92] *Grove City College v. Bell*, 465 U.S. 555 (1984).

[93] Here and below we take civil liberties scores from the Supreme Court Database, using orally argued citation plus split votes as the unit of analysis.

[94] *Swann v. Charlotte-Mecklenburg County Board of Education*, 402 U.S. 1 (1971).

[95] *Planned Parenthood of Southeastern Pennsylvania v. Casey*, 505 U.S. 833 (1992). Reagan nominated O'Connor despite her previous support for abortion rights. The Reagan administration also knew of Kennedy's support for the right to privacy prior to his nomination (Yalof, *op. cit.*, n. 18, *supra*), but desperately needed a confirmable nominee following the Senate rejection of Robert Bork and the administration's withdrawal of Douglas Ginsburg.

[96] *Roe v. Wade*, 410 U.S. 113 (1973).

Amendment,[97] permitted school busing,[98] and accepted race-based affirmative action plans.[99] But as Nixon supported the Equal Rights Amendment and introduced some early affirmative action programs into the executive branch, at least some of these liberal decisions were consistent with Nixon's preferences.

Beyond the cases of Nixon and Reagan, we can more generally examine the success of Presidents in their Supreme Court appointments. Using expert judges to assess presidential ideology,[100] we find fairly strong correlations between presidential preferences and the justices' behavior: 0.45 in civil liberties cases and 0.58 in economic cases. But as was the case with Blackmun, this association is not constant across time. During the first four years of the justices' tenure, their voting behavior correlates at 0.55 with their appointing President's preferences in civil liberties cases and at 0.58 with their appointing President's preferences in economic cases. But for years 11–20 of the justices' tenure, those figures drop to 0.10 and 0.28, respectively.[101]

We can examine the impact of presidential regimes on the Court's behavior in Figure 5.2. We begin with a moderate Eisenhower Court, which decided 58 percent of its civil liberties cases in the liberal direction.[102] As expected, the average score rose during the presidencies of Kennedy and Johnson and decreased during Nixon's and Ford's tenure. With no appointees, Carter had no impact on the Court. Yet Ronald Reagan, perhaps the most conservative President of the twentieth century, oversaw a Court that had only a marginally lower average score than Ford and Carter, despite four appointees.

Influence will depend not just on whom the President places on the Court, but on whom that justice replaces. For example, Reagan placed the extremely conservative Antonin Scalia on the Court, but Scalia took the associate justice seat of William Rehnquist, another extreme conservative. Appointments such as that may have little impact on the Court's decisions.

[97] *Reed v. Reed*, 404 U.S. 71 (1971).

[98] *Swann v. Charlotte-Mecklenburg Board of Education* (1971).

[99] *Regents v. Bakke*, 438 U.S. 265 (1978).

[100] Jeffrey A. Segal, Richard Timpone, and Robert Howard, "Buyer Beware: Presidential Success in Supreme Court Appointments," 53 *Political Research Quarterly* 557 (2000). The expert judges were a random sample of scholars belonging to the presidency section of the American Political Science Association.

[101] *Id.*

[102] Using the U.S. Supreme Court Database, we chose orally argued cases with written opinions by citation plus split votes. Civil liberties cases are those involving criminal procedure, equal protection, First Amendment, due process, privacy, and attorneys.

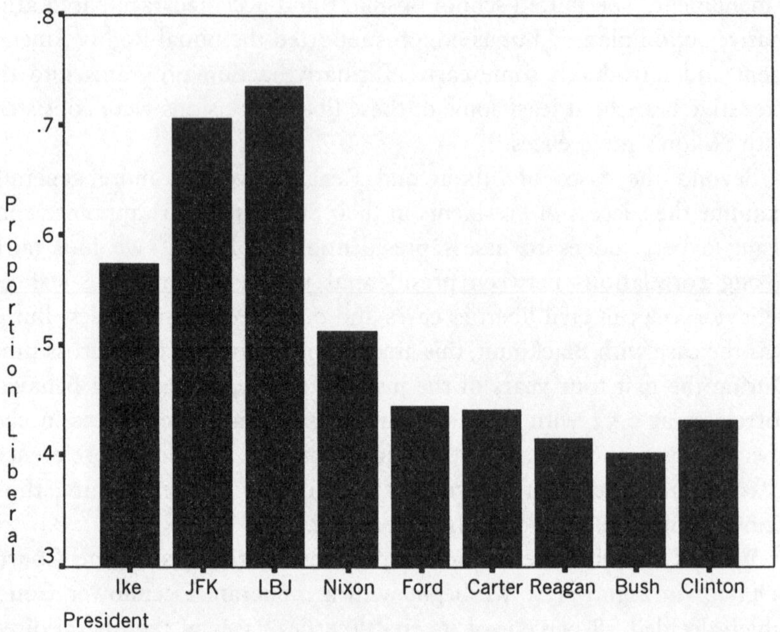

FIGURE 5.2. Proportion liberal in civil liberties during presidential regimes.

Thus, explanations of presidential impact become clear when we examine Figure 5.3, which displays the average annual voting scores of each President's appointees and the justices they replaced.[103]

At the time Richard Nixon took office in 1969, the Supreme Court consisted of Chief Justice Earl Warren and Associate Justices Black, Harlan II, Brennan, Stewart, Fortas, White, Marshall, and Douglas. The average civil liberties score for these nine justices was 68.9. The four justices that President Nixon replaced (Warren, Black, Fortas, and Harlan II) averaged 69.3, almost exactly the same as the Court average. The four justices Nixon appointed in their place averaged 35.2, bringing the Court's average down to 52.9, almost directly in the middle of the civil liberties score. But while Reagan's nominees were as conservative as Nixon's, Reagan's appointees replaced other conservatives, leaving his short-run impact on the High Court fairly negligible.

[103] The data are derived from Lee Epstein, Jeffrey A. Segal, Harold J. Spaeth, and Thomas G. Walker, *The Supreme Court Compendium*, 2nd ed. (Washington, D.C.: CQ Press, 1996).

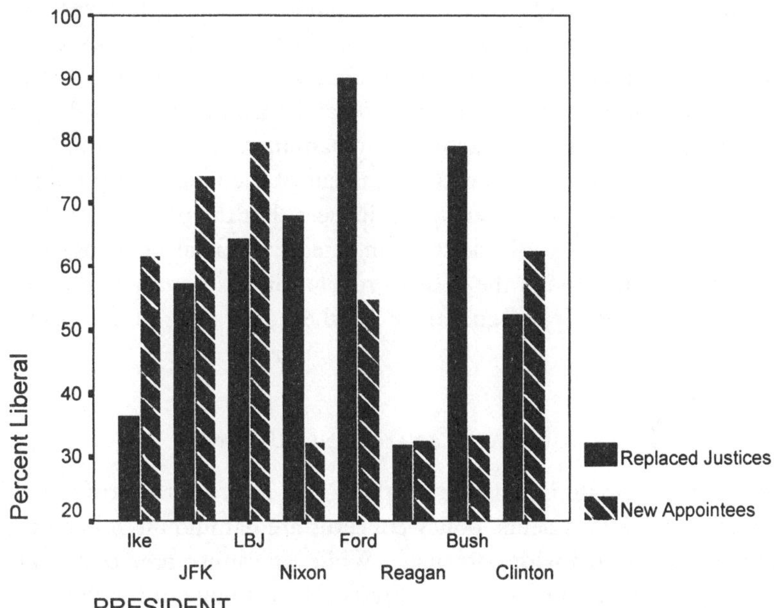

FIGURE 5.3. Liberalism of replaced and new justices in civil liberties cases by presidential regime.

Given the discretion that justices have, and the impact of ideology in shaping that discretion, Chief Justice Rehnquist finds it "normal and desirable for Presidents to attempt to pack the Court."[104] As he explains:

> Surely we would not want it any other way. We want our federal courts, and particularly the Supreme Court, to be independent of public opinion when deciding the particular cases or controversies that come before them. The provision for tenure during good behavior and the prohibition against diminution of compensation have proved more than adequate to secure that sort of independence. The result is that judges are responsible to no electorate or constituency. But the manifold provisions of the Constitution with which judges must deal are by no means crystal clear in their import, and reasonable minds may differ as to which interpretation is proper. When a vacancy occurs on the Court, it is entirely appropriate that the vacancy be filled by the President, responsible to a national constituency, as advised by the Senate.[105]

104 William Rehnquist, *The Supreme Court: How It Was, How It Is* (New York: Morrow, 1987), p. 236.

105 *Id.*

Whether packing the Court is a laudable goal or not, a variety of factors can conspire against Presidents. They may have goals beyond policy when naming Supreme Court justices, as with Eisenhower's pre-election selection of the Catholic Democrat William Brennan or Reagan's redemption of a campaign promise by naming a woman to the Court. And changing attitudes can rob a President of the long-lasting influence he may have wished from one of his justices. But the public that elected Richard Nixon in 1968 desired and received a more conservative Supreme Court. Though the Reagan revolution did not make the Court *more* conservative, it did guarantee another generation of conservative domination.

SUMMARY AND CONCLUSIONS

Presidents nominate individuals to the Court in order to satisfy certain goals. For some Presidents, policy concerns are paramount, while others are more concerned with patronage. While we cannot predict nominees with any overall accuracy, we can predict the ideology of the President's choice. In short, that ideology will be a function of the President's ideology, the ideological composition of the Senate, and the ideological makeup of the Supreme Court.

While the Senate routinely confirms most nominations, it rejects a substantial number. Five nominees failed of confirmation between 1968 and 1987. We find that the senators' votes greatly depend on the ideological distance between senators and the nominee, the perceived qualifications of the nominee, and, crucially, the interaction between the two. In short, a nominee's reception hinges on the characteristics of the nominee and the composition of the Senate.

So, too, the context of a nomination strongly influences the outcome. The strength and popularity of the President emerge as important determinants of individual votes. In addition, the relative mobilization of interest groups around a nominee also has pronounced effects.

The appointment process, in which Presidents typically nominate justices ideologically close to them, and the Senate closely evaluates the nominee's ideology, ensures that even if the justices follow their own preferences, as surely they do, those preferences are usually shared by the dominant political coalition[106] at the time of the nominee's confirmation.

[106] Robert Dahl, "Decision-Making in a Democracy: The Supreme Court as National Policy Maker," 6 *Journal of Public Law* 179 (1957).

6

Getting into Court

Assertions by persons about to initiate a lawsuit, as well as by those who have already lost, that they will take their cases all the way to the United States Supreme Court undoubtedly bespeak their deeply felt intentions, but in most cases their avowals lack credibility. Individuals who wish to file a lawsuit must be proper parties, that is, they must have standing to sue. If they do have such credentials, they must also bring their cases to the proper forum: The court in question must have jurisdiction – the capability to resolve their dispute. Assuming that the plaintiff is a proper party and is in the proper forum, a third hurdle to Supreme Court resolution still remains: The justices themselves must deem the matter worthy of their consideration. The last is by far the most difficult to surmount.

Decisions about access, whether they concern proper parties or the proper forum, have important policy effects. Although such questions do not resolve the merits of the cases before the Court, they serve as a "gate" that litigants must pass through in order to obtain a meritorious resolution of their disputes.[1] The policies that govern access, like decisions on the merits, impact and bind the operation of the judicial system generally. Analyses show that the Warren Court provided relatively open access, a policy that the Burger Court continued during its very early

[1] The original "gate" through which litigants must pass is the justices' decision whether or not to decide the case at all; i.e., whether to grant the petition for certiorari or, in the case of an appeal, to note probable jurisdiction. Absent reconsideration, which almost never occurs, denial ends further Supreme Court consideration of the case. We discuss this "gate" in the section on case selection in this chapter.

years.[2] But by the mid-1970s, the Burger Court had established policies that narrowed access to the federal courts.[3] The cited analyses both show that the individual justices' votes opening or closing access covary with their overall rankings on a general liberal-conservative dimension.[4] Liberals vote to open access; conservatives to close it.

In this chapter, we begin by detailing the legal requirements for getting into federal court by specifying the jurisdiction of the federal courts in general and that of the Supreme Court in particular, and the elements that determine whether a litigant has standing to sue. We also present the procedure whereby cases reach the Supreme Court and the factors that affect the justices' decision to accept a case for consideration. We conclude with a discussion of the Court's caseload.

LEGAL REQUIREMENTS

There are two legal considerations for accessing a court: Does the petitioned court have jurisdiction? Does the petitioning party have standing to sue? These considerations apply to all courts, state and federal. They vary inasmuch as courts differ from one another in the jurisdiction they have; furthermore, state courts are generally much less insistent that plaintiffs meet all the technical requirements of standing to sue.

Jurisdiction

In its broadest sense jurisdiction means the authority by which a court accepts and decides matters brought to its attention. Jurisdiction takes three forms: geographical, hierarchical, and subject matter. Most basic is subject matter because it limits the decision-making capacity of the federal courts. Justice Ginsburg has stated the matter well:

[2] Gregory J. Rathjen and Harold J. Spaeth, "Access to the Federal Courts: An Analysis of Burger Court Policy Making," 23 *American Journal of Political Science* 360 (1979), at 361–64.

[3] Gregory J. Rathjen and Harold J. Spaeth, "Denial of Access and Ideological Preferences: An Analysis of the Voting Behavior of the Burger Court Justices, 1969–1976," 36 *Political Research Quarterly* 71 (1983).

[4] The overall ranking of the justices on a liberal-conservative continuum is taken from David W. Rohde and Harold J. Spaeth, *Supreme Court Decision Making* (San Francisco: W. H. Freeman, 1976), pp. 142–44. Also see Sara C. Benesh, Saul Brenner, and Harold J. Spaeth, "Conditions Associated with the Outcome-Prediction Strategy in Cert Voting on the Supreme Court," paper presented at the 1998 annual-meeting of the American Political Science Association, Boston.

Subject-matter limitations on federal jurisdiction serve institutional interests. They keep the federal courts within the bounds the Constitution and Congress have prescribed. Accordingly, subject-matter delineations must be policed by the courts on their own initiative even at the highest level.[5]

The federal courts organize themselves along state lines, while the state courts basically rely on their counties and the subdivisions thereof – cities, towns, and townships – to separate the geographical jurisdiction of one court from another. Hierarchically, the federal courts have a three-tiered system: trial or courts of first instance, inferior or intermediate courts of appeals, and a Supreme Court. Most states adhere to the same arrangement, although some of the less populous states do without an intermediate court of appeals.

The federal district courts try the vast majority of cases heard in the federal system. Each state has at least one. If a state has more than one, the additional district courts carry a geographical designation, that is, northern, southern, eastern, western, central, or middle.[6] Except for the district court for the District of Columbia, those in the states and other territories of the United States are gathered together into eleven numbered courts of appeals, which are identified as United States Courts of Appeals for the [N]th Circuit. A given circuit court will hear appeals from all of the district courts in the adjacent states that comprise its geographical jurisdiction.[7] The sole exception is the court of appeals for the District of Columbia, which hears appeals only from the District's district court and from various federal agencies, most especially the independent regulatory commissions. Panels of three judges decide the vast majority of the cases in the courts of appeals. Depending on the rules of the specific circuit, some cases may be heard by the full bench (en banc).

[5] *Ruhrgas AG v. Marathon Oil Co.*, 143 L Ed 2d 760 (1999), at 770.

[6] Twenty-six states and the District of Columbia have a single district court: the six New England states (ME, NH, VT, MA, RI, CT), NJ, DE, MD, SC, plus sixteen states west of the Mississippi River (MN, ND, SD, NB, KS, MT, WY, CO, NM, AZ, UT, ID, NV, OR, AK, HI). Twelve states have two: all but one of which (WA) are in the Midwest or South (OH, IN, MI, WI, IA, MO, KY, AR, MS, VA, WV). Seven of the nine states with three are in the South: AL, FL, GA, LA, NC, OK, TN. The other two are IL and PA. Three states have four: NY, TX, and CA. Four territories of the United States each have a district court: Puerto Rico, the Virgin Islands, Guam, and the Northern Mariana Islands.

[7] The states and territories that each Circuit encompasses are as follows: First: ME, NH, MA, RI, PR; Second: VT, NY, CT; Third: PA, NJ, DE, VI; Fourth: MD, WV, VA, NC, SC; Fifth: MS, LA, TX; Sixth: MI, OH, KY, TN; Seventh: WI, IL, IN; Eighth: MN, IA, MO, AR, ND, SD, NB; Ninth: MT, ID, WA, OR, CA, NV, AZ, AL, HI, Guam, N. Marianas; Tenth: KS, OK, WY, CO, NM, UT; Eleventh: AL, GA, FL.

The foregoing courts, plus the Supreme Court, resolve most every matter that the Constitution authorizes the federal courts to resolve. Although their subject matter is thereby limited, within its confines the district courts, courts of appeal, and the Supreme Court may be described as courts of general jurisdiction.[8]

The source of the federal courts' and the Supreme Court's subject-matter jurisdiction is Article III of the Constitution and acts of Congress based thereon. The heart of this jurisdiction consists of federal questions: "all cases, in law and equity, arising under this Constitution, the laws of the United States, and treaties." The federal courts make policy because they authoritatively resolve these questions. Ancillary to federal questions are those arising under diversity of citizenship and supplementary jurisdiction. We discuss each in turn.

Federal Questions

To invoke federal question jurisdiction, parties seeking access to a federal court must demonstrate to the court's satisfaction that the essence of their cases substantially concerns some provision of the Constitution, an act of Congress, or a treaty of the United States. The actions of federal administrative agencies and officials or actions to which the United States is party are, for all practical purposes, also federal questions. Article III also makes reference to suits between states, admiralty and maritime jurisdiction, and cases to which foreign diplomatic personnel accredited to the United States are party. Though such controversies technically constitute federal questions, they infrequently arise. And when they do, their litigation comports more with private disputes than it does with the resolution of matters of public policy that characterizes cases arising under the Constitution, acts of Congress, or treaties.[9]

[8] A number of "specialized" federal courts that have their own judges also exist. Four trial courts: the Tax Court, the Court of Claims, Court of Veterans Appeals, the Court of International Trade, plus the separate court within each branch of the armed forces that reviews decisions of courts martial; and two appellate courts: the Court of Appeals for the Federal Circuit and the Court Appeals for the Armed Forces. The Tax Court hears federal tax cases; the Court of Claims entertains suits for damages against the federal government; and the Court of International Trade decides tariff and related sorts of disputes. The Federal Circuit hears appeals from the specialized trial courts other than the Tax Court and appeals in intellectual property cases. The Court of Appeals for the Armed Forces reviews decisions of the court of each branch of the military service that reviews actions of courts martial.

Congress frequently reconstitutes these courts and their subject matter jurisdiction.

[9] One may argue that suits between states have a public-policy dimension because of the character of the parties to such litigation. Though that is true, these disputes typically

Because the federal courts, as noted, are courts of limited jurisdiction, plaintiffs must show that a right or immunity arising under federal law is an integral element of their causes of action and not merely a collateral issue, or introduced as a defense, or in response to respondents' counterclaims. Two additional conditions must also be met. If the facts alleging federal jurisdiction are challenged, the burden of proof falls on the party seeking access to the federal courts. Second, all federal courts have a continuing obligation to notice a lack of jurisdiction and to dismiss cases on their own motion if either of the parties fails to so move.

Diversity of Citizenship

Because of concern that state courts would be biased in favor of their own residents in cases involving an out-of-state litigant, the Framers authorized the federal courts to decide cases "between citizens of different states" or between citizens of one state and aliens. These cases rarely contain an issue of policy consequence. Instead, they tend to be the kinds of everyday tort, contract, and property cases that predominately find their way into state courts.

To avoid inundating the federal courts with diversity cases, the Supreme Court as well as Congress have imposed conditions on those who would bring them. In an early decision, the Supreme Court ruled that diversity must be complete, that is, that every litigant on one side of the controversy must be domiciled in a state different from those on the other side.[10] Domicile, rather than residence, controls. An individual may have several residences, but only one domicile: the place where he or she currently resides, so long as he or she intends to remain there for some indefinite period of time.[11] Resident aliens are deemed citizens of the state in which they reside. The domicile of the members of unincorporated associations, such as a labor union, controls, which, in the case of a union with members throughout the United States, effectively means that the organization can neither sue nor be sued in diversity. Congress,

involve title to land bordering the states in question or the allocation of water or other resources. As such, they rarely involve more than a dispute over a few acres of real property, e.g., *Georgia v. South Carolina*, 497 U.S. 376 (1990), or a matter of contract, e.g., *Texas v. New Mexico*, 482 U.S. 124 (1987), 494 U.S. 111 (1990). But cf. *Wyoming v. Oklahoma*, 502 U.S. 437 (1992), which delared unconstitutional an Oklahoma statute that discriminated against an out-of-state product.

10 *Strawbridge v. Curtis*, 3 Cranch 267 (1806).

11 *Gilbert v. David*, 235 U.S. 561 (1915); *Mississippi Band of Choctaw Indians v. Holyfield*, 490 U.S. 30 (1989).

however, has exempted corporations from this rule by providing them with citizenship in the state of their incorporation as well as in their primary place of business.[12] Thus, in order for General Motors to be involved in a diversity action, no adverse party may be a citizen of Michigan, its principal business place, or Delaware, its state of incorporation.[13]

Congress has also specified a jurisdictional dollar amount that must be met so that the federal courts may avoid petty lawsuits. It was set at more than $75,000 in 1994. The amount claimed controls.[14] Once a jurisdictionally sufficient amount is established, subsequent events cannot destroy it.[15] Aggregation of claims is permissible so long as one jurisdictionally sufficient claim exists. But a defendant's counterclaim may not be aggregated with the plaintiff's claim in order to meet the jurisdictional amount of $75,000. In multiple-party litigation, aggregation may occur if the relevant party has a joint and common interest in the disputed property (e.g., a $100,000 painting jointly owned by a husband and wife) rather than a several interest (e.g., two passengers in a car each of whom suffers a $40,000 injury).

Congress has excepted class actions and interpleaders from the foregoing requirements. Although every class member must meet the jurisdictional amount,[16] only the named or representative party, not every individual class member, need be diverse from the party or parties on the

[12] 28 *United States Code* 1332(c). Federal courts differ about the location of a corporation's "principal place of business." Some hold it to be its home office; others where the bulk of its activity occurs. See *Kelly v. United States Steel*, 284 F.2d 850 (1960); *Egan v. American Airlines*, 324 F.2d 565 (1963).

[13] Note the fictional character of corporate citizenship. The Supreme Court had originally ruled that for diversity purposes the citizenship of the individual stockholders controlled access to the federal courts. *Bank of the United States v. Deveaux*, 5 Cranch 84 (1810). Subsequently, the increasing geographical spread of corporate stockholders began to preclude corporations from suing in federal court because of a want of complete diversity. The Court rectified the matter in 1845 by qualifying *Deveaux* and limiting corporate citizenship to its place of incorporation. *L.C. & C. RR. Co. v. Letson*, 2 Howard 497. As a result, "every one of the shareholders of the General Motors Corporation is a citizen of Delaware despite the fact that there are more stockholders than there are Delawareans." John P. Frank, *Justice Daniel Dissenting* (Cambridge, Mass.: Harvard University Press, 1964), pp. 51–52.

[14] If the plaintiff's cause of action does not allege a dollar amount, as in an injunction, nuisance abatement, or specific performance of a contract, the court will determine the jurisdictional amount either by the value of the relief to the plaintiff or by the cost that the respondent would incur if the relief is granted.

[15] 28 *United States Code*, 1331(a), 1332(a). *St. Paul Mercury Indemnity Co. v. Red Cab*, 303 U.S. 283 (1938).

[16] *Zahn v. International Paper Co.*, 414 U.S. 291 (1973).

other side of the controversy. With regard to interpleader – an action whereby a stakeholder who does not claim title to property, such as a bank or an insurance company, deposits the proceeds with a court when ownership or title is in question, thereby forcing the claimants to resolve the matter without subjecting the stakeholder to multiple liability – diversity is satisfied as long as at least two claimants have citizenship in different states and the amount in controversy exceeds a mere $500.[17]

Supplementary Jurisdiction

This pertains to pendent and ancillary jurisdiction, which largely result from decisional rather than statutory law. Both arise in the context of multiple claim litigation and permit a federal court to hear an entire case and not just the federal portion of it. Invocation requires the presence of at least one claim sufficient to establish either federal question or diversity jurisdiction. If all the claims in the case "derive from a common nucleus of operative fact," the entire dispute may be heard.[18] Pendent jurisdiction allows a question of state law over which the federal court has no jurisdiction – for example, aspects of employment discrimination that do not violate federal law – to be adjudicated along with the federal question that occasioned the parties' dispute, while ancillary jurisdiction allows parties other than the original plaintiff to join their jurisdictionally insufficient claims – for example, a multiple-party accident where some of the victims suffer injuries less than $75,000 – with that which is sufficient so that a single proceeding may resolve them all.

The purpose of supplementary jurisdiction – to promote judicial economy and preclude piecemeal litigation – was undermined in *Finley v. United States*[19] when the Court appeared to rule that the federal courts lack pendent jurisdiction absent explicit congressional legislation that says they do. Congress responded by codifying supplemental jurisdiction, thereby overriding *Finley* and preventing erosion of the federal courts' authority to resolve an entire case or controversy.[20]

[17] Strictly speaking, only statutory interpleader, 28 *United States Code* 1335, 1397, 2361, is exempt from the ordinary jurisdictional requirements. Not so interpleader arising under Rule 22 of the Federal Rules of Civil Procedure.

[18] *United Mine Workers v. Gibbs*, 383 U.S. 715 (1966), at 725.

[19] 490 U.S. 545 (1989).

[20] In the Federal Courts Study Committee Implementation Act of 1990, 28 *United States Code* 1367. Also see T. M. Mengler, S. B. Burbank, and T. D. Rowe, Jr., "Recent Federal Court Legislation Made Some Noteworthy Changes," *National Law Journal*, December 31, 1990 – January 7, 1991, pp. 20–21; T. M. Mengler, "The Demise of Pendent and Ancillary Jurisdiction," 1990 *Brigham Young Law Review* 247 (1990).

Summary and Conclusion

In exercising their jurisdiction, the federal courts, including the Supreme Court, depend not only on Article III of the Constitution, but also on acts of Congress. Indeed, the lower federal courts owe their very existence to Congress, to say nothing of their subject-matter jurisdiction. And although the Constitution established the Supreme Court, it specifies only its original jurisdiction. It receives all of its appellate jurisdiction – the heart of its policy-making capacity – from Congress, and what Congress grants, Congress may revoke. In our discussion of national supremacy in Chapter 1, such congressional legislation – particularly section 25 of the Judiciary Act of 1789 – played a key role in checking the centrifugal force of states' rights. In the twentieth century, Congress relieved the federal courts of the power to issue labor injunctions, thereby presaging the ultimate victory of organized labor, a few years later, to bargain collectively. More recently, Congress has recently limited federal court jurisdiction to review state death penalty cases.

To function as effective policy makers, courts depend on their subject-matter jurisdiction. The federal courts, however, are not free agents in this regard. Congress determines which courts, if any, should exercise which segments of the constitutionally provided subject-matter jurisdiction. As a result, Congress has the power to check judicial decision making on and about matters of which it disapproves.

Standing to Sue

The mere appearance of a plaintiff before the proper federal court does not guarantee access. Litigants must be proper parties, that is, they must have standing to sue. Unlike the state courts, the federal courts are quite finicky in this regard. Whether a plaintiff is a proper party turns on a number of constitutional and prudential considerations. We discuss each element separately, paying special attention to the one that has dominated access policy making since the beginning of the Burger Court: the presence of personal injury.

Case or Controversy

The words of Article III limit the federal courts to deciding "cases" or "controversies." The difference between them is purely technical. Compatibly with legal definitions generally, the requirement does not admit of precise specification: a legal dispute between two or more persons whose interests conflict. As such, the federal courts may not decide hypothetical questions, render advisory opinions, or resolve collusive, or feigned, cases.

Hypothetical questions typically result when a live dispute becomes moot because of changes affecting a litigant's contentions. Thus, an out-of-court settlement moots further proceedings; the repeal of a law precludes a challenge to its constitutionality. If, however, the controversy is sufficiently short-lived through no fault of the plaintiff, it may be "capable of repetition, yet evading review."[21] This is especially likely because "[t]he usual rule in federal cases is that an actual controversy must exist at stages of appellate or certiorari review, and not simply at the date the action is initiated."[22] If such be the situation, as when individuals challenge a denial of their right to vote, or a woman challenges an antichoice abortion statute, the matter does not become moot because the election is over or the woman is no longer pregnant. Even in matters where mootness can be avoided, the Court can find a way around the doctrine if it so desires. A good example is the 1986 homosexual sodomy case where Michael Hardwick brought his challenge to the Georgia statute to the Supreme Court even though the state refused to prosecute Hardwick after his arrest.[23] The Court accepted his fallacious claim that he was in imminent danger of arrest.

An advisory opinion typically results when a governmental official requests a court's opinion about a hypothetical matter, for example, the constitutionality of a bill introduced but not yet enacted by the legislature or the legality of certain proposed administrative action. Not only do advisory opinions lack liveliness, they also force the courts to trench on separation of powers. Nonetheless, a number of states do permit their supreme court to respond to them if the governor or attorney general so request.

Collusive disputes most often occur in the guise of a stockholder's suit. When, for example, shareholders seek to enjoin their corporation from complying with a tax, the interests of the parties do not conflict; they coincide. Collusion is not always apparent, however. The decisions that voided the federal income tax and applied the contract clause to actions of a state legislature were brought by nonadversarial parties.[24] On the other hand, the parties need not necessarily disagree formally. Courts may accept guilty pleas and enter default judgments.

[21] *Southern Pacific Terminal Co. v. Interstate Commerce Commission*, 219 U.S. 498 (1911), at 515.

[22] *Roe v. Wade*, 410 U.S. 113 (1973), at 125.

[23] *Bowers v. Hardwick*, 478 U.S. 186.

[24] *Pollock v. Farmers' Loan & Trust Co.*, 157 U.S. 429, 158 U.S. 601 (1895); *Fletcher v. Peck*, 6 Cranch 87 (1810).

Legal Injury

Access requires more than a mere conflict of interest. The conflict must also pertain to a right that is statutorily or constitutionally protected or to some personal or property interest that the law recognizes. A business, for example, has no right to avoid ordinary commercial competition. Traditionally, only injuries susceptible of liquidation were actionable. Today, the courts also recognize aesthetic, conservational, recreational, cultural, and religious interests. In large part because of the immunity that surrounds government officials, a clear-cut injury may not be redressible, for example, persons found innocent after serving their sentence or property whose value declines because of a change in a zoning ordinance. The gravity of injury does not necessarily determine whether it is legally protected. Under the common law, such trifles as a single footstep on another's land, unwanted touching, or a threatening gesture constitute trespass, battery, and assault, respectively, even though no discernible damage may have resulted.

Personal Injury

Closely related, but nonetheless separate and independent from legal injury, is the requirement that plaintiffs show they have suffered or are threatened with personal injury. Individuals may not sue solely on behalf of third persons who themselves are competent to bring their own lawsuits. Nonindividuals, however, may sometimes bring action on behalf of others. Thus, a group may represent its members and a state may occasionally sue in a parens patriae capacity for persons fully competent to bring their own lawsuits.[25] The rule does not prohibit class actions, of course, where an individual sues to vindicate his or her own rights, plus those of similarly situated persons. The prohibition of taxpayer's suits best illustrates the rigor with which the federal courts – though not the state courts – adhere to this prudential aspect of standing. On the rationale that a person subject to a federal tax does not suffer an injury more severely or more peculiarly than taxpayers generally, but suffers only in an indefinite way along with millions of others, individuals may not initiate a judicial challenge to the constitutionality of a

[25] *United Automobile Workers v. Brock*, 477 U.S. 274 (1986), which permitted the union to sue for benefits for members laid off because of import competition; and *Snapp & Son, Inc. v. Puerto Rico*, 458 U.S. 592 (1982), which allowed the Commonwealth to seek an injunction against apple growers who were discriminating against migrant Puerto Rican farm workers.

TABLE 6.1. *Disposition of Standing to Sue Cases, 1953–2000 Terms*

	Warren Court			Burger Court			Rehnquist Court		
Access	Pro	Anti	% pro	Pro	Anti	% pro	Pro	Anti	% pro
Personal injury	8	3	72.7	18	34	34.6	9	15	37.5
Other aspects	23	11	67.6	14	9	60.9	12	18	40.0
TOTAL	31	14	68.9	32	43	42.7	21	33	38.9

federal tax.[26] The Court subsequently limited the scope of this precedent when it excepted from the ban on taxpayer's suits those that allege the challenged tax exceeds some specific limitation on the power of Congress to tax or to spend money.[27] Examples in which the plaintiffs were denied standing include an organization of taxpayers dedicated to the separation of church and state who sought to contest the no-cost transfer of government property to religious educational institutions, and the parents of black school children who wished to challenge the action of the Internal Revenue Service granting tax exemptions to racially discriminatory schools.[28]

Table 6.1 shows that the antiaccess decision making of the Burger Court resulted from its treatment of cases raising claims of personal injury, an element of standing with which the Warren Court was little concerned and which the Rehnquist Court decided no differently from its other access issues.[29] Thirty-four of the Burger Court's 43 antistanding decisions pertained to personal injury (79 percent), as compared with only 15 of the Rehnquist Court's 33 (38.9 percent). Moreover, only 11 of the Warren Court's 45 standing cases pertained to personal injury

[26] *Frothingham v. Mellon*, 262 U.S. 447 (1923). Of course, taxpayers may refuse to pay a tax and, having been indicted, defend their nonpayment on the ground that the tax violates the Constitution. If they lose, they will likely incur a markedly more severe sanction than if they merely lost a taxpayer's suit brought while the tax was held in abeyance.

[27] *Flast v. Cohen*, 392 U.S. 83 (1968). The challenged expenditure provided aid to parochial schools.

[28] *Valley Forge Christian College v. Americans United for Separation of Church and State*, 454 U.S. 464 (1982); *Allen v. Wright*, 468 U.S. 737 (1984).

[29] These data span the Warren and Burger Courts, plus the 1986–2000 terms of the Rehnquist Court. The unit of analysis is docket number and excludes memorandum decisions.

claims (24 percent), as compared with 52 of the Burger Court's total of 75 (69 percent) and 24 of the Rehnquist Court's 54 (44 percent).

Within the various aspects of standing, the Burger Court and, to a lesser extent, the Rehnquist Court, have together disproportionately addressed private or implied causes of action. The Warren Court, by contrast, decided nary a one. These cases present the question of whether an identifiable group of litigants have standing under various federal statutes. For example, does the Parental Kidnapping Prevention Act allow parents to determine in federal court the validity of state child custody orders? Does the Civil Service Reform Act of 1978 authorize federal employees to sue their unions for breach of the duty of fair representation?[30] Overall, the Court has been markedly unsympathetic toward such claims. The Burger Court denied access in 17 of 23 such cases (74 percent), the Rehnquist Court in eight of nine (89 percent). Indeed, the Rehnquist Court has not upheld one since its first term (1986).

Political Questions

If the Supreme Court believes it inappropriate for the federal courts to resolve the merits of a controversy, it labels the matter a "political question," thereby sending a message to the other branches of government, including the state courts, that they, rather than the judiciary, should resolve it. History records few such decisions. Among them are the ratification of a constitutional amendment, the legitimacy of two competing state governments, the boundary between the United States and Spain, the adequacy of national guard training, and what constitutes a trial for purposes of impeachment.[31] One matter that the Court initially refused to adjudicate, but now finds justiciable, is legislative apportionment and districting.[32] In so ruling, the Court devised a set of criteria for determining whether a question is political that raised the nebulosity level of legal definitions to new heights:

> Prominent on the surface ... is found a textually demonstrable constitutional commitment of the issue to a coordinate political department; or a lack of judi-

[30] The Court unanimously answered "no" to both questions. *Thompson v. Thompson*, 484 U.S. 174 (1988); *Karahalios v. National Federation of Federal Employees*, 489 U.S. 527 (1989).

[31] *Coleman v. Miller*, 307 U.S. 433 (1939); *Luther v. Borden*, 7 Howard 1 (1849); *Foster v. Neilson*, 2 Peters 253 (1829); *Gilligan v. Morgan*, 413 U.S. 1 (1973); and *Nixon v. United States*, 506 U.S. 224 (1993).

[32] *Colegrove v. Green*, 328 U.S. 549 (1946); *Baker v. Carr*, 369 U.S. 186 (1962).

cially discoverable and manageable standards for resolving it; or the impossibility of deciding without an initial policy determination of a kind clearly for nonjudicial discretion; or the impossibility of a court's undertaking independent resolution without expressing lack of the respect due coordinate branches of government; or an unusual need for unquestioning adherence to a political decision already made; or the potentiality of embarrassment from multifarious pronouncements by various departments on one question.[33]

Prior to *Bush v. Gore*, one might have thought that one of the clearest examples of a "textually demonstrable constitutional commitment of [an] issue to a coordinate political department" would be disputes over presidential electors, which the Constitution explicitly declares shall be judged by Congress, not by the Supreme Court.

Notwithstanding the inherent subjectivity of the foregoing criteria, one should not overlook the utility of the label "political question." It formally bespeaks a decision qualitatively different from those that courts render and rhetorically asserts that courts avoid intruding themselves into the unprincipled domain of bureaucrats and politicians. As such, the political question doctrine has thus far helped to preserve the mythology of judging discussed in Chapter 1: that it is objective, dispassionate, and impartial.

Finality of Decision

To avoid any diminution of the authoritativeness of their decisions, courts scrupulously avoid controversies where their decisions may be overruled by nonjudicial decision makers. As we pointed out in our discussion of jurisdiction above, Congress must provide the federal courts with the authority to decide the cases they hear. Only the Supreme Court's original jurisdiction is activated by the Constitution directly. Congress, however, has not seen fit to bestow on the various federal courts all of the subject-matter jurisdiction that the Constitution contains. Instead, it vests some of it in various nonjudicial agencies and officials. The classic example dates from the Court's fifth reported case and governs eligibility for veterans' pension and

[33] 369 U.S. at 217. The nebulosity of these criteria was perhaps best illustrated by the failure of the majority's opinion in *Bush v. Gore* to provide any discussion whatsoever that the case might be a political question. The four dissenters, however, in their separate opinions all lambasted the majority's total disregard of this matter. One may also note that the Court has regularly taken pains to establish its jurisdiction whenever the question is fairly raised. But then, as *Bush v. Gore* so indisputably illustrates, the activistic Rehnquist Five make their own rules as they go along to insure the realization of their personal policy preferences.

disability benefits, where the final and binding decision was originally made by the War Department and until 1988 was made by the Veterans' Administration.[34]

The ability of a court to make the final and binding decision is not precluded because a higher court may overturn it. Or Congress, at some time in the future, may amend a statute adverse to the construction that a court had put on it. The same applies to proposed constitutional amendments. The rule requires only that at the time of decision, the court's judgment bind the parties and not be susceptible to alteration administratively or legislatively.

Estoppel

State as well as federal courts rather rigorously limit litigants to a single bite of the apple, to but one figurative day in court. Because estoppel is so thoroughly entrenched throughout the judicial system, few cases involving it reach the Supreme Court. It takes two general forms. Res judicata, or claim estoppel, precludes a party from relitigating the same cause of action against the same party if it was resolved by a final judgment that addressed the merits of the controversy. As an example, consider the Court's decision in *South Central Bell Telephone v. Alabama*.[35] The justices unanimously rejected the state's contention that res judicata barred the plaintiff's challenge to its franchise tax. The justices pointed out that the plaintiffs in the previous case were different, as was the tax year; neither case was a class action; and no privity existed between the two plaintiffs.

Although the common law defined causes of action narrowly, most court rules, including the Federal Rules, require the merger and joinder of claims today. This "transactional" definition of cause of action is designed to avoid piecemeal litigation and to promote judicial economy. The same party requirement governs those in privity with the relevant party, as well as employment and agency relationships and successors in

[34] *Hayburn's Case*, 2 Dallas 409 (1792). Questions about the constitutionality of a veterans' benefits statute or the meaning of the words therein are, of course, matters for judicial determination. E.g., *Traynor v. Turnage*, 485 U.S. 535 (1988), which presented the question of whether Congress statutorily authorized a Veterans' Administration regulation disqualifying alcoholic veterans from education benefits under the G. I. Bill. In 1988, Congress passed the Veterans Judicial Review Act, which created the Court of Veterans Appeals whose decisions could be reviewed by the Supreme Court. See *Brown v. Gardner*, 513 U.S. 115 (1994).

[35] 143 L Ed 2d 258 (1999).

interest. Res judicata does not bar relitigation if the cause of action lacks meritorious resolution. Thus, dismissal for want of subject-matter jurisdiction does not bar relitigation in the proper forum.

The other component, collateral estoppel, or issue preclusion, may be invoked only on a showing that an earlier proceeding actually decided the identical issue, and that it had to be decided in order to resolve the original case. Although the doctrine of mutuality prevented the assertion of collateral estopped against nonparties to the original proceeding, most jurisdictions have discarded this doctrine. Consequently, a party may be collaterally estopped from raising an issue if the original proceeding fully and fairly litigated it. The concept of full and fair litigation is increasingly limited to issues whose relitigation was reasonably foreseeable at the time of the original action. Thus, the second of two passengers in an automobile may not relitigate the driver's negligence if the other passenger had previously lost her suit for damages for injuries suffered in the resulting accident. If, however, the first passenger had won, the driver may not relitigate his negligence in the case of the second passenger.

Estoppel's preclusion of multiple lawsuits serves several purposes. In addition to enhancing the efficient use of judicial time and energy, it enables litigants to rely on a court's final judgment and thereby plan for the future. It also prevents the judicial system from being used as a tool for harassment.

Exhaustion of Administrative Remedies

To avoid trenching on other methods of dispute resolution, the Court requires potential litigants to exhaust any administrative remedies that may exist before gaining access to the federal courts. Exhaustion occupies a position with regard to agency action similar to the relationship of the abstention doctrine to state court action, a matter discussed in the last major section of Chapter 2. They differ in that abstention applies only if state court proceedings have commenced, whereas exhaustion applies regardless of the onset of agency action.[36] If a state has not initiated proceedings, persons may take their grievances – assuming the

[36] Exhaustion should be distinguished from the doctrine of primary jurisdiction. While both seek to thwart the courts from impinging on agency resolution of disputes, exhaustion applies only where an agency has exclusive primary jurisdiction over a matter. Primary jurisdiction, by contrast, is a form of abstention that a court may exercise even though it and the agency have concurrent jurisdiction.

existence of federal jurisdiction – directly to the proper federal court. That is not true of agency action. Because exhaustion applies whether or not the agency has launched proceedings, exceptions exist. These include inadequate agency remedies, an unduly dilatory agency, irreparable injury, or an agency acting ultra vires.

The Utilities of Standing

The elements of standing determine whether litigants are proper parties, thereby enabling the federal courts to avoid hypothetical, officious, and redundant decisions, and unnecessary conflicts with other decision makers. The rules governing standing enable judges to avoid issues they prefer not to resolve and to cite good legal form to justify their doing so.

The policies that govern access to the federal courts necessarily have substantive as well as procedural effects. Denial of access may equally readily produce conservative or liberal effects, depending on the orientation of the nonjudicial decision makers who serve as the justices' surrogates. Conversely, opening access may again produce liberal or conservative effects, depending on the justices' policy preferences about the substantive matters that cases gaining access contain.

Jurisdiction over the Parties

A final legal requirement that governs getting one's case into court concerns the question of whether the court has jurisdiction over the respondent. By initiating lawsuits, plaintiffs voluntarily subject themselves to the court's jurisdiction. Not so, the party who is sued. Due process of law requires that the court have the power to act on defendants or their property.[37] Courts have such power if defendants have "minimum contacts" with the state in which the court is located, "such that the maintenance of the suit does not offend 'traditional notions of fair play and substantial justice.'"[38]

[37] Due process, of course, also requires that the respondent receive notice of the pendency of legal action, and a hearing.

[38] *International Shoe Co. v. Washington*, 326 U.S. 310 (1945), at 316.

With some relatively minor exceptions, the federal courts are treated as though they are courts of the state in which they sit for purposes of determining the territorial reach of their jurisdiction. This is especially true of cases that raise a federal question.

Minimum contacts obviously exist if the respondent resides in or is domiciled in the forum state. It similarly exists in actions about property located in the state (e.g., to quiet title to real estate) or a status granted individuals by the state in question (e.g., dissolution of a marriage).[39] Nor is there any question of minimum contacts if the respondent voluntarily agrees to suit in a given state's courts. The test's application becomes crucial only over an unwilling out-of-state respondent. For such persons, the effect may be enormous. If, at one extreme, the Court construes minimum contacts to require that the defendant be resident or domiciled in the forum state, individuals could avoid legal responsibility by merely crossing the state line.[40] At the other extreme, a loose definition of minimum contacts could paralyze commercial activity if a retailer or other small business could be required to defend itself in a distant state's courts solely on the basis of an injury involving its product that occurred within that state. Such a policy would deter sellers from doing business with nonresidents, because liability to suit would travel with every item sold.

Collectively, the Court's decisions have staked out a position more or less midway between these extremes. In its most instructive decision, the Court rejected foreseeability of an injury as a permissible criterion for suit and focused instead on the defendant's conduct and connections with the forum state. Did it solicit business there, close sales, perform service, or avail itself of the benefits of the forum state's laws to the extent that it "should reasonably anticipate being haled into court there"?[41] More recent decisions require a "substantial connection" between the defendant and the forum state, which, according to at least four of the justices, "must come about by *an action of the defendant purposefully directed toward the forum State.*"[42]

39 In addition to jurisdiction over persons (*in personam*) and jurisdiction over things (*in rem*), the Court has also subjected *quasi in rem* jurisdiction to the minimum contacts test. See *Shaffer v. Heitner*, 433 U.S. 186 (1977). *Quasi in rem* actions attempt to seize the defendant's tangible or intangible property in order to satisfy a judgment. They are brought in a state where the defendant has property but the plaintiff lacks sufficient contacts to establish *in personam* jurisdiction over the defendant.

40 This was effectively the Court's original policy. *Pennoyer v. Neff*, 5 Otto 714 (1877). "Process from the tribunals of one State cannot run into another State, and summon parties there domiciled to leave its territory and respond to proceedings against them." 5 Otto, at 727. Also see *Harris v. Balk*, 198 U.S. 215 (1905). *Shaffer v. Heitner*, 433 U.S. 186 (1977), overruled them both. 433 U.S., at 212, note 39.

41 *World-Wide Volkswagen Corp. v. Woodson*, 444 U.S. 286 (1980), at 297.

42 *Burger King Corp. v. Rudzewicz*, 471 U.S. 462 (1985), at 475; *Asahi Metal Industry Co. v. Superior Court*, 480 U.S. 102 (1987), at 112.

CASE SELECTION

While the requirements of jurisdiction and standing apply to all federal courts, the process by which cases come to court differs across the federal judiciary. We, of course, focus on the Supreme Court.

The procedure that the Court employs to select the cases that it wishes to decide is formally uncomplicated. But because the justices provide very little information about this stage of their decision making, we do not know whether its formal simplicity also characterizes its operation. However, we can infer that the procedure the Court uses to choose its cases does work efficiently. The justices manage to stay abreast of their docket, unlike the vast majority of courts, state and federal. Little time elapses between receipt of a case and its disposition: A decision not to hear a case may be made within a week or two, but not for several months if the case reaches the Court during the summer when it is not in session. Cases that the Court agrees to review are almost always heard and decided within a year. Finally, lay and professional criticism is notable by its absence, which assuredly would not be true if an affected public considered the Court dilatory or ducking important issues.

The Court has authority to adopt rules governing its own operations, and a goodly number of these rules lay out the processes whereby losing litigants bring cases to the Court's attention and the criteria that govern the justices' decision to review the lower court's judgment.[43]

For all practical purposes, the justices are free to accept or reject cases brought to their attention as they see fit. That is to say, the Court has full control over its docket.[44] But that is not to say that the Court has no obligation to decide certain sorts of cases.[45] The justices would not likely refuse to review a decision by a lower federal court that voided a major act of Congress, nor would it decline to consider a state court's

[43] *The Rules of the Supreme Court of the United States* are published at periodic intervals in the *United States Reports*. The most recent compilation appears at 515 U.S. 1197 (1995).

[44] Especially since 1988 when Congress eliminated virtually all of what remained of the Court's mandatory jurisdiction. See Lynn Weisberg, "New Law Eliminates Supreme Court's Mandatory Jurisdiction," 72 *Judicature* 138 (1988).

[45] The most authoritative treatise on the procedures that govern the practice of law before the Supreme Court are the various editions of *Supreme Court Practice*, published in Washington by the Bureau of National Affairs. Robert L. Stern and Eugene Gressman were its original authors, aided in more recent editions by others.

On the workload of the Supreme Court, see Gerhard Casper and Richard A. Posner, *The Workload of the Supreme Court* (Chicago: American Bar Foundation, 1976).

decision that substantially redefined the scope of the First Amendment, absent extenuating circumstances.

Procedure

Because the Court had far less control over its docket in the nineteenth and early twentieth centuries than it does now, a remnant of this situation still persists in the technical distinction between the two major methods for accessing the Court: the writ of certiorari and the writ of appeal.[46] Within one to three months from the date the highest state or federal court with authority to hear the matter has entered its judgment, the losing litigant may petition the Supreme Court for a writ of certiorari if the case is one which Congress has not required the Court to review. If Congress has mandated review, the losing litigant files a writ of appeal. Although the effect of a denial differs, the Court uses the same procedure to grant either writ: the vote of four of the nine justices, three if only six or seven participate.[47]

Statutes and court rules specify the time within which losing litigants must petition the Court to review their cases. In all but the most exceptional circumstances, petitioning parties must have exhausted the remedies provided by the lower courts. Most often, this is either a final judgment of a state supreme court or a federal court of appeals. Many states, however, permit their supreme courts to deny a litigant leave to appeal, in which case the loser may petition the Supreme Court on the issuance of a judgment or decree by the inferior court of appeals or the trial court, as the case may be. The Supreme Court's rules specify the format that petitions for writs of certiorari and appeal must take, the information they shall include, and the number of copies to be filed.

[46] Litigants may petition the Court through other writs, such as certification, mandamus, injunction, stay of execution, or rehearing. The Court also accepts cases under its original jurisdiction and has authority to entertain various motions and to issue such orders on its own motion as it deems appropriate. These alternative routes are rarely used and, except for the exercise of original jurisdiction, are almost always handled summarily.

The Court does not consider itself obliged to hear all cases arising under its original jurisdiction. *Illinois v. City of Milwaukee*, 406 U.S. 91 (1972); *Arizona v. New Mexico*, 425 U.S. 794 (1976). If it grants leave to file a complaint thereunder, it almost always appoints a special master to hear the issues of fact and file a written report for the justices' consideration.

[47] According to the opinion of Justice Douglas in *Pryor v. United States*, 404 U.S. 1242 (1971), at 1243.

Other parties to the litigation are notified and provided an opportunity to submit briefs in opposition to Supreme Court review.

Additionally, interested third parties or interest groups have the opportunity to file amicus curiae (friend of the court) briefs supporting or opposing a petition for certiorari.[48] Nongovernmental entities may do so with the consent of both parties or, failing that, with the consent of the Court. National, state, and local governmental units are automatically granted the right to file briefs. The Court will occasionally ask third parties, usually the United States or a state, to file amicus briefs.

On receipt of a petition and the winning party's brief in opposition, plus an optional reply by the petitioner, the clerk of the Supreme Court compiles and reviews the documents, along with the lower court's record of the case. If the clerk deems the petition "frivolous" – undeserving of review – he so informs the chief justice, who, in turn, has his clerks prepare a digest of the case. If the chief justice and his clerks agree that the case does not merit review, it is "deadlisted." The material and recommendations pertaining to the case are sent to the other justices who, assisted by their clerks, review the file. If all the justices agree with deadlisting, the case will not be discussed in conference and will automatically be denied review. This fate apparently befalls well over half the petitions. But if any justice objects to deadlisting, the case will be discussed in conference.

The Court's conduct of its conferences, according to an on-the-scene professional, Stephen Wermiel, who covered the Court for the *Wall Street Journal* and is now a law professor at American University in Washington, D.C., "has followed a well-established, set-your-watch-to-it pattern of behavior for many years":

– when regular conferences were scheduled (Wednesday afternoon and Friday morning)
– when order lists would be released from those conferences (Monday mornings until the last few years when the practice started to include certiorari grants on Friday afternoons and certiorari denials on Monday mornings during the time when the Court was filling its calendar for oral argument)

48 See, e.g., Lucius Barker, "Third Parties in Litigation: A Systemic View of the Judicial Function," 29 *Journal of Politics* 41 (1967); Lee Epstein, *Conservatives in Court* (Knoxville: University of Tennessee Press, 1985); and Karen O'Connor, *Women's Organizations Use of the Courts* (Lexington, Mass.: Lexington Books, 1980).

– certiorari grant announcements during the week before the Court's term begins on the first Monday in October.[49]

But early in the 1999 term, episodes occurred that deviated from this set-in-concrete procedure.[50] Of course, the justices have occasionally had midnight conference calls to consider stays of execution and have undoubtedly held other unscheduled meetings, but, according to Wermiel, "they didn't produce certiorari grants, except in the most rare circumstances."

> What has changed this term is an outward manifestation: all of a sudden, a handful of cases are granted in mid-September when there is no information that the Court has held an unscheduled conference. Does this prove there was no conference? Absolutely not! But is it a change in an otherwise almost entirely predictable routine? Yes. The outward manifestations for the ADA and qui tam cases [*Vermont Agency of Natural Resources v. United States ex rel. Stevens*, 146 L Ed 2d 836 (2000)] is that they, too, came out of cycle. They were not announced as part of any set of orders, either on a Friday afternoon or a Monday morning that . . . grew out of a known, scheduled conference. Could they have come from an unscheduled conference? Absolutely! But is it highly unusual for the Court to be having an unscheduled conference during the term to talk about certiorari grants? Yes![51]

Cases not deadlisted are further considered in each justices's chambers, where memos are prepared by the clerks. To cut down on the work of the clerks, several justices have instructed their clerks to form a "cert pool," where the participating clerks divide the petitions among themselves. Other justices have their clerks write memos on each case or those considered important.[52] In conference the justices discuss the cases and vote on the basis of seniority. If, following discussion, at least four justices support review (three if seven or fewer participate) (the Rule of Four), the petition is granted and the case is scheduled for oral argument. Out of the 8,000 or so petitions the Court receives per term, approximately 100 or less are granted and become candidates for formal

[49] E-mail correspondence between Wermiel and Spaeth, February 9 and 10, 2000.

[50] Joan Biskupic, "Full Court Press, Justices in Conference: A Tradition Wanes," *Washington Post*, February 7, 2000, p. A15. The reporter covering the Court for the *New York Times*, Linda Greenhouse, has also alluded to altered conference procedure: "Justices to Weigh Constitutionality of Key Element of Whistle-Blower Law," November 30, 1999, p. A10.

[51] Wermiel, *op. cit.*, n. 49, *supra.*

[52] Jan Palmer, *The Vinson Court Era* (New York: AMS, 1990), pp. 24–30.

decision.[53] One third of the petitions for review are cases in which the Court's filing fee is paid and the requisite number of copies are filed, and two thirds are *in forma pauperis* petitions in which the filing fee and the requirement of multiple copies are waived.[54] The vast majority of these are filed by incarcerated indigents. The justices accept and decide only a handful of these cases per term, well under 1 percent of the total submitted.[55]

Criteria for Selection

In adumbrating the criteria for granting a writ of certiorari,[56] the justices give heaviest emphasis to decisions "in conflict" with another court of appeals, with a state court of last resort, or with "relevant decisions" of the Court.[57] The other two stipulated criteria are decisions which have "departed from the accepted and usual course of judicial proceedings, or sanctioned such a departure" and those which have "decided an important question of federal law that has not been, but should be, settled by this Court." Although conflict may be amenable to objective determination, the Court does not limit itself only to the enumerated considerations which, according to Rule 10, are "neither controlling nor fully measuring the Court's discretion."[58]

Although no comparable rule addresses the granting of writs of appeal, the rules provide indirect guidance by instructing appellants and appellees about the kind of arguments and considerations their briefs should contain. The fact that the Court uses the same procedure – the Rule of Four, described above – to dispose of petitions for certiorari as well as writs of appeal suggests that their criteria for selection may be fungible.[59]

[53] Granting a petition does not necessarily preclude a summary decision on the merits without the benefit of oral argument and a formal opinion of the Court. Rule 16.1 specifically so provides.

[54] 518 U.S. 1059 (1995).

[55] Linda Greenhouse, "'Pauper' Cases Reshape High Court's Caseload," *New York Times*, January 28, 1991, p. A13.

[56] Most of the data in this and the remaining sections of this chapter date from the beginning of the Warren Court in 1953 because highly reliable data are available for this period. We certainly do not intimate that nothing of importance in this – or other – regard occurred between the time of Chief Justices Marshall and Warren.

[57] Rule 10, 515 U.S., at 1204. [58] *Id.*

[59] Robert L. Stern and Eugene Gressman, *Supreme Court Practice*, 5th ed. (Washington: Bureau of National Affairs, 1978), pp. 374–77. Justice Stevens, joined in dissent by Ginsburg and Breyer, offered the following advice about certiorari petitions in *O'Sullivan v.*

That four or more justices agree to review a case does not necessarily ensure a decision on the merits of the controversy. After oral argument, a majority may rule that the writ was improvidently granted or dismiss an appeal for lack of jurisdiction, for want of a substantial federal question, or some other nonmeritorious reason.

But that does not end the story. Consider the following: An attorney tells his client who has been convicted of a capital offense and who has petitioned the Supreme Court for review that he has good news and bad news. The good news is that four justices voted to grant certiorari. The bad is that five have not voted to stay his execution pending review of his case. The upshot: He was executed (by Texas, not surprisingly). Justice Brennan explains: "[F]our Members of this Court have voted to grant certiorari in this case, but because a stay cannot be entered without five votes, the execution cannot be halted."[60] Normally in such cases, "one of the five justices who does not believe the case certworthy will nonetheless vote to stay; this is so that the 'Rule of Four' will not be rendered meaningless by an execution that occurs before the Court considers the case on the merits."[61] In earlier terms, Justice Powell was willing to provide the fifth vote to stay executions when cert had been granted. But in the Hamilton case, not Rehnquist nor White nor O'Connor nor Scalia nor Kennedy was willing to issue the stay.

From the beginning of the Warren Court through the end of the 2000 term, the justices addressed the advisability of a nonmeritorious decision after oral argument in 140 cases. In almost 90 percent, the justices did deny the plaintiffs access notwithstanding their initial decision to the contrary (125 of 140). In only fifteen cases did the justices reconfirm the grant of access. Ten denied the states' contentions that their decisions rested on adequate nonfederal grounds (out of a total of twenty cases, as Table 6.2 indicates). Three reconsidered cases requesting the state supreme court to answer certain questions of law, while the other two sought determination of the basis for the state court's decision.

Reconsideration following a grant of access does not necessarily undermine the integrity of the Rule of Four. But, as Justice Douglas

Boerckel, 144 L Ed 1 (1999) at 18: "The most helpful and persuasive petitions . . . usually present only one or two issues, and spend a considerable amount of time explaining why those questions of law have divided or confused other courts. Given the page limitations that we impose, a litigant cannot write such a petition if he decides, or is required, to raise every claim that might possibly warrant reversal in his particular case."

60 *Hamilton v. Texas*, 497 U.S. 1016 (1990) at 1016–17.

61 *Straight v. Wainwright*, 476 U.S. 1132 (1986) at 1135 (Brennan, dissenting).

TABLE 6.2. *Nonmeritorious Reconsideration of Orally Argued Cases, 1953–2000 Terms*

Nonmeritorious action	Warren Court	Burger Court	Rehnquist Court	Total
Writ improvidently granted	34	32	22	88
Want of adequate federal question	7	2	2	11
Want of jurisdiction	1	2	1	4
Adequate nonfederal grounds	14	6	0	20
To determine basis of state decision	3	2	5	10
Miscellaneous	2	2	3	7
TOTAL	61	46	32	140

pointed out: "If four can grant and the opposing five dismiss, then the four cannot get a decision of the case on the merits. The integrity of the four-man vote rule . . . would then be impaired."[62] The justice who most assiduously subverted the rule was Frankfurter. In workers' compensation cases, he regularly refused to address the merits after he had voted to deny cert. He rationalized his position as follows:

> The right of a Justice to dissent from an action of the Court is historic. . . . Not four, not eight, Justices can require another to decide a case that he regards as not properly before the Court. The failure of a Justice to persuade his colleagues does not require him to yield to their views, if he has a deep conviction that the issue is sufficiently important. . . . Even though a minority may bring a case here for oral argument, that does not mean that the majority has given up its right to vote on the ultimate disposition of the case as conscience directs. This is not a novel doctrine. As a matter of practice, members of the Court have at various times exercised the right of refusing to pass on the merits of cases that in their view should not have been granted review.[63]

If, however, one or more of those voting to dismiss originally voted to grant, no impairment of the Rule of Four results.

[62] *United States v. Shannon*, 342 U.S. 288 (1952), at 298.

[63] *Rogers v. Missouri Pacific R. Co.*, 352 U.S. 500 (1957), and *Ferguson v. Moore-McCormick Lines*, 352 U.S. 521 (1957), at 528. Also see Glendon Schubert, *Quantitative Analysis of Judicial Behavior* (Glencoe, Ill.: Free Press, 1959), pp. 210–67, and Glendon Schubert, "Policy Without Law: An Extension of the Certiorari Game," 14 *Stanford Law Review* 284 (1962). Other than Frankfurter, only five dissenters from certiorari appear to have voted to dismiss in five cases since the beginning of the Warren Court in 1953.

Effects of Denial or Dismissal

The Court's refusal to decide a case arising on certiorari whether or not the petition had been granted has no precedential effect. With regard to appeals, unqualified assertions that "[d]ismissal and affirmance are treated legally as decisions on the merits of cases, and they have some weight as precedents for future cases" are not quite correct.[64] Affirmation, with or without opinion, whether on certiorari or appeal, clearly has precedential value. So also when an appeal is dismissed for want of a substantial federal question as distinct from lack of jurisdiction. When the Court rules a question insubstantial, it says something about the merits of the case. But when it dismisses for want of jurisdiction, it has "no occasion to address the merits of the constitutional questions presented in the jurisdictional statements."[65]

Although peripheral to the denial and dismissal of petitions, reference should be made to the justices' practice of "holding" one or more of a number of cases that raise similar issues until the one that has been granted review has been decided. The justices' docket books, which contain the votes and other actions taken prior to final disposition, are rife with references to cases being held. Once the Court makes its decision in the case selected for full review, the justices decide the disposition to be made of the held case(s). Although we lack systematic data on these cases, we may safely conclude that most all of them are either conjoined with the formally decided case or are otherwise subjected to grant-vacate-remand (GVR) treatment, that is, certiorari is granted; the decision of the lower court is vacated; and the case is remanded for further consideration in light of the Court's decision in the formally decided case. Cases receiving GVR treatment are neither briefed nor orally argued but rather are "an appropriate exercise of our discretionary certiorari jurisdiction."[66] They are treated the same as cases in which certiorari is denied, except that the decision of the court that last decided them is not final. Further proceedings will occur.

The Court has stated the utility of the GVR: . . . A GVR order conserves the scarce resources of this Court that might otherwise be expended on plenary consideration, assists the court below by flagging a particular issue that it does not

[64] Lawrence Baum, *The Supreme Court*, 2nd ed. (Washington: Congressional Quarterly, 1985), p. 89.

[65] *Hopfmann v. Connolly*, 471 U.S. 459 (1985), at 460–61.

[66] *Lawrence v. Chater*, 516 U.S. 163 (1996) at 166.

appear to have fully considered, assists this Court by procuring the benefit of the lower court's insight before we rule on the merits, and alleviates the "[p]otential for unequal treatment" that is inherent in our inability to grant plenary review of all pending cases raising similar issues. . . .[67]

The facts of *Lawrence v. Chater* and its companion[68] illustrate well the applicability of GVRs. *Chater* concerned the rejection of a minor's claim for survivor's social security benefits by a federal court of appeals. Subsequent to the decision, the Social Security Administration changed its policy. The Court told the lower court to reconsider its decision in light of the new policy. *Chater*'s companion case instructed a lower court to apply the Court's newly established precedent permitting the late filing of an appeal for "excusable neglect."

Distinct from held cases are those that are "relisted." This practice apparently began in the early 1970s and has the effect of postponing – that is, delaying – action on petitions to review decisions of lower courts. References to relisting are found in the docket sheets of both Brennan and Powell. Brennan makes no mention of it prior to the 1971 term, Powell's first. According to H. W. Perry, the only source who apparently makes reference to relisting,[69] any justice may request that a case be held over until the next conference (usually one week later). The reasons for relisting vary. Sometimes a justice wishes to persuade his colleagues to grant cert. Other times a justice wants more time to consider the case. Not uncommonly, one justice's request may be followed by another's. Although most such requests do not extend beyond a week, some run on for months. Thus, for example, Powell requested that *Snepp v. United States* be relisted five times between October 26, 1979, and January 11, 1980, and that its companion, *United States v. Snepp*, be relisted six times between October 5, 1979, and January 11, 1980. Thereafter, Stevens had both cases relisted on January 18, 1980.[70]

Although Perry quotes a justice in support of his assertion that with a couple of exceptions "relisting is not a favored practice,"[71] Brennan's and Powell's docket sheets identify well over 2,000 relisted cases during

[67] *Id.* at 167. Scalia and Thomas would limit GVRs to cases where an intervening factor bearing on the decision has arisen; where a question of the Court's jurisdiction over a matter decided by a state court exists; or where the respondent confesses error.

[68] *Stutson v. United States*, 516 U.S. 193 (1996).

[69] *Deciding to Decide* (Cambridge, Mass.: Harvard University Press, 1991), pp. 49–51.

[70] 444 U.S. 507 (1980). The cases were decided per curiam without oral argument on February 19, Stevens, Brennan, and Marshall dissenting.

[71] *Op. cit.*, n. 69, *supra,* p. 51.

TABLE 6.3. *Cases Filed, 1880–1995*

Term	Cases filed
1880	417
1890	636
1900	406
1910	516
1920	565
1930	845
1940	977
1950	1,181
1960	1,940
1970	3,419
1980	4,175
1985	4,421
1990	5,502
1995	6,597

Source: Excerpted from Epstein et al., *The Supreme Court Compendium*, 2d ed. (Washington: Congressional Quarterly, 1996), Table 2-2.

the last fifteen terms of the Burger Court. Though many relisted cases end with certiorari being denied, a substantial number do receive full treatment. The effect obviously is to delay the Court's productive process, with what cost we will not know, absent a systematic analysis of these cases and the behavior of the individual justices.

THE SUPREME COURT'S CASELOAD

Tremendous growth has occurred in the Supreme Court's caseload over time. As shown in Table 6.3, little change occurred in the number of cases filed between 1880 and 1920. Small increases occurred between the 1930s and 1950s, with explosive growth since. Between 1789 and 1950 the number of cases filed climbed from under ten per term to slightly over 1,000. By 1961 the Court faced 2,000 filings. It took only six years after that to reach 3,000, and but another six to reach 4,000. Between 1950 and 1995 the total number of filings almost sextupled.

Cases filed are either paid or unpaid. The latter are placed on the *in forma pauperis* docket, which was known as the miscellaneous docket until the 1977 term. Through 1958 the paid cases annually exceeded the unpaid cases. During the Warren Court, the number of unpaid cases grew substantially and exceeded the paid cases every year from 1959 until 1978. They then held steady through the early 1980s but began to grow dramatically at the end of the decade, reaching more than 4,500 by the mid-1990s.[72]

The Supreme Court can review only a small percentage of the cases filed. Indeed, the Court reviews only about 5 percent of the paid cases and well under 1 percent of the *in forma pauperis* cases. Moreover, not all of these cases receive full treatment by the Court: oral argument and written opinions; the remainder result in summary dispositions. The early Warren Court decided less than 100 cases per year, but the early Burger Court heard as many as 153 cases in the 1972 term. That appears to be close to the Court's institutional limit, for since then the Court has never decided more than 155 cases in a single term. The 1989 term of the Court, which made headlines for the rate at which it rejected petitions for review,[73] decided but 130 cases, the lowest total since 1980. Since then the number has dropped precipitously. In the 1998 term, counting case citations, it formally decided only 80 cases, and fell to 76 in the 1999 term and to 72 in the 2000 term.

The broad issues contained in the Warren, Burger, and Rehnquist Court's cases through the 1998 term are presented in Table 6.4. Again we count by citation, not docket. As can be seen, continuity characterizes the issues decided. Criminal procedure was most frequently litigated in the Burger and Rehnquist Courts, and was second only to economic cases in the Warren Court. Economic activity, civil rights, judicial power, and the First Amendment have received substantial attention from all three Courts. Yet, while economic activity is second overall in type of case heard, it occupies a decreasing share of the Court's agenda. A full quarter of the Warren Court's cases dealt with economic activity as compared with less than a fifth of the Burger and Rehnquist total. Also showing a substantial decrease are cases dealing with unions and federal taxation, now with less than half the proportion they had in the Warren Court. Alternatively, issues of federalism are substantially more frequently litigated by the Rehnquist than its two predecessor Courts. A likely explanation for these trends may be the justices' perception that business, labor, and tax matters have relatively little salience, as com-

72 518 U.S. 1059 (1996).

73 Linda Greenhouse, "As Its Workload Decreases, High Court Shuns New Cases," *New York Times*, November 28, 1989, p. A1.

TABLE 6.4. *Case Selection by Issue Area Controlled for Court*

	Warren 1953–68	Burger 1969–85	Rehnquist 1986–2000	Row total
Criminal procedure	352 (19.6%)	517 (21.5%)	377 (24.4%)	1,246 (21.7%)
Economic activity	448 (25.0%)	427 (17.8%)	274 (17.7%)	1,149 (20.0%)
Civil rights	224 (12.5%)	496 (20.6%)	233 (15.1%)	953 (16.6%)
Judicial power	228 (12.7%)	269 (11.2%)	217 (14.0%)	714 (12.4%)
First Amendment	155 (8.6%)	208 (8.7%)	114 (7.4%)	477 (8.3%)
Unions	127 (7.1%)	108 (4.5%)	47 (3.0%)	282 (4.9%)
Federalism	81 (4.5%)	87 (3.6%)	92 (6.0%)	260 (4.5%)
Federal taxation	115 (6.4%)	68 (2.8%)	49 (3.2%)	232 (4.0%)
Due process	37 (2.1%)	128 (5.3%)	68 (4.4%)	233 (4.1%)
Attorneys	10 (0.6%)	32 (1.3%)	26 (1.7%)	68 (1.2%)
Privacy	2 (0.1%)	40 (1.7%)	24 (1.6%)	66 (1.1%)
Interstate relations	9 (0.5%)	17 (0.7%)	12 (0.8%)	38 (0.7%)
Miscellaneous	5 (0.3%)	7 (0.3%)	12 (0.8%)	24 (0.4%)
Column total	1,793	2,404	1,545	5,742

pared with increased autonomy for the state and local governments. If we combine the six areas commonly lumped together as civil rights and liberties – criminal procedure, civil rights, First Amendment, due process, attorneys, and privacy – we find that over half the Court's formal output concerns these matters. Finally, while the content of the cases heard might give some guide to the type of questions the Court deems important, it is not foolproof. Criminal procedure covers a wide array of constitutional issues, including Fourth, Fifth, Sixth, and Eighth Amendment rights. Privacy, on the other hand, has largely dealt with contraception and abortion. This does not necessarily make privacy a less important issue to the Court.

WHICH CASES FOR DECISION

Analyses of whether to grant review, with but a couple of exceptions, are limited to cases arising on writ of certiorari and exclude writs of appeal. Cert studies of Courts predating Rehnquist consequently omit approximately a quarter of the Court's cases.[74] Although the Court gives no stated reason for review of noncert cases, other factors that account for much of the Court's behavior are knowable, for example, the "cues" that the cases contain, the direction – whether liberal or conservative – of the lower court's decision, whether any judges on this court dissented, and whether the Supreme Court affirmed or reversed the decision of the lower court. Only the analyses reported below that use the Supreme Court Judicial Database and Jan Palmer's masterful work on the Vinson Court[75] include appeals. We examine first those factors linked with individual-level decisions to grant certiorari and then examine the aggregate decisions of the Court itself.

Individual-Level Models

Despite tremendous scholarly interest,[76] award-winning books,[77] clever research strategies,[78] and sophisticated statistical analyses,[79] no consen-

[74] Excluding cases on the original docket and using docket number, 25 percent of the Warren Court's cases did not arise on cert, 27 percent of the Burger Court's, but only 9 percent of the Rehnquist Court's through the end of the 2000 term. The difference results because Congress markedly reduced the number of cases to be heard on appeal shortly after the start of the Rehnquist Court.

[75] *Op. cit.*, n. 52, *supra*, ch. 6. Though Palmer finds similarity in how the justices voted between granting cert and noting jurisdiction on appeals, the model he formulates to explain cert voting does not adequately explain appeals voting. *Id.*, p. 95.

[76] H. W. Perry, Jr., "Agenda Setting and Case Selection," in John Gates and Charles Johnson, eds., *American Courts: A Critical Assessment* (Washington, D.C.: Congressional Quarterly Press, 1991).

[77] Perry, *op. cit.*, n. 69, *supra*.

[78] Saul Brenner, "The New Certiorari Game," 41 *Journal of Politics* 649–55 (1979).

[79] Jan Palmer, "An Econometric Analysis of the U.S. Supreme Court's Certiorari Decisions," 39 *Public Choice* 387–98 (1982).

sus exists among scholars of individual-level voting behavior as to what factors influence the granting of certiorari. Some view the process as essentially legalistic, while others see it as essentially political or policy-based. Furthermore, among the policy-based school, dissent exists as to whether the justices are forward-thinking in their certiorari votes, that is, whether they consider the likelihood that they will win on the merits when voting to grant review. However surprising this disagreement may be, it is all the more so when one realizes that most of the individual-level analyses are based on the same data: the docket books of Harold Burton, who served from the 1945 through 1957 terms of the Court.

We assess the literature and use data from the Vinson-Warren Court Judicial Database to examine the factors motivating the justices' certiorari voting.[80]

Reversal Strategies

A major premise behind most prior work on certiorari is the assumption that the justices prefer to hear cases they wish to reverse. Given a finite number of cases that can be reviewed in a given term, the Court must decide how to utilize its time, the Court's most scarce resource. Certainly, overturning unfavorable lower court decisions has more of an impact – if only to the parties to the litigation – than affirming favorable ones. Moreover, reversal of erroneous or malfeasant lower courts can help keep those courts in line.[81] Thus, the justices should hear more cases with which they disagree, other things being equal.

The first person to actually test this simple reversal strategy in cert voting was S. Sidney Ulmer.[82] He proposed that justices who voted for cert would support the applicant on the merits, while justices who voted against cert would not. Ulmer found a significant relationship between the cert vote and the vote on the merits for eight of eleven justices,[83] but the proportional reduction in error statistic he used, lambda, was quite low, ranging from 0.00 to 0.157.

[80] This database, along with others funded by the National Science Foundation that pertain to the Supreme Court, is freely available, along with its documentation, at the website of the Michigan State University Judicial Center: www.ssc.msu.edu/~pls/pljp.

[81] We develop this argument more fully in the section on aggregate certiorari models.

[82] S. Sidney Ulmer, "The Decision to Grant Certiorari as an Indicator to Decision 'On the Merits,'" 4 *Polity* 429 (1972).

[83] Ulmer's study, like most of the individual-level studies that follow, relies on the eventual outcome as a predictor of what justices will do at cert. Thus, they necessarily examine only cases where the Court actually grants cert.

Ulmer used his evidence of a reversal strategy to suggest a policy-based approach to certiorari voting, but his low reported correlations helped lead Doris Marie Provine to the conclusion that justices do not pursue policy goals in their certiorari voting.[84] Her assumptions about policy-based voting led her to deduce that justices would virtually always vote to hear cases whose result they would reverse and deny review to decisions they would affirm. This in turn would lead to few unanimous cert decisions. We discuss the appropriateness of these hypotheses below, but note for now, not surprisingly, that she finds little support for them.

Additionally, Perry supports the essence of Provine's claim.[85] He argues that certiorari is essentially a legal process, not a political one. Based on interviews with justices and clerks, Perry asserts that error correction is of minor importance,[86] and even then is limited to "egregious" decisions by the lower courts.[87]

Alternatively, we wonder how any higher court could possibly keep any form of hierarchical control over lower courts if its justices did not engage in a substantial amount of error correction. We thus reexamine the arguments over reversal strategies both empirically and theoretically.

Empirically, we begin by noting that Ulmer's meager reported findings, based as they were on a proportional reduction of error statistic, should not be surprising given the skew of the dependent variable. But that does not mean that there is not in fact a strong relationship between voting on cert and voting on the merits. Our own tests (see Table 6.5) using Vinson Court data show that the relationship between the vote on the merits and the vote on cert is quite strong.

Every justice on the Vinson Court was *much* more likely to vote to reverse when he had voted to grant the petition than he was to reverse when he had voted to deny the petition. The reversal rate for justices who voted to deny ranges from 29 percent for Clark to 46 percent for Douglas. But the reversal rates for justices who voted to grant range from 55 percent for Reed to 74 percent for Black. The gammas, a measure of association ranging from −1.0 (perfect negative relationship) to 0 (no relationship) to 1.0 (perfect positive relationship), range from 0.38 (Reed) to 0.72 (Black) and are all significant at $p < 0.001$. Thus, reanalysis of the same justices examined by Ulmer demonstrates beyond cavil that to a significant extent the vote to grant is in fact a preliminary vote on the merits.

[84] "Deciding What to Decide: How the Supreme Court sets Its agenda," 64 *Judicature* 320 (1981).

[85] *Op. cit.*, n. 69, *supra.* [86] *Id.*, p. 36. [87] *Id.*, p. 265.

TABLE 6.5. *Reversal Rate by Certiorari Vote in the Vinson Court, 1946–1952 Terms*

Justice	Deny	Grant	γ
Black	31.5 (197)	73.5 (611)	0.72
Burton	29.6 (216)	56.7 (603)	0.51
Clark	29.2 (65)	56.9 (262)	0.52
Douglas	45.8 (120)	68.5 (568)	0.44
Frankfurter	37.3 (255)	58.4 (551)	0.41
Jackson	32.8 (235)	58.4 (476)	0.49
Minton	37.7 (151)	59.7 (181)	0.42
Murphy	41.7 (48)	71.6 (324)	0.56
Reed	35.7 (199)	55.4 (607)	0.38
Rutledge	36.9 (65)	72.6 (318)	0.64
Vinson	30.6 (232)	62.8 (497)	0.59

Note: Numbers in parentheses are total number of votes to deny or grant. Thus, Black voted to reverse in 31.5% of the 197 cases where he voted to deny and 73.5% of the 611 cases where he voted to grant.

Moreover, unanimity in cert decisions does not indicate that reversal strategies are not paramount. The overwhelming majority of unanimous cert denials occur in *in forma pauperis* petitions submitted by convicted criminals. As they incur virtually no cost in filing such petitions, largely frivolous appeals result.[88] If the majority of trials do comport with due process, from an attitudinal perspective we would expect unanimous denials. Presumably, even liberal justices don't want to free criminals just because they disapprove of incarceration.

Prediction Strategies

While reversal is a major premise determining which cases to review, one ought not consider it the only factor guiding the cert votes of policy-minded justices. First, with approximately 8,000 cases confronting the Court annually, justices who voted to review every case with which they disagreed would generate institutional paralysis. Salience will obviously matter. Moreover, even if the Court could hear all cases with which a justice disagreed, it is not necessarily in that justice's best policy interest

[88] The Court is cognizant of this problem and has taken steps to alleviate it. See *In re Demos*, 500 U.S. 16 (1991).

to have all such cases reviewed. If the justice will likely lose on the merits, it is preferable that the case not be heard at all.

A series of obscenity cases during the 1970s exemplifies. By a 5-to-4 vote in *Miller v. California*,[89] the majority decided that states and local governments could ban sexually explicit patently offensive work that lacked serious literary, artistic, political, or social value and which violated contemporary local community standards. The four dissenters preferred constitutional standards more protective of freedom of communication. When lower courts upheld convictions based on *Miller*, three of the dissenters – Brennan, Stewart, and Marshall – voted to grant certiorari. Justice Stevens, who replaced Justice Douglas, also opposed *Miller*, but nevertheless voted to deny cert:

> Nothing in Mr. Justice Brennan's opinion dissenting from the denial of certiorari in this case persuades me that any purpose would be served by such argument. For there is no reason to believe that the majority of the Court which decided *Miller v. California*... is any less adamant than the minority. Accordingly, regardless of how I might vote on the merits after full argument, it would be pointless to grant certiorari in case after case of this character only to have *Miller* reaffirmed time after time.[90]

Alternatively, justices who favored a particular lower court decision might vote to grant cert if they were confident of affirmation.

Thus, while reversal clearly is a part of the justices' strategy, adequately determining whether a policy-based focus can explain certiorari voting requires more sophisticated strategies.

Glendon Schubert's "Certiorari Game"[91] represents the first systematic attempt to explain the justices' behavior in game-theoretic terms. Schubert examined the strategies of the four-member liberal bloc of the 1942 term: Wiley Rutledge, Frank Murphy, Hugo Black, and William Douglas. According to Schubert's analysis, the bloc voted to grant cert in thirteen of the fourteen cases in which an appellate court overturned a lower court decision favorable to the employee. The bloc apparently eschewed a simple reversal strategy of voting to hear every antiworker appellate court decision by focusing instead only on those where the appellate court reversed a trial court decision favorable to the worker. Unfortunately, Schubert's analysis was limited by the fact that he could only infer the justices' conference votes from the actual granting of cert;

[89] 413 U.S. 15 (1973). [90] *Liles v. Oregon*, 425 U.S 963 (1976), at 963–64.
[91] *Quantitative Analysis of Judicial Behavior* (Glencoe, Ill.: Free Press, 1959), pp. 210–54.

he had no data on how they actually voted. Indeed, Provine has since contested his specific conclusions.[92]

Strong support for strategic certiorari voting can also be found in the early work of Saul Brenner.[93] He assumed that justices will be more likely to behave strategically when only four vote to grant cert, because then each vote is essential. He therefore argues that a justice who wants to affirm will not provide the fourth vote unless he or she is quite certain that the Court will in fact affirm. As he predicts, when a four-person certiorari bloc includes justices who want the court to affirm, the affirmance-preferring justices in that bloc will be more likely to prevail than the reversal-preferring justices. He also finds the justices to be less forward concerned with eventual outcomes when more than four vote for cert, because in these cases each justice's vote does not affect the decision to hear the case. Voting for cert in such cases neither aids nor hinders the justice's policy designs, making predicted outcomes irrelevant to the decisional outcome. In a later study, Brenner and John Krol found, consistent with policy-based models, that justices were more likely to vote for cert if they wanted to reverse, if their side would win on the merits, and if they were liberals on a liberal Court or conservatives on a conservative Court.[94]

Similarly, Caldeira, Wright, and Zorn find that during the 1982 term of the Court, justices who were more likely to win on the merits were more likely to vote for cert.[95] These results coincide with the findings of Jan Palmer, who found that the justices' votes on cert correlate with their vote on the merits and whether their side wins on the merits.[96] More recent work by Palmer extends these findings to the appeals docket and finds overwhelming evidence for reversal strategies, but little evidence that those who vote for cert are overall more likely to win on the

[92] Doris Marie Provine, *Case Selection in the United States Supreme Court* (Chicago: University of Chicago Press, 1980), ch. 5. Brennan did not follow Schubert's strategy. The other liberal justices adhered to it between 62 and 100 percent of the time. One can dispute the criterion of success, but we consider Schubert's model reasonably accurate empirically.

[93] Brenner, *op. cit.*, n. 78, *supra.*

[94] Saul Brenner and John F. Krol, "Strategies in Certiorari Voting on the United States Supreme Court," 51 *Journal of Politics* 828 (1989); also see John F. Krol and Saul Brenner, "Strategies in Certiorari Voting on the United States Supreme Court: A Reevaluation," 43 *Political Research Quarterly* 335 (1990).

[95] Gregory A. Caldeira, John R. Wright, and Christopher J. W. Zorn, "Strategic Voting and Gatekeeping in the Supreme Court," 15 *Journal of Law, Economics and Organization* 549 (1999).

[96] *Op. cit.*, n. 79, *supra.*

merits.[97] According to Brenner, though, a "prediction" strategy is only likely to be followed under the circumstances described above.[98]

Thus, similar to reversal strategies, scholars have disputed the notion and prevalence of prediction strategies. Provine claims that the justices are not motivated by what she called outcome-oriented concerns. Rather, she claims that "a shared conception of the proper role of a judge prevents the justices from exploiting the possibilities for power-oriented [i.e., strategic] voting in case selection."[99] Moreover, Perry claims, "even if one concedes that some cert votes are preliminary votes on the merits, that does not imply that a cert vote involves any strategic or 'sophisticated' voting." Nevertheless, Perry does not deny the existence of strategic voting, merely its prevalence. "All of the justices act strategically on cert at times, and much of the time none of them acts strategically."[100] Justices on occasion engage in "defensive denials" – voting to deny petitions from disfavored lower court decisions in order to prevent probable affirmance by the Supreme Court – and "aggressive grants" – voting to grant petitions from favorable lower court decisions in order to achieve probable affirmance by the Supreme Court. Blurring the lines in this debate, Saul Brenner, an early proponent of strategic certiorari voting, claims in his work with John Krol that when justices who switch their votes between the conference vote on the merits and the final or report vote on the merits are eliminated from consideration, evidence of strategic voting shrinks to statistically significant but substantively meaningless levels. Moreover, they find no evidence whatsoever for defensive denials. They conclude that their research "buttresses the view that . . . error-correction . . . is extant in certiorari voting but undermines the perception that the prediction strategy is also present."[101]

We attempt to resolve this set of contradictory findings by examining the votes on certiorari by the justices during the Warren Court, paying special attention to the difference between affirm- and reverse-minded justices.[102]

[97] *Op. cit.*, n. 52, *supra*, ch. 6.

[98] *Op. cit.*, n. 78, *supra*. Also see Sara C. Benesh, Saul Brenner, and Harold J. Spaeth, "Aggressive Grants by Affirm-Minded Justices," 30 *American Politics Research* (2002).

[99] *Op. cit.*, n. 92, *supra*, p. 172. [100] *Op. cit.*, n. 69, *supra*, pp. 270, 198.

[101] *Op. cit.*, n. 94, *supra*, p. 342. Cf. *op. cit.*, n. 48, *supra*.

[102] We base this section on Robert L. Boucher, Jr., and Jeffrey A. Segal, "Supreme Court Justices as Strategic Decision Makers," 57 *Journal of Politics* 824 (1995), and Jeffrey A. Segal, Robert Boucher, and Charles M. Cameron, "A Policy-Based Model of Certiorari Voting on the U.S. Supreme Court," paper presented at the 1995 meeting of the Midwest Political Science Association, Chicago, Ill.

The justice's preferred outcome on the merits of the case is the first factor that should determine whether or not he or she will support a grant of certiorari. As there is more value in reversing an unfavorable lower court decision than upholding a favorable one, justices who vote to reverse on the merits should be more likely to have voted for certiorari than should justices who vote to affirm on the merits.

The second variable entails the level of support that a justice receives for his or her position on the merits of the case. A basic strategic calculus suggests that those who will win on the merits should be more likely to vote for certiorari than those who will lose on the merits, regardless of whether one wishes to affirm or reverse. We operationalize the support that the justice will gather by utilizing the percent of the Court, including the justice himself, that adopts the justice's position on the merits in the final report vote.

To this point, we simply have a model that seeks to explain certiorari as a function of the vote on the merits and the level of support that the justice can expect. Justices, however, might engage in different strategies when they are reverse-minded than when they are affirm-minded. Since voting to grant and wishing to affirm is a riskier strategy than voting to grant and wishing to reverse, and since reversal is the more likely outcome, affirmance-minded justices need to pay much more attention to probable outcomes than do reversal-minded justices. In other words, we should find a positive interaction between desire to affirm and support on the merits.

We test our model on the certiorari votes of the justices in the Warren Court, as contained in the Vinson–Warren Court Judicial Database (see Table 6.6). We use docket as the unit of analysis. Where several certiorari, conference, or report votes exist on the same docket, we use the final one of each.

As each justice's decision on certiorari is a dichotomous dependent variable, we estimate our model using logistic regression. The predictors of the justices' certiorari votes are (1) the justice's report vote (0 to reverse, 1 to affirm), (2) the percent support the justice receives for his position in the report vote, and (3) the interaction term for percent support when voting to affirm.

By estimating this model, we can judge the extent to which justices appear to exhibit strategic behavior when voting on writs of certiorari. The coefficient for the affirm variable should be negative, as a vote to affirm should associate with a vote against certiorari. Given the interaction term between "support" and "affirm," "support" is the impact of support for judges wishing to *reverse*. This measures the extent of

TABLE 6.6. *Logit Estimates of Certiorari Voting on the Warren Court, 1953–1968 Terms*[a]

Justice	Constant	Affirm	Percent support	Affirm percent support	−2*LLK
Black	2.926***	−3.479***	−0.014	0.027***	1,362.0
(n = 1,434)	(0.3547)	(0.4397)	(0.0042)	(0.0054)	
Brennan	2.810***	−2.334***	−0.011	0.027***	892.1
(n = 1,133)	(0.4810)	(0.8136)	(0.0056)	(0.0101)	
Burton	1.965***	−2.262***	−0.011	0.023***	551.2
(n = 451)	(0.6584)	(0.7527)	(0.0075)	(0.0091)	
Clark	1.258***	−2.300***	−0.005	0.024***	1,601.9
(n = 1,276)	(0.4257)	(0.4886)	(0.0049)	(0.0059)	
Douglas	2.210***	−2.989***	−0.010	0.023***	1,518.8
(n = 1,430)	(0.2659)	(0.3559)	(0.0032)	(0.0045)	
Fortas	2.136***	−2.072**	−0.004	0.016	227.2
(n = 249)	(0.8857)	(1.156)	(0.0104)	(0.0147)	
Frankurter	2.878***	−4.089***	−0.0221	0.0399***	923.7
(n = 758)	(0.5344)	(0.6085)	(0.0061)	(0.0073)	
Goldberg	2.758**	3.394	−0.003	−0.044	106.5
(n = 191)	(1.3120)	(3.7207)	(0.0152)	(0.0402)	
Harlan	3.021***	−3.554***	−0.021	0.035***	1,488.7
(n = 1,251)	(0.5077)	(0.5397)	(0.0056)	(0.0063)	
Jackson	5.536*	−7.633**	−0.040	0.091**	40.1
(n = 61)	(3.478)	(3.891)	(0.0373)	(0.0448)	
Marshall	2.327*	−2.822	−0.008	0.033	74.4
(n = 84)	(1.7683)	(2.6256)	(0.0202)	(0.0316)	
Minton	1.489*	−2.341**	−0.010	0.017*	316.6
(n = 240)	(0.9317)	(1.0767)	(0.0105)	(0.0126)	
Reed	2.567***	−3.411***	−0.015	0.035***	302.9
(n = 261)	(0.9723)	(1.0654)	(0.0109)	(0.0125)	
Stewart	1.021***	−2.078***	−0.003	0.020***	1,161.1
(n = 898)	(0.4524)	(0.5274)	(0.0051)	(0.0065)	
Warren	2.707***	−3.400***	−0.009	0.030***	1,155.7
(n = 1,374)	(0.4048)	(0.5756)	(0.0048)	(0.0071)	
White	1.585***	−2.055***	−0.003	0.020**	591.0
(n = 545)	(0.6144)	(0.7669)	(0.0069)	(0.0095)	
Whittaker	1.482***	−2.666***	−0.014	0.028***	542.8
(n = 407)	(0.5821)	(0.6920)	(0.0068)	(0.0088)	

[a] One-tailed sig tests, with: *$p \leq 0.10$; **$p \leq 0.05$; and ***$p \leq 0.01$. Cert vote coded 1 if grant, 0 if deny.

defensive denials. The coefficient for the interaction term then measures the change in the impact of support for judges wishing to *affirm*. This measures the extent of aggressive grants.

The column labeled "Affirm" measures the impact of wishing to affirm on the likelihood of voting to grant. It is negative and significant at $p < 0.01$ for virtually every justice. This confirms the existence of reversal strategies for the overwhelming majority of Warren Court justices.

The column labeled "percent support" represents the change in the likelihood of voting to grant for justices wishing to reverse as one's support on the Court increases. Surprisingly, it is not positive for a single justice, thus casting some doubt on the notion of defensive denials.[103]

Alternatively, consider the coefficient for "affirm percent support," which measures the change in the likelihood of voting to grant for justices wishing to affirm as one's support on the Court increases. The coefficient is positive and significant for the vast majority of Warren Court justices. Overall, these findings replicate almost precisely findings by Boucher and Segal on the Vinson Court.[104]

To give some sense of the impact of these coefficients, Figure 6.1 presents the probability of Justice Black voting to grant when he wishes to affirm and reverse, as the percent of justices who will support him on the merits increases. As can be seen, there is virtually no impact of percent support when Black wishes to reverse; but when he wishes to affirm, support is crucial to his likelihood of voting to grant.

These results make a fair amount of sense, as one formal model of the certiorari process demonstrates.[105] A justice wishing to reverse has less to lose than a justice wishing to affirm. More important, a justice wishing to reverse can also count on a fairly high prior probability of reversal for any case that is actually granted. But we nevertheless caution that these results are based only on cases in the Court granted cert. Only the Caldeira, Wright, and Zorn study, among those examining prediction strategies, includes both grants and denials.[106] While the authors

[103] We are hesitant about drawing firmer conclusions about defensive denials because cases where defensive denials successfully keep the Court from hearing the case do not show up in our data set.

[104] Boucher and Segal, *op. cit.*, n. 102, *supra.*

[105] Segal, Boucher, and Cameron, *op. cit.*, n. 102, *supra.*

[106] *Op. cit.*, n. 95, *supra.* They get around the problem of predicting how justices will vote on the merits in cases that are denied cert by using past votes on the merits as an indicator of how the justices would have voted had cert been granted. This requires the assumption that granted and denied cases are homogenous.

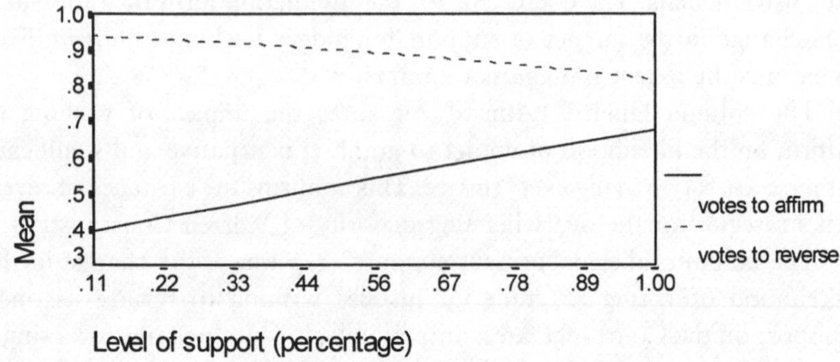

FIGURE 6.1. Expected probability Justice Black votes to grant writ of certiorari (given final report vote and level of support).

clearly show that the justices take probable outcomes into account, the study does not separate out affirm- and reverse-minded justices to see whether both groups consider probable outcomes.[107]

Given the foregoing results, and the limits thereon, we deem it advisable to consider the findings of aggregate-level models of certiorari voting.

Aggregate-Level Models

If the members of the Supreme Court are motivated by their policy preferences, then they would presumably want justice done – as they perceive it – not just to the litigants before it, but to the hundreds of thousands of litigants whose decisions the Court cannot review. It would do the Court little good to require the exclusion of evidence illegally obtained against Dollree Mapp only to have lower courts flout this decision.

Unfortunately, the Supreme Court has few of the traditional mechanisms available to hierarchical superiors for controlling judicial subordinates.[108] It can neither hire nor fire lower court judges, promote nor demote them, raise their salary nor dock their pay.

107 There is no reason for them to have done so, as this distinction was not part of their model. But, unfortunately, from our perspective, this leaves a crucial question unanswered.

108 Charles M. Cameron, Jeffrey A. Segal, and Donald R. Songer, "Strategic Auditing in a Political Hierarchy: An Informational Model of the Supreme Court's Certiorari Decisions," 94 *American Political Science Review* 101 (2000).

TABLE 6.7. *Affirmation and Reversal by Court*

	Warren 1953–68	Burger 1969–85	Rehnquist 1986–99	Row total
Affirm	775 (35.9%)	995 (35.7%)	719 (43.4%)	2,489 (37.7%)
Reverse	1,382 (64.1%)	1,795 (64.3%)	939 (56.6%)	4,116 (62.3%)
Column total	2,157	2,790	1,658	6,605

There is one tool available to it, though: It can reverse lower court decisions. This act, we believe, is costly to lower court judges in terms of their professional status and policy preferences. Thus it is crucial for a policy-based Court to use the primary hierarchical tool at its disposal, reversal, as a mechanism for controlling lower court behavior.

We report the extent to which the Supreme Court reverses lower court decisions for the Warren, Burger, and Rehnquist Courts in Table 6.7.[109] As can be seen, these Courts all reversed more cases than they affirmed, though the proportion is markedly smaller for the Rehnquist Court (57 vs. 64 percent). When we break the data down by term (see Table 6.8), we find that except for the first term of the Warren Court and the 1987, 1988, and 1993 terms of the Rehnquist Court, reversals invariably outnumber affirmances. Reversals peaked in the 1962 and 1963 terms at 75 and 76 percent, respectively. It is noteworthy that no Rehnquist Court term exceeds 65 percent.

[109] Our data consist of all orally argued cases decided from the 1953 through the 1998 terms except those that arose on original jurisdiction. This period includes the Warren and Burger Courts and the 1986–98 terms of the Rehnquist Court. We use docket number as our unit of analysis because the Court does not necessarily dispose of all cases decided by a single opinion in the same fashion. We also count as separate cases the handful that contain split votes, in the sense that one or more of the justices voted with the majority on one aspect or issue of the case and dissented on another. We include these to avoid making an arbitrary judgment of whether the Court affirmed or reversed the lower court's decision.

Because the Court's formal disposition of the cases it decides does not unerringly indicate affirmation or reversal, we focus instead on whether the petitioning party prevailed in whole or in substantial part or not. If the petitioning party prevailed, we count the case as a reversal of the lower court. If the petitioning party did not prevail, we count the case as affirmed.

TABLE 6.8. *Reversal Rate by Term*

Term	Rate	Term	Rate	Term	Rate	Term	Rate	Term	Rate
53	48.2	62	74.7	71	61.2	81	65.0	91	64.5
54	66.7	63	76.2	72	68.2	82	62.6	92	61.7
55	53.3	64	72.5	73	67.5	83	72.1	93	44.0
56	66.0	65	71.1	74	68.1	84	63.6	94	59.6
57	56.6	66	69.9	75	65.5	85	58.3	95	59.6
58	57.1	67	68.0	76	64.6	86	60.8	96	65.2
59	60.3	68	72.1	77	68.7	87	48.2	97	51.6
60	53.1	69	64.5	78	66.9	88	49.4	98	63.1
61	68.9	70	60.1	79	61.5	89	55.2	99	55.3
				80	66.7	90	60.8	00	54.8

Conflict with Supreme Court Preferences

A focus on reversal rates allows us to make inferences about the cases the Court chooses to hear, but it does not allow for inferences about cases the Court chooses not to hear. For instance, the above data are consistent with a Supreme Court that consciously seeks hierarchical control through reversal, but they are also consistent with a Court oblivious to such concerns facing lower courts whose preferences and behavior diverge from those of the Court. Without any certiorari strategy a majority of cases would be reversed under such conditions. If the Court's certiorari behavior is consciously policy-based, those cases that are granted should be more likely to be reversed than those cases that are denied. This is not the same as stating that a majority of cases that are granted will be reversed.

S. Sidney Ulmer provides initial support for this hypothesis by showing that conflict between lower court decisions and *his* assessment of Supreme Court preferences is the most important factor affecting the grant of certiorari. Among the cert petitions he sampled, review was granted in only 12 percent. Breaking the percentage into conflict and no-conflict categories reveals grants of cert in 44 percent of the conflict cases, but only 7 percent of those without. Thus, if we accept Ulmer's subjective operationalization of conflict with contemporary Supreme Court preferences, such conflict appears almost a necessary condition for review.[110]

[110] S. Sidney Ulmer, "The Supreme Court's Certiorari Decisions: Conflict as a Predictive Variable," 78 *American Political Science Review* 901 (1984).

In a related work, Donald Songer found that presumed conflict with lower court decisions in economic cases was a crucial factor in cert decisions during the four years he analyzed: 1935, 1941, 1967, and 1972.[111] Similarly, Armstrong and Johnson found that the Burger Court was more likely to grant cert in civil liberties cases when the decision below was liberal than when it opposed individual rights.[112]

While these studies certainly suggest that the Court is more likely to choose cases it wishes to reverse, the Court's preferences are presumed, not estimated. To our knowledge only one study statistically estimates the likelihood of reversal and uses that to assess the likelihood of certiorari.[113] That study finds that the likelihood of reversal has an enormous impact on the probability of granting cert. For example, when the likelihood of reversal is below 10 percent, the probability of granting certiorari is near zero, even when other factors such as the presence of the United States as petitioner is present. But when the likelihood of reversal is over 80 percent, the probability of granting cert can jump to 0.5 or greater. This is a remarkable increase in a population where the mean probability of a grant is 0.05 or less. Thus, a substantial increase in the likelihood of reversal can increase by a factor of ten or more the probability that cert is granted.

Information and Lower Court Ideology

While these studies support the notion that a policy-minded court uses its certiorari jurisdiction to control the lower court, they do not suggest how the Court might most efficiently go about doing so. After all, losing litigants appeal thousands of cases to the Court each year, and the limited information available in certiorari briefs means that the Court can't know with certainty whether a decision was doctrinally deviant or not until it actually hears the case.[114]

One useful piece of information available to a Supreme Court seeking doctrinal compliance is the ideology of the lower court. Consider a

[111] "Concern for Policy Outputs as a Cue for Supreme Court Decisions on Certiorari," 41 *Journal of Politics* 1185 (1979).

[112] Virginia Armstrong and Charles Johnson, "Certiorari Decision Making by the Warren and Burger Courts: Is Cue Theory Time Bound?," 15 *Polity* 141–50 (1982).

[113] Jeffrey A. Segal, Charles M. Cameron, and Donald R. Songer, "A Rational Actor Model of Supreme Court Decisions to Accept Cases for Review," paper presented at the 1993 meeting of the American Political Science Association, Washington, D.C.

The authors use a fact-pattern analysis (see Chapter 8) to assess the likelihood that the Supreme Court would reverse any lower court decision.

[114] This section is based on Cameron, Segal, and Songer, *op. cit.*, n. 108, *supra*.

conservative Supreme Court reviewing lower court decisions in search and seizure cases. If the lower court is moderate or liberal and it issues a conservative decision (i.e., one upholding the admission of seized evidence), there is little reason for the Supreme Court to grant review, for if a conservative decision is acceptable to a more liberal court, it would certainly be acceptable to the more conservative Supreme Court. This finding should hold regardless of the apparent facts of the case,[115] which in the search and seizure example would mean the apparent intrusiveness of the search. Similarly, the Supreme Court would have little reason to second guess a liberal decision by a lower court more conservative than it is.

Alternatively, if a moderate lower court facing a conservative Supreme Court renders a liberal decision, that decision is going to warrant a fair amount of scrutiny. At a high level of apparent intrusiveness, the Supreme Court might believe that a liberal decision was in fact called for, but those cases without extremely intrusive searches should face a high probability of review. For a liberal lower court, any liberal decision might be inherently suspect, and thus regardless of the apparent facts, petitions in those cases will face the strictest scrutiny.

Models similar to this help explain a wide variety of political events. For example, many conservatives accepted Nixon's opening to China, believing that if a staunch anti-Communist like Nixon thought it was in our national interest to do so, then perhaps it was okay. Of course, had a moderate Democrat attempted such a move, cries of treason would have been heard.

More relevant to our concerns, an informational model along these lines does an extremely good job explaining certiorari decisions in search and seizure cases during the Burger Court. For example, the Court, which was at least as conservative in the area of search and seizure as almost any lower court panel under it, almost never reviewed conservative decisions by liberal, moderate, or conservative Courts of Appeals. It would, however, generally review liberal decisions by moderate to conservative lower courts except when the apparent facts showed a sufficiently intrusive search. In such cases, the Court was willing to deny cert. But when liberal courts reached liberal decisions, the Court frequently

[115] Cameron et al., *ibid.*, distinguish between the "apparent" or "publicly observable" facts of the case – those it learns prior to the cert vote – and the true facts of the case – the complete rendering of the details – which it learns following a grant of cert through the merits briefs and oral argument.

granted cert and did so regardless of the apparent intrusiveness of the search. The Court viewed such decisions to be inherently untrustworthy. Thus the data support the model's hypothesis that the Court uses certiorari grants and merits reversals to keep control of the lower courts, and most efficiently does so by considering the interactions of case facts, decisions, and lower court ideology.

The model featured above relies on the Court's role of ensuring doctrinal compliance in the lower courts. But that is only a partial view of the certiorari process. Certainly, the well-supported notion of aggressive grants suggests that much more than doctrinal compliance motivates the Court. Moreover, the Court is also involved in law creation for issues that have not yet reached the Court. Thus, a sizable number of cases that don't conflict with Court preferences do in fact get heard. We examine explanations of these different types of behavior next.

Cue Theory

The major theoretical focus of studies examining aggregate cert decisions is cue theory, first applied to judicial behavior by Joseph Tanenhaus and associates.[116] Arguing that the justices can give petitions no more than cursory consideration, they hypothesize that certain cues will merit further consideration while those without any cues will be dropped. The cues they examined were the parties involved, the subject area of the case, and conflict in the court below.

Parties and Groups as Cues for Review

Various parties might have an effect on the grant of review. One party who might particularly be advantaged is the United States, whose cases are usually briefed and argued by the office of the Solicitor General. The Solicitor General appears before the Court more than any other attorney and appears to benefit from this repeat experience.[117] As Chief Justice Rehnquist observed: "[W]e depend heavily on the Solicitor General in deciding whether to grant certiorari in cases in which the government is a party. . . ."[118] According to one justice, "the ablest advocates in the U.S.

[116] Joseph Tanenhaus, Marvin Schick, Matthew Muraskin, and Daniel Rosen, "The Supreme Court's Certiorari Jurisdiction: Cue Theory," in Glendon Schubert, ed., *Judicial Decision-Making* (New York: Free Press, 1963), pp. 111–32.

[117] See, generally, Marc Galanter, "Why the 'Haves' Come Out Ahead: Speculations on the Limits of Legal Change," 9 *Law and Society Review* 95 (1974), and, specifically, Provine, *op. cit.*, n. 92, *supra*, pp. 86–92.

[118] *Alvarado v. United States*, 497 U.S. 543 (1990), at 546.

are the advocates in the Solicitor General's Office."[119] The office has been considerate of the Court's caseload, appealing only one tenth or so of the cases that the government loses.[120] These are presumably the most meritorious ones.

Tanenhaus et al. find that between 1947 and 1958, when the United States sought review, cert was granted 47 percent of the time, but when the United States did not seek review and no other cues were present, cert was granted only 6 percent of the time. After controlling for the presence of other cues, they estimate that if the United States favored review, the probability of cert being granted increased by about 0.38. Provine's data, which cover the same period as Tanenhaus's, show the United States was granted review 66 percent of the time.[121] This discrepancy probably results because Provine includes cases containing multiple cues. Ulmer and associates found that if the United States requested review, the probability of cert being granted in the 1955 term increased from 32 percent to 66 percent after deadlisted cases were dropped.[122]

Analyses of more recent terms confirm and extend these findings. Studies by Teger and Kosinski and Armstrong and Johnson show that the United States as a party, alone or together with other cues, greatly increased the probability of review in the 1967–68 and 1975–77 terms.[123] Results reported by Caldeira and Wright for the 1982 term demonstrate that when the Solicitor General requested review, the probability of cert being granted increased, depending on the other variables present, between 0.36 and 0.64.[124]

Humphries et al. compared the characteristics of cases decided by the federal courts of appeals that the Supreme Court reviewed with those in

[119] Karen O'Connor and Lee Epstein, "States Rights or Criminal Rights: An Analysis of State Performance in U.S. Supreme Court Litigation," paper presented at the 1983 meeting of the Northeastern Political Science Association, Philadelphia. Quoted in Jeffrey A. Segal and Cheryl Reedy, "The Supreme Court and Sex Discrimination: The Role of the Solicitor General," 41 *Political Research Quarterly* 553 (1988), 556.

[120] Robert Scigliano, *The Supreme Court and the Presidency* (New York: Free Press, 1971), p. 169.

[121] Provine, *op. cit.*, n. 92, *supra*, p. 87.

[122] S. Sidney Ulmer, William Hintze, and Louise Kirklosky, "The Decision to Grant or Deny Certiorari: Further Consideration of Cue Theory," 6 *Law and Society Review* 637 (1972).

[123] Stuart H. Teger and Douglas Kosinski, "The Cue Theory of Supreme Court Certiorari Jurisdiction: A Reconsideration," 42 *Journal of Politics* 834 (1980); Armstrong and Johnson, *op. cit.*, n. 112, *supra.*

[124] Gregory A. Caldeira and John Wright, "Organized Interests and Agenda Setting in the U.S. Supreme Court," 82 *American Political Science Review* 1109 (1988).

which the losing party did not seek certiorari and also with those in which certiorari was denied. Paramount among specific characteristics were actions of the Solicitor General.[125] In sum, the evidence is overwhelming: Solicitor General requests for review enormously increase the probability of acceptance. While such success is not predicted by the attitudinal model, the reasons for such success have not been closely examined.

Additionally, the existence of a repeat player can signal the Court as to the importance of a case.[126] One-shot attorneys representing clients who lost below have little to lose by insisting to the Court that their case is of the utmost importance. Even if the Court grants cert and eventually discovers that the case is not earth-shaking, the attorney has lost little. Not so for the repeat player, whose credibility in future cert briefs is decidedly at stake.

Influences on cert decisions are not limited to the parties. As noted above, interest groups and various organizations can file amicus curiae briefs. These briefs, in addition to providing legal arguments that the parties themselves might not make, may enable the Court to judge the importance of the litigation. Indeed, in one recent case, Justice Stevens in dissent buttressed his view that the case was an unimportant one that never should have been reviewed, noting that "not a single brief *amicus curiae* was filed."[127] If amicus curiae briefs signal a case's importance, then briefs both in favor and in opposition should further enhance review. This is exactly what Caldeira and Wright found.[128] Cert was granted in 36 percent of the cases they examined that had at least one brief, but in only 5 percent of those without any. While briefs favoring review produced stronger effects, briefs opposed also increased the probability of review.

Lower Court Conflict

When circuits conflict with one another, or when state supreme courts conflict with one another on national questions, "federal law is being administered in different ways in different parts of the country; citizens

[125] Martha Anne Humphries, Tammy A. Sarver, and Donald R. Songer, "Going All the Way: How to Seduce the Supreme Court into Granting Cert," paper presented at the 1998 meeting of the American Political Science Association, Boston, Mass.

[126] Kevin T. McGuire and Gregory A. Caldeira, "Lawyers, Organized Interests, and the Law of Obscenity: Agenda Setting in the Supreme Court," 87 *American Political Science Review* 717 (1993).

[127] *United States v. Dalm*, 494 U.S. 596 (1990), at 612.

[128] *Op. cit.*, n. 124, *supra*.

in some circuits are subject to liabilities or entitlements that citizens in other circuits are not burdened with or otherwise entitled to."[129] Thus the Court should review such cases even though they otherwise would not merit review. Indeed, Rule 10 of the Supreme Court specifically lists conflicts between or among lower courts as a reason for granting cert.

Not all justices agree that sufficient credence is paid to lower court conflicts. In a dissent to a denial of review on the final day of the 1989 term, Justice White pointed out that he had dissented from denial of certiorari sixty-seven times during the term:

> My notes on these dissents indicate that on 48 occasions I dissented because in my view there were conflicts among courts of appeals sufficiently crystallized to warrant certiorari if the federal law is to be maintained in any satisfactory uniform condition. In 7 other cases, there were differences on the same federal issue between courts of appeals and state courts; in another case state courts of last resort differed with each other. Finally, there were 11 cases that did not involve a conflict but in my view presented important issues that had not been settled but should be settled by this Court.[130]

White admitted that though some of these conflicts may not have been "real" or "square," in most cases the court of appeals "expressly differs" with another court.

> ... yet certiorari is denied because the conflict is "tolerable" or "narrow," or because other courts of appeals should have the opportunity to weigh in on one side or another of the unsettled issue, or for some other unstated reason.[131]

At the other extreme, the Court sometimes manufactures a conflict in order to justify review. Thus, in a suit for equitable recoupment of a time-barred tax refund, the majority asserted that the "approach taken" by two courts of appeals conflicted with that "adopted" by another.[132] The dissenters, however, persuasively documented the absence of conflict.[133] Significantly, the majority made no effort to refute the dissenters' assertions.

Systematic analyses find White's concerns somewhat overstated. Though Ulmer et al. found little evidence that conflict affected the grant of cert in the 1955 term,[134] Ulmer's more extensive treatment of the issue indicates the cruciality of intercircuit conflict to cert decisions of the

[129] *Beaulieu v. United States*, 497 U.S. 1038 (1990), at 1039. [130] *Id.* [131] *Id.*
[132] *United States v. Dalm*, 494 U.S. 596 (1990), at 601.
[133] *Id.* at 614, n. 2, 620–21, 623. [134] *Op. cit.*, n. 122, *supra*.

Vinson and Warren Courts, but less to Burger Court decisions, after controlling for other factors.[135] Caldeira and Wright also show conflict to have significant effects, but, unfortunately, they do not distinguish between conflict among lower courts and conflict with the prevailing direction of the Supreme Court's decisions on the issue that the case concerns.[136] The importance of intercircuit conflict suggests some level of rule-bound behavior at cert.

Tanenhaus et al. studied a variant of the conflict hypothesis: whether disagreement within the court below or disagreement between different courts in the same case affected the likelihood of review. They found that the Court granted review 13 percent of the time when there is dissension between or within lower courts and no other cues present, versus 6 percent of the time when these cues are absent.[137] They estimate that conflict between or within lower courts in the same case increases the probability of review by 0.11 after controlling for other cues.

Subject Matter

Although much evidence shows that conflict with Supreme Court preferences, conflict between and among lower courts, the presence of the United States as a party, and activity by interest groups as amici curiae affect cert, less evidence indicates that the type of case does also. Scholars have inquired whether civil liberties or economic claims are more likely to be reviewed than other types of cases. The evidence that they are is underwhelming. Tanenhaus et al. found that the Vinson and Warren Courts were more likely to hear noncriminal civil liberties cases than other types of cases, but were only marginally more likely to hear economic cases.[138] Ulmer found no effect for either civil liberties or economic cases after controlling for other factors,[139] while Caldeira and Wright similarly found that a civil liberties cue did not significantly increase the probability of review after other factors were considered.[140] Issue as a cue was found to be significant in the Teger–Kosinski and Armstrong–Johnson studies, but these do not fully control for other factors.[141]

Petition Type

We note again that the Court is more likely to grant review to paid petitions than to unpaid ones. Less than 5 percent of the former gain review

[135] *Op. cit.*, n. 110, *supra.* [136] *Op. cit.*, n. 124, *supra.* [137] *Op. cit.*, n. 116, *supra.*
[138] *Id.* [139] *Op. cit.*, n. 110, *supra.* [140] *Op. cit.*, n. 124, *supra.*
[141] *Op. cit.*, n. 123, *supra.*

in a given year, as opposed to only a fraction of a percent of the latter. While this might suggest a bias against indigent petitioners, the lack of filing fees no doubt produces a large number of completely frivolous claims.[142]

Entirely apart from the factors we have addressed are questions of standing and jurisdiction. Perry argues that the clerks who review the thousands of petitions the Court receives each year need some quick way of discarding as many petitions as possible.[143] Procedural defects such as standing, jurisdiction, or the like provide the clerks with a valid justification for recommending denial, one that only a handful of petitions survive. Though all but unexamined by other political scientists, these factors obviously affect the Court's decisions concerning review.

FUTURE CHANGES

The system that the First Congress created in 1789 exists today with only a few significant structural changes. The most important occurred in 1891 when Congress created nine circuit courts of appeals and in 1925 when the Judges' Bill of that year drastically reduced the Court's obligation to decide certain cases. Many reasons seem to mitigate reformist inclinations.

First, the justices do not sit from late June or early July until the first Monday in October.[144] Because they may visit their offices, hire staff, and evaluate petitions for certiorari and writs of appeal during this time, they are not totally duty free.[145] But though it may not be accurate to view the interterm recess as a three-month vacation, it is markedly lengthier than that of the average full-time worker.

Second, the burdens of office do not preclude the justices from speaking at bar and other associational meetings, granting interviews, and writing books and articles. The same year he became chief justice,

[142] E.g., *In re Demos*, 500 U.S. 16 (1991). [143] *Op. cit.*, n. 69, *supra.*

[144] Special sessions in 1958 and 1972 cut into this hiatus. The justices issued half a dozen orders between August 28 and September 17, 1958, in addition to hearing arguments and deciding the school desegregation ruckus in Little Rock, Arkansas: *Cooper v. Aaron*, 358 U.S. 1. In 1972, they reconvened on July 7, a week after adjournment, to stay three judgments of the D.C. Circuit concerning the seating of delegates to the Democratic National Convention. *O'Brien v. Brown*, 409 U.S. 1.

[145] Their clerks are certainly busy. See Stuart Taylor, Jr., "When High Court's Away, Clerks' Work Begins," *New York Times*, September 23, 1988, p. A12.

Rehnquist published a book on the Court,[146] and throughout his tenure, Chief Justice Burger heavily involved himself in matters of judicial administration. Frankfurter and Fortas closely advised Presidents Roosevelt and Johnson. Warren served as head of the commission that investigated the assassination of President Kennedy, and Justice Jackson left the country for over a year to preside at the Nuremburg Trials of Nazi war criminals.

Third, notwithstanding generous retirement benefits, recent Courts have been among the most aged in history. The presence of sitting justices who are in their eighties belies an overburdened bench.

Fourth, the most time-consuming portion of the justices' work consists of writing opinions. The justices equally divide the task of writing opinions of the Court among themselves, which currently requires each to write an average of ten or twelve per term. At their own volition, the Warren Court justices also wrote an average of one and a quarter special opinions (concurrences and dissents) per orally argued case; the Burger Court justices averaged 1.6.[147] Table 6.9 displays the frequency with which the Rehnquist Court justices have written opinions in the formally decided cases of the 1986–99 terms.[148] The difference between 11 percent – the share of the opinions of the Court that each justice is expected to bear – and the percentages that appear in Table 6.9 indicates the extent to which each of them engages in special opinion writing. Except for the Chief Justice and Blackmun, they all write approximately twice the minimum required, with Stevens more than three times the minimum, and Brennan slightly less. Overworked justices would hardly display such behavior.

Finally, Congress effectively eliminated the last vestiges of the Court's obligatory jurisdiction in 1988. No longer must the Court hear appeals

[146] William H. Rehnquist, *The Supreme Court: How It Was, How It Is* (New York: Morrow, 1987).

[147] Harold J. Spaeth and Michael F. Altfeld, "Influence Relationships within the Supreme Court: A Comparison of the Warren and Burger Courts," 38 *Political Research Quarterly* 70 (1985).

[148] We count citations to orally and nonorally argued cases appearing in the front portion of the *Lawyers' Edition* of the *United States Reports*. Nonparticipations are excluded. Coauthoring counts as an opinion. Note that an undercount results for each justice because the unsigned per curiam opinions are authored by the assigned justice. The 2000 term produced little change in the justices' behavior. The percentage for each is: Rehnquist 15.6, Stevens 35.5, O'Connor 20.0, Scalia 35.1, Kennedy 15.6, Souter 22.4, Thomas 24.7, Ginsburg 22.1, Breyer 28.9.

TABLE 6.9. *Frequency and Percentage of Total Opinion Writing by Justice by Term*[a]

	1986	1987	1988	1989	1990	1991	1992	1993	1994	1995	1996	1997	1998	1999	Total
Blackmun	41	30	48	32	24	32	33	25							265
	26.1	20.4	32.2	23.2	19.2	26.7	27.5	27.2							25.3
Brennan	48	40	45	46											179
	30.0	27.4	30.6	33.3											30.3
Breyer									17	19	25	28	23	27	139
									19.3	21.8	26.0	28.3	25.0	31.8	25.4
Ginsburg								27	21	19	15	22	18	17	139
								28.7	23.1	21.6	15.6	22.2	19.6	20.0	21.6
Kennedy		14[b]	29	32	28	26	24	21	15	18	12	20	19	18	276
		20.9	19.7	23.4	23.0	21.7	20.0	22.3	16.3	20.5	12.5	20.2	20.7	21.2	20.3
Marshall	37	29	32	32	32										162
	23.1	19.7	21.6	23.2	25.6										22.6
O'Connor	43	36	34	28	25	37	31	28	29	14	22	17	15	14	373
	27.0	24.8	23.6	20.4	20.0	30.8	25.8	30.1	31.5	15.9	23.2	17.3	16.5	16.5	23.5

Powell	39														39
	24.5														24.5
Rehnqust	26	24	23	22	19	22	22	16	16	16	15	17	19	15	251
	16.3	16.6	15.5	15.9	15.2	18.3	28.3	17.0	17.4	18.2	15.8	17.2	20.7	17.6	17.0
Scalia	42	43	44	41	43	42	32	33	22	28	29	34	22	23	478
	26.9	29.9	29.7	29.7	34.7	35.0	26.7	35.1	24.2	31.8	30.2	34.3	23.9	27.1	30.0
Souter					12	23	26	27	18	19	19	21	15	27	208
					10.8	20.1	21.7	28.7	19.6	21.6	19.8	21.2	16.3	31.8	20.9
Stevens	62	45	55	57	44	47	45	36	36	39	35	36	44	37	618
	39.0	30.6	37.4	41.3	35.2	39.2	37.5	38.3	39.6	45.3	36.5	36.4	47.8	43.5	38.6
Thomas						21	24	21	23	22	15	17	24	23	190
						21.2	20.0	22.3	25.0	25.3	15.6	17.2	26.1	27.1	22.0
White	40	44	33	29	29	25	24								224
	25.2	29.9	22.1	21.0	23.2	20.8	20.2								23.4

[a] Percentages are percent of cases in which each justice writes an opinion.
[b] Partial term.

in which a state court voided an act of Congress or upheld a state law against a challenge to its constitutionality. Although these cases comprised less than 5 percent of the Court's docket, the justices had complained that they usurped too much of their time and resources.[149]

SUMMARY AND CONCLUSIONS

Unlike the vast majority of American courts, state and federal, the justices remain abreast of their docket. Notwithstanding a substantial increase in the number of cases the Court has been petitioned to review over the past half-century, the justices make their decisions to grant or deny review within a few weeks of their receipt, with the notable exception of "relisted" cases, which may remain in limbo for months. If accepted during the first four months of the Court's term, the case will likely be decided before adjournment, otherwise during the following term. Because of the currency of its docket, the luxury of a three-month summer vacation, and the justices' failure to speak with a single unequivocal voice, the likelihood of appreciable change in the Court's jurisdiction or procedures is slight.

The link that connects the various factors that determine who gets into the Supreme Court are the individual justices' personal policy goals. Given the freedom to select for review such cases as they wish, the factors that govern selection and the strategies that the various justices employ in voting to review a case are matters of individual determination.[150]

Although analyses of case selection have primarily focused on petitions for certiorari rather than writs of appeal, a fairly detailed picture of the considerations that enter into the justices' choice has emerged.

We have demonstrated that even the two legal requirements for getting into Court – jurisdiction and standing to sue – are subject to the justices' control, although Congress, compatibly with the provisions of Article III

[149] Weisberg, *op. cit.*, n. 44, *supra*, p. 138. The number of clerks to which each justice is entitled has increased with the growth in the Court's caseload, from one to two following World War II to three in the 1960s and to four in the 1970s. "Rx for an Overburdened Supreme Court," 66 *Judicature* 397 (1983).

[150] Lee Epstein, who has examined the justices' papers as extensively as anyone we know, has found absolutely no examples of logrolling (personal communication, February 11, 2000). Moreover, no systematic evidence exists that junior justices cue on signals from senior justices during conference votes on cert. See, e.g., Perry, *op. cit.*, n. 69, p. 48. But Burger did pass at conference and merits votes – especially the latter – far more than any of his colleagues. We assume he did so to control the assignment of the Court's opinion.

of the Constitution, determines the Court's jurisdiction.[151] As with other congressional legislation, however, the Court interprets the language and intentions of Congress. So also here. And though some of the elements of standing to sue are constitutionally grounded, while decisional law has produced others, the precedents governing both kinds are no less subject to judicial manipulation than are those governing other areas of the law, as we documented in Chapter 1.

As for the nonlegal factors that govern case selection, although a fully explainable model remains to be constructed, we do know that in addition to amicus curiae briefs and the presence of the United States as a party, the justices are concerned with (1) a desire to reverse errant lower court decisions, and (2) the likelihood of winning on the merits (at least for affirm-minded justices).

With the exception of the informational model above (pp. 265–67), which was derived from a formal model, these results do not clearly distinguish between attitudinal and rational choice approaches. While attitudinalists were the first to assess the likelihood of winning on the merits as a predictor of certiorari votes,[152] such behavior is only implied from the attitudinal model; it is not formally derived from it. Alternatively, while rational choice cert models can, of course, look forward to the decision on the merits as the endpoint of the game,[153] that is not necessarily the case. In policy-based rational choice models winning on the merits might not be important if the endpoint of the game – so often the case in judicial rational choice models – is Congress. Under such models, a justice might prefer losing on the merits in order to induce a congressional override that would improve the policy to one better than the Court could or would do on its own.[154]

Moreover, under rational choice theory, the goals of the justices could include legal values such as intercircuit consistency. Thus, a justice might

[151] We no longer vouch for the accuracy of the statement that Congress determines the Court's jurisdiction, given the Court's current penchant for indiscriminately declaring acts of Congress unconstitutional. See the discussion in Chapter 1 at pp. 32–6. Also see *Felker v. Turpin*, 518 U.S. 651 (1996).

[152] Schubert, 1959, *op. cit.*, n. 63, *supra*; Schubert, 1962, *op. cit.*, n. 63, *supra*. For recent work, see Boucher and Segal, *op. cit.*, n. 102, *supra*.

[153] Caldeira, Wright, and Zorn, *op. cit.*, n. 95, *supra*.

[154] Pablo T. Spiller and Emerson H. Tiller, "Invitations to Override: Congressional Reversal of Supreme Court Decisions," 16 *International Review of Law and Economics* 503 (1996); Lori Hausegger and Lawrence Baum, "Inviting Congressional Action: A Study of Supreme Court Motivations in Statutory Interpretations," 43 *American Journal of Political Science* 162 (1999).

rationally prefer that a law be interpreted uniformly throughout the United States rather than that it be interpreted compatibly with his or her preferred position in only part of the country. In such a model, resolving intercircuit conflicts would be key and winning on the merits of lesser importance.

The clearest divide between the legal model, the attitudinal model, and the rational choice model rests on the decision on the merits, which is where we next focus our attention.

7

The Decision on the Merits

The Legal Model

Chapters 7 and 8 begin where Chapter 6 left off: with the considerations that apply once the Court has agreed to hear a litigant's case. Accordingly, we start with a discussion of the stages that follow the decision to decide a case and the considerations that govern the disposition of these cases. We especially emphasize the legal and political factors that affect the justices' decisions. In this chapter we focus on the process of deciding cases and the influence of legal factors; in the next chapter we focus on the attitudinal and rational choice explanations.

PROCESS

Cases that receive full treatment from the Court – that is, those that are orally argued and decided with a full opinion (which are also referred to as formally decided cases)[1] – are typically subject to three votes. We considered the first of these – the decision to decide – in the previous chapter. If the Court votes to grant cert or to note probable jurisdiction, the other two votes occur following oral argument. These are the original vote on the merits and the final vote on the merits. Palmer refers to them more accurately and descriptively as "conference votes on the merits" and "report votes on the merits.[2] We know relatively little about the former vote, a great deal about the latter. First, though, we present a discussion of oral argument.

[1] But a formally decided case need not be decided on the merits of the controversy, as we pointed out in Chapter 6.

[2] Jan Palmer, *The Vinson Court Era: The Supreme Court's Conference Votes* (New York: AMS Press, 1990), p. 97.

Oral Argument

Oral argument is the only publicly visible stage of the Court's decision-making process. The extent to which it affects the justices' votes is problematic. The justices aver that it is a valuable source of information about the cases they have agreed to decide,[3] but that does not mean that oral argument regularly, or even infrequently, determines who wins and who loses. Justice Powell's docket sheets, which systematically summarize the position taken by each justice in conference, make virtually no reference to oral argument. Presumably, if oral argument proved pertinent, Powell would have reported it.[4] The conference vote on the merits occurs within 72 hours of oral argument; hence, it is likely to be fresh in the justices' minds. On the other hand, the Court rigorously limits the time for argument to 30 minutes for each side, with a few exceptions when an hour is allotted.[5]

The Court devotes fourteen weeks per term to oral argument, two weeks each during the months of October through April. During this time, it sits in public session on Mondays, Tuesdays, and Wednesdays, from 10 A.M. to noon, and from 1 to 3 P.M. This schedule provides an upper bound for the number of orally argued cases that the Court will consider during a term: four per day for three days over each of fourteen weeks, for a normal maximum of 168 cases. The clerk of the Court schedules oral argument; it typically occurs between four and six months after the justices have agreed to review the case. Several weeks before the date of argument, the justices receive the briefs filed by the parties to the litigation, along with those that interested nonparties may have submitted (amici curiae). Such nonparties receive permission from the parties themselves or they may motion the justices for permission to file a brief stating their view of the proper resolution of the controversy. The parties' consent need not be had for the Solicitor General to file a brief

[3] Robert L. Stern and Eugene Gressman, *Supreme Court Practice*, 5th ed. (Washington: Bureau of National Affairs, 1978), pp. 730–35; William H. Rehnquist, *The Supreme Court: How It Was, How It Is* (New York: Morrow, 1987), pp. 271–85.

[4] Justice Powell's docket sheets are housed in the law library of the Washington and Lee Law School in Lexington, Virginia. We greatly appreciate the unstinting assistance – far beyond the call of duty – provided by John N. Jacob, the Law School's archivist, in making these documents available to us and to Lee Epstein.

[5] Rules limiting the time of oral argument are a modern phenomenon. They did not exist early in the Court's history. Previous to the current time limits, the Court allowed each side an hour in important cases, 30 minutes in the remainder. Rehnquist, *op. cit.*, n. 3, *supra*, pp. 274–75.

on behalf of the United States, or for the authorized official of a federal agency, state, territory, or political subdivision of a state or territory to file on its behalf.[6] Nongovernmental interests generally have little trouble gaining permission from the Court to file briefs. Between 1969 and 1981, only 11 percent of motions for leave to file amicus briefs were denied.[7] Most frequently participating as amici are states, followed by corporations and business groups, and citizen organizations. Individuals rarely file.[8]

Lawyers filing amicus briefs on behalf of organized interests are not allowed to present oral argument except "in the most extraordinary circumstances."[9] Nevertheless, interest groups are often parties, in which case their lawyers may engage in the oral argument. For instance, the NAACP Legal Defense Fund (LDF) sponsored the historic case of *Brown v. Board of Education*[10] with the plaintiff represented by the LDF's chief counsel, Thurgood Marshall. For public interest lawyers representing groups such as the NAACP or the ACLU, the Supreme Court serves as a forum not just for winning clients' cases but for promoting the cause that the group espouses.[11]

While we know of no systematic information indicating the influence of oral argument on the justices' decisions, we do know what interests the justices most about oral argument: the policy implications of potential decisions. Over 40 percent of the justices' questions at oral argument involve policy, whereas less than 10 percent involve either precedential or constitutional issues.[12]

The Conference

No one is permitted to attend the justices' conferences except the justices themselves. At these meetings, the justices decide whether or not to hear the cases they have been asked to review; they discuss and vote on

[6] Rule 37 of the *Rules of the Supreme Court of the United States*, 515 U.S. at 1244–46.

[7] Karen O'Connor and Lee Epstein, "Court Rules and Workload: A Case Study of Rules Governing Amicus Curiae Participation," 8 *Justice System Journal* 35 (1983).

[8] Gregory Caldeira and John Wright, "Amici Curiae Participation Before the Supreme Court: Who Participates, When, and How Much," 52 *Journal of Politics* 782 (1990).

[9] Supreme Court Rule 28, 515 U.S. at 1233.

[10] 347 U.S. 483 (1954).

[11] Jonathan Casper, *Lawyers before the Warren Court* (Urbana: University of Illinois Press, 1972).

[12] Timothy Johnson, "Information, Oral Arguments, and Supreme Court Decision Making," *American Politics Research* [forthcoming].

whether to affirm or reverse the cases before them; and assignments are made to write the opinion of the Court. What transpires in the conference is often described as Washington's best-kept secret. What little we know we learn long after the fact, apart from an occasional statement in an opinion, the justices' private papers, or their off-the-bench communications.

According to Chief Justice Rehnquist, conferences convene on Wednesday afternoons following oral argument and on Friday mornings. The Wednesday conference votes on the cases at which oral argument was heard the preceding Monday, while the Friday conference disposes of the orally argued cases from Tuesday and Wednesday. The second part of the conferences that dispose of orally argued cases is devoted to the consideration of cases the Court has been asked to review.[13]

At one time, the process apparently involved two stages, with the chief justice speaking first, followed by the others in descending order of seniority. The second stage, in which the justices voted to affirm or reverse, proceeded in the opposite order: the most junior voted first, the chief justice last. Sometime between the Vinson Court (1946–52) and the Warren Court (1953–68), the process became a single stage, with the justices speaking and voting in order of seniority.[14]

The Court follows basically the same procedure with regard to the decision to decide a case, except that the discussion on the merits "is much less elaborate."[15] Chief Justice Rehnquist reports that "[w]ith occasional exceptions, each justice begins and ends his part of the discussion without interruption from his colleagues." He further states:

> When I first went on the Court, I was both surprised and disappointed at how little interplay there was between the various justices during the process of conferring on a case. Each would state his views, and a junior justice could express agreement or disagreement with views expressed by a justice senior to him earlier in the discussion, but the converse did not apply; a junior justice's views were seldom commented upon, because votes had been already cast up the line. Like most junior justices before me must have felt, I thought I had some very significant contributions to make, and was disappointed that they hardly ever seemed to influence anyone because people did not change their votes in response to my contrary views. I thought it would be desirable to have more of a round-table discussion of the matter after each of us had expressed our views. Having now

[13] Rehnquist, *op. cit.*, n. 3, *supra*, pp. 287–88, 289.

[14] Saul Brenner and Jan Palmer, "Voting Order in Conference on the Vinson Court," unpublished manuscript, 1991.

[15] Rehnquist, *op. cit.*, n. 3, *supra*, p. 289. For a description of the Court's decision to decide practices during the Vinson Court, see Palmer, *op. cit.*, n. 2, *supra*, pp. 26–30.

sat in conferences for fifteen years [as of 1987], and risen from ninth to seventh to first in seniority, I now realize – with newfound clarity – that while my idea is fine in the abstract it probably would not contribute much in practice, and at any rate is doomed by the seniority system to which the senior justices naturally adhere.[16]

Justice Scalia has echoed Rehnquist's sentiments, but without endorsing Rehnquist's approval of the lack of interchange among the justices. In response to questions following a speech at the George Washington University Law School, Scalia said that "not very much conferencing goes on" in conference. He used "conferencing" in the sense of efforts to persuade others to change their minds by debating matters of disagreement. "In fact," he said, "to call our discussion of a case a conference is really something of a misnomer. It's much more a statement of the views of each of the nine Justices, after which the totals are added and the case is assigned." He went on to say that he doesn't like this: "Maybe it's just because I'm new. Maybe it's because I'm an ex-academic. Maybe it's because I'm right." He concurred with Rehnquist's observation that his own remarks "hardly ever seemed to influence anyone because people did not change their votes in response to my contrary views."[17] However, Powell's annotated docket sheets report many instances of a justice acceding to or being persuaded by the views of another justice. Not uncommonly, vote changes did result. Admittedly, most such instances resulted when the changing justice was initially ambivalent: "not at rest," to use Powell's phrase.

On the other hand, according to a former clerk for Justice Blackmun, the give and take of conference is so unimportant to the justices that Justice Stevens would sometimes phone his votes in from his winter home in Florida.[18] Justices absent from the conference do commonly cast a vote, usually via a written memo.

Although the other branches of government have opened their proceedings to a degree of public scrutiny, the Supreme Court has adamantly refused to follow this trend. On the other hand, unlike Congress and the executive branch, the Court has provided the public with all relevant materials pertaining to its decisions: briefs, transcripts of oral argument,

[16] *Op. cit.*, n. 3, *supra*, pp. 290–91.

[17] "Ruing Fixed Opinions," *New York Times*, February 22, 1988, p. 20; reprinted in Harold J. Spaeth and Saul Brenner, eds., *Studies in U.S. Supreme Court Behavior* (New York: Garland, 1990), pp. 256–57.

[18] Edward Lazarus, *Closed Chambers: The First Eyewitness Account of the Epic Struggles Inside the Supreme Court* (New York: Times Books, 1998), p. 279.

the record of lower court proceedings, as well as the opinions of the justices themselves. The Court justifies its refusal to open its conferences to public examination on the ground that it would jeopardize its effectiveness as an authoritative policy-making body. While still an associate justice, Rehnquist provided what appears to have been the first full-blown defense of the practice. He gave four reasons for the secrecy.

First, "[a] remarkably candid exchange of views" occurs. "No one feels at all inhibited" about being quoted out of context or that "half-formed or ill conceived ideas" might subsequently be "held up to public ridicule." Second, each justice is required to do his or her own work. Unlike members of the President's Cabinet, who are "generally flanked by aides," the justices are forced to prepare themselves personally for the conference. Third, public scrutiny or press coverage could subject the Court to "lobbying pressures" intended to affect the outcome of decisions. Fourth, "occasionally short-tempered remarks or bits of rancorous rhetoric" are uttered which might transcend the cordiality that exists among the justices if they became part of a public record.[19]

THE CONFERENCE VOTE ON THE MERITS

We know precious little about conference voting, not only because of an historic lack of information, but also because much of what was communicated lacked accuracy. For instance, Professor J. Woodford Howard contended that changes in the justices' voting between the original and final votes on the merits were "so extensive in empirical reality as to pose very serious problems of classification and inference."[20] Yet support for his assertion that voting fluidity belies the validity of the attitudinal model as the explanation for the justice's behavior rests exclusively on anecdotal evidence. We falsify Howard's assertion below.

The justices' docket books contain the records of their conference voting.[21] The justices are provided these books at the beginning of each term so that they may individually keep a record of the votes cast in conference, the dates of votes, and to whom the opinion of the Court was assigned, by whom, and when. Although these books become the private

[19] Mort Mintz, "Rehnquist Strongly Defends Secrecy in Supreme Court," *Washington Post*, January 28, 1977, p. A2.

[20] "On the Fluidity of Judicial Choice," 52 *American Political Science Review* 43 (1968), at 44.

[21] Jan Palmer and Saul Brenner, "Working with Supreme Court Docket Books," 81 *Law Library Journal* 41 (1989); Palmer, *op. cit.*, n. 2, *supra*, pp. 34–49.

property of the justice to whom they are issued, several have made them available to posterity along with their other private papers. Seven of the eleven justices who served on the Vinson Court opened their docket books to the public, as well as several who served on the Warren Court.[22]

Fluidity and the Attitudinal Model

Not until 1980 did the first scientific analysis of the original vote on the merits appear: Professor Saul Brenner's reexamination of Howard's assertions about voting fluidity.[23] Brenner found that the Vinson Court justices voted the same way at the original and final votes on the merits 86 percent of the time overall, and 91 percent of the time in major cases. In 8.6 percent of the cases, a voting change transformed a minority or a tie into a majority. Similar findings resulted from his study of the latter portion of the Warren Court.[24]

Apart from the incidence of fluidity, current work has directly assessed the compatibility of the attitudinal model with changes between the original and final votes on the merits. Not only do these studies find no incompatibility, they also show that the attitudinal model explains those that do occur, while the role and small-group explanations favored by other scholars do not. Thus, ideological voting on the Vinson Court did not decrease between the original and final votes on the merits, which would clearly be the case if nonattitudinal variables intervened.[25] When minimum winning coalitions on the Warren Court broke up, they most often did so when the marginal justice in the majority was ideologically

[22] Palmer, *op. cit.*, n. 2, *supra*, contains a meticulous compilation of conference voting on the Vinson Court, with a complete case-by-case record of the justices' voting and opinion assignments, along with an assortment of other pertinent identifying information. As a result of Palmer's work, scholars now have a highly accurate record of at least three voting data points for each of the Court's formally decided cases: the vote whether or not to accept the case for review, conference voting, and the report vote. Palmer's Vinson Court data includes every available vote, not just those cast in the formally decided cases. These data are available in machine-readable form as "The Vinson-Warren Database" at www.ssc.msu.edu/~pls/pljp.

[23] "Fluidity on the United States Supreme Court: A Re-examination," 24 *American Journal of Political Science* 526 (1980); reprinted in Spaeth and Brenner, *op. cit.*, n. 17, *supra*, pp. 53–60.

[24] Saul Brenner, "Fluidity on the Supreme Court, 1956–1967," 26 *American Journal of Political Science* 388 (1982); reprinted in *op. cit.*, n. 17, *supra*, pp. 61–65.

[25] Saul Brenner, "Ideological Voting on the Vinson Court: A Comparison of the Original Vote on the Merits with the Final Vote," 21 *Polity* 102 (1989).

closer to a dissenting justice than he was to any member of the majority.[26] Attitudinal factors also accounted for majority-minority voting shifts by members of the Warren Court when the original vote coalition did not break up. Conversely, a set of nonattitudinal factors did not explain these voting shifts: the length of service of the shifting justice,[27] the importance of the case, whether the Court affirmed or reversed the decision of the lower court, whether dissent occurred on the lower court, whether the original vote coalition was large or small, whether the Court declared action unconstitutional or overruled one of its precedents.[28]

The foregoing pattern continues through the Burger Court (1969–85 terms). In 7.4 percent of its cases, the direction of the Court's decision changed between the final merits vote and the published report vote. The issue areas of these 225 cases bear approximately the same proportion as do those in the Burger Court's formally decided dockets overall. But when we examine the most drastic reversals, that is, where no more than a single justice dissents from the final result (32 percent), we find that the area of judicial power accounts for more than any other, 27 percent.

[26] Saul Brenner and Harold J. Spaeth, "Majority Opinion Assignments and the Maintenance of the Original Coalition on the Warren Court," 32 *American Journal of Political Science* 72 (1988); Saul Brenner, Timothy M. Hagle, and Harold J. Spaeth, "The Defection of the Marginal Justice on the Warren Court," 42 *Political Research Quarterly* 409 (1989).

[27] Howard posits the existence of a so-called freshman effect as the first of his nonideological intervening variables. He defines it as "unstable attitudes that seem to have resulted from the process of assimilation to the Court. It is not uncommon for a new Justice to undergo a period of adjustment, often about three years in duration, before his voting behavior stabilizes into observable, not to mention predictable, patterns." *Op. cit.*, n. 20, *supra*, p. 45. Most recent studies discount the existence of a freshman effect. See Edward V. Heck and Melinda Gann Hall, "Bloc Voting and Freshman Justice Revisited," 43 *Journal of Politics* 852 (1981); John M. Scheb II and Lee W. Ailshie, "Justice Sandra Day O'Connor and the 'Freshman Effect,'" 69 *Judicature* 9 (1985); Thea F. Rubin and Albert P. Melone, "Justice Antonin Scalia: A First Year Freshman Effect?," 72 *Judicature* 98 (1988); Albert P. Melone, "Revisiting the Freshman Effect Hypothesis: The First Two Terms of Justice Anthony Kennedy," 74 *Judicature* 6 (1990). Cf. Timothy M. Hagle and Carolyn I. Speer, "A New Test for the Freshman Effect: Justices Scalia and Kennedy," paper presented at the 1991 meeting of the American Political Science Association, Washington, D.C.

[28] Timothy M. Hagle and Harold J. Spaeth, "Voting Fluidity and the Attitudinal Model of Supreme Court Decision Making," 44 *Political Research Quarterly* 119 (1991). Cf. Forrest Maltzman and Paul Wahlbeck, "Strategic Considerations and Voting Fluidity on the Burger Court," 90 *American Political Science Review* 581 (1996), who find evidence that fluidity is more likely to occur in complex cases, defined as those with multiple issues, legal provisions, and opinions. *Id.* at 587. They also find that dissenters, and particularly solo dissenters, are likely to suppress dissent.

TABLE 7.1. *A Typology of Supreme Court Decision-Making Models on the Merits*

	Temporal influence	
Source of influence	**Past**	**Present**
Legislators	Legal model: text and intent	Rational choice model: separation of powers
Judges	Legal model: precedent	Attitudinal model

By comparison, only 12 percent of the Burger Court's cases overall concern the exercise of judicial power. Moreover, half of these extremely altered judicial power cases pertain to the low salient matter of mootness. Hence, we may preliminarily conclude that strong fluidity – altering the outcome of a case – rarely occurs, and when it does it disproportionately happens because most of the justices switch their votes to avoid a decision on the merits of the controversy.

THE REPORT (OR FINAL) VOTE ON THE MERITS

At any point between the conference vote on the merits and the day a decision is announced, justices are free to change their votes. Their position when the decision is announced constitutes the final vote on the merits.

In Table 7.1 we present a typology of the most prominent models of Supreme Court decision making (see Chapters 2 and 3) as applied to the vote on the merits. Sources of influence include legislators and judges. When the justices rely on the rulings of past judges, they are following precedent. But when justices follow their own (present) preferences, they behave attitudinally. When justices rely on the text and intent of the constitutions and statutes, they follow text and intent. But when they strategically defer to the constraints imposed by current legislative majorities, they behave consistently with the rational choice separation-of-powers model.

In this chapter we begin our examination of the factors that influence the final vote on the merits with the most important component of the legal model, stare decisis, or precedent. We then conclude this chapter with a shorter section on text and intent.

Stare Decisis[29]

According to political scientist Ronald Kahn, Supreme Court decision making can best be understood as a *constitutive* process, by which "members of the Supreme Court believe that they are required to act in accordance with particular institutional and legal expectations and responsibilities."[30] Thus, "justices must be principled in their decision-making process."[31] "Respect for precedent and principled decision making are central to Supreme Court decision-making."[32]

Kahn's prime example of principled, precedential decision making is the plurality opinion in *Planned Parenthood v. Casey*,[33] the 1992 abortion decision that reaffirmed, in part, *Roe v. Wade's*[34] right to abortion.

Certainly, the plurality's explanation of why it voted the way it did focused heavily on the doctrine of stare decisis. Opening with the stirring claim that "[l]iberty finds no refuge in a jurisprudence of doubt,"[35] the Court declared that "[a]fter considering the fundamental constitutional questions resolved by *Roe*, principles of institutional integrity, and the rule of stare decisis, we are led to conclude this: the essential holding of *Roe v. Wade* should be retained and once again reaffirmed."[36] While noting that stare decisis in constitutional questions is far from an inexorable command,[37] the Court explained why *Roe* differed:

> Where, in the performance of its judicial duties, the Court decides a case in such a way as to resolve the sort of intensely divisive controversy reflected in Roe and those rare, comparable cases, its decision has a dimension that the resolution of the normal case does not carry. It is the dimension present whenever the Court's interpretation of the Constitution calls the contending sides of a national controversy to end their national division by accepting a common mandate rooted in the Constitution.
>
> The Court is not asked to do this very often, having thus addressed the Nation only twice in our lifetime, in the decisions of Brown and Roe. But, when the Court does act in this way, its decision requires an equally rare precedential force to counter the inevitable efforts to overturn it and to thwart its implementation. Some of these efforts may be mere unprincipled emotional reactions; others may

[29] Parts of this section derive from Harold J. Spaeth and Jeffrey A. Segal, *Majority Rule or Minority Will: Adherence to Precedent on the U.S. Supreme Court* (New York: Cambridge University Press, 1999).

[30] Ronald Kahn, "Interpretive Norms and Supreme Court Decision Making: The Rehnquist Court on Privacy and Religion," in Cornell W. Clayton and Howard Gillman, eds., *Supreme Court Decision Making: New Institutionalist Approaches* (Chicago: University of Chicago Press, 1999), p. 175.

[31] *Id.* at 176. [32] *Id.* at 178. [33] 505 U.S. 833. [34] 410 U.S. 113 (1973).

[35] 505 U.S. 833 at 843. [36] *Id.* at 845–46. [37] *Id.* at 854.

proceed from principles worthy of profound respect. But whatever the premises of opposition may be, only the most convincing justification under accepted standards of precedent could suffice to demonstrate that a later decision overruling the first was anything but a surrender to political pressure, and an unjustified repudiation of the principle on which the Court staked its authority in the first place. So to overrule under fire in the absence of the most compelling reason to reexamine a watershed decision would subvert the Court's legitimacy beyond any serious question.[38]

In further support of his thesis, Kahn quotes from the opinion: "Our obligation is to define the liberty of all, not to mandate our own moral code."[39] Kahn declares that "the joint opinion in *Casey* emphasizes that a continuing commitment to *stare decisis* requires a reaffirmation of *Roe*."[40]

Kahn's view is far from unique. Journalists and scholars alike were quick to accept the triumvirate's explanation that stare decisis influenced its decision. Linda Greenhouse's analysis of the decision accepts at face value the claim that adhering to *Roe v. Wade* was necessary even for justices who continued to have doubts about the decision.[41] The *Chicago Tribune* declared that the "decision relied on the time-honored doctrine of respecting legal precedent."[42]

With all due respect, we couldn't disagree more.[43] We begin with the basic notion that those wishing to assess systematically the influence of precedent must recognize that in many cases Supreme Court decision making would look exactly the same whether justices were influenced by precedent or not. Consider the Court's decision in *Roe v. Wade*. The majority found a constitutional right to abortion that could not be abridged without a compelling state interest. The dissenters found no such right. In subsequent cases, Justices Blackmun, Brennan, Marshall, and others continued to support abortion rights. While we could say that

[38] *Id.* at 866–67. [39] Kahn, *op. cit.*, n. 30, p. 180. [40] *Id.*

[41] Linda Greenhouse, "A Telling Court Opinion," *New York Times*, July 1, 1992, p. A1.

[42] William Neikirk and Glen Elsasser, "Top Court May Face Backlash," *Chicago Tribune*, July 1, 1992, p. 1. Also see Erin Daly, "Reconsidering Abortion Law: Liberty, Equality and the Rhetoric of *Planned Parenthood v. Casey*," 45 *American University Law Review* 77 (1995); C. Elaine Howard, "The Roe'd to Confusion: *Planned Parenthood v. Casey*," 30 *Houston Law Review* 1457 (1993); and Earl M. Maltz, "Abortion, Precedent and the Constitution: A Comment on *Planned Parenthood v. Casey*," 68 *Notre Dame Law Review* 11 (1992).

[43] Evidenced in part by our prediction of the outcome of *Planned Parenthood* on the day before the decision was announced, Interview with Gene Healy, WJR Radio, Detroit, June 28, 1992. The prediction correctly specified how each of the justices would vote, largely for the reasons specified in the remainder of this section.

choices in these cases were based on the precedent set in *Roe*, it is just as reasonable – arguably, more so – to say that those justices would have supported abortion rights in subsequent cases even without the precedent in *Roe*. Thus, even in a system without a rule of precedent, Justice Scalia would continue to support the death penalty, nonracial drawing of congressional districts, limited privacy rights, and so on. When prior preferences and precedents are the same, it is not meaningful to speak of decisions as being determined by precedent. For precedent to matter as an *influence* on decisions, it must achieve results that would not otherwise have obtained.[44] As Judge Jerome Frank stated, "Stare decisis has no bite when it means merely that a court adheres to a precedent that it considers correct. It is significant only when a court feels constrained to stick to a former ruling although the court has come to regard it as unwise or unjust."[45]

Did the plurality opinion in *Casey* give any indication that its authors considered the ruling in *Roe* to be unwise or unjust? For the most part, the answer is "no." While the authors pointed out that "time has overtaken some of *Roe*'s factual assumptions,"[46] and that some parts of *Roe* were unduly restrictive, the decision "has in no sense proven unworkable,"[47] has facilitated "the ability of women to participate equally in the economic and social life of the nation,"[48] and fits comfortably with doctrinal developments before and after 1973.[49] Indeed, the Court refers to *Roe* as an "exemplar of Griswold liberty."[50]

While it is true that there are instances where the Court finds fault with *Roe*, each and every time it does it substitutes its own judgment for that of *Roe*! Thus the Court supplants the trimester framework with viability[51] and exchanges the compelling interest standard for an undue burden standard.[52] Additionally, the Court reversed holdings in *Akron*

[44] An appropriate example may be Chief Justice Rehnquist's vote and opinion in *Dickerson v. United States,* 147 L Ed 2d 405 (2000), reaffirming *Miranda v. Arizona*, 384 U.S. (1966). Except for four unanimous decisions, Rehnquist had unfailingly voted against *Miranda* in his other thirty participations in which it was at issue. On the other hand, his opinion did declare unconstitutional an act of Congress that would have replaced the Miranda warnings with a case-by-case assessment of the voluntariness of a confession. Rehnquist, therefore, had to choose between *Miranda* and congressional action infringing on the Court's assertedly exclusive capacity to interpret the Constitution. Arguably, Rehnquist considers the Court's monopoly on judicial review of greater moment than ridding the nation of *Miranda*.

[45] *United States ex rel. Fong Foo v. Shaughnessy*, 234 F.2d 715 (1955), at 719.

[46] 505 U.S. 833 at 860. [47] *Id.* at 855. [48] *Id.* at 856. [49] *Id.* at 857–58.

[50] *Id.* at 857. [51] *Id.* at 870. [52] *Id.* at 876.

v. Akron Center for Reproductive Health[53] and *Thornburgh v. American College of Obstetricians and Gynecologists.*[54] In sum, in no place in the plurality opinion does the Court clearly substitute *Roe*'s judgment, or that of any other case, for its own contemporary preference.

Our answer about the *influence* of *Roe* changes a bit if we look to the past for the views of the justices. Undoubtedly, an arguable case for precedential impact can be made for Justice Kennedy. In 1989, Kennedy joined Rehnquist's opinion in *Webster v. Reproductive Health Services*, which, among other things, questioned why the "State's interest in protecting human life should come into existence only at the point of viability."[55] But as a federal court of appeals judge, Kennedy "only grudgingly upheld the validity of naval regulations prohibiting homosexual conduct," citing *Roe v. Wade* and other privacy cases very favorably.[56] According to the dossier Deputy Attorney General Steven Matthews prepared on Kennedy for the Reagan Justice Department, "This easy acceptance of privacy rights as something guaranteed by the Constitution is really very distressing."[57] Thus, it is difficult to categorize Kennedy as an opponent of *Roe*, notwithstanding his subsequent dissenting opinion in *Stenberg v. Carhart*[58] in which the Court voided a loosely worded Nebraska statute prohibiting late-term abortions regardless of their effect on the mother's health.

Even more ambiguous is the position of Justice Souter. Though appointed by a purportedly prolife President,[59] Souter had sat on the board of directors of a New Hampshire hospital that performed voluntary abortions, with no known objections from Souter. Without any clear indications of his prior beliefs about *Roe*, it is nearly impossible to determine the extent to which *Roe* influenced his position in *Casey.*

Alternatively, no ambiguity surrounded Justice O'Connor's preferences. O'Connor supported abortion rights while a legislator in Arizona[60] and, once on the Court, frequently found problems with the trimester format of *Roe* but never doubted that a fundamental right to

[53] 462 U.S. 416 (1983). [54] 476 U.S. 747 (1986).

[55] 492 U.S. 490 at 519. As we note, though, the *Casey* plurality adopted precisely that position.

[56] David Yalof, *Pursuit of Justices* (Chicago: University of Chicago Press, 1999), p. 211.

[57] *Id.* [58] 147 L Ed 2d 743 (2000).

[59] Bush supported abortion rights until Ronald Reagan nominated him to be vice-president in 1980. He had even been an active supporter of Planned Parenthood.

[60] "It's About Time," *Los Angeles Times*, September 13, 1981.

abortion existed.[61] Indeed, *Casey*'s attacks on *Roe*'s trimester framework and its adoption of the undue burden standard come directly from O'Connor's *dissent* in *Akron v. Akron Center for Reproductive Services*.[62] So, too, *Casey*'s overruling of *Akron* and *Thornburgh* comport perfectly with her dissents in those cases.

We summarize these points in Table 7.2, which, for each issue in *Casey*, presents the established doctrine or precedent of the Court, O'Connor's prior position on the issue, and the result in *Casey*. It is extraordinarily difficult to argue that stare decisis influenced O'Connor in any manner in this purported paragon of precedent. Where precedent and her previously expressed preferences met, she followed precedent. But where any majority opinion in any abortion case differed from her previously expressed views, she stuck with her previously expressed views. Justice O'Connor "followed" precedent to the extent that she used precedent to justify results she agreed with, but there is no evidence whatsoever that these precedents influenced her positions.

Measuring the Influence of Precedent

While we believe our position on the justices' votes to be reasonable, we are struck by a lack of hard evidence as to how, for example, Justice Souter might have felt about *Roe* as an original matter. Thus, the best evidence about whether justices are influenced by a precedent would come not from justices who joined the Court after the decision in question, for we usually cannot be certain about what their position on the case would have been as an original matter. Nor can we gather such evidence from those on the Court who voted with the majority, for the precedent established in that case coincides with their revealed preferences (whatever their cause). Rather, the best evidence for the influence of precedent must come from those who dissented from the majority opinion in the case under question, for we *know* that these justices disagree with the precedent. If the precedent established in the case influences them, that influence should be felt in that case's progeny, through their votes and opinion writing. Thus, determining the influence of precedent requires examining the extent to which justices who disagree with a precedent move toward that position in subsequent cases.

[61] E.g., *Webster v. Reproductive Health Services*, 492 U.S. 490 (1989), and *Thornburgh v. American College of Obstetricians and Gynecologists*, 476 U.S. 747 (1986).

[62] 462 U.S. 416 (1983).

TABLE 7.2. *Impact of Precedent versus Preferences on the O'Connor et al. Judgment in* Casey

Issue	Court's prior ruling (precedent)	O'Connor's prior view	*Casey* result
Framework	Trimester (*Roe*)	"Neither sound constitutional theory nor our need to decide cases based on the application of neutral principles can accommodate an analytic framework according to the 'stages' of pregnancy" (*Akron* I, O'Connor dissent, at 452).	"We reject the trimester framework" (at 872).
Standard	Compelling interest (*Roe*)	"A lawful abortion is not unconstitutional unless it unduly burdens the right" (*Akron* I, O'Connor dissent, at 453).	"The right protects the woman from unduly burdensome interference" (at 874).
Spousal notice	Unconstitutional (*Danforth*)	None	Unconstitutional
Informed consent	Unconstitutional (*Akron I*)	Informed consent provisions "impose no undue burden" (*Akron* I, O'Connor dissent, at 472).	"To the extent that *Akron I* and *Thornburgh* find a constitutional violation when the government requires, as it does here, the giving of truthful and nonmisleading information . . . , those decisions are overruled" (at 882).
24-hour waiting	Unconstitutional (*Akron I*)	"Although the waiting period may impose an additional cost on the abortion decision, this increased cost does not unduly burden the availability of abortions" (*Akron* I, O'Connor dissent, at 473).	"We consider [*Akron*'s decision striking the waiting period] to be wrong" (at 885).
Parental consent	Valid (*Akron II*)	O'Connor joined the *Akron II* majority opinion.	Valid (at 899).
Record keeping	Valid (*Danforth*)	None	No "substantial obstacle" (at 900).

This is not an unobtainable standard. For example, in *Griswold v. Connecticut* (1965),[63] Stewart rejected the creation of a right to privacy and its application to married individuals. Yet in *Eisenstadt v. Baird* (1972)[64] he accepted *Griswold's* right to privacy and was even willing to apply it to unmarried persons. And while Justice Rehnquist dissented in the jury exclusion cases *Batson v. Kentucky* (1986)[65] and *Edmonson v. Leesville Concrete* Co. (1991),[66] he concurred in *Georgia v. McCollum* (1992), providing an explicit and quintessential example of what it means to be constrained by precedent: "I was in dissent in *Edmonson v. Leesville Concrete* Co. and continue to believe that case to have been wrongly decided. But so long as it remains the law, I believe it controls the disposition of this case. . . . I therefore join the opinion of the Court."[67]

Moreover, meeting this type of standard does not require that a justice follow precedent, as we have operationalized it, in any given case. Obviously, dissenting justices may legitimately dispute the application of a precedent to a progeny (though as we find below, justices in the original majority almost never do). By focusing on a large number of cases, we only require a "gravitational force"[68] of precedent, such that in some meaningful percent of cases precedent has an impact.

We believe that our operational definition of precedent is both reasonable and, unlike other definitions, falsifiable. Compare our definition to one that counts a justice as following precedent as long as she cites some case or cases that are consistent with that justice's vote. Since there are always some cases supporting both sides in virtually every conflict decided by the Court, such a definition turns stare decisis into a trivial concept, at least for explanatory purposes.

Analyzing precedent from this perspective should yield important substantive and theoretical insights into the nature of judicial decision making. Certainly, systematic evidence supports the notion that stare decisis permeates the decisional process at the Supreme Court. For the briefs on the merits, previous decisions typically outweigh constitutional provisions, statutes, regulations, and all other sources combined in the Table of Authorities.[69] Moreover, justices frequently make appeals to

[63] 381 U.S. 479. [64] 405 U.S. 438. [65] 476 U.S. 79.

[66] 500 U.S. 614. [67] 505 U.S. 42 at 52.

[68] Ronald Dworkin, *Taking Rights Seriously* (Cambridge, Mass.: Harvard University Press, 1978).

[69] Jack Knight and Lee Epstein, "The Norm of Stare Decisis," 40 *American Journal of Political Science* 1018–35 (1996).

precedent in their private conference discussions.[70] Additionally, justices more frequently cite precedents in their written opinions than any other source of information.[71]

But with all this attention to stare decisis, we still need to know whether previously decided cases influence the decisions of Supreme Court justices. That is, does precedent actually cause justices to reach decisions that they otherwise would not have made? Of course, as we have shown, in some cases the answer clearly appears to be "yes." The real question is not whether such behavior exists at all, for surely it does, but whether it exists at systematic and substantively meaningful levels.

Sampling Precedents

If our goal is to examine the decisions of the justices in the progeny of established precedents, we must sample the precedents that we examine.

We initially limit our search for progeny to those that pertain to the Court's major decisions. We do so because major cases are most likely to be cited as precedents and hence most likely to spawn progeny. We operationalize major cases quite simply as those listed in the Congressional Quarterly's *Guide to the U.S. Supreme Court* as "major decisions."[72] Common alternatives, such as constitutional law books, almost completely ignore statutory cases. We exclude from Witt's list unanimously decided cases. Only dissenters can be conflicted between their stated preferences and the precedent the majority established in that case.

Because the number of landmark cases on Witt's list is manageable, we sampled 100 percent of the cases with dissent. We next add to our study a stratified random sample of ordinary decisions with dissent.[73]

Identification of Progeny

With our 100 percent sample of landmark cases with dissent and our random sample of ordinary cases with dissent, we must now determine what the progeny of these cases are.

[70] *Id.*

[71] *Id.* See also Glenn A. Phelps and John B. Gates, "The Myth of Jurisprudence: Interpretive Theory in the Constitutional Opinions of Justices Rehnquist and Brennan," 31 *Santa Clara Law Review* 567–96 (1991).

[72] Elder Witt, ed., *CQ Guide to the U.S. Supreme Court*, 2nd ed. (Washington, D.C.: Congressional Quarterly, 1990), pp. 883–929.

[73] See Harold J. Spaeth and Jeffrey A. Segal, *Majority Rule or Minority Will: Adherence to Precedent on the U.S. Supreme Court* (New York: Cambridge University Press, 1999), for details.

Only formally decided cases are treated as progeny. We identify progeny by finding citations in the case syllabus, or summary, that pertain to the issue the case concerns. Such citations qualify as precedents. Absent a syllabus reference, we consult *Shepard's Citations* to ascertain the precedents of our cases. We examine all citations in *Shepard's* analysis column as well as all cases that are cited at least twice. A case may be precedent for certain progeny, and for those progeny to serve as precedents for still other progeny. Issue discrepancy between putative progeny and precedents requires verbal dependence on the precedent, a lesser amount where issue identity prevails.

If these criteria create progeny of the original decisions, we evaluate the behavior of all justices who dissented from the original decision. We assess each dissenter's opinion and voting behavior to determine whether or not the dissent adheres to the precedent. We do so by dividing precedential and preferential behavior into three exclusive categories: strong, moderate, and weak. Strong precedential behavior formally accedes to the precedent in question. Moderate precedential behavior sees a justice writing or joining an opinion that specifically supports the precedent as authority for his or her vote. Weak precedential behavior involves a vote that supports the direction of the precedent's decision where the progeny's issue is effectively identical to that of the precedent. Preferential voting parallels that which supports precedent. Thus, a weak preferential vote occurs when a dissenter from a precedent writes or joins an opinion opposite in direction from that of the precedent. Moderate preferential voting occurs when justices support their original position by dissenting from or concurring with the prevailing opinion in a progeny that cites the precedent as authority. Justices vote strongly preferentially when they reassert adherence to their disapproval of the precedent either in approximately so many words or by citing a dissent from the precedent as their authority.

In designing our research strategy, we recognize that a switch in judicial behavior following the establishment of a precedent toward the position taken in that precedent merely establishes a rebuttable presumption that the switch was due to the precedent. Undoubtedly, we code some votes as precedential when other factors may have intervened. Nevertheless, we later compare the precedentially consistent switching we observe to a baseline of precedentially inconsistent switching (i.e., voting with the majority and then opposing the precedent in future cases), so as to derive an aggregate estimate of an appropriate deflation factor.

Alternative Approaches

We also recognize that alternative approaches to assessing precedential impact might exist, both narrowly and broadly. Narrowly, alternative approaches to our coding of the cases clearly exist. In our view, though, proffered alternatives do not accord with the realities of the Court's decision making. Thus, we could have counted justices as supporting precedent any time they agreed with an opinion that cited it as authority. This, of course, completely ignores the strategic ability of justices to use (and misuse) precedents for their own ideological purposes as well as the Court's institutional rules for writing and forming opinions. To illustrate: The Court standardly uses language from the World War II internment cases to void racial discrimination: for example, racial categorizations are "by their very nature odious to a free people,"[74] and "courts must subject them to the most rigid scrutiny."[75] If the *Korematsu* dissenters had still been alive to participate in the unanimous opinion that voided bans on interracial marriage,[76] is it likely that joining the majority would have signified support for the *Korematsu* precedent? Hardly.

On other occasions, the justices so severely limit or distinguish precedents that they become irrelevant to a succeeding decision. To count such behavior as precedentially supportive countenances frigidity as a temperature less than 70 degrees Fahrenheit. Given the reluctance of a court to overturn a precedent unnecessarily, litigants realize they need not ask the Court to do so when they can win if an objectionable precedent is held inapplicable. Thus, the Legal Defense Fund's initial strategy focused on the inequality of segregated Southern schools before it sought overruling of the separate but equal doctrine.[77] Judicial statements that various systems could not meet the separate but equal standard hardly meant, on the eve of *Brown v. Board of Education*,[78] that they accepted that doctrine.

Furthermore, although justices disagree with a precedent, they will commonly write that in the case at hand their policy preferences are accommodated "even under" the objectionable precedent. Thus, for example, no rational person would allege that Justices Rehnquist and White ever supported *Roe v. Wade*.[79] With one debatable exception, they

[74] *Hirabayashi v. United States*, 320 U.S 81 (1943), at 100.

[75] *Korematsu v. United States*, 323 U.S. 214 (1944), at 216.

[76] *Loving v. Virginia*, 388 U.S. 1 (1967).

[77] *Plessy v. Ferguson*, 163 U.S. 537 (1896).

[78] 347 U.S. 483 (1954). [79] 410 U.S. 113 (1973).

have invariably voted against a woman's right to abortion.[80] In doing so, they follow a simple strategy: If *Roe* sustains the decision, attack *Roe.* If the case does not implicate *Roe*, assert that even *Roe* does not support the prochoice position. Thus, in *Harris v. McRae*[81] the Court permitted states to terminate Medicaid funding for abortions, holding that the cutoff did not violate *Roe.* That certainly does not imply that the majority opinion writer and those acceding to it supported *Roe* as a precedent for this decision.

Data Description and Summary

Our sample resulted in 2,418 votes and opinions, of which 285, or 12 percent, fall into one of our precedential categories,[82] while 2,133, or 88 percent, fall into one of our preferential categories.[83] We break these down below into landmarks versus ordinary cases, and apportion them among a number of other factors. Though there may be some subset of justices or some types of issues or some periods of time within our sample where precedential behavior might be greater, we can state our overall conclusion straightforwardly: The justices are rarely influenced by stare decisis. This holds even without comparisons to changing behavior by justices who originally supported the precedents in question (see below). The levels of precedential behavior that we find in the U.S. Supreme Court are simply not consistent with the sort of arguments we find, for example, in Dworkin, Kahn, or any of the other legalists that we have discussed here or in Chapter 2.

Nor can the levels of precedential behavior we find allow us to agree with C. Herman Pritchett's famous statement that "[j]udges make choices, but they are not the 'free' choices of congressmen."[84] Indeed, given the extraordinary constraints on representatives imposed by con-

[80] Rehnquist's vote in *Bellotti v. Baird*, 443 U.S. 622 (1979), in which the Court required judicial bypass for minors seeking parentally unapproved abortions. He adhered to the position he took in *Planned Parenthood v. Danforth*, 428 U.S. 52 (1976), that a state could constitutionally impose a blanket parental consent requirement, but willingly joined the *Bellotti* opinion limiting *Danforth* by allowing a judicial bypass as a parental alternative.

[81] 448 U.S. 297 (1980).

[82] We find 2.6 percent in our strong precedential category, 7.4 percent in our moderate precedential category, and 1.9 percent in our weak precedential category.

[83] We found 25 percent in our strong preferential category, 22 percent in the moderate preferential category, and 41 percent in the weak preferential category.

[84] C. Herman Pritchett, "The Development of Judicial Research," in Joel Grossman and Joseph Tanenhaus, eds., *Frontiers of Judicial Research* (New York: Wiley, 1969), p. 42.

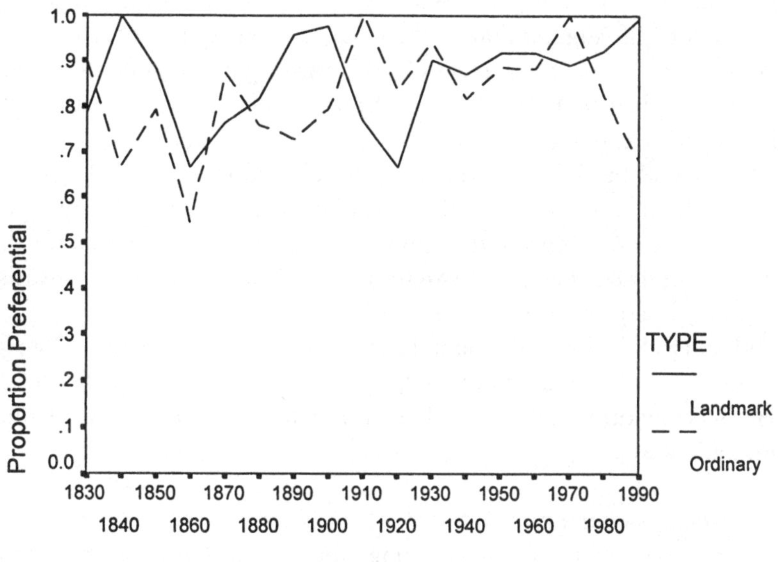

FIGURE 7.1. Precedential/preferential behavior by decade.

stituents[85] and party,[86] we would argue, conversely, that members of Congress make choices, but they are not the free choices of Supreme Court justices.

Precedent over Time

We present our findings diachronically in Figure 7.1. Here we aggregate cases by decade according to the year of the progeny, with five landmarks and four ordinary cases from before 1830 coded with the 1830s. As can readily be seen, while levels fluctuate around the mean levels, there is not much of a pattern over time. Preferential behavior in landmark cases peaks in the 1840s (100 percent), in the first decade of the twentieth century (98 percent), and again at the end of the twentieth century (99 percent). Precedential behavior in landmarks peaks at fairly moderate levels during the 1860s (33 percent precedential),[87] and again in the

[85] Morris Fiorina, *Representatives, Roll Calls, and Constituencies* (Lexington, Mass.: D. C. Heath, 1974).

[86] Gary W. Cox and Matthew D. McCubbins, *Legislative Leviathan: Party Government in the House* (Berkeley: University of California Press, 1993).

[87] The *n* here is only six cases, compared with 17 in the 1850s and 46 in the 1870s.

1920s (again 33 percent). The sharp rise in preferential behavior during the 1930s might suggest that as the Court gained control over its jurisdiction in the 1920s, the percent of cases with legal discretion increased, but this is belied by the low levels of precedential behavior in virtually all previous decades.

Preferential behavior in ordinary cases peaked in 1910, and again in the 1970s, at 100 percent.[88] Precedential behavior in ordinary cases peaks at 46 percent during the 1860s, suggesting that the results for the landmarks during that decade were not accidental, and peaks, surprisingly, at 32 percent during the 1990s.

What is clear beyond doubt is that the modern Supreme Courts, heavily criticized for their activism, did not invent or even perfect preferential behavior; it has been with us since Washington packed the Court with Federalists.

The Justices' Behavior

Table 7.3 presents the summary voting scores for each justice who served during the Rehnquist Court era for whom we have at least one vote to consider in either a landmark or ordinary case.[89] We label justices "preferential" if their preferential scores are above 67 percent, "moderately preferential" if their scores are between 33 and 67 percent, and "precedential" if their scores are below 33 percent. In landmark cases, for justices deciding ten or more cases, no justice can be labeled a precedentialist, but Lewis Powell (65 percent preferential) can be labeled a moderate. Alternatively, Brennan (99 percent), Marshall (99 percent), O'Connor (100 percent), and Rehnquist (96 percent) each voted preferentially over 95 percent of the time.

In ordinary cases, no justice with ten or more votes can be labeled a "precedentialist" but John Paul Stevens (62 percent preferential) can be labeled a moderate. At the other end of the spectrum, Brennan and Marshall are 100 percent preferential, with Powell, surprisingly, reaching 90 percent preferential.

Overall, if we categorize precedents as being liberal or conservative, something we are able to do for all civil liberties and economics cases

[88] Again, we have only six cases in the 1910s. The preferential perfection demonstrated in the 1970s is based on 52 cases.

[89] To allow time for progeny to develop, we ended our sampling of precedents in 1989. Thus we do not have votes for Souter, Thomas, Ginsburg, or Breyer.

since the 1937 term,[90] we find that dissenters from conservative landmarks switched their positions in those cases' progeny only 15 times out of 640 opportunities (2.3 percent). Alternatively, dissenters from liberal landmarks switched their positions 99 times out of 711 opportunities (14 percent). It is hard to escape the descriptive conclusion that in these cases for these years the old canard is apparently true: Conservative justices are more restrained, toward precedent at least, than are liberal justices.

Establishing a Baseline

We have found that when a newly established precedent diverges from a justice's previously revealed preferences, the justice will shift positions and support the precedent about 12 percent of the time in subsequent cases. About 10 percent of the total cases represent the strongest manifestations of precedential behavior (strong or moderate), whereby justices either explicitly accede to the precedent they had dissented from or sign opinions explicitly citing the original precedent as authority for their opinion. But this amount of changing behavior could readily occur due to a series of other factors that need not have anything to do with the establishment of the precedent. That is, some proportion of the changing behavior we have observed would have happened anyway. The question is, how much?

We answer this question by examining the behavior of those justices who originally joined the majority opinion of the established precedent. To establish a baseline of normal behavioral changes by justices, we took a random sample of 30 percent of our cases and assessed the future behavior of the justices who sided with the majority in the established precedents. Compared with dissenting justices who *explicitly* switched positions 10 percent of the time, justices who sided with the majority explicitly switched positions only 0.9 percent of the time. This quasiexperiment, holding the cases, the progeny, and the time periods constant, and "manipulating" which side of the case the justice was on, demonstrates that the overwhelming majority of strong precedential behavior that we find is in fact precedential. Though the absolute levels are low,

[90] From the 1946 term forward, we use Spaeth's U.S. Supreme Court database, as expanded to cover the Vinson Court. For the 1937–44 terms, we use data from a separate project (NSF grant SBR9320509, Lee Epstein, Carol Mershon, Jeffrey Segal, and Harold Spaeth, principle investigators) to categorize cases from the 1937 through 1945 terms.

TABLE 7.3. *Justices' Precedential Behavior by Case Type*

Justice		Type: Landmark	Ordinary	Total
Blackmun	Precedential	13	3	16
		20.0%	21.4%	20.3%
	Preferential	52	11	63
		80.0%	78.6%	79.7%
	Total	65	14	79
		100.0%	100.0%	100.0%
Brennan	Precedential	2		2
		1.4%		1.2%
	Preferential	146	25	171
		98.6%	100.0%	98.8%
	Total	148	25	173
		100.0%	100.0%	100.0%
Kennedy	Preferential	4		4
		100.0%		100.0%
	Total	4		4
		100.0%		100.0%
Marshall	Precedential	2		2
		1.3%		1.1%
	Preferential	154	28	182
		98.7%	100.0%	98.9%
	Total	156	28	184
		100.0%	100.0%	100.0%
O'Connor	Precedential		3	3
			60.0%	9.4%
	Preferential	27	2	29
		100.0%	40.0%	90.6%
	Total	27	5	32
		100.0%	100.0%	100.0%
Powell	Precedential	8	1	9
		34.8%	10.0%	27.3%
	Preferential	15	9	24
		65.2%	90.0%	72.7%
	Total	23	10	33
		100.0%	100.0%	100.0%
Rehnquist	Precedential	5	3	8
		3.9%	11.5%	5.2%
	Preferential	122	23	145
		96.1%	88.5%	94.8%
	Total	127	26	153
		100.0%	100.0%	100.0%

Justice		Type: Landmark	Type: Ordinary	Total
Scalia	Precedential		1	1
			100.0%	16.7%
	Preferential	5		5
		100.0%		83.3%
	Total	5	1	6
		100.0%	100.0%	100.0%
Stevens	Precedential	4	8	12
		9.8%	38.1%	19.4%
	Preferential	37	13	50
		90.2%	61.9%	80.6%
	Total	41	21	62
		100.0%	100.0%	100.0%
White	Precedential	22		22
		13.5%		13.3%
	Preferential	141	3	144
		86.5%	100.0%	86.7%
	Total	163	3	166
		100.0%	100.0%	100.0%

justices who dissent from a precedent are much more likely to explicitly change positions than are those justices who originally supported the precedent.

At the same time, we must take a more cautious view if we try to examine all manifestations of precedential behavior. Here we find justices in the original majority switching positions 9.7 percent of the time, compared with 12 percent of the time for justices who dissented. While these differences are statistically significant,[91] suggesting a small but statistically significant impact of precedent, the results suggest that we should at least be wary of the small percentage of our cases that fall into the weak precedential category.

Toward an Explanation of Precedential Behavior

At this point, we might be tempted to conclude that we have relatively clear evidence of low levels of precedential behavior and leave it at that.

[91] $p < 0.05$.

On the other hand, even though precedential behavior seems fairly rare, it is important enough to attempt to inquire why it exists at all.

To be sure, we would not have predicted anything but low levels of precedential behavior. Yet if such behavior does exist, even at low levels, it should be *relatively* more likely to exist in low salience cases. Conversely, preferential behavior, though conceivably dominating all aspects of the decision on the merits, might be *relatively* more dominant in high salience cases. The low salience case would obviously include ordinary cases over landmark cases. Among cases not designated as landmarks, this might include statutory cases over constitutional cases and, since the Roosevelt Court, economic cases over civil liberties cases.

We begin with the distinction between landmark and ordinary cases. Of our 2,418 votes and opinions, 1,822 were from our population of landmark cases from Witt. The remaining 596 come from our stratified random sample of ordinary Supreme Court cases with dissent. Cumulatively, in cases where the justices' preferences conflicted with the relevant precedent, the justices supported the precedent in just 9.9 percent of landmark cases and 18 percent of ordinary cases. The results are significant at $p < 0.001$. This relationship holds through much of the Court's history. The exceptions, as Figure 9.1 demonstrates, are the 1830s, the 1870s, the 1910s–1930s, and 1970s.

We next examined the justices' behavior as a function of the level of interpretation. We expect that precedential behavior should be higher in statutory cases, where the stakes are typically lower, than in constitutional cases, which make up the core of the Court's policy-making powers. This hypothesis coincides, though for slightly different reasons, with some of the Court's rhetoric about precedent. As the Court noted in *Patterson v. McLean Credit Union*, "Considerations of stare decisis have special force in the area of statutory interpretation, for here, unlike in the context of constitutional interpretation, the legislative power is implicated, and Congress remains free to alter what we have done."[92]

Similarly, Justice Scalia echoed Justice Douglas's statement that "[a] judge looking at a constitutional decision may have compulsions to revere past history and accept what was once written. But he remembers above all else that it is the Constitution which he swore to support and defend, not the gloss which his predecessors have put on it."[93]

[92] 491 U.S. 164 (1989) at 172–73.
[93] *South Carolina v. Gathers*, 490 U.S. 805 (1989) at 825.

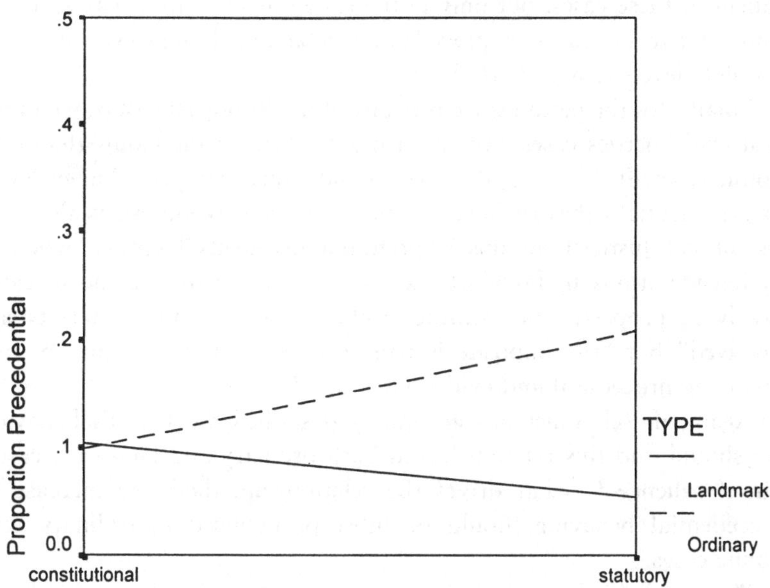

FIGURE 7.2. Precedential behavior by level of interpretation (cases prior to 1830 coded as 1830).

We distinguish our explanation from the Court's in that under the Court's explanation the difference between statutory and constitutional cases should hold regardless of whether we are dealing with landmark or ordinary cases. But if salience is the key to the difference, then landmark statutory cases may be just as preferentially driven as landmark constitutional cases; ordinary statutory cases may be where precedential behavior is maximized.

Figure 7.2 presents our results. Among landmark cases, there is little difference between precedential levels in constitutional and statutory cases; indeed, the relationship is in the opposite direction of what we predicted (and the Court claims). Alternatively, we see a substantial increase in precedential behavior in statutory decisions of ordinary litigation. The precedential level of 21 percent is significantly higher than the constitutional level of ordinary litigation (9.9 percent)[94] and the statutory level of landmark litigation (5.5 percent).[95] That is, in the least

[94] $p < 0.001$. [95] $p < 0.001$.

salient of these cases, but only in the least salient of these cases, do we find relative increases in precedential behavior, though even here the absolute levels remain fairly low.

Finally, for the period since the start of the Roosevelt Court, we know that civil liberties cases have been more salient to the Court than economic cases. If this is so, then we should expect relatively higher levels of precedential behavior in economic cases. This hypothesis is also consistent with Justice Rehnquist's "preferred precedents doctrine," whereby "[c]onsiderations in favor of stare decisis are at their acme in cases involving property and contract rights, where reliance interests are involved" but "the opposite is true in cases such as the present one involving procedural and evidentiary rules."[96]

Again, if Rehnquist has accurately described the Court's behavior, we should find this relationship in both ordinary and landmark cases, but if salience is what drives the relationship, then any increase in precedential behavior should be most pronounced in ordinary economic cases.

We tested this hypothesis by categorizing cases involving civil liberties or economic issues using Spaeth's U.S. Supreme Court Database for the Vinson through Rehnquist Courts, and data from a separate project to categorize cases from the 1937 through 1945 terms. We present the results in Figure 7.3.

Again, there is no difference in precedential behavior between economic (11 percent precedential) and civil liberties cases (8.3 percent precedential) among the progeny of landmark decisions ($p < 0.6$). But among the progeny of ordinary decisions, the difference is striking: 21 percent for economic cases versus 9.2 percent for civil liberties ($p < 0.02$).

In sum, to the (minor) extent that precedential behavior exists, it is more likely to be found in cases of the lowest salience: ordinary cases compared with landmark cases and, among ordinary cases, statutory cases over constitutional cases and modern economic cases over modern civil liberties cases. The influence of precedent appears to be quite minor, but it does not appear to be completely idiosyncratic.[97]

In *Dickerson v. United States*, the Supreme Court upheld *Miranda v. Arizona*,[98] striking a congressional attempt (section 3501) to overturn it.

[96] *Payne v. Tennessee*, 501 U.S. 808 (1991) at 828.

[97] Spaeth and Segal, *op. cit.*, n. 73, found no support for a variety of other potential explanations for the behavior we observe, including changing judicial preferences and changing political environments.

[98] 384 U.S. 486 (1966).

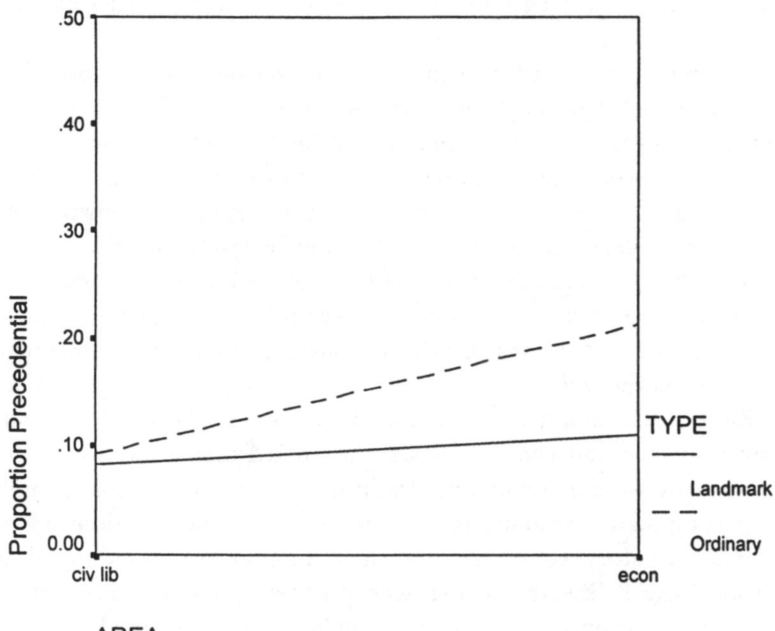

FIGURE 7.3. Precedential behavior by issue area.

In response to the majority opinion, Justice Scalia declared, "I dissent from today's decision, and, until 3501 is repealed, will continue to apply it in all cases where there has been a sustainable finding that the defendant's confession was voluntary."[99] This explicit refusal to abide by the Court's precedent distinguishes Scalia in words, but not deeds, from what the justices do day in and day out.

Crisis Stare Decisis

Dickerson aside, perhaps stare decisis doesn't constrain justices in their everyday decisions, where fact freedom abounds. Maybe its constraint is felt only in crisis, in the most extreme of circumstances, when justices must confront overruling a previous decision. As Chief Justice Rehnquist recently noted, "While *stare decisis* is not an inexorable command, particularly when we are interpreting the Constitution, even in constitutional cases, the doctrine carries such persuasive force that we have

[99] 147 L. Ed. 2d 405 (2000), at 434. Dissenters almost always "respectfully" dissent. Scalia did not so state.

always required a departure from precedent to be supported by some 'special justification.' "[100]

Certainly, the Court rather infrequently overrules its prior decisions. According to the leading authorities on such overruling, the Supreme Court overturns merely 2.5 cases per year or so.[101] In any given decade, the Court overturns less than 0.002 percent of its previous decisions![102]

Thus, unlike the everyday stare decisis examined above, where deference to precedent was found at only minimal levels, the gravitational force of stare decisis should be relatively greatest when the doctrine is pushed to its outermost limit, that is, when justices must confront overturning previous decisions. Arguably, if justices don't defer to precedent here, they never will.

We test this using the research strategy first used to test for judicial restraint in the mid-1960s.[103] Spaeth first noted that while justices frequently cast votes that could be classified as "restrained" – for example, supporting state economic regulations or upholding the decisions of federal regulatory commissions – such support was conditional on the ideological direction of the agency decision. For example, Justice Frankfurter, the purported paragon of judicial restraint, voted to uphold 60 percent of National Labor Relations Board decisions during the first seven terms of the Warren Court. But breaking down the data by ideological direction of the agency's decision reveals that while Frankfurter upheld 88 percent of the agency's antiunion decisions, he upheld only 29 percent of the agency's prounion decisions. Frankfurter's voting behavior was consistent with economic conservatism, not judicial restraint.

Similarly, to conclude that a justice generally upholds precedent in the face of a decision to overturn, she must generally defer both when that precedent is in a liberal direction and when that precedent is in a conservative direction.

We test this by examining the votes of the justices overturning precedent during the Rehnquist Court (see Table 7.4).[104] A preliminary version

[100] *Id.* at 419. Internal cites omitted.

[101] Saul Brenner and Harold J. Spaeth, *Stare Indecisis: The Alteration of Precedent on the U.S. Supreme Court, 1946–92* (New York: Cambridge University Press, 1995).

[102] Knight and Epstein, *op. cit.*, n. 69, *supra.*

[103] Harold J. Spaeth, "The Judicial Restraint of Mr. Justice Frankfurter – Myth or Reality," 8 *American Journal of Political Science* 22 (1964).

[104] Lacking access to conference discussions, it is not always clear when justices consider overturning a precedent. Thus, we examine every case in which at least one justice votes

TABLE 7.4. *Justices' Votes on Overturning Precedents*

	Liberal precedents			Conservative precedents		
	Uphold	**Overturn**	**% overturn**	**Uphold**	**Overturn**	**% overturn**
Marshall	14	4	22.2	0	5	100.0
Brennan	10	5	33.3	0	4	100.0
White	4	18	81.0	2	4	66.7
Blackmun	15	9	37.5	1	5	83.3
Powell	2	3	60.0	1	1	50.0
Rehnquist	6	24	80.0	9	4	30.8
Stevens	23	7	23.3	2	10	83.3
O'Connor	8	22	73.3	9	4	30.8
Scalia	2	28	93.3	4	9	69.2
Kennedy	6	17	73.9	1	9	90.0
Souter	8	7	46.7	4	5	55.6
Thomas	1	11	91.7	3	5	62.5
Ginsburg	6	2	25.0	1	6	85.7
Breyer	5	1	16.7	2	5	71.4

of Benesh and Spaeth's "flipped" database[105] contains these data, defined as any case in which one or more justices say in so many words that one or more of the Court's own precedents should be overruled or are "disapproved," "no longer good law," or something equivalent. Note that cases that the justices "distinguish" alter no precedents. In no way does such language alter the scope of a precedent. However, a subsequent decision may state that an earlier one overruled a precedent, even though the earlier one nowhere says so. For example, the majority in *Patterson v. McLean Credit Union* said that a 1973 decision overruled a 1948 precedent.[106]

The results could not be more clear. When the Court votes on overturning liberal precedents, liberals such as Brennan and Marshall insist that the precedents be upheld. But when conservative precedents are attacked, they show no inclination to uphold them. Marshall's statement that stare decisis " 'is essential if case-by-case judicial decision-making is

to do so. Nevertheless, our findings are similar to Segal and Howard, who examined every brief filed over a ten-year period in order to find every request that the Court overturn a precedent. See Jeffrey A. Segal and Robert M. Howard, "The Systematic Study of Stare Decisis," paper presented at the 2000 meeting of the American Political Science Association, Washington, D.C.

105 NSF grant SES-9910535. 106 485 U.S. 617 (1988) at 618.

to be reconciled with the principle of the rule of law'"[107] appears in his case only to apply to liberal precedents.

The situation for conservatives, though, is not so clear-cut. Rehnquist, for example, rarely votes to overturn conservative precedents (31 percent) but is quite willing to overturn liberal precedents (80 percent). But Scalia, Kennedy, and Thomas defer to neither conservative nor liberal precedents. Overall, not one justice on the Rehnquist Court exercised deference to precedent by voting to uphold both liberal and conservative precedents.

Text and Intent

While the new "systematic study of stare decisis"[108] has yielded a wealth of information about this most fundamental legal doctrine, there has been virtually no systematic information gathered about the influence of two of the other main components of the legal model: text and intent. One study in progress, though, has examined legal arguments based on text and intent made by litigants in briefs on the merits over six Court terms.[109] Briefly, the authors find that none of the justices is significantly influenced by arguments over text or intent. While this one paper, of course, does not prove a lack of influence for these factors, at the very least we can state that there exists no systematic evidence to date to support the force of these factors, and that preliminary evidence clearly goes in the opposite direction.

SUMMARY

We began this chapter with a description of the process by which the Court reaches decisions on the merits. We then focused on the influence that stare decisis has on the Court's decisions. First, examining what we can call "everyday" stare decisis, we see that justices rather easily avoid supporting precedents with which they disagree. Though support for stare decisis here is minimal, we do find an intriguing increase in support for stare decisis in the least salient of the Court's cases. Second, exam-

[107] *Payne v. Tennessee,* 501 U.S. 808 (1991) at 849. Of course, Marshall may be (properly) responsible for more precedents being overturned than any other litigator in the twentieth century.

[108] Segal and Howard, *op. cit.*, n. 104.

[109] Robert M. Howard and Jeffrey A. Segal, "An Original Look at Originalism," 36 *Law and Society Review* [forthcoming] (2002).

ining what we can call "crisis" stare decisis, we see that the decision to overturn precedent is conditioned on the ideological direction of the precedent being overturned.

This chapter finds virtually no evidence for concluding that the justices' decisions are based on legal factors. The evidence does support the inference that the justices' decisions are policy-based, but, so far, this is an inference and nothing more. In the next chapter we provide direct evidence on the role the justices' policy goals have on the decision on the merits, comparing the attitudinal model with the rational choice separation-of-powers model.

8

The Decision on the Merits

The Attitudinal and Rational Choice Models

In Chapters 2 and 3 we examined three models of Supreme Court decision making: legal, attitudinal, and rational choice. While there potentially may be any number of ways for rational choice theorists to model the decision on the merits, overwhelmingly, the most prominent application is the separation-of-powers model. We continue our look at the Court's decision on the merits with examinations of the attitudinal and separation-of-powers models.

THE ATTITUDINAL MODEL

Recall from Chapter 3 that the attitudinal model holds that the justices base their decisions on the merits on the facts of the case juxtaposed against their personal policy preferences. We thus examine the influence of case facts (or case stimuli), which are central to both attitudinal and legal models; attitudes, which are central only to the former; and the interaction between the two.

Facts

Case stimuli or facts are central to the decision making of all judges. Trial judges and juries must determine, for example, whether criminal suspects committed the deeds alleged by the prosecution. Appellate courts often must decide, based on the facts of the case as determined by the trial court judge and jury, whether the defendant's conviction was obtained in violation of the Constitution. Determinations of whether a given conviction or a given law violates constitutional rights necessarily depend on the facts of the case. Speaking out against the President is not the same as exposing nuclear secrets. Nor is libeling the President the same as libeling a private individual. Prohibiting abortion after conception is not the same as prohibiting abortion after viability.

To phrase the matter from the standpoint of attitude theory, behavior may be said to be a function of the interaction between an actor's attitude toward an "object" (i.e., persons, places, institutions, and things) and that actor's attitude toward the situation in which the object is encountered.[1] Insofar as judicial decision making is concerned, attitude objects are the litigants that appear before a court, while attitude situations consist of the "facts," that is, what the attitude object is doing, the legal and constitutional context in which the attitude object is acting. The examples in the preceding paragraph illustrate the situational context. "Objects," on the other hand, include indigents, businesses, persons accused of crime, women, minorities, labor unions, juveniles, and so on. As far as the Supreme Court is concerned, research has shown that situations predict behavior much better than objects.[2] Indeed, matters could hardly be otherwise. Responses to a survey of people's attitudes toward students, for example, lack meaning unless the inquiry is placed in a specific context: Students doing what? Rioting in the streets or studying in the library?

To a greater extent than attitude objects, situations are subjectively perceived. Justices not uncommonly dispute the facts of a case. Sometimes the justices accept as true what is empirically false. Consider the Court's acceptance of the lower court's finding in *Buck v. Bell*[3] that the Buck family had produced three generations of imbeciles. Contrary to the "facts" of the case, Carrie Buck was a woman of normal intelligence

[1] Milton Rokeach, *Beliefs, Attitudes, and Values* (San Francisco: Jossey-Bass, 1968), pp. 112–22.

[2] Harold J. Spaeth and Douglas R. Parker, "Effects of Attitude toward Situation upon Attitude toward Object," 73 *Journal of Psychology* (1969), 173–82; Milton Rokeach and Peter Kliejunas, "Behavior as a Function of Attitude-toward-Object and Attitude-toward-Situation," 22 *Journal of Personality and Social Psychology* (1972), 194–201; Harold J. Spaeth et al., "Is Justice Blind: An Empirical Investigation of a Normative Ideal," 7 *Law and Society Review* (1972), 119–37.

Bush v. Gore serves as the most prominent example of the attitude-toward-object (presidential contenders Bush and Gore) dominating the attitude-toward-situation (court-ordered recounts under a feigned equal-protection argument). So, too, the First Amendment appears to have lesser protections for antiabortion protesters. See, e.g., *Madsen v. Women's Health Center*, 512 U.S. 753 (1994).

[3] 274 U.S. 200 (1927).

whose daughter made the first-grade honor roll.[4] Conversely, what is empirically true the justices may assert to be false. Consider, for example, its unanimous decision that Long Island is not an island but an extension of the mainland.[5]

With these caveats in mind, we examine the role of case stimuli or facts in the decisions of the Supreme Court. We choose search and seizure as our substantive area of investigation, and we do so for two reasons. First, the situational context – the facts – in which law enforcement authorities conduct searches are readily identifiable and limited in number. Second, search and seizure is one of the many areas about which justices and scholars bewail the Court's alleged inconsistencies.[6] The question of whether a given search or seizure violates the Fourth Amendment is also of great substantive importance, for as of this writing, evidence seized in violation of the Constitution may not be used in criminal trials.[7] Thus, in the immortal words of Benjamin Cardozo, "the criminal is to go free because the constable has blundered."[8]

Specification

In determining what variables to include for analysis, we consider those facts that relate to the prior justification for the search (warrant and probable cause), the place of the intrusion (e.g., home or car), the extent of the intrusion (full searches vs. lesser intrusions, such as frisks), and various exceptions to the warrant requirement, including searches incident to arrest.[9]

The most basic requirements for the reasonableness of a search are a warrant and probable cause. Probable cause is generally required whether there is[10] or is not a warrant,[11] though evidence from warrants issued without probable cause can be used in court if the police officers acted in good faith.[12]

[4] Stephen Jay Gould, "Carrie Buck's Daughter," *Natural History*, July 1984, p. 14.

[5] *United States v. Maine*, 469 U.S. 504 (1985).

[6] See Jeffrey A. Segal, "Predicting Supreme Court Cases Probabilistically: The Search and Seizure Cases, 1962–1981," 78 *American Political Science Review* 891 (1984), at 891.

[7] *Mapp v. Ohio*, 367 U.S. 643 (1961). But see *United States v. Leon*, 468 U.S. 897 (1984), creating a "good-faith" exception to the exclusionary rule.

[8] *People v. Defore*, 242 N.Y. 13 (1926), at 21.

[9] See Segal, *op. cit.*, n. 6, *supra*.

[10] *United States v. Harris*, 403 U.S. 573 (1971).

[11] *Chambers v. Maroney*, 399 U.S. 42 (1970).

[12] *United States v. Leon*, 468 U.S. 897 (1984).

For a search to be unreasonable it generally must occur at a place where the accused has an expectation of privacy.[13] The greatest expectation of privacy is in one's home. "At the very core [of the Fourth Amendment] stands the right of a man to retreat into his own home and there be free from unreasonable governmental intrusion."[14] Commercial premises are likewise given great protection. "The businessman, like the occupant of a residence, has a constitutional right to go about his business free from unreasonable official entries."[15] Yet, "commercial premises are not as private as residential premises."[16] Still receiving protection, but to a lesser degree, are one's person[17] and one's car (or other motorized vehicle),[18] but the protection afforded them is nevertheless great compared with places where one has no property interest,[19] such as the home of a third party.

The type of search can be as determinative of reasonableness as the place of the search. Limited intrusions such as stop and frisks or detentive questioning require less prior justification than do full searches.[20]

Finally, there are well-established exceptions to the warrant requirements. The most important of these is the right to search incident to a lawful arrest.[21] This right generally extends to immediate searches of the arrestee and the area under his or her control. Lesser authority exists for arrests that follow upon but are not incident to lawful arrests.[22] Other exceptions include searches of evidence in plain view,[23] searches with the permission of those having a property interest in the area being searched,[24] searches after hot pursuit,[25] searches at fixed or functional borders,[26] searches explicitly authorized by Congress,[27] and searches for evidence to be used at noncriminal trials or hearings.[28]

[13] *Katz v. United States*, 389 U.S. 347 (1967).
[14] *Silverman v. United States*, 365 U.S. 505 (1961), at 511.
[15] *See v. Seattle*, 387 U.S. 541 (1967), at 543.
[16] Wayne LaFave, *Search and Seizure* (St. Paul: West, 1978), I, 338.
[17] *Davis v. Mississippi*, 394 U.S. 721 (1969).
[18] *Carroll v. United States*, 414 U.S. 132 (1925).
[19] *United States v. Calandra*, 414 U.S. 338 (1974).
[20] *Terry v. Ohio*, 392 U.S. 1 (1968). [21] *Chimel v. California*, 395 U.S. 752 (1969).
[22] *Chambers v. Maroney*, 399 U.S. 752 (1970).
[23] *Coolidge v. New Hampshire*, 493 U.S. 443 (1971).
[24] *Schneckloth v. Bustamonte*, 412 U.S. 218 (1973).
[25] *Warden v. Hayden*, 387 U.S. 294 (1967).
[26] *United States v. Ramsey*, 431 U.S. 606 (1977).
[27] *Colonade Catering v. United States*, 397 U.S. 72 (1970).
[28] *United States v. Calandra*, 414 U.S. 338 (1974).

Methods and Results

We examine all Supreme Court decisions dealing with the reasonableness of a search or seizure from the beginning of the 1962 term through the end of the 1998 term (*N* = 217). The independent variables are the facts of the case discussed above. We note here that it may be improper to rely on the Supreme Court's written opinion to ascertain the facts of the case. Thus, the Court may assert that certain variables are or are not present, such as probable cause, in order to justify its decision. Occasionally, opinions even differ about "objective" determinations, such as where the search took place. For instance, in *California v. Carney* the California Supreme Court considered the warrantless search of the respondent's motor home to be akin to a search of a home,[29] while the U.S. Supreme Court considered it closer to a search of a car, and thus found the search reasonable.[30] To guard against the possibility that the Supreme Court's statement of facts is influenced by the decision it desires to reach, we use the lower court record to determine the facts of each case.[31]

Our dependent variable is the decision of the Supreme Court whether or not to exclude evidence or find a search unreasonable. A liberal decision is one that prohibits the use of questionably obtained evidence; a conservative decision is one that admits such evidence. Overall, the Court ruled in a liberal direction in 36 percent of the cases.

We begin by examining the percentage of liberal or conservative decisions based on the presence or absence of the fact in question. We initially consider the nature of the search, which involves the locus of the search and the extent of the intrusion. As expected, the Court gave greatest protection to one's home, upholding only 53 percent of the searches conducted there. Less protection is given to places of business, where 59 percent of searches have been upheld. One's person receives still less protection (65 percent upheld), while searches of one's car or other motor vehicle are very likely to be upheld (74 percent). The least protection is

[29] 668 P.2d 807 (1983). [30] 471 U.S. 386 (1985).

[31] Certain facts cannot be ascertained independently of the Court's decision, such as whether the case concerns statutory construction or constitutional interpretation. Similarly, unobserved preferences that underlie the justices' decisions, such as whether the decision supports or opposes considerations of federalism (i.e., state action) or upholds or overturns administrative agency action. Although such factors have an ideological component that exists independent of and prior to any given decision, they can be measured only concomitantly with that decision. See Timothy M. Hagle and Harold J. Spaeth, "The Emergence of a New Ideology: The Business Decisions of the Burger Court," 54 *Journal of Politics* (1992), 120–34.

given to places where the suspect does not have a property interest (81 percent upheld).

The extent of the intrusion involves the difference between full searches and lesser intrusions, such as detentive questioning or a stop and frisk. Overall, 61 percent of full searches have been upheld, as compared with 81 percent of limited intrusions.

Against the nature of the search the Court must consider the prior justification for the search, that is, a warrant and probable cause. Even though cases with warrants typically involve questions as to the validity of that warrant, the Court still upholds more cases with warrants (72 percent) than without (63 percent). Alternatively, the lower court's decision as to whether probable cause exists negatively correlates with the Supreme Court's decisions. Some 61 percent of cases with probable cause are upheld, as compared with 66 percent without. This suggests that the Supreme Court views lower court probable cause decisions rather subjectively.

Next, we consider the exceptions to the warrant requirement, the most important of which is a search incident to a lawful arrest. The Supreme Court upheld 90 percent of the searches that the lower court ruled took place incident to a lawful arrest. Surprisingly, the Court did not uphold more searches after, but not incident to, a lawful arrest (63 percent) than it did searches after arrests that the lower court considered unlawful (67 percent).

Other exceptions to the warrant requirement rarely occurred; so we simply note that the Court upheld all of the nine searches when two or three exceptions were present, 75 percent of those containing one exception, and only 57 percent of those without any exceptions.

More interesting than the bivariate effect of facts on the Court's decision is the independent influence of each fact when the influence of every other fact has been controlled. To examine this, we conducted a logit analysis of the Supreme Court search and seizure decisions. We used the decision of the Court in each case as our dependent variable and the facts of the case identified above as our independent variables. Because of the Court's tendency to reverse the decisions it reviews, we include the direction of the lower court decision as a control variable that should negatively associate with the Supreme Court's decision. The results are presented in Table 8.1.

The coefficients show the change in the log of the odds ratio for a conservative decision given the presence of each variable. As this is not readily interpretable to those unaccustomed to logit analysis (and even

TABLE 8.1. *Logit Analysis of Search and Seizure Cases*

Variable	Maximum likelihood estimate	Standard error	Impact[a]
House	−2.96***	0.83	−0.45
Business	−2.45**	0.87	−0.42
Person	−1.84**	0.77	−0.36
Car	−1.74**	0.82	−0.35
Search	−1.24**	0.56	−0.28
Warrant	1.82***	0.56	0.36
Probable cause	−0.09	0.42	−0.02
Incident arrest	3.13**	1.19	0.46
After arrest	0.75*	0.55	0.18
After unlawful	0.43	0.56	0.11
Exceptions	1.45***	0.38	0.31
Lower Ct Dec	−1.42***	0.35	−0.31
Constant	3.45***	1.04	–
% predicted correctly	77		

[a] Impact equals change in probability of a liberal decision when the fact is present for a search with a 50% chance of being upheld. *$p < 0.10$; **$p < 0.01$; ***$p < 0.001$; $n = 216$.

to most who are accustomed to it), we provide under the column "impact" the estimated increase or decrease in the probability of a conservative decision when the variable in question is present. The impact estimate assumes that the search otherwise has a 50–50 chance of being upheld. Note that the places where searches occurred are all compared with a search where one does not have a property interest, and that the arrest estimates are all compared with a search that was not preceded by an arrest. Thus, a search that the lower court found to be after, but not incident to, an arrest, has a 0.18 greater probability of being upheld than a search that did not follow an arrest.

We see from the maximum likelihood estimates (MLEs) that every variable has a significant impact on the likelihood of a search being upheld except probable cause and unlawful arrest. All four places we examine (home, business, person, and car) decrease the probability of a search being upheld when compared with a search where one does not have a property interest.[32]

[32] Though logit's S-shaped specification suggests that the impact of home is not much different than the impact of the other "place" variables, measuring the impact at prior levels higher than 50–50 would show a much stronger effect.

The only substantive difference between the bivariate and multivariate results is that the latter show a clear ordering in terms of searches following arrests: Searches incident to arrest receive the most leeway; searches after lawful arrests receive less leeway; while searches after unlawful arrests receive virtually no additional leeway.

The model predicts 77 percent of the Court's cases correctly for a 30 percent reduction in error over the null model.[33] Though the facts presented do strongly influence the Court's decisions, obviously, other considerations also enter the equation. One problem with pure fact-based models is that they are static. That is, they do not consider how changing membership on the Court influences decisions. For instance, if we add a variable that counted each time a Warren Court appointee was replaced by a Nixon, Ford, or Reagan appointee,[34] we get a highly significant variable (MLE = 0.20, $p < 0.01$) that indicates that the current Court evaluates search and seizure cases much more leniently than did the Warren Court. This suggests that the exclusionary rule may soon be overturned directly or simply made irrelevant because so few searches are ruled unreasonable. This also betokens a need to explicitly consider the attitudes and values of the justices as a factor affecting their decisions.

Facts obviously affect the decisions of the Supreme Court, but on that point the attitudinal model does not differ from the legal model. The models differ in that proponents of the legal model conjoin facts with legalistic considerations such as the intent of the Framers, the plain meaning of the law, and prior decisions of the Court, while proponents of the attitudinal model describe the justices' votes as an expression of fact situations applied to their personal policy preferences. Unfortunately, there exists virtually no systematic evidence for the legal model, as we demonstrated in the previous chapter.

Focusing on facts to evidence the operation of the attitudinal model has its own set of problems, however. First, we do not know for certain that facts explain the justices' behavior except in those areas where they have been identified. Outside of search and seizure, only a handful of other subjects have successfully been put to such a test.[35] Whether facts

[33] For these data, the null model is that every decision is decided conservatively.

[34] We also subtract one for the replacement of Blackmun, a Nixon appointee, with Stephen Breyer, a Clinton appointee.

[35] Sara C. Benesh, "Principal Agency in American Courts: Perspectives on the Hierarchy of Justice," Ph.D. diss., Michigan State University, 1999, pp. 58–72 (involuntary confession cases); Timothy M. Hagle, "But Do They Have to See It to Know It? The Supreme

cause the justices to vote as they do in areas such as antitrust litigation, state taxation, national supremacy, First Amendment, and so on has not been determined. Furthermore, certain justices in certain areas may deem "facts" irrelevant. Justice Harlan, for example, never once supported a judicially imposed legislative apportionment plan, asserting that it was a matter that the Supreme Court had no authority to resolve.

Attitudes

Measuring the attitudes of political elites is a difficult task, as senators, justices, and Presidents are unlikely to fill out survey questionnaires provided by scholars, no less fill them out honestly. One type of solution, commonly used to this day in the congressional literature, is to use either interest group ratings from selected votes, as is done by the Americans for Democratic Action (ADA), or data reduction techniques from all votes, as in the NOMINATE scores, which are derived from the totality of nonunanimous congressional roll-call votes. In either case, these scores are then frequently used to "explain" the congressmen's votes in particular subsets of cases. Thus, Senator Ted Kennedy is measured as a liberal because he votes liberally, and he votes liberally because his ideology, as measured by his vote-derived ADA or NOMINATE scores, identifies him as a liberal. While such scores can provide a useful description of congressional behavior, the circularity inherent in using such scores should properly prevent their use as an explanation of such behavior.

One potential resolution to the circularity problem uses *past* votes as a measure of the justices' ideology.[36] While this does, in fact, resolve the

Court's Obscenity and Pornography Decisions," 45 *Political Research Quarterly* 1039 (1992); Tracey George and Lee Epstein, "On the Nature of Supreme Court Decision Making," 86 *American Political Science Review* 323 (1992)(death penalty cases); Robin Wolpert, "Explaining and Predicting Supreme Court Decision-Making: The Gender Discrimination Cases, 1971–1987," paper delivered at the 1991 annual meeting of the Midwest Political Science Association, Chicago, Ill.; Joseph A. Ignagni, "Explaining and Predicting Supreme Court Decision-making: The Establishment Clause Cases, 1970–1986," Ph.D. diss., Michigan State University, 1990; Kevin McGuire, "Obscenity, Libertarian Values, and Decision Making in the Supreme Court," 18 *American Politics Quarterly* 47 (1990); Jeffrey Segal and Cheryl Reedy, "The Supreme Court and Sex Discrimination: The Role of the Solicitor General," 41 *Political Research Quarterly* 553 (1988).

[36] Lee Epstein and Carol Mershon, "Measuring Political Preferences," 40 *American Journal of Political Science* 261 (1996).

circularity question, and provides useful tests for the stability and predictability of judicial attitudes (see below), it nevertheless begs the question as to what explains the justices' past votes. If justice A votes liberally in the 1999 term while justice B votes conservatively, their past preferences, as measured by the 1999 term, may well predict their behavior in the 2000 term. But we still don't have independent evidence as to what caused their behavior in the 1999 term. Thus, though past votes may offer an excellent description of the justices' current preferences, they cannot qualify as an explanation of the justices' behavior.

Our attempt to create an exogenous measure of the justices' attitudes independent of their votes focuses on the judgments in newspaper editorials that characterize nominees prior to confirmation as liberal or conservative insofar as civil rights and liberties are concerned.[37] Although this measure is less precise than past votes, it nonetheless avoids the circularity problem, is exogenous to the justices' behavior, and is reliable and replicable. As a result, it provides crucial evidence in testing the behavioral existence of the attitudinal model.

Segal and Cover originally created this measure by analyzing editorials about nominees from selected newspapers that appeared between the time of their nomination by the President until their confirmation by the Senate.[38] The scores of the confirmed justices are reprinted in Table 8.2.

We believe that the scores accurately measure the perceptions of the justices' values at the time of their nomination. While not everyone would agree that every score precisely measures the perceived ideology of each nominee, Fortas, Marshall, and Brennan are expectedly the most liberal, while Scalia and Rehnquist are the most conservative. Harlan and Stewart come out liberal because the debate about them centered around their support for the overriding issue of the day, segregation. Goldberg is not perceived to be as liberal as Fortas or Marshall because of an evenhandedness at the Department of Labor that even

[37] David Danelski suggested coding the qualitative content of speeches made by Justices Brandeis and Butler prior to their appointment to the Court as a measure of their attitudes. He found that support for or opposition to laissez-faire correlated with the direction of these two justices' dissents in economic cases. "Values as Variables in Judicial Decision-Making: Notes Toward a Theory," 19 *Vanderbilt Law Review* 721 (1966).

[38] Jeffrey A. Segal and Albert D. Cover, "Ideological Values and the Votes of U.S. Supreme Court Justices," 83 *American Political Science Review* 557 (1989). See Chapter 6 for details.

TABLE 8.2. *Justices' Values and Votes*

Justice	Values[a]	Votes[b]	Justice	Values[a]	Votes[b]
Warren	0.50	78.6	Powell	−0.67	37.4
Harlan	0.75	43.6	Rehnquist	−0.91	21.8
Brennan	1.00	79.5	Stevens	−0.50	64.2
Whittaker	0.00	43.3	O'Connor	−0.17	35.5
Stewart	0.50	51.4	Scalia	−1.00	29.6
White	0.00	42.4	Kennedy	−0.27	36.9
Goldberg	0.50	88.9	Souter	−0.34	59.9
Fortas	1.00	81.0	Thomas	−0.68	25.7
Marshall	1.00	81.4	Breyer	−0.05	61.1
Burger	−0.77	29.6	Ginsburg	0.36	64.4
Blackmun	−0.77	52.8			

[a] Updated from Segal and Cover, *op. cit.*, fn. 38 *supra*. The range is −1.00 (extremely conservative) to 1.00 (extremely liberal).
[b] Percentage liberal in civil liberties cases, 1953–99 terms.

the conservative *Chicago Tribune* could support. O'Connor comes out as a moderate, given her previous support for women's rights and abortion. Indeed, the only hint of opposition to her nomination came from right-wing interest groups and the arch-conservative senator Jesse Helms (R-N.C.).

Measures of perceived attitudes are obviously imperfect measures of those the justices actually possess. Given the impossibility of surveying the justices themselves (even if one rashly assumed that such surveys would be scientifically valid and reliable), content analysis has its place. To the extent that measurement error exists in the data, we will undoubtedly find weaker correlations than would otherwise be the case.[39] Therefore, the correlation between ideological values and votes that we present is almost certainly lower than the true correlation.

Because statements in newspaper editorials deal almost exclusively with support by the justices for civil liberties and civil rights, we use as our dependent variable the votes of all justices appointed since the beginning of the Warren Court in all formally decided civil liberties cases from the beginning of the 1953 term through the end of the 1999 term, as derived from the Original U.S. Supreme Court Judicial Database. Civil

[39] William D. Berry and Stanley Feldman, *Multiple Regression in Practice* (Beverly Hills: Sage, 1985).

liberties issues are those involving criminal procedure, civil rights, the First Amendment, due process, and privacy. Liberal decisions are (1) pro-person accused or convicted of crime, (2) pro-civil liberties or civil rights claimant, (3) proindigent, (4) pro-Indian, and (5) antigovernment in due process and privacy, except for takings clause cases.[40] The data are presented in Table 8.2.

The results are straightforward: The correlation between the ideological values of the justices and their votes is 0.76 ($r^2 = 0.57$, adjusted $r^2 = 0.55$). Regressing votes on our measure of values yields a constant of 53.4 and a slope of 23.5 ($t = 5.06$). The largest residuals belong to Goldberg, who is 23 percentage points more liberal than expected, and Harlan, who is 27 points more conservative than expected. Alternatively, Scalia and Powell are less than one point from their expected scores. Given the fact that our correlation is attenuated by the measurement error that no doubt exists in the independent variable, the results supply exceptional support for the attitudinal model as applied to civil liberties cases.

Critics of the attitudinal model might present the following alternative scenario: If judges and justices base decisions on legal values (e.g., precedent or the intent of the Framers) and not political values, editorials on nominees with lower court experience would be based on those legal values. Our measures will correlate with their votes on the Supreme Court because as justices they are again basing their votes on their legal values. But if this were the case, lower court experience would provide crucial information that does not exist for those without such experience: the legal (as opposed to political) values of the nominees. If the editorials provided information on legal values and if such values were relevant to the justices' decisions, the correlation for those with such information should be higher than the correlation for those without such information. This is clearly not the case. Though the *N*s are small, the correlation between values and votes for those with lower court experience is 0.67 (adjusted $r^2 = 0.40$), while the correlation

[40] This specification of direction (i.e., liberal or conservative) is determined by reference to the issue variable to which the case pertains. Hence, anti–affirmative action plaintiffs who successfully allege that the program deprives them of civil rights does not make them or the case outcome liberal since a pro–affirmative action outcome is defined as liberal. See Harold J. Spaeth, *The Original United States Supreme Court Judicial Database, 1953–1999 Terms* (East Lansing, Mich.: Program for Law and Judicial Politics, Michigan State University, 2000), pp. 51–53.

for those without lower court experience is 0.92 (adjusted $r^2 = 0.81$). If anything, the voting record of lower court judges, who *are* bound by Supreme Court precedents, might constitute *disinformation* about their true values and thus their likely voting behavior once on the Supreme Court.

Prediction

As we noted in Chapter 3, an attitude is a relatively enduring set of interrelated beliefs. Thus, if attitudes are the proximate cause of the votes of Supreme Court justices, their votes must be relatively stable and consistent. Quite a bit of research has demonstrated the stability and predictability of judicial attitudes. For example, Spaeth was able to predict accurately 88 percent (92 out of 105) of the Court's decisions between 1970 and 1976 and 85 percent of the justices' votes.[41] In a looser test, we accurately predicted the majority and dissenting coalitions in 19 of 23 death penalty cases, and similar percentages of other civil liberties cases.[42]

Combining Facts and Attitudes

Consistent with the attitudinal model, we have seen that both facts and attitudes affect the decisions of the Supreme Court. The attitudinal model, though, does not hold that these are separate influences on the Court's decisions. Rather, it holds that facts or case stimuli are juxtaposed against the attitudes of the justices in determining how any particular justice reaches a decision in any particular case.

We thus come to our most specific test of the attitudinal model by using as our dependent variable the decision of each justice in each search and seizure case from the 1962 through 1998 terms (N = 1,900). The independent variables are the facts of each case plus each justice's attitudes.

We first entered only attitudes into the equation and achieved a 70 percent prediction rate, for a 32 percent reduction in error over the justices' mean of 56 percent. We then entered just the twelve fact-based variables described above and achieved a 62 percent prediction rate, for a relatively low 14 percent reduction in error. This suggests that in pre-

[41] Harold J. Spaeth, *Supreme Court Policy Making: Explanation and Prediction* (San Francisco: W. H. Freeman, 1979), pp. 122–23, 154–64.

[42] Jeffrey A. Segal and Harold J. Spaeth, *The Supreme Court and the Attitudinal Model* (New York: Cambridge University Press, 1993), ch. 6.

TABLE 8.3. *Logit Analysis of Search and Seizure Cases with Attitudes*

Variable	Maximum likelihood estimate	Standard error
House	–1.53***	0.24
Business	–1.43***	0.26
Person	–1.27***	0.23
Car	–1.24***	0.24
Search	–0.87***	0.17
Warrant	0.86***	0.17
Probable cause	0.09	0.13
Incident arrest	1.05***	0.28
After arrest	0.21	0.18
After unlawful	0.11	0.17
Exceptions	0.83***	0.10
Attitudes	–1.35***	0.08
Constant	1.75***	0.26
% predicted correctly	71	

*$p < 0.10$; **$p < 0.01$; ***$p < 0.001$; $n = 1{,}900$.

dicting votes, one is clearly better off knowing the attitudes of the justices than the facts of the case. Finally, we combined the attitude measure with the fact variables into a single model. The results are presented in Table 8.3. Some 71 percent of the individual justices' decisions were predicted correctly for a 34 percent reduction in error. Nine of the twelve variables were significant at $p < 0.001$.

Results from the model can be presented in visual form as in Figure 8.1, which places the case stimuli and justices' values in attitudinal space. Any justice should vote to uphold any search to the left of his or her indifference point and will vote strike any search to the right of his or her indifference point. For instance, the search for evidence in *Mapp v. Ohio* at 0.65 would be allowed in court by Rehnquist (1.23), but not by Breyer (0.07) or Brennan (–1.35).[43] As this is an empirical model, prediction errors will occur. Nevertheless, with 71 percent of the

[43] Scale points for the justices are created by multiplying their factor scores by the slope coefficient for attitude in Table 8.3. Scale points for case stimuli is –1 times the predicted log of the odds ratio of upholding the search given the facts of the case and an attitude score of 0.

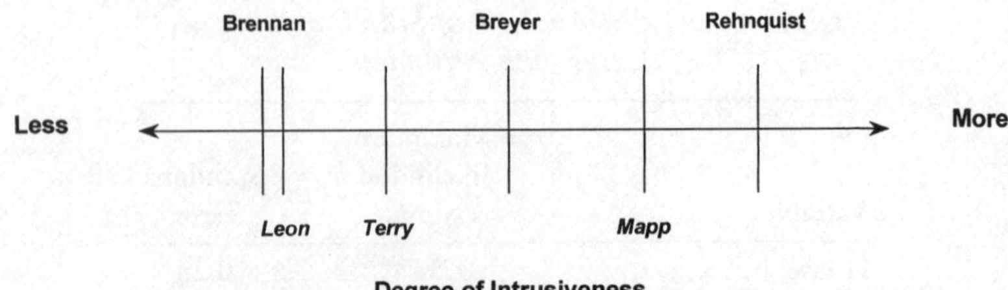

FIGURE 8.1. Justices and cases in ideological space.

individual-level votes predicted correctly, the model demonstrates the overall validity of the attitudinal model.[44]

THE SEPARATION-OF-POWERS MODEL

Applications of rational choice theory to the Supreme Court, as noted in Chapter 3, may be divided into an internal program, which focuses on intra-Court strategies, and an external program, which focuses on constraints imposed by other political actors. For the decision on the merits, internal models have concentrated on voting fluidity, the changing of votes from the conference vote to the report vote. As we report in Chapter 7, most voting fluidity is completely consistent with attitudinal considerations. We also are not aware of any equilibrium-based formal models of voting fluidity.

The external program, on the other hand, has focused on the so-called separation-of-powers model. Recall from Chapter 3 that this model posits that the Supreme Court will often need to defer to congressional/presidential preferences in order to prevent its decisions from being overturned. Because these models are equilibrium-based (typically, Nash equilibria, in that the Court's behavior is a best response to Congress and the President's best response), because numerous articles claim empirical support for the model, and because these models directly contradict the attitudinal model's claim of rationally sincere behavior on the

[44] There are several causes of error in the model, including measurement error on the attitudinal variable, incomplete specification of relevant case stimuli, and measurement error of case stimuli (caused by measuring case stimuli by the lower court record). Others sources of error might include excluding nonattitudinal factors, such as the presence of the United States as a party to the suit or excluded role values. To the extent the first set of problems exists, the attitudinal model is stronger than our empirical model demonstrates.

merits, we carefully investigate the empirical literature. We divide our efforts between qualitative and quantitative analyses.

Qualitative Analyses and Case Studies

Unlike the strong support that exists for the attitudinal model, empirical support for the separation-of-powers model, though frequently claimed, is substantially more problematic. Many articles are content with providing a model and leaving real-world concerns to others. That is fine, but such articles cannot answer the question of whether the Supreme Court actually does behave as is posited. More typically, scholars will find a case that seems to satisfy the expectations of the model. This, too, will not do, for as Lee Epstein has so cogently noted, "the modus operandi of the theorem provers who have studied these questions will not suffice. The standards of social science simply require more than reading some cases (*e.g., Grove City* seems to be a favorite), developing a model, and then testing the model against the same cases used to develop it (again, *Grove City* comes to mind)."[45]

Some case studies, though, can illuminate aspects of cases that were otherwise undetectable. Recent game-theoretic works on *Marbury v. Madison*, for example, clarify the strategic choices facing President Jefferson and Chief Justice Marshall in that epic struggle.[46] Nevertheless, the ability to generalize from one particular case remains problematic.

Measurement

The standards of social science to which Epstein refers to above also demand a degree of reliability and validity in the measurement of preferences that is not found in many separation-of-powers studies. For example, William Eskridge argues that the early Burger Court kept its civil rights decisions to the left of center because of a Congress that was substantially to the left of the Court and a series of Presidents who were often to the left of Congress.[47] The fact that Richard Nixon, and the

[45] Cited in Jeffrey A. Segal, "Separation of Power Games in the Positive Theory of Congress and Courts," 91 *American Political Science Review* 28 (1997), p. 33.

[46] Robert Lowry Clinton, "Game Theory, Legal History, and the Origins of Judicial Review: A Revisionist Analysis of *Marbury v. Madison*," 38 *American Journal of Political Science* 285 (1994); and Jack Knight and Lee Epstein, "On the Struggle for Judicial Supremacy," 30 *Law and Society Review* 87 (1996).

[47] William N. Eskridge, Jr., "Reneging on History? Playing the Court/Congress/President Civil Rights Game," 79 *California Law Review* 613 (1991), p. 650.

President who devised the "Southern strategy" for capturing the Wallace vote, the President who activated that policy by nominating G. Harrold Carswell to the Supreme Court, and the President who campaigned to end school busing, must be categorized as a civil-rights liberal to make the model work suggests the possibility of alternative explanations. The same can be said of President Ford, who in his last fifteen years in Congress never had an ADA score greater than 17.[48]

Additionally, Eskridge places the gatekeeping committees to the left of Congress, yet the Senate Judiciary Committee median was to the right of the full Senate median every year between 1970 and 1977. He also places the committees to the left of Congress in the 1981 through 1990 period, but again, the Senate Judiciary Committee median was to the left of the Senate median three times during this era, was to the right four times, and was tied three times.[49] So, too, must we question Gely and Spiller's placement of Congressman John ("Dirty Air") Dingell (also known as the congressman from General Motors) as a strong supporter of government safety regulation of the automotive industry.[50]

Leverage

We next reiterate the point made in Chapter 3 that a nearly limitless array of behavior can be interpreted consistently with rational action.[51] Consider, for example, the Court's actions in *Ex parte Milligan*,[52] as discussed by Epstein and Walker. In the case, the Supreme Court declared that "Milligan, a Confederate sympathizer living in Indiana, could not be arrested and tried by the military when civilian courts were in full operation and the area was not a combat zone."[53] In April 1866, the

[48] Nixon's average ADA scores were 14 in the House and 27 in the Senate. See Michael J. Sharp, *The Directory of Congressional Voting Scores and Interest Group Ratings* (New York: Facts on File Publications, 1988).

[49] Segal, *op. cit.*, n. 45, *supra.*

[50] Rafael Gely and Pablo T. Spiller, "A Rational Choice Theory of Supreme Court Decision Making with Applications to the *State Farm* and *Grove City* Cases," 6 *Journal of Law, Economics and Organization* 263 (1990).

[51] See also Lawrence Baum, *The Puzzle of Judicial Behavior* (Ann Arbor: University of Michigan Press, 1997), ch. 4.

[52] 4 Wallace 2 (1866).

[53] Lee Epstein and Thomas G. Walker, "The Role of the Supreme Court in American Society: Playing the Reconstruction Game," in Lee Epstein, ed., *Contemplating Courts* (Washington, D.C.: CQ Press, 1995), pp. 315–16.

Supreme Court issued a little-noticed order, without an opinion, releasing Milligan. It was not until December of that year, after the Radical Republicans made monumental gains in the November elections, that the Court issued its opinion rendering Congress unable to create military tribunals remote from the actual theater of war. While April's order seems rational enough given the contemporary political environment, December's opinion does not. Moreover, the December opinion need not have been so harsh. The Court, for example, might have averted a crisis by adopting the more moderate opinion of Justice Chase.[54] The Chase concurrence, and not the Davis majority, is arguably the action that the Court should have taken had it been behaving strategically. Indeed, had the Chase opinion been the majority, it would have been easy for Epstein and Walker to write that the Court readily and clearly saw what the results of the 1866 election meant.

The Civil Rights Game

Undoubtedly, the most extensive and widely cited qualitative analysis of the separation-of-powers game is Eskridge's study of the Court's decisions in civil rights cases.[55] It may thus be useful to compare separation-of-powers and attitudinal models of Supreme Court decision making during the three periods that Eskridge studies: 1962–72, 1972–81, and 1981–90. During the first period, there is no conflict between the two. Eskridge remarks that the Court was able to vote its sincere preferences because the legislative gatekeepers protected the Court from remedial legislation.

During the second period, Eskridge argues that the Court voted more liberally than it otherwise would have due to fear of override by a liberal President and Congress. As noted above, the notion that Richard Nixon and Gerald Ford were liberals is just not supported by the evidence. Moreover, a Senate Judiciary Committee chaired by the unreconstructed Mississippi Democrat James Eastland undoubtedly would and could have protected the Court from whatever conservative decisions it might have wanted to make. A more likely scenario for the Court's moderate course was its composition. Through 1975 the Court consisted of three hard-core liberals (Douglas, Brennan, and Marshall) and three justices who had always been moderate on civil rights (White, who stayed

[54] 4 Wallace 2 (1866), at 132. [55] Eskridge, *op. cit.*, n. 47, *supra.*

moderate on civil rights even after he moved rightward on most other issues;[56] Stewart, who was strongly opposed during his nomination by Southern conservatives because of his progressive views on civil rights;[57] and Blackmun, who was never as conservative on civil rights as he originally was on criminal procedure).[58] In 1975, Stevens replaced Douglas, but Stevens was to the left of Stewart, so this did not change the median.[59] Thus, we conclude that the Burger Court was moderate in civil rights not because a liberal Congress and President pushed them in that direction, but because the moderate wing had a clear working majority.

Crucial to Eskridge's argument that the Court was constrained in the 1970s is the Court's purported shift to the right in civil rights immediately following the election of Ronald Reagan. Eskridge provides summary data of voting shifts for the Court as a whole that seem to back his claim.[60] The data, though, are not consistent with data derived from the U.S. Supreme Court Database.[61] If we compare the moderates and conservatives on the Court from the appointment of Stevens in 1975 until the retirement of Burger in 1986, we ought to find, following Eskridge, that these justices, who purportedly were constrained in the 1970s, moved to the right beginning in 1981 as Reagan protected them from override. The results, presented in Table 8.4, show nothing of the sort. First, O'Connor's replacement of Stewart, as Eskridge suggests, had little effect. Next, the Court as a whole, and the three justices with liberalism scores below 50 percent during this period (Burger, Powell, and Rehnquist), collectively moved slightly (but insignificantly) to the left during this period. Finally, two of the three justices who had scores in the 50 to 60 percent range moved to the left (Blackmun, whose move

[56] Lee Epstein, Jeffrey A. Segal, Harold J. Spaeth, and Thomas G. Walker, *The Supreme Court Compendium* (Washington, D.C.: CQ Press, 1994), pp. 453–54.

[57] Segal and Cover, *op. cit.*, n. 38, *supra*.

[58] Epstein et al., *op. cit.*, n. 56, *supra*, pp. 442–43. [59] *Id.*, pp. 449–51.

[60] William N. Eskridge, Jr., "Overriding Supreme Court Statutory Interpretation Decisions," 101 *Yale Law Journal* 331 (1991), pp. 395–97.

[61] We choose all formally decided cases, whether per curiam or with signed opinions. For unit of analysis, we originally included, in addition to the standard citation plus split votes, records in the database corresponding to multiple legal provisions (or multiple issues/legal provisions), as numerous cases with statutory content could nevertheless show a constitutional issue in the first record. We then selected all records where the Court's stated authority for its decision was interpretation of a federal statute, treaty, court rule, executive order, regulation, or rule. Next, we deleted duplicate records from the same case dealing with the same value area, unless the direction of the decision differed from one record to the next. Finally, we selected all cases dealing with civil rights.

TABLE 8.4. *Proportion of Liberalism Voting of Supreme Court Justices in Civil Rights Cases, 1975–1986*

Justice	1975–80	1981–86	*p*	*n*
Court	0.52	0.51	0.85	200
Brennan	0.85	0.77	0.18	196
Stewart/O'Connor	0.44	0.52	–	84/95
White	0.53	0.51	0.73	200
Marshall	0.84	0.79	0.43	197
Burger	0.37	0.39	0.72	199
Blackmun	0.54	0.68	0.03	195
Powell	0.42	0.39	0.69	185
Rehnquist	0.22	0.28	0.31	197
Stevens	0.51	0.56	0.54	187

Source: Derived from U.S. Supreme Court Judicial Database.

was statistically significant, and Stevens), while one moderate (White) moved ever so slightly to the right.[62] Interestingly, only the liberals, Brennan and Marshall, show a directional move to the right, but by all accounts they should not have been constrained in either period, and, indeed, their changes are insignificant.

Finally, in the 1987–90 period, following Democratic control of the Senate, the Court issued a series of hard-core conservative decisions. Eskridge readily admits that the Court was far more conservative than it should have been during this period. He argues that the Court, consistent with the separation-of-powers and rational choice models, was "mistaken about the congressional median" or was trying to shift congressional preferences.[63] But with these escape hatches, the separation-of-powers model becomes completely unfalsifiable.

Given these problems, we next focus on quantitative analyses of the separation-of-powers games.

Quantitative Analyses

Beyond a doubt, the seemingly most impressive support for the separation-of-powers model comes from Spiller and Gely, who find in

[62] Stewart's half-term while Reagan was President showed him moving to the right as well, but it's hard to make much of half a term.

[63] Eskridge, *op. cit.*, n. 47, *supra*, pp. 658–59.

their sophisticated econometric analysis that changes in the ideal points of relevant congresspersons influence Court decisions in National Labor Relations Act cases to the same extent that changes in the ideal points of the Supreme Court do.[64] Bergara, Richman, and Spiller find similar results.[65]

Before we accept these findings, a few points need to be examined more fully. First, Spiller and Gely find that under open rule,[66] "for most observations the set of nonreversible decisions included almost the whole range of feasible outcomes."[67] In other words, if we accept open-rule models as appropriate, then the Court is almost never constrained. Are open-rule models more appropriate than closed-rule models? Yes. Empirically, the Senate almost always acts under open rule and the House usually does.[68] But, theoretically, the closed-rule assumption is inappropriate even in situations when the rule is more frequently granted, for the provision of the closed rule is endogenous to the committee's proposal. As Ferejohn and Shipan note, "Congress is unable to commit itself to the use of a closed rule in advance of a committee proposal. Thus, once a legislative proposal comes before it, Congress will be faced with a temptation to amend it even if the committee has been promised a closed rule."[69] Thus, according to Ferejohn and Shipan, we are likely to see a closed rule only in situations where committees affirm chamber preferences, that is, when closed rule mimics open rule. The ability to find positive results under clearly inappropriate assumptions suggests that something may be amiss, and, indeed, something is.

Statistical Bias

The second problem that we note in the quantitative literature is absolutely crucial: *Biases in the regime-change, switching regression*

[64] Pablo T. Spiller and Rafael Gely, "Congressional Control or Judicial Independence: The Determinants of U.S. Supreme Court Labor-Relations Decisions, 1949–1988," 23 *RAND Journal of Economics* 463 (1992).

[65] Mario Bergara, Barak Richman, and Pablo T. Spiller, "Judicial Politics and the Econometrics of Preferences," paper presented at the 2000 Annual Meeting of the American Political Science Association, Washington, D.C.

[66] Under open rule, amendments to committee proposals are allowed. Under closed rule, committees can offer take-it-or-leave-it proposals.

[67] Spiller and Gely, *op. cit.*, n. 64, *supra*, p. 470, fn. 24.

[68] Walter J. Oleszek, *Congressional Procedures and Policy Process*, 3rd ed. (Washington, D.C.: CQ Press, 1989), pp. 123, 186.

[69] John Ferejohn and Charles Shipan, "Congressional Influence on Bureaucracy," 6 *Journal of Law and Economics* 1 (1990).

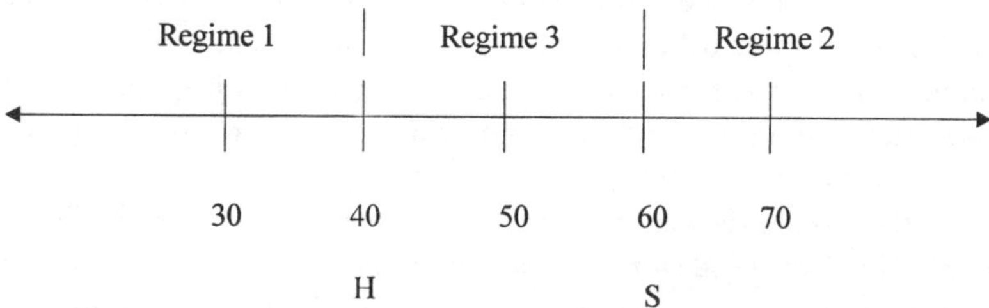

FIGURE 8.2. Regime change model. Adapted from Spiller and Gely (1992).

models as used in the Spiller articles mean that the articles completely fail to distinguish sincere from sophisticated behavior by the Court. Because the biases are so fundamental, we believe it necessary to take the space necessary to demonstrate them. These results are also necessary for our own tests that follow. While our description of the biases must be read carefully to be understood, they do not require technical expertise beyond a comprehension of simple regression analysis.

We start with three players, a House, a Senate, and a Court. The Court reaches decisions in policy space, subject to oversight by the House and Senate. An important aspect of this game is that the Court has some leeway as to where it sets policy. That is, there exists more than one point in the policy space at which the Court cannot be overturned. This protected area is sometimes referred to as the Win set, the set of irreversible decisions (SID), and – not always accurately – the Pareto set. We refer to such space as the SID.

Figure 8.2 presents hypothetical preferences of the congressional chambers, with the House (H) at 40 and the Senate (S) at 60. The following strategic situation exists: If the Court (C) makes policy either below 40 or above 60, both H and S will prefer some outcomes between 40 and 60 to what the Court has done.[70] Alternatively, if the Court places the decision in the set of irreversible decisions [40, 60], that decision cannot be overturned, as there exists no alternative that both H and S prefer to what the Court has done.

[70] If the Court places its decision at $40 - x$, the eventual outcome will be between 40 and the lesser of either $40 + x$ or 60, for this range contains those decisions that both H and S prefer to $40 - x$. Similarly, if the Court places its decision at $60 + y$, the eventual outcome will be between the greater of 40 and $60 - y$, for that range contains those decisions that both H and S prefer to $60 + y$.

The strategy for the Court under such a model is clear. If the Court's ideal point is below the minimum (H, S), then set policy at that minimum (40). That is the point closest to the Court's ideal point that cannot get overruled and replaced with something worse (from the Court's perspective). If the Court's ideal point is above the maximum (H, S), then set policy at that maximum (60), as that is the point closest to the Court's ideal point that cannot get overruled and replaced with something worse. Finally, if the Court's ideal point is greater than the minimum but less than the maximum of the set of irreversible decisions, then it should choose its ideal point, as that point cannot be overturned.

The setup of this model suggests three regimes that influence the Court's decision. Following Spiller and Gely, we label the situation where the Court is to the left of the set of irreversible decisions "regime 1," the situation where the Court is to the right of the set of irreversible decisions "regime 2," and the situation where the Court is within the set of irreversible decisions as "regime 3."

Consider the comparative statics for the Court in different regimes, that is, the change in the Court's decision given a change in the relevant minimum, maximum, or ideal point. For a Court in regime 1, the relevant variable is the minimum: If the minimum is at 40, the Court should rule at 40; if the minimum is at 39, the Court should rule at 39; and so on. Thus, in equilibrium, a one-unit change in the minimum leads to a one-unit change in the Court's decision. Thus, if the Court acts strategically, we should observe a slope coefficient of 1.0 for the Court in regime 1.

The story is precisely the same for the Court in regime 2, where the relevant variable is the maximum. If the maximum is at 60, the Court should rule at 60; if the maximum is at 61, the Court should rule at 61; and so on. Again, in equilibrium, a one-unit change in the maximum leads to a one-unit change in the Court's decision. Thus, if the Court acts strategically, we should observe a slope coefficient of 1.0 for the Court in regime 2.

Consider, finally, the Court in regime 3. Here the only relevant variable is its own preference. If its preference is at 45, it should rule at 45; if its preference is at 55, it should rule at 55. This suggests that for a Court in regime 3, in equilibrium, we should once again observe a slope coefficient of 1.0, for a one-unit change in its preference results in a one-unit change in its behavior.

Testing the Model

As this generic model creates a set of mutually exclusive independent variables (the min, the max, and the Court ideal point for regimes 1, 2, and 3, respectively) and since the expected slope coefficient in all three regimes is the same,[71] the model is tested in the Spiller papers by a regime-change switching regression model of the form

$$Y = \alpha + \beta_{123} X_i + \varepsilon_i$$

where X = min if regime 1; max if regime 2; and I if regime 3, where I equals the ideal point of the Court and the subscript 123 represents the fact that β is estimated across regimes 1, 2, and 3.[72]

One set of problems with this approach involves testing a null hypothesis of $\beta_{123} = 0$ against an alternative hypothesis of $\beta_{123} > 0$.[73] As noted above, the appropriate expectation in the policy model, as in Bergara et al., is that $\beta_{123} = 1$, not simply that it is greater than 0.

But far more important, perfectly sincere (i.e., attitudinal) behavior across all three regimes can return a slope coefficient for β_{123} that is not only greater than 0, but can readily approach 1.0. In other words, this model generally fails to distinguish sincere behavior – that is, voting at one's ideal point – from sophisticated behavior – that is, voting off of one's ideal point in order to achieve the best possible final result. One reason for this, though not the only reason, is that in regime 3, the prediction from a sincere model (voting one's ideal point) is exactly the same as the prediction from the strategic model (voting one's ideal point).

We demonstrate the problem with a very simple simulation, which demonstrates what happens to tests of strategic (separation-of-powers) behavior when the Court acts only sincerely (attitudinally). Consider the Supreme Court over six different time periods, 1–6, with median justices whose ideal points range from 25 to 75, respectively, in increments of 10, facing a set of Houses and Senates such that the SID over time runs from [50, 70] to [40, 60] to [30, 50]. Now assume that the Courts vote only their sincere preferences. We present these simulated data in Table 8.5.

[71] Because Spiller and Gely test a probability model, the predicted coefficient is not 1.0. Nevertheless, the probability model should still provide a similar slope coefficient across regimes. See Spiller and Gely, *op. cit.*, n. 64, *supra*, p. 487.

[72] Note that the Spiller papers use the data to scale the Court to congressional preferences and add probabilistic assessments as to which regime the Court is in. We turn to the problems created by this type of scaling in the next section.

[73] See Bergara, Richman, and Spiller, *op. cit.*, n. 65, *supra.*

TABLE 8.5. *Simulated Data for Figures 8.2–8.4*

Pref[a]	Policy[b]	Min[c]	Max[d]	Regime[e]	Equil[f]	Court[g]
25	25	30	50	1	30	1
35	35	30	50	3	35	2
45	45	30	50	3	45	3
55	55	30	50	2	50	4
65	65	30	50	2	50	5
75	75	30	50	2	50	6
25	25	40	60	1	40	1
35	35	40	60	1	40	2
45	45	40	60	3	45	3
55	55	40	60	3	55	4
65	65	40	60	2	60	5
75	75	40	60	2	60	6
25	25	50	70	1	50	1
35	35	50	70	1	50	2
45	45	50	70	1	50	3
55	55	50	70	3	55	4
65	65	50	70	3	65	5
75	75	50	70	2	70	6

[a] Pref: Court's ideal point.
[b] Policy: policy set by Court, which is set at Court's ideal point.
[c] Min: minimum of set of irreversible decisions (SID).
[d] Max: maximum of SID.
[e] Regime: 1 = left of min; 2 = right of max; 3 = inside SID.
[f] Equil: equilibrium prediction from strategic model.

Figure 8.3 presents the fit of the separation-of-powers model to these data, that is, data in which the Court acts only sincerely. The x-axis represents the separation-of-powers equilibrium predictions: the min for regime 1 Courts, the max for regime 2 Courts, and the Court's ideal point for regime 3 Courts. The y-axis represents the Court's behavior, which we set to be at its ideal point. Even though the Court is ignoring Congress and voting its sincere preferences, and even though regime 3 cases make up only one third of the data, the data (falsely) appear to fit the separation-of-powers model very well. Note that this is a rather conservative simulation, as regime 3 cases make up only one third of our data, whereas they represent the vast majority of cases in the Spiller data sets.[74]

[74] Moreover, these results and those that follow hold up for more sophisticated simulations. See Jeffrey A. Segal and Cheng-Lung Wang, "Inducing Apparently Strategic Behavior in Models of Bounded Discretion: The Case of Regime-Change Switching

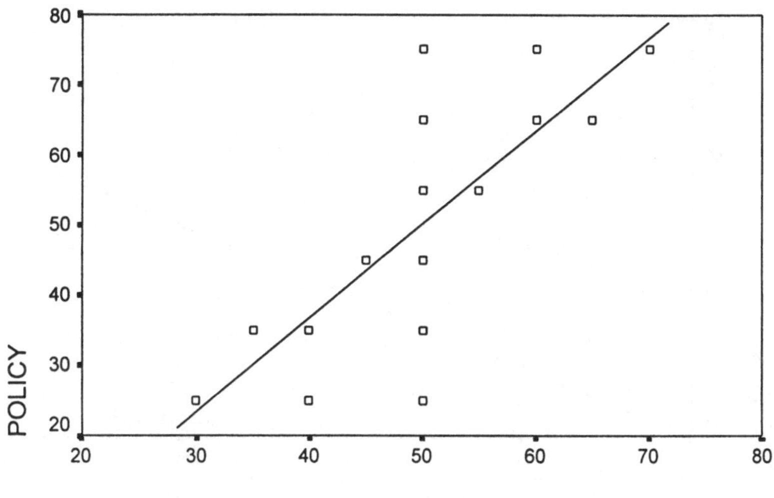

FIGURE 8.3. Fit of strategic model across regimes to sincere behavior.

Thus, whether or not regime 3 cases dominate a series, if the Court always votes its sincere preferences, one could find not only that $\beta_{123} > 0$, but that β_{123} is not statistically different from 1. Moreover, as we demonstrate below, the reason for this is not just the overlap in predictions between the sincere and strategic models for regime 3 cases, but because of a further bias in testing regime 1 and regime 2 cases in the standard regime-change, switching-regression model.

At this point we leave Bergara, Richman, and Spiller behind, for they do no more than test β_{123}, which means that they are completely incapable of distinguishing sincere from strategic behavior. This conclusion applies as well to all of the Spiller and Gely work prior to their table 6.[75]

Spiller and Gely then provide a separate test for what we call β_1 and β_2, which represent, respectively, the impact of the minimum for regime 1 Courts and the impact of the maximum for regime 2 Courts.[76] Under this approach, the expectations for β_1 and β_2, unlike those for β_3, differ from that of sincere behavior.

Regressions," paper presented at the 2001 meeting of the American Political Science Association, San Francisco, Calif.

[75] *Op. cit.*, n. 64, *supra*, p. 487.

[76] While the Spiller and Gely work provides tests of six different models in tables 1–5, their crucial test, which occurs in table 6, tests only their committee median model.

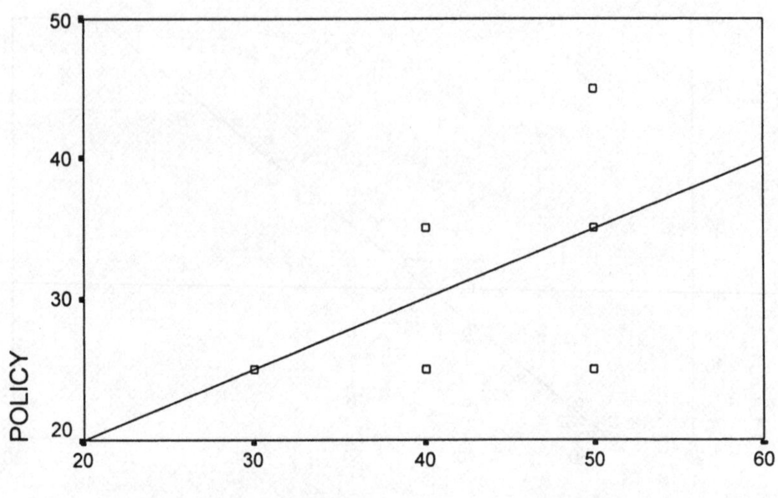

FIGURE 8.4. Test of strategic model given sincere behavior, regime 1 cases.

Unfortunately, testing this model still results in biased estimates for β_1 and β_2, in that even if the Court is acting sincerely and is not paying any attention to which regime it is in (i.e., a change in the value of the relevant regime has no change in its behavior), the regression will still return positive estimates for not only β_3 but β_1 and β_2 as well.

To see this, consider again the data from Table 8.5. Assume again that the Court votes only its sincere preferences. Presumably, we should observe a positive slope for the Court in regime 3, as the separation-of-powers model predicts sincere behavior there. But in regimes 1 and 2, if the Court is behaving sincerely, then a change in the relevant min or max should have no impact on its behavior. Intuitively, we should observe that, but let's look at what we actually observe.

Figure 8.4 plots the data points for justices in regime 1. For Court 1, whose ideal point is at 25, we observe court decisions at 25 when the min is at 50 (the bottom right data point), 25 when the min is at 40 (the bottom center data point), and 25 when the min is at 30 (the bottom left data point). A flat line that could connect these three points at the bottom of the figure is what we expect. Next we add Court 2, whose ideal point is at 35. We observe court decisions at 35 when the min is at 50, 35 when the min is at 40, and, crucially, we don't find Court 2 in regime 1 when the min is at 30, for Court 2 is now in regime 3 (see the

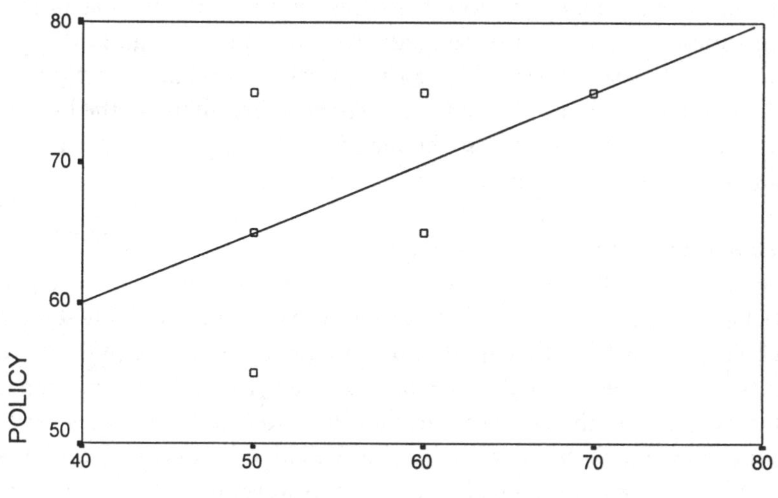

FIGURE 8.5. Test of strategic model given sincere behavior, regime 2 cases.

two data points in the middle row of the figure). Finally, we add Court 3, whose ideal point is at 45. We observe court decisions at 45 when the min is at 50, but we don't observe Court 3 in regime 1 when the min is at 40 or 30, for Court 3 is now in regime 3 (see the top point in the figure). Thus when we fit a regression line through the observed points for regime 1 Courts only, we observe an upward slope (here, of 0.5) even when there is no impact of the relevant regime on the Court. The true impact of a one-unit change in the min is 0; the estimated impact is 0.5.[77] At the other end of the scale, we find the same result for regime 2. As long as the Court's preferences change over time, this result follows.

The explanation for this should now be clear: As the relevant minimum decreases in regime 1 cases, we only find more conservative Courts in regime 1. And when the relevant maximum increases in regime 2 cases, we only find more liberal Courts in regime 2 (see Fig. 8.5).

Thus, even when separate regimes are tested, as Spiller and Gely do (though only for one out of the six models they examined), the

[77] This figure will change a bit with different distributions of data. With normally distributed data, the observed slope is about 0.64. See Segal and Wang, *op. cit.*, n. 74, *supra*.

regime-change model provides biased estimates of the impact of Congress on the Court. The reason, simply put, is that in regimes 1 and 2 the sincere preferences of the Court positively correlate with the value of the minimum and maximum, respectively.[78] To eliminate the bias, the preferences of the Court *must* be included in tests of the impact of the minimum and maximum in regimes 1 and 2.

Scaling Revisited

Finally, the scaling scheme used by Spiller and Gely (and Bergara, Richman, and Spiller) is worthy of more than a little scrutiny. Like all scholars in this field, they need to find a manner of placing judicial preferences and congressional preferences on a single scale. They accomplish this by allowing the computer to find the imputed ADA scores for the Court that best fit the data, so that the median of a Court with x number of Democrats will be equivalent to a congressperson with an ADA score of y. What is notable about this technique, though, is that it allows the imputed ADA score for a given Court to change dramatically given different specifications of congressional behavior. For example, in their Floor Median model, the median Supreme Court justice's imputed ADA score is equal to $-46.13 + 1.9 \cdot \text{SCDEM}$, where SCDEM equals the number of Democrats on the Court. Thus, this model finds a significant impact for Congress by giving the Court median during the later Vinson Court (Reed or Minton) an imputed ADA score of 122.97, a fantastic result given that ADA scores theoretically range from 0 (most conservative) to 100 (most liberal) and that Ted Kennedy (D-Mass.), as liberal as anyone could expect, only averages a 95.[79] So, too, the imputation finds the post-Douglas Burger Court median (Stevens) to have an imputed ADA score of 16.57. Alternatively, in the Committee Median model, the model finds a significant impact for Congress by giving the Reed/Minton Vinson Court median an imputed ADA score of 109.71, and the Stevens Burger Court median an imputed ADA score of 30.75. Thus, the conclusion to be drawn from the estimation is that for most models of congressional decision making, there exists a distinct mapping of Supreme Court preferences onto congressional preferences that, com-

[78] This is true whether justices are placed into different regimes deterministically or, as Spiller and Gely do, stochastically. Segal and Wang, *op. cit.*, n. 74, *supra*.

[79] See Sharp, n. 48, *supra*, for the source of ADA scores. Note that Spiller and Gely code Frankfurter as a Democrat for purposes of calculating the Court's percent Democratic.

bined with the biases discussed above, result in the finding of a significant congressional coefficient across regimes. While this is problem enough, the actual mappings are such that no scholar of the U.S. Supreme Court would find them plausible, much less reasonable.

Reexamining the Separation-of-Powers Model

Because of the theoretical and empirical concerns noted above and in Chapter 3, we undertake an examination of whether the voting patterns of the justices of the Supreme Court change as the political environment changes. Just what shifts in the political environment, though, should lead to changes in the behavior of Supreme Court justices is not entirely clear, for the constraints faced by the justices depend crucially on who has control over the legislative process in Congress. Yet this is not the place to answer longstanding arguments over committee and/or leadership power. Rather, we hope to achieve consistent results regardless of which model we use.

We examine two models of the legislative process: a committee power model and a party caucus model. Briefly, the committee power model resembles the Eskridge and Gely/Spiller models that explicitly allow committee preferences to differ from their parent chambers and grant committees agenda control. Alternatively, the party caucus model assumes that agenda setters act as relatively faithful agents of their party caucus.[80]

The tests for these models follow a similar procedure. Specifically, we attempt to place Supreme Court justices and members of Congress on a consistent ideological dimension and measure the preferences of the Court vis-à-vis the set of irreversible decisions established by the relevant model. As noted above, the crucial and distinct equilibrium predictions for the separation-of-powers model concern the impact of the maximum when the justice is above the set of irreversible decisions and the impact of the minimum when the justice is below the set of irreversible decisions. As demonstrated above, these predictions must be

80 We do not present results for the multiple-veto model originally presented in Jeffrey A. Segal, "Separation-of-Powers Games in the Positive Theory of Congress and Courts," 91 *American Political Science Review* 28 (1997). While our results from this model are perfectly consistent with the results below, we accept the criticism by Bergara et al. (n. 65, *supra*) that this model overstates the protection given the Court. Those wishing to see these results may contact us.

We also find no impact for the filibuster-veto model suggested by Bergara et al.

significant after controlling for the preferences of the justices. For example, in regime 2, as the maximum increases, we are likely to see increasingly liberal behavior from the justices. That could be because the maximum is increasing, as the separation-of-powers model predicts, or, rather, because as the maximum increases, we place only increasingly liberal justices in regime 2. Thus, the model we test is a regime-change switching regression of the form

$$Y_i = \alpha + \beta_1\text{Preference} + \beta_2\text{Regime}_{12} + \beta_3\text{Equilibrium} + \varepsilon_i$$

where

Y_i is each justice's percent liberal in statutory decisions for the relevant year;
"Preference" is a measure of the justice's ideological preferences;
"Regime_{12}" is a dummy variable representing whether the justice is in either regime 1 or regime 2, the constrained regimes;
"Equilibrium" is the regime-switching variable that takes on the value of the minimum of the set of irreversible decisions if the justice is in regime 1 and the maximum of the set of irreversible decisions if the justice is in regime 2;
α is the constant;
βs are parameters to be estimated; and
ε_i is the error term.

Measurement

We need to measure the preferences of each justice for two separate tasks. First, we need a descriptive measure so that we can place each justice into regimes 1, 2, or 3 for each year he or she was on the Court. Second, we need a preference measure as an independent variable in the estimation equation. This will allow us to determine whether observed changes in the behavior of regime 1 and regime 2 justices are due to changes in the equilibrium predictions, as expected by the separation-of-powers model, or are simply due to the preferences of the shifting set of justices who are placed in those regimes, as expected by the attitudinal model.

To place the justices in one regime or another, we begin by relying on the "Constitutional" measure of the justices' preferences: the justices' predicted, annual liberalism support scores in nonunanimous civil liberties constitutional cases, as derived from the U.S. Supreme Court Judicial Database.[81] This provides what we hope to be a reliable and valid

[81] See Segal, *id.*, and Bergara et al., *op. cit.*, n. 65, *supra*. We use these instead of the Segal-Cover editorial scores, as the Segal-Cover scores are not the best *description* of the justices' preferences. See Epstein and Mershon, *op. cit.*, n. 36, *supra*. Thus, we include the

description of the justices' ideological preferences. The overall scores range from a high of 93.3 (Douglas) to a low of 5.0 (Rehnquist).

We measure the (revealed) ideological preferences of members of Congress using the support scores provided by Americans for Democratic Action. While ADA scores have marked deficiencies, most notably, the fact that nonvoting congresspersons are counted as voting against the ADA position, this should have very little influence on chamber and committee medians. Moreover, research demonstrates the reliability, validity, and stability of ADA scores as a measure of congressional preferences.[82]

The next step is to scale the constitutional scores comparably to ADA scores.[83] There is no clear way of doing so, so we sought expert

more direct constitutional measure, one derived from the justices' votes, but only after purging those scores of any plausible influence from the political environment. We accomplished this as follows.

First, and for obvious reasons, we exclude statutory decisions. While Epstein and Mershon argue that the justices' votes in *all* past cases are the best measure of their sincere preferences, this can be true only if the separation-of-powers argument is false. Thus, the Epstein/Mershon measure is not an appropriate measure for testing separation-of-powers hypotheses. Instead, we use the votes of the justices in constitutional cases. Overwhelmingly, the averages of these votes should be independent of congressional preferences, even if on rare occasions the justices do defer to congressional preferences. Even Eskridge (*op. cit.*, n. 47, *supra*) is willing to use votes in constitutional cases, "where there was little chance of being overridden" (p. 652), as a valid baseline against which to measure votes in statutory cases.

Second, we chose civil rights and liberties cases because the House and Senate judiciary committees have jurisdiction over almost all of the Court's civil liberties decisions. While this decision might limit generalizability, it does so over an area that encompasses a majority of the Court's docket.

Third, we use nonunanimous decisions only. We do so to enhance the ability to scale these decisions with the ADA measure of congressional preferences (see below).

Fourth, we use annual support scores, not aggregates across an entire career, as some justices may exhibit long-term changes in their sincere preferences.

Fifth, we use predicted annual support scores, not actual annual support scores, as derived from a regression of each justice's support score over time. This further helps ensure that the preference measure is independent of short-term contemporary congressional preferences and short-term fluctuations due to changes in case stimuli.

82 Richard Herrera, Thomas Eperlein, and Eric R.A.N. Smith, "The Stability of Congressional Roll-Call Indexes," 48 *Political Research Quarterly* 403 (1995).

83 Needless to say, our ideological support scores for the justices are not created in a manner similar to ADA scores for congresspersons. Our goal, though, is not to replicate ADA scores but to come up with scores that measure liberalism for both justices and congresspersons. While interest group support scores for justices would be nice if they existed, following ADA ranking procedures is not essential, and could even be harmful, to our purposes. E.g., counting absentee votes of the justices as conservative would produce an obviously inferior measure of the justices' ideology. Moreover, even if ADA procedures could be followed precisely for the justices, that would not relieve the need to ensure that the votes were similarly scaled.

judgments from three highly regarded public law colleagues. The question we asked them was how these scores related, in their judgments, to ADA scores. That is, is 93.3 about where Douglas would be if he had real and comparable ADA scores, or is it too high or too low? Is 5.0 about where Rehnquist would be if he had real and comparable ADA scores, or is it too high or too low? The three scholars who answered our queries unanimously stated that it was better to keep the scores as is than rescale them higher, lower, or more toward the middle, or more toward the extremes.[84] As this is our view as well, we use the scores as is. While this is obviously not a textbook example of scaling, the results have, we believe, a fair amount of face validity, and seem superior to the arbitrary placement and nonsensical scaling of players that one sometimes finds in the separation-of-powers literature.

We next determine for each model the set of irreversible decisions that the Court faced for each year, such that decisions mapping within that set could not be reversed. We present the derivation of these data in Appendix 8.1.

Finally, we need to control for the justices' sincere preferences. To test the robustness of our findings, we use two measures: the Segal-Cover editorial scores and the constitutional scores discussed above. The dependent variable consists of the justices' annual votes in all statutory decisions in civil liberties cases rendered by the Supreme Court between the beginning of the 1946 term and the end of the 1992 term. We derive the data from the U.S. Supreme Court Judicial Database, as backdated by Harold Spaeth to cover the Vinson Court era.[85] This selection procedure yields 412 annual voting scores over thirty justices.[86]

Results

We present the results in Table 8.6. While the preference measure, whether using the constitutional score or the Segal-Cover score, is significant in every model at $p < 0.001$, what is really of significance at this point is the influence of the variable "Equilibrium." This represents

[84] Thanks to Larry Baum, Greg Caldeira, and Tom Walker.

[85] See n. 61 for derivation of the data. Here, we use all civil liberties cases, not just civil rights cases.

[86] Because observations across justices and observations across terms will not be independent of each other, we estimate a least squares dummy variable linear regression model, with dummy variables for different years and justices.

TABLE 8.6. *Influence of Separation-of-Powers Equilibrium Predictions on Justices' Votes in Statutory Cases*

	Constitutional preference measure		Segal-Cover preference measure	
Variable	Committee power model	Party caucus model	Committee power model	Party caucus model
Constant	9.11 (7.30)	13.29 (7.29)	20.04 (7.86)	25.23 (7.83)
Preference	0.53 (0.07)	0.51 (0.07)	44.22 (8.76)	41.87 (8.79)
$Regime_{12}$	6.99 (3.45)	1.63 (3.50)	5.18 (3.58)	0.05 (3.64)
Equilibrium	−0.08 (0.07)	−0.06 (0.07)	−0.02 (0.07)	−0.03 (0.07)

Notes: $n = 412$ for all models. Standard errors in parentheses. Preference significant at $p < 0.001$, all models. Equilibrium not significant, all models.

the influence of the SID minimum for justices in regime 1 or the SID maximum for justices in regime 2. The separation-of-powers prediction is that this coefficient should be significantly greater than 0 and not significantly different from 1. Whether we use the committee power model or the party caucus model, the constitutional preference score or the Segal-Cover preference score, the "Equilibrium" coefficient is in the wrong direction and not significantly different from 0.

As an additional test of the separation-of-powers model, we perform a test on a crucial subset of justices: those who occupy the median position on the Court in any given term. These justices, by themselves, might have the capability to keep the Court's preferences consistent with Congress's. The attitudinal position, though, is that the democratic appointment process, combined with extra scrutiny for policy-critical nominations,[87] means that these justices, more than any others, might frequently fall inside the set of irreversible decisions, and thus could only infrequently be constrained. And even if they fall outside the set, factors such as the ability to manipulate issues, the ability to review congressional overrides, or the high cost of passing legislation can still lead to rationally sincere voting.

[87] Peter H. Lemieux and Charles H. Stewart III, "Advice? Yes. Consent? Maybe. Senate Confirmation of Supreme Court Nominations," paper presented at the 1989 annual meeting of the Law and Society Association, Madison, Wisc.

TABLE 8.7. *Influence of Separation-of-Powers Equilibrium Predictions on Justices' Votes in Statutory Cases with Median Interactions*

	Constitutional preference measure		Segal-Cover preference measure	
	Committee power model	**Party caucus model**	**Committee power model**	**Party caucus model**
Constant	10.04 (7.37)	14.24 (7.32)	20.59 (7.90)	26.27 (7.86)
Ideology	0.53 (0.07)	0.51 (0.07)	44.37 (8.75)	41.99 (8.78)
$Regime_{12}$	6.67 (3.48)	1.35 (3.53)	4.90 (3.60)	−0.36 (3.67)
Equilibrium	−0.07 (0.07)	−0.06 (0.07)	−0.02 (0.07)	−0.03 (0.07)
Median dummy	−1.15 (1.95)	−2.20 (1.93)	−1.24 (2.07)	−2.81 (2.08)
Median equilibrium	−0.08 (0.10)	−0.11 (0.14)	−0.12 (0.11)	−0.07 (0.15)

Notes: $n = 412$ for all models. Standard errors in parentheses. Ideology significant at $p < 0.001$, all models. Separation-of-powers equilibrium not significant, all models. Equilibrium predictions for median interactions insignificant in all models.

These results (see Table 8.7) are no more favorable to the separation-of-powers model. The equilibrium predictions are again all negative and insignificant, and the median interactions are also negative and insignificant.

Recent Findings

Beyond our own previously published articles[88] and the works discussed above, recent years have witnessed an explosion in quantitative analyses of the separation-of-powers model. The findings are overwhelming in their lack of support for the model.

Melissa Marschall and Andreas Broscheid's award-winning work turns the Downsian space of the typical separation-of-powers model into

[88] See Jeffrey A. Segal, "Separation-of-Power Games in the Positive Theory of Congress and Courts," 91 *American Political Science Review* 28 (1997), and Jeffrey A. Segal, "Supreme Court Deference to Congress: An Analysis of the Marksist Model," in Cornell W. Clayton and Howard Gillman, eds., *Supreme Court Decision Making* (Chicago: University of Chicago Press, 1999).

Bergara et al. make the claim that Segal's 1997 results are biased. For a refutation, see Jeffrey A. Segal, "Separation of Power Games in the Positive Theory of Congress and Courts Revisited," typescript, State University of New York at Stony Brook, 2001.

the binary "Schubertian" space that arguably better represents judicial decisions.[89] They nevertheless find no support for the separation-of-powers model.

Sara Schiavoni replaces raw ADA scores with "inflation-adjusted" ADA scores. She nevertheless finds no support for the separation-of-powers model.[90]

Joshua Clinton's award-winning work resolves the scaling problem between Supreme Court and congressional preferences by using the presidency as a bridge between them.[91] The President takes a stand on many bills before Congress and the Supreme Court takes a stand on positions supported by the President's representative in Court, the Solicitor General. Under an extraordinary array of tests, he finds no support for the separation-of-powers model.

Andrew Martin uses a two-level hierarchical probit model to test the influence of the separation-of-powers model on the justices' behavior.[92] Despite ample evidence that Court preferences strongly influence congressional decisions, Martin finds no significant impact of either Congress or the President on the Court's statutory decisions.[93]

Two studies examining narrower sets of U.S. Supreme Court decisions find no support for separation-of-powers hypotheses: McGuire finds that strategic behavior does not account for the Supreme Court's support for the Solicitor General,[94] while Spriggs and Hansford find that congres-

[89] Melissa Marschall and Andreas Broscheid, "A NeoMarksist Model of Supreme Court/Congress/President Interaction: The Civil Rights Cases, 1953–1992," paper presented at the 1995 meeting of the American Political Science Association, Chicago, Ill., and winner of the 1996 Congressional Quarterly Press Award.

[90] Sara Schiavoni, "Constraints on the Court, Congressional Preferences, and the Spinal Tap Fallacy," paper presented at the 1997 Conference on the Scientific Study of Law and Courts, Atlanta, Georgia.

[91] Joshua Clinton, "An Independent Judiciary? Determining the Influence of Congressional and Presidential Preferences on the Supreme Court's Interpretation of Federal Statutes: 1953–1995," paper presented at the 1998 meeting of the American Political Science Association, Boston, Mass., and winner of the 1999 Congressional Quarterly Press Award.

[92] Andrew D. Martin, "Decision Making on the Supreme Court and the Separation of Powers," typescript, Washington University, 2000. Unlike the Marschall and Clinton papers, no award yet for this manuscript, but the dissertation from which the paper derives won the political economy section award for best dissertation written in 1998.

[93] Nor does Martin find any influence of Congress in the Court's constitutional decisions. He does, however, find influence of the President in constitutional cases, a finding consistent with the well-established impact of the Solicitor General (see Chapter 10).

[94] Kevin T. McGuire, "Explaining Executive Success in the U.S. Supreme Court," 51 *Political Research Quarterly* 505 (1998).

sional preferences have no impact on the Court's decision to overturn precedent.[95]

One requirement of the separation-of-powers model is that the justices know the preferences of members of Congress. The most obvious signal of such preferences would be amicus curiae briefs filed by members. Yet, Heberlig and Spill find that unlike the Solicitor General (see Chapter 10), members of Congress fare no better than chance as amici, winning only 48 percent of the time.[96] Most important, they find no relationship with a slew of amici-related factors that should signal an increase in the likelihood of congressional override. While statutory decisions are *much* easier to override than constitutional decisions, members of Congress saw their side prevail only 32 percent of the time in statutory cases. Nor do Heberlig and Spill find any relationship between committee or leadership position and winning as amicus. Moreover, members of Congress are not helped as more members join the brief, as the brief becomes bipartisan, or as the brief crosses Chambers; again, all factors that should make override more likely. In sum, the Court's reaction to the costly revelation of congressional preferences is a collective yawn.

Why does the Court fail to heed congressional preferences? Beyond the reasons discussed in Chapter 3, an analysis of congressional overrides by Virginia Hettinger and Christopher Zorn suggests it would be counterproductive for the Court to do so, because *Supreme Court decisions outside of the congressional set of irreversible decisions are no more likely to be overridden than decisions that fall into the set.*[97] Why this might be is subject to speculation,[98] but, regardless, deferring to Congress makes little sense if such deference does not decrease the likelihood of override. The obvious implication of this work is that sincere behavior may almost always be the rational alternative for the Court.

Against all of these findings we find one limited exception. Hansford and Damore test six hypotheses about the influence of

[95] James F. Spriggs II and Thomas G. Hansford, "Explaining the Overruling of U.S. Supreme Court Precedent," 63 *Journal of Politics* 1091 (2001).

[96] Eric S. Heberlig and Rorie L. Spill, "Congress at Court: Members of Congress as Amicus Curiae," 28 *Southeastern Political Review* 189 (2000).

[97] Virginia Hettinger and Christopher Zorn, "Explaining the Incidence and Timing of Congressional Responses to the U.S. Supreme Court," typescript, Indiana University, 2000.

[98] One relevant factor may be that, in even-numbered years, at least, the contemporary Congress will soon be replaced.

Congress on the justices' decision making and find support for two of them.[99]

For our final piece of evidence, we turn to William Eskridge, one of the foremost advocates of the separation-of-powers model:

> The Court that decided *Patterson* and the other 1989 decisions was producing results that did not reflect current legislative preferences. However, this was also true of the Warren Court (which thrived on such independence and never got overruled) and was often true of the Burger Court (which in almost every instance was promptly overruled). Therefore, again, ignoring legislative preferences is nothing new. Finally, the Rehnquist Court approached *Patterson* and the other 1989 decisions from a perspective substantially more conservative than that of Congress. But that has been true of the Court since 1972, when Justices Rehnquist and Powell started voting.[100]

If the overwhelming majority of statistical models find no support for the separation-of-powers model, if the few statistical models supporting the separation-of-powers model are seriously flawed, and if the model's foremost advocate concludes that the Warren, Burger, and Rehnquist courts all ignored legislative preferences, there is little need to say more.

CONCLUSIONS

The failure of the separation-of-powers model as applied to the U.S. Supreme Court should not be seen as the categorical failure of the separation-of-powers model per se. The federal judiciary was designed to be independent, so we should not be surprised that it in fact is. Courts in diverse institutional settings, though, might evidence precisely the type of behavior predicted by the model. One might readily imagine a spectrum along which the separation-of-powers model might be relatively true (a parliamentary system with strong party control over members and a single majority party, a judiciary without constitutional powers, judges without life tenure) or relatively false (a

[99] Thomas Hansford and David F. Damore, "Congressional Preferences, Perceptions of Threat, and Supreme Court Decision Making," 28 *American Politics Quarterly* 490 (2000). The authors claim that Congress matters when it is more conservative than the justice, but not when it is more liberal; that credible threats from Congress matter when Congress is more liberal than the justice but not when it is more conservative. Finally, they find no influence of congressional amici under conservative or liberal congressional regimes.

[100] Eskridge, "Reneging on History," *op. cit.*, n. 47, *supra*, p. 683.

congressional system with decentralized power, a constitutional court, judges with life tenure). In sum, it should hardly surprise that institutional structures matter. Comparative studies of other nations or American state courts, whose institutional features vary dramatically, could prove consequential.[101]

Moreover, as we saw in Chapter 6, justices are capable of engaging in sophisticated behavior in arenas where sophisticated voting clearly makes sense. For example, in certiorari voting, where justices *know* that a grant almost invariably leads to a decision on the merits, where they know that the people who voted on cert will almost precisely be those who vote on the merits, and where they have a very good idea about how those people will vote, sophisticated voting may operate. Needless to say, the structure of the merits decision and the informational environment in which such decisions are made are far different for the Court, allowing the justices to engage, in almost all cases, in rationally sincere behavior.[102]

According to Oliver Wendell Holmes, law is nothing more than "the prophesies of what the courts will do in fact."[103] By this he meant that statutes and constitutional commands do not give citizens a fair understanding of what the law permits and what the law prohibits. It is a judge's decision that tells us what we may and may not do. Since decisions about the legality of today's activity will be made by judges tomor-

[101] See, e.g., Paul Brace and Melinda Gann Hall, "Studying Courts Comparatively: The View from the American States," 48 *Political Research Quarterly* 5 (1995).

[102] Thus, we do not say that the Supreme Court *never* engages in sophisticated behavior on the merits. Rather, given the difficulty of passing legislation in Congress, given the Supreme Court's rather incomplete information about congressional preferences, the salience of Court decisions to members of Congress, and the short-lived duration of whatever Congress the Court is facing, we argue that the Court virtually never defers to presumed congressional preferences in the first instance. Rather, the justices will routinely vote their sincere preferences. If and when Congress ever mounts a clear and imminent threat to the Court's institutional policy-making powers, then and only then will the Court respond and back down. But given the extraordinary difficulty of striking at the Court's powers, such times will be rare, indeed. Of course, this model fits well with the overwhelming majority of Court decisions that appear to be based on sincere preferences, as well as the few well-known examples when the Court arguably has backed down in the face of real danger from Congress, such as *Ex parte McCardle*, 7 Wallace 506 (1869), *Barenblatt v. United States* 360 U.S. 109 (1959), and the New Deal cases. It also explains the clear findings in this chapter that the justices do not change their behavior as the political environment changes in the manner predicted by the existing separation-of-powers models.

[103] Oliver Wendell Holmes, "The Path of the Law," 10 *Harvard Law Review* 457 (1897), 460–61.

row, law becomes the prophesies of what judges will do. "The object of our study, then, is prediction."[104]

As political scientists, though, we require more than prediction; we require explanation. The legal model, the attitudinal model, and the separation-of-powers model all attempt to provide explanations of what the Court actually does. Only the attitudinal model's explanation, though, is well supported by systematic empirical evidence. The fact that the attitudinal model has been successfully used to *predict* the Court's decisions further confirms its status as the best *explanation* of the Court's decisions.

APPENDIX 8.1 DERIVING THE SETS OF IRREVERSIBLE DECISIONS

In this appendix we explain the derivation of the set of irreversible decisions for the committee power and party caucus models. We begin with a generic gatekeeping model, extend it, and then adapt it to conform to the expectations of the two models.

The Basic Model

We begin with a Court (C), a legislature (L), and a gatekeeper (G). Under the separation-of-powers game, the Court selects a policy in one-dimensional (liberal-conservative) space. A legislative gatekeeper (such as a committee) can propose an alternative. If the gatekeeper proposes an alternative, The legislature can consider an override of the Court decision under open rule (i.e., with amendment).

Figure 8.6 presents potential preferences of the Court, the gatekeeper, and the legislature. Additionally, the point labeled G(L) represents the position where the gatekeeper is indifferent to the position favored by the legislature.[105]

Working backward, we note the following results. If the legislature receives a bill from the gatekeeper, it will amend the bill to L and pass it. The gatekeeper will then propose legislation only if G is closer to L than G is to the policy chosen by the Court. Thus the set of irreversible decisions (SID) is the set [G(L), L], in that any decision within that set could not be overruled. For any Court decision within that set, the gate-

[104] *Id.* at 457.

[105] That is, the distance between G(L) and G is the same as the distance between G and L.

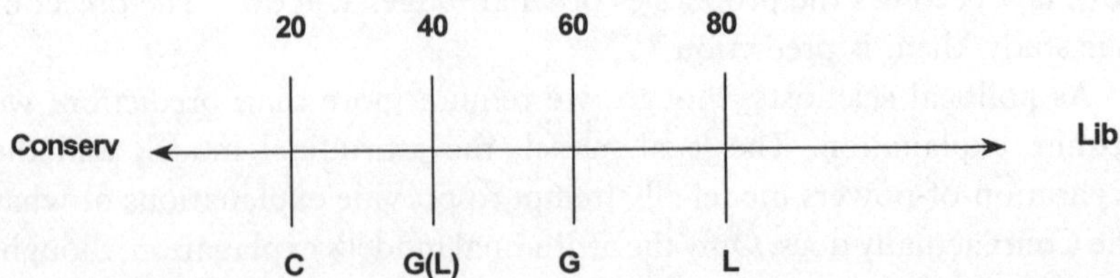

FIGURE 8.6. Preferences of Court (C), gatekeeper (G), legislature (L), and gatekeeper's indifference point (G(L)).

keeper prefers what the Court has done to what the legislature would do and thus does not introduce legislation.

We now arrive at the crucial stage of the separation-of-powers model. If the Court voted its sincere preferences, it would simply choose C. Such a result, though, would not be rational, for the result of that action is that the gatekeeper would propose legislation that the legislature would amend to L. The Court could get the best possible outcome if it placed its decision at G(L). At this point the gatekeeper is indifferent between the Court's position and the legislature's ultimate outcome. Just to the left of G(L), the gatekeeper prefers the legislative outcome to the Court's decision and thus introduces legislation. To the right of G(L), the Court is not overturned but the policy is not as good – from the Court's perspective – as G(L). Thus, G(L) is the point closest to the Court's ideal point that does not result in a legislative override. Thus, for any Court to the left of G(L), the equilibrium outcome is G(L). Alternatively, if the Court is anywhere to the right of L, the best position for the Court is L, as any decision to the right of L gets overturned and any decision to the left of L surrenders more than is necessary. Finally, if the Court is between G(L) and L, the Court should simply set policy at its ideal point. That policy would fall within the set of irreversible decisions, for the gatekeeper prefers the Court's decision to the legislature's and thus would not introduce override legislation.

The Extended Model

We next extend the model to include bicameralism and presidential veto.[106] We start with bicameralism. Bicameralism extends the set of irre-

[106] This section follows Tim Groseclose and Sara Schiavoni, "Rethinking Justices' and Committees' Strategies in Segal's Separation of Powers Game," 106 *Public Choice* 121 (2001).

versible decisions because override legislation must pass through two separate chambers. Now, for override legislation to pass, the gatekeeper in each chamber must propose legislation; each chamber (the House (H) and the Senate (S)) must pass the legislation; the chambers, through a conference committee (CC), must compromise over the eventual outcome; and both chambers must support the compromise. We set CC's preference at the average of the House and Senate medians. The conference committee, if it receives a bill, will choose the policy closest to its ideal point subject to the constraint that both H and S prefer the bill to the Court's position. Thus, the gatekeepers must look forward to this result.

Finally, we add presidential veto. Assume a rating scale such as ADA scores, where higher numbers represent greater liberalism. We assume that Democratic Presidents are more liberal than the 67th percentile House and Senate members, and that Republican Presidents are more conservative than the 33rd percentile House and Senate members.[107] This means that a Democratic President would be willing to veto any conservative override (i.e., an override that makes the result more conservative) that Congress would sustain and that a Republican would be willing to veto any liberal override that Congress would sustain.

This changes the strategies of both the conference committee and the gatekeeping committees. The conference committee, as before, will not write a bill at any spot where legislation would not pass, or now, where a veto could be sustained. Consider the situation with a Republican President and a conservative Court decision below the SID. The conference committee will write a bill at its most favorite policy subject to the constraint that H_{33} and S_{33} would vote to uphold it. This also means that if the gatekeeper is above the minimum of H_{33} and S_{33}, the gatekeeper's indifference point doesn't matter in calculating the minimum, for the gatekeeper knows that the conference committee will not propose legislation below the minimum of H_{33} and S_{33}.

For a liberal Court decision (again with a Republican President), the conference committee will write a bill at its most favorite policy subject to the constraint that H and S would vote to uphold it. This also means that if the gatekeeper is below the max (H, S), the gatekeeper's

[107] Nolan McCarty and Keith Poole, "Veto Power and Legislation: An Empirical Analysis of Executive-Legislative Bargaining from 1961–1986," 11 *Journal of Law, Economics, and Organization* 282 (1995).

indifference point doesn't matter in calculating the maximum, as the conference committee will not propose legislation above the max (H, S). Complementary rules hold for Democratic Presidents.

Application

We apply the model to two different models of congressional decision making. The first, the committee power model, is consistent with the specific derivation of the separation-of-powers model by William Eskridge. Here, the House and Senate Judiciary Committees act as gatekeepers for any override legislation.

Alternatively, recent models of congressional lawmaking provide theoretical and empirical evidence that policy making typically represents neither independent committee preferences nor independent leadership preferences, but the preferences of the majority party caucus.[108]

To test the party caucus model, we operationalize potential gatekeepers as representing the preferences of the median member of the House and Senate majority party caucuses.

We provide an example using 1982 and the committee power model. The preferences of the players are presented in Figure 8.7. The set of irreversible decisions is [15, 45]. If the Court rules between 15 and 45, any liberal override (of a conservative decision) makes H_{33} worse off and thus would lead to a sustainable presidential veto, while any attempt at a conservative override (of a liberal decision) would fail because it would make the Senate worse off.

Why is the minimum 15? For any Court decision below 15, the pivot player is H_{33}, who can vote to sustain a Republican veto. The conference committee thus sets the override at the point where H_{33} is indifferent to or weakly favors the override over the Court decision. So if the Court rules at 10, the bill is written at 20 (minus some minute amount). Reagan could veto such a bill, but the veto would be overridden, as H_{33} weakly favors the override at 20 to the Court policy at 10. If the Court rules at 14, the bill is written at a shade below 16, for precisely the same reason.

[108] D. Roderick Kiewiet and Matthew D. McCubbins, *The Logic of Delegation: Congressional Parties and the Appropriations Process* (Chicago: University of Chicago Press, 1991); Gary W. Cox and Matthew D. McCubbins, *Legislative Leviathan: Party Government in the House* (Berkeley: University of California Press, 1993).

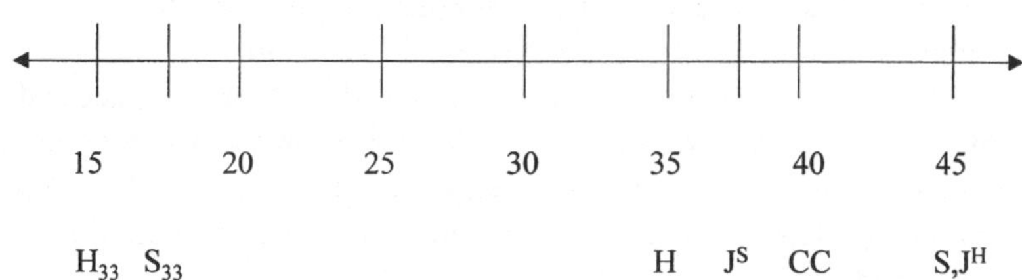

FIGURE 8.7. The set of irreversible decisions (15, 45) in Congress, 1982. H_{33}: House 33rd percentile; S_{33}: Senate 33rd percentile; H: House median; J^S: Senate judiciary median; CC: conference committee; S: Senate median; J^H: House judiciary median.

The maximum of the SID is 45. The pivotal players are the Senate median (S) and the House Judiciary Committee (J^H), both at 45. If the Court's decision is above 50, the conference committee sets policy at its ideal point, which all players favor to the Court decision. If the Court decision is between 45 and 50, the conference committee can write the bill to the left of 45 such that S (and J^H) is indifferent to or weakly favors the bill to the Court's decision. For example, consider a Court decision at 48. Working backward, the conference committee, if it received a bill, would place the bill at 42, the spot closest to its ideal point that both H and S (weakly) prefer to 48. Knowing this, both chambers would approve legislation, and both judiciary committees would introduce legislation. The Court is thus overridden at 42. If the Court ruled at 46, the conference committee would write the bill at 44. Note that while the House Judiciary Committee's indifference point from the conference committee is 50, the indifference point doesn't matter in this regime because S constrains CC from setting policy too far to the left.

Alternatively, if the House Judiciary Committee were just one point to the right of S, at 46, the maximum of the SID would move from 45 to 52, the spot where the committee would be indifferent to CC's preference. For example, if the Court ruled at 51 and CC received a bill, it could set policy at its ideal point, 40, just as above, as both chambers prefer the bill to the Court's ruling. But this action makes the House Judiciary Committee worse off, so it would not introduce the bill.

For 1982, the predicted preferences of White (35), Burger (21), Powell (35), and O'Connor (15) fall within the set of irreversible decisions. These justices should be affected by their own preferences, and not congressional preferences. Of the five remaining justices, the predicted preferences of four fall above the maximum (Marshall at 93, Brennan at 91, Stevens at 64, and Blackmun at 51), and thus their vote, according to the separation-of-powers model, is dependent on the SID maximum, and not on their own preferences. Alternatively, Rehnquist (6) falls below the minimum. His vote should depend on the SID minimum, and not on his own preferences.

9

Opinion Assignment and Opinion Coalitions

The decision on the merits merely indicates whether the ruling of the court whose decision the Supreme Court reviewed is affirmed or reversed and, consequently, which party has won and which has lost. The opinion of the Court, by comparison, constitutes the core of the Court's policy-making process. It specifies the constitutional and legal principles on which the majority rests its decision; it guides the lower courts in deciding future cases; and it establishes precedents for the Court's own subsequent rulings – even if such decisions and their supporting opinions can be overturned by future Supreme Courts.

Justice Dooley of the Vermont Supreme Court, concurring in the first state supreme court decision to void state marriage laws because they exclude same-sex partnerships – *Baker v. State*, No. 98-03 (1999) – states the matter very well:

> I recognize to most observers the significance of this decision lies in its result and remedy. In the cases that come before us in the future, however, the significance of this case will lie in its rationale – that is, how we interpret and apply . . . the Vermont Constitution. Moreover, in this, the most closely-watched opinion in this Court's history, its acceptability will be based on whether its reasoning and result are clearly commanded . . . and whether it is a careful . . . exercise of the Court's . . . powers. I do not believe that the majority's rationale meets this . . . standard, and I fear how it may be applied – or ignored – in the future.

Although the opinion of the Court is controlling and authoritative, the nonmajority opinions that the justices write – concurrences and dissents – are by no means exercises in futility. Concurring opinions punctuate over- or understated aspects of the Court's opinion, indicate its scope insofar as the concurring justice is concerned, address related matters, and exhibit the extent to which the members of the majority coalition are in agreement. More important, concurring opinions can control the holding of the Court when a majority opinion fails to form and the concurrence contains the viewpoint of the median member of the Court.[1]

Dissenting opinions obviously express disagreement with the majority's holding. They may also provide a rationale whereby the majority's opinion may be undermined and/or eventually qualified or overruled. Thus, the first Justice Harlan's dissent in *Plessy v. Ferguson* formed the basis for its overruling in *Brown v. Board of Education*,[2] and opinions dissenting from the Court's refusal to apply portions of the Bill of Rights to state criminal procedure during the 1940s and 1950s laid the groundwork for the liberal Warren Court majority to do so during the 1960s.[3] Charles Evans Hughes – later chief justice – probably stated best the function of the dissenting opinion:

> ... an appeal to the brooding spirit of the law, to the intelligence of a future day, when a later decision may possibly correct the error into which the dissenting judge believes the court to have been betrayed.[4]

In this chapter, we initially identify the patterns of assignment and the reasons for their existence. We then investigate opinion coalitions – who joins with whom and why – and the reasons why such coalitions may fail to form.

OPINION ASSIGNMENTS

Although the justices are free to write concurring and dissenting opinions as they individually see fit, that is not true of opinions of the Court. If the chief justice is among the majority in the original (conference) vote on the merits, he almost always determines who will write the Court's opinion. If he is not a member of this group, the senior justice who is typically makes the assignment. (By definition, the chief is considered most senior even though, like Warren, he initially was the most junior.)

[1] The holding of the Court may be viewed as "that position taken by those Members who concurred in the judgments on the narrowest grounds." *Gregg v. Georgia*, 428 U.S. 153, 169 n. 15 (1976).

[2] 163 U.S. 537 (1896), at 552; 347 U.S. 483 (1954).

[3] See the discussion of these matters in Chapter 4.

[4] Charles Evans Hughes, *The Supreme Court of the United States* (New York: Columbia University Press, 1928), p. 68.

Although the Court's published Reports name the author of the Court's opinion, we cannot accurately infer who assigned the opinion from those the Reports list as being in the majority; and, furthermore, we have no idea if there may have been earlier assigners or assignees. Except for Palmer's study of the Vinson Court,[5] and various journal articles and papers written by Forrest Maltzman, James Spriggs, and Paul Wahlbeck,[6] other analyses of opinion assignment have been based on membership in the final vote coalition – the one provided in the Reports – rather than membership in the final conference vote on the merits.

Hence, we go to the source: the justices' private papers, specifically, the assignment sheets prepared by the chief justice and the memoranda that supplement these sheets. Each justice is provided with a copy of these materials. To determine the membership of conference vote coalitions, which is where opinion assignments are made, we rely on the docket books of justices who have made them available for scholarly research.

Because the justices are free to change their votes between the conference vote and the report vote, we do not know for a fact that the ostensible assigner was a member of the final conference coalition at which the opinion of the Court was assigned. Although the justices' private papers make occasional reference to their changing sides,[7] Saul Brenner's systematic comparison of the justices' conference votes with their final votes shows switching to be fairly unusual, and that when it does occur it tends to increase the size of the final coalition rather than to transform the conference majority into either a minority or a smaller majority.[8] If, however, the original majority opinion coalition does break up and the author of a dissenting or a concurring opinion gains a majority, he or she is by that fact automatically reassigned the opinion of the

[5] Jan Palmer, *The Vinson Court Era* (New York: AMS Press, 1990).

[6] E.g., "May It Please the Chief?: Opinion Assignments in the Rehnquist Court," 40 *American Journal of Political Science* 421 (1996). References to most of their other related work can be found in their book, *The Collegial Game* (New York: Cambridge University Press, 2000).

[7] Walter F. Murphy, *Elements of Judicial Strategy* (Chicago: University of Chicago Press, 1964), pp. 68–73; J. Woodford Howard, "On the Fluidity of Judicial Choice," 62 *American Political Science Review* 43 (1968), at 44–49; S. Sidney Ulmer, "Earl Warren and the Brown Decision," 33 *Journal of Politics* 689 (1971).

[8] Saul Brenner, "Fluidity on the United States Supreme Court: A Reexamination," 24 *American Journal of Political Science* 526 (1980); Saul Brenner, "Fluidity on the Supreme Court, 1956–1967," 26 *American Journal of Political Science* 388 (1982); Saul Brenner, "Strategic Choice and Opinion Assignment on the U.S. Supreme Court: A Reexamination," 35 *Political Research Quarterly* 204 (1982).

Court without another conference vote.[9] Moreover, if the chief justice switches to the majority prior to the report vote, he also may reassign the Court's opinion without taking another conference vote. Chief Justice Warren exemplified this practice in a memo to the Court:

> You will recall that when we discussed No. 24 – *Halliburton Oil Well Cementing Co. v. Reily* – I did not vote because I was uncertain as to what my decision would be, and Justice Black assigned the case further. I have decided to vote to reverse. I am, therefore, reassigning the case to myself.[10]

Given the variegated volatility that may, and sometimes does, characterize the justices' voting behavior between the conference vote on the merits and their published Report votes, we use the chief's assignment sheets, supplementary memoranda, and the docket books of those justices that are available to scholars. We are thereby enabled to determine the specific justices involved in all cases in which majority opinion assignments are made. These documents, then, enable us to resolve situations such as the following: a chief justice whom the Reports indicate specially concurred – that is, agreed with the majority's decision but not its opinion – may or may not have assigned the Court's opinion. If the justice who appears to have made the assignment joined the prevailing coalition after the conference vote, said justice would not have made the assignment. Similarly, a dissenting justice may have actually made the assignment because he was the senior member of the winning conference vote coalition.

Hence, we rely on the chief justice's assignment sheets and accompanying memos, which are distributed to each of the associate justices, to determine the opinion assigner.[11] These documents indicate that assigners occasionally make mistakes[12] and that the Court sometimes ignores its seniority rule. Thus, Justice White once informed Chief Justice Burger, "I appreciate the opportunity to see the light, but my notes show

[9] Palmer, *op. cit.*, n. 5, *supra*, p. 127.

[10] Quoted in David M. O'Brien, *Storm Center*, 2nd ed. (New York: Norton, 1990), p. 287.

[11] The assignment sheets are not completely errorless. Most egregious, perhaps, is the omission of the federal flag-burning case, *United States v. Eichman*, 496 U.S. 310 (1990).

[12] Justice Stewart justified his self-assignment of two opinions early in the 1976 term given "[his] dismal track record as an assigner." Memorandum to the chief justice, William J. Brennan's docket books, Library of Congress, Washington, October 8, 1976. As evidence of his self-declared ineptitude, Stewart's memo refers to *United States v. Glaxco Group Ltd.*, 410 U.S. 52 (1973), in which Justice White wrote the opinion for a six-member majority, with Stewart, Rehnquist, and Blackmun dissenting.

that I was in the minority. . . . Someone else should perhaps take this one."[13] As for deviations from the seniority rule, consider: Justice O'Connor self-assigned a case to herself even though only Scalia had less seniority.[14] With only Scalia and Kennedy junior, she self-assigned *Penry v. Lynaugh*, involving execution of the mentally retarded.[15] Justice Stevens, sixth in seniority, assigned *Tompkins v. Texas*;[16] Justice Blackmun, fifth in seniority, assigned the famous Christmas display case, *Allegheny County v. ACLU*;[17] and Justices Brennan and White jointly assigned *Missouri v. Jenkins*.[18]

Although the Reports identify the author of the Court's opinion, irregularities nonetheless occur. The aggregation and disaggregation of docket numbers complicates matters. A single assignment of two or three dockets may appear in the Reports as so many separate opinions. For example, the 1974 decisions *Pell v. Procunier*, *Procunier v. Hillery*, and *Saxbe v. Washington Post Co.*[19] ended as two separate opinions by Justice Stewart. Conversely, multiple assignments sometimes collapse into a single assignment. Companion cases, necessitating a single author, as well as separate citations, may also upset the distributional balance. For example, the four reapportionment cases that Warren assigned to himself on November 26, 1963, comprised one third of that day's total number of assignments. Per curiam assignments, which the assignment sheets separately identify, sometimes result in signed opinions, and vice-versa.[20]

As noted above, with a few scattered exceptions the chief justice assigns the Court's opinion when he is among the majority at the conference vote on the merits.[21] If he is not, the senior associate justice typically makes the assignment. The operation of this rule has meant that chief justices have assigned the great majority of the Court's opinions: Vinson 77 percent, Warren 80 percent, Burger 87 percent, and

[13] Memorandum to the chief justice, William J. Brennan's docket books, Library of Congress, Washington, November 16, 1976. The case referred to is *Ingraham v. Wright*, 430 U.S. 651 (1977).

[14] *Boos v. Barry*, 485 U.S. 312 (1988). [15] 492 U.S. 302 (1989).

[16] 490 U.S. 784 (1990). No opinion resulted because of a tied vote.

[17] 492 U.S. 573 (1989). [18] 495 U.S. 33 (1990).

[19] 417 U.S. 817, 417 U.S. 817, and 417 U.S. 843.

[20] E.g., *Fuller v. Oregon*, 417 U.S. 40 (1974); *Van Lare v. Hurley*, 421 U.S. 338 (1975); and *Vance v. Universal Amusement Co.*, 445 U.S. 308 (1980).

[21] E.g., Warren's assignment sheets report that Black assigned the opinion in six cases in which he and Warren were in the majority on the first assignment day, October 19, 1953, after Warren became chief justice.

Rehnquist 81 percent over the first five terms of his Court (1986–90).[22] The remaining percentage is divided among the two or three senior associate justices.[23]

Assignment Patterns

We start our analysis with a complete listing of all opinion assignments made during the Vinson, Warren, Burger, and the first five terms of the Rehnquist Courts. Tables 9.1–9.4 contain these data.

The most obvious feature of the tables is that, as noted, the chief justice makes most of the assignments. Burger's proportion exceeds his fellows because his assignment sheets identify the assigner and assignee in the orally argued per curiams. And inasmuch as these per curiams tend to be decided unanimously, the chief assigns them.

On the Vinson Court, Black, the senior associate, made almost all assignments Vinson did not, 17 percent. During the Warren Court, Black made proportionately far fewer assignments because he overwhelmingly

[22] These data are drawn from Chief Justice Vinson's and Warren's assignment sheets and supplementary memoranda, and Justice Brennan's copy of the assignment sheets provided him by Burger and Rehnquist. We have none beyond the 1990 term. Those we have include not only the original assignment, but also any subsequent ones that supplanted the original except for a second assignment by the same assigner to the same assignee. These we count as a single assignment. The data also include orally argued dockets that were decided per curiam. Not uncommonly, assignments are made in these cases. However, orally argued per curiams which specify no assignee are excluded from the data in Tables 9.1–9.4. Assignments are made by docket, with the assignment sheets noting those that the assigned justice was to treat as a single assignment. We count these as such. Because of sequential assignments in a given case, the total number of assignments exceeds the number of orally argued citations. The Vinson and Warren courts required 103 and 107 assignments, respectively, to produce 100 percent of their orally argued citations, the Burger and Rehnquist courts only 101 and 101, respectively. Thus, the Burger and Rehnquist courts rarely required a second assignment in a case, while the Warren Court most often did. These differences are misleading, however. The Burger Court typically identified the assignee in its orally argued per curiam cases; the Warren Court rarely did. Inasmuch as these cases are appreciably less complex than the signed opinion decisions, multiple assignments are rare, and thus increase the proportion of one assigner–one assignee cases. The Rehnquist Court's one-to-one relationship results from signed opinions rather than per curiams, however. Hence, we conclude that the Rehnquist Court is the most efficient of the four courts in this aspect of the decisional process.

[23] Palmer, *op. cit.*, n. 5, *supra*, p. 125; S. Sidney Ulmer, "The Use of Power on the Supreme Court: The Opinion Assignments of Earl Warren, 1953–1960," 30 *Journal of Public Law* 49 (1970), at 53; Harold J. Spaeth, "Distributive Justice: Majority Opinion Assignments in the Burger Court," 67 *Judicature* 299 (1984), at 301; Sue Davis, "Power on the Court: Chief Justice Rehnquist's Opinion Assignments," 74 *Judicature* 66 (1990).

TABLE 9.1. *Opinion Assignment in the Vinson Court*

Majority opinion writer	Majority opinion assigner					
	Vinson	Black	Reed	Frankfurter	Douglas	Total
Vinson	80					80
Black	88	33				121
Reed	64	11	11			86
Frankfurter	47	14	6	8		75
Douglas	81	20	5	2		108
Jackson	71	12	2	1		86
Burton	40	13	2	2	1	58
Minton	31	7	2	1		41
Clark	39	5	1	1		46
Murphy	25	12		1		38
Rutledge	23	6	1			30
TOTAL	589	133	30	16	1	769

TABLE 9.2. *Opinion Assignment in the Warren Court*

Majority opinion writer	Majority opinion assigner							
	Warren	Black	Reed	Frankfurter	Douglas	Clark	Harlan	Total
Warren	178[a]	2[b]						185
Black	159	28						187
Reed	15	3	16					34
Frankfurter	50	4	7	30				91
Douglas	176	13		4	2			195
Jackson	2	1	4					7
Burton	25	3	4	5				37
Minton	18	5						23
Clark	133	12	3	21	2	7		178
Harlan	106	20	5	24	2	3	2	162
Brennan	139	5	2	9	4	5	2	166
White	38	3		6				47
Stewart	107	13		18	2	2		142
White	75	9			1	1	1	87
Goldberg	39	3			1	1		44
Fortas	42	1			2		1	46
Marshall	22	1					1	24
TOTAL	1328	127	41	117	16	19	7	1655

[a] Plus four opinions assigned by Warren, but assignee unspecified.

[b] Plus one opinion assigned by Black, but assignee unspecified. Black also assigned two opinions delegated to him by Warren.

TABLE 9.3. *Opinion Assignment in the Burger Court*

Majority opinion writer	Majority opinion assigner								
	Burger	Black	Douglas	Brennan	Stewart	White	Marshall	Blackmun	Total
Burger	289[a]								289
Black	18	12							30
Douglas	65	4	13						83[b]
Harlan	20	2	2						24
Brennan	162	1	23	85					271
Stewart	173	1	11	11	10				206
White	270	2	7	11	2	7			299
Marshall	227	1	3	16	2		1		250
Blackmun	197		2	25	1		1	1	227
Powell	229		6	13	2	1			251
Rehnquist	251		3	6	3		1		264
Stevens	144			12	4	1	1		162
O'Connor				2		4			6
TOTAL	2045	23	70	181	24	13	4	1	2362[c]

[a] Includes five assignments to a "write team" in a set of death penalty cases.
[b] Includes a "conference" assignment.
[c] Includes an assignment jointly made by Burger and Brennan.

TABLE 9.4. *Opinion Assignment in the Rehnquist Court, 1986–1990 Terms*

Majority opinion writer	Majority opinion assigner							
	Rehnquist	Brennan	White	O'Connor	Stewart	Marshall	Blackmun	Total
Rehnquist	85							85
Brennan	26	39						65
White	75	7	8					90
Marshall	57	13						70
Blackmun	48	15				1	2	66
Powell	18	2						20
Stevens	63	10	2		1			76
O'Connor	73	3	2	3				81
Scalia	58	7	2					67
Kennedy	37	6	4					47
Souter	7							7
TOTAL	547	102	18	3	1	1	2	676[a]

[a] Includes two joint assignments: Brennan-White and Rehnquist-Marshall.

sided with Warren on the merits. Felix Frankfurter, who was fourth in seniority (including the chief justice) through 1957 and third until his retirement in 1962, assigned 117 opinions during his nine Warren Court terms, only ten less than Black, who served as senior associate during the entirety of the Warren Court. These patterns, limited though they be, emphatically establish justice ideology as the explanatory variable. Black proportionately assigned more than twice as many opinions on the Vinson Court than he did on the Warren Court because his quasiliberalism put him in agreement with Warren on almost all matters other than civil rights. But when the conservative Vinson dissented, Black almost never did.

Note also that Black preferred, other than himself and Douglas, conservative and nonliberal assignees: Harlan, Stewart, Clark, and White. This further evidences that when Warren dissented, Black found himself in coalitions comprised of the nonliberal members of the Court. Most of these assignments occurred in the latter half of the Warren Court when civil rights became a major component of the Court's agenda.

Although Frankfurter was fourth in seniority during all of the Vinson Court and for all but the last four years of his tenure, he assigned seven times as many opinions on the Warren Court as he did on the Vinson Court (117 vs. 16). This resulted because when Vinson was not part of the majority, neither was Frankfurter. On the early Warren Court, when Black was aligned with the chief, Frankfurter was the senior conservative after Reed's retirement in February 1957 and made the assignments in conservatively decided cases thereafter in which Warren and Black dissented.

Brennan, fourth in seniority at the start of the Burger Court, assigned an appreciably higher number of cases than any other justice on this Court. His elders, Black and Douglas, served only two and six years, respectively. On the Rehnquist Court, he assigned a higher percentage of cases than any associate justice (15) since Black on the Vinson Court (17).

Unlike the chief justices, who retained for themselves between 13 and 16 percent of the opinions, the senior associates, except for Douglas, had a penchant to self-assign. While retaining only 13 and 19 percent on the Warren and Burger courts, Douglas assigned approximately twice his retained portion to Brennan. Other than Douglas, only Black on the Warren Court exercised restraint in this regard (22 percent). But he self-assigned more than half of his 23 Burger Court opinions and almost a quarter on the Vinson Court. At the other extreme, Brennan self-assigned

85 of 181 Burger Court opinions and 39 of 102 during his four years on the Rehnquist Court. Reed, 11 of 30 and 16 of 41 on the first two Courts; Frankfurter, eight of 16 and 30 of 117. On the Warren Court, Clark self-assigned seven of 19; Harlan, two of seven. On the Burger Court, Stewart kept 10 of 24; White, seven of 13; Marshall, one of four; and Blackmun, one of one. On the Rehnquist Court, White retained eight of 18, while the other four assigners kept all seven of their opinions for their respective selves. Needless to say, self-assignment by these associate justices means that in those cases, they will have added influence over the Court's policy output.

Eight of the thirteen justices on the Burger Court made opinion assignments, including one unlikely assignment by Blackmun, who at the time was fifth in seniority.[24] Douglas assigned more than any other associate (70) until his resignation in 1975; Brennan thereafter made virtually every associate assignment until his retirement at the end of the 1989 term. In less than 1 percent of all cases did Douglas or Brennan dissent along with Burger.

Equality

An unwritten rule of the Court decrees that each justice should receive an equal share (one ninth) of the Court's opinions, deviation from which apparently produces disharmony.[25] As Chief Justice Warren phrased it:

> I do believe that if [assigning opinions] wasn't done . . . with fairness, it could well lead to gross disruption in the Court. . . . During all the years I was there . . . I did try very hard to see that we had an equal work load.[26]

The equality to which the norm refers is absolute equality, not that which is conditioned on the frequency with which any given justice is a member of the conference vote coalition. Thus, if justice A is available for assignment in fifty cases and justice B in twenty-five, and A receives the assignment in ten and B in five, equality would not result even though the frequency with which they were assigned opinions when members of the conference vote coalition was identical: 1 in 5.

[24] In *Williams v. United States*, 458 U.S. 279 (1982).

[25] Alpheus T. Mason, *Harlan Fiske Stone: Pillar of the Law* (New York: Viking, 1956), pp. 602–3, 793; Nina Totenberg, "Behind the Marble, Beneath the Robes," *New York Times Magazine*, March 16, 1975, pp. 64–65.

[26] Anthony Lewis, "A Talk with Warren on Crime, the Court, the Country," *New York Times Magazine*, October 19, 1969, p. 130.

Efforts to achieve an equal apportionment of opinions among the justices are more complicated than the literature indicates.[27] Although the chief justice assigns the vast majority of the opinions, equal distribution also depends on the behavior of the senior associate justices.

> With respect to the assignments, it is a particularly difficult matter at this time of the year, since it is the last opportunity to strike a balance for all the Brethren. For that reason, in those cases in which I am in the majority, I will not undertake to make the assignments until after all the other cases are decided in Conference.[28]

A memo by a petulant Burger further documents the matter: "Just as I was about to send the current assignments out, I received Bill Brennan's assignment of cases. This requires me to do a total and complete revision, and it will not be out today."[29]

Vote changes in the aftermath of the conference also make equitable assignment difficult. In reference to several cases with uncast votes, Burger wrote: "I am not in a position to make these final assignments until all votes are firmly in hand. Even one change has a 'domino' impact on all other assignments – especially at this time of the Term."[30]

Although previous work has used the term of the Court as the unit of analysis to determine the number of assignments made to each justice,[31] we focus on the point where the assigner controls selection: the periodic assignment days – typically, eight per term – at which the chief justice compiles an "assignment sheet" that lists the docket number of the case and the names of the assigning and the assigned justice. Scattered assignments – usually a day or two later – are combined with those of the proximate assignment day. Use of assignment day as our measure of equality in the distribution of opinions has one shortcoming: the two or three opinions per term that are assigned weeks removed from a regular assignment day. We exclude such cases from our analysis simply

[27] *Op. cit.*, n. 6, *supra*; Spaeth, *op. cit.*, n. 23, *supra*; and Elliot E. Slotnick, "Who Speaks for the Court? Majority Opinion Assignment from Taft to Burger," 23 *American Journal of Political Science* 60 (1979).

[28] Memorandum of Burger to W. O. Douglas, William J. Brennan's Assignment Books, Library of Congress, Washington, April 25, 1974.

[29] Memorandum to the Conference, William J. Brennan's Assignment Books, Library of Congress, Washington, April 4, 1977.

[30] Memorandum to the Conference, William J. Brennan's Assignment Books, Library of Congress, Washington, April 28, 1978.

[31] *Op. cit.*, n. 23, *supra*. The remainder of this section and the following one are based on Sara C. Benesh, Reginald S. Sheehan, and Harold J. Spaeth, "Equity in Supreme Court Opinion Assignment," 39 *Jurimetrics* 377 (1999).

because they are not part of our unit of analysis. Consider *Lefkowitz v. Newsome*,[32] which Douglas assigned to Stewart on December 30, 1974. The next assignment day did not occur until January 27, 1975. Omission of such cases from analysis skews our results away from distributional equality. In the *Lefkowitz* situation, Stewart was the only underassigned justice on the assignment day following his receipt of *Lefkowitz*.

The number of assignments made per assignment day typically ranges from ten to twenty and includes those made by associate justices as well as the chief. They are otherwise uncontaminated by events beyond the chief's control. Retention of an opinion obviously depends on the assignee's continued membership in the majority vote coalition. If he or she departs, a new assignment is made to one of the members of the new coalition. However, analysis has shown that the original assignee retains the opinion almost 60 percent of the time – at least on the Warren Court.[33] When a reassignment occurs within three days of the original assignment, we disregard the first one. Reassignments made more than three days later we count separately. Only 4 percent of all assignments in the forty-one terms we analyze (1950–90) fall into this category (116).

Assignments are made during the week in which oral argument occurs. We measure equality of opinion distribution by dividing the total number of assignments (A), excluding those assigned as per curiam opinions, by the number of participating justices (J). Only one apportionment achieves equal distribution regardless of the number of participating justices:

$$A/J = ErX$$

where X is the remainder resulting from the division of A by J. If X = 0, each justice receives the same number of assignments. A justice whose assignments do not fit perfectly into this pattern is scored as deviating by that number. Thus, assume thirteen opinions are distributed among nine justices as follows: A = 4; B, C, and D = 2; E, F, and G = 1; and H and I = 0. A, H, and I are deviant; A is overassigned by two cases and H and I underassigned by one, since the most equitable division of

[32] 420 U.S. 283 (1975).

[33] Saul Brenner and Harold J. Spaeth, "Majority Opinion Assignments and the Maintenance of the Original Coalition on the Warren Court," 32 *American Journal of Political Science* 72 (1988).

TABLE 9.5. *Deviation of Assignments per Assignment Day from Distributional Equality, by Term*

	Deviation from mode						
Term	**0**	**1**	**2**	**3**	**4**	**% 0**	***N***
Vinson Court							
1950	48	12	3			76.2	63
1951	59	11	1	1		81.9	72
1952	60	11	1	–		83.3	72
TOTAL	167	34	5	1		80.7	207
Warren Court							
1953	74	6	1			91.4	81
1954	41	11	6			70.7	58
1955	62	18	1			76.5	81
1956	61	19	2			74.4	82
1957	68	19	3			75.6	90
1958	67	11	3			82.7	81
1959	64	12	5			79.0	81
1960	46	28	7			56.8	81
1961	47	8	3			81.0	58
1962	55	13	4			76.4	72
1963	81	6	2	1		90.0	90
1964	51	18	2	1		70.8	72
1965	45	22	5			62.5	72
1966	39	19	5			61.9	63
1967	43	16	4			68.3	63
1968	47	12	4	–		74.6	63
TOTAL	891	238	57	2		75.2	1,188
Burger Court							
1969	67	14	7			76.1	88
1970	45	18	9			62.5	72
1971	47	17	7	2		64.4	73
1972	46	15	2			73.0	63
1973	64	8				88.9	72
1974	51	7	1			86.4	59
1975	47	12		1		78.3	60
1976	49	11	3			77.8	63
1977	58	11	3			80.6	72
1978	60	2				96.8	62
1979	48	14	1			76.2	63
1980	64	6	2			88.9	72
1981	66	5	1			91.7	72
1982	57	13	2			79.2	72
1983	49	11	3			77.8	63

Term	Deviation from mode					% 0	*N*
	0	1	2	3	4		
1984	57	10	3			81.4	70
1985	51	15	6			70.8	72
TOTAL	926	189	50	3		79.3	1,168
Rehnquist Court							
1986	59	2	2			93.7	63
1987	67					100.0	67
1988	72					100.0	72
1989	61	2				96.8	63
1990	57	5	1			90.5	63
TOTAL	316	9	3			96.3	328
GRAND TOTAL	2,300	470	115	6		79.6	2,891

Sources: Benesh et al., *op.cit.* fn. 31, *supra*, pp. 382–84.

thirteen among nine recipients is for five to receive one and four to receive two.

Table 9.5 lists by term the deviation from perfect equality that each assignment day during that term produced.[34] Thus, the 1950 term shows that of the 63 assignments made, 48 were equally apportioned on the relevant assignment day, 12 assignments deviated from equality by one assignment (six on the first assignment day, and four on the fifth), and three assignments deviated from equality by two assignments (all on the second assignment day, along with the other two single deviation assignments). Accordingly, 76 percent of the term's assignments were equally distributed.

Over the 41 terms displayed in Table 9.5, a remarkable level of distributional equality results, notwithstanding the conditions – specified above – portending inequality: 2,300 of 2,891 assignments (80 percent) reflect equal distribution; 471 deviated from equity by a single assignment (16 percent). Thus, less than 5 percent of all assignments deviated from parity by more than a single assignment. At the opposite extreme, only six assignments deviated from the pertinent day's equal distribution

[34] Because of their unavailability, we lack assignment sheets for the first four terms of the Vinson Court and the post-1990 terms of the Rehnquist Court.

by three assignments (0.2 percent), with an additional 115 deviating by two (4.0 percent).

Most equitable are the first five terms of the Rehnquist Court, a somewhat surprising result, given the contentiousness that afflicted it during this time.[35] Over 96 percent of its assignments met distributional equality. Three adjacent terms, 1987–89, beat the other 38, two at 100 percent equity. Only nine of its 328 assignments deviated from equality by a single assignment; three by two. The other Courts diverge but little from one another in equity: Vinson, 81; Burger, 79; and Warren, 75. In only six terms (four Warren, two Burger) did assigners achieve less than 70 percent equality.

No correlation exists between deviation and the number of assignments made on any given day. Few assignments, as well as days with more than twenty, produce equally disproportionate deviations, and vice-versa. Neither do deviations increase as the end of the term nears. Approximately as many terms show an increase in end-of-term deviations as show fewer. Nor does the number of assignments made at the end of the term increase. Assignments made at the final two assignment days of the three Vinson Court terms numbered barely half those of the overall term average. On the Warren and Rehnquist Courts, end-of-term assignments slightly exceed the term average, with the Burger Court the opposite. Clearly, neither of these end-of-term variables produces a systematically significant effect.[36]

In sum, the equalization of opinion assignments demonstrates the operation of organizational goals in one crucial aspect of the Court's decisions.[37] Yet, as we see below, the maintenance of organizational goals does not necessarily preclude the simultaneous attainment of policy goals.

Ideology

Determining the distribution of opinions by assignment day does not preclude assigners from favoring certain of their colleagues. They may give ideological confreres the more important or salient cases and, when

[35] William Lazarus, *Closed Chambers* (New York: Times Books, 1998).

[36] The term-by-term breakdown of these data may be found in Benesh et al., *op. cit.*, n. 31, *supra*, pp. 385–86.

[37] See, most notably, Lawrence Baum, *The Puzzle of Judicial Behavior* (Ann Arbor: University of Michigan Press, 1997).

TABLE 9.6. *Cumulative Number of Deviations from the Most Equal Distribution of Assignments per Assignment Day per Justice per Term*

	Court			
Justice	**Vinson**	**Warren**	**Burger**	**Rehnquist**
Black	3.33 [10/3]	0.25 [4/16]	3.50 [7/2]	
Blackmun			–0.75 [–12/16]	–1.00 [–5/5]
Brennan		0.00 [0/13]	–0.35 [–6/17]	1.20 [5/4]
Burger			0.76 [13/17]	
Burton	–2.33 [–7/3]	–2.60 [–13/5]		
Clark	–0.33 [–1/3]	1.43 [20/14]		
Douglas	1.67 [5/3]	1.13 [18/16]	–1.29 [–7/5.43]	
Fortas		–0.75 [–3/4]		
Frankfurter	–1.33 [–4/3]	–0.22 [–2/9]		
Goldberg		–1.00 [–3/3]		
Harlan		–0.46 [–7/15]	–0.50 [10/2]	
Jackson	–1.00 [–3/3]	1.00 [1/1]		
Kennedy				–0.59 [–2/3.4]
Marshall		0.50 [1/2]	–0.59 [–10/17]	0.00 [0/5]
Minton	–1.00 [–3/3]	–2.33 [–7/3]		
O'Connor			0.20 [1/5]	1.80 [9/5]
Powell			0.76 [11/14.5]	4.00 [4/1]
Reed	0.67 [2/3]	–0.86 [–3/3.5]		
Rehnquist			1.72 [25/14.5]	0.80 [4/5]
Scalia				0.00 [0/5]
Souter				–3.00 [–3/1]
Stevens			–0.48 [–5/10.5]	0.80 [4/5]
Stewart		–0.18 [–2/11]	0.83 [10/12]	
Vinson	–0.67 [–2/3]			
Warren		–0.69 [–11/16]		
White		–0.42 [–3/7.14]	1.53 [26/17]	3.40 [17/5]
Whittaker		–1.60 [–8/5]		

Source: Benesh et al., *op. cit.*, fn. 31, *supra*, p. 387.

X > 0, the remainder may be assigned to justices attitudinally aligned with the assigner.

Table 9.6 addresses this possibility. To determine which, if any, of the justices were over- or underassigned during a given term, we separately summed the assignments (*j*) made each justice (*i*), the difference between the most equitable division of assignments (*E*) and the number actually made (*A*):

$$\sum_{ij}(E_{ij} - A_{ij})$$

As an example, on the eleven assignment days during the first term of the Burger Court in 1969–70, Justice Marshall received the most equitable number on five days, fell one below on three, one above on two, and two above on one, for a net of one extra assignment.[38] Following this procedure for each of the sixteen other terms of the Burger Court – on all of which Marshall served – produces a net of −10 assignments for the seventeen terms, an average of −0.59 per term.

The contents of Table 9.6 reveal that the overall distribution of assignments among the justices does not vary much, which comes as no surprise given the equity displayed in Table 9.5. Least variant are the Vinson and Warren Courts. Only four of the nine Vinson Court justices deviated by more than a single assignment per term, along with five of the sixteen Warren Court justices. Moreover, the Vinson-Warren imbalance, such as it is, occurs randomly, but not that of the Burger and Rehnquist Courts.

Specifically, the two liberals on the later Vinson Court – Black and Douglas – were favored, +3.33 and +1.67, respectively. Black's imbalance largely resulted from self-assignment. Least favored was Burton (−2.33), very likely because he was a sluggish writer.[39] Vinson neither favored himself nor his fellow conservatives: Minton, Clark, Jackson, and Frankfurter. Except for Black, Burton, and Douglas, term deviation never exceeded a per term average of 1.33. These assignment patterns appear random, that is, non-strategic.

So also the Warren Court. Three briefly serving justices appear most deviant: Whittaker, Minton, and Burton. Minton's underassignments all occurred in his final term and may have resulted from the lengthy illness that forced his retirement.[40] Burton again was least favored, being underassigned thirteen opinions. Whittaker, who retired on his physician's advice after five terms on the Court, averaged 1.6 opinions less than the norm per term. No other justice was underassigned more than one opinion per term. Warren behaved the same as Vinson, underassigning himself at −0.69, Vinson at −0.67. Most favored were Clark at +1.43

[38] Previous research has relied on the coefficient of relative deviation (CRV), which divides the standard deviation by the mean in order to control for the total number of opinions in a term. E.g., assume the standard deviation in each of two terms was 1.1. Further assume that the mean in one was 14, twice the mean of the other. The CRV for the term with a mean of 14 is more equal than one whose mean is 7. We do not use the CRV because, given our approach, CRV is superfluous.

[39] William O. Douglas, *The Court Years* (New York: Vintage Books, 1980), pp. 247–48.

[40] N. E. H. Hull, "Minton, Sherman," in K. L. Hall, ed., *The Oxford Companion to the Supreme Court of the United States* (New York: Oxford University Press, 1992), p. 552.

and Douglas at +1.13. Given that Clark was ideologically most distant from Warren on most, if not quite all, issues dealing with freedom and equality, the treatment accorded him does not comport with the liberal orientation of Warren's Court. Clark, though, was in fact underassigned in civil liberties, but overassigned in economics cases, where he was ideologically close to Warren.[41] Not only did Warren not favor himself, neither did the senior associate, Black, appreciably do so: +0.25. Other liberals also received less than equitable treatment: Brennan, 0.00; Fortas, −0.75; and Goldberg, −1.00. By contrast, some of the nonliberals were less disfavored: Frankfurter, −0.22; White, −0.42; and Harlan, −0.46.

Randomness, however, does not characterize the assignments of the Burger and Rehnquist Courts. The resulting patterning evidences a definite ideological orientation: Conservatives were favored, liberals disfavored. Thus, the five reputed liberals on the Burger Court all received negative scores, notwithstanding that two of them functioned as the senior associate: Douglas (1970–74 terms), −1.29; and Brennan (1975–85 terms), −0.35. Joining them were Marshall at −0.59, who was underassigned four opinions in the 1971 and 1983 terms and three in 1984; Stevens, −0.48; and Blackmun, −0.75. Blackmun fell into disfavor once he separated himself from Burger, his Minnesota twin. He was underassigned two opinions in the 1982 and 1983 terms and four in 1985. By contrast, the conservatives all received more than their share, except Harlan, who served only two years on the Burger Court during which time he received one less opinion than equity decreed.

Burger preferred himself, +0.76; Stewart and Powell were similarly favored: +0.83 and +0.76, respectively. Most advantaged – other than Black, who served only two years – were White (+1.53) and Rehnquist (+1.72).

These findings withstand multivariate scrutiny. Controlling for a host of other factors, Burger was more likely to assign to those ideologically closest to him.[42]

Like his conservative predecessor, Rehnquist also preferred his ideological allies, but did so while achieving almost perfect equity during his first five terms: a deviation of only 0.3, with two terms perfectly equitable. He most advantaged White (+3.40), providing him with four extra

[41] Gregory Rathjen, "Policy Goals, Strategic Choice and Majority Opinion Assignment: A Replication," 18 *American Journal of Political Science* 714 (1974).

[42] *Op. cit.*, n. 31, *supra*, pp. 388–89.

assignments in three successive terms (1986–88), two in 1989, and three in 1990. Rehnquist's behavior reciprocated that of Burger, who favored Rehnquist most, followed by White. Rehnquist also overassigned to O'Connor (+1.80) and himself (+0.80). Surprisingly, perhaps, he did not overassign to either Scalia (0.0) or Kennedy (–0.59). On the other hand, Stevens did better than expected (+0.80), while Marshall could have anticipated less than his share rather than perfect equity. Brennan received a decidedly positive score (+1.20), but only because of self-assignment.

Complicating Factors

Although the remarkably equal distribution of opinions that the Court has achieved between 1950 and 1990 may suggest that apportionment is an easy task, decided complexity exists.

The chief justice, responsible for an overwhelming proportion of the assignments, must be ever alert to the assignment practices of the senior associates who will typically locate at the other end of the Court's ideological spectrum. If they do not, then, like Black on the Warren Court (see Table 9.2), their alignment with the chief will substantially decrease their assignment opportunities. As Tables 9.1–9.4 indicate, the senior associate justices grossly self-assign, Douglas alone excepted. Such behavior impedes the attainment of equality.

Absent the norm of equal distribution, the assigning justice would be expected to assign opinions disproportionately to himself or to the justice whose policy preferences most closely approximated his own, thereby insuring congruence between his preferences and the contents of the majority opinion. As we have noted, associate justices do just that. But chiefs are markedly more constrained inasmuch as the responsibility for equal distribution rests far more heavily on their shoulders.

Another complicating factor is the variant frequency with which the individual justices find themselves in the majority vote coalition. Douglas, for example, was a member of Burger's majority vote coalition less than 50 percent of the time (in 303 of 613 cases), while White was available for a Burger assignment in almost 90 percent of the cases during the first twelve terms of the Burger Court (1,126 of 1,279 occasions).[43] Thus, though infrequent membership in majority vote coalitions does not preclude attainment of equal distribution, it certainly exacerbates the

[43] Spaeth, *op. cit.*, n. 23, *supra*, p. 301.

assigner's task. Similarly, ideological distance makes assignment a bit more difficult, but it does not preclude achievement of absolute equality, if a chief justice is so inclined.

A final factor that may occasionally limit equal assignments is the tendency to give fewer assignments to newcomers. From 1950 through 1990, of the eleven justices who either began their service with the start of a term or took their seat sufficiently late so that no opinions were assigned to them until their first full term (i.e., Stewart and Blackmun), only one received extra assignments: Brennan in the 1956 term, and then only one more than equity decreed. Of the other ten, Clark and Minton each received one less in the 1950 term; Goldberg, Fortas, Blackmun, O'Connor, and Scalia, two less; and Souter, three less. Stewart and Marshall were treated completely equitably. As for the two chiefs, Warren took only an equal share, while Burger took an extra opinion.

Important Cases

Within the goal of equality of assignment, assigners are free – and the chief justice is expected – to retain important cases for themselves.[44] This guarantees that in these cases the opinion will conform as closely as possible to the chief's personal policy preferences. Arguably, all the Court's cases are important inasmuch as they are culled from the 8,000 or so petitions that the Court annually receives and which at least four of the justices have agreed warrant review and decision. Nonetheless, external indicators may be employed to enable analysts to establish degrees of importance. We use two such indicators: citation in either the Congressional Quarterly's *Guide to the U.S. Supreme Court* or *The Supreme Court Compendium*.[45] We begin with the Vinson and Warren Courts, as we have assignment sheet and docket book records that provide direct evidence of who assigned which cases to whom.

Of the 32 Vinson Court cases that our sources list, Vinson assigned 26 (81 percent), a proportion 5 percent higher than his assignments overall. He self-assigned 10 of these 26 (39 percent), a rate almost three

[44] Slotnick, "The Chief Justices and Self-Assignment of Majority Opinions," 31 *Political Research Quarterly* 219 (1978), p. 225. David W. Rohde, "Policy Goals, Strategic Choice and Majority Opinion Assignments in the U.S. Supreme Court," 16 *American Journal of Political Science* 652 (1972), at 656–57.

[45] Elder Witt, ed., 2nd ed. (Washington: Congressional Quarterly, 1990), pp. 906–15. Lee Epstein, Jeffrey A. Segal, Harold J. Spaeth, and Thomas G. Walker, *The Supreme Court Compendium* (Washington: Congressional Quarterly, 1994), pp. 81–99.

times as high as his self-assignments overall (14 percent: 80 of 589). He distributed the remainder fairly evenly: from four to one among nine of his eleven colleagues. By comparison, Warren assigned 87 percent of his Court's "important" cases, some 6 percent higher than his assignments overall. Unlike Vinson, he retained only 18 of 84 (21 percent), a rate that nevertheless is more than 50 percent higher than his overall proportion of 14 (182 of 1,328).

Markedly less equity characterized Warren's assignments to his colleagues in important cases. Brennan received the most, 14, followed by Stewart with 10, and Black and Douglas with 9 and 8, respectively. The Court's most conservative member, Harlan, received only five of these cases, even though he sat for all but the Court's first two terms. Clark, almost as ideologically far from Warren as Harlan except on economic issues, also received five cases, though he sat for all but the Court's last two terms. The moderate White got one during his seven-plus terms, while the liberals, Goldberg and his successor, Fortas, who together served a few months less than White, each got four.

Using other measures, analyses of the Burger and early Rehnquist Courts produce similar findings.[46] The chiefs prefer to self-assign important cases to themselves, while disproportionately bestowing others on their ideological kin. Opponents are disadvantaged.[47]

Issue Specialization

Another consideration that impacts opinion assignments is the disproportionate assignment of certain types of cases to specific justices. One may credibly demur that disproportionate assignment amounts to issue specialization. Given the norm of equal distribution and assigners' policy preferences, it makes perfect sense to assign unattractive cases to one's ideological opponents. Hence, Marshall found himself on the Burger Court writing the Court's opinion in essentially unanimous low-salience Indian cases, Blackmun in those construing the language of the Internal Revenue Code.[48] Conversely, assigners prefer colleagues who share a

[46] The findings for Burger more or less hold up under Maltzman's and Wahlbeck's (*op. cit.*, n. 6, *supra*) multivariate analysis. Specifically, Burger tends to overassign in politically important cases, though not in legally important cases.

[47] Spaeth, *op. cit.*, n. 23, *supra;* Davis, *op. cit.*, n. 23, *supra.*

[48] Saul Brenner, "Issue Specialization as a Variable in Opinion Assignment," 46 *Journal of Politics* 1217 (1984); Saul Brenner and Harold J. Spaeth, "Issue Specialization in Majority Opinion Assignment on the Burger Court," 39 *Political Research Quarterly* 520 (1986).

similar vision on issues deemed important, for example, civil rights and liberties or criminal procedure. To characterize such justices as specialists seems a misnomer; better to describe them neutrally as "frequent authors."

Unlike self-assignment in important cases, the concentrated bestowal of opinions on certain subjects to specific justices does not characterize the assignment patterns of all chief justices. Palmer reports that Hughes, Stone, and Vinson did not allow it.[49] But it apparently did occur on the Warren and Burger Courts.[50]

"Issue specialization" seems to serve three important purposes. Given its work load, the division of labor that frequent authorship allows may increase the Court's productivity. Some areas of the law are complex – for example, tax, energy, transportation – and efficiency may warrant assignment of the Court's opinions to a specific justice. However, rarely does the specialist write more than half the opinions, even when he or she is a regular member of the majority coalition.[51] Second, certain justices may prefer to write on certain subjects. Third, specialization may facilitate the development of judicial expertise, which enhances the credibility and legitimacy of the Court's decisions.[52]

Despite claims that Warren expressly disapproved of issue specialization,[53] analysis of the Warren Court's civil liberties decisions shows that in approximately two thirds of the narrowly defined issues into which civil liberties are divided, a particular justice wrote the Court's opinion significantly more frequently than any of his colleagues. The specialists, moreover, were justices who attitudinally positioned themselves close to Warren, who made most of the assignments.[54] Thus, for example, Brennan frequently authored First Amendment, right to counsel, and discovery and inspection cases; Douglas courts-martial and indigents. A more inclusive study of the 1969–83 terms of the Burger Court displayed similar results. In 63 percent of the civil liberties issues and in 62 percent of those that did not concern civil liberties, at least one justice wrote sufficiently frequently to qualify as a frequent author. As on the Warren Court, the Burger Court's civil liberties' authors are the ideological allies

[49] *Op. cit.*, n. 5, *supra*, p. 125.

[50] On the Burger Court, see Maltzman and Wahlbeck, *op. cit.*, n. 6, *supra*, p. 48.

[51] Brenner and Spaeth, *op. cit.*, n. 48, *supra*, pp. 525–27.

[52] Burton Atkins, "Opinion Assignment on the United States Courts of Appeal: The Question of Issue Specialization," 27 *Political Research Quarterly* 409 (1974).

[53] David M. O'Brien, *Storm Center* (New York: Norton, 1986), p. 246.

[54] Brenner, *op. cit.*, n. 48, *supra*.

of the chief justice, for example, Rehnquist in double jeopardy and confrontation, Powell in commercial speech and attorneys' fees, White in jury trial and reapportionment. In areas of arguably less substantive importance, justices attitudinally distant from Burger – Douglas (judicial review of agency action), Brennan (arbitration and priority of federal fiscal claims), and Marshall (state jurisdiction over Indians and non-governmental tort liability) – emerged as "specialists."[55]

This research seems to indicate that the achievement of equal distribution does not preclude opinion assigners from realizing their personal policy preferences. The chief justice can overassign to ideological clones, knowing that his opponents will get more than their share of cases assigned by associate justices. Further, by disproportionately retaining the important cases, opinion assigners insure maximum congruence between enunciated policy and their personal preferences. The existence of frequent authors in the highly salient area of civil liberties who are attitudinally aligned with the chief justice further enables him to correlate equal distribution and the realization of his own policy preferences. On the other hand, the appearance of specialists in only two thirds of the issues into which the Court's decisions are apportioned suggests that division of labor, the presumed desire of a justice to write on certain subjects, and the development of expertise sufficient to enhance the credibility and legitimacy of the Court's decisions are secondary objectives, at best.[56]

While policy goals safely coexist with organizational constraints in opinion assignments, the extent to which formal, rational choice theories will add to our understanding of opinion assignment is still unclear. Spiller, working under the questionable assumption that the majority opinion necessarily represents only the views of the median justice (see Chapter 11), argues that opinion assignment is thus a chore that justices would rather avoid, rather than an opportunity to make

[55] Brenner and Spaeth, *op. cit.*, n. 48, *supra*.

[56] Two other factors appear to have had some limited impact on opinion assignment: perceived competence and the time justices take to write majority opinions. A study of competence found that of the 32 justices who served between 1921 and 1967, those whom law professors considered less competent received fewer assignments. Saul Brenner, "Is Competence Related to Majority Opinion Assignment on the United States Supreme Court?," 15 *Capital University Law Review* 35 (1985). With regard to time, an analysis of the Vinson Court's opinion assigners showed them to be partial to those who wrote most quickly. Saul Brenner and Jan Palmer, "The Time Taken to Write Majority Opinions as a Determinant of Opinion Assignments," 72 *Judicature* 179 (1988). Also see Palmer, *op. cit.*, n. 5, *supra*, pp. 132–49.

policy.[57] Hammond et al. suggest a series of spatially based opinion-assignment hypotheses, but these have not yet been tested.[58]

OPINION ASSIGNMENTS AND OPINION COALITIONS

The Court delivers an opinion only if a majority agrees on an explanation for its decision. If less than a majority do so, then the plurality view becomes a "judgment" of the Court, not an "opinion," and lacks precedential value. For example, in *Houchins v. KQED*,[59] four of the seven participating justices voted to reverse an appellate court ruling granting the press expansive rights to investigate prison conditions. The three-member plurality declared that the press has no special access to prisons. The three dissenters argued that the media have such entrance under the First Amendment. Justice Stewart's special concurrence regarded the lower court's ruling as too broad, but nevertheless upheld limited access. Hence, the plurality's view of no special access lacked a majority and has no authoritative bearing on future decisions. Because a majority opinion usually depends on the approval of the marginal (usually fifth) justice, he or she receives a greater share of assignments.[60]

Thus, David Danelski asserts that "the selection of the Court's spokesman may be instrumental in . . . holding the . . . majority together in a close case," and that the assignment of the opinion to the justice "whose views are closest to the dissenters" might increase the size of the majority.[61] Unfortunately, both assertions are false.

With regard to the former, inspection of the minimum winning coalitions on the Warren Court shows that though the marginal justice – the one attitudinally closest to the dissenters on the narrowly based

[57] Pablo T. Spiller, "Review of *The Choices Justices Make*," 94 *American Political Science Review* 943 (2000).

[58] Thomas H. Hammond, Chris W. Bonneau, and Reginald S. Sheehan, "Toward a Rational Choice Spatial Model of Supreme Court Decision Making: Making Sense of Certiorari, the Original Vote on the Merits, Opinion Assignment, Coalition Formation and Maintenance, and the Final Vote on the Choice of Legal Doctrine," paper presented at the 1999 meeting of the American Political Science Association, Atlanta, Ga.

[59] 438 U.S. 1 (1978).

[60] David W. Rohde and Harold J. Spaeth, *Supreme Court Decision Making* (San Francisco: W. H. Freeman, 1976), ch. 8.

[61] "The Influence of the Chief Justice in the Decisional Process," in Sheldon Goldman and Austin Sarat, eds., *American Court Systems* (San Francisco: W. H. Freeman, 1978), p. 514; in Walter F. Murphy and C. Herman Pritchett, eds., *Courts, Judges, and Politics*, 4th ed. (New York: Random House, 1986), p. 574. Murphy and Howard, *op. cit.*, n. 7, *supra*, essentially make the same allegations.

cumulative scale to which the case pertains – was hugely advantaged in the number of assignments received (more than twice the random expectation), his selection did not increase the probability that the coalition would survive.[62] Neither self-assignment nor assignment to the justice in the middle of the conference coalition enhanced its preservation. "Apparently, whenever a justice decided to leave the original coalition, he did so, and the fact that he had been assigned to author the majority opinion did not forestall his defection."[63]

With regard to the latter of Danelski's assertions that we quoted above – assignment so as to increase the size of either the final vote or the final opinion coalition – analysis of the Warren Court shows that the marginal justice's authorship of the Court's opinion does not increase the size of either coalition.[64]

If the justice attitudinally closest to the dissenters cannot increase the size of minimum winning decisional coalitions when assigned to write the opinion of the Court, why then is this justice so disproportionately favored with assignments?

First, the probability that the majority opinion will have to be reassigned to another justice because the conference vote coalition breaks up is lessened. Breakups occur when the vote coalition shifts from affirm to reverse, or the converse. The reassignment of the opinion obviously takes time and slows the Court's productive process.[65] Research, however, has shown that once assigned the Court's opinion, the marginal member of the vote coalition retains it, regardless of whether or not the coalition breaks up. But when nonmarginal members receive the assignment, they are much less likely to retain it when the coalition breaks up.[66]

Other considerations that may cause assigners to favor the marginal justice include an opinion of moderate content that should help retain

[62] Brenner and Spaeth, *op. cit.*, n. 33, *supra*. This study used conference vote data from the justices' docket books to determine the membership of the original (conference) vote coalition.

So, too, as conference size becomes minimum winning, Burger was much less likely to assign to those ideologically close to him. See Maltzman and Wahlbeck, *op. cit.*, n. 6, *supra*, p. 48.

[63] Brenner and Spaeth, *id.*, p. 80.

[64] Saul Brenner, Timothy M. Hagle, and Harold J. Spaeth, "Increasing the Size of Minimum Winning Coalitions on the Warren Court," 23 *Polity* 309 (1990). This study also utilized the justices' docket books to ascertain membership in the final conference vote coalition.

[65] Saul Brenner, "Reassigning the Majority Opinion on the United States Supreme Court," 11 *Justice System Journal* 186 (1986).

[66] Brenner and Spaeth, *op. cit.*, n. 33, *supra*, p. 78.

support for the Court's position in future cases. Tension may also be reduced between the majority and minority.[67] And because the marginal justice is attitudinally closer to the minority than any other member of the majority, assigning the opinion to this justice may keep the original coalition intact.

One may ask why assignment to the marginal justice does not attract those who dissented at the conference vote. The answer seems to be that the main task of assignees, whether they are marginal or not, is to write an opinion that garners the votes of the other members of the original vote coalition. This job is especially important in the minimum winning situation. It does not make sense to attempt to satisfy justices who voted the other way at the final conference vote when such attempts might cause one or more of the original majority to refuse to join the Court's opinion.[68]

OPINION COALITIONS

In arriving at their decisions, the individual justices are free actors in two separate senses. First, they may vote as they see fit: either as a member of the majority vote coalition or in dissent. Second, except for the opinion of the Court, the justices may write such opinions as they desire to explain their individual votes. As a consequence, a justice may be a member of a particular voting coalition, but not a member of the opinion coalition that supports that vote. For example, a justice may specially concur by agreeing with the disposition the Court makes of the case, while disagreeing with the reasons the majority gives for its disposition. We preface our discussion of opinion coalitions with a systematic listing of the nine voting and opinion options available to the justices.

Voting and Opinion Options

1. A justice may be assigned to write the opinion of the Court. As noted in our discussion of opinion assignment, a justice does not freely decide to write the opinion of the Court, with the possible exception of the assigning justice.

[67] William P. McLauchlan, "Ideology and Conflict in Supreme Court Opinion Assignment, 1946–1962," 25 *Political Research Quarterly* 16 (1972), at 26.

[68] Brenner, Hagle, and Spaeth, *op. cit.*, n. 64, *supra*, p. 318.

2. A justice who is assigned to write the opinion of the Court fails to get a majority of the participating justices to agree with the contents of the opinion. In which case, the justice's opinion becomes a "judgment of the Court." Because only a plurality instead of a majority of the participating justices join it, the opinion – unlike an opinion of the Court – lacks precedential value.

3. A justice may be a voiceless member of the majority (or plurality) vote and opinion coalitions, that is, the justice writes no opinion, but simply agrees with the opinion or judgment of the Court.

4. A justice may write an opinion notwithstanding membership in the majority or plurality opinion coalition. Such an opinion is a regular concurrence. It manifests itself only by the writing of an opinion or the joining of one written by another justice. Absent the writing or joining of such an opinion, the justice has exercised option 3, willy-nilly.

5. A justice may agree with the disposition made by the majority or plurality, but disagree with the reasons contained in its opinion. Unlike a regular concurrence, this option may occur with or without opinion. At least one justice must cast such a special concurrence to produce a judgment of the Court.

6. A justice may dissent. Like a special concurrence, a dissent may be coupled with an opinion. A dissent indicates that the justice in question disagrees with the disposition that the majority has made of the case.

7. A justice may dissent from a denial or a dismissal of certiorari, or from the summary affirmation of an appeal. Such votes, plus any accompanying opinion that a justice may see fit to write, pertain only to cases that the Court refuses to hear and decide.

8. A justice may render a jurisdictional dissent, which, like the preceding action, may or may not be accompanied with an opinion. This type of dissent disagrees with the Court's assertion of jurisdiction or with the Court's failure to afford the parties time for oral argument.

9. Finally, a justice may refuse to participate in a case. The justices most commonly recuse themselves because of illness. Other reasons, which the justices exercise at their own discretion, include previous involvement in a case or with a party thereto. Thus, justices promoted from a lower court will not participate in cases in which they previously voted. Justices will typically recuse themselves if they hold stock in a company before the Court. Because he served as Solicitor General before he was appointed to the Court, Justice Marshall recused himself from all of the cases in which his office had represented the United States. For this and perhaps other reasons, he failed to participate in 98 of the 171

TABLE 9.7. *Behavioral Options Exercised by the Rehnquist Court Justices, 1986–1998 Terms*

	Behavior[a]							
Justice	1	2	3	4	5	6	7	8
Blackmun	9.3	0.3	51.2	4.0	8.7	25.5	0.3	0.7
Brennan	10.9	0.6	46.3	3.7	6.4	31.0	0.1	0.9
Breyer	9.1	1.3	56.8	8.1	5.1	18.2	0.2	1.3
Ginsburg	10.8	0	59.3	6.6	5.1	17.8	0.2	0.2
Kennedy	9.8	0.2	66.0	5.3	5.5	8.0	0	5.3
Marshall	9.6	0.4	48.2	2.5	5.8	32.9	0.2	0.4
O'Connor	11.3	0.8	59.5	6.2	6.1	14.7	0.1	1.4
Powell	12.6	0.5	68.1	5.8	2.1	9.9	0	1.0
Rehnquist	11.4	0.2	68.0	1.6	2.7	15.9	0	0.2
Scalia	9.7	0.2	55.6	5.9	10.3	16.8	0.2	1.2
Souter	9.9	0.3	64.1	5.7	4.2	14.2	0.2	1.3
Stevens	10.1	0.7	48.9	4.6	7.9	27.1	0.2	0.6
Thomas	8.7	0.1	55.2	5.7	8.3	18.8	0.1	3.0
White	12.3	0.6	66.0	2.4	4.7	13.4	0.1	0.6

[a] 1: opinion of the Court; 2: judgment of the Court; 3: member, majority or plurality coalition; 4: regular concurrence; 5: special concurrence; 6: dissent; 7: dissent from certiorari denial or jurisdictional dissent; 8: nonparticipation.

docketed cases that were formally decided during the 1967 term (57 percent).

The frequency with which the justices engaged in these behaviors during the first thirteen terms of the Rehnquist Court (1986–98) is displayed in Table 9.7. The unit of analysis in this table is orally argued docketed cases, excluding decrees.[69] The rare single docket that required more than one vote to decide are also included.[70]

The table shows that silent membership in the majority vote coalition is by far the most common action of each of the justices, accounting for 58 percent of the total. Brennan and Marshall so behaved the least, 46 and 48 percent, respectively; Powell and Rehnquist, the most. Not surprisingly, ideological closeness to both the opinion writer and the

[69] Decrees typically ratify, automatically and without any named justice authoring an opinion, the report of the special master whom the justices chose to hear a dispute that arose under the Court's original jurisdiction.

[70] E.g., *Denver Area Educational Television v. FCC*, 518 U.S. 727 (1996); *Allentown Mack Sales v. FCC*, 522 U.S. 359 (1998).

emerging opinion coalition dramatically add to the likelihood that a justice will join the majority.[71] Marshall and Brennan, the Court's liberals, lead in proportion of dissents, with 33 and 31 percent, followed by Stevens (27 percent) and Blackmun (26 percent). Kennedy locates at the other extreme, with 8.0 percent, almost two points lower than the next justice, Powell.

Although commentators now accept the propriety of judicial dissent,[72] many disapprove of concurrences as unnecessary nitpicking.[73] Most culpable from this point of view is Scalia, 10 percent of whose votes are special concurrences. Blackmun and Thomas follow, with 8.7 and 8.3 percent, respectively. The two Clinton justices, Breyer and Ginsburg, lead in proportion of regular concurrences at 8.1 and 6.6 percent, respectively. The chief justice set the best example by far among frequently participating justices, casting only 1.6 and 2.7 percent of his votes as regular and special concurrences. This percentage is also markedly lower than Rehnquist's percentage during his tenure as an associate justice, suggesting a special level of institutional concern for the chief justice.[74]

Note should be made of how infrequently the justices recuse themselves. It is likely that the Rehnquist Court has an appreciably better record in this regard than any of its predecessors. Kennedy alone accounts for almost 38 percent of the total (75 of 198). This largely results because he took his seat midway through the 1987 term after many cases had been argued, thus requiring his recusal. By comparison, seven of the other twelve justices recused themselves less than 1 percent of the time.

The other behaviors account for markedly less than 1 percent of the justices' votes (judgment of the Court and the two types of jurisdictional dissent). Indeed, collectively they amount to only half a percent of their total votes.

Not surprisingly, the coalition behavior of the justices depends in substantial part on their policy preferences. Those who join the majority opinion are ideologically closer to the opinion writer than those who

[71] Maltzman and Wahlbeck, *op. cit.*, n. 6, *supra.*

[72] Thomas G. Walker, Lee Epstein, and William Dixon, "On the Mysterious Demise of Consensual Norms in the United States Supreme Court," 50 *Journal of Politics* 361 (1988).

[73] E.g., Robert W. Bennett, "A Dissent on Dissent," 74 *Judicature* (1991), 255–60.

[74] Ellen R. Baik, "Distinguishing Chief: An Analysis of Justice Rehnquist, 1971–1997 Terms," paper presented at the 2000 meeting of the Midwest Political Science Association, Washington, D.C.

write regular concurrences; regular concurrers, in turn, are ideologically closer to the majority opinion writer than special concurrers; and to complete the picture, special concurrers are ideologically closer to the majority opinion writer than are justices who dissent.[75] We further examine the politics of coalition formation below.

THE POLITICS OF COALITION FORMATION

Substantively, among the most important decisions a justice makes is whether or not to join the majority opinion coalition. If fewer than a majority of the justices do so, judgments of the Court result, precluding an authoritative resolution of the controversy at issue.

To a markedly greater extent than earlier Courts, the Burger and Rehnquist justices have failed to produce opinions of the Court to explain their decisions and guide affected publics and lower courts in the resolution of all similar cases. Typically, the number of judgments is not large – 4.2 percent of the Burger Court's signed opinions and 3.3 percent of those of the Rehnquist Court during its first thirteen terms (1986–98) – as opinion writers often attempt to accommodate conference coalition members.[76] Nevertheless, these figures compare unfavorably with the Warren Court's 2.3 percent.[77]

[75] Chad Westerland, "Attitudes and Institutions: Understanding Opinion Writing Behavior on the U.S. Supreme Court," typescript, SUNY Stony Brook, 2001.

[76] Lee Epstein and Jack Knight, *The Choices Justices Make* (Washington, D.C.: Congressional Quarterly, 1998), ch. 3; and Maltzman, Spriggs, and Wahlbeck, *op. cit.*, n. 6, *supra*, ch. 4.

[77] For analytical purposes, we consider all orally argued signed opinion cases using docket number, rather than case citation, as the unit of analysis.

We scrupulously define a judgment according to the Court's own language. Though only a small part of the prevailing opinion may comprise the "opinion of the Court," we exclude the case from consideration. Thus, the convoluted statement in *Arizona v. Fulminante*, 499 U.S. 279 (1991), at 281 constitutes an opinion, not a judgment:

> WHITE, J., delivered an opinion, Parts I, II, and IV of which are for the Court, and filed a dissenting opinion in Part III. MARSHALL, BLACKMUN AND STEVENS, JJ. joined Parts I, II, III, and IV of that opinion; SCALIA, J., joined Parts I and II; and KENNEDY, J., joined parts I and IV. REHNQUIST, C.J., delivered an opinion, Part II of which is for the Court, and filed a dissenting opinion in Parts I and III, *post*, p. 302. O'CONNOR, J., joined Parts I, II and III of that opinion; KENNEDY and SOUTER, JJ., joined Parts I and II; and SCALIA, J., joined Parts II and III. KENNEDY, J., filed an opinion concurring in the judgment, *post*, p. 313.

Although this is an extremely cumbrous example, by no means is it *sui generis* for either opinions or judgments of the Court.

The vast majority of these cases concern civil rights and liberties: 85 percent of the Burger Court's and 80 percent of the Rehnquist Court's (as compared with 57 and 54 percent of the cases decided by an opinion of the Court). Almost 41 percent of the Burger Court's judgments concern criminal procedure, with an additional 16 percent pertaining to the First Amendment. Both of these proportions approximately double the percentage of cases decided by an opinion of the Court. On the Rehnquist Court, the proportion of the judgments accounted for by First Amendment and due process cases each comprised two and a half times the proportion decided by an opinion of the Court. This rather clearly indicates that judgments occur in cases the justices deem highly salient. Supporting their importance is the inordinate number of opinions they contain, an average of 4.5 in the Burger Court and 4.0 in the Rehnquist Court.

The justices' behavior indicates that they vote their attitudes – their personal policy preferences – in cases decided by a judgment with at least as much regularity as they do overall. What characterizes these cases is the unusual amount of overt conflict they engender – an inability to compromise and resolve differences. An appropriate focus, therefore, from which to analyze these cases is conflict of interest theory.[78] Although we do not formally apply the theory here, we do focus on the three key actors who – given the Court's rule structures – bear most responsibility for judgments: justices who specially concur, the justice assigned to write the opinion of the Court, and the opinion assigner. Thus, failure to form a majority opinion coalition may result because the policy preferences of one or more of the members of the majority vote coalition are insufficiently satisfied, resulting in a special concurrence. Conversely, the fault may lie with the opinion assignee who fails to bargain effectively because he or she gives primacy to his or her own policy preferences, or, alternatively, the opinion assigner may have selected an assignee unable to effect the necessary compromises.

Special Concurrences

Although the frequency with which the justices specially concurred varies little relative to the number of times each held membership in majority

78 See Robert Axelrod, *Conflict of Interest* (Chicago: Markham, 1970). David W. Rohde applied conflict of interest theory to the formation of majority opinion coalitions in the civil liberties decisions of the Warren Court. See "Policy Goals and Opinion Coalitions in the U.S. Supreme Court," 16 *American Journal of Political Science* 208 (1972).

vote coalitions, frequencies tell us nothing about the cruciality of a justice's special concurrences insofar as the preclusion of a majority opinion coalition is concerned. Clearly, a justice who specially concurs when the Court splits between a four-member plurality and an equal number of dissenters more crucially affects the formation of the majority opinion coalition than a justice who is one of several special concurrers, only one of whom is needed to form a majority opinion coalition.

What we need, therefore, is a measure that will specify the cruciality of each special concurrence to the preclusion of a majority opinion. Such a measure may readily be formulated. Simply divide the number of special concurrences into the number of votes needed to form a majority opinion coalition in a given case. Thus, if the plurality opinion coalition contains four votes, and four justices dissent, the specially concurring justice receives a score of 1. Similarly, if the plurality has three members, while three others specially concur, only two of their votes are needed. Cruciality thus becomes 0.67. This measure may range from 1.00 to 0.20. The latter obtains in a case where a four-member plurality confronts five special concurrers.[79]

Table 9.8 displays the application of this measure to the special concurrences cast in the 157 cases decided by a judgment of the Court during the 1969–98 terms. Viewed solely from the standpoint of each justice's special concurrences on the preclusion of a majority opinion coalition, the measure may be labeled the culpability index. Except for Ginsburg and Breyer, the two briefest-serving justices – each of whom cast only one special concurrence – we deem the measure indicative of the extent to which each justice allows his or her policy preferences to ride roughshod over judicial norms supporting cohesion and the enunciation of binding policy.

Not much differentiation occurs among the justices. Apart from Ginsburg and Breyer, with their single special concurrence, Douglas appears the most culpable, with a ratio of 0.92. The other sixteen justices

[79] E.g., *Texas v. Brown*, 460 U.S. 730 (1983). Other unanimous decisions, though containing concurrences with slightly greater weight, are *United States v. Mandujano*, 425 U.S. 564 (1976), and *McDaniel v. Paty*, 435 U.S. 618 (1978), both decided 8 to 0, with four special concurrences; *Ballew v. Georgia*, 435 U.S. 223 (1978), in which a two-member plurality was arrayed against seven special concurrences written by three different justices; and *Burnham v. California Superior Court*, 495 U.S. 604 (1990), in which a three-member plurality confronted six special concurrences written again by three different justices.

TABLE 9.8. *Culpability Index*

Justice	Number of special concurrences	Weight
Breyer	1	1.00
Ginsburg	1	1.00
Douglas	8	0.92
Black	7	0.75
Powell	17	0.74
Scalia	21	0.73
Harlan	10	0.73
White	33	0.72
Rehnquist	21	0.69
Burger	21	0.68
O'Connor	25	0.67
Stevens	22	0.66
Stewart	17	0.66
Blackmun	43	0.65
Brennan	38	0.61
Souter	5	0.60
Kennedy	11	0.60
Marshall	29	0.59
Thomas	12	0.58

collectively occupy a space of only 0.17 points. We may consider those scoring in the mid- to upper 0.60s less culpable than those above them, with those between the low 0.60s and upper 0.50s the least culpable. Coupling the small variance in the justices' scores with the unpatterned ideological order suggests that attitudinal considerations have little to do with the justices' behavior. More likely are individual personality characteristics.

Opinion Assignees

Although the foregoing results provide an indication of responsibility for the Court's failure to produce opinions of the Court, we should also assess the behavior of the other actors in the process: the assignees and their assigners. Assignees may bear responsibility because they may bargain ineffectively or because they may disregard the preferences of one or more of the members of the majority vote coalition. On the other hand, as Table 9.8 shows, the justices do vary – albeit slightly – in the

TABLE 9.9. *Assignee Difficulty in Cases Resulting in Judgments of the Court as Measured by the Culpability Scores of Special Concurrers*

Justice	Number of assignments	Difficulty
Marshall	4	0.799
Scalia	4	0.727
Blackmun	12	0.708
Black	7	0.696
Stewart	10	0.686
Brennan	18	0.685
Burger	11	0.669
Stevens	20	0.667
Powell	14	0.667
O'Connor	10	0.665
Rehnquist	15	0.660
Harlan	1	0.650
Souter	3	0.647
Kennedy	3	0.639
White	21	0.625
Thomas	1	0.603
Breyer	3	0.592

Note: Douglas and Ginsburg wrote no judgments of the Court.

extent to which they are willing to subordinate their views in the interests of institutional loyalty. Moreover, institutional considerations matter. Overall, opinion writers are more willing to accommodate when they are ideologically distant from the conference majority, when the conference majority is ideologically heterogeneous, and when the conference coalition is minimum winning.[80] Hence, the task of a given assignee may correspondingly vary depending on the members and number of members in the majority vote coalition. Table 9.9 contains an index that specifies the degree of difficulty assignees faced in their unsuccessful efforts to write an opinion of the Court.

In calculating this index, we used the culpability scores of Table 9.8. If only a single justice precluded formation of a majority opinion, that justice's culpability score indicates the difficulty the assignee had in arriving at an opinion of the Court in that case. Where several justices

[80] Maltzman, Spriggs, and Wahlbeck, *op. cit.*, n. 6, *supra*, ch. 4.

specially concurred, we total their culpability scores and divide by their number in order to specify the difficulty the assignee had in producing the Court's opinion. The score for each assignee's cases is totaled and divided by the number of assignments made to that justice.

Among the seventeen Burger and Rehnquist Court justices whose assignments failed to produce an opinion of the Court, Marshall faced the greatest difficulty in forming a majority, followed at some distance by Scalia and Blackmun. Given that Marshall was among the least culpable among special concurrers, we judge his inability to generate opinions of the Court to result from his dependence on stubborn special concurrers. Inspection of his assignments indicates this to be the case: Douglas, the most culpable of the frequent special concurrers, made Marshall's task difficult. Scalia, however, seems to be his own worst enemy. His high score on the culpability index suggests an unwillingness to accommodate the views of the members of his vote coalitions. Blackmun's difficulties in forming majority opinion coalitions occurred on the Burger rather than the Rehnquist Court, a result perhaps of his shift from an initially staunch conservative to a liberal moderate by the end of the Burger Court. At the other extreme, Thomas with his single judgment and Breyer with his three had the easiest task in holding their original vote coalitions. From an absolute standpoint, of course, Douglas and Ginsburg were the most effective assignees: During their six terms, they invariably produced an opinion, rather than a judgment, of the Court. Given Douglas's position as the most intransigent justice on our culpability index (Table 9.8), this finding is surprising.

The bulk of the justices (11) vary but little from one another, occupying a space of only 0.57 points on Table 9.9. The two chief justices locate in the middle of this group, a mere 9 points apart. Inasmuch as no chief can be assignee without simultaneously being the opinion assigner, their rank likely results as much from their abilities as assigners as from their ability to hold a vote coalition together.

Opinion Assigners

To complete the picture, we investigate the performance of opinion assigners. We add Jan Palmer's Vinson Court data, which includes all data since its start in 1946, to our own. This enables us to complete our set of the chief justice's assignment sheets, which date only to 1950.[81] As

[81] *Op. cit.*, n. 5, *supra*, pp. 163–285.

TABLE 9.10. *Proportion of Majority Opinion Coalitions Achieved by Assigners, 1946–1990 Terms*

Justice	Number of assignments made	Number of judgments of the Court	Proportion of majority opinions
White	13	0	100.0
Harlan	7	0	100.0
Blackmun	2	0	100.0
Frankfurter	131	2	98.5
Warren	1,328	25	98.1
Vinson	589	16	97.3
Reed	71	2	97.2
Burger	2,045	75	96.3
Rehnquist	547.5	22.5	95.9
Clark	19	1	94.7
Douglas	87	5	94.3
Black	273	20	92.7
Brennan	283	22	91.9
Stewart	24	2	91.7
Marshall	4.5	0.5	88.9
O'Connor	3	1	66.7
Stevens	1	1	0.0

Note: Includes one Rehnquist-Marshall and two Burger-Brennan joint assignments.

we noted previously, the four chief justices made the vast majority of the assignments, followed by Brennan, the senior associate for the fifteen terms following Douglas's retirement in 1975, and Black, the senior associate on the Vinson and Warren Courts. These six justices account for 93 percent of the 195 judgments handed down during this time, as Table 9.10 indicates.

Very little difference exists among the justices who made more than a dozen assignments. Ratios of opinions to judgments exceed 95 percent for seven of these twelve justices. The five immediately below 95 percent all comfortably surpass 90 percent. Notwithstanding these high proportions, we consider whether self-assignment or the failure of the assigning justice to join the resulting coalition may have impacted assigners' effectiveness.

First, among the six leading assigners, both Black and Brennan self-assigned more than two and three times the proportion of their cases that resulted in judgments – 45 and 61 percent, respectively – than the

TABLE 9.11. *Frequency with Which Assigners Failed to Join the Final Vote Coalition*

Justice	Number of assignments	Number of unjoined coalitions	%
Clark	1	1	100
Marshall	1[a]	1	100
Douglas	5	3	60.0
Reed	2	1	50.0
Burger	76[a]	28	36.8
Black	20	7	35.0
Brennan	23[a]	7	30.4
Rehnquist	23[a]	6	26.1
Vinson	15	3	20.0
Warren	25	3	12.0

[a] Split assignments counted as one.

highest chief: Warren at 20 percent. Rehnquist was the lowest at 8.9 percent, followed by Burger (17) and Vinson (19). We may therefore conclude that Black and Brennan might have enhanced their low assigner rank if they had eschewed their proclivity for self-assignment.

Second, one may expect an assigner to join the opinion of his assignee. The justices, however, shatter this expectation by failing to do so almost 30 percent of the time. Among the six major assigners, Burger has the worst record, 37 percent, followed by Black and Brennan at 35 and 30 percent, respectively. Rehnquist (26), Vinson (20), and Warren (12) are least culpable (see Table 9.11).

Although the Court's rule structures badly skew assigner data, they nonetheless clearly show that performance is lessened when assigners either disproportionately self-assign or remove themselves from the plurality opinion coalition by specially concurring. Indeed, 107 of the 197 judgments that the Court produced between the 1946 and 1990 terms were characterized by one or the other of these two types of behavior. Disproportionately responsible were Burger and the two long-serving senior associates, Black and Brennan.

PATTERNS OF INTERAGREEMENT

Although the joining of the majority opinion coalition provides a possible basis for identifying who agrees and disagrees with whom, the extent to which individual justices join one another in their special opinions (regular and special concurrences, and jurisdictional and regular dissents) comprises a much richer source of information about judicial relationships. We focus on these opinions here because, as noted above, the justices are completely free actors insofar as concurrences and dissents are concerned. That is, no justice can be forced to or prevented from concurring or dissenting, nor can any justice be required to or prevented from joining a special opinion of another justice. This, of course, is not true of opinions and judgments of the Court. To the extent that the justices value the opportunity to write the Court's opinion, the opinion assigner possesses something akin to a coercive instrument, as do other members of the opinion coalition, especially when the coalition is minimum winning in size: One or more may withdraw from the coalition, thus precluding formation of a majority opinion.[82]

The writing and joining of special opinions bespeak an ability to persuade or convince another of the correctness of one's position in that case. Such an effect occurs without the use of coercion, authority, or political control. As such, it constitutes what Webster defines as "influence,"[83] and as such is distinct from the related construct of power, which does involve the use of coercion, authority, or control.[84] Note also that the writing and joining of special opinions occur in a context in which side payments are not made. That is, justices do not do something to induce others to do something they would not otherwise do. The fact that a justice may be motivated to write a special opinion for reasons other than to exert influence – to curry favor with a segment of the public, to enhance one's reputation, or to express disapproval of certain conduct – does not gainsay the absence of side payments. We view influence as an effect, not as a motivation. As a result, concurrences and dissents reflect the strongly held policy views of their authors. And because those who join such opinions may be said to be "persuaded" – or at least

[82] We could have divided each justice's special opinions between concurrences and dissents and analyzed them separately. We chose not to do so because no theoretical reasons support one rather than the other as a vehicle for the expression of personal policy preferences. Suffice it to say that the justices write dissents much more often than they do concurrences, except for Scalia and Kennedy, as the data in Table 9.7 indicate.

[83] *Webster's Seventh New Collegiate Dictionary* (Springfield, Mass.: G. and C. Merriam, 1972), p. 433.

[84] See Michael F. Altfeld and Harold J. Spaeth, "Measuring Influence on the U.S. Supreme Court," 24 *Jurimetrics* (1984), 236–47; and Bernard Schwartz, *Super Chief: Earl Warren and His Supreme Court* (New York: New York University Press, 1983), pp. 302–3, 352–53, 381, 437, 719–20.

accepting – of the correctness of the positions they espouse, one may, given our operationalization, easily infer who is influencing whom.

In what follows, we focus on the patterns of interagreement that occur in the justices' special opinions as a form of influence. Such a focus warrants comparing each justice with his and her colleagues. We begin by paralleling the frequency with which each justice joins another's special opinions – that is, dissents and concurrences – and the frequency with which other justices join such opinions of the authoring justice.

Table 9.12 presents these data for the first thirteen terms of the Rehnquist Court. The rows represent the frequency with which the named justice functioned as a joinee, or a joiner of the opinions of another justice. The columns represent the frequency with which the various justices joined the opinions of the named justice. Thus, Marshall joined Brennan's special opinions 90 times, Stevens's 53 times, and Rehnquist's not at all. Conversely, Brennan joined Marshall only half as frequently (44 times) as Marshall joined him. Stevens joined Marshall only 23 times, while Rehnquist reciprocated Marshall's failure to join him. The bold-faced entries specify the number of special opinions each justice wrote during the first thirteen terms of the Rehnquist Court. The figure at the foot of each column indicates the number of joiners each justice got per authored special opinion. This number can theoretically range from 0.0 to 4.0. The former indicates a situation where no one ever joined the authoring justice, while a range exceeding 4.0 is not possible, because beyond that point a special opinion becomes an opinion of the Court.

Table 9.12 presents several interesting results. First, very little interagreement occurs. Brennan got the most, a mere 1.5 votes per opinion; Rehnquist slightly less (1.44). At the other extreme, Stevens on average got 0.81 votes per opinion, Thomas 0.84. Brennan's high rank totally depends on Marshall's willingness to join him; he provided Brennan with 90 of his 164 "joins." Thomas would have fared even worse without Scalia, who joined him 33 times; his other nine colleagues did so on only 40 occasions. And if we also exclude Rehnquist, the other eight joined him only 22 times. An even more extreme pattern afflicts Marshall and Brennan: White, O'Connor, and Scalia joined Marshall only once; Souter, Powell, Kennedy, and Rehnquist not at all. Brennan obtained three joins from White, two from O'Connor, and one from Kennedy, and none at all from Powell, Rehnquist, and Scalia.

The table also shows that the interagreement that does occur tends to be among like-minded individuals. Thus, for example, the liberal

TABLE 9.12. *Interagreement in Special Opinions, 1986–1998 Terms*

Justice	Marshall	Brennan	Blackmun	Stevens	Ginsburg	Breyer	Souter	White	O'Connor	Powell	Kennedy	Rehnquist	Scalia	Thomas
Marshall	**72**	90	46	53	–[a]	–	1	10	5	2	3	0	9	–
Brennan	44	**111**	39	33	–	–	–	6	6	3	1	0	6	–
Blackmun	29	43	**160**	71	5	–	14	21	15	1	9	9	9	2
Stevens	23	25	31	**347**	16	13	25	18	17	1	9	5	9	4
Ginsburg	–	–	1	24	**62**	13	17	–	3	–	6	1	5	2
Breyer	–	–	–	18	12	**55**	15	–	9	–	3	1	2	2
Souter	0	–	9	20	17	12	**89**	3	15	–	11	5	10	2
White	1	3	2	17	–	–	5	**109**	7	1	7	18	14	0
O'Connor	1	2	15	19	2	11	7	17	**185**	9	19	23	37	7
Powell	0	0	2	0	–	–	–	3	4	**18**	–	1	1	–
Kennedy	0	1	2	5	2	1	2	7	16	–	**125**	10	37	3
Rehnquist	0	0	2	9	5	2	5	26	34	5	24	**80**	50	18
Scalia	1	0	2	7	1	2	5	11	35	2	22	23	**288**	33
Thomas	–	–	1	5	0	1	4	1	19	–	8	19	71	**87**
Joiners/ opinion	1.38	1.49	0.95	0.81	0.97	1.00	1.12	1.13	1.00	1.33	0.98	1.44	0.90	0.84

[a] –: not on the Court together.

Note: Rows represent the frequency with which the named justice functioned as a joinee: a joiner of the opinions of another justice; columns represent the frequency with which the various justices joined the opinions of the named justice; bold-faced entries specify the number of special opinions each justice wrote.

Marshall joined his fellow liberal, Brennan, and the next two justices ideologically closest to him – Blackmun and Stevens – 189 times, but joined the other seven justices with whom he served a grand total of only 30 times. The Court's conservatives behaved reciprocally, joining their ideological neighbors – Thomas, Scalia, Rehnquist, Kennedy, Powell, O'Connor, and White – much more frequently than they did the other justices. Thus, Scalia joined O'Connor, Thomas, Rehnquist, and Kennedy 113 times, the remaining justices only 31 times. Thomas joined O'Connor, Scalia, and Rehnquist 109 times, the others with whom he served only 20.

It seems reasonably clear, therefore, that the justices exert little influence on one another, except for those with whom they most commonly vote. Bloc voting, accordingly, results. And bloc voting arguably results from like-mindedness, not influence.

Our earlier research indicates that the pattern displayed by the Rehnquist Court does not appreciably deviate from its predecessors.[85]

The rules specified in the preceding footnote produce 1,821 Warren Court cases that contain 2,251 special opinions (1,475 dissents and 776 concurrences), an average of 1.24 special opinions per case. For the Burger Court, there are 2,440 cases which contain 3,698 special opinions (2,191 dissents, 1,507 concurrences), an average of 1.52 per case. For the first thirteen terms of the Rehnquist Court, there are 1,553 cases with 1,788 special opinions (963 dissents, 825 concurrences), an average of 1.14 per case. While the frequency of special opinions has remained relatively stable across the three Courts, it is interesting to note a steady increase from one Court to the next in the proportion of concurring opinions at the expense of dissents: from 34.5 to 40.8 to 45.5.

[85] Jeffrey A. Segal and Harold J. Spaeth, *The Supreme Court and the Attitudinal Model* (New York, Cambridge University Press, 1993), pp. 281–82. We defined a special opinion as we did in Table 9.8: an author's specification of the reason for his or her vote. A mere citation of a precedent or a simple statement that the author supports the rationale of the court below suffices. Joint authorship counts as an opinion for each author. (No jointly written opinions have occurred in any formally decided Rehnquist Court case to date.) Where a justice states that the opinion governs an additional case or cases, it is multiply counted. E.g., Brennan's and Marshall's opinions in *Mobile v. Bolden*, 446 U.S. 55 (1980), also apply to *Williams v. Brown*, 446 U.S. 236 (1980). The unit of analysis is the same as before: orally argued cases by citation, excluding tied votes and decrees. As we did with the Rehnquist Court, a small handful of Warren and Burger Court cases in which one or more of the justices concurred in some of the majority's holdings and dissented in others was counted compatibly with the smallest whole number necessary to account for the variant behavior of the justices involved.

Is there something about judicial conservatives that causes them to haggle about the details of opinions that support conservatively decided outcomes?

Who "Influences" Whom?

Previous efforts to measure influence have indicated that the construct is best captured by focusing on the behavior of particularized individuals.[86] Because influence may be one-sided or mutual, a measure that centers on pairs of justices needs to be formulated. Accordingly, we consider the number of times each justice joins a given author's special opinions as a percentage of the number of opportunities that the justice has to join. Thus, if A joins B in 10 of 20 opportunities, while C joins B in 15 of 45, A's ratio is 0.5 and C's is 0.33. The use of opportunities automatically corrects for justices who were not on the Court for the full period under analysis and also for recusals by sitting justices. To assess the mutuality of the pairwise relationship, we calculate the number of times B joined each colleague's special opinions as a percentage of B's opportunities to do so. Extending the preceding example, assume B joined A 45 percent of the time and joined C 10 percent of the time. We would characterize the A-B relationship as mutual, and that of B-C as one-sided, with B influencing C but not vice-versa.

Table 9.13 presents these data. The columns represent the influencer, the rows the influencee. The blank entries indicate pairs of justices who never served together. The entry at the bottom of each justice's column specifies the average pairwise relationship for each justice: the proportion of the time the other justices who served with the columnar justice joined the author's special opinions.

Several interrelated results emerge from this table. First, the mean percentage with which any justice joined another is quite low overall. Highest are Marshall's 38.3 percent with the like-minded Brennan and Thomas's 31.0 percent with the like-minded Scalia. Next highest is Marshall's 19.3 percent with Blackmun. Of the total of 152 pairs displayed on Table 9.13, only 33 exceed 10 percent. Six justices agree with Stevens above this level, and four with Ginsburg and Scalia. By contrast, among the seven conservative justices (the rightmost), only Scalia garners a 10 percent level of agreement with four justices.

[86] Michael F. Altfeld and Harold J. Spaeth, "Measuring Influence on the U.S. Supreme Court," 24 *Jurimetrics Journal* (1984), 236–47.

TABLE 9.13. *Dyadic Influence Matrix, 1986–1998 Terms*

Special opinion joiner	Special opinion writer													
	Marshall	Brennan	Blackmun	Stevens	Ginsburg	Breyer	Souter	White	O'Connor	Powell	Kennedy	Rehnquist	Scalia	Thomas
Marshall		38.3	19.3	18.9	–[a]	–	0.2	7.3	1.8	3.2	3.4	0.0	3.2	–
Brennan	18.7		16.6	14.0	–	–	–	2.6	2.6	4.6	0.6	0.0	2.6	–
Blackmun	12.2	18.3		19.0	12.5	–	8.0	6.3	4.0	1.9	2.8	2.4	2.4	1.5
Stevens	8.2	10.6	8.3		11.4	10.6	13.1	9.9	4.8	0.0	4.2	1.9	2.0	1.4
Ginsburg	–	–	2.5	17.1		9.8	12.1	–	2.1	–	4.3	0.7	3.6	1.4
Breyer	–	–	–	14.6	10.6		12.2	–	7.3	–	2.4	0.8	1.6	1.6
Souter	0.0	–	5.1	10.5	12.1	9.8		4.4	7.7	–	7.2	3.4	3.7	1.0
White	0.7	1.3	0.9	9.4	–	–	7.4		3.9	2.9	4.9	9.9	7.7	0.0
O'Connor	0.4	0.9	4.0	5.3	1.4	8.9	3.6	9.4		17.3	8.8	6.5	10.6	4.0
Powell	0.0	0.0	3.8	3.6	–	–	–	8.6	7.7		–	3.6	3.6	–
Kennedy	0.0	0.6	0.6	2.3	1.4	0.8	1.3	4.9	7.4	–		4.6	17.1	2.3
Rehnquist	0.0	0.0	0.5	3.4	3.6	1.6	3.4	14.4	9.6	17.9	11.9		18.6	13.8
Scalia	0.4	0.0	0.5	1.6	0.7	1.6	1.9	6.1	9.8	7.1	10.4	8.7		14.4
Thomas	–	–	0.7	1.8	0.0	0.8	2.1	2.3	10.8	–	6.2	14.6	31.0	
Average	4.1	7.8	5.2	9.3	6.0	5.5	5.9	6.9	6.1	6.9	5.6	4.4	8.3	4.1

[a] –: not on Court together.

Notes: Entries are the proportion of the time the row justice joined columnar justice's special opinions.

At the other extreme, 29 pairs agree with less than 1 percent of the author's special opinions, 12 of them not at all. An additional 60 pairs agree between 1 and 5 percent. Because we arranged the justices ideologically, low percentages should concentrate in the upper right and lower left segments of the table, the higher ones in the opposite corners. This is what we find, further evidencing the operation of attitudinal considerations. When a justice does agree with another's special opinion, it tends to be that of an ideologically aligned colleague.

The pattern displayed on the Rehnquist Court also manifested itself on the Warren and Burger Courts as our previous research has shown.[87] The only appreciable difference among the three Courts is the steady decline in the frequency of interagreement: the average pairwise interagreement on the Warren Court was 12.5 percent, 9.1 percent on the Burger Court, and but 6.2 percent on the Rehnquist Court. As on the Rehnquist Court, like-minded pairs tended to agree appreciably more than those ideologically distant.

Does not this decrease in interagreement further evidence the breakdown in consensual norms, alluded to above?[88] Recent research indicates that the lack of consensus may result from either legal or attitudinal factors or both. Analysis of the contents of the Rehnquist Court's special opinions shows that such opinions do not disagree with the majority over what the case is about. That is, the justices agree with one another – whether they be members of the majority opinion coalition or not – on the basic ground rules that the case concerns: legal provisions, issues, and the basis for decision (e.g., constitutional, statutory, common law). Disagreement occurs only on case outcome, not about what the case involves. Hence, dissensus appears to be attitudinal, rather than legal, notwithstanding the many opportunities for the latter to manifest itself.[89]

Note may also be made of Rehnquist's behavior. Of the other thirteen justices on his Court, four have joined less than 1 percent of his special opinions; five others less than 5 percent. Only Thomas reaches double digits. This lack of association with the chief also characterized the Warren and Burger Courts.[90] In all three Courts, the relationships were

[87] Segal and Spaeth, *op. cit.*, n. 85, *supra*, pp. 282–90. [88] *Op. cit.*, n. 72, *supra*.

[89] Sara C. Benesh and Harold J. Spaeth, "Disagreement on the Court: Have All Consensual Norms Collapsed?," paper presented at the 2000 meeting of the Southern Political Science Association, Atlanta, Ga.

[90] Segal and Spaeth, *op. cit.*, n. 85, *supra*, pp. 282–83.

mutual. Thus, the seven justices who agreed least with Rehnquist were reciprocally joined the least by Rehnquist. This failure to join the chief supports the absence of side payments, to which we alluded above. One such payment would involve joining the chief's special opinions in return for future majority opinion assignments.

The gist of these results is that few pairwise relationships involve a substantial degree of influence, least of all on the Rehnquist Court. Indeed, most special opinions appear to be exertions without discernable effects on the other justices.

Notwithstanding the pairwise relationships that may warrant the label influential (those reaching double digits), only 22 of 34 (65 percent) are mutual. This, however, markedly exceeds the proportion on the Warren and Burger Courts (43 percent): 26 of 60. These proportions suggest that to some extent the justices do differ in their ability to persuade others of the correctness of their views and that joining special opinions is not solely a matter of scratching each other's back. Also note that on all three Courts, mutual relationships predominate among the minority cluster. Thus, 14 of the 23 nonliberal relationships (61 percent) on the Warren Court are mutual, as compared with but four of 12 among the liberals. Conversely, on the Burger and Rehnquist Courts, the conservative majority mutually influences one another to a lesser extent than the other justices. These findings suggest that mutuality may be a function of a group's loss of power (as distinct from influence). As personnel changes shrink a group's domination of the Court's decisions, ideological reinforcement (via agreement in special opinions) occurs.

Within the bifurcated ideological structure of the earlier Courts, Warren and Brennan were most influential on the Warren Court. Brennan retained this position in the shrunken liberal cluster on the Burger Court, along with Douglas. On the nonliberal side of the Warren Court, Clark appeared most influential,[91] with Burton and Harlan pivotal therein. Interestingly, the two justices most influential within their respective clusters were uninfluenced by anyone else: Brennan and Clark. On the Burger Court, Powell was the most influential conservative. He

[91] Notwithstanding the judgment of the President who nominated him – Truman – that he was "such a dumb son of a bitch." Merle Miller, *Plain Speaking* (New York: Berkley, 1973), p. 226.

By contrast, Frankfurter, deemed by many to be highly influential – e.g., Wallace Mendelsion, *Justices Black and Frankfurter: Conflict on the Court* (Chicago: University of Chicago Press, 1961); G. Edward White, *The American Judicial Tradition* (New York: Oxford University Press, 1976), p. 325 – actually influenced only Harlan.

also was uninfluenced by any justice. Brennan, however, was.[92] On the Rehnquist Court, Scalia clearly exercises the most influence among his conservative colleagues, Stevens among the remaining justices. Given the overall low level of interagreement, note that six justices reached double-digit agreement in Stevens's special opinions, four with Scalia. No other justice reached these numbers except Ginsburg, but her joiners barely attain 10 percent. Note also that every justice agreed to at least 1 percent of Stevens's and Scalia's special opinions. The same may be said of White and O'Connor, but neither of them has the double-digit numbers of Scalia and Stevens.

Finally, seniority (or the lack thereof) appears to have little, if any, effect on what we consider influence. This further supports the exclusion of side payments from the operational definition of influence, and further substantiates the dominance of like-mindednes. Burton, Clark, and Harlan, highly influential members of the Warren Court, were relatively junior. Burton began the Warren Court sixth in seniority, and ended as fourth. Clark rose from seventh to third, Harlan from junior to fourth. On the liberal side, Marshall was junior and Brennan rose no higher than fifth. Other junior members, by contrast, exerted relatively little influence: Goldberg, Fortas, Stewart, and White – none of whom exceeded the sixth position. As for the most senior members – Black, Reed, Frankfurter, and Douglas – only Reed influenced as many as two of his colleagues. Similar patterns (or lack thereof) characterize the Burger and Rehnquist Courts. Stevens began as fifth senior on the Rehnquist Court, rising to first associate with Blackmun's retirement at the end of the 1993 term. Scalia began his service on the Rehnquist Court as the junior justice, rising to third associate with Blackmun's retirement.

SUMMARY AND CONCLUSIONS

Insofar as opinion assignment is concerned, the four Courts we consider – Vinson, Warren, Burger, and Rehnquist – have achieved aggregate equality, in spite of the ideologically based opinion assignments by the chief justices and, even more notably, the senior associates. Bias from the left counterbalances bias from the right. The various chiefs have further enhanced their ideological goals through retention of a disproportionate segment of the important cases for themselves.

[92] Segal and Spaeth, *op. cit.*, n. 85, *supra*, p. 287.

A modicum of what may loosely be termed specialization manifests itself, with certain justices – usually those closest to or most distant from the opinion assigner – called upon to write the Court's opinions in certain issue areas. (Justices distant from the opinion assigner don't necessarily view the areas in which they "specialize" a mark of distinction, however.) Thus, while the Court does achieve remarkably equal workloads, even though some justices write much more than the others on certain issues, neither of these results impedes ideologically based opinion assignments by individual assigners.

Unlike the decision on the merits, coalition formation takes place in an inherently interactive environment, as both attitudinal[93] and rational-choice based works[94] have demonstrated. Nevertheless, the sincere preferences of the justices go a long way toward explaining their decisions, while interactive factors such as influence do not. And while formal (i.e., equilibrium-based) models of coalition behavior abound, the few falsifiable tests of these models as applied to the Supreme Court have demonstrated them to be, in fact, false.[95]

Indeed, when we consider the formation of special opinion coalitions, our analyses demonstrate such activity to be notable for its absence, notwithstanding the emphasis that the conventional wisdom gives to judicial bargaining and negotiation.[96] The frequency with which the justices write special opinions, which barely average a single joiner, bespeaks a lack of persuasive interaction. "Influence" seems to be a function of like-mindedness, for example, the Brennans and Marshalls, the Frankfurters and Harlans, and the Scalias and the Thomases.

The Court's ability to arrive at decisions efficiently – the vast majority of which are supported by an opinion in which a majority of the justices concur – evidences healthy institutional characteristics. Nevertheless, as Justice Powell pointed out, the Court

93 Glendon Schubert, *Quantitative Analysis of Judicial Behavior* (Glencoe, Ill.: Free Press, 1959), sec. 4, and David W. Rohde and Harold J. Spaeth, *Supreme Court Decision Making* (San Francisco: W. H. Freeman and Co., 1976), ch. 9.

94 Maltzman, Spriggs, and Wahlbeck, *The Collegial Game*, *op. cit.*, n. 6, *supra*; Epstein and Knight, *op. cit.*, n. 76, *supra*.

95 R. W. Hoyer, Lawrence S. Mayer, and Joseph L. Bernd, "Some Problems in Validation of Mathematical and Stochastic Models," 21 *American Journal of Political Science* 381 (1977); Micheal Giles, "Equivalent vs. Minimum Winning Opinion Coalition Size," 21 *American Journal of Political Science* 405 (1977).

96 Though formation of the majority opinion is an inherently interactive situation, a majority of cases involve no bargaining statements at all between the opinion writer and any other member of the Court, at least in the 1983 term. Epstein and Knight, *op. cit.*, n. 76, *supra*, p. 74.

is perhaps one of the last citadels of jealously preserved individualism. To be sure, we sit together for the arguments and during the long Friday conferences when votes are taken. But for the most part, perhaps as much as 90 percent of our total time, we function as nine small, independent law firms.[97]

More recently, Chief Justice Rehnquist[98] and Justice Scalia have echoed Powell's remarks:

Justice Scalia says one thing has disappointed him . . . the absence of give and take among the Court's members . . . efforts to persuade others to change their views by debating points of disagreement.

. . . he said his own remarks "hardly ever seemed to influence anyone because people did not change their votes in response to my contrary views."

But he added that he now realized that his initial hope for "more of a round-table discussion" would probably not contribute much in practice and "is doomed by the seniority system."[99]

[97] Lewis F. Powell, Jr., Report to the Labor Law Section of the American Bar Association, Atlanta, Georgia, August 11, 1976.

[98] *The Supreme Court: How It Was, How It Is* (New York: Morrow, 1987), pp. 289–95.

[99] "Ruing Fixed Opinions," *New York Times*, February 22, 1988, p. 20. In Harold J. Spaeth and Saul Brenner, eds., *Studies in U.S. Supreme Court Behavior* (New York: Garland, 1990), pp. 256–57.

10

The Supreme Court and Constitutional Democracy

Not only do the justices serve lifetime appointments, as we pointed out in Chapter 1, they also bear primary responsibility for safeguarding the nation's fundamental law: the Constitution. Therefore, expectations that the Supreme Court should be responsive to the vagaries of public opinion bespeak either woeful ignorance or arrogant disregard of the character of the American judicial system. On the other hand, no one credibly alleges that the Court should lightly upset the actions of the other branches of the federal government or those of the state and local governments. Rather, the Court should lard its policy making with restraint.

The wisdom of such a course rests on several postulates. Judges, especially those holding lifetime appointments, are insulated and remote from the public's wishes and sentiments. Hence, they should – when the Constitution does not clearly mandate the contrary – defer to publicly accountable decision makers. Deference should also be accorded to state and local governmental officials because of the federal character of the constitutional system. Not all political wisdom (oxymoronic though the phrase be) emanates from Washington, and the bit that does may occasionally originate elsewhere than from the justices' marble palace. Furthermore, many issues, especially those of an economic, environmental, and technological sort, are highly and increasingly complex. Such matters require expertise for optimal resolution. Judges, consequently, should defer to the experts and not impose their amateurish judgments on the professionally competent. In sum, the Court should not declare unconstitutional congressional or executive action, except in the most blatant and wanton circumstances; the Court should uphold the decisions of state and local officials; and the rules and regulations of the federal bureaucracy – especially those of the federal regulatory commissions – should receive the Court's support.

The remainder of this chapter empirically assesses the extent to which the Court shares its policy-making capabilities with the other branches and levels of government, along with an explanation for its behavior.

The normative appeal of judicial restraint, such as it is, does not guarantee its empirical operation, however. Moreover, an opposite persuasion shares the normative spotlight: The Court should make policy precisely to curb and check the unconstitutional actions of those government officials who possess the coercive capability of purse and sword. Thus, a posture of judicial activism better protects the integrity of the constitutional system than does the laissez-faireism of judicial restraint. Currently, however, the activist persuasion is rarely articulated.[1] And when it is, lower courts tend to take the lead. Consider the following language from the eloquent opinion of Justice Denise Johnson of the Vermont Supreme Court in the landmark decision requiring that the same guarantees be afforded same-sex couples as heterosexual marriage provides:

> One line of opinion contends that this is an issue that only ought to be decided by the most broadly democratic of our governmental institutions, the Legislative, and that the small group of men and women comprising this Court has no business deciding an issue of such enormous moment. . . . this is simply not so. This case came before us because citizens of the state invoked their constitutional right to seek redress through the judicial process. . . . The Vermont Constitution does not permit the courts to decline to adjudicate a matter because its subject is controversial, or because the outcome may be deeply offensive to the strongly held beliefs of many of our citizens. We do not have, as does the Supreme Court of the United States, certiorari jurisdiction, which allows that Court, in its discretion, to decline to hear almost any case. To the contrary, if a case has been brought before us, and if the established procedures have been followed, as they were here, we must hear and decide it.[2]

Obviously, it is much more prudent and politic for judges to affect a posture of restraint rather than activism when confronted with a "hot

[1] But see Arthur S. Miller, "In Defense of Judicial Activism," in Stephen C. Halpern and Charles M. Lamb, eds., *Supreme Court Activism and Restraint* (Lexington, Mass.: Lexington Books, 1982), pp. 167–99; Christopher Wolfe, *Judicial Activism: Bulwark of Freedom or Precarious Security?* (Pacific Grove, Calif.: Brooks/Cole, 1990); Marcia Coyle, "Campaign 2000 Focus Is 'Judicial Activism,'" *National Law Journal*, August 21, 2000, p. A1.

[2] *Baker v. State*, Entry Order, docket no. 98–032 (1998), at 50–51.

potato," just as it is for politicians who oppose the Court's ideological orientation to mouth demands for the seating of "strict constructionists," or whatever the code words for judicial restraint happen to be at a given point in time. Use of the word "affect" in the preceding sentence states the matter accurately. Words need not correlate with behavior. The mere fact that justices may wrap themselves in the mantle of restraint does not mean that they actually practice what they preach.

Indeed, to a substantial extent, activism and restraint are used as epithets to bludgeon legal and political opponents. Thus, Robert Bork in an op-ed piece declared: "Far from forsaking activism, American courts, enforcing liberal relativism, are leading the parade to Gomorrah." Citing state court decisions on homosexual unions, school vouchers, and obscenity, he writes:

> The truth is that these are not constitutional rulings but moral edicts, and the morality enforced is a minority morality, one directly contrary to the morality of a majority of Americans. . . . That activism prevails in [state] courts, even though many of them are manned by elected judges, suggests either that the public is ill-informed about the shift in power from democratic institutions to authoritarian bodies or that there is a general weariness with democracy and the endless struggle it entails.[3]

From the opposite pole, Anthony Lewis, a *New York Times* columnist and author of the acclaimed *Gideon's Trumpet*, assailed conservatives for labeling liberal judges as "activists." He chided the Court's five states' rightists – Rehnquist, Scalia, O'Connor, Kennedy, and Thomas – for creating the constitutionally baseless doctrine "that states must have sovereign immunity to maintain their 'dignity' " by suits filed by their own citizens. Such decisions, says Lewis, "throw a cloud of hypocrisy over conservative statements that judges who construe the Constitution should respect the text, the intention of the framers, and so on."[4]

Indeed, even the most nodding acquaintance with the real world ought to make apparent that such instrumental values as activism and restraint do not operate in an even-handed fashion.[5] A decision maker may indeed

[3] "Activist Judges Strike Again," *Wall Street Journal*, December 22, 1999, p. A18.

[4] "No Limit but the Sky," *New York Times*, January 15, 2000, p. A17. The Eleventh Amendment applies to suits filed by "Citizens of another State, or by Citizens or Subjects of any Foreign State." Only by judicial fiat does it apply to a state's own citizens.

[5] Indeed, in the hands of skilled, attitudinally inclined justices, restraint can be morphed into activism, and vice-versa. Consider Scalia's concurrence in *Christensen v. Harris County*, 146 L Ed 2d 621 (2000), at 632–34, in which he renders a paean to judicial

defer to the judgment or action of others when subject to their hierarchical control or persuasive influence. But absent such, as is the case with the justices, rational people do not goose-steppingly defer. Nonetheless, not all are convinced. Consider the hagiolatrous piety of the following quotation:

> Some have made uncertainty the servant of selected business interests. Others have been guided by more generous considerations. In Mr. Justice Frankfurter's view this "sovereign prerogative of choice" is not for judges. He would resolve all reasonable doubt in favor of the integrity of sister organs of government and the people to whom they must answer. . . . He is wary of judicial attempts to impose Justice on the community; to deprive it of the wisdom that comes from self-inflicted wounds. . . . In his view, humanitarian ends are served best in that allocation of function through which the people by a balance of power seek their own destiny.[6]

And more recently: "Today's justices . . . are unwilling to look for the meaning of the law beyond the words of the Constitution." "The current majority decides only the case before it . . . rather than . . . treading where the rest of the nation has not yet gone." "The legislatures are where the action should be, according to this majority."[7]

Though the foregoing passages deal with conservative justices, readers should be disabused of the notion that restraint correlates with conservatism, and activism with liberalism. Beyond conservative support for the right to contract or, more recently, sovereign immunity, one highly salient example should suffice: the affirmative action case *Metro Broadcasting, Inc. v. Federal Communications Commission*, in which the Court upheld FCC policies that give preference to minorities in the licensing of broadcasters.[8] The liberals adopted a restraintist rationale to uphold the affirmative action:

restraint while summarily voting judicially activist because the position taken by a division of the Department of Labor – though supported by the Solicitor General – was not "reasonable."

[6] Wallace Mendelson, *Justices Black and Frankfurter: Conflict on the Court* (Chicago: University of Chicago Press, 1961), pp. 130–31. Sad to say, but reputable scholars have accepted as gospel the pseudologue of Frankfurter's restraint. E.g., "Frankfurter . . . who would become one of the most ardent and consistent advocates of judicial restraint. . . ." Henry J. Abraham, "Line-Drawing between Judicial Activism and Restraint: A Centrist Approach and Analysis," in Halpern and Lamb, *op. cit.*, n. 1, *supra*, p. 207. Ardent? Perhaps. Consistent? Not at all. See Harold J. Spaeth, "The Judicial Restraint of Mr. Justice Frankfurter – Myth or Reality," 8 *American Journal of Political Science* 22 (1964).

[7] Joan Biskupic, "A Look at the Rehnquist Court; They Want to Be Known as Jurists, Not Activists," *Washington Post*, January 9, 2000, p. B3.

[8] 497 U.S. 547 (1990).

. . . we are "bound to approach our task with appropriate deference to the Congress, a coequal branch charged by the Constitution with the power to 'provide for the . . . general Welfare' . . . and 'to enforce . . . the equal protection guarantees of the Fourteenth Amendment.' . . . We explained that deference was appropriate in light of Congress' institutional competence as the national legislature. . . ."[9]

Further, deference should be paid not only Congress, but also the FCC: "we must pay close attention to the expertise of the Commission and the factfinding of Congress when analyzing the nexus between minority ownership and programming diversity."[10] Why? Because "both Congress and the Commission have concluded that the minority ownership programs are critical means of promoting broadcast diversity. We must give great weight to their joint determination."[11]

The conservative dissenters – O'Connor, Rehnquist, Scalia, and Kennedy[12] – wrapped themselves in the mantle of constitutional activism: "The Court's application of a lessened equal protection standard to congressional actions finds no support in our cases or in the Constitution."[13] They concluded:

The Court has determined . . . that Congress and all federal agencies are exempted, to some ill-defined but significant degree, from the Constitution's equal protection requirements. This break with our precedents greatly undermines equal protection guarantees, and permits distinctions among citizens based on race and ethnicity which the Constitution clearly forbids.[14]

Justice Kennedy separately observed: "in upholding this preference, the majority exhumes Plessy's deferential approach to racial classifications."[15]

In what follows, we assess the extent to which the Rehnquist Court justices have displayed judicial activism and restraint in matters where it ought to be most relevant: support for the Solicitor General, declarations of unconstitutionality, administrative agency action, access to the federal courts, comparisons of the justices' behavior between federal and state economic regulation and that involving civil rights and liberties, and public opinion. We place the behavior of the Rehnquist Court jus-

[9] *Id.* at 563 (citations omitted). [10] *Id.* at 569. [11] *Id.* at 579.

[12] These are the same four justices – plus Thomas, who had not yet been appointed – who constitute the Rehnquist Five and the Court's states' rights bloc referenced above.

[13] 497 U.S., at 603. [14] *Id.* at 631.

[15] *Id.* at 632. The reference is to the separate but equal doctrine formulated in *Plessy v. Ferguson*, 163 U.S. 537 (1896).

tices in the context of earlier courts whose behavior was reported in this book's predecessor.[16]

SUPPORT FOR THE SOLICITOR GENERAL

We begin our examination of activism and restraint with the one clear example of real restraint: support for the Solicitor General. As noted in Chapter 6, the Solicitor General is the President's representative before the Supreme Court. As the President (along with the vice-president) is the only official elected by the entire country, justices might show restraint by supporting the policies supported by his representative in Court.

Previous research has amply documented Supreme Court support for the Solicitor General. Scigliano's sample of cases shows that the United States won about 62 percent of its cases in the nineteenth century and 64 percent in the twentieth.[17] The search and seizure data set provides evidence that the United States as a party significantly affects the Court's decisions even when the facts of the case are controlled. Adding the United States to the model presented in Table 8.1 increases the reasonableness of a search by 0.20.

Many times the United States is not a direct party, but nevertheless has a substantial interest in the outcome of the case. For instance, in *Brown v. Board of Education*,[18] the famous racial desegregation suit, the Solicitor General filed only an amicus brief. It was in the government's brief in the second *Brown* case that the Court found the "all deliberate speed" proposal.[19]

Looking at the amicus cases more generally, it becomes clear that despite the government's success as a litigant, it "has an even better record as amicus curiae."[20] For the years 1943, 1944, 1963, and 1965, Scigliano reports that the party supported by the Solicitor General won 87 percent of the time. Such results comport with more recent findings.[21]

[16] Jeffrey A. Segal and Harold J. Spaeth, *The Supreme Court and the Attitudinal Model* (New York: Cambridge University Press, 1993).

[17] Robert A. Scigliano, *The Supreme Court and the Presidency* (New York: Free Press, 1971).

[18] 347 U.S. 483 (1954).

[19] Lincoln Caplan, *The Tenth Justice* (New York: Knopf, 1987), p. 31.

[20] Scigliano, *op. cit.*, n. 17, *supra*, p. 179.

[21] Karen O'Connor, "The Amicus Curiae Role of the U.S. Solicitor General in Supreme Court Litigation," 66 *Judicature* 256 (1983); Steven Puro, "The Role of the Amicus

Again, preliminary evidence suggests that these results hold after controlling for the facts of the case. One tested area is the sex discrimination cases heard by the Supreme Court between 1971 and 1984.[22] The Court supported the Solicitor General 64 percent of the time when it favored a conservative (antiequality) decision and 90 percent of the time when it favored a liberal (proequality) decision. After controlling for several case facts, changes in the Court's membership, and the Court's tendency to reverse, the position taken by the Solicitor General still had a large influence, affecting the probability of a liberal or conservative decision by as much as 0.28. Evidence of Solicitor General influence has also been found in death penalty cases.[23]

Finally, our own research has shown that virtually every justice serving between 1953 and 1982 supported the party favored by the Solicitor General in amicus curiae briefs over half the time.[24] This, of course, suggests some degree of nonattitudinal influence. Nevertheless, such support was largely conditioned on the ideological position of the party being supported. Fifteen of the twenty justices examined demonstrated significantly different levels of support when the Solicitor General favored the liberal side than when he favored the conservative side. Rehnquist, for example, supported the Solicitor General 77 percent of the time in conservative briefs but only 39 percent of the time in liberal ones, the largest difference among the Court's conservatives. We further examine the success of the Solicitor General when we examine the Supreme Court's support for federal agencies, below.

DECLARATIONS OF UNCONSTITUTIONALITY

While the Court's responsiveness to national policy making has been extensively studied,[25] less attention has been paid to the Court's solici-

Curiae in the United States Supreme Court," Ph.D. diss., State University of New York at Buffalo, 1971; Steven Puro, "The United States as Amicus Curiae," in S. Sidney Ulmer, ed., *Courts, Law and Judicial Processes* (New York: Free Press, 1983); and Jeffrey A. Segal, "Amicus Curiae Briefs by the Solicitor General during the Warren and Burger Courts," 41 *Political Research Quarterly* 135 (1988).

22 Jeffrey A. Segal and Cheryl Reedy, "The Supreme Court and Sex Discrimination: The Role of the Solicitor General," 41 *Political Research Quarterly* 553 (1988).

23 Tracey George and Lee Epstein, "On the Nature of Supreme Court Decision Making," 86 *American Political Science Review* 323 (1992).

24 Segal, *op. cit.*, n. 21, *supra.*

25 Robert Dahl, "Decision-Making in a Democracy: The Supreme Court as National Policy Maker," 6 *Journal of Public Law* 179 (1957); Jonathan Casper, "The Supreme Court

tousness toward state legislatures. One recent study, though, found that, since Reconstruction, state laws struck by the Supreme Court pertained to the most salient of the issues that had produced contemporary electoral realignments. Moreover, laws that the Court voided tended to be those enacted by state legislatures under partisan control different from the Court's majority.[26] Indeed, one may readily note that the resolution of such convulsing controversies as employment discrimination, affirmative action, and the rights of persons accused and convicted of crime do not depend on the action of either congressional or state legislative kakistocrats. As these matters became burning issues in the early 1970s, legislators, as is their wont, avoided them like a social disease. Instead, prevailing policies have been forged by judges and bureaucrats, under the direction of the justices of the U.S. Supreme Court.[27]

Fitting this work into the attitudinal model leads to the following hypotheses: (1) The Supreme Court will generally support policies passed by the dominant law-making coalition. (2) Such support will be produced not by deference or restraint toward the law-making coalition, but rather by the shared values that the appointment process produces. (3) When the values of the justices conflict with the values of the relevant law-making coalition, little restraint will be apparent. We examine these hypotheses in the following section.

Certainly, the most dramatic instances of a lack of judicial restraint – or, conversely, the manifestation of judicial activism – are decisions that declare acts of Congress and, to a lesser extent, those of state and local governments unconstitutional.[28] Here the conflict between an unelected,

and National Policy Making," 70 *American Political Science Review* 50 (1976); David Adamany, "Legitimacy, Realigning Elections and the Supreme Court," 1973 *Wisconsin Law Review* 790 (1973); Richard Funston, "The Supreme Court and Critical Elections," 69 *American Political Science Review* 795 (1975); and Bradley Canon and S. Sidney Ulmer, "The Supreme Court and Critical Elections: A Dissent," 70 *American Political Science Review* 1215 (1976).

26 John B. Gates, "Partisan Realignment, Unconstitutional State Policies, and the U.S. Supreme Court, 1837–1964," 31 *American Journal of Political Science* 259 (1987).

27 See our discussion of these matters in Chapter 4 and, in addition, Isabelle Katz Pinzler, "A Major Change in Bias Law for the Workplace," *National Law Journal*, August 21, 1989, pp. S5, S12; Paul Gewirtz, "Discrimination Endgame," *The New Republic*, August 12, 1991, pp. 18–20, 22–23. Also cf. *Griggs v. Duke Power Co.*, 401 U.S. 424 (1971), with *Wards Cove Packing Co. v. Atonio*, 490 U.S. 642 (1989).

28 In declaring unconstitutional federal and state action, a case will strike one or the other, not an action of both. However, in *Saenz v. Roe*, 143 L Ed 2d 689 (1999), the Court did void a state law that limited new residents' welfare benefits, as well as the federal law that authorized the state's action. How unprecedented this simultaneity is, we know not.

lifetime judiciary and the public's representatives is most acute. Absent a constitutional amendment, the Court's decision is final.

The Supreme Court first declared an act of Congress, or portion thereof, unconstitutional in the 1803 case of *Marbury v. Madison*.[29] Over fifty years passed before the Court again did so.[30] Following the Civil War, though, the Court began using its power of judicial review on a more regular basis. Peaks of activism occurred "during the late 1860s; during the administration of Theodore Roosevelt; after World War I; during the 1920s and 1930s; and during the 1960s, a cycle that has not yet begun to decline."[31] Indeed, as we document below, it has intensified under the direction of Chief Justice Rehnquist and his fellow conservatives.

Of the several dozen acts of Congress declared unconstitutional in the half-century preceding the millennium – somewhat less than two per term – only one has been reversed by congressional action: the eighteen-year-old vote. Because the Court so rarely strikes federal laws, these Courts, as well as all their predecessors, may accurately be characterized as restraintist. Nonetheless, marginal differences in deference may be specified. Thus, the Burger Court, notwithstanding its reputation for restraint, declared proportionately more federal laws unconstitutional than the reputably activist Warren Court: 28, an average of 1.65 per term. The comparable figures for the Warren Court are 22 and 1.38,[32] while the fourteen terms of the Rehnquist Court preceding the millennium produced 29, for an average of 2.07 per term.

These Courts display much more activism when confronted with the actions of state and local governments. By our subjective count, of 180 state and local ordinances and constitutional provisions challenged as unconstitutional during the 1986–98 terms of the Rehnquist Court, the justices voided 77, or 43 percent. This contrasts with 37 percent for federal enactments. But from February 22, 1995, until the end of the 1998 term, the Court, incredibly, voided federal statutes in 16 of the 21 cases in which their constitutionality was at issue: 76 percent!

As it did toward federal legislation, the Burger Court declared that of the state and local governments unconstitutional at a higher frequency than the Warren Court: 13 per term (225 total), as compared with

29 1 Cranch 137. 30 *Scott v. Sandford*, 19 Howard 393 (1857).

31 Gregory A. Caldeira and Donald J. McCrone, "Of Time and Judicial Activism: A Study of the U.S. Supreme Court, 1800–1973," in Halpern and Lamb, *op. cit.*, n. 1, *supra*, p. 113.

32 Segal and Spaeth, *op. cit.*, n. 16, *supra*, p. 320.

8.7 per term (139 total). The Rehnquist Court, much more active in declaring federal legislation unconstitutional, ranks last where state and local statutory provisions are concerned: an average of 7.9 per term (111 total). Note also that the Warren Court's liberally activist reputation rested primarily on its opposition to state action with regard to persons accused of crime, First Amendment freedoms, and race discrimination.[33]

We examine the individual justices' votes for and against declaring actions unconstitutional. A preliminary version of the Benesh and Spaeth "flipped" database[34] contains these data, defined as any case in which one or more justices say in so many words that they would void a legislative enactment or a provision of a state constitution or municipal charter. Note that many declarations of unconstitutionality do not pertain to legislation. Rather, they concern such matters as the ultra vires activity of unduly zealous police officers for whom the means justifies the end, the unauthorized action of an administrative agency, or the ruling of a lawless jury. Although such activities are usually not legislatively authorized, in many cases it is far from clear whether the Court has voided a statute or some other legislatively enacted provision. The inherent subjectivity in such judgments gives us pause. Thus the database and we, by extension, limit ourselves to the definition of unconstitutionality with which this paragraph begins.

Table 10.1 displays the votes of the thirteen Rehnquist Court justices who participated in the 170 cases during the 1986–98 terms of the Rehnquist Court in which one or more justices voted to void a federal, state, or municipal law. With the exception of Byron White and William Rehnquist,[35] every justice displays an attitudinal pattern: They vote to uphold either conservative laws or liberal laws, but never both. While Marshall, for example, voted to strike only 21 percent of the liberal laws under consideration, he voted to strike 96 percent of the conservative ones. Alternatively, Thomas not only voted to strike 80 percent of the liberal laws, but also 40 percent of the conservative ones. Neither the Rehnquist Court nor its immediate predecessors respect the legislative activity of Congress or the state and local governments.

[33] *Id.*

[34] NSF grant SES-9910535, Sara C. Benesh and Harold J. Spaeth, principal investigators. The "flipping" involves recreating the database with the individual justice as the unit of analysis, rather than the case.

[35] This finding about Rehnquist is consistent with the findings of Sue Davis, *Justice Rehnquist and the Constitution* (Princeton: Princeton University Press, 1989).

TABLE 10.1. *Justices' Votes on Declarations of Unconstitutionality*

	Liberal laws			Conservative laws		
	Uphold	Strike	% strike	Uphold	Strike	% strike
Marshall	11	3	21.4	3	67	95.7
Brennan	7	4	36.4	2	60	96.8
White	12	8	40.0	58	32	35.6
Blackmun	16	9	36.0	19	76	80.0
Rehnquist	24	16	40.0	98	28	22.2
Stevens	20	19	48.7	31	96	75.6
O'Connor	9	31	77.5	67	61	47.7
Scalia	14	26	65.0	79	48	37.8
Kennedy	10	22	68.8	46	61	57.0
Souter	15	11	42.3	17	49	74.2
Thomas	5	20	80.0	33	22	40.0
Ginsburg	11	9	45.0	10	28	73.7
Breyer	10	5	33.3	8	25	75.8

FEDERAL ADMINISTRATIVE AGENCIES

We proceed to consider evidence of deference to administrative agency action. Here, the rationale for deference differs from that applicable to constitutionality. Courts should yield to agency action because their personnel possess subject matter expertise, while judges do not. Hence, on matters of technical complexity – the grist of most administrative mills – courts should behave deferentially. Moreover, the Supreme Court in 1984 required, as a matter of national law, that whenever Congress has not provided an "unambiguously expressed intent," federal courts must defer to any "permissible" interpretations of the statute by the administrative agency.[36] Additionally, federal agency cases brought before the Supreme Court are almost exclusively argued by the Solicitor General's office, thus adding to the likelihood of deference.

Among administrative agencies, the federal independent regulatory commissions are generally regarded as the most expert in their grasp of highly technical and complex matters.

One of them, the National Labor Relations Board (NLRB), regulates labor-management relationships. Analysis of the first seven terms of the Warren Court (1953–60) reveals that a majority of the justices deferred

[36] *Chevron U.S.A. Inc. v. Natural Resources Defense Council*, 467 U.S. 837, at 843.

either to the pro- or antiunion decisions of the NLRB, but not to both.[37] Furthermore, those who deferred to prounion NLRB decisions opposed the probusiness decisions of the other agencies, while those who supported antiunion NLRB decisions supported only probusiness agency decisions. What explains these results? Again, the ideologically grounded substantive policy preferences of the justices: Liberals support antibusiness and prolabor decisions; conservatives the opposite. Thus, for example, three judicial conservatives – Frankfurter, Harlan, and Whittaker – supported the seven prounion NLRB decisions with 2, 0, and 0 of their votes, respectively; the liberals – Black, Douglas, and Warren – with 6, 6, and 7 of theirs. The pattern reversed when the NLRB rendered an antiunion decision: 80 percent of the three conservatives' votes supported the NLRB, while only 13 percent of the liberals' votes did so. Similar behavior occurred where agencies regulatory of business were concerned. When the agency supported business, so also did the three conservatives, with 82 percent of their votes. The liberals, however, did so with only 19 percent of theirs. The proportions reverse when the agencies rendered an antibusiness decision. Then the conservatives supported the agency with 31 percent of their votes, the liberals with 84 percent.

Needless to say, these patterns do not occur by chance. The consistently selective pattern of support and nonsupport clearly indicates that neither judicial restraint nor judicial activism motivates these justices' votes.[38] Notwithstanding the conclusive character of these findings, Warren and Douglas continued to be excoriated as judicial activists, while Frankfurter remained the apotheosis of judicial restraint.

The sharply delineated pattern of the Warren Court no longer persists, however, as Table 10.2 indicates. Apart from the lack of antiunion NLRB decisions, the substantially participating Rehnquist Court justices, with only four exceptions, support agency action whether liberal or conservative with at least 50 percent of their votes. The exceptions: Brennan and Marshall in conservative independent regulatory commission (IRC) business decisions, Thomas in liberal IRC business decisions, and Scalia in liberal non-IRC business decisions. Disproportions do exist between

[37] See Segal and Spaeth, *op. cit.*, n. 16, *supra*, pp. 305–6.

[38] Of the thirteen justices who sat between the 1953 and 1960 terms, only Burton, Reed, Minton, and Jackson evidenced restraint toward the NLRB by casting more than half their votes in support of the agency's pro- and antiunion decisions. Only Minton and Burton supported pro- and antibusiness agency decisions with more than half their votes. See Spaeth, *op. cit.*, n. 6, *supra.*

TABLE 10.2. *Voting Behavior toward Federal Agency Cases, 1986–1999 Terms*

	Independent regulatory commissions								Other federal agencies regulatory of business			
	NLRB				Business agencies[a]				Agency liberal		Agency conservative	
Justice	Liberal	%	Conservative	%	Liberal	%	Conservative	%		%		%
White	5–1	83.3	1–1	50.0	13–2	86.7	10–2	83.3	17–1	94.4	13–0	100
Breyer	3–1	75.0	–		3–3	50.0	2–0	100	6–2	75.0	2–1	66.7
Stevens	8–4	66.7	2–0	100	23–4	85.2	10–6	62.5	25–4	86.2	10–6	62.5
Rehnquist	10–2	83.3	1–1	50.0	17–10	63.0	13–0	100	15–14	51.7	16–0	100
Ginsburg	4–2	66.7	–		5–4	55.6	0–2	0.0	6–5	54.5	3–0	100
Kennedy	9–1	90.0	–		16–7	70.0	7–2	77.8	17–6	73.9	12–0	100
Souter	7–2	77.8	–		11–0	100	8–0	100	13–2	86.7	5–1	83.3
O'Connor	9–3	75.0	1–1	50.0	17–5	77.3	14–0	100	16–13	55.2	14–1	93.3
Blackmun	4–4	50.0	2–0	100	31–0	100	6–5	54.5	17–4	81.0	11–2	84.6
Scalia	9–3	75.0	2–0	100	27–7	79.4	16–0	100	12–15	44.4	15–0	100
Marshall	4–1	80.0	2–0	100	17–0	100	4–5	44.4	13–1	92.9	8–3	72.7
Thomas	0–1	0.0	–		4–7	36.4	2–2	50.0	7–8	46.7	4–1	80.0
Brennan	3–0	100	2–0	100	15–0	100	2–3	40.0	13–1	92.9	6–3	66.7
Powell	0–1	0.0	1–0	100	4–0	100	2–0	100	2–1	66.6	4–0	100

[a] Federal Communications, Federal Energy Regulatory, Federal Trade, Interstate Commerce, and Securities and Exchange Commissions.

TABLE 10.3. *Federal Agency Action Affecting Civil Rights and Liberties, 1986–1999 Terms*

	Agency liberal			Agency conservative		
Justice	Proagency	Antiagency	% pro	Proagency	Antiagency	% pro
Brennan	16	0	100	9	25	26.5
Marshall	16	0	100	9	30	23.1
Breyer	12	1	92.3	17	4	81.0
Souter	14	2	87.5	22	10	68.8
Blackmun	16	3	84.2	24	22	52.2
Powell	4	1	80.0	8	2	80.0
Ginsburg	12	3	80.0	15	6	71.4
Stevens	25	8	75.8	48	18	72.7
White	12	6	66.7	41	3	93.2
Scalia	18	14	56.3	55	8	87.3
O'Connor	18	14	56.3	55	11	83.3
Kennedy	12	11	52.2	39	8	83.0
Rehnquist	13	19	40.6	58	7	89.2
Thomas	5	11	31.3	22	4	84.6
TOTALS	193	93	67.5	422	158	72.8

liberal and conservative support, however, for such liberally inclined justices as Marshall, Brennan, and Stevens and the conservative Rehnquist Five. We attribute the lack of substantial discrimination to the breakdown of the earlier ideological division, New Deal economics,[39] plus some level of deference to the Solicitor General.

Federal administrative agencies also operate in the area of civil rights and liberties, chief among them the Equal Employment Opportunity Commission and the Departments of Health and Human Services and Housing and Urban Development. But a wide range of other agencies occasionally addresses controversies that directly bear on civil rights and liberties. We accordingly consider all such federal agency action reviewed by the Rehnquist Court during the 1986–99 terms in which Spaeth's database identifies the issue as one involving criminal procedure, civil rights, due process, First Amendment freedoms, privacy, or attorneys. Table 10.3 displays these data.

[39] Timothy M. Hagle and Harold J. Spaeth, "The Emergence of a New Ideology: The Business Decisions of the Burger Court," 54 *Journal of Politics* 120 (1992); "Ideological Patterns in the Justices' Voting in the Burger Court's Business Cases," 55 *Journal of Politics* 492 (1993).

The totals superficially indicate that the justices are deferential to the agencies engaged in such regulation: two thirds of liberal regulation receives support, as opposed to 73 percent of a conservative character. Half of the fourteen justices support liberal agency decisions with 80 percent or more of their votes, with another two at two thirds or more. Only Thomas and Rehnquist are clearly activist, supporting these decisions with less than half their votes. On the conservative side – apart from the fact that 68 percent of the justices' votes occurred in conservative agency decisions – eight of the fourteen justices support these decisions with 80 percent or more of their votes. Three others exceed two thirds. Only Brennan and Marshall are activist, with Blackmun almost so, at 52 percent.

On the other hand, the rank order of the justices does vary systematically enough to give us pause. The tau b correlation coefficient of –0.56 is significant at $p < 0.015$, indicating that agency action does not itself explain the justices' votes. Granted, the three justices ranked in the middle of the Court – Powell, Ginsburg, and Stevens – vary but little (and in Powell's case, not at all) in their support between liberal and conservative decisions. Breyer comes close to joining them, varying 11 percent in his support of these agency decisions.

CONSIDERATIONS OF ECONOMIC FEDERALISM

We next consider cases involving action of the state and local governments, specifically, their efforts to regulate economic activities that allegedly violate the interstate commerce clause, impose taxes, determine tortious liability, and preempt federal court jurisdiction and federal regulation, and whether certain of their activities invades the sphere of national supremacy.

Analysis conducted for this book's predecessor showed the justices even less restrained than in their treatment of the federal regulatory commissions. Only Rehnquist showed a modicum of support for the states. For the others, their substantive attitudes toward economic regulation dominated their behavior. The premillennial behavior of the Rehnquist Court, however, produces behavior orthogonal to that manifest earlier. Rather than treat the state cases as an entity, we divided them into two segments: those involving national supremacy and those that do not. The justices do not particularly vary their pro- and antistate behavior among the aspects of economic federalism or the preemption cases. But they definitely do do so in the highly salient

TABLE 10.4. *Rehnquist Court Voting in Economic Federalism Cases, 1986–1999 Terms*

	Economic federalism			National supremacy		
Justice	Prostate	Antistate	% pro	Prostate	Antistate	% pro
Rehnquist	81	42	65.9	24	12	66.7
Thomas	34	27	55.7	18	5	78.3
Scalia	66	55	54.5	22	14	61.1
O'Connor	63	54	53.8	25	11	69.4
Blackmun	48	42	53.5	1	17	5.6
Souter	36	32	52.9	6	18	25.0
Kennedy	52	49	51.5	19	13	59.4
White	39	37	51.3	2	17	10.5
Powell	9	9	50.0	1	2	33.3
Ginsburg	23	24	48.9	3	14	17.6
Stevens	59	62	48.8	8	28	22.2
Marshall	28	29	49.1	1	11	8.3
Brennan	25	26	49.0	2	9	18.2
Breyer	14	18	43.8	2	15	11.8
TOTALS	577	506	53.2	134	186	41.9

area (at least for the justices) of national supremacy,[40] as Table 10.4 indicates.

Except for Rehnquist, the other justices occupy a narrow 12-point swath on the economic federalism side of Table 10.4 between 56 and 44 percent support for the states. Rehnquist is deviant. If we do not consider his behavior in the preemptive state regulation case, in which he supported the states with only 21 of his 43 votes, his pro-state voting approaches 77 percent (59 of 76). Clearly, then, except for Rehnquist (partially) considerations of federalism do not motivate the justices' behavior.

A different picture emerges from the right side of Table 10.4. Four justices exceed 60 percent support for the states in conflicts with the national government; the other nine, excluding Kennedy, locate at the polar extreme: between 33 and 5 percent pro-state. Evidencing the chasm between the five states' rightists (the Rehnquist Five) and the other justices is the former group's declaring acts of Congress unconstitutional in

[40] Segal and Spaeth, *op. cit.*, n. 16, *supra*, pp. 308–10.

eight of the fourteen national supremacy cases decided between April 1995 and January 2000. Two of the other six voided a state, rather than a federal, law – the two term limits cases[41] – an outcome that resulted because one of the antifederalists, Kennedy, switched sides and supported national supremacy.

Clearly, then, considerations of federalism drive behavior in the national supremacy set, but not in the other components of economic federalism. In doing so, however, only five of the justices pay obeisance to the states. The others could hardly be more antipathetic to them. Whether these five – and perhaps others – defer to the states elsewhere remains to be seen: a matter to which we now turn.

CIVIL LIBERTIES

The remaining area in which we may assess the operation of judicial restraint in the context of considerations of federalism are cases concerning civil liberties. To the extent that the provisions of the Bill of Rights and the various provisions of the federal civil rights acts apply to the state and local governments, they do so in precisely the same fashion as they bind the federal government, with the exception of the size of juries in criminal cases and the need for unanimity in arriving at guilty verdicts.[42] Accordingly, because of the generally accepted view that the states serve as laboratories for political experimentation and innovation, coupled with the principle of state sovereignty and the fact that nothing in the Constitution explicitly makes the Bill of Rights binding on the states, one may expect a restraint-oriented justice to give the state and local governments a bit more leeway than the federal government in their activities affecting civil liberties.

Previous analysis belied the assumption that the Burger Court might be more deferential to state action in four areas of civil liberties than the federal government: First Amendment freedoms, double jeopardy, search and seizure, and poverty law. With only a few exceptions – and those incidental – the justices behaved similarly. A global analysis of the 1981–89 terms also disclosed more support of federal action affecting individual freedom than it did that of the states. Only Rehnquist and

[41] *U.S. Term Limits v. Thornton* and *Bryant v. Hill*, 514 U.S. 779 (1995).

[42] See *Williams v. Florida*, 399 U.S. 78 (1978); *Apodaca v. Oregon*, 406 U.S. 404 (1972); *Ballew v. Georgia*, 435 U.S. 223 (1978); *Burch v. Louisiana*, 441 U.S. 130 (1979). The states, however, need not adhere to the Second, Third, or Seventh Amendments, nor to the requirement that persons be indicted by a grand jury.

TABLE 10.5. *Rehnquist Court Support of State and Federal Action Restricting Individual Freedom, 1986–1999 Terms*

Justice	% state	% federal	Difference
Kennedy	91.3	91.7	–0.4
Powell	89.4	100	–10.6
O'Connor	84.7	84.4	0.3
White	84.2	87.2	–3.0
Rehnquist	77.7	85.2	–7.5
Scalia	77.4	81.8	–4.4
Thomas	77.1	82.7	–5.6
Souter	72.8	86.0	–13.2
Breyer	70.3	84.2	–13.9
Ginsburg	69.1	70.4	–1.3
Blackmun	66.2	64.3	1.9
Stevens	62.6	68.0	–5.4
Brennan	51.0	49.2	1.8
Marshall	46.3	49.3	–3.0

O'Connor on the Burger Court and Rehnquist during the first four terms of his Court supported the states a tad more frequently than they did the feds.[43]

We supplement the foregoing analysis with an examination of all thirteen premillennial terms of the Rehnquist Court. We alter our focus somewhat to increase the possibility that the justices may exhibit deference to the states by considering only constitutionally based decisions. The inclusion of statutorily construed cases causes the federal cases to have a component that the state set lacks (the federal courts having no jurisdiction to construe state enactments apart from their constitutionality, except for cases arising under diversity jurisdiction), with the result that the justices' deference – or lack of it – may be affected by such cases. Our analytical scope again encompasses the issues of criminal procedure, civil rights, First Amendment freedoms, due process, privacy, and attorneys, as specified in Spaeth's database. Table 10.5 displays the results.

Of the fourteen Rehnquist Court justices, only three support the states more than the federal government: O'Connor, Blackmun, and Brennan. Their deference, such as it was, averaged only 1 percent more than that

[43] Segal and Spaeth, *op. cit.*, n. 16, *supra*, pp. 310–12.

they accorded the feds. The other eleven on average supported federal regulation 6.2 points above that of the states. All of the reputedly "strict constructionist" justices locate within this group, with the exception of O'Connor. The same explanation governs this behavior as we specified in the other areas where restraint and deference should putatively be manifest: the justices' individual policy preferences. As evidence: consider that six of the fourteen justices did not cast a single vote in a federal case dissenting counter to their ideological orientation, while two others cast but one such vote; Marshall, Brennan, Souter, Ginsburg, and Breyer cast no conservative dissents to liberal decisions; while White, Powell, and Rehnquist lacked liberal dissents to conservative decisions. Indeed, only Kennedy split his dissents even remotely evenly: four liberal and four conservative. A similar pattern obtains in the much larger number of state cases: Six justices supported an ideologically opposite outcome in dissent no more than once, while four others did so no more than 7.5 percent of the time: Souter (7.5), Scalia (7.4), Blackmun (3.8), and Stevens (2.7).

PUBLIC OPINION

Supreme Court decisions by and large correspond with public opinion.[44] This should not be surprising, as Supreme Court justices are chosen by the President, who in turn is normally selected by vote of the people. Our question of concern is whether public opinion – however defined – directly *influences* the Court.

Theoretically, there is little reason to think so. Institutionally, the justices are immune from majoritarian pressures. The public neither elects nor removes them from office. Nevertheless, scholars often invoke rational choice theories to justify their models. Arguably, the justices might need to react to public opinion in order to keep their decisions from being overturned by elected representatives.[45] We have extensively reviewed the separation-of-powers literature in Chapter 8, so it is not necessary to review these arguments. But if Congress has virtually no

[44] David Barnum, "The Supreme Court and Public Opinion: Judicial Decision Making in the Post-New Deal Period," 47 *Journal of Politics* 652 (1985); and Thomas Marshall, *Public Opinion and the Supreme Court* (New York: Longman, 1989).

[45] James A. Stimson, Michael B. MacKuen, and Robert S. Erikson, "Dynamic Representation," 89 *American Political Science Review* 543 (1995); Roy B. Flemming and B. Dan Wood, "The Public and the Supreme Court: Individual Justice Responsiveness to American Policy Moods," 41 *American Journal of Political Science* 468 (1997).

direct influence on the Court, it is hardly likely that the influence of public opinion will flow indirectly through Congress. Moreover, it is curious that the only measure of public opinion that even correlates with the Court's behavior is Stimson's "public mood."[46] Stimson's "mood" is largely a relative and reactive measure (e.g., should the government be spending more or less on welfare than it currently is?). This means, as scholars have shown, that as the government becomes more liberal, the public mood will grow more conservative.[47] This negative correlation between government actions and public mood means that Stimson's measure is not particularly consistent with these sorts of rational choice models.

Additionally, from a normative perspective, the justices are not supposed to represent majoritarian concerns. As Justice Jackson so eloquently stated in *West Virginia Board of Education v. Barnette*:

> The very purpose of a Bill of Rights was to withdraw certain subjects from the vicissitudes of political controversy, to place them beyond the reach of majorities and officials and to establish them as legal principles to be applied by the courts. One's right to life, liberty, and property, to free speech, a free press, freedom of worship and assembly, and other fundamental rights may not be submitted to vote; they depend on the outcome of no elections.[48]

Conceptually, the question of whether public opinion directly influences the Court is much more difficult than questions as to whether administrative agencies or the Solicitor General do. As Mishler and Sheehan astutely note, this is because the justices are members of the public and the same factors that might influence the public may influence the justices, even if the public itself has no influence on the Court.[49] An example of this relationship is depicted in Figure 10.1.

Briefly, exogenous factors such as the unemployment rate, the crime rate, war, and government spending influence the attitudes of the public at large,[50] which presumably includes judges. Additionally, public opinion may have a direct influence on judges' behavior. But by merely

[46] James A. Stimson, *Public Opinion in America: Mode, Cycles, and Swings* (Boulder: Westview Press, 1992).

[47] Robert H. Durr, "What Moves Policy Sentiment," 87 *American Political Science Review* 158 (1993), and Christopher Wlezian, "The Public as Thermostat: Dynamics of Preferences for Spending," 39 *American Journal of Political Science* 981 (1995).

[48] 319 U.S. 624 (1943), at 638.

[49] William Mishler and Reginald S. Sheehan, "Public Opinion, the Attitudinal Model, and Supreme Court Decision Making: A Micro-Analytic Perspective," 58 *Journal of Politics* 169 (1996).

[50] See Durr (1993) and Wlezian (1995), *op. cit.*, n. 47, *supra.*

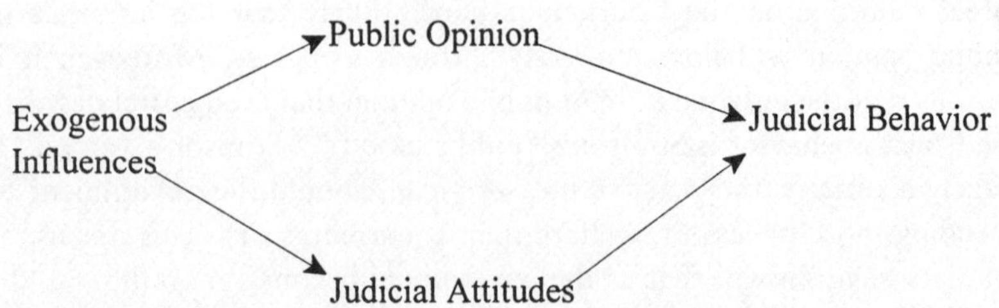

FIGURE 10.1. A conceptual model of the influence of public opinion on Supreme Court decisions.

assessing the correlation between public opinion and judges' behavior, scholars fail to control for the potential spurious nature of that relationship.

A classic example of this is Cook's analysis of draft-dodging cases. Cook shows that as public opinion turned against the Vietnam War, sentencing by federal judges in draft-dodger cases became more lenient.[51] But, needless to say, it's hard to imagine that the same American casualties, the same administration lies, and the same news stories that turned the public at large against the war didn't also by and large turn federal judges against the war. As Herbert Kritzer noted, "while there is some evidence that judicial behavior in the area of sentencing of draft offenders during the Vietnam War moved in a direction consistent with public opinion, there is no evidence that the movement reflected a response to the opinion."[52] Rather, Kritzer argues that the changes were due to changes in "the judges' own doubts about the war."[53]

Similarly, more recent studies claiming a direct influence of public opinion on the Supreme Court fail to account for the factors that move public opinion. As Mishler and Sheehan note, this sort of design makes it impossible to determine whether the Court is reacting to public opinion itself or whether the purported relationship, like that involving draft dodgers, is spuriously influenced by real world factors that influence both the public's and the justices' preferences.[54] Thus, the most appropriate

[51] Beverly B. Cook, "Public Opinion and Federal Judicial Policy," 21 *American Journal of Political Science* 567 (1977).

[52] Herbert M. Kritzer, "Federal Judges and Their Political Environment: The Influence of Public Opinion," 23 *American Journal of Political Science* 194 at 204 (1979).

[53] *Id.*, p. 198.

[54] See Mishler and Sheehan, *op. cit.*, n. 49, *supra*. They note that it is "virtually impossible" to distinguish a causal impact of public opinion from a spurious one. From their theoretical perspective, the counter-majoritarian nature of courts, the causal/spurious

way to characterize the relationship found in most studies between public opinion and judicial behavior is an "association."

The debate over the relationship between public opinion and the Supreme Court began with Mishler and Sheehan's finding of a significant correlation between judicial behavior and public opinion that lagged by five years, but there were no other lags.[55] Norpoth and Segal wondered why the Court, say, in 1967, would be concerned with what public opinion was in 1962, regardless of what had happened in the meantime.[56] The reason they found for Mishler and Sheehan's reported association was simple: Public mood grew much more conservative around 1967, while the Court, due to Nixon's appointments of Burger, Blackmun, Rehnquist, and Powell, grew far more conservative starting around 1972. Thus, public opinion influenced the Court in that a more conservative public elected Richard Nixon, who then got to appoint four conservative justices to the Court.

More recently, Mishler and Sheehan found significant associations between public opinion and the votes of some justices at lags ranging between one and seven years, but they are unwilling to assert any causal relationship, and neither are we.[57] Alternatively, Stimson et al. find no direct, significant association between public opinion and Court decisions.[58] Flemming and Wood do find a significant association between Court behavior and public opinion, but their best model finds that a 29 percent change in public opinion is associated with but a 1 percent change in the Court's decisions.[59] By any reasonable interpretation, this is substantively meaningless.

Of course, these meager findings do not mean that we can conclude that public opinion has no influence on judicial behavior. Public opinion undoubtedly influences elected state court judges. In a compelling demonstration of this, Paul Brace and Melinda Gann Hall show that

question is irrelevant. But for those wishing to understand the causes of judicial behavior, the distinction is far more important.

[55] William Mishler and Reginald S. Sheehan, "The Supreme Court as a Countermajoritarian Institution? The Impact of Public Opinion on Supreme Court Decisions," 87 *American Political Science Review* 87 (1993).

[56] Helmut Norpoth and Jeffrey A. Segal, "Popular Influence on Supreme Court Decisions," 88 *American Political Science Review* 711 (1994).

[57] Mishler and Sheehan, *op. cit.*, n. 49, *supra*. See their quoted statement, n. 54, *supra*.

[58] Stimson, MacKuen and Ericson, *op. cit.*, n. 45, *supra*.

[59] Flemming and Wood, *op. cit.*, n. 45, *supra*. The 1 percent change is based on their generalized least squares (GLS) model. Their "first stage" ordinary least squares model, which shows significant autocorrelation, differs only by rounding error (p. 484) from the more appropriate GLS model.

state supreme court judges who are currently facing reelection are more responsive to public opinion than are less constrained judges.[60] So, too, a wonderfully innovative study by James Kuklinski and John Stanga shows that the mere revelation of public preferences, through a referendum, influenced the behavior of state court judges on the issue in question.[61] But while public opinion might influence state court judges, evidence on unelected, life-tenured lower court federal counterparts shows no such influence.[62]

CONCLUSION

We need not summarize the manifestations of judicial restraint evidenced in the behavior of recent Courts, particularly the Rehnquist Court. Outside of support for the Solicitor General (including agency cases), they are either imperceptible or explained by the justices' substantive policy preferences. One ought neither be surprised nor saddened to find that judicial restraint has so little operational force. It has been pointed out:

> If not to decide is to decide (and it surely is), then even the restrained jurist is promulgating policy decisions when he defers. Can anyone of reason and conviction really believe that someone who has attained the office of Supreme Court justice is able to submerge his politics entirely in deference to vague notions of judicial restraint? One may defer, but never blindly. Justices, like most mere mortals, defer to the ideas and institutions of which they approve. We would not want them on the Supreme Court otherwise.[63]

As the behavior illustrated by our tables shows, hyperactivity, rather than restraint, characterizes the Court that now spans the millennium, a hyperactivity, moreover, that best characterizes the pathetically mislabeled "strict constructionist" justices appointed by Ronald Reagan and

[60] Paul Brace and Melinda Gann Hall, "Neo-Institutionalism and Dissent in State Supreme Courts," 52 *Journal of Politics* 54 (1990). A claim of "influence" is warranted here because there is no plausible reason to suspect that exogenous factors that shape public opinion would influence the attitudes of judges up for reelection, but not those with years to go in their terms. Unfortunately, such tests are not possible of life-tenured federal judges.

[61] James Kuklinski and John Stanga, "Political Participation and Governmental Responsiveness," 73 *American Political Science Review* 1090 (1979).

[62] Micheal Giles and Thomas G. Walker, "Judicial Policy-Making and Southern School Segregation," 37 *Journal of Politics* 917 (1975).

[63] Harold J. Spaeth and Stuart H. Teger, "Activism and Restraint: A Cloak for the Justices' Policy Preferences," in Halpern and Lamb, *op. cit.*, n. 1, *supra*, p. 297.

the first President Bush. We are heartened that other analysts and commentators have begun to target the hypocrisy latent in the cloaking with which the Court lards its opinions. Thus,

> The most startling quality of today's conservative judicial activists is not only the unselfconscious hypocrisy with which they are abandoning the judicial philosophies on which they have staked their careers. It is also their overconfidence and lack of humility – as they blithely substitute their own policy judgments for those of Congress, the president of the United States, and even the states in whose name they claim to speak.[64]

Note that we hold no brief in this book for either judicial activism or judicial restraint. Those normatively inclined are encouraged to debate their position unstintingly. We believe only that candor better serves constitutional democracy – by which we mean structural limitations on the popular will, for example, judicial review, federalism, separation of powers – than the cynical prevarications of partisans in both camps.

As for allegations that our demystification of the Court's role in the political system is itself subversive, we reiterate what we have said in another context: "We hardly think that knowledge of politics is something to fear. As political scientists we should enlighten. To claim that valid social research should not be undertaken in order to protect cherished myths is the most dangerous argument of all."[65]

[64] Jeffrey Rosen, "How the Right Learned to Love Judicial Activism," *The New Republic*, January 20, 2000, p. 22.

[65] Jeffrey A. Segal and Harold J. Spaeth, "Norms, Dragons, and Stare Decisis: A Response," 40 *American Journal of Political Science* 1064 (1996), 1080.

11

Conclusion

If the Supreme Court's decision that handed George W. Bush the election tells us anything, it's that the Supreme Court is more secure and more comfortable than it has ever been in pushing an agenda that is not only activist and conservative, but also blatantly partisan. *Bush v. Gore* illustrates the latter; while the disdain – and frequency – with which the Court demeaningly voids congressional legislation best evidences the former.

Despite the attack on state sovereignty in *Bush v. Gore*,[1] an attack the conservative justices needed to produce Bush's victory, it is federal authority that the Rehnquist Court's guns have primarily assailed and which will continue to be subject to judicial assault.

As of this writing, the most recent manifestation of this assault came in *Board of Trustees v. Garrett*.[2] Patricia Garrett, a nurse recovering from breast cancer surgery, found that her illness had cost her her job at an Alabama state hospital, in clear violation of the Americans with Disabilities Act. Though the Court recognized that the Eleventh Amendment (which applies to in-state suits only through judicial fiat) could be supplanted by the Fourteenth Amendment, and though Congress explicitly acted through its Fourteenth Amendment authority to enforce the equal protection of the laws, and though Congress produced voluminous records of state-sanctioned discrimination against the disabled, the Court's 5-4 decision found the state immune.

As usual, Linda Greenhouse got it exactly right:

[1] 148 L Ed 2d 388 (2000). [2] 148 L Ed 2d 866 (2001).

More clearly than any precedent on which it built, the decision revealed the Supreme Court's real concern with the way power is allocated in the American political system to be less the balance between the federal government and the states than that between the Supreme Court and Congress.

At its core, this is a separation-of-powers revolution, one that happens to be playing out now on the field of states' rights but is not likely to stay confined to that battleground.

The exercise of power is largely a zero-sum game, and the court, defining the rules of engagement to give itself the last word, is winning at the expense of Congress. . . .

[T]he Americans With Disabilities Act, the most important civil rights law of the last quarter-century, was the highly visible product of a bipartisan legislative process, so much so that some people assumed the law might stand as a firewall against the court's further expansion of state immunity.

Before passing the A.D.A. in 1990, Congress spent years compiling a record of the extent of discrimination against people with disabilities, both in society at large and specifically as the result of government policies that created and perpetuated patterns of segregation, exclusion and lack of access to public services.

But Chief Justice William H. Rehnquist said for the majority last week that the evidence was inadequate: "minimal," "anecdotal," unproven and insufficiently tailored to the precise question of whether state governments had unconstitutionally discriminated as employers.

"The court is acting as if Congress is just a bad lower court," Robert Post, a law professor at the University of California at Berkeley and a critic of the recent federalism cases, said. The opinion was remarkable, he said, "for its tone-deafness to the institutional differences between the Court and Congress, almost obliterating a role for Congress as a separate institution."

And as a practical matter, there is little Congress can do about it.[3]

There may have been a time when one could have claimed that the Court was merely supporting honestly held notions about federalism. If the continued abrogation of the adequate-and-independent-state-grounds doctrine doesn't end such pretense, *Bush v. Gore* surely does. Again, Greenhouse:

Looking at the court's behavior through the lens of judicial triumphalism makes it possible to reconcile the apparent contradiction between the solicitude the court showed for the states last week and the same 5-to-4 majority's disregard of the Florida Supreme Court in the presidential election case two months ago.

The decisions were not about states' rights but about the Supreme Court's own role.[4]

[3] Linda Greenhouse, "The High Court's Target: Congress," *New York Times*, February 25, 2001, sec. 4, p. 3.

[4] *Id.*

Judicial ascendency continues. In 2000, the Court declared unconstitutional the Violence Against Women Act, which permitted victims of rape, domestic violence, and other crimes "motivated by gender" to sue their attackers in federal court, despite, again, voluminous congressional evidence that violence aimed at women has a substantial impact on interstate commerce.

But, ultimately, the Court's evisceration of the ADA or the Violence Against Women Act matters less than the strengthening of its position as king of the governmental hill. For the Court majority is concerned not only with ideological purity – that is, functioning unabashedly as hard-core conservatives – but with extending authoritative judicial policy making across the entire governmental spectrum, thus striking the line-item veto,[5] thus voiding the Religious Freedom Restoration Act.[6]

Those who wish to argue that the Court merely follows established legal principles in deciding cases (yes, such views exist, as we have documented in Chapters 2 and 7) certainly have their work cut out for them. But in what may best be categorized as a strategic retreat, postpositivist legalists now argue that all that can be expected of judges is that judges *believe* that they follow legal principles. Howard Gillman well states this position:

> In the version of the argument that might be called "post-positivist," legalists make claims, not about the predictable behavior of judges, but about their state of mind – whether they are basing their decisions on honest judgments about the meaning of law. What is post-positivist about this version is the assumption that a legal state of mind does not necessarily mean obedience to conspicuous rules; instead, it means a sense of obligation to make the best decision possible in light of one's general training and sense of professional obligation. On this view, decisions are considered legally motivated if they represent a judge's sincere belief that their decision represents their best understanding of what the law requires. [Steven J.] Burton [*Judging in Good Faith*, Cambridge University Press] (1992: xi–xii, 44) has persuasively argued that this notion of "judging in good faith" is all we can expect of judges.[7]

Thus, under the postpositivist approach, virtually any decision *can be* consistent with the legal model. And any decision *is* consistent with the

[5] *Clinton v. City of New York*, 524 U.S. 417 (1998).

[6] *City of Boerne v. Flores*, 521 U.S. 507 (1997).

[7] Howard Gillman, "What's Law Got to Do with It? Judicial Behavioralists Test the 'Legal Model' of Judicial Decision Making," 26 *Law and Social Inquiry* 465 at 486 (2001).

model as long as the judge has sincerely convinced him- or herself that the decision is legally appropriate.

The problems with this approach are clear. First, the model is not falsifiable in terms of which decisions judges actually make.[8] Thus, by accepted standards of scientific research, the model cannot provide a valid explanation of what judges actually do.[9]

Second, the postpositivist model fails to appreciate the fundamental influence of motivated reasoning in human decision making. As classic social psychological findings demonstrate, the ability to convince oneself of the propriety of what one prefers to believe psychologically approximates the human reflex.[10] This is particularly true when plausible arguments support one's position, as is invariably the case for the types of issues the Supreme Court decides.

The attitudinal position on motivated reasoning is one of agnosticism. What matters is that the justices' ideology directly influences their decisions. Whether the justices do so with self-awareness or whether, consistent with fundamental human psychological mechanisms, they are capable of convincing themselves that Congress cannot block slavery in the territories,[11] that the due process clause implies a right to contract,[12] that the Civil Rights Act allows race to be a factor in hiring and promotions,[13] that the Eleventh Amendment applies to suits by a citizen of the state being sued,[14] and that – as implausible as it might seem – the Florida recount violated the Fourteenth Amendment, doesn't matter.[15] The fact remains that the ideology of the justices drives their decisions.

[8] *Id.*, p. 485: "Behavioralists want to force legalists into offering testable hypotheses so that beliefs about law's influence can be verified by a kind of scientific knowledge that behavioralists consider more authoritative; however, legalists believe that doing such tests has the effect of changing the concept of 'legal influence' so that it no longer represents what they believe."

[9] See the discussion in *Daubert v. Merrell Dow*, 509 U.S. 579 (1993) at 593.

[10] E.g., Roy Baumeister and Leonard Newman, "Self-Regulation of Cognitive Inference and Decision Processes," 20 *Personality and Social Psychology Bulletin* 3 (1994); and Ziva Kunda, "The Case for Motivated Reasoning," 108 *Psychological Bulletin* 480 (1990).

Of course, humans are also motivated to find correct answers. Baumeister and Newman refer to this as the "intuitive scientist" model. They refer to the search for preferred answers as the "intuitive lawyer" model (p. 4). We have little doubt that Supreme Court justices are better represented as lawyers than as scientists.

[11] *Scott v. Sandford*, 19 Howard 393 (1857).

[12] *Lochner v. New York*, 198 U.S. 45 (1905).

[13] *Steelworkers v. Weber*, 443 U.S. 193 (1979).

[14] *Board of Trustees v. Garrett*, *op. cit.*, n. 2, *supra*.

[15] *Bush v. Gore*, *op. cit.*, n. 1, *supra*.

But at the same time, to the extent that the justices' ideological values determine their legal views,[16] then there may be some unexpected overlap between the attitudinal model and the postpositivist position. Under both the attitudinal model and a motivated-reasoning understanding of the postpositivist position, justices may typically reach decisions that approximate their personal policy preferences. Nevertheless, because a priori expectations cannot be made and, indeed, are not desired, under the postpositivist position, it cannot provide us with what we seek: an explanation for what the justices actually do.

The rational choice model, on the other hand, holds greater promise. If the next decade provides us with empirically verified, equilibrium-based predictions, the model will have gone where the attitudinal model has not gone and cannot go.

We provide some examples of questions that conceivably could be well answered by equilibrium analysis (demonstrating that the proposed strategies are optimal) and empirical tests (demonstrating that the justices act consistently with the proposed strategies):

- Does the sequential process of certiorari voting lead to a signaling game? For example, if a liberal justice wishes to grant cert to a conservative lower court ruling, but sees three conservative justices vote to grant, does he or she then conclude that the conservatives do so because they believe that they have the votes to affirm, and does he or she then vote to deny?
- Are majority opinions written at the median of the Court (or perhaps at the median of the decision coalition), or does the opinion writer have special influence? If the opinion writer has special influence, is it because he or she has the final option of making a take-it-or-leave-it proposal?
- If the opinion writer has special influence and can write opinions off the Court median, what, if anything, constrains a lower court whose preference is closer to the median from ignoring the opinion of the Court and tailoring its decisions to the preferences of the Court median?

[16] Richard A. Brisbin, "Slaying the Dragon: Segal, Spaeth and the Function of Law in Supreme Court Decision Making," 40 *American Journal of Political Science* 1004 (1996); and Howard Gillman, *The Constitution Besieged: The Rise and Demise of Lochner Era Police Power Jurisprudence* (Durham: Duke University Press, 1993).

- Alternatively, is the median justice preferred because of the "narrowest grounds" doctrine,[17] whereby the holding of the Court in a plurality judgment is the holding of the median justice, regardless of whether or not that justice is part of the judgment of the Court? This would seem to provide special bargaining power to the median, who can always threaten to concur. If he or she thus breaks the majority, his or her position becomes the holding of the Court.
- Can the structural features of the American political system lead to a compelling formal model of rationally sincere behavior on the merits for the justices, even in statutory cases?

While it remains to be seen whether these questions can be answered, we would be remiss if we did not point out examples of behavior that appear to violate strategic hypotheses: Given a rather good ability to assess how the other justices will vote on the merits, why do four-person cert coalitions frequently include justices who will lose on the merits? Since four can grant cert, while five can dismiss, why don't we see far more cases dismissed as improvidently granted (DIG)? Given the enormous advantage of speaking first and voting last, why in the world did the chief justice ever begin voting first?

If we observed far more DIGs, for example, scholars would certainly label such behavior strategic. Since we don't observe them or, at least, seldom do, what does that mean for strategic behavior?

Of course, these problems pale in comparison to the problems of the rational choice model on the merits. The essence of the separation-of-powers model is captured by Mr. Dooley's quote that "th' supreme coort follows th' iliction returns." Not quite. These days, as predicted by the attitudinal model, th' iliction returns follow the supreme coort.

[17] *Gregg v. Georgia*, 428 U.S. 153, at 169. See also Maxwell Stearns, *Constitutional Process: A Social Choice Analysis of Supreme Court Decision Making* (Ann Arbor: University of Michigan Press, 2000).

Case Index

General Index